CELLULOID ACTIVIST

CELLULOID ACTIVIST

THE LIFE AND TIMES
OF
VITO RUSSO

═══ MICHAEL SCHIAVI ═══

The University of Wisconsin Press

The University of Wisconsin Press
1930 Monroe Street, 3rd Floor
Madison, Wisconsin 53711-2059
uwpress.wisc.edu

3 Henrietta Street
London WC2E 8LU, England
eurospanbookstore.com

1   3   5   4   2

Printed in the United States of America

Library of Congress Cataloging-in-Publication Data
Schiavi, Michael R.
Celluloid activist: the life and times of Vito Russo / Michael Schiavi.
p.   cm.
Includes bibliographical references and index.
ISBN 978-0-299-28230-1 (cloth: alk. paper)
ISBN 978-0-299-28233-2 (e-book)
1. Russo, Vito.   2. Film historians—United States—Biography.
3. Gay activists—United States—Biography.
4. Homosexuality in motion pictures—History—20th century.
5. Gay & Lesbian Alliance Against Defamation (New York, N.Y.)—History—20th century.
6. ACT UP New York (Organization)—History—20th century.
I. Title.
PN1998.3.R885S35   2011
791.43092—dc22
[B]
2010044627

For
Arnie Kantrowitz

Contents

Acknowledgments

"Well, it's about fuckin' time!"

In the early stages of research for this book, I phoned playwright Doric Wilson for an interview. I had barely announced my intention to write a biography of Vito Russo when the above response came booming back through the receiver. Doric's endorsement, though more bluntly phrased than most, was typical. For the past four years, I have been astounded by the generosity of people who had never heard of me but trusted me to tell the story of this beloved gay icon.

I never met Vito. But I was fascinated by him by the time I was seventeen. As a closeted and frightened freshman at American University, I spent innumerable hours in Bender Library, secretly researching my two favorite topics: homosexuality and film. In September 1987, *The Celluloid Closet*'s second edition arrived at Bender just as I did. Studying the book's spine, I was savvy enough to understand the "closet" allusion, and Vito's Italian names made me feel a kinship with him.

When I took the book off the shelf and saw the subtitle, *Homosexuality in the Movies*, stamped on its cover, I slid to the floor and spent the next several hours hypnotized. I'd had no idea of the damage that Hollywood had done to gays and lesbians. Some of the titles that Vito mentioned were familiar; most went right past me. That afternoon I received my first inkling that some gays not only liked themselves but fought like hell when insulted.

Three years later, as an out and proud senior, I opened a copy of the *Washington Blade* and felt a rush of tears sting my eyes. "*Celluloid Closet* author Vito Russo dies at 44." It was like losing a favorite uncle.

Flash-forward fifteen years. At the 2005 Northeast Modern Language Association conference in Boston, Damion Clark chaired a panel on the *Closet*'s relevance to film studies today. I delivered a paper that I hoped might grow into a journal article.

Angling for a personal perspective on Vito and his work, I wrote a letter to Vito's best friend, Arnie Kantrowitz, and Arnie's partner, Larry Mass. Both men gave me hours of phone time and insight. Larry also gave me an inadvertent grail. "It's nice that you're writing an article on *The Celluloid Closet*, but somebody really should write a full biography of Vito."

The notion seemed heaven-sent, but I was very nervous. Vito was a one-name phenomenon. He knew everyone in gay culture and politics. He numbered

Lily Tomlin and Bette Midler among his friends. He epitomized two generations of gay activism, from Stonewall through the first decade of AIDS. And he had any number of colleagues far more qualified and knowledgeable to write his story.

Trying to muster self-confidence, I applied for fellowships under the careful guidance of David Román and my dear friend Robert Gross. I then spent several months poring over Vito's papers in the Manuscripts and Archives Division of the New York Public Library (NYPL), where Arnie had deposited them ten years earlier. (Yale wanted them, too. Bless Arnie for giving first dibs to the scholars of Vito's favorite city.) There I received boundless help from head of manuscripts processing Melanie Yolles; reference archivists Laura Ruttum and Thomas Lannon; archivists Don Mennerich, Megan O'Shea, and Susan Waide; and technical assistant John Cordovez. These people know from primary sources, and they know how to advise in the friendliest, most efficient manner imaginable.

I am also indebted to Lodi Memorial Library's Barbara Frank and Artie Maglionico, who introduced me to local history that brought Vito's adolescence to vivid life. At Fairleigh Dickinson University, Okang McBride, director of Alumni Relations, and Professor Martin Green, chair of English, gave me detailed background on Vito's undergraduate career. I must thank Suzanne Dmytrenko, university registrar of San Francisco State University, for shedding light on Jeff Sevcik's training as a poet. I offer deep gratitude to Maxine Wolfe and Marwa Amer of Brooklyn's Lesbian Herstory Archives, a peerless resource where I received my first glimpses of *Our Time* and the 1973 Gay Pride debacle.

Before digging deeply into Vito's life, I never expected to learn much about his earliest education. His elementary-school days at Holy Rosary were nearly fifty years past, and his NYPL files contained no papers from his childhood. To my amazement, Holy Rosary (renamed Mt. Carmel-Holy Rosary School) still occupies the same Pleasant Avenue building that Vito knew. Principal Suzanne Kasynski and director of development Andrea Arce have been extremely generous with their time and assistance. Andrea even managed to locate Vito's P.S. 80 kindergarten records. Her sleuthing skills are unmatched.

As I started sketching Vito's childhood, I realized that I couldn't proceed without the cooperation of the Russo family. Before meeting Charlie Russo, Vito's closest living relative, I had heard that he wanted to write his own memoir about his brother. I was very nervous about approaching him. As a quick glance at my notes reveals, Charlie proved completely receptive to this project. He invited me to his home for dinner and long conversations with him and his lovely wife, Linda. He gave me unrestricted access to family photos, letters, school records, Vito's baby book, *Celluloid Closet* rough drafts, and his own memories, the painful along with the exhilarating. He answered entirely too many e-mails containing my nitpicky queries about family history. He also paid me the highest possible compliment during our first interview when, in the middle of a sentence, he broke off and remarked, "You know, looking at you is like looking at my brother."

I wish I had space to thank individually each member of the Russo and Salerno clans. They all welcomed me as one of the family. Several, however, require particular mention. Vito's eighty-eight-year-old aunt and godmother, Jean Tramontozzi, not only gave me reams of Salerno backstory unknown to younger relatives; she also treated me to a scrumptious Italian lunch the likes of which I hadn't enjoyed since my grandmother died. Charlie's oldest daughter, Vicki, photocopied and mailed to me the lengthy journal that Annie Russo kept after Vito's death. Charles Russo Jr. met with me in San Francisco to pass on a wealth of his uncle's personal papers, many of them untouched since Vito's death. Vito's cousin, Vin Tozzi, provided me with dozens of photos, videos, and written memories.

The extended family of Vito's friends has been equally magnanimous. Without my having to ask, I received unpublished interviews of Vito conducted by Richard Berkowitz, Leslie Cohen, Esther Newton, and Nancy Stoller. Jay Blotcher and Don Shewey sent me private journal entries that they had written about Vito. Larry Mass dropped into my lap seven years' worth of journals that he had not opened since writing them. A few months later, he donated the entire stash to NYPL—meaning that I got the first read. I'll be forever grateful to Larry for his trust and kindness.

Other personal writings began flooding in. Howard Cruse, Dorian Hannaway, and Charles Silverstein shared unpublished memoirs that offered unique perspectives on Vito's life and activism. Allen Sawyer lent me two volumes of Jeff Sevcik's unpublished poetry, left to him by Vito. Lily Tomlin sent me several letters that Vito had written to her along with video of his "Celluloid Closet" lecture. (I also thank Lily for the two hours of uproarious interview she gave me—and I thank her assistant, Janice Frey, and John "Lypsinka" Epperson for helping me to contact Lily in the first place.) Vito's physician, Ron Grossman, gave me several letters brimming with information on Vito's battles with AIDS.

Stephen Conte, Robert Leuze, Rick Mechtly, and Charles Silver provided me with rare documents illuminating Vito's career. James Cascaito and Stephen Soba wrote to me, respectively, about Vito's participation within ACT UP and his Public Theatre presentations of "The Celluloid Closet." Eileen Bowser put me in touch with Vito's Museum of Modern Art colleagues. With extraordinary generosity, Michael Musto advertised my book on his *Village Voice* blog and urged anyone with Vito memories to contact me. I am indebted to Michael for information I could never otherwise have learned.

I conducted nearly two hundred interviews for this book. As with Vito's family, I cannot honor all these people with individual mention. Everyone who spoke with or wrote to me about Vito has my heartfelt thanks. But I must give explicit nods to several heroes, beginning with Vito's surviving partners, Steve Krotz and Bill Johnson. Steve granted me untold hours of phone interview and a vivid description of Vito's Gay Activists Alliance (GAA) days. Bill allowed me to spend several days in his Cleveland home, where I transcribed dozens of letters that Vito had sent him during their courtship. Bill and his assistant, Lorraine Cogan, made my trips to Ohio extraordinarily pleasant and productive.

Vito's famous friends—New York state senator Tom Duane, Rob Epstein, Jeffrey Friedman, Valerie Harper, Larry Kramer, Dean Pitchford, Howard Rosenman, Craig Zadan—were incredibly giving with their time, memories, and connections. Other friends provided carte blanche access to precious materials. Jay Blotcher lent me the entire run of *Our Time* on VHS, sparing me many tedious hours of transcription at NYPL. NYPL's Kevin Winkler, an archive unto himself, gave me dozens of Vito's *Advocate* articles and rare Bette Midler footage. Patrick Pacheco kindly lent me the run of *After Dark* issues on which Vito worked. Despite illness, Fred Goldhaber journeyed into Manhattan both to be interviewed and to give me a complete audio recording of Vito's 1987 appearance with the New York City Gay Men's Chorus. Hal Offen entrusted me with two overstuffed binders of GAA papers that are, in toto, an unrivaled overview of the early gay-rights movement in New York. Arthur Evans, Ron Goldberg, Jim Hubbard, and Tom Steele generously assisted me in the securing of permissions. Hugh Van Dusen and Cynthia Merman helped me to flesh out Vito's interactions with Harper & Row.

As I was preparing to write the book, I received expert advice from Michael Denneny, Karla Jay, Eric Myers, Sarah Schulman, and Ed Sikov on the minefields of gay publishing. Eric was the first person to refer me to the University of Wisconsin Press, where this project has benefited from the impeccable stewardship of senior acquisitions editor Raphael Kadushin, his assistants Nicole Kvale and Katie Malchow, managing editor Adam Mehring, copyeditor Barb Wojhoski, copy chief Will Broadway, marketing intern Ellen Maddy, director Sheila Leary, and electronic publishing manager Krista Coulson. As *Celluloid Activist*'s peer reviewers, David Bergman and Anthony Slide provided invaluable commentary on the book's focus and accuracy.

Without the help of Patrick Merla, this book would never have reached print. A ferociously intelligent editor, agent, and writer, Patrick advised me through several proposal drafts and contract negotiations. He provided these services for free, out of love for Vito and a belief in my abilities. I can never repay him.

Several colleagues at New York Institute of Technology deserve special thanks. Provost Richard Pizer and Dean Roger Yu granted me course release time and a year's sabbatical so that I could focus on my research and writing.

Within the Manhattan English Department, I am especially grateful for the encouragement of my friends, chair Kathy Williams and professors Cathy Bernard and Jennifer Griffiths. Our tireless administrative assistant, Maggie Albright, has made my life easier every day for eight years.

My family has supported me in this project from the start. I thank my parents, Judy and Joe Schiavi, for always checking in on my progress, and my aunt and uncle, Clorine and Nino Patete, for tutoring me in the nuances of Italian ballads.

I save my deepest gratitude for three men at the center of my life. Chris Collette, my best friend, is a vital part of this book. Back in olden days, when we were a couple, Chris bought me my first copy of *The Celluloid Closet* as a birthday gift. Since then, he has listened to more rambling about Vito Russo than any human should have to endure. He has also provided unstinting technical support and reassuring back pats. If E. M. Forster's Margaret Schlegel existed as a twenty-first-century gay man, she'd be Christopher William Collette.

My former partner, Scott Stoddart, is the kindest soul I know. In our ten years together, Scott helped me over countless personal and professional hurdles. His sage counsel saw me through this book's drafting. During my sabbatical year, Scott fed me, printed my chapters, kept me in office supplies, listened patiently to my research and writing woes, and got me out of the house on days when I hadn't budged from my computer since dawn. His love and encouragement made this project possible. (Special thanks also to Suzanne Richardson, Scott's administrative assistant at Fashion Institute of Technology, for her kindness.)

And finally, the man to whom I dedicate *Celluloid Activist*: the incomparable Arnie Kantrowitz. Like Charlie Russo, Arnie had planned to write his own biography of Vito. Instead, he turned the project over to me without a backward glance. Like far too many gay men of his generation, Arnie has lost hundreds of friends and acquaintances to AIDS. But not once in our dozens of conversations did he flinch from a painful memory. He opened his mind, his heart, and his home to me. He lent me copies of Vito's journals to facilitate my drafting. He also lent me twenty years' worth of datebooks that kept a far more meticulous record of Vito's life than Vito himself ever managed. Arnie embodies the term "mensch." I love him and thank him from the bottom of my heart.

When I first contacted Arnie and Charlie about this book, I promised to do justice to the man who was a brother to them both. I hope they feel that I have kept my promise.

New York City
September 2010

Celluloid Activist

Introduction

In May 2009, author and activist Jay Blotcher asked to interview me about this book. Along with Jeffrey Schwarz's forthcoming documentary, *The Times of Vito Russo*, *Celluloid Activist* seemed to indicate a resurgence of interest in Vito's life and legacy.

When Jay's article appeared in *Pride '09*, I was jolted to see "Who in the World Is Vito Russo?" plastered across the first page. The next time I spoke to Jay, he was furious. The title, he told me, had been imposed by *Pride*'s editor, who didn't think that Vito's name would be familiar to current readers. I conceded the point and went back to my manuscript, more determined than ever to fill that gap in history.

Vito Russo (1946–90) is the pioneering activist whose book, *The Celluloid Closet: Homosexuality in the Movies* (1981; rev. ed. 1987), almost single-handedly invented the field of gay and lesbian media studies. By documenting the hundreds of homicides, suicides, and stereotypes that typified filmed representation of homosexuals throughout the twentieth century, *The Celluloid Closet* taught gay readers that the bigotry they suffered offscreen correlated directly to the lies perpetuated about them onscreen. Never before had watching movies, the unofficial gay pastime, entailed such political urgency.

Both before and after *Closet*'s publication, Russo toured widely with a lecture presentation of his work, which introduced the notion of gay imaging to audiences in over two hundred colleges, universities, museums, and community centers throughout the United States as well as Canada, England, Ireland, the Netherlands, Sweden, Germany, Belgium, and Australia. During the 1970s and 1980s, Russo's writing regularly reached thousands of readers in *Esquire*, *Rolling Stone*, *New York*, the *Nation*, *Film Comment*, *Village Voice*, *Moviegoer*, *After Dark*, the *Advocate*, *New York Native*, *Soho Weekly News*, *GAY*, and London's *Gay News*.

But Russo's influence stretched well beyond his lecturing and journalism on film. He was a principal shaper of post-Stonewall gay politics and AIDS activism. A New York City native, he witnessed the Stonewall riots in 1969 and was an early, prominent member of Gay Activists Alliance (GAA), the first organization to lobby city and state government for gay and lesbian rights. As chair of the GAA Arts Committee, Russo introduced the organization's membership to the pleasures of film spectatorship far from the heckling they found in mainstream theaters. Many gays and lesbians who lacked the courage to claim their rights in public attended Russo's phenomenally popular "Firehouse Flicks" and subsequently joined the gay liberation movement.

Russo's political innovations continued into the 1980s, when he cofounded both the Gay and Lesbian Alliance Against Defamation (GLAAD) and the AIDS Coalition to Unleash Power (ACT UP). In late 1985, as AIDS hysteria and gay-bashing swept America, GLAAD became the first group exclusively committed to securing a balanced portrayal of gays and lesbians in the media. A little over a year later, Russo helped to channel ACT UP's theatrical rage against a government that was criminally serene about the deaths of thousands of gay men, drug addicts, racial minorities, and women. As a person with AIDS and an ACT UP warrior, Russo delivered some of the epidemic's angriest, most eloquent speeches against institutionalized neglect.

Writer and publisher Felice Picano proclaimed Russo "one of the epicenters of communication in the gay world." By his early thirties, Russo had become an undisputed hero within the community. Friends who experienced the hagiography of Vito Russo up close depict his public persona as half matinee idol, half guru. Fellow AIDS activist Larry Kramer notes that "people worshiped [Russo]. To walk down the street with him was like being with a star. His fans rushed to him." Arnie Kantrowitz, Russo's best friend, remembers, "If you went out with Vito, you had to be prepared to stand on the sidelines while he greeted five hundred friends and acquaintances. . . . I felt like an adoring . . . First Lady [in his presence]." Kantrowitz also deems Russo a gay "Martin Luther King" during an era when gay people were starved for "stars" and role models. Kantrowitz's partner, Dr. Larry Mass, ascribes to the public Russo "a magnetism that simply transformed people. . . . He had an inner light of personality that you just wanted to reflect on you and be a part of. When Vito gave one of his talks, there was so much love and affirmation exchanged between him and the audience. There are [such] moments when it's just the artist and the audience. [The audience has] to know the artist is putting himself out there in some way. With Vito," Mass avers, "I saw it all the time."

Russo was also well known beyond the worlds of gay and AIDS politicking. At the dawn of gay liberation, he befriended Lily Tomlin, then a struggling comedienne on the verge of *Laugh-In* superstardom. This close relationship endured for the rest of Russo's life and culminated with Tomlin's narrating Rob Epstein and Jeffrey Friedman's film version of *The Celluloid Closet* (1995). Bette Midler, catching fire at the Continental Baths in 1971, also became an early Russo buddy. During an era when most celebrities shunned the gay press, Russo's friendships with Midler and Tomlin made possible his landmark *Advocate* interviews of them in 1975 and 1976.

Eventually, Russo would number among his friends actress Valerie Harper; composer Dean Pitchford; filmmakers Pedro Almodóvar, Rob Epstein, Jeffrey Friedman, and Jim Hubbard; film producers Howard Rosenman and Craig Zadan; former New York City mayor David Dinkins; current New York state senator Tom Duane; former Massachusetts state representative Elaine Noble (the first open lesbian in U.S. history to hold this office); playwrights Charles Busch and Doric Wilson; groundbreaking AIDS doctors Marcus Conant, Ron Grossman, and Howard Grossman; film critics Richard Dyer, David Ehrenstein, and Edward Guthmann; writers Dennis Altman, Arthur Bell, Malcolm Boyd, Christopher Bram, Michael Bronski, Larry Bush, Howard Cruse, Michael Denneny, Karla Jay, Brandon Judell, Jonathan Ned Katz, Armistead Maupin, Patrick Merla, Michael Musto, Esther Newton, Felice Picano, James Saslow, Sarah Schulman, Don Shewey, Ed Sikov, Mark Thompson, and Stuart Timmons—the majority of whom, along with 150 other Russo friends and fans, have lent their reminiscences to this book.

Perhaps the best indicator of Russo's fame came near the end of his life, when Epstein and Friedman's Oscar-winning documentary *Common Threads: Stories from the Quilt* (1989) featured Russo and gave him an international platform for his AIDS activism. While helping to publicize the film, Russo got to meet and work with Elizabeth Taylor. Their photo together has become an iconic image of Hollywood's initial responses to AIDS. At the time, Russo's friend Allen Sawyer related to an acquaintance that he had just spent time with Russo and Taylor. The acquaintance gasped, "You know Vito Russo?"

Russo's is a representative voice for a generation of gay men who found sexual liberation in the 1970s followed by devastation and mature heroism in the 1980s. He was present for the defining moments of his era, many of which bear his stamp. Russo's papers at New York Public Library include a prospectus for a memoir he had tentatively titled "An Activist Life." It is one of AIDS's countless tragedies that he did not survive to write his own life story, from liberation to loss to legacy.

For his contributions to post-Stonewall activism, for his unprecedented work on gays and lesbians in film, for his centrality to the worlds of gay politics and entertainment, for his galvanizing of AIDS activism with one of its first, and most persuasive, voices—a full-length biography of Vito Russo is long overdue.

1

Birth of a New Yorker

Early in 1980, Vito Russo joined the staff of London's *Gay News*. When he confessed his infatuation with British culture and men to his best friend, activist and author Arnie Kantrowitz, he received this tart reply: "Don't think you'll get away with 'cheerio' and 'ring me up' around here. Acquired British accents crack like stale meringue . . . and we haven't forgotten that you were born on a hot night in Manhattan from Sicilian thighs."

Vito wasn't about to forget his heritage. Had Martin Scorsese's *Goodfellas* been gay film critics rather than Mob hit men, he could have joined their circle without missing a wingtipped step. His wide brown eyes, olive skin, and hairy chest bore the stamp of Italy; his frenetic hand gestures crackled with Sicilian snap. And the city of his birth was obvious whenever he opened his mouth. Vito's take-no-prisoners speech patterns sounded the East Harlem honk known universally as New Yorkese.

Twenty years after Vito's death, we remember him as the author of *The Celluloid Closet*, as one of Gay Liberation's angriest agitators, and as one of the earliest, most eloquent voices raised on behalf of people with AIDS. But we must also recognize Vito as the descendent of four struggling Italian grandparents who landed in New York City some fifty years before his birth. The life that they built for their seventeen children set the stage—or screen, as Vito would no doubt have preferred—for a grandson they could never have imagined on arrival at Ellis Island.

The "Sicilian thighs" of Arnie's letter belonged to Angelina (Annie) Salerno Russo. Vito's mother was the youngest of the ten children of Angelina (née Fituccia) and Ciro Salerno, who had immigrated to New York from Messina, Sicily, around the turn of the century. In the Italian enclave of Manhattan's Lower East Side, they settled at 266 Elizabeth Street and had their first child, daughter Sarah, soon afterward. Another four girls and four boys followed before Angelina Jr. was born on October 13, 1922, on East 1st Street. As the last in a line of siblings old enough to be her parents, little Annie barely knew her oldest brothers and sisters.

Angelina and Ciro had little means of support for their rapidly expanding family. Saddled with a new child every other year, Angelina was confined to home and unable to work or acquire education. After decades in the United States, she could understand English but spoke very little of it, and she never did learn the correct spelling of her married name. Annie's next-oldest sister, Jean, instructed their mother to make a cross for her signature.

Though Ciro had no more schooling than his wife, he learned to call himself "Charles" in work settings dominated by Irish immigrants who scorned Italian greenhorns. The new name fooled nobody, but Charles became passably fluent in English from his odd jobs. As a teenager, Jean was startled to find her father selling lemons on Houston Street. She hadn't heard about this latest gig, one of an endless string. A stint working in New York's new subway system cost Charles four fingers and made him realize he would have to be more careful in future employment. His loss of manual ability would mean the family's starvation.

By the time of Annie's birth, her parents were exhausted from decades of child rearing in a culture that never ceased to seem foreign to them. In 1922, Angelina was forty-four, Charles was forty-eight, and they had had enough of the smelly, jam-packed Lower East Side. Charles got his first glimpse of life north of Houston Street when he heard of a super's job at a powerhouse on 10th Avenue and West 59th Street. A move was finally possible, and the Salernos rented a spacious apartment at 313 West 69th Street. Abutting West End Avenue, it was situated in the middle of another Italian slum—but with fresh Hudson breezes and elegant 70th Street townhouses a block west and north, the new digs represented a considerable step up for the family. When Angelina first stepped off the subway at Broadway and West 72nd Street, she flushed to see impeccably dressed ladies in elegant hats crisscrossing the avenue. She, in contrast, was sweaty and disheveled from her long train ride, during which baby Annie had thrown up on her shoulder. Thereafter, Angelina took pains to dress "like a chicken in the house and a queen outside" when she ventured into her new neighborhood.

The first apartment that Annie remembered had six big rooms and, miraculously, a backyard where the family could raise rabbits and chickens. While it provided far more space than the Salernos had ever known, 313 West 69th was also a cold-water building, and Angelina had to make do with a coal-burning stove. Eighty years later, Jean remembers the apartment's blistering heat as her mother cooked vats of spaghetti and pork chops for children and grandchildren. Dinners during the 1920s found fifteen people seated at Angelina's overflowing table while she toiled in the kitchen. Jean's next-oldest sister, Marie, recalled precious little meat at those family dinners. She would later tell her children that a typical meal included pasta, beans, and vegetables. "Once in a blue moon," Marie noted, "your Grandma would throw a thin sliced frankfurter in a pot of beans. Grandma called it 'chumbroth.'"

Charles was working inordinate hours to put even "chumbroth" on the table. Serving as super both in his new building and at the powerhouse ten blocks south, he arose at two o'clock in the morning, when he began apportioning the building's coal. After fifteen years of this grueling double duty, he grew alarmingly weak and thin. In 1939, throat cancer forced retirement on a man who had driven himself to exhaustion. Lying on his deathbed, he told Jean, "If I knew I was gonna die so young, I would have enjoyed myself a little bit more." In his final moments, he sat up and remarked with wonder to Marie, "The angels are coming."

To sixteen-year-old Annie, Charles's death meant the end of a charmed childhood. The baby of the family, she was protected and fawned over by an array of doting older sisters. Blessed with her mother's pug nose and hazel eyes, teenaged Annie was a striking, leggy girl with long black hair and rambunctious spirits. She had begun ninth grade at the prestigious Julia Richman High School, a modern, five-story facility across town in the tony East Sixties, but her father's illness forced her to drop out of school and take work in a button factory. Desperate for diversion, she attended dances on Central Park's Mall. Near the band shell, she began noticing the stylish East Side blades who also came to West Side clubs, where Annie's moves were attracting attention.

Jean watched in shock as Annie pranced off to Central Park and picked up some vocabulary—"Hello, you frig!"—that would never have escaped her own mouth. Annie's audacity made Jean giggle, but she went stone sober when their older sister Sally asked, "Jen, do you know that your sister's going out with a gangster?" Jean took to waiting on the fire escape for Annie to return home from dates with zoot-suited Angelo (Charles) Russo.

Charles was no gangster. He was a sweet-natured East Harlem Lindyhopper whose nimble steps matched Annie's. The youngest of seven children, Charles was born to Vito and Mary Russo (née Tartaglione), natives of Caserta, Naples, on May 21, 1916. He grew up on 1st Avenue between East 114th and 115th Streets in an apartment directly over a bar. The noise downstairs was no problem, since the Russos were so boisterous that the bar's mayhem seemed muted by comparison.

Charles was raised in a neighborhood that had exploded with Italian immigrants shortly before his birth. From 1880 to 1910, New York's Italian population surged from 12,000 to over 340,000. Many found the Lower East Side too crowded and relocated to "Italian Harlem," or what soon became known as East Harlem, where Vito Russo found work as a stonemason. East Harlem Italians received a chilly reception from neighbors. Until 1919, the flagship church Our Lady of Carmel obliged Italians to worship in the basement. Moreover, while job opportunities abounded in the neighborhood's masonry, iron, stone, and rubber factories, the padrone system of labor often forced Italian immigrants to work for starvation wages. Striving for autonomy in this stranglehold economy, Mary Russo opened her own grocery store on nearby Pleasant Avenue.

The store did a decent business but not good enough for the Russo children to remain in school. Charles dropped out in fourth grade to begin supporting his family. His life at home was distinctly Old World. Some fifty years after moving to New York, Mary Russo performed an exorcism on her grandson to cure him of the "evil spirits" that she thought were causing his headaches. Holiday parties at the Russos' featured bawdy songs and jokes, with Charles decked out as a diapered Baby New Year whose buttocks guests and family targeted with canes. The Russos' earthy household defied Annie Salerno's saltiest vocabulary.

Despite their differences, Annie and Charles enjoyed a "real World War II romance." As a small girl, Marie's daughter Phyllis ("Perky") Percoco witnessed her aunt and uncle-to-be's courtship with swoony awe. "Theirs was the only romance in our family of aunts that was just *out there*," Perky recalled with a sigh. Charles loved to sing, and Annie was mesmerized by his Italian repertoire and his crooning of the sentimental '40s favorites "You'll Never Know" and "I'll Be Seeing You." Charles also relished performing for crowds. At a Police Athletic League benefit in Secaucus, New Jersey, Perky's younger brother Vinny beamed to see Uncle Charles's audience expand beyond one lovestruck West Side girl: "He's a hoot and holler kind of singer. The audience claps to 'Shine Away Your Bluesies,' and dances in the aisles to his robust 'Darktown Strutters Ball.' Then he sings 'Mama,' first in Italian, then in English. At the end of 'Mama,' he starts to cry, removes a big white handkerchief from his pocket, wipes his eyes, and keeps on singing, waving the handkerchief in the air. There's not a dry eye in the house."

On the morning of January 10, 1943, Annie's young niece, Anna, watched rapt as her twenty-year-old aunt, shimmering in white satin folds, left her apartment en route to St. Matthew's Church one block south. The opulence of Annie's gown notwithstanding, the strapped young couple settled for a "football wedding" of copious sandwiches prepared by the Salerno and Russo women and served up at the nearby Democratic Club. One expense not spared the reception was the semiprofessional dancers who entertained guests with their renditions of popular steps—no doubt the same ones that had attracted Annie and Charles to each other in the first place.

Shortly after the wedding, Charles enlisted in the army and was stationed in Hays, Kansas. His rendition of "I'll Be Seeing You" took on new resonance for Annie, transplanted across Central Park and living with her in-laws in East

Harlem. Gazing toward sunsets over the Hudson, she missed her family and her husband. Having never ventured past the New York metropolitan area, Annie decided to join Charles in Kansas, where he was fully occupied with his job of clearing airfields so that army planes could land safely. He had neither the time nor the inclination to focus on his homesick bride. Annie soon rushed back to her mother's house. She'd had enough of faraway lands, which, to her mind, meant anywhere beyond New Jersey.

In New York, Annie was delighted to discover that she was pregnant. She took care of her fragile health and dreamed about her future family. But within several weeks, she suffered a miscarriage. After fainting at the sight of blood on the floor, sisters Jean and Josephine struggled to find a doctor for a wartime house call. By the time one finally arrived, Annie lay devastated on the floor. The fetus, a boy, looked to her sisters "like a little doll, a rubber doll; it had the eyes and everything formed."

Annie begged Charles to return to New York. Under the circumstances, he could secure a leave, but he couldn't yet move back permanently. On one of his visits, Annie became pregnant again and held her breath. Her confidence grew as the baby reached full term. When she went into labor and was rushed to New York Hospital on November 10, 1944, she felt secure. This child would survive, and the Russos would begin their family at last.

At work, Jean received a frantic call. Annie had just delivered a baby boy who wasn't expected to live, and Jean was needed to serve as godmother at her nephew's hasty baptism. Upon arrival, she discovered her dazed sister holding an infant with "white, white long fingers; they called him a 'blue baby'—blue blood, or something." Jean gently lifted the child from Annie's arms as the service was pronounced over him. Unnamed, he died in Jean's arms and was buried in a potter's field. Annie lay in a daze, unaware that she had just lost her second child in little over a year.

Annie fell into a dark depression. Her husband was still marooned in some ridiculous backwater, and during an era when a young wife's primary responsibility was the birthing and raising of children, she had suffered two traumatic failures. The V-J Day jubilation that rocked Times Square, just twenty blocks south of the Salerno homestead, barely touched her.

She rallied when Charles returned to New York that fall and rented them their own apartment at 336 East 120th Street. Once more Annie had to leave her family for East Harlem—and this time for a fifth-floor walk-up—but at least the place was hers, with no well-meaning but noisy in-laws to cramp the young bride's style. Efforts to entertain her family in the tiny living/dining area had the Salernos sitting on top of one another and spilling into the kitchen. But bedroom windows allowed Annie to monitor the 120th Street action while gossiping with her neighbors. On the whole, she was pleased with her new home.

Charles, meanwhile, was suffering a string of professional failures. A Bronx diner foundered, as did a fish store just across the Harlem River. On the store's closing night, Annie and Charles walked quietly together across the 3rd Avenue Bridge back to East 120th Street. They had no money and no car to carry them home. They also realized that Charles, unlike his no-nonsense mother, was not cut out for business. In his son's assessment, "if [a customer] came in and gave [Charles] a hard story, he would give in and say, 'You owe me,' and they never paid. . . . He was too easy."

Despite the Russos' financial struggles, Annie began thinking again of motherhood. The postwar nation was in a cautiously expansive mood, and she wanted to join the celebration. In November 1945, secure in her own apartment, with her husband home to stay, she learned that she was pregnant for the third time.

As Arnie Kantrowitz wrote, Vito Anthony Russo was indeed born in Manhattan and of Sicilian lineage, but not on a "hot night." Thursday, July 11, 1946, dawned uncharacteristically cool for a New York summer. When Vito arrived at New York Hospital at 7:49 a.m., the temperature hovered below 70 degrees and climbed only to 72 later in the day. It was an ironically temperate entrance for the man who always preferred broiling New York heat to any other climate.

Nearly a year after the war's end, the country was still wincing with economic pinch. On the day of Vito's birth, *New York Post* headlines screamed with relief, "Senate Keeps Rent Control"—announcing the death of an amendment that would have authorized 5 percent increases in July, November, and March 1947. But prices of household staples continued to creep up. On July 11, buyers staged raucous strikes in more than a dozen cities nationwide. Between lampposts on Broadway and West 46th Street, protesters strung a clothesline from which dangled a "suit with a $199 price tag, a loaf of bread marked at 40 cents, and a sign that warned, 'This will happen without price control and the [Office of Price Administration, which had ceased operation July 1].'"

Vito was born into a war-weary country struggling to regain its footing. But he was also born into a swinging Manhattan infected with a party bug that it hadn't known since the Jazz Age. Spike Jones and His City Slickers were playing the Strand, while Guy Lombardo and His Royal Canadians held court at the Waldorf-Astoria's Starlight Roof. On Broadway, theatergoers had their pick of Laurette Taylor in *The Glass Menagerie*, Ethel Merman in *Annie Get Your Gun*, Orson Welles in Cole Porter's *Around the World*, break-out star Judy Holliday in *Born Yesterday*, or *Wizard of Oz* (1939) veteran Ray Bolger in *Three to Make Ready*. Longer-running shows included the Rodgers and Hammerstein smashes *Oklahoma!* and *Carousel*.

Films were riding a comparable crest. Orson Welles's latest movie, *The Stranger*, opened the weekend of Vito's birth. Already appearing in theaters were

Eleanor Parker—later the star of his favorite film, the lurid prison melodrama *Caged* (1950)—in *Of Human Bondage*, Lana Turner and John Garfield in *The Postman Always Rings Twice*, Bette Davis (as good and evil twins) in *A Stolen Life*, Gene Tierney in *Dragonwyck*, and the epitome of 1946 sex appeal, Rita Hayworth, in *Gilda*, the homoeroticism of which Vito would one day analyze in detail. Manhattan's revival movie houses, where Vito would spend countless hours, offered Laurence Olivier in *Wuthering Heights* (1939) and Fred MacMurray and Barbara Stanwyck—whom Vito would hail for playing America's first fully realized lesbian screen character in *Walk on the Wild Side* (1962)—in *Double Indemnity* (1944). In other entertainment news, future gay porn superstar Jack Wrangler was born in Beverly Hills on the same day as Vito. From a Hollywood perspective, the boys could hardly have picked a more provocative summer for their debut.

On the morning of Vito's birth, the *New York Herald-Tribune* ran a plea from renowned Presbyterian minister Henry Sloane Coffin on behalf of East Harlem youth: "Thousands of young boys and girls living in east Harlem, a congested area of New York City, have never seen the country. They play in dirty hot streets, lounge around street corners at night, and try to sleep in stifling tenement rooms." Coffin urged his readers to send a child—for the steep sum of $7.50 per week—to Bear Mountain Union Settlement. Through this gift, many East Harlem mothers and children could enjoy, for the first time, flowers, trees, lake swimming, and decent food.

It's unlikely that Annie or Charles read Coffin's heart-wringer. And while they would eventually slave to get their children out of East Harlem, matters weren't so dire in 1946. After a loss of five ounces in his first week, baby Vito's eating habits steadied. By his fourth month, he had doubled in weight, and Annie could relax. This child was going to make it.

Annie took pride in Vito's animated antics, which she interpreted as evidence of healthy masculinity. Before his first birthday, Vito was in constant motion, prompting his mother's affectionate observation, "I can surely say he's a real boy. But I love him that way." For his first haircut, Annie remarked, Vito "took it like a major, he sat very still and looked in the mirror at himself. He looks like a real man now. But he's still a baby to me." At nine months, incessantly jumping up and down, Vito fell hard out of his crib and then out of his kiddy car. At his second and third Christmases, toys were ripe for the breaking, and Vito got right to work.

Shortly before he turned three, Vito's world flipped with the arrival of baby brother Charles ("Charlie"), on April 1, 1949. With his parents' attention diverted, the ambulatory toddler was everywhere. Annie rushed to record her older son's adventures in his baby book: "He has every bad habit you can think of. He crosses street's alone, goes down cellers exploring garbage can's, goes in old broken down houses and bury's dead cat's, takes walks around the block. I'll never forget his play day's they are all to full of mischief. Vito got lost a few hours, we had to go look for him, he came around the block as tho nothing happened. He also follows fire Engines and crossed the street to get to them. He said he had to tell the firemen how to put out the fire." By this point, Vito's reputation preceded him among the Salerno cousins. Before his visits, cousin Joanie would announce to her mother, "Batten down the hatches! Here comes Vito!" Aunt Marie half-dreaded the invasion of the "one-man army" who would arrive at her West End Avenue apartment to "disrupt the whole house" and "consume the whole conversation."

Vito showed a rebellious streak at age five, when he pulled a 1st Avenue fire alarm. When the huge red trucks showed up, lights ablaze and sirens screaming, he hid in the apartment, trembling over his mother's admonition that all the commotion was a manhunt for him. He didn't budge for two days. But he forgot his fear of authorities sufficiently to begin turning in false alarms whenever he got the chance. He was also twice arrested on scorching summer afternoons for opening hydrants with a stick and a piece of wire.

Eventually Vito decided to use the police in a different sort of ploy for attention. During the 1950s, East Harlem boys and men crowded brownstone stoops with nonstop games of pinochle and blackjack. Vito gave them a wide berth. To him stoops were places to read the *New York Times*, purchased with nickels that other kids his age were spending on candy. Still, he wasn't going to be ignored. Knowing that his father was playing craps with some buddies in a nearby alley, Vito flagged down a cop car and led officers to the game. After busting the players, the police kept their higher bills as booty. Charles thrashed his son, astounded that the boy would turn in his own father.

Vito inherited his audacity from Annie. One afternoon, skipping along the street while blowing bubbles, he collided with the neighborhood drunk and her baby carriage. When the impact knocked some of Vito's liquid soap into the carriage, the woman slapped Vito hard enough to mark his cheek. Watching the scene from her apartment window, Annie tore down five flights of stairs and into the street, where, as she reported to nephew Vinny, "I beat the SHIT out of that woman." Vito learned that survival in East Harlem required a certain fearlessness.

Armed with his mother's bravado, Vito found courage in unfamiliar surroundings. On visits to Aunt Marie's, he introduced cousin Perky, nine years his senior, to neighborhood sights she had never seen, dragging her off to explore the nearby railroad so that he could see grounded trains. In his neighborhood, the 3rd Avenue El, the New York Central, and the New Haven Railroad rattle-slammed high above the streets and didn't lend themselves to easy scrutiny even from 336's roof, which he and little Charlie turned into their own beach, party room, and sports arena. Perky, a ground-floor dweller, had never thought to visit her own roof until Vito took her up for a closer look at the sky. Nor had it ever occurred to her to stroll down 79th Street toward the Hudson for a glimpse of the Boat Basin. In shock, Perky could only ask, "'How do you *know* all this stuff?' I mean, he was an amazing, amazing little boy."

In his own neighborhood, Vito began to branch out. By early adolescence, he had become "the Pied Piper of the neighborhood" and was happy to play tour guide for less enterprising peers. June 1960 saw the opening of Freedomland USA, an amusement park in the Baychester section of the Bronx. The jingle "Mommy, Daddy, take my hand! Take me out to Freedomland!" clamored over the radio waves. Vito rounded up a gang of ten from his block and trooped them over to the IRT line at 125th Street and Lexington Avenue—having failed to mention his plan to a single adult. At the park, everyone paid his or her $3.95 for all-day admission and access to the new rides. For poor East Harlem kids who could never afford a trip to Disneyland, and for whom Coney Island required long, sweaty rides on multiple trains, Freedomland was like having Pleasure Island at their fingertips. When the group reached the park, Charlie recalls, "each one of us resembled the kids in *Pinocchio*, running from ride to ride; the theme towns, [the] old-time cars we drove—it was a magical time that none of us wanted to have end." They stayed the full day and night, finally clambering back on the subway well after ten o'clock, chanting the Freedomland theme all the way back home. On arrival at 120th, they discovered an army of frantic parents waiting out in the sweltering heat. Charlie got a single swat on the bottom while his brother was beaten for organizing the journey. Vito didn't mind. Seeing new sights justified any punishment.

Vito's favorite place to go was always the movies. Splashed across the silver screen were colors, fashions, music, and emotions not available at home. When he wasn't leading Perky to the Boat Basin, he was cajoling her to take him to the Lincoln, the Colonial, or the Beacon, grand old movie palaces near her apartment. Whenever Perky planned a screening with her girlfriends, Vito made the rounds to his aunts and uncles, gathering nickels and pennies. A few years later, boys eager to impress Perky would take her to the swankier Paramount and Roxy theaters in Times Square—and boys who *really* wanted to impress her would allow little cousin Vito to accompany them. "*Awestruck* by the lights of Broadway," Vito rocked violently in his seat while memorizing the actors' lines and costumes in order to regale relatives with everything he'd seen. Listening to his perfect imitation of James Stewart in *It's a Wonderful Life* (1946), Perky shook her head and asked, "How do you *remember* what he said?" In response, Vito would bear hug his beloved cousin for taking him where he most wanted to be.

Annie and Charles generally indulged Vito's passion for the movies. Charles enjoyed a good action picture, so when the family attended a film together, it was along the lines of *Somebody Up There Likes Me* (1956), starring the young Paul Newman as boxer Rocky Graziano, or *The Guns of Navarone* (1961), with Gregory Peck and David Niven as Allies wiping out German artillery in World War II. These macho films didn't much interest Vito, but any movie was better than none. By age five, he was spending all his free time in theaters. As Annie remembered, "He practically lived at the movies. Saturdays, he never came home. We had to go look for him, that's where he was. He'd be there seeing the same movie over and over again." Any dimes earned by running errands instantly went into the admission-and-junk-food fund. As a child, Vito later joked, he developed an aversion to natural light.

Vito's parents sometimes found his total disappearance into the movies alarming. Once he discovered 3-D films, he was never home. In his own delirious retelling: "I was nine years old, and thanks to 3D the girl in my lap was Rita Hayworth. The picture was *Miss Sadie Thompson* [1953] and even though I was hours late for supper, I was sitting through it for the third time that day." At *Charge at Feather River* (1953), he "didn't even flinch when Guy Madison aimed a tomahawk at [his] scalp." In fact, the film only got scary "when a hand suddenly shot out of the darkness at [his] throat" and Vito "merely thought, 'Hey, this one's pretty good.' But in the next instant, my old man had me by the back of the neck and dragged me screaming up the center aisle. I wasn't allowed to go to the movies for a month." Though the "big traumatic experience of [his] life was not being allowed to go to the movies," Vito defiantly refused to learn his lesson. Soon after *Feather River*, he accompanied some older kids over to far West 125th Street for a *House of Wax* (1953) screening. Vito noted his cool nonreaction when "Vincent Price tossed a severed head [his] way." Unfortunately, "[my mother] somehow found out where I was and came down the aisle and dragged me out of the theater screaming and I couldn't go to the movies for two weeks. But for a horror movie, I'd go anywhere."

And horror films he saw by the gross. Annie and Charles were happy to subsidize Vito's weekend sojourns to the Cosmo, a 116th Street movie house where Charles had worked as an usher in the thirties. During the 1950s, Vito took little Charlie along with him. With a dollar in Vito's jeans, the brothers traipsed off to double and triple features, especially repeat viewings of *Creature from the Black Lagoon* (1954), *Invasion of the Body Snatchers* (1956), and *The Blob* (1958). Admission cost a quarter each; the rest of the dollar was to be divided between treats and, following the movies, a hot dog or knish and soda at a luncheonette. Vito always blew his lunch money on SnoCaps, Raisinettes, and Mello-Rolls. Charlie had to guard his own quarters against his spendthrift big brother, who had no scruples about muscling in on Charlie's share. When the smaller boy held his ground, Vito dubbed him "Cheap Charlie" and took revenge by terrorizing him at night with *Snatchers*-style warnings: "Don't go to sleep! You're gonna turn into one of them!" Poor Charlie would remain awake all night, praying that a pod doppelgänger wouldn't claim his life.

But even in childhood, Vito's tastes extended well beyond horror. At age ten, he adored *The Bad Seed* (1956), not for Patty McCormack's turn as killer-in-pinafores Rhoda Penmark, but for Eileen Heckart as the alcoholic, grief-stricken mother of one of Rhoda's victims. Equal parts hilarious, harridan, and heart-breaking, Heckart delivered one of "those old fashioned star performances" that would obsess Vito for the rest of his life. Heckart had some competition from Leslie Caron, whom Vito claimed as his "first girlfriend" when he saw her play the title ballerina in *Gaby* (1953). Musicals caught his fancy—as befitting the little boy who, seated in the Peanut Gallery at a taping of *The Howdy Doody Show*, forgot to yell, "It's Howdy Doody Time!" because he was busy humming "Sophisticated Lady." One of his favorite musicals was *The Glenn Miller Story* (1954), starring James Stewart as the legendary band leader. Other gay kids, such as future friend and playwright Doric Wilson, spent the forties and fifties mooning over such smoking-jacket icons as Leslie Howard, Cary Grant, or Noël Coward, but Vito "always hated all those wimps." He'd far sooner catch *Glenn Miller* every day until his exasperated father put a stop to it. When Vito and Charlie got older, they took the 2nd Avenue bus down to East 86th Street, where Loew's and RKO brought back an occasional musical oldie like *Yankee Doodle Dandy* (1942). Vito's enthusiasm was so infectious that even Charlie, already on his way to becoming a gold-letter jock, memorized George M. Cohan tunes right alongside his brother.

The pubescent Vito was also bewitched by a range of melodramas. David Lean's *Summertime* (1955) was perhaps the most lasting, so much so that nearly twenty years later, Vito would reference the film in his courting of a new lover. Katharine Hepburn's lovesick spinster, wooed by suave Rossano Brazzi in Technicolor Venice, somehow spoke to the precocious boy. Adult movies alerted him to the existence of bigotry, as when Constance Ford, playing Sandra Dee's hyper-repressed mother in *A Summer Place* (1959), numbered Italians and Catholics among her many hated groups—though the real draw was watching Dee and Troy Donahue buck social convention right up to their teen pregnancy. Vito cemented his lifelong love of sexual outlaws with a screening of *Where the Boys Are* (1960). Tottering blindly from one Lothario's motel room, "loose" coed Yvette Mimieux gave what Vito deemed "the greatest performance I'd ever seen." At age fourteen, anyway.

Following this sun-drenched triple header, Vito sparked to the amorous cowboys of Howard Hawks's *Red River* (1948). In early adolescence, he gaped to see Montgomery Clift work himself into a lather over John Wayne and enjoy a homoerotic round of shooting with John Ireland. Vito later drew on this moment in an effort to define his burgeoning gay consciousness: "I want to track down what is the sensibility that exists where I could be 14 and sit in a movie house looking at Montgomery Clift in *Red River* and know that there was something different there that I couldn't put my finger on." Naming that ineffable "something" wouldn't happen for many years. For now, Vito simply swallowed movies whole and didn't think much about their hidden meanings.

During the midfifties, Annie and Charles saved up to buy Vito the best possible Christmas gift: his own film projector. Now viewings were possible at 336 East 120th, where Vito could be curator, projectionist, and critic all at once. Naturally, screenings were no fun without an audience, and the same kids who were willing to follow Vito up to Freedomland filled his apartment for free weekend matinees. Vito began to collect short clip reels of the Three Stooges, the Little Rascals, and excerpts from *The Invisible Man* (1933) and *Abbott and Costello Meet Frankenstein* (1948). Across his living-room wall scrambled Bud and Lou, frantic to elude Frankenstein as he pelted them with oil cans. While the reels turned, Vito stood back and studied his friends carefully, gauging their reactions, noting what they found funny or frightening, preening in the knowledge that without his efforts, they would never have discovered these images.

Vito had established his lifelong passion of imposing favorite performances on others. His choice of subject matter wasn't always as jovial as Abbott and Costello. At fourteen, he insisted that Perky and Aunt Marie watch with him the *Twilight Zone* episode "Twenty-Two," starring Barbara (*Where the Boys Are*) Nichols as a harried hospital employee endlessly reminded by a sinister nurse that there is "room for one more" in the basement morgue. Afterward, Vito wrote out on some fifty slips of paper, "Room for one more, honey!" and hid them all over Marie's apartment—"in her bras, in her underwear, in her stove, in her oven, in her pots"—anywhere not available for immediate discovery. The notes were a gift that kept on giving. Marie "would open up something that she didn't use [often], like at holidays, she'd take out a tablecloth that she hadn't taken out for six months," only to find yet another "Room for one more, honey!" her nephew's cackly imitation ringing in her ear.

Ever scouting talent, Vito became Charlie's "agent" and built regular family showcases for his little brother. Charlie liked to imitate Elvis Presley, so Vito helped him decorate his cardboard guitar with rhinestones and fashioned his long blond hair into a DA cut. The boys then presented Charlie lip-synching to Elvis 45s. Another favorite impersonation of Charlie's was Al Jolson, whose records Annie had in abundance. Vito enjoyed putting blackface on his brother for performances of "Mammy" and other Jolson standards. As Charlie now wryly comments, "You do that today and you'd get arrested—but [such] was the entertainment" for the Russos during the 1950s.

Vito didn't confine his agenting to home. Immediately west of their building was a Mafia-owned candy store complete with old-time marble counter and elaborate stools. It also featured a jukebox blaring Dean Martin, Louis Prima, Frank Sinatra, the Coasters, Teresa Brewer's "Music! Music! Music!" Patti Page's "Tennessee Waltz"—a constant, pulsating soundtrack of fifties pop. Vito was the only kid who dared interrupt the beat. He had taken a professional interest in a neighborhood girl named Louise Messina, whose sweet soprano voice he admired and wanted to share with others. Vito's own coins paid for the operatic tunes that brought a rare change of program to the jukebox's Hit Parade. As Louise trilled a succession of crystalline high notes, Vito beamed from a leather stool and tried to ignore the dangerously sour faces of Louise's older brother Johnny and his gang, the Lords. Charlie couldn't resist this golden clowning opportunity: "Louise was getting ready to hit her high note for a big finish. She drew a deep breath and I spun around on one of the counter stools and yelled, 'Can I please have a chocolate ice cream cone?'"

Johnny and the Lords brayed laughter. They'd only kept silent during Louise's aria because she was family and because Vito made a strangely compelling emcee. But Charlie's interjection broke the spell. Mortified, Louise flushed and took flight. Vito rounded on his brother in a rage. Relieved to be delivered from Maria Callas, Johnny and his buddies leapt into the fray, ruffling Charlie's hair and offering to pay for his cone. Vito threw Charlie a scorching glance and stalked off to comfort his wounded client.

Vito enjoyed promoting Louise. But this wasn't his first run-in with Johnny. He no longer felt secure in a neighborhood where his intelligence and indifference to athletics made him a very visible target.

During his infancy, Vito's advanced verbal skills had Annie reaching for the baby book: "At six months, he knew where the radio is, when you ask him where it is he looks right at it, also the light." As he moved into toddler days, Annie noted, "Vito doesn't like to play with his toy's very much, he prefers book's, paper's, and pot's and pan's." With baby Charlie squalling in her arms, Annie decided it was time to send her older son to kindergarten at P.S. 80. Just two months past his fourth birthday, Vito made a smooth adjustment to his new routine. Full of melancholy pride, Annie remarked of Vito's first school day, "he loves it and didn't even miss me."

But school didn't agree with Vito for long. During his first year, he missed 37 days and had to repeat kindergarten. For his second year, he was absent a whopping 73 of 190 days. Vito's teacher expressed grave concern about his social skills, noting that he required an "inordinate amount of attention," was "moderately aggressive," "usually not dependable," "usually restless, hyperactive," had "numerous nervous habits," did "not possess leadership qualities," and "frequently seem[ed] unhappy." The cause of these problems is unclear. Vito suffered a bout of ringworm that may have kept him home and crotchety; he may also have resented the attention that Annie was lavishing on the noisy new stranger in their apartment. In any case, by the end of his second kindergarten year, Annie and Charles decided to take Vito out of P.S. 80 and enroll him at Holy Rosary, a parochial school around the corner from their apartment.

Founded in 1949 by the Pallottines, Holy Rosary School sat on Pleasant Avenue between 119th and 120th streets, less than a minute's walk from the Russos' building. Tuition cost three dollars per month per child—not a minor amount when the family's rent was twenty-eight dollars per month. But the neighborhood was changing. Annie and Charles were determined to keep their boys in Catholic school because it kept them at a distance from the racial tensions then starting to simmer in East Harlem's public schools.

Vito soared at Holy Rosary, bringing home a series of stellar report cards. As soon as possible, he became an altar boy by memorizing lengthy prayer cards in Latin. Spurred by his new success, he befriended the nuns and priests and began spending as much time as possible at school. He found a close friend in Sister Jane Francis, a progressive nun who, before Vito's eighth-grade graduation, came to a party at his apartment in "civilian" clothes. She had left the order and gave Vito his first glimpse of an intellectual life outside the church. She was also among the teachers who encouraged him to follow his dream of being a writer. At age eleven, Vito taught himself how to type on an old manual by transcribing, verbatim, his favorite novel, Bram Stoker's Dracula (1897). The nuns may have been less than thrilled by his choice of text, but they blessed his professional ambition with a doctrinaire nudge: "We need good Catholic journalists to teach the world about Catholicism."

Charlie, meanwhile, was beginning to realize a truth that became inescapable as the boys grew up. "If ever there were two brothers that were complete opposites, it was Vito and I." Vito looked forward to reaching Holy Rosary each morning; little Charlie considered school "prison." He had no ambitions to be an altar boy, much less a devotee of language and literature. Long before puberty, Charlie discovered the joys of sports. He spent his days at Holy Rosary "getting into trouble and waiting for 3:00" so that he could escape to the streets and Central Park for any available game. In school, Charlie seldom kept his vocabulary to parochial standards. His first-grade teacher was a "short, wire-rimmed linebacker" named Sister Benigna ("Italian for ballbuster," the adult Charlie speculates), who, at the end of each day, marched her paired charges out to Pleasant Avenue with military precision. One afternoon in May, six-year-old Charlie spotted Annie waiting for him and raised aloft the Mother's Day gift that he had belatedly collected from Sister Benigna. "Ma, now she gives me the fucking thing!" rang out over the street. Annie decided on the spot that Vito was old enough to walk his little brother home. She didn't realize that in the short distance from Holy Rosary, Vito needed far more protection than Charlie.

With his barbed vocabulary and love of sports, Charlie was a natural fit on East 120th. His teacher's-pet brother wasn't so lucky. Once Annie relinquished the job of shepherding her sons home from school, the journey became a daily gauntlet for Vito. Immaculate in his uniform of pressed dark slacks, crisp white shirt, and blue tie embossed with a gold HRS, Vito was an irresistible target to Johnny Messina and the teenage Lords. For Charlie's sake, he worked hard to ignore the taunts of "faggot" and "queer" that chased him down the street. One day, however, his smart mouth got the better of him.

When Johnny spied the uniformed Russos trotting along 120th, he yelled to his buddies, "Look, here come the Girl Scouts." Vito's patience snapped. There were too many shameful associations bound up with this particular jibe. He'd tried to be a Boy Scout and found it an agony. "I was always the one who, when they gave wrestling lessons . . . would sneak behind the screen and try to play the piano. Then they would come and drag me out and say, 'You're supposed to be in boxing class.'" The Scouts were also filled with boys who would readily fool around with each other on camping trips but refuse to talk about it afterward, never admitting that they liked each other in ways that were starting to obsess Vito.

He stopped dead on 120th and turned to face Johnny. "And your mother's a Campfire Girl" emerged. Not the most prudent comeback, and enough to propel Johnny up off a parked car while his greaser friends egged him on. "You gonna take that from that faggot?!" The answer was an unequivocal no. "You fuckin' homo! I'll kick your faggot ass!" Johnny knocked Charlie over and lunged for Vito. Grabbing his prey by the neck, he slammed the boy against the nearest building and lifted him off the ground head first. Vito's first challenge to homophobia might have been his last if news of the fracas had not reached his father.

Between construction gigs, Charles was home in the middle of the day and in no mood for nonsense. Clad in a tank top, muscles bulging and eyes on fire, he barreled down five flights of stairs and into the street, tearing Johnny off Vito with a powerhouse yank. Vito clutched his injured throat and collapsed to the sidewalk. Charles began to throttle Johnny with such force that several burly men had to be summoned from the corner candy store to free the teenager. The enraged father issued Johnny a parting warning: "If you go near either one of my kids again, I'm gonna wipe the fuckin' streets with you." For a time, Johnny and the Lords kept their distance. But they would be back, and they were far from alone in their attacks on Vito.

The East Harlem of Vito's youth was a crucible of troubled Italian machismo. The Italian Americans once considered immigrant scum by Irish squatters had come to dominate the area by World War II. Pleasant Avenue and its surrounding streets were dotted with Italian social clubs that served as neighborhood anchors. Between 3rd Avenue and the East River, 104th to 120th streets became known as "Little Italy" and took on a flavor familiar to anyone who has seen Scorsese's early films. When Vito watched *Mean Streets* in 1973, he recognized the trappings of his own youth transposed 120 blocks south to the "real" Little Italy. Scorsese's characters, he wrote, "are products of the candy store Italian store-front generation whose mothers iron their handkerchiefs and shirts but otherwise don't exist. They come from scapulars around the neck, blue confirmation suits, envelopes for Sunday Mass, football weddings, Friday night novenas, and flowered print wallpaper. . . . They sat on the stoop at night, opened the fire hydrant in the summer, wore strap T-shirts, made scooters out of wooden boxes, a two-by-four and the front and back of a roller skate. As they grew up they wore silk suits and acted like big shots, mouthing off a lot for the children they used to be. Big fish in a little pond doomed to die without a piece of the real action in life."

Vito knew the authenticity of *Mean Streets*' characters from observation of his own family and neighbors. His uncle, Tony Russo, had been a rodeo rider and amateur boxer at Madison Square Garden, albeit under an assumed Irish name, as Italians weren't allowed to box for money. With dreams of a flashier life, Tony got involved with the Mob, which was omnipresent in the uptown Little Italy of the early to mid-twentieth century. Along with a couple of his brothers, Tony drew a short prison stretch—"went away to college," the family called it.

Vito grew up with plentiful Mob presence in his own building. In February 1957, he and Charlie barely missed a hit in their lobby. After returning from a visit to Grandma Salerno's, they discovered that East 120th Street was crawling with lights and sirens. As they pushed past police barricades, they saw that the action was centered at 336. On the lobby floor lay a bullet-riddled body in a pool of blood. The victim was Tony De Simone, manager of the corner candy store and father of the boys' good friends Donald and Philip. The De Simones lived on three, the Russos on five; on many evenings, Vito and Charlie entered the building with Tony and climbed with him to his apartment before continuing on up to theirs. His body was found in front of an alcove where Vito and Charlie often played hide-and-seek. Spotting the cigarette butts littering the area, the boys realized that the killers had been awaiting Tony for some time. They wondered what might have happened if they'd skipped their visit to Grandma's that day and decided to play in their own building. Or what if Tony had been coming home at the same time they were, as he had on so many other nights? Would he have been spared, or would they all have been killed?

Bullet holes remained in the lobby wall.

Unlike his brothers, Charles did his best to steer clear of the Mob. He had offers to join, but having seen the risks up close, he focused on construction work with his brother Tony. As city planner Robert Moses busily turned New York into his personal Monopoly board, jobs were plentiful. One of the Russos' biggest projects was helping demolish the legendary Astor Hotel in Times Square and build what is today the Minskoff Theater.

At home, Charles was beginning to share his wife's dislike of their sur-roundings. The neighborhood's violence only underscored the family's more routine problems. Even for relatively young parents, bundling two children and groceries up five flights of stairs every day wore on the calves and the lungs—particularly for Annie, a heavy smoker. Also, given Annie's Sicilian volatility, it wasn't always easy for the family to tolerate each other's moods in such close quarters. When Vito and Charlie were young, Annie took a job making artificial flowers at home and enlisted the boys' help. With his mother's taste for the verbal kill, Vito began teasing her about this frou-frou job. Annie repeatedly warned him to back off, but he persisted until reading imminent doom in her face. Although he took flight, the heavy pair of scissors she hurled at him ended up embedded in his leg. Tending to the wound, Annie begged her sons not to report what had happened to their father.

Overrun by two active boys, the apartment became impossible to navigate. Charlie and Vito were forced to share a "very, very small room that today wouldn't even be called a bedroom." With space for only one bed, the brothers doubled up. The room itself wasn't conducive to quiet sleeping; over their bed was an opening through which kitchen noises carried easily, competing with the oath-laden stickball and card matches that dominated East 120th day and night. The boys certainly didn't sleep the night their father hid Joey D, a professional boxer, in the tiny closet behind their bed. Running from the law or a jealous hus-band, Joey arrived over the roof at 336 and directly into the Russos' apartment. Vito rolled over in bed and thought about nearby 2nd Avenue, where downtown buses whisked people away from the craziness of East Harlem.

For now, the only escape was further down the block, to 318 East 120th. The parents-in-law of Annie's niece Camille owned this brownstone and invited the Russos to take up residence one floor above them, on the second floor. Though Annie and Charles agonized over the doubling of their monthly rent—from $28 to $60—the brownstone meant big improvements for the family. They were leaving behind tenement housing in favor of French doors, parquet floors, ample light, and a break from suffocating top-floor summer heat. Unlike 336, 318 had a fire escape, so the boys' play space increased as well.

The Russos' move occurred at a time of tremendous social and architectural change in East Harlem. In the aftermath of World War II, the neighborhood's predominantly Italian composition shifted as Puerto Ricans began arriving en masse. With the area's unofficial Italian border fixed at East 104th Street, Puerto Rican immigrants generally stayed further south, between 97th and 103rd streets, and further west along Lexington Avenue, where each block was "its own self-sufficient world, with its own bodega, *cuchifritos* stand, beauty salon, Laundromat, bar, and church." In 1940, public housing came to East Harlem and inaugurated a trend that would stretch into the 1950s as tenements were bulldozed in favor of the projects that African Americans began to fill. Tensions soon smoldered between the disparate groups, particularly as tenement dwellers, largely Italians and Puerto Ricans, looked with envy on the brand-new accommodations enjoyed by neighborhood newcomers. According to resident Thomas L. Webber, the East Harlem social hierarchy of the fifties put tenement dwellers one step above "homeless junkies." Tenants who contributed to their buildings' upkeep earned grudging respect, but their image plummeted as tenements became rat- and roach-infested and suffered devastating burglaries and fires. Projects, meanwhile, enjoyed regular heat, hot water, fewer if any rats, reliable maintenance, and even occasional gardens. White East Harlem residents were bitterly aware of who had access to this gracious lifestyle and who did not.

As hostility mounted, East Harlem blocks became sharply segregated. Webber recalls that in the 1950s, though an occasional Puerto Rican moved into the predominantly African American projects, he never saw either group spending time on Italian blocks, nor did Italians spend much time in Puerto Rican or African American sections. Boys in the neighborhood parsed themselves in rigidly territorial terms: "Your block or project is part of your identity. It's your turf, where you're from. When guys introduce themselves, it's first name, short pause, block number or project name, as in I'm Freddie . . . Freddie from 105th, or I'm Ray Ray . . . Ray Ray from Carver Houses, or You know Moody . . . Moody from 100th Street."

East Harlem boys came together in two places: the Boys' Club on East 111th Street, and the new Wagner Community Center, which appeared directly opposite the Russos' when the entire north half of East 120th Street between 1st and 2nd avenues was razed. Vito much preferred the Boys' Club, where contact and competitive sports were available but far from obligatory. In addition to basketball, ping-pong, billiards, and knock-hockey in the game room, boys could learn how to play chess or swim in a pool where nudity, oddly, was mandatory. Charlie won medals for his freestyle and backstroke prowess and was named New York City's champion ping-pong player in the eleven-to-twelve-year-old set. Vito hung back while his little brother excelled. At the pool, he cautiously watched the action and kept his telltale reactions in check. He found far greater safety in the drama club, where he could express himself through someone else's words. The young "agent" who preferred to oversee other performers' showcases finally reached the spotlight himself as orphan Sparky, the resourceful lead in Charlotte B. Chorpenning's children's drama *Radio Rescue* (1938). One adult admirer praised Vito for his "enthusiastic responses to telling scenes."

Upon leaving the Boys' Club, Charlie and especially Vito entered much more dangerous territory. Punks lining the nine blocks between the Club and 120th Street remained eternally vigilant for boys wandering onto "their" turf. "Many times coming up 1st Avenue from the 111th Street Boys' Club," Charlie recalls, "I remember us running home, trying to get away from bad things."

Homophobia dogged Vito back to his home block, where he found an equally unwelcome reception at the Wagner Center. Puerto Rican boys loudly branded him a faggot, though with a Spanish epithet that escaped Charlie: "I can still hear them using the word *maricón*; every time he passed by, they would say, '*Maricón*, here comes *maricón!*' and he would just kind of sulk away" to a neighborhood library, where he scored "shopping bags full of books." An inveterate reader, Vito treasured the library both for its holdings and for its shelter from abuse.

Though Charlie frequently witnessed his brother's victimization, he didn't understand its roots. To him, Vito was just Vito; he didn't see whatever it was that other boys saw and attacked. Charlie received an abrupt education when *Radio Rescue* director Carole Schwarts slapped him across the mouth for calling one of Vito's friends, fellow actor Anthony Cuomo, "Cuomo the Homo." In bewilderment, Charlie turned to Vito for clarification. "What's that? Everybody says that." Vito knew the definition but didn't elaborate beyond a gentle rebuke. "You don't understand; it's not something you should say." To his little brother, he wasn't yet ready to admit the sting he felt every time such names blasted him. As far as Vito knew, only one gay man lived on his block: an overweight, brassy platinum blonde named Charles. Even as a child, Vito found Charles hard to miss, so he laughed over the following exchange between an upstairs neighbor girl and her mother:

> DAUGHTER: Why doesn't Daddy dye his hair if it's going gray?
> MOTHER: Men don't dye their hair.
> DAUGHTER: Oh yes, Charles down the street does.
> MOTHER: Oh, that's glandular.

The mother's ignorance was funny, but the realization that Vito might be linked with such a ridiculous figure was not.

In any event, he did not focus long on his fey neighbor. Racial tensions were tearing the neighborhood apart. The new apartments, unsupported by proper city maintenance, were falling into disrepair. Charles Russo's sister Yetta and her two children became rare white residents in one project. Charlie remembers enviously visiting his aunt and cousins when they moved in. Their building had elevators, large rooms, and outside lighting that illuminated the structure at night and made it glow in the dark. Within a few years, things had changed. The elevators stank of urine, and drugs were omnipresent on nearby streets. As white

East Harlemites watched the buildings they'd once coveted deteriorating into slums, they blamed African American residents for bringing down "their" neighborhood. War was on the horizon.

When Vito became friendly with an older black boy named Lucky, he invited him home for a visit. Lucky responded, "Oh, no," and would not elaborate. Vito persisted until Lucky relented and accompanied him to 336. Annie and Charles took pains to make him comfortable, but the boy sat rigid on the edge of the living-room sofa, too tense in a white household and on a staunchly white block to let himself relax. He spent only a few minutes at the Russos' and did not return. Though sensing there was something amiss, Vito did not understand what fueled Lucky's discomfort. The experience provided one of his first glimpses of bigotry beyond homophobia.

Charlie learned the same lesson, if much more violently. At Wagner, he cultivated a friendship with a black boy who shared his love of basketball. He was immediately branded a "nigger lover" and began to suffer regular taunting from his peers. One day the ridicule became too much to bear. In one seething second, he remembered his father's advice: "If anybody bothers you, pick up anything near you and use it on them." Charlie heaved a metal milk crate at one heckler and smashed a stickball bat across the back of another. The blow was so severe that he thought he had killed the boy. Neighborhood parents instructed their sons to avoid Charlie. For the Russos, East Harlem had lost its cozy cohesion. The safe neighborhood of Charles Russo's childhood had degenerated into a battleground.

Charles reluctantly recognized this change after he moved the family to 318. Though he, Annie, and the boys loved the extra space, their second-floor vista put them much closer to the street. Racial confrontations became impossible to overlook. Once as Charles watched from his window, he witnessed a couple of thugs beating a cop. When he barked at them to turn the officer loose, they hollered back, "Shut up or we'll come up there." Despite Charles's obviously muscled physique, he realized that he was unable to protect his family. Annie took the hoods' threat as an ultimatum. "That's it. We're gettin' outta here. This is *bad*. This is gettin' *bad*, this neighborhood."

In Thomas L. Webber's memory, those at the top of the East Harlem social ladder were the ones most eager to abandon the neighborhood. Residents of all races looked up to the "favored few who [had] saved enough money to move out of El Barrio altogether [to] honest to God one-family houses on Long Island or in Jersey." Annie shared this grail view of New Jersey. For years, as their only vacations, the Russos had taken day-trips to the Old Mill picnic grounds and swimming hole in Paramus. Charles got the family up shortly after dawn on summer Saturdays and Sundays and drove them out to the country, where the extended Russo and Salerno clans gathered by 8 a.m. Starting with morning eggs and continuing on through a hearty lunch and dinner, Charles treated the entire group to a day's lavish meals. The party ended only when the park closed at 10 p.m. Throughout those lazy, languid days, Annie looked about the woods and sighed, "Oh, I want to die in New Jersey! I love New Jersey. This is where I want to be. I don't want to be looking out a tenement window; I want to be in New Jersey with the trees!" Fear for her sons' safety on East 120th Street made it easy to forget that her one exposure to "nature," in wartime Kansas, had sent her running back to Manhattan's grime and crime.

Joe Mortillo, an army buddy of Charles, lived in Lodi with his wife and children. During the Russos' occasional visits, Annie realized that Lodi was where she wanted to transplant her family. The Mortillos began to search their neighborhood for available housing and soon discovered a modest Cape Cod at 24 Blueridge Road. A lifelong apartment renter, Annie fell in love with this sprawling new property. It boasted front *and* backyards, separate bedrooms for the boys, a proper dining room, and an unfinished game room in the basement. The $18,000 price tag was staggering but ultimately immaterial. Annie *had* to own this house, had to offer her boys a safer, more civilized life than they could ever enjoy in East Harlem. She set about raising the $500 down payment—nearly nine months' rent in the brownstone. Weeks of begging and borrowing from Russos, Salernos, and friends finally produced the coveted sum. The Russos became the first among their extended families to own a home in the suburbs.

Quite out of nowhere, Annie and Charles fulfilled the postwar American dream. Three members of the family were overjoyed. The fourth left New York in a funk.

2

Jersey Boy

On the afternoon of Sunday, October 1, 1961, the Russos left Manhattan for the last time. Three of them would never live there again. One was already plotting his return.

With one ear tuned to the Yankees broadcast, twelve-year-old Charlie gazed westward. The young jock couldn't wait to ditch East Harlem's cramped streets for the fresh green grass of the Jersey fields. As Charlie watched the Palisades swell through the windshield, the radio suddenly squawked in triumph: right-fielder Roger Maris had just shattered Babe Ruth's record by hitting his sixty-first homerun of the season. Charlie whooped with joy over Maris's achievement—sixty-one homers in '61. The youngest Russo sailed over the Hudson and into Jersey on a cloud.

In the front passenger seat, Annie grinned at her younger son's glee and congratulated herself on giving him access to a world that her hometown could never offer. She glanced away from the Palisades and swiveled in her seat, her gaze drifting over Charlie's head to the receding Manhattan skyline. Craning to the far right, Annie peered 110 blocks down the Henry Hudson Parkway to West 69th Street. For two years, the residential blocks of the West Sixties had been tumbling like dominoes in order to make room for the gleaming marble complex that would soon be Lincoln Center, the Juilliard School, and Fordham Law School. Annie's eyes welled as she thought of the song that she and her sisters sang to each other while their homestead vanished. They borrowed the melody of "Back to Hawaii," but their adapted lyrics were pure West Side:

> It won't be long before those little dumpy flats on 69th Street
> Will be thrown down and then they'll be no more.
> Well I'm just a little Italian . . . a homesick ginny goil,
> I wanna go back to my pasta and oil.

I wanna go back to my little dumpy flat on 69th Street.
With the bookies and the big mouths and the people I love so well.

Annie wiped her eyes. There was no point in getting sloppy. She was doing her duty. No more "nigger lover" taunts for Charlie; no more hoods to terrorize Vito. So what if she had never learned how to drive? Charles could chauffeur her anywhere she needed to go. She mustered a smile and turned back in her seat.

Charles fixed his eyes on the road and tried to concentrate. The pro-Yankees yelps echoing from the backseat were distracting, but Charles shared his younger son's excitement and was overjoyed by the boy's athletic gifts. He was less sanguine about this move. With the exception of his tour in Kansas, Charles had never lived beyond the five-block walk between his apartment and his mother's in East Harlem. He could scarcely imagine how it would feel to fall asleep on a street that wasn't still hopping with fistfights and craps games well past midnight. Still, the move offered irresistible advantages. For years now, on every late-night ride back from Paramus, Annie had badgered Charles with her wish to live and die in New Jersey. After nearly nineteen years of marriage, Charles still adored his wife and strove to do whatever he could to please her. He also had no desire for his sons to see him helpless as cop-hassling punks invaded their old block.

Which brought him to the matter of Vito. Now fifteen, the boy was a model student and had begun expressing himself with a literate vocabulary that Charles sometimes found impenetrable. That was okay; he was proud of the sharp mind that would guarantee his son a bright professional future. But there were other sides to Vito that Charles didn't want to ponder at all. He shook his head, trying to clear his mind. Vito was a good, healthy boy. He just needed a new environment away from certain influences.

From the backseat, Vito squinted at the Hudson glare while trying to ignore both the radio and his brother's hysteria. Roger Who? Like Annie, he turned in his seat and stared through the rear window at his vanishing hometown. He tried to look on the bright side. He had always wanted to live in a house where he and Charlie could run down the stairs on Christmas morning to find presents awaiting them under the tree. Now that dream could become a reality.

Big deal. This move was a disaster. Jersey meant endless days in Paramus without a single subway to whisk him off to parts unknown. It also meant incurring the wrath of crabby neighbors when he innocently plucked flowers from their yards. What was all the commotion about? Nature, when you cared to notice it at all, was there for everyone's enjoyment. Hadn't these yahoos ever been to Central Park?

Then there was the change of schools. A year earlier, Vito had celebrated his eighth-grade graduation from Holy Rosary. That June, in his school keepsake book, he recorded his professional ambition: to become a journalist after attending West Point. "Attending West Point" was code for "surrounding myself with handsome men"—a goal he achieved the following September. He enrolled as a freshman at the all-male Catholic high school Power Memorial Academy (PMA), where he would have been completely unimpressed to learn that one of his new school's future alums was basketball great Kareem Abdul-Jabbar. As far as Vito was concerned, PMA gave him a passport out of East Harlem and a daily excuse to explore Columbus Circle, where Lincoln Center's construction kept everyone in a state of high anticipation. As an added bonus, just when Vito started at PMA, the *West Side Story* (1961) production team was setting up camp on his school's very street to film the Sharks and Jets opening ballet sequence. For a filmstruck kid, no place outside Hollywood could be more exciting.

During his year at PMA, Vito often walked over to Central Park to share a lunch of hard-boiled eggs with his cousin Anna Romanello, who worked at nearby ABC. At their meals, she found him "always smiling" and "always happy" about his successes at school, where he made friends and flourished academically. After years of ducking home from Holy Rosary, Vito had finally found peace. He had no wish to leave it behind.

The Russos' car was exiting the George Washington Bridge. Christmas was nearly three months off. Vito closed his eyes.

A few years before the Russos' move, Lodi historian Lawrence C. Toscano composed a paean to his hometown. Here are two of eight stanzas from "Mister—We Are Proud of Lodi":

> Maybe your ancestors came on the Mayflower to our shores,
> And you feel that gives you the privilege to judge our criteria.
> But may I remind you that many of our people settled on San Salvadore.
> They came long ago on the ships, Nina, Pinta, and the Santa Maria.
>
> But you see Mister, we claim no greatness of that age and Era.
> So cast no stones upon us and do not be too harsh and critical,
> Because we respect all people, love our country, our great America.
> Instead, extend to us your hand without being snobbish or cynical.

Toscano must have seen Vito coming.

By the late 1950s, Lodi had a population of approximately twenty-one thousand, many of whom were employed at the nearby Wright Aeronautical Plant. When not at work, Lodi's residents had at their disposal a wide range of social clubs (American Legion, Lodi Rotary, Lodi Kiwanis, Lodi Women's Club, Lodi Boys' Club) that interested Vito not in the slightest. He was aghast at his new town's lack of diversion. In order to see a film, he had to endure a forty-minute bus ride to the nearest theaters, in Passaic or Hackensack. The closest live musical entertainment was accessible only by car. When the Russos arrived in New

Jersey, future Catwoman Julie Newmar was "pitch[ing] curves" in *Damn Yankees* at Cedar Grove's Meadowbrook Dinner Theater; she was followed that season by Jack Carson in *The Music Man*, and Mamie Van Doren in *Wildcat*. This wasn't Broadway by a long shot.

The Russos' new home sat roughly a mile from the town's commercial center. This distance presented no problem during clement weather, but as autumn froze into winter, it meant a bitter walk to the area's shops and to Vito's own sanctuary, the public library. He escaped for hours into reading, trying to forget that he'd landed, in his brother's phrasing, in "*Ozzie and Harriet* and [*Leave It to*] *Beaver* territory." In the weeks prior to the Russos' arrival, Lodi's two hottest news items had been "Police Issue More Than 300 [Parking] Tickets" and "Mayor Warns Young Main St. Loiterers," that is, the teenage boys who sometimes congregated opposite Borough Hall after midnight, to go home. This was news? Vito couldn't help summoning up Thelma Ritter as the caustic nurse in Hitchcock's *Rear Window* (1954): "I've handled enough of [these] red pills to put everyone in Hackensack to sleep for the winter." As far as Vito could tell, everyone in Lodi was still asleep from *last* winter, without the benefit of Nurse Ritter's meds.

Luckily, Vito found plenty of excitement at home. Starting in October 1961 and stretching over the next twenty years, 24 Blueridge Road served as party central for the Russos, the Salernos, and countless friends of Vito and Charlie. By taking the suburban plunge, Charles and Annie gave their city-bound families access to a world they had only read about in *Life* or *Good Housekeeping*. Cars from the Bronx, Queens, and Manhattan started lining up early Saturday morning. As guests piled out and wandered toward the dining room or backyard stone patio, they were greeted by the distinctly Italian stylings of Jimmy Roselli, Jerry Vale, Lou Monte, Louis Prima, Connie Francis, Dean Martin, "and of course the king, MR. SINATRA."

As he had at the Old Mill picnic grounds, Charles served as principal chef. Summertime lunches were barbecue feasts of sausage and peppers, ribs, hot dogs, and hamburgers accompanied by a huge mozzarella, tomato, and red onion salad. Beer and wine flowed through the afternoon and into dinner, when Charles outdid himself weekly: linguine with white clam sauce and baked clams, platters of fried flounder filets, fried shrimp by the basket, spaghetti with tangy crab sauce, and, on special occasions, lobster gravy made fresh from Tommy Russo's fish store in the Bronx. Even when Charles suffered layoffs, he was determined to share his new home in style. Parties lasted until after midnight, when younger visitors often didn't want to accompany their parents back to New York. They begged to spend summer weeks at Aunt Annie's, which was fine by her.

Nieces and nephews weren't the only children present. The Russos' house was located on a friendly block of small, look-alike Cape Cod homes whose tidy lawns teemed with kids around Vito and Charlie's ages. Next door lived Dianne

Wondra, who was two years behind Vito in school, and whose best friend, Carol De Simone, came to consider the Russos' her second home once she began dating Charlie. Carol spent many an afternoon dancing with him to Dion and the Belmonts records in the basement game room, which Charles had pieced together from eclectic materials picked up on construction jobs. She considered Annie a second mother, always ready to offer advice, and none of her other friends' fathers could crack her up like Charles could.

For a time, Carol didn't notice the fourth member of the household. In her mind, Vito was only her beau's big brother, hardly worth a second glance—until the afternoon that he burst from his bedroom, one of Annie's skirts draped over his shoulders, and came careening down the stairs, declaiming at the top of his lungs verses that he had lifted from some unidentified play or movie. Carol and Dianne looked up in wonder at this impromptu performance, realizing that a unique force had entered Lodi society. How would other kids respond to him?

In October 1961, Vito restarted his sophomore year at Lodi High School (LHS). The school was a rambling, relatively new (1934) structure with imposing Doric columns and a handsome white cupola atop the entrance. High, plentiful windows looked out on a wide green lawn sprinkled with young trees. Situated above the Saddle River, LHS gave Vito his first taste of a school not completely ringed by concrete.

He entered a class of 240 students, 2 of whom were black, the vast majority of whom were Italian, including 4 Russos. Lodi's own Mayor Focarino was a member of the English department. LHS took pride in its well-educated faculty. During Vito's junior year, 13.3 percent of New Jersey's teachers lacked certification. At LHS, however, all thirty-two instructors held bachelor's degrees, while nineteen had also earned their masters'.

If Vito was impressed by his new school's academics, he gave a wide berth to its extracurricular activities and is notably absent from his sophomore and junior yearbooks. His eleventh-grade portrait shows a pale, scrawny boy in a black suit and tie. Disheveled hair and an extremely tentative grin give the impression that he arrived breathless at school and didn't want to be photographed in the first place. His next appearance, shockingly, is as the newly crowned king of the junior prom, held at the upscale Bow and Arrow Manor in nearby West Orange. Charlie, who ended up prom king for his own sophomore and junior years, isn't sure whether LHS students chose their royalty by election or random drawing, but he does remember that the honor made Vito and their parents very happy. It must have been a surprise to the boy who had kept a deliberately low profile for two years.

At the LHS of the early sixties, jocks ruled the roost, and it didn't take them long to discover the new bookworm in their midst. It might be perfectly okay for athletes to don cheerleader drag for the Thanksgiving pep assembly, but woe to any other boy who seemed less than a total he-man in gym class. Vito took considerable abuse, but he also found champions who protected him, ordering would-be tormentors, "Leave that guy alone." His ethnicity may have earned him some safety. Carol De Simone jokes that "LODI" stands for "Lots of Dumb Italians," who often vented their hostility on kids of other nationalities. As Vito's Irish Mexican classmate Ronnie Giles recalls, "I was the only kid with red hair and freckles in a town filled with Guidos, Giuseppes, and Anthonys—and those were just the women. So I got the crap beat out of me regularly." As a full-blooded Italian American, Vito may have accrued some default security. He may also have benefited from being Charlie Russo's brother. What jock would attack anyone related to the little dynamo whose picture was already dominating local newspapers?

Vito began to emerge from his shell in jealous response to his brother's phenomenal athletic successes. At his first basketball game, three seconds from the final buzzer, Charlie sank the winning basket and was engulfed by fans. At his first football game, he similarly scored the winning touchdown and was carried off the field on teammates' shoulders. Lodi Thanksgivings meant ritual attendance at Charlie's football games, with Annie and all the aunts decked out in corsages. Vito chafed at these massive shows of support for Charlie and shunned his brother's games. He also resented bitterly the attention that Charlie earned from their father. More than a decade later, the wound still stung. "One thing I've seen very clearly," he wrote, "is no matter how much I accomplish, it's hard to let go of a need to be appreciated (approved of) by my father (who always expressed all his pride in my brother the athlete, coach, champ, etc.) . . . it's . . . a nagging, pissed off feeling which manifests itself in a certain reckless hostility." As a teenager, he struggled to tug some of the spotlight back from his little brother.

During his senior year, Vito became the exchange editor of the *Jefferson News*, LHS's student paper. Assuming this position required some courage. One year earlier, the *News* editorial staff had been entirely female, while its business staff boasted one lone boy in a sea of girls. During Vito's tenure, the numbers were slightly more balanced: five boys and seventeen girls on editorial, three boys and thirteen girls on business. Vito refused to let sexism keep him from his first byline.

After submitting a favorable review of William Golding's novel *The Lord of the Flies* (1955), he discovered that working on the *News* gave him a professional excuse for returning to Manhattan. He wangled the plum assignment of reviewing the new Broadway musical *Oliver!* In his virgin effort, Vito tried to engage readers' senses directly: "The musical score makes you want to tap your feet and it literally puts you in just the right mood for the right scene." Other features in the same issue do not carry Vito's name but do bear his stamp: a note that Richard Burton, soon to open in *Hamlet* on Broadway, is filming *Night of the Iguana* in

New Mexico (actually Mexico); a survey seeking students' opinions on the most popular movies of 1963 (the choices *Lawrence of Arabia* and *To Kill a Mockingbird* are flanked by *Call Me Bwana, What Ever Happened to Baby Jane?*, and *Gidget Goes to Rome*) and the most popular TV variety show of 1963 (*Judy Garland* heads the list of choices). Another question in the survey doesn't sound at all like Vito but offers a vivid snapshot of Cold War paranoia distilled for high school consumption: "What do you think 1964 will bring to the United States?" Possibilities include "world leadership," "we will get a man on the moon," "we will be communistically controlled," and "World War III."

Vito's work on the *News* made him more outgoing and better able to express himself orally as well as on paper. On the day of President Kennedy's assassination, he raced through LHS corridors, pausing briefly at classroom doors to deliver the news. A few teachers got angry, thinking he was playing a tasteless joke. But most took it seriously because Vito had a reputation for reliability and intelligence. In Ronnie Giles's Sales and Advertising class, nobody doubted what Vito had to say. As Ronnie puts it, "It was like those old . . . commercials: 'When [E. F. Hutton] talks, people listen.'" By his senior year, Vito had accumulated enough credibility that his journalism teacher chose him as the sole LHS student to see the brand-new World's Fair site in Flushing Meadow, Queens. Vito reported back to classmates on the beauty of the fair's iconic Unisphere.

As his prominence grew, Vito nonetheless despaired of fitting in among Lodi youth whose tastes differed wildly from his. On the night of the Beatles' February 1964 arrival in New York, he sat home, indifferent to the white-hot quartet. To his ears, the pop music that enthralled his classmates—anything by the Fab Four, the Kingsmen's "Louie Louie," the Angels' "My Boyfriend's Back," Frankie Valli and the Four Seasons' "Candy Girl," Bobby Rydell's "Swingin' School"— could not compete with Garland's torchy wail in "The Man That Got Away." Still, eager to establish a playboy image, he threw a couple of decadent parties and got himself hauled into court when one of his guests damaged a neighbor's property. The judge, a close friend of one of Charlie's coaches, tossed the case out. On the surface, Vito was relieved, but the outcome troubled him. How many times would he have to depend on his little brother to get him out of a jam? When would he be able to defend himself without anyone's assistance?

In the hermetically sealed world of 1964 Lodi, self-reliance was not easy for a gay adolescent. For the yearbook blurb accompanying his senior portrait, Vito listed as his likes "weekends, N.Y., vacations, and girls." The latter was by no means wholly untrue; Vito was often more comfortable with female friends than he was with other males. But in deliberate echo of many boys in his class, he included "girls" in his roster in order to promote his heterosexuality among peers. In reality, his physical experience with girls was confined to some enjoyable "doctor" sessions with a neighbor and two "steady" years with a classmate at Holy Rosary. "If that wasn't love," he insisted, "then there's no such thing. I hung on this woman's every word."

In twelfth-grade homeroom, alphabetical order placed Vito Russo one seat ahead of Lucille Sanzero. Like Vito, Lucille was a Lodi transplant. She had come to Jersey at age twelve, when her family moved from Scranton, Pennsylvania. Also like Vito, Lucille considered herself a misfit. Younger than the majority of her classmates, she was a shy, bookish girl who deemed her time at LHS "some of the worst years of [her] life." Lucille quickly learned that "the popular kids were very vocal towards those of us . . . who weren't." LHS girls were intensely cliquish and given to wearing initial-embossed sweaters to indicate who was socially acceptable and who wasn't. Lucille's darkly exotic, heavily Italian features cut her no slack with the school's princesses, who scorned her avid study habits and turned study-hall periods into a nonstop nightmare of teasing. Her extremely strict parents also won her no points.

Shooting through this adolescent gloom, "the sun" entered Lucille's life at the beginning of her senior year. When Vito took his homeroom seat in front of her, Lucille found herself fascinated by this painfully thin boy who always seemed to wear his pants too short and too tight. "He was enthusiastic, had boundless energy, had a zest for life—nothing bothered him; he was always happy. . . . People used to tease him. . . . I think they probably used the word 'fag' . . . and he outwardly brushed it off. It didn't appear to bother him. That was another thing that impressed me about him. He was just his own person." For his part, Vito was happy to chat up an articulate girl, particularly one who shared his aversion to "people who won't let you argue," the sole dislike that Lucille cited for her senior yearbook portrait. Vito was charmed by this smart cookie whose father, an employee of the *Newark Star Ledger*, inhabited the professional orbit to which Vito aspired. He and Lucille soon exchanged class rings.

Annie and Charles, no doubt relieved to see evidence of Vito's interest in girls, welcomed Lucille and her parents into their home. Up in his bedroom, Lucille admired the wide-eyed Margaret Keane "waif" prints adorning Vito's walls. She listened patiently to recitals of stories he had written and enjoyed his impressive collection of Garland albums, which he played, imitated, and dissected at length. How passionately Vito sang along to his records! "I can just see his ebullient personality talking about Judy. . . . He could do a *fabulous* impersonation with gestures—I can [still] see his broad, grand gestures of Judy singing." Vito and Lucille's relationship never quite reached an exchange of "I love you"s, but they did discuss the possibility of living in Manhattan after marriage. Vito also promised to squire Lucille to the Academy Awards when he got nominated for Best Original Screenplay.

Looking back on his relationship with Lucille, Vito—always more conversant in the dates of his favorite films than in the dates of his personal milestones—stretched the time of their dating from one to three years. He also claimed that they had sex. Lucille places their entire relationship within senior year and insists, with a laugh, that they "never got past first base." Shortly after their graduation from LHS, Vito escorted Lucille home from a date. When she invited him in, they began kissing in a vestibule just past the front door. Emboldened, they climbed up to Lucille's bedroom and continued making out, unaware that Mr. Sanzero had spotted them. Bedlam ensued. "My father tore open the door, began shouting at us, and threw Vito out. It was *mortifying* for both of us, and pretty much right after that was when he broke up with me." Lucille was beyond bewildered; she could only assume that Vito's embarrassment drove him away. Heartbroken, she wanted the relationship to continue.

Vito told a different story. Following the breakup, he turned to Carol De Simone for comfort. In Carol's memory, Vito sobbed convulsively in her bedroom, devastated that Lucille had dumped him. Carol took his shattered word for it. Like Lucille, she never questioned what he was doing with a girl in the first place.

There is no reason to doubt Lucille's version of events. There is, however, every reason to doubt Vito's. By June 1964, on the eve of his eighteenth birthday, Vito realized that his future did not include heterosexual dating or marriage. He genuinely liked Lucille, but her father's inopportune entrance gave him an excuse to end a relationship that he could not pursue. Fully aware of his homosexuality, Vito had become involved in gay circles both in and outside LHS. While dating Lucille, he was living the double life of most pre-Stonewall gay men. Typical of Vito, he did it with a flair that would have put men twice his age to shame.

Whenever Vito told the story of his coming-out, he invariably began with praise for New York City. He recognized that there were gay people living all over Manhattan and counted himself lucky that he "never had the experience that you always hear from so many lesbians and gay men of growing up in a small town where there were no other gay people and thinking that you were the only one in the world." But even if he had not spent his first fifteen years in New York, Vito would not have suffered the isolation common to his gay generation. In his family were two older, openly gay cousins who provided him with the invaluable knowledge that gays were "we" rather than alien "they." The family might not have spoken approvingly about these cousins, but they *did* speak about them—often—and language breeds reality.

As a little boy, Vito loved to toss water bags off the rooftop at 336 East 120th. His accomplices were cousins Maria "Chickie" Salerno, daughter of Annie's brother Tony, and Vinny Percoco, Aunt Marie's son. Annie whipped all three for the infraction, but Vito was willing to take any punishment for adventures with Chickie. Eleven years older than Vito, teenage Chickie "scandalized" her family with her butch appearance and the switchblade in her back pocket. Vito, on the other hand, "was just *fascinated* by her; [he] thought she was *great*!" He looked up to Chickie as "the classic '50s dyke. You know, tough, black leather jacket, duck-tail hairdo, slicked back with grease." He listened with relish to tales of Chickie's exploits in a girl gang and gleaned that she'd spent some of her adolescence in jail, though he was not quite sure of the cause. Her permanent decampment to California in 1957, when Vito was barely eleven years old, made it impossible for him to grill her for details.

Chickie's full story is far more dramatic. When violence forced her out of the house at age fifteen, she took to the streets. Looking "like a little boy," she lived in subways and hallways until a friend took her in. Chickie didn't realize that this friend was hiding drugs in the apartment. She also didn't know that said friend had packed drugs in the suitcase that she gave Chickie to take with her when she moved out. Subsequently arrested for not wearing three articles of women's clothing, as per New York State law, Chickie slashed a cop with her switchblade when he began beating her female companion. Between the drugs, the assault on an officer, and clothing violations, she was remanded to the Bedford Hills Correctional Facility for Women, where she spent the next three years. Whether Vito ever learned the particulars of Chickie's tale is unclear. But without question he adored this unapologetically lesbian cousin who asserted herself during a time when women of all orientations generally deferred to men.

Born in 1940, Vinny was six years older than Vito and a far greater influence on him. Omnisexual from puberty, at fifteen he nearly became a father (false alarm), contracted gonorrhea, and experimented, guilt free, with male friends. With his "overt distaste for authority," Vinny wore a Star of David, gift of a trick, in the Italian Catholic West Sixties and sported hickeys, gifts of various tricks, all over his neck. Detectives caught Vinny with another boy and an older man, prompting beatings with a broom handle and a belt buckle from both his parents. Throughout the ordeal, Vinny maintained that he was not "molested," that he genuinely liked his sex partners, and that whatever he did with them was absolutely "normal."

Shortly after this confrontation, Vinny moved out of his parents' apartment and in with his first boyfriend—in the same building, five stories below. His place became a nonstop party palace, one of whose most frequent visitors was little cousin Vito, agog at the clutch of sailors fresh off the Hudson and more gay men than he had ever seen in one place at one time. Among the throng was drag legend Lynne Carter, whom Vinny proudly introduced to Vito with the epithet, "It's not a she; it's a he!" By 1960, Carter was a fixture on the drag circuit. He numbered Pearl Bailey and Josephine Baker among his fans, had starred in New

York's notorious Jewel Box Revue drag show, and later played the Apollo, the Bon Soir, and Long Island's Town and Country. He would eventually be the first female impersonator to sell out Carnegie Hall. When he met Vito, Carter favored the teenager with a rendition of "Leave Transylvania," a vampire spoof from his latest show. The crowd at Vinny's roared, and Vito realized he had found a second home.

Having openly gay relatives and acquaintances made it easier for Vito to acknowledge what he had already known about himself for years. He first realized his attraction to boys at age four and began scoping out Manhattan's male scenery as soon as possible. Though he enjoyed shepherding Charlie to Freedomland and Yankee Stadium, once Vito realized that the subway ran downtown as well, he left his little brother behind to go exploring on his own.

One of his first destinations was the Museum of Natural History on West 77th Street, where he stared for hours at the dinosaurs and the famous battling squid and whale diorama. Of greater interest, however, was the unmistakable gay scene on adjacent Central Park West. In the early sixties, pioneering activist Dick Leitsch attested that the avenue from 59th to 86th streets "was one long bench from corner to corner, solid with gay men. Hundreds and thousands of them walked back and forth singularly, in couples, and in groups." Frequent harassment from patrol cars—"Keep moving, faggots. Keep moving"—did not much dissuade the men, who simply pretended to vacate the area until the police had left. Some gay men, such as Vito's future friend and fellow activist John Paul Hudson, found the scene too intimidating to join. "I would hunker down beneath the [museum's] equestrian statue of Teddy Roosevelt in the protective shadow of his mighty steed's magnificent balls and wistfully watch the big boys bravely promenading across the street on Central Park West. But I wouldn't haul ass over, CPW being too close to the unknown for comfort." Longing for connection, teenaged Vito stepped into the fragile community. "I would see men that I was interested in [and] talk to them and sometimes give them my phone number, but I was always too scared to do anything." At least twice Vito approached men not because he found them attractive, but because they were clearly gay and he wanted to make contact. Spotting him for jailbait, the men remained aloof. When he confessed his age, they fled and left him feeling more cut off than ever.

During his last year at Holy Rosary, Vito found a confidant in Sister Jane Francis, the teacher who eventually left the order and the Catholic Church. He felt that he could talk with her about any issue. Except one. For weeks he wrestled with how to tell Sister Jane about a personal "problem" that he could not share with anyone else. But even with her, he could only hint at the problem; he lacked the language to name homosexuality beyond a dirty joke or a parkside proposition. Ultimately, he didn't have to say anything. On one of their many walks from Holy Rosary back to Vito's apartment, Sister Jane abruptly remarked, "I got up in the middle of the night last night and I figured out what you were talking about and I said, 'Oh, my God!'" Though she was no more direct than he, they knew that they were discussing the same topic. Realizing that it was probably "the first time she had ever even considered such a thing," Vito marveled at Sister Jane's ability to perceive his "terrible sin" without a single criticism. She was, as he commented with understatement, "pretty openminded" for a 1960 nun.

Sister Jane provided Vito with badly needed adult sympathy. His parents reacted with horror when he began to explore his sexuality, especially since Annie suspected that a priest had already molested Vito. Extremely young at the time, Charlie remembers many heated conversations between Annie and her sisters over "that sonofabitch" and what he had allegedly done to her son. He more clearly remembers a later episode in which his father discovered that a stepnephew living in their building had had sex with Vito. Charles had to be physically restrained after attacking the man on the street. This is surely the incident to which Vito was referring when he related that Charles "went out with a hatchet to look for some guy because [Vito] had sex with him."

The notion of Vito's homosexuality was simply more than Charles and Annie could accept. As an adult, Vito recalled, "[I had] a lot of confrontation with my parents, a lot of hurt, around that issue. Every time when I was ever sexual with another man . . . they found out about it . . . [and] it was incredibly traumatic." The worst instance occurred when Charles discovered Vito with an older boy who had taken him to the movies and spent the night. At eleven, Vito was only "experimenting," but to Charles, relative degrees of sexual involvement did not lessen the crime. Both Vito and his partner "got the shit kicked out of [them]," and Vito received "hysteria and screaming and lectures from [his] father about how dreadful this was and lectures from [his] aunt about how these people were the scum of the earth. . . . All these confrontations had this ominous ring to them: 'These people' were cursed by God and it was a sin and it was sick and 'these people' were perverted and how could [Vito] have anything to do with them?" For the time being, Vito didn't answer such questions.

But he was developing a defiant insistence about his sexuality. No matter the pitch of his father's rhetoric or violence, Vito refused to stop having sex with men. Thanks to an experience at church, he soon stopped honoring Catholic doctrine as well. "I went to confession and told this priest that I was having sex with this guy. And of course he recognized my voice because, you know, every week he was hearing me say this, so he says finally, 'Look! Enough is enough! Next time I'm not giving you absolution.'" That did it. Vito thought to himself, "Who the hell cares if he doesn't give me absolution? This is absurd!" He recognized that even when he had followed Church directives to "'confess' these 'awful' feelings, on some level [he] couldn't believe a *word* of it." With serene self-confidence, Vito realized that "there was nothing wrong with being gay, that [the church] was full of shit and this was all just a guilt trip." He came to understand that if being gay "could be so natural to who [he] was, then it had to be okay. [He] also knew that [his] only real choice was whether to express it openly." For a working-class, Italian Catholic teenager, this was a stunningly precocious conclusion to reach nearly a decade before Stonewall.

When Vito arrived in Lodi, he found no equivalent to Central Park West or Vinny's apartment. In his isolation, he turned to his most reliable source of comfort: the movies. As luck would have it, American and British filmmakers were finally ready to deal openly with homosexuality. Of 1961's cinematic output, Vito merrily noted: "The movies obviously grew up just in time for me."

On February 23, 1962, an anguished shot of Shirley MacLaine appeared on the cover of *Life* magazine with the caption "A Tortured Role in a Daring New Movie." The movie was *The Children's Hour*, an adaptation of Lillian Hellman's landmark play (1934) about two schoolteachers accused of lesbianism by a malicious student. When the story had been previously filmed as *These Three* (1936), the scandal was diluted to an allegation of heterosexual adultery. By 1962, Hollywood was ready to take Hellman's story on its own terms. *Life* spotted similar boldness in the recent films *The Mark* (1961), the story of a heterosexual child molester (Stuart Whitman), and the British film *Victim* (1961), about a closeted lawyer (Dirk Bogarde) and his attempts to bring blackmailers of gay men to justice.

Vito devoured the article in a single gulp and shoved it under Aunt Marie's nose for her reaction. She didn't disappoint. "Three sick movies, none of which you should see." He didn't need an embossed invitation. With gay-themed films popping up everywhere and family disapproval guaranteed, Vito practically sprinted to the theater.

First up was *Victim*, which gave him an excuse to return to Manhattan. The import was confined to the artsy Paris Theatre, opposite the Plaza Hotel. Its distributor had scorned Production Code warnings to cut the word "homosexual," which had never been heard in an English-language film. Mainstream release was forbidden. That was fine by Vito, who knew that he was watching a film that Hollywood didn't want him to see. *Victim* shows its gay protagonist, Melvin Farr (Bogarde), in a sympathetic light. Though married and deeply ashamed of his homosexuality, he takes extremely risky legal action as one man after another falls prey to a blackmail ring. Vito squirmed in his seat when the blackmailers, trying to scare Farr off, painted "Farr Is Queer" in huge white letters on his garage door. "Queer" was a word that Vito had heard all too often directed at him; seeing it broadcast so boldly from the silver screen was almost unendurable. But he listened with wonder as a police captain defended gays to a bigoted colleague: "If the law punished every abnormality, we'd be kept pretty busy, son!" And his jaw dropped to hear Farr's tortured roar to his wife that he had "wanted" the young man whose suicide sets the story in motion. Despite the character's audible self-disgust, Vito recognized in Farr his first "homosexual hero," one who implied that "maybe it was okay to be gay."

A game stretch, but one that warmed Vito up while he waited for the bus back to Lodi that cold February night. Winter 1962 introduced another homo-erotic film to heat his blood: Sidney Lumet's *A View from the Bridge,* based on Arthur Miller's play (1955), which gave Vito his first sight of two men kissing on screen. The kiss comes as an assault when longshoreman Eddie Carbone (Raf Vallone) plants one on unwitting pretty-boy Rodolpho (Jean Sorel) in order to "prove" the youth's homosexuality. Eddie's accusation "burned a hole" in Vito, but the moment contained an undeniable erotic charge. And the clean-cut blond Rodolpho was Vito's physical ideal.

A few months later, he caught *Advise & Consent* (1962), which director Otto Preminger adapted from Allen Drury's bestseller. This film required a hike to Passaic's Capitol Theatre, but it was worth the trip for a glimpse inside a gay bar—a notorious first in mainstream American film. Senator Brigham Anderson (Don Murray) goes hunting for his blackmailing ex-lover at Club 602, where a male throng listens to Frank Sinatra's queasy crooning as swirling lights pinpoint their haunted faces. Vito's eyes bugged to see the handsome Brig cruised by three pinched queens who give him an unmistakable once-over. They bugged harder still to see Brig take flight from the bar, pursued by the hunky blond, whom he shoves face first into a puddle. Later, when Brig drew a straight razor across his own throat, Vito sat "horrified." He recalled, "[The film] impressed upon me that homosexuality was something so terrible that you committed suicide. I came home on the bus after seeing it, in shock. I had seen a character whom I identified with—I knew what I was—and this is what happened to him."

The fatalism of these movies was terrifying. Vito had left Manhattan positive that homosexuality was acceptable. Now in Lodi, he needed to find friends to convince him that he was right. There was no way he would let himself end up like the suicides and outcasts populating the new gay screen. He began scanning LHS's male population with furtive interest.

Looking back, Carol De Simone realizes that the boys of the LHS crowd she shared with Vito were gay. Along with Vito's neighbor Dianne, Carol happily dated several of them after she and Charlie broke up. Despite the pronounced homophobia at LHS, she never suspected the boys' homosexuality. She and Dianne, Carol remarked with a shrug, "never judged [their] friends that way."

Vito and his gay friends discovered one another much as Vito had recognized men on the streets of Manhattan. "Gaydar" was alive and well in 1963 Lodi. Nearly every day after school, the quartet would meet at wooded railroad tracks in town to discuss the two topics that mattered most to them: reading and boys. For their first meeting, one boy instructed Vito to "bring anything [he thought was] interesting" to share with the group. Typically, "anything interesting" meant a letter one of them had received or an article they could discuss. The themes of their texts weren't important; the boys simply wanted an opportunity to converse in a manner that their peers would have found bizarre outside a classroom. Safe in the woods, they also had the chance to light up Marlboros and review their crushes on straight boys in town.

Vito didn't share any overtly gay-themed literature with his buddies. But his constant library visits had unearthed a pulpy trove of it. At age twelve, he introduced himself to literary scandal via Polly Adler's memoir *A House Is Not a Home* (1953). Manhattan's most successful madam in the twenties and thirties, Adler spun a yarn to which Vito could well relate. Through hard work and indifference to social mores, she rose from desperately poor immigrant roots to a social network that included film stars and politicians. Given her line of work, much of Adler's narrative is necessarily heterosexual, but she touches on a number of topics already growing dear to Vito's heart: a casual friendship with boozy torch singer Helen Morgan, a tantalizing hint that one of her former employees has ascended to Hollywood royalty, an improbably chaste romance with Oscar winner "Wally" Beery. It endeared Adler to Vito even more when, at the Times Square opening night of the *House* film adaptation (1964), he got to sit behind Sophie Tucker and collect autographs from several starlets who played Adler's "girls." His date, Dianne Wondra, marveled at Vito's unself-conscious ability to approach celebrities as if they were just anybody.

Adler's memoir and the film reassured Vito that sexual "morality" is a more flexible concept than society generally acknowledges. She accounts for her career choice with an unruffled aplomb that Vito adopted for himself on the spot: "I am not apologizing for my decision, nor do I think, even if I had been aware of the moral issues involved, I would have made a different one. My feeling is that by the time there are such choices to be made, your life has already made the decision for you." Adler casts her professional decision in terms of inevitability that anticipate gay pride rhetoric by nearly twenty years. She also expresses a comfort with homosexuality that is extraordinary for a book published during the McCarthy era. Some of her employees, she acknowledges, are lesbian. Some are "troublemakers," some are "very peaceful souls," but in Adler's placid estimation, lesbianism simply "occurs in every walk of life." Gay men bother Adler not in the least; in fact, she is delighted by the antics of "three queer boys" in drag, and she adores her dishy hairdresser, who is "regarded by [her] girls as the ultimate authority on matters of appearance, taste, style and grooming" and is, more importantly, "the only real friend" Adler's employees have. Vito could hardly have hoped for more compassionate treatment of his emerging identity.

The first overtly gay novel that Vito read was *Maybe—Tomorrow* (1952) by "Jay Little" (aka Clarence Lewis Miller). As an adult, Vito recalled liking the book for its happy ending: protagonist Gaylord Le Claire lands himself a quarterback hunk. He apparently didn't remember what an agonizing path "Gay"—who seems a refugee from some pre-Stonewall *Pilgrim's Progress*, so allegorical is his sexual development—must endure before finally snagging Bob Blake, jock of his dreams.

At the novel's opening, Gay is a high school senior fraught with "melancholia, emotional frigidity, [and] feminine symbolisms." A tormented teen who likes trying on his emasculating mother's wedding dress, he spends entire paragraphs wishing he'd been born a girl. When Gay escapes tiny Cotton, Texas, for New Orleans, he gets an education in camp humor and vocabulary that Vito eagerly imbibed. Like Vito, Gay mistakes his first drag queen for a woman; he also learns the terms "crabs," "sixty-nine party," and "glory hole." Gay's lover, Paul, warns him about closeted quacks who promise heterosexual "cures" while lusting after their patients and counsels Gay that although homosexuality makes for a "hard life," they are but two of countless gay men stretching back to "the beginning of time." Like his unnamed ancestors, Gay must follow his heart and do "what seems natural" for him. Ultimately, Gay does just that, moving to New Orleans with Bob and deciding that "if loving Blake was a crime for which society would never forgive him he didn't care." Despite its considerable hand-wringing, *Maybe—Tomorrow* introduced Vito to the possibility of gay self-respect. All he had to do was follow the protagonist's example and ditch his small town to find it.

While stuck in Lodi, however, Vito continued to pursue his fascination with the world's oldest profession. Kenneth Marlowe's *Mr. Madam: Confessions of a Male Madam* (1964) appeared the year of Vito's high school graduation. He devoured it at once, thrilled to learn "that there was also such a thing as a loose man." *Mr. Madam* opens with all the misery of *Maybe—Tomorrow*. In his introduction, Dr. Leonard A. Lowag labels Marlowe's life "degrading" and "pathetic," while Marlowe argues in his own preface (plaintively titled "Why?") that "homosexuality is not a convenience. It's a hell of a problem. Homosexuals are what they are because they have confused sex for love." But Marlowe's boyhood aversion to baseball and his failure at Boy Scouts were reassuringly familiar, and Vito snapped to attention on reading that in boyhood Marlowe turned himself into a "size queen" by test-driving a wide range of peers. He also felt a surge of recognition at Marlowe's description of his new gay friends: "There's an immediate acceptance by them. You've shared forbidden experiences, forbidden lusts. You have a kinship." From daily talks with his LHS friends, Vito appreciated this brand of camaraderie.

And he couldn't miss the book's nascent politicking. Repeatedly arrested in bar raids and for running a stable, Marlowe gets fired from a hairdressing job when his boss discovers that he moonlights as a drag queen: "We don't want any of *your kind* here" (emphasis in original). He attacks gay men who take out female "beards" twice a week while dating men every other night. Most strikingly, he informs skeptical readers, "Homosexuals aren't lepers, you know. We're people." Echoing rhetoric of the early homophile organizations, Marlowe declares homosexuals "a minority group who are denied their human rights!" and argues, with conservative prescience, "If homosexuals ever organized, banding together for mutual protection and rights, like other minorities, they could exist without bondage as long as they publicly behaved themselves as thinking adults."

Vito wasn't ready to organize for rights. Oppression meant enduring his father's rage, not losing a job or an apartment. Yet Marlowe's seedy, campy milieu felt very comfortable. Before he finished high school, Vito had already begun to find gay friends well past the literate trio he met at the tracks.

Two acquisitions broadened Vito's social life beyond LHS and Blueridge Road. The first was a fake ID, procured for the express purpose of getting into gay bars. The second was his own wheels, obtained when Charles bequeathed to him a finned old rattletrap. Where the backseat should have been were yawning holes through which exhaust fumes rose into the faces of Vito's passengers. Carol De Simone's mother gave Vito some old sofa cushions to cover the holes, et voilà! He had his own means of transportation, which enabled him to disappear for long stretches outside his parents' vision and explore a very different social life than that offered in Lodi.

Vito's first drag-queen contemporary was a fellow student who could have given Kenneth Marlowe lessons in flash. Standing six feet two inches under a bleached-blond mane, Billy knew how to make a striking entrance—particularly when bombing around Lodi in his pink Cadillac convertible. Contact with Billy meant automatic social ostracism. "If you hung around with him," Vito asserted, "that was it; your reputation was ruined. You were gay." The majority of the student body gave Billy plenty of space. But Vito, amazed by his nerve, "moved immediately to become his friend because [he] knew that [he] had something in common with this person." Billy invited Vito to a New Year's Eve party held at the home of "the most outrageous drag queen in Bergen County." At this party, Vito met the men who would become his best friends for the next several years and introduce him to gay life.

Billy's friends were working-class drag queens from Lodi and the nearby towns of Garfield, Bloomfield, Hackensack, and Paterson. Like Billy, these men were wildly out of the closet, almost unwittingly so: they were "identifiable on the street whether they liked it or not. They couldn't hide it even if they tried." From them, Vito got his first lessons in gay survival. He listened attentively to their tutorials on "how to take care of [himself] on the streets and be funny and get out of a raid and go through a window in a bathroom and all that stuff you had to know in the '60s." The older queens had suffered at length for their appearance and responded with a gutsy sass that Vito immediately adopted. "Honey," one growled, "I'm from the old school; me and the queens from downtown Paterson came up the hard way. Anybody tries to mess with this bitch'll be teasing a bald head."

The older queens were only too happy to introduce an eager novitiate to the local bar scene. From *Mr. Madam*, Vito had some sense of gay life on the Jersey Shore. Bradley Beach was hustler heaven; the Asbury Park Y hopped all weekend long. But he didn't know how to find these places, and anyway, where could he just hang out with friends and have fun? He soon learned that Asbury Park, like Seaside Heights, boasted an impressive array of gay bars. Another favorite haunt was Danny's in Fort Lee, where the group went to see "Bella from the Bronx," a drag queen whose act consisted of traditional Italian families' reactions to the revelations of their gay children. For obvious reasons, Vito found this routine uproarious and went every weekend. He was also enamored of the headliner at Fran Bell's in Nyack, New York. Fran herself, a more stylized rendition of cousin Chickie, donned a tuxedo and top hat and crooned "Just a Gigolo" à la Dietrich. Then there were the drag balls at Newark's Robert Treat Hotel. Vito's social life was like a page from *Mr. Madam* come to life.

From his friends, Vito learned a campy affect that he would cherish all his life. After the buttoned-down years of Catholic school and serving as LHS's star journalist, it was exhilarating to go "'riding around' at night with the other gays and proposition[ing] truck drivers on the highway out of an open window at 60 mph: 'Hey, wanna fuck an Italian actress?'" The new slang Vito was learning could fill several dictionaries. He quickly caught on when the queens addressed him as "Mary," and nothing was funnier than tales of the nearly deaf, ninety-year-old Arthur Cohen, who, stopped by a highway patrolman demanding to see his license and registration, turned to his friends in the car and shrieked, "Who's she calling a cocksucker?" These queens, who fought with fists flying, forever shattered for Vito any equation of effeminacy with weakness. Typical exclamations at each other's apartments included, "Listen, bitch, how would you like to eat pastina for the rest of your life?" and "Don't fuck with my man, you tacky cunt, or I'll put your lights out."

Through this circle, Vito discovered a place he had read about but never thought to visit on his own. In one of his favorite novels, Auntie Mame tells her nephew Patrick that a visit with the snooty Upsons is costing her a weekend "out at Fire Island with some of the most amusing boys." Vito was certain he knew who Auntie Mame's "boys" were and why they congregated on Fire Island. The picture sharpened when he read Polly Adler's assertion that "the island was popular with the long-haired boys and the short-haired girls, and they showed up in swarms." Vito tucked these nuggets away for future reference.

One Friday night in the summer of 1966, a group of friends picked Vito up on Blueridge Road. He told Annie he was off to Seaside Heights for the evening and piled into the car. After riding some distance, Vito realized that the car was headed east, not south. He asked the driver, his buddy Joey Foglia, "Don't we have to get on the Garden State Parkway?" Joey responded, "We're not going to Seaside Heights; we're gonna go to Fire Island!" Vito's reply, informed by Auntie Mame and Polly Adler, was an unqualified "Oh, *great!*"

When Vito stepped off the Cherry Grove ferry for the first time, he realized that the "world" didn't exist on Fire Island. He gasped at the male smorgasbord spread out before him. "I never realized there was a totally gay place before. I mean, I'd heard that Fire Island was gay, but a place where you could do any-thing, and not be bothered by the straight world?" Here the woods didn't con-tain just four gay students cautiously dishing their latest boy-crushes; they contained hundreds of barely clad gay men openly seeking the same sport in the moonlight. None of his reading had prepared Vito for the orgiastic sight of the wooded "Meat Rack" that separates Cherry Grove from the Pines. Cruising guys in the shoreside bars was one thing; cruising them under the stars for im-mediate sexual gratification was something else altogether. This was galaxies away from the covert hunting on Central Park West just a few years earlier. Vito had never felt so safe in nature or so at home in his own body.

On arrival, Joey hooked up with a Montreal native who offered lodging to the entire Jersey gang. Vito was secretly relieved. He was willing to sleep on the beach if necessary, but the great outdoors was never his favorite setting, and ac-cess to a bathroom meant being able to clean up for the Ice Palace. In pre-disco 1966, the hall was an unadorned oasis. With a floor made of "old, shiny wood worn away by dancers, it was very rustic, very beach-y." Cool ocean breezes blew through the open doors while the DJ spun, over and over, Chris Montez's ballad "The More I See You." But there was also an unexpected throwback to Annie and Charles's courting days. To Vito's delight, some of these guys liked to Lindy. Looking back in 1987, long after the island had become outrageously ex-pensive and the Ice Palace impossibly noisy, Vito remembered its 1966 incarna-tion as "nothing fancy. There were no amenities the way there are now; there [were] no poolbar and cabanas and organized doody-doos. . . . [There were] just a lot of people having a good time." In the arms of innumerable male cuties, the pounding Atlantic surf echoing his steps, Vito was overjoyed to be one of those people.

Three frenzied days later, duty called. The Jerseyites dragged themselves down to the dock and caught the last possible ride back to Sayville, Long Island, where Joey had left his car. Their boat wasn't the sleek ferry that would later ease transportation between Long Island and Fire Island; it was a so-called bucket, named for its resemblance to "a bucket of blood." In this rickety sloop, Vito sagged, sun scorched, his feet aching, "The More I See You" still ringing in his ears. Joey and another friend, Greg, slumped at Vito's sides. Across the aisle, their lesbian cohort Jo Jo grinned at this spent gay portrait. "Look at these three; they don't want to go home, do they?" Vito looked up. "No." Jo Jo asked, "You guys want to stay out here all summer?" "Yeah" was Vito's immediate reply. Jo Jo smiled. "You're exhausted. You should go home and get some sleep." Vito knew she was right. But as he headed toward New York, Vito realized that the weekend had been "a revelation." He could now imagine the idyllic world that gay men and lesbians might create on their own.

Back in Lodi, Annie was a wreck. Vito was twenty years old, no longer a baby, but he was still living under her roof, and this three-day vanishing act just wasn't acceptable. She was fairly sure that he hadn't gone to Seaside Heights as he had said. But where? With whom? And why didn't she ever meet these friends who occupied his every weekend?

Vito approached Lodi with a twinge of guilt. As revelatory as the weekend had been, he had no desire to worry his parents. On the whole, he reasoned, Annie and Charles "put up with a *lot* from [him] that a lot of parents simply would not have put up with." Considering their conservative background and lack of education, they gave Vito "virtually no trouble at all." His years of being caught in bed with boys were past, and in any case, Charles was too exhausted by twelve-hour workdays to notice what Vito was up to. When he arrived home after 6:30, all he wanted to do was eat his dinner and collapse on the couch.

Annie, however, was not so encumbered. Her part-time job at the local Modell's department store left her plenty of time to worry about her kids. She issued an ultimatum: either Vito introduce her to these mysterious friends or stop seeing them. He readily complied. He loved his friends and wanted his mother to meet them. On the other hand, he couldn't help but wonder how she would respond to a group of guys who, even when they weren't in drag, tooled about New Jersey in full make-up. He invited his friend George, better known as Brandy, home for a visit. Stunned, Brandy replied, "Do you know you're the only friend I have who ha[s] the nerve to bring me in their house and introduce me to their family? Everyone else is ashamed of the way I look." Vito swallowed hard, grimly determined to show Brandy a hospitable time and prove that at least one of his friends was proud to know him. When they arrived at the Russos', Annie greeted Brandy warmly but then recoiled. She maintained composure throughout the visit but rounded on Vito the second Brandy left. "He was wearing make-up!" she screamed. Vito remained cool. "So?" As his mother sputtered, Vito decided to up the ante. At the next visit, Brandy wouldn't be the only drag queen on Blueridge Road.

A few months later, Vito invited a bunch of friends to share Christmas Eve with his family. Annie and Charlie settled into the living room with everyone while Vito played bartender. Realizing that his friends would be nervous, he poured with a heavy hand and distributed lethal cocktails all around. Joey took a sip of his and announced, pointing at Vito, "Boy! When she makes a drink, she really makes a fuckin' *drink*!" The room fell dead silent. Annie might have been offended by the profanity on Christmas Eve, but under these circumstances, she barely noticed it. That kid had just called her son "she." Unmistakably.

Vito shot Joey a look and steered the conversation in a different direction. The room buzzed, glad to bury the gaffe, while Vito studied his friends. He realized that he would have had no social life without them for the past few years. These were the same guys with whom he had just met Barbra Streisand in Philadelphia, where, when her outdoor concert was rained out, the diva proved accessible at her trailer door. And they were all planning a trip together to Montreal's massive Expo '67 the following summer. But Vito also knew that in certain important ways he was outgrowing these men. They didn't share his interest in education, and they had no desire ever to leave New Jersey. The Shore/Fire Island circuit was more than enough for them. Vito saw a very different future for himself.

Ironically, he was building that future in the heart of New Jersey. Following his graduation from LHS, Vito enrolled as an English major at Fairleigh Dickinson University (FDU) in Rutherford. The last place he wanted to be was stuck at home with his parents, but Annie and Charles couldn't afford to send him anywhere that would require tuition and housing. The mortgage payments at 24 Blueridge were high, and Charles's work situation remained precarious. He did, however, manage to pay one full year of Vito's tuition on a fluke. Reading the *Daily News* one morning, he spied the number 310 on a license plate in the comic strip *Smitty*. With a "what-the-hell" attitude, he called up a bookie and told him to play the number. It hit. Charles raced home, threw his paper in the air, and yelled through the house, "We got the tuition!" Otherwise, Vito was on his own, which meant substantial student loans and choosing a college within quick driving distance of home.

At FDU, Vito summoned the courage to do something he had avoided since his days back at the East Harlem Boys' Club: get up in front of an audience to perform. FDU offered a Play Production class that had been under the energetic guidance of Bertha Ayres since 1948. Ayres assigned Vito prominent roles in such "sophisticated" plays as Luigi Pirandello's *Six Characters in Search of an Author* (1923), Terrence Rattigan's *Separate Tables* (1954), Brian Friel's *Philadelphia, Here I Come* (1964), and J. B. Priestley's *An Inspector Calls* (1945), starring Vito as Inspector Goole.

He became active in FDU campus life by joining the Film Arts Club and getting himself elected the Student Council Fine Arts Board chairman. Vito found his student council work especially rewarding. The board secured Dr. Martin

Luther King Jr. and F. Lee Bailey as campus speakers. For entertainment they engaged Jack Jones, The Four Tops, The Happenings, and The Magnificent Men. In his Film Arts capacity, Vito cautiously brought gay-themed movies to a campus that found such subject matter deeply shocking. During a single semester, he screened *The Children's Hour* and Kenneth Anger's intensely homoerotic *Scorpio Rising* (1963) three times—occasioning his surmise that although he wasn't officially out on campus, he probably "wasn't that difficult to spot."

Of necessity, Vito remained closeted at FDU. But he tried to take on homophobia in a sociology course. After months of discussing every minority save his own, Vito put up his hand and asked the professor, "What about homosexuals?" In the Rutherford, New Jersey, of the mid-1960s, this was a nitroglycerine question. "The class went crazy. Crazy. And the teacher said, 'Wait a minute, wait a minute—all right, homosexuals are a minority.'" Then, gazing directly at Vito, he asked, "Why did you bring it up?" Vito flushed, gulped, and answered, "Because I know a lot of people who are gay." Recounting this experience more than a decade later, he commented, "[It] stands out in my memory more vividly than anything else I've ever done. I don't think I've ever been ashamed of anything as much as I was ashamed of that. And it hurt me so much to have to sit there and deny" being gay. On the spot, he vowed, "[I] would never, ever do that again, I would never, ever deny—that if anybody asked me, I would always admit [my sexuality]. Because it hurt so much not to be able to stand up in front of that class and say, 'I'm in your class; I've been in your class for two semesters now, and you're talking around me.'"

Vito's silence was understandable given the climate at FDU. He didn't find comrades even where he might reasonably have expected them. In Play Production, he knew of "several gay men and at least one gay woman . . . but nobody talked about it. *Nobody* talked about it to each other." Vito "slept with all of [his] English teachers" and "had some disastrous encounters with women who wanted to prove something," but by this point, he knew that he was otherwise inclined.

Vito visited his first Manhattan gay bar with an FDU friend during the World's Fair (April 1964–October 1965). In an effort to "clean up" the city for mobs of tourists, Mayor Robert F. Wagner posted in the windows of gay bars big, white cardboard signs proclaiming in bold black letters, "This Is a Raided Premises [*sic*], New York City Police Department." Many of the bars also suffered a policeman standing guard at the door in a clear attempt to intimidate patrons. Vito recognized the degree to which his sexuality put him at odds with city government. He also understood that the Mafia's widespread control of Manhattan gay bars made for a complicated relationship between crime, justice, and the simple desire to enjoy a drink with his own kind.

During other escapes from FDU, Vito visited his first bathhouse, the St. Marks, on East 8th Street. As a college sophomore, he had gathered some sense of the East Village as the "capital of hippiedom," which seemed to promise a certain degree of sexual tolerance. With a friend in tow for moral support, Vito trudged up the dingy marble staircase, paid his three-dollar entrance fee, and entered the "dilapidated old fire trap." If he had hoped to find a bevy of cute young things like himself reclining on sparkling tile, he was sorely disappointed. The hallways were filthy and crawling with "lost souls and seedy drunks" who made Vito wonder why he'd bothered to take the trip in from Rutherford. The St. Marks didn't even afford its customers the privacy of rooms; it offered instead dank cubicles so tight that "you couldn't bend over . . . in any way." Men lurked inside these tiny spaces, hoping to lure in passersby, until, as frequently happened, "there would be a great crashing and stomping of feet and six men in suits would come rampaging down the hallway, slamming all the doors shut and screaming 'Keep those doors shut, you queers.'" Vito cowered inside his cubicle. His caution notwithstanding, he still got swept up with all other patrons during a raid. Terrified to contact Annie, he allowed himself to be bailed out by a friend's mother who, he suspected, would be more understanding than his own.

Following his visits to 24 Blueridge with the Jersey queens, Vito did not tell his mother about his sexuality. He had learned this lesson from one queen who counseled him, "If your mother asks if you're gay, deny it left and right. They can't prove a thing." Despite the Jersey circle's flamboyance in wardrobe and affectation, they did not endorse the notion of honesty with families. They instructed Vito that if by some tragic turn his parents *did* find out that he was gay, he should move to New York immediately so as not to "disgrace" them. In this milieu, Vito could not conceive of romance between two men. When Chuck, an FDU friend, confessed his love, Vito shot back that "he was full of shit: 'You don't love me.'" Even with his ever-widening circle of gay friends and acquaintances, Vito went through much of college in emotional lockdown.

He realized that he couldn't survive in this mode. He had to begin relating to other gay men as more than tricks. Ever since his eureka moment in the confessional, Vito had accepted that being gay was an immutable facet of his identity — and a central one at that. He had too much self-respect to allow a repeat of his performance in class or to sleep with professors who couldn't face him on campus.

At an FDU New Year's Eve party, Vito met a sweet guy, Lenny, who invited him home not just for the night but for the weekend. Like his first trip to Fire Island, this experience showed Vito a new element of gay rapport. Prior to Lenny, Vito had never pondered spending time with a man after sex. The goal was to meet, enjoy each other's bodies, and then get back to the "real," respectable world as soon as possible. Lenny showed him that physical pleasure could be combined with emotional connection. Vito was astonished to realize that such kinship between two men could be "the most natural thing in the world." And what a relief that their shared weekend "was not fraught with any kind of meaning about what it is to be 'queer' and to be doing this kind of thing for the first time." The weekend made Vito recognize his own capacity for affection and kindness toward another man. It also made him determined to find other men who thought that being gay meant more than a shared, shameful orgasm.

During his trips to New York, Vito discovered the tiny but tenacious world of gay publishing. On Thanksgiving weekend in 1967, Craig Rodwell opened the world's first gay bookstore, the Oscar Wilde Memorial Bookshop, at 291 Mercer Street in Greenwich Village. With only twenty-five titles to offer, Rodwell refused to sell pornography and was "determined to have a store where gay people did not feel manipulated or used." On opening day, signs in the window and inside the store proclaimed "Gay Is Good" at the "Bookshop of the Homophile Movement." At Oscar Wilde, it was possible to purchase the gay magazine *ONE*, which had been founded in Los Angeles in January 1953. Though the publication eschewed any overt politicking on behalf of gay rights, its national distribution did provide countless gay men with their first understanding that they were not alone. Featuring articles on entrapment, gay sexuality, bar life, and even fiction (including one story by Norman Mailer), *ONE* helped give "an oppressed minority the chance to express thoughts that had previously been barred from public discourse." Through *ONE*, Vito became aware of the Mattachine Society New York (MSNY), an East Coast offshoot of Los Angeles' Mattachine Society, one of the country's first gay-rights organizations, founded in 1951 by Harry Hay. He also became aware of MSNY's president, Dick Leitsch, the man who would plant in him the seeds of gay militancy.

At twenty-nine, Leitsch was a well-to-do Kentucky native with no particular interest in gay politics. Believing that the "only three significant letters in the word 'homosexual'" were "*s*, *e*, and *x*," Leitsch "entered the [gay] movement 'dick first'" with the philosophy that "homosexuality is 10 percent cause and 90 percent fun." But when Donald Webster Cory (aka Edward Sagarin), the author of *The Homosexual in America* (1951), ran for MSNY president despite his contention that homosexuals are "disturbed individuals" who "tend to be goofers" if not "borderline psychotics," Leitsch decided to enter gay politics full force. He ran against Cory on the platform that "homosexuality is *not* a sickness, disturbance, or other pathology in any sense, but is merely a preference, orientation, or propensity on par with and not different in kind from heterosexuality." Leitsch vowed to end police entrapment of gays and to eradicate their suffering under homophobic law. He won the MSNY election over Cory by a margin of two to one.

New York's fledgling gay-rights advocates were ready for a charismatic leader. In April 1966, Leitsch went on the attack against police harassment of gay bars. He decided to stage a theatrical "sip in," in which he, bookstore owner Rodwell, and MSNY officer John Timmons, trailing reporters from the *New York Times*, the *New York Post*, and the *Village Voice*, dared Village bartenders to honor the State Liquor Authority (SLA)'s prohibition against serving liquor to known homosexuals. Less than a year later, the SLA lost its legal ability to "revoke [a bar's] license on the basis of homosexual solicitation." Leitsch and MSNY had begun to defang the laws that targeted gays in public places. His media-friendly successes earned him a spot on *The David Susskind Show* in February 1967.

As MSNY president, Leitsch extended the organization's educational outreach to American colleges and universities. A coordinator at City College of New York thanked him for providing "a friendly discussion rather than a rote lecture," noting, "I learned much about the function of the Mattachine Society and of laws concerning homosexuality." Denison, Ohio State, and Hofstra, where Leitsch proposed to discuss sodomy law reform, requested visits as well. As his reputation grew, students from across the country began contacting him. A Grinnell senior, terrified of the draft, confessed to Leitsch, "The prospect of donning those dismal army khakis without the masterful touch of Balenciaga or Schiapparelli leaves me frigid."

Vito decided to put Fairleigh Dickinson on Leitsch's tour of duty. He paid several visits to Leitsch at his Upper West Side apartment, often in the company of Madolin Cervantes, MSNY's heterosexual vice president. It was, Vito later declared, "the first time I ever heard gay people talk politics. Gay politics. . . . They were simply talking about being allowed to live without being subject to attack." Besides, Leitsch's banter had a familiar ring; his free application of "she" and "auntie" to other men sounded very much like the Jersey queens. Vito had to share this funny, brave man with his benighted classmates and professors. He persuaded FDU's Student Activities to pony up one hundred dollars for Leitsch to come lecture on campus. With the force of an atomic explosion, Leitsch arrived in Rutherford at 10 a.m. on March 6, 1968.

For the occasion, Vito managed to gather an audience of roughly one hundred—not bad, he thought, considering FDU's terror of the subject matter. In the crowd, he spotted "the inevitable closet queens (about whom everyone 'knew' anyway), several 'interested' professors and scores of ostentatiously heterosexual couples in tight physical embrace." After receiving Vito's decorous introduction, Leitsch shattered the pomp by branding himself a "good old fashioned cocksucker." The remark was intended to disarm, but the FDU audience had no idea how to take it. Leitsch's term was one seldom voiced in public, much less in an academic forum. Out in the throng, Vito noticed "a *lot* of hostility . . . a lot of laughter. A lot of disdain." Later at lunch, Vito's political science professor—"a droll, quick-witted woman from the Joan Blondell school of classroom technique"—pulled him aside to remark, "Some day, cookie, they'll shoot you in the streets if you push this thing."

Vito bristled at the recommendation of self-censorship. Near the start of his college career, he had promised himself that he would never hide again. Now with graduation approaching, Vito renewed that promise with a resolve to put both Jersey and the closet behind him for good.

3

Return of the Native

Vito sat stunned in a Village dive. It was shortly after 3 a.m. on June 5, 1968, and Senator Robert Kennedy had just been assassinated in Los Angeles. The news settled over the assortment of drag queens, transsexuals, leathermen, Warhol superstars, and gay transients who regularly swamped Mama's Chick'N'Rib, the restaurant where Vito was working as a counterman and waiter. In light of the assassination, his graduation from FDU three days later seemed very small potatoes. He asked for eight hours off to celebrate with his family.

Following the ceremony, a Russo tornado was brewing at 24 Blueridge. Nineteen-year-old Charlie had just finished his freshman year of college and was about to become a first-time father. He was understandably distracted when the local bakery delivered a vast whipped-cream sheet cake for Vito's party. It was too big for the kitchen refrigerator. How to keep it cold? Lightbulb! Charlie laid the basement refrigerator on its back and slid the cake inside. A perfect solution. Then his father arrived home and began screaming. "You stupid fucking sonofa—you coulda blown the house up!" "But I saved your cake for you!"

As his father and brother vented their Italian passions, Vito climbed the stairs, rubbing his temples. RFK had just been murdered—two months after Dr. King—and these two were yelling about cake? He thought about his arriving guests. The Russos and the Salernos were used to such scenes; no doubt they'd be chiming in momentarily. But Vito's professors were a different story. He didn't want them seeing his family at their most volatile. Out in the yard, he joked to his former teachers, "I don't know how I got into this family." Everyone chuckled, but Vito felt a flash of guilt. He knew the remark was bitchy and not fair to his parents, who had spent a fortune they didn't have on this party. He also knew that his father had been cooking for days when he should have been resting after work.

Vito realized that Jersey brought out the worst in him. It was one of several reasons why he began plotting his escape. He also wanted to flee his family's indifference to events beyond their backyards. Late in life, he marveled to Aunt Marie that elephants would be extinct by the time her great-grandchildren reached adulthood. Baffled, she shot back, "What the *fuck* do I care about *elephants* disappearing off the face of the earth when I have a grandson who needs to go to the dentist and I can't afford to send him?" As ever, Vito's mind was on problems that eluded many of his relatives.

This trend stretched back to his childhood. He was never satisfied with his parents' commitment to voting Democrat simply because a district leader had instructed them to do so, or because they believed that rich Republicans couldn't possibly represent their interests. Vito expected Annie and Charles to base their votes on careful consideration of issues that didn't interest them. When he learned about Ferdinando Nicola Sacco and Bartolomeo Vanzetti, he sought his parents' opinion on these Italian immigrant anarchists unjustly condemned under American law. Despite their shared heritage, Vito "never got the sense that [his] parents knew what the hell those men believed in, or why they went to jail . . . or why they were treated the way they were."

Vito's parents considered television a source of pure entertainment, the conduit that brought them *Your Hit Parade* and the first implicitly gay character Vito had ever seen (Milton Berle's huggy male friend—"I'm with you tonight!"—on *Texaco Star Theatre*). News items, like comedies and musicals, were digested without reflection. Steeped in Senator Joseph McCarthy's anti-Communist bluster, Annie and Charles pronounced him "a great man who was crucified," a message they passed along to their boys. As a teenager, Vito confronted his parents over the misinformation: "You know, you taught me this man was a hero, and this man was like the worst creature who ever lived!" Unfazed by their son's accusation, the Russos offered no apologies. Vito reached the difficult realization that to his parents, it was "not important to worry your mind over [political matters]. . . . They [were] only concerned with their own lives and how things affect[ed] them personally." Invested in local and world news, Vito had no patience for uninformed politics.

In 1968, Main Street Court House bore an enormous sign proclaiming, "Lodi Supports Our Boys in Vietnam." Three native sons had been lost in battle. Vito staunchly opposed U.S. involvement in the war. In his first stirrings of political activism, he marched for peace and participated in FDU antiwar rallies. When the topic of the draft arose at a weekend party on Blueridge Road, confrontation loomed. Knowing well his conservative audience, Vito decided to test his skills as provocateur and announced, "If I'm called, I will not go." Perky's husband Joey, an ex-Marine and Purple Heart awardee, bit. "How *dare* you? What do you mean you won't go?!" When Vito denounced the "bogus war," Joey approached his younger, considerably less muscled in-law with righteous fury in his eyes. The two men went nose-to-nose until Charles physically separated them. To his surprise, Charlie found himself agreeing with his brother.

The conflict was generational. The older relatives trusted their government, while the baby boomers, who had been impressionable teenagers at the time of President Kennedy's assassination, "questioned everything."

Vito could not stomach dogma. Following his disillusionment with confession, he considered "hypocrisy" the only lesson he took away from his Catholic education. He accepted the notion of a force greater than humans but wasn't at all certain that force came "in the form of an old man with a white beard." He was, of course, only too willing to share these views at large family gatherings. His niece Leslie recalls the shrieks of outrage that Vito elicited from relatives by announcing over dinner, "I don't believe in Jesus, but I think he was a very nice man." In grade school at the time, Leslie laughed to see the adults in a sudden uproar over an obviously flippant remark.

Vito loved to make trouble, but he needed an environment where doing so didn't necessarily risk bodily harm. Manhattan was his only logical home base. The island was a liberal stronghold, and it offered cultural riches that Lodi sorely lacked.

When Vito lived in East Harlem, Broadway lay beyond his reach. Annie and Charles had no particular interest in theater and couldn't afford to send their stagestruck son. As a Lodi teenager, however, Vito devoured revivals of hit shows. While still a junior at LHS, he sneaked into Manhattan for a City Center matinee of *Wonderful Town* with Kaye Ballard and future *Chorus Line* author James Kirkwood. When he began acting in college, he caught Maureen Stapleton re-creating the role that had made her famous, Serafina Delle Rose, in Tennessee Williams's *The Rose Tattoo*. With Polly Adler still on his mind, Vito dragged his cousin Robert to the Broadway transfer of Ann Corio's *This Was Burlesque*. For a steep nineteen dollars each, the boys sat enthralled in the balcony of the Hudson Theatre and ogled Sally Rand's legendary fan dance.

But Broadway was a rare treat. When Vito came to Manhattan, he usually hooked a right off the George Washington Bridge and headed straight downtown to the Village, where talent was plentiful, cover charges were more affordable, and openly flirtatious men were everywhere. His lifelong love of pinspot divas was born on one such visit, when, at sixteen, he caught the act of a kooky twenty-year-old singer just beginning to wow the cabaret cognoscenti. "You had to stand in the darkness of a club called the Bon Soir on 8th Street . . . [listening to] . . . Barbra Streisand belt 'Who's Afraid of the Big Bad Wolf?' wearing a white sheet for a dress." Hearing the predominantly male audience cheer Streisand's assertion that the first little pig was "very gay," Vito felt right at home.

He had to come back to New York—not just for the occasional show or visit to the bars, but for good. Although Vito had sworn for years that he would leave Lodi the day he turned eighteen, such a neatly timed exit wasn't possible. For one thing, Annie and Charles wouldn't hear of it. Children left home when they got married, period. While it was already clear to them that marriage wasn't in Vito's future, they dug in their heels and objected vociferously when he informed them that he was Manhattan bound.

Parents and son could have saved themselves the drama. Vito couldn't afford to leave home until the start of his junior year at FDU, when he began dating a guy who lived at 77 East 12th Street, mere steps from the East and West Villages. What better way to get back to Manhattan and begin living the gay life to which he was more drawn every month?

True, he was faced with a nasty bus commute to and from Rutherford for his last two years at FDU. And the cost of tuition combined with Manhattan rent would keep him in debt for years. But living 24/7 in Gay Central more than compensated. While attending day classes, Vito sought night work in order to support himself. Waiting tables was an obvious option, and he got hired near the top of the food chain, at Longchamps. The elegant restaurant had sprouted locations all over Manhattan, including on the corner of 5th Avenue and 12th Street, a minute's walk from Vito's new apartment. With no experience, he fast installed himself in the profession's upper tiers. Boasting classic French service, Longchamps sent its waiters to school to learn the elaborate division of labor between kitchen and table. Keeping quiet about his private life, Vito settled in, thrilled to be working in a genteel setting while earning "a lot of money." Soon afterward, when Charlie married high school sweetheart Linda Chepauskas, Vito served as best man and took his little brother and new sister-in-law to an upscale restaurant in the Empire State Building, where everybody seemed to know him. Though Linda's pregnancy was causing tension in both families, Vito took the news in stride and used his new affluence to treat the scared young couple to an evening's honeymoon in Manhattan.

The silence required for such luxury was toxic. Vito had come to New York to be openly gay, not to strangle in a tux while coddling bluehairs who would have fainted into their bouillabaisse had they realized who was serving them. A quick glance around the Village turned up any number of joints—The Pilgrim, Aldo's, The Finale—where Vito could wait on his own people. The managers of these places didn't flinch at gay clientele, which, Vito averred, "was a big thing in those days; if you were allowed to congregate someplace, it didn't matter how bad the food was or the drinks or whatever." Feeling as free as his customers, Vito set about increasing his tips. His trim torso, bright brown eyes, and toothy grin attracted plenty of attention. Soon he was matching his Longchamps earnings while staying true to his emerging values as a gay man.

Vito's Village education began when he answered a plea issued by an elderly woman addressing passersby at the corner of Greenwich Avenue and Charles Street: "My boy, my boy, why you no work Sundays for Mama?" Mama was the eponymous Greek owner of Mama's Chick'N'Rib, a downtown fixture that one employee dubbed "the gay hangout of the world." In the late 1950s, it served as a welcome alternative to Mob-owned gay bars, where weak drinks and hassling were inevitable. On slow nights, Mama left the place to her boys, who would lock the doors, feed their friends for free, and fog the windows with unsupervised kissing and dancing. Mama took a certain amount of heat for her clientele. On "brown-bag Fridays," local cops blackmailed business owners who were friendly to gay men: "You want your windows broken? . . . Well, you let all these fags hang out in here." Eager to avoid trouble, Mama paid up.

Vito was charmed by his new boss, who "called everyone 'my boy' regardless of age or apparent gender." Mama's world was filled with gay men to mother. Financial generosity, however, did not figure among her virtues. She paid employees a bare forty cents an hour, lived in mortal terror of the word "union," and exercised serving practices that might have made Upton Sinclair flinch. Food dropped on the floor got returned to a customer's plate; too-large shrimp portions found Mama's bare fingers plunged, before customers' astonished eyes, into served plates to retrieve the surplus. As Vito later laughed, "Mama was a class act." But the waiters adored her, going so far as to adopt her inevitable black-dress-and-pearls ensemble on Halloween.

Through his employment at Mama's, Vito picked up knowledge "that you didn't get in a New Jersey classroom." On the graveyard shift from 6 p.m. to 6 a.m., he stood behind the counter, sucked down gallons of cherry Coke, and tended the colorful parade that marched through Mama's doors. The usual suspects included "baby faced hustlers from Iowa, overweight chorus boys from off-Broadway, transsexual prostitutes from uptown, babbitty [sic] schoolteachers from the suburbs and a few actual stars of stage and screen." One such star was Warhol drag institution Jackie Curtis, whose play *Glamour, Glory, and Gold: The Life and Legend of Nola Noonan, Goddess and Star* enjoyed a healthy off-Broadway run in 1968 with an unknown Robert De Niro playing four different roles. Spending roughly half his day toiling at Mama's, Vito loved Nola's reminiscence of her former life as a waitress: "I slung hash when hash was hash and slingin' was slingin'!" A future "star" who frequented Mama's was Don McLean, better known by his drag name, "Lori Shannon." A decade later, he landed the recurring role of Beverly LaSalle, Edith Bunker's martyred transvestite friend on *All in the Family*. A rotund, acerbic queen, Lori liked sitting at Vito's counter and pointing at her mouth whenever she wanted another cherry Coke. In infrequent male drag, Don earned the nickname "Tommy Taffy" for his unconvincing toupee.

Despite her many years on the Village front lines, Mama "sometimes crossed herself very quickly when somebody really freaky walked in." Someone "really freaky" was Lenore, a transsexual "given to scaring straight tourists by lifting her skirt over her head and showing everybody her 'new cunt.'" Vito reveled in this outré new environment. He got to fulfill his lifelong ambition of playing Eve Arden, wisecracking restaurant hostess in *Mildred Pierce* (1945)—though he also fancied himself Ann Sheridan, noir diva of *They Drive by Night* (1940), "dispensing black coffee, cherry cokes and occasional sarcasm across the lunch counter." Customers got these film references and could slam them back over the napkin dispensers. They formed a tight, safe nucleus for one another in the chaotic summer of 1968, particularly on the night of RFK's assassination. The report reached Mama's in predawn hours through the staticky transistor radio of a leatherman and a drag queen in miniskirt and stilettos, mascara tears zigzagging down her face. Exhausted from a shift that still had three hours to go, Vito listened in shock. Mama, always dressed for mourning, stood by and shook her head, aghast at the craziness of a country where heroes were so expendable. Watching customers too grief stricken to move, Vito recognized the haven that Mama's represented. "We couldn't close early and go home. We were home. We needed each other. Everyone sat in Mama's until it was light outside again."

Fifteen years before New York would open its first LGBT center, Vito found gay community at Mama's. The customers at Mama's also reminded Vito of his Jersey crew, whose jokes and banter seemed transplanted across the Hudson. But as in Jersey, Vito knew that he stood out from this crowd. As the only college student employed at Mama's, he earned the alternating nicknames "smart queen" or "Betty Co-Ed." He tolerated both, even though the latter irked him because "it always made me think of Betty Grable in eyeglasses and I hated her." He began to scrutinize his surroundings. Mama's provided a retreat for people who had nowhere else to congregate, but Vito couldn't accept such crumbs with the gratitude of his compatriots. The Village "ghetto" was starting to seem oppressive. Vito resented "being herded into dark, smelly places being controlled largely by organized crime and being exploited. . . . a perception which [he didn't] think many of [his] friends shared." They did not yet recognize their need for a civil-rights movement of their own.

Matters were far worse in Lodi. If the crowd at Mama's seemed politically indifferent, the Jersey queens were locked in self-loathing. They regularly patronized "seedy bars in bad neighborhoods, ramshackle diners like Brookies in Paterson and rest stops on the Garden State Parkway like the Brookdale Howard Johnson's. Nobody ever complained that the surroundings were dirty, the prices too high, or the help sneering and derisive. Nobody complained that the straights would sometimes wait outside the bar to beat [them] up on [their] way home ('Miss Thing, I'm not going out there alone; come with me.'). This was [their] place in society." At any rate, it was *his friends'* place in society. Vito's belligerent mother had taught him too much fight to be a straight man's punching bag.

Vito was also tired of his friends' worship of the same men who beat them up. He had swooned over his share of unattainable jocks, but that was in high school. The Jersey gang continued to pine for "a straight 'lover' because that was the highest compliment a queen could get." Vito couldn't see that the prize was much worth attaining. And the queens' worship of maleness made them openly distrustful of lesbians. They instructed Vito "that you should never hang around with dykes because they fought all the time and they would throw beer cans, and that if you let them come into your bar, they would start fights." Older lesbians were acceptable, almost motherly to gay men, but their younger counterparts were considered brutal "truck drivers" best left alone. Vito didn't question this sexism until he met politically informed lesbians who made him realize that his friends feared women who asserted a masculinity that they lacked.

After graduating from FDU, Vito decided that he needed a more intellectual atmosphere than Mama's or the Jersey circuit. Yet he also knew that he was most comfortable in a gay milieu. He found a reasonable compromise at the restaurant where he waited tables for the next decade. Located at 57 West 10th Street, the Omnibus drew a tony crowd. Theater folk and literati, including Paul Krassner, editor of the underground magazine *The Realist*, were regulars. Owner and chef Ed McDonald had performed on *Horn and Hardart's Children's Hour*, which helped launch the careers of Rosemary Clooney and Bernadette Peters. The restaurant's décor could have been designed by Vito himself. Echoing Joe Allen's Theater District staple, the Omnibus's walls were plastered with posters of Broadway flops, and the jukebox, in the approving words of one devotee, "was not subject to current musical fads." Patrick Merla recalls a roster of which Vito must have heartily approved: Barbra Streisand's "The Summer Knows," Herb Alpert and the Tijuana Brass's "Lonely Bull," and, a particular favorite, Nina Simone's "Break Down and Let It All Out." The menu, in Patrick's recollection, "consisted only of casserole dishes, which for some reason was considered very gay. (Those were the days before we all became gourmet cooks.)" In cuisine and tone, the Omnibus was a decided step up from Mama's.

Vito spent considerable time harping to his coworkers on a favorite theme. "I would rant and rave and complain and bitch and moan and piss about the thing that bothered me the most, which was that most people that you meet in gay bars are not concerned with anything in the world except, 'What time are you going to the bar tonight?'" Nobody paid the slightest attention, however, since Vito himself was as big a barfly as anyone in his circle. In the late 1960s, he proudly numbered himself among the "gay party people at the height of the gay explosion." With other Village waiters and bartenders, Vito regularly finished night shifts by heading for after-hours bars and clubs, where he caroused until dawn. In retrospect, he justified those crawls as a kind of social networking that helped sustain the Village economy. "Everybody who worked in gay restaurants or gay bars would, after they got off work, go to *other* gay restaurants and gay bars. It was like, bartenders [went] to spend money at other people's bars as a courtesy and [made] the rounds. . . . It was like this tight gay society of bar people and restaurant people." Ironically, the clientele with whom Vito fraternized at the Gold Bug and the Washington Square were precisely those whose political obliviousness he was trying to escape: young, often flamboyantly effeminate men whom "people used to call Greenwich Village Trash." No matter his disagreements with them, Vito still very much enjoyed his friends' arch sensibilities. Insisting that he "didn't have a political thought in [his] head," he tried to keep the party going.

The phone shrilled. Vito rolled over and squinted at the clock. Who in hell was calling on a Sunday morning? One thing was certain: it couldn't be any of the queens from last night's crawl.

He was wrong. The caller was Jackie Curtis's roommate, Kevin Brattigan, one of few contemporaries whose Judy fixation exceeded Vito's. In 1969, when young gay men were besotted with Diana Ross and Joni Mitchell, Garland-love risked turning off potential lovers: "If you went home with a guy who liked Judy Garland, you'd say, 'I'm getting outta *here*!'" Undaunted, Kevin hitchhiked nationwide so as not to miss a single concert appearance of his idol. Even Vito thought this degree of devotion extreme, but he could relate to the passion that fueled it.

On the morning of Sunday, June 22, 1969, Kevin didn't bother with a hello. "Judy Garland died in London." Vito sat up as the boys quietly took in the news. Decades of drug and alcohol abuse had led to the singer's death at forty-seven.

Kevin spoke again. "I want to do something with you today. What should we do?" The two friends arranged to meet in the West Village, where they rented bicycles and rode up to Central Park without speaking a word to each other.

In the park, Vito played on mental loop the Garland images that he had been collecting for a decade. Chief among them was the concert he had attended, almost exactly a year earlier, at the Garden State Arts Center in Holmdel, New Jersey. Garland had been in horrendous shape. The recent assassination of her dear friend Robert Kennedy had shaken her deeply. She was also enmeshed in the financial and chemical woes that had long since tattered her reputation. In no condition to perform, she hacked through her repertoire until reaching "What Now, My Love?" during which she fell asleep onstage. At a later performance, she fell down the set's staircase and had to be rushed to a hospital.

Through Garland's stumbles and slurring, Vito sat riveted. Like many gay men, he "wanted to hold her and protect her because she was a lost lamb in a jungle and yet be held by her and protected by her because she was a tower of strength, someone who had experienced hell but continued to sing about bluebirds and happiness." Even before gay liberation, Vito tried to dissociate himself from the cult image of "frail, young, pale homosexual men [who] would stand in the aisles of Carnegie Hall and cry and wring their hands while Judy Garland sang 'The Man That Got Away.'" But he was sufficiently unashamed of his own diva worship that he sought to enliven one boring tryst by thumbing through a Garland biography while his partner gamely carried on.

After the Garden State show, Vito bulldozed backstage and managed to gain entry into Garland's dressing room, where she was sipping from water glasses filled with what seemed to be either vodka or gin. In view of her obvious frailty, he didn't linger, staying only long enough to hear her opinion that Katharine Hepburn's portrayal of a morphine addict in *Long Day's Journey into Night* (1962) was obviously uninformed by personal experience. On that astonishing near-confidence, Vito fled.

A year later, Garland lay in state at Frank Campbell's Funeral Home on the Upper East Side. For the first time since Rudolph Valentino's funeral in 1924, the public was allowed to pay its final respects to a celebrity inside the parlor. Vito was among twenty-one thousand fans who braved the sweltering outdoor wait on Friday, June 27. He arrived to find a line stretching from the Madison Avenue entrance to and up 5th Avenue. A large majority of the mourners, he noted with little surprise, were also gay men, many of whom played Garland's records on portable phonographs until her daughter, Liza Minnelli, asked them to stop. Vito waited for hours in the heat before being admitted to the chapel, where he found his diva looking "gorgeous"—"I swear, *exactly* like the old Judy Garland from the MGM musicals," courtesy of Charles Schram, her makeup man from *The Wizard of Oz* thirty years earlier. With soft organ strains of "Over the Rainbow" filling the chapel, Vito slowly approached the coffin, positioned under an enormous floral rainbow tribute. He gazed down through the protective glass at Garland in her pale gray chiffon gown, a cool contrast with the light blue velvet lining that cushioned her. After his interminable wait in the heat, the moment passed quickly, and Vito filed back outside, where he spotted Lauren Bacall and Mickey Rooney in the crowd. As pallbearers carried Garland's coffin, awash in yellow roses, from the chapel, Vito remembered the long shift that awaited him at the Omnibus. He headed back downtown.

After midnight, Vito was exhausted from being on his feet since morning. As he and Ed McDonald closed the restaurant, news reached them that tension was bubbling between patrons and cops at the Stonewall, a deeply déclassé bar off Sheridan Square where Vito spent many after-work hours. The details were sketchy. Police had been performing what at first seemed like a routine raid—the most recent one had occurred four days earlier—but tonight's customers were actually protesting. Ed caught enough of the drift to warn his young employee, "Don't go to Christopher Street. There's a lot of trouble there, and it's totally bad news. These people are rabble-rousers, radicals; they shouldn't be doing this. . . . There's gonna be bloodshed. Stay away from there." As usual, Vito needed no further invitation than prohibition to see the action for himself.

Of his many after-work haunts, the Stonewall was Vito's favorite. The "place everyone loved to hate," it seemed to Vito "seedy, loud, obvious, and sheer heaven." Located at 53 Christopher Street, the former straight nightclub and restaurant fell under Mob control in 1966, when "Fat Tony" Lauria, along with two associates, reopened the Stonewall Inn as a two-room gay bar. Despite—or perhaps because of—Fat Tony's obvious homosexuality, homophobic rhetoric flew around the bar. Jazz great Dawn Hampton, who supplemented her income by working at the Stonewall's hatcheck, heard her bosses mention "their hatred for the 'faggot scumbags' who made their fortunes." The Stonewall underscored its impression as a vice den with blackened, doubly reinforced windows, the better to prevent an untimely police entrance. Multilocked oak and steel doors did their part to keep out the law as well; patrons were admitted only after being scrutinized through a peephole.

With just one front-door exit, the Stonewall flagrantly disregarded fire regulations. And the atmosphere in which customers were risking their necks was hardly inviting. The bar's faint lighting filtered through a smoky haze trapped under low ceilings and poor ventilation. Temperatures varied widely, from "hot as hell" to "like a tomb." All this squalor cost customers plenty. Mandatory coat-check often resulted in stolen garments. Admission was one dollar on weekdays, three dollars on weekends, for which customers received a complimentary drink ticket—but subsequent drinks, which cost a pricey dollar apiece, were watered down and generally dispensed from bottles marked with high-end brand names to disguise the "swill" sloshed into customers' glasses. Patrons did well not to inspect those glasses too carefully. Lacking sinks behind the bar, bartenders "washed" glasses in two tubs of dirty water before sending them back into circulation. By evening's end, the water was "murky and multicolored" and may, in fact, have caused a hepatitis outbreak among gay men in 1969.

So what drew Vito to a bar that he deemed "a regular hell hole"? Part of the attraction was Stonewall's reign as "the hottest dance bar in Greenwich Village." In 1969 it was the only bar where gay men were allowed to dance together unmolested, which provided a very welcome contrast with other gay clubs, such as the nearby Tenth of Always, where Mafia thugs "were very gruff about telling you not to dance; they'd really treat you like queers, like you were disgusting." Stonewall dancers freely practiced the Boston Jerk, the Monkey, and the Spider under pinspots that made them feel like stars. What Vito remembered as "the best music" in town included, on the backroom jukebox, the soul of Otis Redding and, in the front room, the lush pop harmonies of the Beach Boys, Aretha Franklin, the Beatles, and Elvis Presley, offset by the Motown mellowness of Marvin Gaye, Junior Walker, the Temptations, even the schmaltzy "Love Theme" from Franco Zeffirelli's *Romeo and Juliet* (1968). Poised above the dancers were "teenaged go-go boys from the Tennessee mountains and Pennsylvania farms" who, clad in "paisley bathing suits and soiled silver g-strings," writhed in cages while psychedelic light designs splashed over their taut bodies.

For Vito, the Stonewall's chief allure was its democracy. A fan of "very low-class bar[s]," he appreciated an atmosphere where "people who were too young, too poor or just too much to get in anywhere else" could enter with little hassle. Unlike the majority of his coworkers, Vito fit in at more conservative bars, such as the uptown Candy Store, when he chose to visit them. But loyalty to his friends kept him patronizing downtown dives where gay self-hatred was kept to a comparative minimum. The Stonewall was not the sort of place where, as happened at nearby Julius', a male couple would be forbidden to sit together with the admonition, "Ladies and gentlemen only!" If for no other reason, Vito treasured this bar as a flawed oasis in vast and hostile territory. When it fell under siege, he had to be present.

The timing of Vito's arrival at the Stonewall, no more than a five-minute walk from the Omnibus, is obscure. He claimed that the restaurant closed "about midnight" on the morning of Saturday, June 28, and that he and Ed McDonald had already heard about the riot in progress. When Vito arrived at Christopher Park, directly across from the Stonewall, he was "pissed off" to note that he'd already missed some of the action. As he strolled up, "various person-ages of grand demeanour and exotic affectation were exiting the premises to the whistles and cheers of a large gathering." However, police didn't arrive at the bar until 1:20 a.m., at which time they were surprised by the verbal resistance of transvestite and lesbian patrons. Roughly fifteen minutes passed before they began to march prisoners out of the bar.

This sets Vito's arrival in Christopher Park at roughly 1:35 a.m., not the 12:15 that he approximated. Whether he left work later than he thought or stopped anywhere en route is unclear. What is certain is that given his first glimpse of theatrical exits from the Stonewall, he witnessed considerably more than "half the story" of the Stonewall riots, as he later demurred.

Upon reaching Christopher Street, Vito caught a spectacle worthy of "an Academy Award red carpet walk." The summer heat, the unannounced raid's occurrence during peak hours, and the cops' tearing apart of Stonewall prop-erty made for a combative scene both inside and outside the bar. Rebellion was rising. In contrast with typical raids, arrestees were not departing the bar with their faces covered. The Stonewall patrons, delighted to find an audience await-ing them on Christopher Street, "took the opportunity to strike instant poses, starlet style, while the onlookers whistled and shouted their applause-meter ratings." As he left the bar, one mincing youth vamped the officer guarding the door: "Hello there, fella!"

Like many onlookers, Vito found this hilarious, a benign "good show. Gays answering back to the police was unique but it was all so camp it seemed harmless." But the tone began to darken as cops loaded patrons into vans rather than simply forcing them to leave the bar. When one spectator screamed out, "Why don't you people leave us alone for a change?" Vito agreed. It was a sentiment he'd also felt but never shouted. Watching patrons' forced march into the vans, Craig Rodwell felt a surge of rage and screamed out, "Gay Power!" and "Get the Mafia out of our bars!"; others began to sing "We Shall Overcome."

Then the scene turned ugly. All too familiar with police abuse, the crowd began screaming for friends whom they suspected to be in danger inside the bar. The decisive moment arrived when police roughly escorted a butch lesbian, who remains unidentified, out of the bar and toward a patrol car. "Kicking, cursing, screaming, and fighting," she escaped the car twice and ran back to the bar in an increasingly dangerous game of cat and mouse. When she yelled at the gay men watching the scene, "Why don't you guys do something!" shouts of "Police brutality!" and "Pigs!" filled the air, as did coins hurled at the cops. Heavier missiles soon replaced the pennies as cobblestones, bricks, and bottles went whistling over Christopher Street and trapped cops against the Stonewall entrance. They took terrified, baffled refuge inside the bar as the crowd exulted in its unprecedented fury. Years of abuse from the police, from government, from religious institutions, and from families finally exploded into vocal and physical revolt. As one participant remarked, "We all had a collective feeling like we'd had enough of this kind of shit. . . . Everyone in the crowd felt that we were never going to go back. It was like the last straw. It was time to reclaim something that had always been taken from us. . . . There was something in the air, freedom a long time overdue, and we [were] going to fight for it."

Well, not quite "everyone." Though mesmerized by the crowd's newfound courage, Vito was also terrified by the melee erupting before his eyes. As the first objects flew past him, he trotted over to Christopher Park and shinnied up an elm tree. From his safe perch, he watched as a small group of men slammed a parking meter-turned-battering ram against the Stonewall's stout front doors while screaming, "Liberate the bar!" and "We're the pink panthers!" His eyes widened to see a wire-mesh garbage can and Molotov cocktails hurtled through the busted doors and broken windows. Now humiliated as well as panicked, the cops readied their attack. Though Inspector Seymour Pine ordered his men not to fire their guns, one was heard to declare, "We'll shoot the first motherfucker that comes through the door."

Hopelessly outnumbered by the mob, Pine called for backup forces at 2:55 a.m. Angry red lights and screaming sirens flooded Christopher Park as the Tactical Police Force (TPF) arrived minutes later. Brandishing nightsticks, the enraged TPF shoved the crowd away from the Stonewall and back toward Sheridan Square. Vito had seen enough. He scrambled down from his tree and beat a quick, if consciously filmic, retreat: "Like Aunt Pittypat in *Gone With the Wind*, I grabbed the smelling salts and hitched up the buggy as soon as the Yankees reached Atlanta." Keeping a safe distance from the nightsticks, he witnessed some of the dispersed crowd racing back around Christopher Street to taunt the TPF from behind. Camp returned in force as a Rockette-style kick line of men threw their arms around one another and began singing with gleeful faggotry: "We are the Stonewall girls / We wear our hair in curls / We wear no underwear / We show our pubic hair!" Vito giggled but decided to take his leave while the TPF was occupied with this latest assault on their dignity.

As he departed Christopher Park, it struck him that he was far from alone in his passivity during the riots. "Most of the people I knew," he asserted, "did not fight back. I was in the majority of the curious but timid who lent numbers to the brave few who dared act." But the spirit of rebellion had touched him. Rumors began to circulate that Judy Garland's death had worked the queens' last nerve and prompted the uprising. Vito repeatedly dismissed this theory as nonsense, a skepticism supported by the fact that Garland goes unmentioned in all contemporary gay accounts of the riots. He developed a far likelier explanation from years of toiling in the gay ghetto, where he "watched gay people get paid shit in restaurants by straight owners, get paid a dollar an hour and no medical expenses and all off the books, and working for nothing all their lives and growing old . . . and being really exploited by a gay ghetto, by a gay community, which is owned lock, stock and barrel by straight people." Vito was starting to chart a continuum of oppression that began with Mama's union-busting and ended with Mob-owned bars where customers might be tolerated but never truly welcomed. Though not ready to jump into the fray, he returned to the Stonewall for the successive evenings' fireworks. The battle had just begun.

By Saturday night, the community's dander was way up. Dawning defiance appeared in signs all over the Stonewall façade: "We Are Open," "Support Gay Power—C'mon in, Girls," "They Want Us to Fight for Our Country [but] They Invaded Our Rights," "Gay Prohibition Corrupt$ Cop$ Feed$ Mafia," "Legalize Gay Bars and Lick the Problem." Vito returned to the scene as shouts of "Liberate Christopher Street!" echoed over the park. With a growing conviction that "Christopher Street belongs to the queens," the second-night rioters literally took the block, declaring it off-limits to heterosexuals. Further up Christopher, prisoners in the Women's House of Detention acknowledged the revolution by igniting toilet paper and wafting it down to the streets in flaming tribute.

Here was a response to which Vito could well relate. Polly Adler had served time in the grim House of D; now her successors were cheering on Vito and his new compatriots. The prisoners' enthusiasm, along with the stepped-up street action, emboldened him. No more watching the action at elm's remove. Tonight he sat with other gay men on Christopher Street stoops until ordered by the TPF to move on. For a while, he and his friends enjoyed the game of pretending to relocate only to circle the block and plop themselves right back where they'd started. How long could they play before getting arrested? When all that running around in the heat grew tiresome, the men stayed put and began sassing the cops. Ten years later, Vito would proudly recall of that moment: "Most of us had a great mouth on our shoulders in those days and there were many spirited exchanges." Actually, Vito had never before opened his mouth to public authorities. He did so that Saturday night for the first time.

He got his second chance the following Wednesday, July 2, when Lucian Truscott IV's article "Gay Power Comes to Sheridan Square" was published in the *Village Voice*. In an era when objective reporting about homosexuality did not exist, Truscott referred to the weekend's rioters as "fags," "a dyke," and the "forces of faggotry." Sunday night's fizzled protests Truscott dismissed as mere "fag follies." In response, newly galvanized activists plotted to burn down the *Village Voice* office, located five doors west of the Stonewall. In their budding rage, they ignored Truscott's implicit support for protests designed "to assert presence, possibility and pride" in the suddenly vocal gay community. Truscott also quoted, with positive editorial spin, a line that would epitomize a turning-point in gay consciousness: Allen Ginsberg's private assertion, "'You know, the guys [at the Stonewall] were so beautiful—they've lost that wounded look that fags all had 10 years ago.' It was the first time," Truscott averred, that he "had heard that crowd described as beautiful."

Like most of the crowd, Vito zeroed in on the phrase "forces of faggotry" and joined the *Voice* protest. Sensing useful unrest, Black Panthers and Yippies joined the Wednesday night demonstration, raising the crowd total to a thousand and bringing days of rioting to a frighteningly violent climax. The more practiced nongay activists spurred on the Stonewall crowd as trash cans were set on fire, bottles flew, and cries of "Pig motherfuckers!" "Fag rapists!" and "Gestapo!" incited an already-enraged TPF. Nightsticks vengefully cracked bodies and left behind bloody and broken wreckage. Eyewitness Dick Leitsch described "young people, many of them queens . . . lying on the sidewalk, bleeding from the head, face, mouth, and even the eyes. Others were nursing bruised and often bleeding arms, legs, backs and necks."

Not everyone perceived the brutality as a clarion call for revolution. Mattachine Society New York sought to quell uprisings by painting a neatly stenciled, block-letter message on the Stonewall facade: " We homosexuals plead with our people to please help maintain peace and quiet conduct on the streets of the Village." Mattachine executive director Leitsch, just sixteen months earlier the daring rebel who introduced himself as a "good old-fashioned cocksucker" to Vito's FDU audience, now emerged as the burgeoning movement's grumpy grandfather. The young queens who had lain battered and bleeding on

Christopher Street did not appreciate his dismissal of their courage, which he coded in the fey terminology of an earlier gay generation as "The Hairpin Drop Heard around the World."

Leitsch found himself and Mattachine hopelessly eclipsed by "the new wild and undefined world of gay liberation: it was louder, more demanding and less forgiving than the homophile movement" led by Mattachine. A month after the riots, a group of radicalized men and women formed Gay Liberation Front (GLF), whose name linked "Gay"—never before lettered into the banner of a gay-rights advocacy group—with the Viet Cong's National Liberation Front, suggesting GLF's commitment to liberating not just gays but "all the oppressed: the Vietnamese . . . the third world, the blacks, the workers."

Vito was nowhere to be found at GLF meetings. He had heard of the group and had a vague sense of GLF's noisy presence on the Village landscape, but he didn't learn until considerably later where it held its meetings. The Stonewall riots had captured his imagination, but only fleetingly. In the summer and fall of 1969, he was "still slinging hash and dancing around the fringes of the battle." He recalled, "Like most people, I just wanted to be left alone. I wanted the right to face exploitation in a fire trap like the Stonewall without having to worry about a vice cop spilling my drink." GLF meetings weren't his style anyway. Their formidable mixture of "drag queens, bar dykes, street people, feminists, radical students, leftists, socialists, Marxists, Maoists, anarchists, libertarians, hippies, and former Yippies" led to discussions so chaotic that chair Karla Jay wielded a softball bat to restore order. GLF's aggressively leftist, doctrinaire politics also chafed Vito. He had little use for those who wielded jargon as a weapon of intimidation.

In mid-1969, Vito's mind was on other matters. Shortly before Stonewall, he had moved to the apartment where he would spend the rest of his life. A year's stay in Jackson Heights, Queens, had strengthened his resolve never to leave Manhattan. Though the West Village had become the center of the gay universe, Vito spent more than enough time there during work and play hours—particularly because he had recently matriculated in the graduate cinema program at New York University (NYU). For down time, he needed a location removed from the nonstop carnival south of 14th Street. Chelsea seemed the perfect compromise. It was a working-class (i.e., affordable) district within walking distance of the Village. Predominantly Puerto Rican, the neighborhood featured, in Edmund White's recollection, T-shirted men lounging on stoops, "listening to Latin music and drinking beer." Chelsea was also saturated with film history. Between 1905 and 1915, its lofts and theaters had housed several motion-picture studios, such as Adolph Zukor's Famous Players, whose alums included Mary Pickford and John Barrymore. Nostalgia was alive and well at the nearby Elgin Theatre, a revival film house that Vito visited religiously, and at his beloved Empire Diner, a black and chrome fifties throwback.

Vito established his new home at 401 West 24th Street, a modest orange-brick building erected in 1904 on the corner of 9th Avenue. The ground floor reeked of the superintendent's cat box, and the creaky stairs ascending to Vito's apartment didn't prettify the picture. Like the building itself, apartment no. 1 wasn't much to look at, even after Charles and the extended family pitched in to make it habitable. One flight off the street, it offered a connecting living room and bedroom just big enough for a platform bed and, eventually, a jerry-rigged office space. The tiny kitchen featured French copper pots (Vito had inherited his father's cooking genes) and "a few discreetly placed mousetraps." The apartment received very little natural light, which was just as well for a home that doubled as a theater. In no time, Vito mounted a movie screen on his living-room wall and began showing his expanding collection of 16mm movies on a projector set up between the living room and the bedroom. (In case anyone missed the apartment's raison d'être, empty film reels dotted the exposed brick.) Garland prints blossomed over every wall, including those of the bathroom.

The best feature of Vito's new home sat beyond its lavishly decorated walls. Leaving 401's front door, he could turn left, walk a few steps to the northwest corner of Twenty-fourth and Ninth, pivot slightly to his left, and take in one of the city's most breathtaking views of the Empire State Building. Towering ten blocks north in Art Deco splendor, it became Vito's favorite icon of the island that he now inhabited permanently.

The edifice loomed over the Village and gave Vito a touchstone for his walks home from work. On the night of Sunday, March 8, 1970, it stood out in a clear winter sky as he trudged north, his feet aching from a long shift. Hunching his shoulders against the cold, he kept his eyes fixed on Empire State's soaring antenna and counted the long blocks remaining between him and home. At West 11th Street, his attention was pulled back to the pavement. Directly across from St. Vincent's Hospital, he spotted hundreds of obviously gay, candle-bearing individuals listening to a pastor's somber prayer for the recovery of Diego Vinales, a young Argentine who lay upstairs in a coma. Vito approached the vigil. A wiry, dark-haired young man thrust into his hand a leaflet:

Gay Activists Alliance—691-2748
"Snakepit" raided, 167 arrested—
One boy near death . . . at St. Vincent's . . .
either fell or jumped out precinct window,
landed and was *impaled* on a metal fence!
Any way you look at it—
that boy was PUSHED ! !
We are ALL being pushed.

———————

Fighting gays and any of you who
call yourselves HUMAN BEINGS with guts

> to stand up to this horror —
> Gather at Sheridan Square tonight
> March 8 at 9:00 to march on the Sixth Precinct.
> Stop the Raids! Defend *Your* Rights!
> There will be a DEATH WATCH VIGIL
> at St. Vincent's immediately after protest!

Vito glanced up at the hospital. He knew the Snake Pit, all right. It was a dank West 10th Street basement bar so nondescript that some area residents didn't even know it existed. Vito occasionally went after work and tried to ignore the awful black lighting that picked up the lint on everyone's sweaters.

Mr. Leaflet introduced himself as Marty Robinson, a Brooklyn carpenter and member of the newly formed Gay Activists Alliance (GAA). He filled Vito in on the reason for the vigil. Early that morning, Inspector Seymour Pine, who had led the Stonewall raids the previous summer, burst into the Snake Pit, where he found almost two hundred men in an area built for a crowd less than half that size. Pine's pretext for the raid was the bar's illegal status as well as its disregard of city fire codes. When customers became belligerent, Pine envisioned another Stonewall. This time he wouldn't let matters escalate. He arrested everyone at the bar and hauled them over to the Sixth Precinct on Charles Street.

Among those arrested, Diego Vinales had special reason to be afraid. He was living on an expired tourist visa in East Orange, New Jersey, and feared deportation. At the precinct, according to one of the other prisoners, "Nobody told us about our rights or why we were being arrested." When this man inquired about his rights, he was ordered by a cop, "Shut your fucking mouth." Another officer called him a "faggot" and a "prick." In this environment, Vinales panicked, bolted up the steps, and tried to leap from a second-story window to an adjacent rooftop. He missed his target and plunged to street level, where six fourteen-inch railing spikes gored his groin and thigh. Unable to free him, fire department rescuers were forced to blowtorch the fence and transport the victim, still impaled, to St. Vincent's.

Hearing the news that morning, members of New York's emerging gay liberation organizations spent the day spreading the word. GAA distributed some three thousand copies of Marty's leaflet to bars all over Manhattan. Members of GLF, the Homophile Youth Movement, and Homosexuals Intransigent joined GAA for a rally in Sheridan Square before marching to the precinct and finally to St. Vincent's.

His voice low, mindful of the silent vigil going on around them, Marty finished his story. Chilled, Vito returned his gaze to the pamphlet in his hand. What it said was true. Diego Vinales had indeed been "pushed from that window: he was pushed by society." Vito "realized that if [Vinales] didn't have to be so scared of being deported, he wouldn't have jumped." And if he hadn't been patronizing a gay bar, he would not have been arrested. Just like the crowd at Stonewall last summer. Just like the guys at the St. Marks Baths five years earlier. These were not isolated injustices. Gay people were perpetual targets of the law.

The crowd at St. Vincent's marched once around the block, their anger building. According to one participant, "We are silent but we are seething. The demonstration cannot end" at the hospital. The protesters pivoted east and flooded down Greenwich Avenue toward the Women's House of Detention, where GLF members planned to show support for their imprisoned sisters. Cries of "Hey, hey, ho, ho, House of D has got to go" nearly drowned out a shout that GAA, dedicated exclusively to gay rights, should not involve itself in this ancillary protest. GAA members swerved away from the House of Detention and spilled onto Christopher Street, the movement's symbolic birthplace. From Christopher the GAA contingent detoured through Gay Street, "stunning the residents of the quiet by-way" with throat-ripping screams of "Gay Power!" Arriving back in Sheridan Square, GAA's Jim Owles pled for donated blood and thanked the crowd for mounting what was, to date, "the largest and angriest planned gay demonstration thus far in the history of the homosexual movement in this country."

Vito left Sheridan Square and walked back up 7th Avenue. Now he barely noticed the cold. It was pure coincidence that he hadn't been at the Snake Pit with Vinales. He pulled Marty's flyer out of his back pocket and scanned the top, noting GAA's phone number and wondering idly where the group met. Maybe it was time for him to meet people like Marty and Jim, guys for whom being gay meant more than campy chatter in seedy Village bars and restaurants.

And yet this screaming-in-the-streets business was alarming. Vito had only heard the word "gay" shouted publicly once before, at Stonewall some eight months earlier. Another young man present at the Snake Pit demo, GLF member Allen Young, remarked of the evening: "Going into the streets and chanting as an openly gay man was something entirely new to me, and rather scary." In 1970, "gay" meant sexual pleasure, a specific circle of friends, a less-than-reputable nightlife. It wasn't something you yelled in public.

Vito folded the leaflet and returned it to his pocket.

I've been going to these meetings of the Gay Activists Alliance; why don't you come?" Two months after the Snake Pit demo, Vito was sitting in a Charles Street restaurant with his friend Michael Morrissey, listening to him hold forth about the group of militants from St. Vincent's back in March. He took a drag on his cigarette and exhaled with an impatient sigh. "I don't go to meetings, leave me alone."

That cold night seemed a long time ago. Now it was the middle of May, and Vito was looking forward to fun in the sun, not a third act of screechy street theater.

Yet Vinales had undergone several operations and was still lying in agony at St. Vincent's, where two cops guarded his door (he remained a prisoner for resisting arrest). And when Vito looked back on the protests, one conspicuous absentee leapt to mind: Dick Leitsch. Mattachine had loudly declined to support GLF, GAA, and the other new groups as they gathered before the hospital. Leitsch argued that a "death watch," as Marty had advertised the demo on his flyer, was an inappropriate tribute to a man not yet gone. "The whole affair," Leitsch complained, "looked as though the demonstrators were wishing [Vinales] dead to give them a martyr, an issue, and a weapon. Instead, MSNY sent wishes for a speedy recovery and an offer to help with whatever immigration problems the man might have." "Wishes for a speedy recovery"? Vito expected a far bolder response from the man who had shown such guts before homophobes at FDU. And while Vinales's immigration problems were important, they were the symptom, not the illness. Shouldn't gays be fighting the system that created such problems in the first place?

Feeling Vito's resistance weaken, Michael hammered away. Their shared history made him tough to resist. Michael was also from New Jersey, the product of a conservative Catholic family and parochial-school upbringing, and "had an amazing knowledge of films." His "movie star face and body" ensured constant admiration, which lent him special powers of persuasion. Plus, he informed Vito, GAA held its meetings and dances at the Church of the Holy Apostles at 28th Street and 9th Avenue, just four blocks from Vito's apartment.

The pitch worked. After nearly a year of flirting with the gay liberation movement, Vito attended his first GAA meeting.

Father Robert Weeks, the same Episcopal priest whom Vito had heard praying for Diego Vinales in front of St. Vincent's, donated his church's annex to GAA for its weekly Thursday-night meetings. On the evening of May 21, 1970, Vito walked up 9th Avenue toward Holy Apostles with some trepidation. GAA's tactics were still unnerving. But Michael had told him that tonight's meeting promised a special guest: Bella Abzug, who was seeking election to the U.S. House of Representatives. A congressional candidate courting the gay vote? This Vito had to see.

Abzug's reputation in progressive politics preceded her. On a vehemently antiwar platform, she had worked to get New York City mayor John Lindsay elected. She had also formed the Metropolitan Council on Peace Politics, designed to marshal Democratic clubs throughout the city against President Johnson's support of the war. As a civil-rights attorney, Abzug had fought racial discrimination in arenas as disparate as upscale Westchester County and rural Mississippi, where she reported in 1952, while pregnant, to defend a poor black boy who was "living a legal lynching." By 1970, as a West Village resident, Abzug was known for her liberal politics in the Seventeenth Congressional District, which included the Lower East Side, Little Italy, Chinatown, Greenwich Village, and part of Chelsea. She came to Holy Apostles seeking the votes of a group that most of her colleagues shunned.

Vito wedged his way into Holy Apostles' packed annex. By late March, in the wake of the Snake Pit demo, GAA membership had swelled to 150; in May over 200 people came to hear Abzug. The meeting began with the election of Jim Owles as president and Arnie Kantrowitz as secretary. The Political Affairs Committee announced that it was preparing a suit to address the false arrest of men detained at the Snake Pit. Then, "looking for all the world like a candidate for the Dolly Levi role in a Rego Park production" of *Hello, Dolly!* the magnificently chapeau'd Abzug took the stage. The annex went berserk. Along with the rest of the room, Vito leapt to his feet in a standing ovation that illustrated how long gays had yearned to be heard.

Abzug beamed and barked in her smokiest New York tones, "I'm quite overwhelmed by the reception!" She then got down to gay politicking. Having provided a lawyer for two GAA members arrested for loitering on a Christopher Street stoop, she declared police harassment of gays an "outrage." She also lambasted the discrimination suffered by gays at work, in federal security clearances, and under state sodomy laws. She graced gay liberation with badly needed legitimacy by likening it to contemporary civil-rights movements: "I think that all the liberation movements relate to each other, whether it's women's liberation or black liberation or gay liberation. They show people determined to assert their political power over the institutions that are discriminating against them and that are not responding to them. What people are saying right now is that they want to have an active role, an activist role."

The room exploded and awarded Abzug a second standing ovation. Vito was back on his feet, clapping wildly and knowing full well that he was "hooked." Abzug made him realize that gays had influential straight allies committed to helping them. He was equally moved by GAA members who introduced him to the possibility of progay political analysis. At the meeting, he recalls, "[I] heard people, for the first time in my life, saying all the things that I had never said to myself. I heard people explain what happened at the Stonewall in terms that I could understand." Street demonstrations might be frightening, but they were necessary. Straight society was all too willing to bulldoze over meek gays who took their lumps and kept their mouths shut. Anybody who didn't like loudmouthed gays would now have to deal with them in ever-growing force. Vito joined GAA on the spot.

For a short period, he sat back and observed. GAA members were "much, *much* more sophisticated than [he] was politically." Many of them had a history of antiwar activism that far exceeded his FDU rallies; several of the principal GAA architects had also been active in GLF before leaving to form their own gay-rights organization. In early June, from the sidewalk at 86th Street and Broadway, Vito watched impressed but passive as his new comrades confronted gubernatorial hopeful Arthur Goldberg. When they demanded the politician's position on sodomy laws and police entrapment of gays, Goldberg frostily replied, "I think there are more important things to talk about." Pelted with shouts of "Answer homosexuals!" and "Crime of silence!" Goldberg dove into his limo, on the hood of which activists scrawled "Gay Power!" To a *New York Times* reporter, President Owles remarked of Goldberg, "I'd like to see [him] go up to Harlem and tell the blacks up there that [he's] got more important things to talk about than their civil liberties."

Later in the month, Vito joined an East Side picket line when roughly ten GAA members stormed the Republican State Committee headquarters in an effort to force Governor Nelson Rockefeller's support for gay rights. When Rockefeller failed to materialize and an assistant refused their request for an appointment, demonstrators plopped down on committee floors to wait out the day. Beneath an American flag, Marty Robinson snuggled up with his lover, Tom Doerr, the artist who designed GAA's Lambda logo (symbolizing the exchange of energy). Picketers outside created their own spectacle by holding hands, kissing, and hugging, which was, participant Arthur Bell notes, "quite a sight for East Fifty-sixth Street." So much so, in fact, that one man lunged for a protester and was pulled away by police. The picket lasted until 7 p.m., when five of the demonstrators upstairs were arrested for criminal trespass. The "first homosexuals ever arrested for a gay sit-in in New York," the self-proclaimed "Rockefeller Five" appeared for arraignment at Criminal Court that evening and found forty GAA members standing and holding hands in solidarity. Vito was beginning to realize that homosexuality, politics, and friendship were vitally intertwined.

He wasn't yet ready to be arrested. He did, however, want to contribute his gifts to GAA. The first opportunity arose at the end of June, when GAA helped organize a weeklong celebration commemorating Stonewall's first anniversary. The week promised to be far more cultural than political. The festivities kicked off on Monday with an erotic art show featuring "live nude sculptures—two men in front of a fireplace, 'at home.'" On Friday the GAA membership and several hundred of their friends crammed the sub-basement of NYU's Weinstein Hall. Swathed in purposely tacky decorations that "looked like the remainders of Bloomingdale's Valentine's Day windows," revelers boogied the night away while ogling go-go boys and preparing for the world's first Gay Pride march on Sunday.

These were variations on a gayness to which Vito could easily relate: campy, sexy, great fun. The only thing missing was movies. He asked the GAA officers to ante up sixty dollars—they had already blown one hundred dollars on the dance—so that he could rent 16mm prints of the Laurel and Hardy short *Twice Two* (1933) and the backstage musical *Gold Diggers of 1933*. The screening was a financial flop. Scheduled on Tuesday evening, it fell early in Pride Week and received scant publicity. But Vito's small audience howled as the comedy team played each other's "wife" in drag, and as Ginger Rogers and crew brightly screeched "We're in the Money" while tripping through Busby Berkeley's surreally ornate choreography. Vito cast an appreciative eye over the group. He had never witnessed the charged reactions of an exclusively gay film audience. If Sunday's marchers proved this electrified, they would present the most imposing gay front the world had ever seen.

Sunday, June 28, dawned warm and crystal clear, with "the sun a blowtorch in a sky bluer than any New York had boasted since the horseless carriage—no gay would remain in the shadows [today]." A playful "Suzy Parker breeze" ruffled the shaggy coifs, navy blue GAA T-shirts with bright gold Lambdas, and homemade cardboard signs ("Hi, Mom," "Better Blatant Than Latent," "I Am a Lesbian, and I Am Beautiful") beginning to fill the West Village's Waverly Place shortly after noon.

Before this day, gays' only public demonstrations had been the Mattachine-organized Annual Reminder, a picket in which a few dozen tastefully dressed, sign-toting gay men and lesbians silently circled Philadelphia's Liberty Bell on the Fourth of July. In the wake of Stonewall, the Annual Reminder seemed an inappropriately decorous response to oppression. In July 1969, Craig Rodwell returned from Philadelphia with visions of a far grander and louder affair. The Christopher Street Liberation Day (CSLD) march, stretching over fifty blocks from the Village to Central Park, would be a "bold demand for equality," not a silent plea for tolerance.

In theory, it sounded wonderful. In practice, it was terror inducing for marchers, who anticipated miles of vulnerability in that long walk up 6th Avenue. Gay-bashings had already tainted Pride Week. At the Elgin on Thursday night, members of the Cuban Venceremos Brigade threatened to rape GLF members when the two groups were mistakenly booked for benefits the same night. On Friday and Saturday mornings, two groups of gay men were ambushed by thugs on Village streets. Police advised Saturday morning's victims to forget about pressing charges lest they find themselves slapped with disorderly conduct. Mindful of these physical and legal dangers, the CSLD Committee distributed to marchers a printed reminder: "Degrading remarks by hecklers or observers are not important enough to interfere with our goal and don't deserve a reaction." Parade marshals also directed marchers to take off any dangling ornament—scarves, jewelry, ties—that could be grabbed by cops or other assailants. GLF member Jerry Hoose was only half-kidding when he remarked of the day, "We don't call it 'The First March'; we call it 'The First Run.'" The only thing that mattered, many marchers felt, was arriving safely in Central Park.

At first, it didn't look as though the day would promise safety in numbers. As Vito arrived at Waverly Place, an occasional egg rained down on the crowd from surrounding rooftops. It was far from encouraging to see gay people "sprinkled in small knots, waiting to see who was going to march and who wasn't before they committed themselves." Marty Robinson shrugged and said that he would be happy to see a few hundred people end up on 6th Avenue. Arrest at any moment seemed perfectly possible.

Shortly after 2:00, marchers swung north off Waverly Place and onto 6th Avenue's far left lane, the only space granted them on the wide boulevard. After progressing a few blocks, they began to feel more secure. Helping to tote GAA's banner, Vito marched at the front of the procession and had a clear view of the groups that followed. Craning his neck, he could see GLF flanked by Mattachine, the venerable lesbian group Daughters of Bilitis, the more radical sisters of Lavender Menace, and student representatives from Yale, Rutgers, and NYU. Gay organizations from Baltimore, Washington, and Philadelphia swelled the march's ranks to roughly twenty groups.

With these numbers crammed into a narrow lane, marchers were forced to proceed four or five abreast. As they started to feel less vulnerable, they raised V peace signs to observers and began chants that would carry them all the way uptown. "2-4-6-8, Gay is just as good [later to be replaced with "*twice* as good"] as straight!" and "Say it loud, gay and proud!" echoed over 6th Avenue as the march reached the Village's northern border.

As their sense of safety grew, marchers grew cheekier in their slogans. "Give us your sons!" earned some chuckles from spectators, as did a randy adaptation of John Lennon's wartime hit: "All we are saying / is give piece a chance." "Hey, hey, whadaya say? Try it once the other way!" turned a few observers pale. But aside from a Black Panther protester at 8th Street, a "Sodom + Gomorrah" sign-waver at 14th, and a reminder at 57th that "Jesus Saves," spectators remained remarkably respectful, if not celebratory. "Middle-aged, middle-class high-rise parent types smiled tolerantly at us," one participant noted, "looking for their sons and daughters in our crowd." Streamers showered down at 22nd Street; at Radio City Music Hall, a group of men staged a Rockettes kick line that recalled last summer's cop-tease on Christopher Street. The *New York Times*, which put the march on page 1, recorded "little open animosity" from onlookers, who giggled nervously and took a plethora of photos but didn't launch any of the attacks feared back on Waverly Place.

A party atmosphere took hold as the marchers neared Central Park. Vito laughed aloud to see one man in full *Wizard of Oz* Glinda drag. Tricked out in a frothy gown, tall golden crown, and magic wand, he lacked only the Good Witch's pink bubble to float him into the park. Crossing Central Park South, the throng devised a new chant for brothers having covert fun in the foliage: "Out of the bushes and into the streets!" This slogan was soon reversed by men flying on the testosterone of holding another guy's hand all the way up from the Village: "Out of the streets and into the bushes!"

Marchers poured into Central Park's Sheep Meadow. From the craggy elevation of its southeastern tip, GAA was in a perfect position to turn around and see the river of gay humanity trailing back to the park's entrance and beyond, sprawling over fifteen blocks. Lovers Jack Nichols and Lige Clarke recorded their reaction on arrival: "Our eyes filled to the brim with tears as we stood together in [the] Sheep Meadow, hugging each other, cheering wildly, applauding." Scanning the park, GAA secretary Arnie Kantrowitz spied a dauntingly diverse gay and lesbian roster on which he embodied the strutting final figure: "We were leathermen and Latino queens . . . black transvestites and young Asians and a few old faces . . . questing wanderers, fierce feminists, revelers and rioters, seers, politicians, artists, cowboys, philosophy teachers, husbands and lovers, loners, pot heads and patriots. We were transsexuals and opera queens and Judy Garland fans and hardhats and hairdressers and poets and fops, and we were totally honest poseurs. We were panhandlers and executives, mothers, anarchists, veterans, bank robbers, barflies, Catholics, and at least one twenty-nine-year-old Jewish Assistant Professor of English from Newark, who was having the time of his life."

Finally seeing their numbers in the sunlight, the celebrants had no patience for old labels. A misguided WNEW radio reporter opened his broadcast by invoking the title of Mart Crowley's smash play (then in its third year off-Broadway) about the miseries of homosexuality: "Ladies and gentlemen, here we are with the boys and the girls in the band." Roaring responses of "That's exactly the image we don't want" and "Fuck you!" sent WNEW censors scrambling for their antacid.

Vito seconded the protests. But with the tang of pot pervading the air and the sight of so many shirtless hunks, he had no desire to denounce politically incorrect imagery. At the playful announcement, "Anyone who's standing is straight," five thousand gay and lesbian backsides hit the dirt. Exhausted and amorous marchers took advantage of their sudden recline. In one tight circle, "two guys were going down on each other. They must have felt very liberated. Or very stoned." In the southeast corner of the Sheep Meadow, two male couples from GAA were in the process of breaking the world's kissing record. Their efforts perfectly embodied Vito's conception of GAA as an "army of lovers." In open air, vulnerable to attack, the four men maintained unbroken erotic contact for nine hours. Multiplied by fifty, the GAA membership seemed an invincible "group of people who truly believed that [they] could love each other and win, that an army of lovers could not fail."

Vito had joined an army that didn't believe in covert fighting. His nights in after-hours Village bars, dangerous Jersey honky-tonks, and political obliviousness were over. Looking about the Sheep Meadow, he noticed that the vast majority of gays and lesbians looked like he did—"young, political, and freak." If older, more conservative gays "still wanted to keep their homosexuality private, still saw their sex life nonpolitically, and were hesitant to share it with TV cameras, tourists, employers, and families," that was their business. Vito, for one, would never shut his mouth again.

The sun was setting over Central Park West. Vito followed its arc and caught the IRT back to Chelsea. Some of his new buddies were due at 24th Street to relive the celebration from start to finish.

4

Birth of an Activist

Michael Morrissey couldn't wait to introduce Vito to Arnie Kantrowitz. Given the secretary's razor wit and love of Hollywood arcana, the two seemed a preordained match. Arnie was a Staten Island Community College professor of English who had only recently accepted his homosexuality after two suicide attempts. When he attended the Snake Pit demo, he realized that the nascent gay movement could save his life. In May 1970, after two months in GAA, he followed Michael to the Omnibus, where he met the manic Italian waiter who would be his best friend for the next twenty years. Once Vito joined GAA, he and Arnie became the "Bobbsey twins of gay liberation."

Arnie's images of Vito from that era are blurry. As Vito immersed himself in GAA, he was in constant motion, endlessly speeding from the Omnibus "to political meetings to gay rights [demonstrations] with his fringed shoulder bag flying in the breeze behind his wiry body." When not waiting tables or attending GAA functions, Vito ran to the movies, which "he digested whole at the rate of several a day." Arnie was charmed by this young man whose "brown eyes brightened with fervor at the mention of Judy Garland" and who bubbled with "easy sentiment for all the celebrities who had acted and sung the fantasies [Kantrowitz] had grown up on." Vito and Arnie shared a campy, film-laden vocabulary more typical of the gay generation that preceded theirs. Nonstop references to Garland and Bette Davis, Arnie's icon of choice, helped cement their friendship. So did their passionate involvement in the first organization created expressly to reform antigay legislation. It was a remarkable transformation for two young men who, less than a year earlier, were peeking at the incipient struggle from behind a professor's tweeds and the elm branches of Christopher Park.

Vito met Arnie during the most exciting period of his life. While active in GAA, he found his first serious lover, his first full-time professional job, and the first friends who were his intellectual and political equals. He took on administrative duties within GAA, got involved in city government, and became, almost by accident, a writer. With fond nostalgia, Vito came to look on his time in GAA as "high school," but this understates the organization's importance in his life. GAA brought Vito into adulthood and launched his career as an activist.

Vito loved GAA from his first meeting. Bella Abzug's charisma helped, but the organization played directly to his sensibilities. The preamble to GAA's constitution proclaimed members' "right to feel attracted to the beauty of members of [their] own sex and to embrace those feelings as truly [their] own, free from any question or challenge whatsoever by any other person, institution, or 'moral authority.'" It also asserted, as Vito witnessed at the first Gay Pride March, the "right to express [their] feelings in action, the right to make love with anyone, anyway, anytime." GAA's explicit linkage of these rights with freedoms guaranteed in the U.S. Constitution and its Bill of Rights surpassed any political utopia that Vito had ever envisioned. He was equally drawn to GAA's definition of *activism* as "the commitment to bring about change in the present, rather than theorize about change in the distant future." After years of Mattachine caution and accommodation, Vito was more than ready to see change for gays put into practice.

GAA's commitment to nonviolence was particularly attractive to the neophyte activist. He was reassured by GAA architects who had left Gay Liberation Front partly because of its willingness to align with organizations, such as the Black Panthers, that considered violence integral to political progress. President Jim Owles, along with his friends Marty Robinson (who had handed Vito the Snake Pit leaflet) and Columbia Ph.D. candidate Arthur Evans, abandoned GLF in November 1969 to create an organization focused exclusively on gay rights, not the hodgepodge of leftist causes that scattered GLF's energies. Jim had tired of courting black, feminist, and Yippie radicals who were, at best, embarrassed by gays and lesbians. He'd had his fill of homophobic rejection in the peace movement, where, he remembered, "they kept telling me that there were greater things to work for than my own oppression and maybe I could be taken care of after the revolution." Neither he nor Marty appreciated GLF's trashing of their penchant for uninhibited anonymous sex—a right that Vito also valued.

Gay Activists Alliance was born on December 21, 1969, in the 1st Avenue apartment of Arthur Bell, Arthur Evans's lover and the *Village Voice*'s first openly gay columnist. The group's thirteen founders also included Marty's lover Tom Doerr, activist chronicler Donn Teal, and a lone woman, Kay Tobin, whose lover, Barbara Gittings, had founded the New York chapter of Daughters of Bilitis, the nation's first lesbian-rights group. The new members finalized their constitution and adopted *Robert's Rules of Order* in hopes of avoiding the anarchy that hampered GLF meetings.

When Vito showed up five months later, he met the men who fast became, second only to Arnie, his dearest friends. A shared love of B actresses endeared him to Arthur Bell, whose poison pen earned more than its share of enemies. Arthur was nearly fourteen years older than Vito, but they clicked as few contemporaries do. Born in Coney Island, Arthur spent most of his youth in Montreal, far from his beloved New York and therefore compelled to invent glamour. While America salaamed to *The Best Years of Our Lives* (1946) and other wartime flag-wavers, fourteen-year-old Arthur wrote to Hollywood stars in the guise of an armless veteran lonely for connection. He received sympathetic letters from Jane Wyman, Elizabeth Taylor, Vera-Ellen, and Vera Hruba Ralston—but Sophie Tucker reported him to the postal authorities when her emissary found not a wounded vet but a teenaged Noël Coward wannabe.

Twenty-five years later, Arthur was exactly Vito's kind of friend: someone who would call him up and, without even a hello, shriek, "Quick! Channel 5! Martha Raye and Frances Faye in *Double or Nothing!*"—or advise him in hot weather, "Think very Miriam Hopkins [;] think nasty, insincere thoughts about people and it'll cool you right off"—or invite him for a stroll down Christopher Street so they could "cast aspersions on people." For all his bile, Arthur adored Vito and introduced him to GLF and GAA member Jim Fouratt as "this young queen who [knew] even more about Hollywood movies" than Arthur himself. Vito met Arthur just as the columnist stopped using a pseudonym and began publishing, with gay pride, under his own name.

Vito was equally impressed by Jim Owles, a pale, delicate-featured Chicago native who, Vito later thought, resembled Princess Di. Jim's slight stature and schoolboy appearance belied a wild streak of rebelliousness that attracted Vito immediately. At thirteen, Jim ran a one-boy Kennedy campaign while his Nixon-loving parents fumed. He dropped out of Illinois State Teachers' College after a year and joined the U.S. Air Force, where he dispensed antiwar literature, received a court-martial, and was ultimately tranquilized and shipped to a Montana base for psychiatric observation. Shortly after moving to New York in April 1969, Jim joined the Gay Liberation Movement. Within a year, at age twenty-three, he had accrued such charisma that his address at one GAA meeting gave Arnie his final shove through the closet door.

Watching Jim get pitched by police down the front steps of City Hall, only to see him rush back up in order to speak with the mayor about gay rights, Marty Robinson dubbed his ex-lover "the scrappiest little faggot in New York." Devoting all his time to GAA, Jim lived in desperate poverty, with only two laundry bags of possessions and a roomy West Point overcoat handy for the stashing of shoplifted steaks. Luckily, diva worship didn't cost much. Jim added Greta Garbo to Arnie and Vito's scrapbook, forming twin trios of Hollywood deities and actress-addled young gay men. A college dropout, Jim sometimes felt insecure around his new friends with their university educations, but shared memorization of *Gone with the Wind* (1939) smoothed over any bumps.

During the summer of 1970, another Illinois native entered Vito's life through GAA. Like Jim, Steve Krotz had served in the air force, but footlight dreams brought him to Manhattan, where he found occasional work playing Pontius Pilate and Joseph of Arimathea in traveling productions of the *Oberammergau Passion Play* for audiences of up to fifteen thousand. Offstage, the sturdy vet with the authoritative bass voice was considerably less confident. As an aspiring actor, he wasn't comfortable with his homosexuality. Steve cruised Christopher Street bars with a wary eye out for homophobic producers or directors who might recognize him and deny him work. One night shortly after his twenty-sixth birthday, he was walking along Christopher and suddenly found himself swamped by cajoling marchers. "Come and join us!" Steve stood rooted to the pavement. "The fact that all these guys were marching down the street shouting at the top of their voices that they were gay and proud of it scared the hell out of me." But he followed them to GLF headquarters, where he began chatting with Jim and a few other men who were planning to start their own group. Steve decided to join them.

It took him several months to work up the nerve to attend a GAA meeting. When he finally did, he was a "nervous wreck," pacing back and forth before the tall iron fence ringing Holy Apostles. After summoning the courage to enter, Steve spotted an "incredibly sexy" guy with a "big, welcoming smile" heading straight for him.

"'Hi. I'm Vito.'

"I couldn't say anything right away. I just kept looking at him.

"'Are you here for the meeting?' he asked, unfazed by my stupor.

"'Hi, I'm sorry, I'm Steve . . . and I think so.'

"His voice and demeanor put me at ease almost right away and I felt that somehow I had always known this person. That I could totally trust this person. . . . Vito took my hand and said, 'Come on, let's go inside. The meeting will be starting in a couple of minutes.' He could have said 'Come on, let's go jump in front of a bus.' And I would have done it."

In short order, Steve began spending most of his time on West 24th Street with Vito, awkwardly sharing his new boyfriend's narrow twin bed. Within several months, they were ready to call the relationship "official," and Steve moved his belongings to Chelsea. As his love for Vito grew, he also became "obsessed" with GAA. From the start, the couple's devotion to each other and to gay liberation were two halves of the same coin.

Despite his bravado with Steve, Vito wasn't comfortable speaking up among activists who were so politically attuned and articulate. Though he was passionate about gay rights, the very notion seemed unreal, and Vito had no experience creating or changing legislation. For the first few months, he attended weekly GAA meetings in silence. He was awed by the courage of the Rockefeller Five, who planned to declare at their trial that they had and would "continue to commit acts of sodomy in order to encourage prosecution so that the constitutionality of the sodomy laws may be tested." He was also tickled by GAA's recourse to old-guard camp to achieve political aims. Male members were encouraged to apply for jobs as Radio City Music Hall Rockettes (no law specified that a Rockette had to be anatomically female), and plans were made to bear a transvestite on a litter, Cleopatra-style, down Lexington Avenue. His head whirling, Vito accepted an appointment as assistant to the secretary but bungled his first job, printing membership cards that read Gay Activist—rather than "Activists"—Alliance.

What most radicalized Vito were GAA's public displays of affection. Encouraged by Arthur Evans to show straight society their tenderness and attraction for one another, GAA members "kissed hello and goodbye wherever [they] went; [they] held hands and embraced as lovers and friends." This was, in fact, Vito's manner of coming out to his brother. Accompanying Charlie, Linda, and their two small daughters on a Village stroll, Vito suddenly stopped in the middle of the street to greet a male buddy with a passionate liplock. Though he had never heard the words "I'm gay" from his brother, Charlie wasn't especially shocked.

Even in the heart of the Village, such open affection wasn't uniformly applauded. In August 1970, Vito lost his job at Tor, a Greenwich Avenue restaurant where he supplemented his Omnibus income, by smooching Jim Owles goodbye after dinner. Informed that he could be fired for such behavior in front of customers—the majority of whom were gay men—Vito directed his boss to "shove it" and exited with Jim. He could always find another waiter job. More importantly, he learned GAA's principal lesson of gay self-respect. He was ready to join the organization as it took to the streets at the top of its collective lungs.

In Vito's words, "[GAA's] chief goal was to focus media attention on our issues because we felt that [the] underlying problem in terms of gay rights had been invisibility for years. It was a step forward just to begin to make ourselves and our issues visible." GAA had the good fortune to be creating itself in the media capital of the United States. If it could get the *New York Times*, the major news magazines (*Time, Newsweek, U.S. News & World Report*), and local and national television to cover demonstrations, the philosophies of gay liberation could spread worldwide. With "an odd mixture of dead earnestness and high camp," GAA mounted public "zaps," protests designed to bring maximum embarrassment to homophobes and maximum exposure to gay issues.

In October 1970, GAA descended on Broadway's Imperial Theatre, where Mayor John Lindsay and his wife were attending the first preview of Richard Rodgers's musical *Two by Two*. Vito was one of approximately six zappers who followed Mr. and Mrs. Lindsay into the lobby, where another six GAA men, including Steve, awaited them. The first contingent bustled the Lindsays toward their comrades, locked arms, and trapped the couple inside a circle of protesters. Screams of "Homosexuals need your help" and "End police harassment" careened off the lobby's polished walls and sent Mrs. Lindsay into a panic. A lifelong claustrophobe, Vito watched with a twinge of sympathy as she "started screaming and carrying on and pounding people" in her effort to break the ring that held her and her husband captive. In her flailing, Mrs. Lindsay slammed Arthur Evans in the chest and shins with her fists and feet and eventually summoned enough sheer physical strength to send the whole group reeling into an adjacent wall. Silent, Lindsay maintained a "smile plastered on his face the entire time"—even when energized theatergoers with no apparent connection to GAA joined in the chanting.

Not everyone in the gay community supported anti-Lindsay zaps. Many gays, remembering the brutal raids, harassment, and entrapment that typified the administration of Lindsay's predecessor, Robert F. Wagner, considered Lindsay a friend. The editors of the newly formed newspaper *GAY* denounced self-serving "gay 'liberationists'" who sought, by zapping Lindsay, to "advance their 'radical' aims at the expense of the city's homosexual community."

What some considered the mayor's do-nothing charm was open to a range of interpretations, but GAA found far less ambiguous bigotry in publications and policies attacking gays nationwide. Vito labeled the early zaps "reactive" rather than remedial. In 1970–71, he noted, "we were simply reacting to society's wrongs—in other words, virtually all of our demonstrations were in reaction to some homophobic thing that had happened and we needed to go after [it]." Two weeks after Vito's firing at Tor in August 1970, *Harper's Magazine* published Joseph Epstein's eleven-page essay "Homo/Hetero: The Struggle for Sexual Identity." It occasioned GAA's first nonpolitical zap.

Epstein begins the piece by recounting his childhood nightmare of a male ghoul who reached "a bony, long-nailed index finger out to touch my little brother's bared genitals. I woke up screaming." After fighting off the washroom advances of a lecherous southern mayor and invoking the "long daisy chain of failed queers" who have dominated American letters, Epstein laments that he has "very little idea" of how to prevent homosexuality in his four sons. Declaring homosexuality "anathema," he marvels at this "medieval"-style "curse" that science cannot fathom. When a party hostess remarks of two departing male guests that they are a closeted couple, Epstein recoils in revulsion while feigning embarrassment over his lack of sophistication: "How middle-class, how irretrievably square, how culture-bound, how unimaginative—I cannot get over the brutally simple fact that two men make love to each other." After averring that he has "never done anything to harm any single homosexual," Epstein thunders that given "the power to do so, [he] would wish homosexuality off the face of this earth." His essay reaches a sonic-boom conclusion with the claim that nothing his sons could do "would make [him] sadder than if any of them were to become homosexual. For then [he] should know them to be condemned to a permanent state of niggerdom among men, their lives, whatever adjustment they might make to their condition, to be lived out as part of the pain of the earth."

Epstein's hysterical rhetoric courted dismissal. One gay reader wrote off "Homo/Hetero" as "just a stupid nowhere article about some straight guy who didn't seem very connected to his own balls." But GAA realized that the piece could net prime publicity. Before orchestrating an all-out zap, four GAA members sent *Harper's* their own essays discussing homosexuality from overtly gay perspectives. All four were summarily rejected. *Harper's* also rejected GAA's proposal that the magazine commission an "unprejudiced article" in response to Epstein's. Executive editor Midge Decter refused to meet with GAA representatives to discuss their demands. She remarked that the magazine had received "hundreds of protests," twelve of which would be published in the November issue. That would have to suffice.

Not by far. A sit-in zap at *Harper's* offices was planned for the morning of October 27. It was to be "a breakfast party celebrating homosexuality, a sort of teach-in, be-in. Have a cup of coffee and a prune Danish and meet and rap with a living, breathing homosexual." Forty zappers arrived at 9 a.m. at 2 Park Avenue. Outside the building, participants distributed a flyer asking, "What are homosexuals like?" and inviting readers to join protesters on the eighteenth floor, where they could compare Epstein's argument against the words of actual homosexuals. Upstairs Vito snickered at the sight of his acerbic friend leaning on a cane and introducing himself to passersby: "Hello, I'm Arthur Bell; I'm a homosexual." Behind him, zappers set up an enormous coffee machine flanked by plates of donuts and bagels. One demonstrator volunteered two boxes of Israeli cookies and a quart of milk. As more employees arrived, zappers pushed the booty along with GAA literature. Most of the workers at 2 Park proved receptive to GAA's invasion and sympathetic to its argument. Many employees left their office doors open and gave zappers free use of their phones, enabling them to summon an army of New York press.

Not all *Harper's* personnel were so friendly. In her office, Midge Decter sat in an iron gray dress behind a cloud of cigarette smoke and defended her author. Epstein's article was, she claimed, "serious, honest, and misread. It [did] not reinforce anti-homosexual prejudices. The narrator [found] himself not liking queers and wonder[ed] about his difficulties since he [was] a liberal eager to insure political and social rights for homosexuals." Arthur Evans lost all patience. Before reporters from WBAI radio, ABC-TV, and WNEW-TV, he screamed at Decter, "You knew that that article would contribute to the suffering of homosexuals—you knew that! And if you didn't know that, you're inexcusably naïve and should not be an editor. If you [knew] that those views contribute to the oppression of homosexuals, then damn you for publishing it. . . . You are a bigot, and you are to be held responsible for that moral and political act!" A month later, as a guest on the *Dick Cavett Show*, Evans justified the *Harper's* zap by telling a national audience that Jews or blacks so maligned would rightly have torched the office. In the wake of all this publicity, *Harper's* devised a "new pro-homosexual policy" that would provide its editors with "open channels to the gay community."

Soon after the *Harper's* zap, Vito got a chance to answer bigotry directly. As GAA's corresponding secretary, his chief duties included establishing a mailing list of gay organizations, communicating with other GAA chapters that were beginning to spring up around the United States, and sending GAA information to anyone requesting it. But the position took on a far darker cast when he received a letter in response to the *Cavett* appearance of Arthur Evans, Dick Leitsch, and Marty Robinson. A Tulsa mother wrote that she and her seventeen-year-old son were "repelled" by the show. Leitsch, she asserted, "bore an actual physical resemblance to all the pictures I've seen of Satan, except for his tail," while all three men "were apt subjects for a painting depicting Dante's Inferno." Vito needed little further provocation to hit the streets yelling.

The early months of 1971 provided him with plenty of opportunities. In January, Gertrude Unser, chair of New York City's Board of Examiners (BOE), announced that she "considered homosexuals unfit to teach because they represented a moral, physical, and psychological danger to students." When a zap at Brooklyn's Board of Education opened no dialogue on discrimination suffered by gay teachers, GAA targeted the BOE offices on April 13. Outside, activists distributed "certificates" labeling Unser the "Bedroom Busybody of the Week." Inside Vito listened proudly as Steve, in his booming bass, read a statement demanding that the BOE declare a nondiscrimination policy toward homosexuals, that it rehire or relicense gay teachers already under attack, and that Unser either resign the BOE chair or retract her statement on gays. GAA distributed coffee, sang liberation songs, and "rapped" with high school students on what they considered "natural" and "unnatural" sexual acts.

Demonstrations often provided entertaining theater for participants and spectators. Nowhere was GAA's playfulness more evident than at the Fidelifacts "quack-in." Fidelifacts, Inc. was a private investigation agency whose president, Vincent Gillen, declaimed that "the problem of homosexuality seem[ed] to be increasing" among corporate ranks. Rest assured, though, he could ferret out deviants for the low sum of $12.50: "I like to go on the rule of thumb that if one looks like a duck, walks like a duck, associates only with ducks, and quacks like a duck, he probably is a duck." On the freezing afternoon of January 18, some twenty GAA protesters, armed with squeaky duck toys and led by Marty Robinson in a fluffy white duck suit, marched before Fidelifacts' West 42nd Street office. With Steve immediately behind him, Vito carried a sign promising "Sex Life Exposé $12.50." The moment was immortalized by Hollywood when director Gordon Parks, filming a Times Square scene for *Shaft*, tracked actor Richard Roundtree strolling through the picket line. GAA hardly blinked. "Accustomed to cameras at their protests, the Activists paid Shaft no mind as he sauntered by giving them a 'What the hell!?' look. Only the GAA could rattle 'the cat who won't cop out when there's danger all about.'"

Upstairs things were far less jolly. Gillen had locked himself in the men's room and refused to talk to GAA. When Jim Owles offered $12.50 to investigate Gillen's private life, he was told by a minion, "We don't handle *your* business." Another Fidelifacts employee warned the activists, "Don't fuck with me, 'cause I'm going for ass here. You're messing with private files here." When a seventeen-year-old demonstrator yelled back, "You're messing with private lives!" the employee knocked him to the ground while a local TV camera recorded the assault. Luckily, Bella Abzug was on hand, as she had been at *Harper's*, to ensure maximum media attention.

The next day, Gillen sent Jim a chutzpah-heavy letter accusing GAA of invading Fidelifacts' privacy and stealing materials from the office. He also extended a withered olive branch: "May I close by assuring you again of my sympathetic understanding, so far as a straight person can understand homosexuality?" One week later he was indicted for buying arrest records from the police.

In late spring, GAA issued an unexpected invitation:

> The Honorable Herman Katz,
> City Clerk, invites you
> to an engagement reception for
> Messrs. John Basso and John G. Bond
> Messrs. Steve Krotz and Vito Russo
> at his office,
> Room 265, Municipal Building,
> Friday, June 4, 1971
> at 10:00 a.m
> All welcome. Dress optional.
> Sponsored by
> Gay Activists Alliance

Katz had raised GAA's hackles when he condemned, in the *New York Post*, the "illegitimate" gay union ceremonies performed by Father Robert Clement at his Church of the Beloved Disciple. GAA decided an engagement party was in order.

John Basso, aka Wojtowicz or "Little John," had been pestering the organization to host his "weddings." GAA balked, unsure whether gays should be imitating heterosexual marriages. They didn't have to hold off Little John for long; in August 1972, he was arrested for robbing a Brooklyn bank in the hopes of paying for his lover's sex change, a story dramatized in the film *Dog Day Afternoon* (1975). Despite its qualms over marriage for gays, GAA knew a theatrical zap opportunity when it saw one.

Twenty-five activists set up camp in Katz's office with coffee, donuts, and a wedding cake bearing an enormous gold Lambda. Atop the cake were a pair of tiny plastic grooms and a pair of tiny plastic brides. "Gay Power to Gay Lovers" screamed block-letter icing on the borders. While ten activists distributed flyers throughout the building, Arthur Evans commandeered Katz's phone: "Hello, Gay Activists Alliance. A marriage license? Yes, this is the place. We're specializing in gay marriages today. Are you gay? Stop by and have a piece of cake at our engagement party." Dialogue with city employees ran smoothly until one man flailed his way through the activists, sputtering, "Let me out of this garbage!" Gay Power asserted its voice: "Hey you, buddy. Are you calling gay people garbage? Come back here and say that to a gay person's face!" The employee scrambled for the door. Dancing, folksinging, and mass cake consumption resumed.

When later asked for his memories of this day, Steve laughed. He recalled neither the zap itself nor any plans that he and Vito might have had to "marry" that summer. They were passionately committed to each other and to their shared activism, but "it was a different world then. [Marriage] wasn't even an option." Merely living in openly gay cohabitation was accomplishment enough.

When he joined GAA, Steve was giving his parents time to adjust to his homosexuality. After moving in with Vito, however, he wanted them to know his lover. At their initial meeting, Vito strode over to Steve's father with a big grin, shook his hand, and warmly welcomed him to "our apartment." It took Vito no time to set up his 16mm projector and begin screenings of TV clip reels and movies. Mr. and Mrs. Krotz thoroughly enjoyed themselves while Steve sat back, admiring "the incredible exuberance and strength of Vito's gregarious personality." What could have been a brutally awkward visit went without a hitch. Vito was completely unself-conscious about being gay and about living with another man.

He displayed the same openness with his own family. When Vito introduced Steve to the Russo clan, he made it clear that they were not "friends," as per the era's euphemism, but a couple. Steve, in turn, felt completely welcomed by his new in-laws. At a Thanksgiving dinner given by one of Annie's sisters, he was just one of the few dozen guests at the folding tables snaking their way around the apartment. After five hours of antipasto, salad, turkey, smoking breaks, and rounds of musical chairs, Steve felt like one of the family. Many of Vito and Steve's GAA cronies were estranged from families who couldn't accept their homosexuality. In his pre-GAA days, Vito had felt "guilt about having to be secretive" with his family. With Steve in his life, he gathered the courage to come out and never look back. None of Charlie's three children remembers learning of Vito's homosexuality; it was simply a given, along with the other "uncles" he brought to Lodi.

At the same time, Vito's homosexuality was sometimes difficult for his father to tolerate. Aunt Jean recalls Charles's boasting about Charlie's achievements until she reminded him, "You know, Vito's your son, too." As Vito's star rose and he began appearing on television to promote gay rights, Charles often left the room. He took considerable jeering from construction-worker colleagues who had seen his volcanic gay son in newspaper or television accounts of demonstrations. But Charles welcomed Vito's friends and lovers into his house without question or comment, always treating them kindly and offering them the same lavish hospitality that had characterized all the Russo family gatherings.

Charles also accompanied Annie into Manhattan to tend to Vito in illness. On one visit, he got a taste of his son's dicey neighborhood and his surprisingly violent temper. Vito and Steve had contracted a case of hepatitis so severe that for several days Steve was delirious, unsure whether it was night or day. Annie and Charles drove in on weekends to nurse the invalids and run errands. On their final visit, the Russos decided to scrub the apartment from floor to ceiling to remove any remaining germs. With the rooms reeking of disinfectant, they opened the windows and front door before retiring to the living room. As they chatted, the foursome heard the click of the bathroom door down the hall. Who could possibly be in the john? Still woozy, Vito staggered to the door and rattled the locked knob. From within a young woman's voice emerged. "Just a minute, just a minute!" The intruder soon appeared and leapt for the front door, leaving a mound of feces on the bathroom rug. Just outside the apartment, she called back, "At least I didn't use your toilet!" Annie and Charles had to restrain Vito, who was screaming for blood and lunging to throw the girl down the stairs. Steve had never before seen Vito's "pit bull" qualities, which resurfaced when their home suffered a second invasion. This time a robber sauntered down the street past the couple, bearing away his haul in Steve's crammed air force bag. A deadbolt and window gates were no deterrent to Manhattan burglars, particularly not when 401's front door remained unlocked.

GAA helped distract Vito and Steve from their neighborhood's problems. Though still more a follower than a leader, Vito began to assert himself during the 1970 GAA elections. Steve's position as chair of the Elections Committee gave Vito confidence and prompted him to question the presidential candidates about one of his key concerns: "GAA is at present a nonviolent organization. Would you change that at all?" Vito wasn't interested in running for office, but he encouraged Steve to nominate himself for secretary. Arnie asked Vito to nominate him for the vice presidency. Steve won by a landslide—though two write-in votes went to Vito (and one to Donald Duck). Arnie trounced Marty

Robinson, while Jim Owles soundly defeated Arthur Evans and Cary Yurman, one of the previous summer's record-breaking kissers in Central Park, for the presidency.

In 1971, the country's premiere gay-rights organization was headed by Vito's two best friends and his lover. It was time for him to make his own mark.

At home and at GAA, Vito's life was ideal. Professionally, he was spinning his wheels. Pushing twenty-five, he was still waiting tables. He decided, once and for all, that it was time for him to grow up and stop being a "Greenwich Village faggot" whose life revolved around ghetto bars and restaurants. GAA helped him realize that homosexuality implied "not only . . . sex, but also politics and art." He took charge of his gay film education by seeking out the underground staples *Lot in Sodom* (1933), *Chant d'Amour* (1950), *Flaming Creatures* (1963), and *Pink Narcissus* (1971). In NYU's graduate cinema program, he studied with several "wonderful crackpots" who taught him the language of film criticism, which had recently become a legitimate academic discipline. The program's director was George Amberg, a chain-smoking former Museum of Modern Art (MoMA) theater curator who, in 1950, established the first university course in experimental film. Future *Time* magazine film critic Richard Corliss was among Vito's classmates. Their heavy-hitting professors included Andrew Sarris, who had just published the influential *American Cinema: Directors and Directions, 1929–1968* (1968) and was on his way to a legendary career in *Village Voice* criticism; Annette Michelson, an editor of *Artforum* and co-founding editor of *October*; and William K. Everson, author of several books on film and owner of an FBI-hunted underground-film stash that must have given Vito no end of collector's envy.

The NYU curriculum tended toward the giants—*Birth of a Nation* (1915), *Potemkin* (1925), *Citizen Kane* (1941)—and afforded Vito an introduction to film aesthetics. Through his coursework, he learned how to read film formally and developed an understanding of palette, sound, acting style, and auteur stamp. More personally, Vito used his time at NYU to practice politicking. A then-closeted classmate, John Kane, retains a vivid picture of Vito sailing into a classroom auditorium wearing a GAA T-shirt and working the room, kissing everyone hello while tossing out liberation bons mots. John was struck by Vito's courage in asserting himself before peers and professors alike.

Now what to do with all the knowledge he was accumulating? It guaranteed good banter with the Omnibus clientele, but Vito wanted to apply what he was learning to a professional future. Opportunity knocked at the beginning of 1971, when he bagged the pleasantly nebulous title of editorial production manager at *After Dark*. First published in 1968, the magazine was the brainchild of William Como, an Italian American World War II veteran who had begun his career at *Dance Magazine* and *Ballroom Dance Magazine* before transforming the latter into *After Dark*. With one eye on revenue and the other on the male form, Como stuffed the pages of his new publication with showbiz gossip and copious nudes. Staff writer and future theater critic Patrick Pacheco discovered *After Dark* in Los Angeles as a recently out ex-seminarian. Spying an issue on a friend's coffee table in 1971, he recognized in it a world of New York glamour that he wanted to join: Stephen Sondheim, Alexis Smith, Angela Lansbury, Sylvia Miles—all flanked by Kenn Duncan's and Jack Mitchell's lush, black-and-white photos of male nudes and partial nudes. Patrick had never visited New York, but he flew east and landed a job at the magazine of his dreams.

When Vito joined the staff, *After Dark*'s gay allure was well established. The first issue on which he worked offered fawning features on Broadway goddess Helen Gallagher, Metropolitan Opera diva Dorothy Kirsten, and the Tony Awards' twenty-fifth anniversary. Stunning portraits of drag queen Holly Wood-lawn, Rudolf Nureyev, Leonard Bernstein, and Leonard Whiting's bare butt (in *Romeo and Juliet*) were tossed in for good measure. The full-page ad preceding the table of contents pitched the clothing store Michael's Closet, "For Those Who Live in . . . and Frequent the West Village." With good reason, associate editor Craig Zadan called *After Dark* "the gayest magazine ever published."

Why, then, did Vito denounce his five-month tenure as "the most horrifying experience [he had] ever had in [his] life"? Principally because this ultra-gay magazine wasn't gay at all. Eager to obtain lucrative advertising, publisher Jean Gordon aggressively pursued liquor and automobile accounts, which, she surmised, would shy away from an overtly gay publication. So *After Dark* resorted to transparent indirection. Como's ad copy read, "In keeping with the new freedom, *After Dark* (a magazine of entertainment) publishes relevant coverage of all that is new, exciting, controversial—and even established—in the broad, changing world of entertainment." Though the ambiguous "new freedom" is trumped by two awkward references to "entertainment," the subtextual demographic eluded no one. But Gordon refused to acknowledge the mainstay of her readership, instructing her staff, "You are to say that we are not a homosexual magazine. It's not our fault that homosexuals read this magazine. We are an entertainment magazine." Not a homosexual magazine when the chief editorial decision each month was "To penis or not to penis"?

Vito tried to look the other way. The magazine was, after all, offering him his first shot at professional writing. The more ambitious of his two film reviews reveals some callow prose ("Watching *The Panic in Needle Park* is like being at the scene of an accident—you can't bear to look, but you can't look away") along with the direct-address tactic ("some [lovers] are just tragic and they live on the same streets as you do") that would soon typify his journalism. Focused on his own work, he disregarded the issue's profile of Murray Head and Jon Finch, playing a bisexual artist and a gay hustler in John Schlesinger's new film *Sunday Bloody Sunday* (1971). The article contained not a word on the film's casual treatment of homosexuality.

But Vito couldn't overlook his coworkers' self-hatred. The timid, predominantly gay staff could not have differed more sharply from the GAA crew with whom Vito spent his free time. An early warning came in the form of watercooler whispers: *"'PSSSST, are you going to F.I. this weekend?' 'F.I.?' 'SHHHH—Fire Island!!!!'* There wasn't a soul in sight. The mind boggled." This was an atmosphere in which Bill Como, who sported caftans, mascara, and a pet poodle named Cesare, threw teary diva fits that suggested Kay Thompson crossed with Blanche DuBois. Como's own reputation, combined with that of his staff, was so notorious that drag queen Craig Russell dubbed the office the domain of the "Comosexuals." But it was also an atmosphere in which publisher Gordon "dated" male employees tricked out in "let's-dress-straight-enough-to-take-the-boss-out-outfits." Amid screamingly obvious gayness, the closet ruled.

Vito's astonishment turned to anger when Steve dropped by the office one day to pick him up for lunch. After a quick peck on the cheek, they were off. When Vito returned, the office "temperature was zero." The receptionist motioned him over and instructed him not to kiss Steve when he visited. When Vito asked why, she regarded him "with the patience that comes only from fear and hiding and having learned to live with daily hypocrisy and said, 'You don't shit where you eat, understand?'" He was appalled. "Yes, I understood perfectly and it made me sick."

He hung on a few months longer, until Gordon dropped two final insults. Vito's friend, vocalist Steve Grossman, attempted to place an ad that promoted him as "A Gay Singer." Gordon accepted the ad with the provision that Grossman change its copy to "A Different Kind of Singer with a Different Kind of Song." Then the *Advocate*, a national gay newspaper, submitted an ad with two men overlooking the Golden Gate Bridge: "These two men are in love. They're trying to build a life together without fear or guilt or shame, and America's #1 homosexual newspaper, the *Advocate*, is trying to help them." Gordon turned the ad down flat. Vito promptly directed all his friends to cancel their subscriptions to *After Dark* and to write letters to Gordon explaining their dissatisfaction. Following a barrage of negative mail, Gordon hauled Vito into her office and asked if he were responsible for the wholesale cancellations—and accompanying loss of revenue. He readily owned up, and a screaming match followed. To Vito's amazement, Gordon did not fire him. But he knew he couldn't remain in such a closeted atmosphere—not for a measly $125 a week, which he could easily best by waiting tables. By July 1971, he was ready to move on, both politically and professionally.

GAA gathered political clout throughout 1970 and 1971. One of the organization's principal goals was to force city, state, and federal candidates to articulate their positions on gay issues, thereby creating a voting bloc capable of swinging elections. In 1970, New York State assemblyman Antonio Olivieri won his Upper East Side district—the first Democrat to do so in over fifty years—by the narrow margin of five hundred votes out of more than eighty-six thousand. He acknowledged to the press that gays, whose rights he publicly supported, may well have ensured his victory.

As GAA's corresponding secretary, Vito enthusiastically canvassed politicians' views on gay rights. In his communications with other activists, he endorsed the publishing of candidates' opinions as a way to politicize apathetic gays: "They're grateful when you take the trouble to find out who's for them and who's against them and they realize that the movement may be for *them* as well as others. Right on with this vital work."

GAA began distributing questionnaires. Candidates were directed to check yes or no to questions asking whether they would support progay policies in housing, employment, and military service. In keeping with its philosophy, GAA promised no endorsement of candidates regardless of their positions, but it indicated that all answers, or lack thereof, would "receive maximum publicity in both the gay and the straight press." The return on questionnaires was approximately 25 percent, far better than the GAA leadership expected. Responses were a predictable mixed bag. Late June seemed an extremely popular vacation time for politicians; virtually all respondents sent their regrets for the Gay Pride March. Future New York mayor Ed Koch checked "yes" to all legislative questions, as did Representative Shirley Chisholm (the first black woman elected to Congress), Senator Eugene McCarthy, and presidential candidate (for the People's Party) Dr. Benjamin Spock. Governor Nelson Rockefeller failed to respond. Other candidates were entirely forthcoming in their homophobia. Bronx representative Robert N. Schneck wrote, "No one should be forced to hire someone that he feels is unqualified because of emotional aberrations," while his colleague Rose Anne Leitenberg opined, "I feel homosexuals are 'sick' people and need help. I don't feel the law intends to harass so much as help the homosexuals. I think it is an unhealthy and undesirable state and feel it should be alleviated rather than expanded or continued."

This brand of official bigotry inspired GAA to draft progay legislation for New York City. The city already offered antidiscrimination protections in housing, public accommodation, and employment based on race, color, creed, national origin, ancestry, physical handicap, and sex. In June 1970, Jim Owles and Arnie Kantrowitz called on Councilman Eldon Clingan to add "sexual orientation" to the city's roster of protected minorities. On January 6, 1971, Clingan and fellow councilman Carter Burden announced their sponsorship of Intro 475, which would insert "sexual orientation" into each clause of the city's Human Rights Law. Having lost one job because of homophobia and soon to quit another for the same reason, Vito was overjoyed at the news.

Intro 475 helped inspire Vito's first demonstration for gay rights outside New York City. On the weekend of March 14, busloads of GAA demonstrators joined some three thousand other gay activists from all over New York State as they marched on the state capitol in Albany. In addition to antidiscrimination legislation for employment and housing, marchers demanded an end to New York State's sodomy, solicitation, loitering, and impersonation laws. John Paul Hudson joked that the "scene on the Capitol steps was like something out of a Cecil B. DeMille epic choreographed by Florenz Ziegfeld—people in every kind and color of dress and costume sweeping up level after level of stairs, [with] banners, and banner carriers." Despite the camp pageantry, parade organizers counseled marchers on how to handle a mace attack and advised that they not carry anything that might be construed as a weapon. Even stick handles for signs were verboten.

Ultimately, the day's only violence came from the speakers. Jim Owles took the podium and informed the crowd that Albany was just the beginning; soon they'd be storming Washington. Southern Pentecostal minister Troy Perry, founder of the Los Angeles Metropolitan Community Church, brought brimstone theatrics to his demand for gay rights. Kate Millett, author of the influential *Sexual Politics* (1970), earned deafening cheers by remarking about her recently uncloseted sexuality: "Today it feels so damn good to say it out loud." Elated, Vito coordinated the entertainment for the bus ride home. "We sang till we were hoarse, led by Vito, who should be a cruise director," John Paul enthused. Still, he wondered, "how could Steve sleep so contentedly with all that screeching?"

Back in Manhattan, Intro 475 ground to a standstill. City Council Democratic majority leader Thomas Cuite, an entrenched Brooklyn conservative, refused to schedule the General Welfare Committee hearings required for the bill to reach full council vote. Nor would he meet with GAA representatives to discuss the stalemate. By Friday, June 25, two days before the second Christopher Street Liberation Day March, GAA had had enough. Vito was one of fifty demonstrators who swarmed City Hall in an effort to reach Cuite's office. Cops at the main doors claimed that the building was "closed to the public," even as obviously nongay people were permitted to come and go. Watching from the street, Arthur Evans scooped up fresh droppings left by police horses, bellowed, "This city administration is horseshit!" and launched his reeking missile at City Hall. When Jim and Arnie attempted to sit on the building's top step, officers shoved them down to the street. Jim ran back up the steps and was immediately arrested. Mounted police charged onto the scene, "attempting to knock the gays aside with their horses and herd them away from the front of the building." When Steve, standing with Arnie, asked an officer how GAA's activities were illegal, both men were arrested on the spot. Vito watched helplessly as his lover and his best friends were led under guard into City Hall.

Conditions inside were less oppressive. In total, nine activists were arrested, including four of GAA's five officers. Arnie commented, with customary drollness, "Seven hours with my hands cuffed behind me in the Fifth Precinct station house is not my idea of a pleasant afternoon." But he and Steve both found the police to be friendly, not at all the fag-bashing rapists they expected. Instead, the cops serenely asked the activists why they were demonstrating. The afternoon also provided some unexpected humor when the prisoners were taken to be photographed by the Red Squad. "Red Squad?" Arnie chuckled. "I'm saying cocksucking, and they're hearing communism." All nine were released on their own recognizance. That night, GAA played video of the day's events, reliving the protest over and over. Vito felt sick with the emotions churning inside him: lingering fear over the day's violence; profound concern for Steve, Arnie, and Jim; relief at their release; most of all, rage that any of it had been necessary in the first place.

Cuite met with GAA shortly afterward. But Councilman Saul Sharison, chair of the General Welfare Committee, refused to schedule a committee hearing on Intro 475. On September 18, GAA sent Sharison a written demand that he announce a hearing date by the thirtieth. His response: "I don't take any shit." Shortly after midnight on October 3, approximately one thousand activists marched to Sharison's luxury apartment building. Vito was at the forefront of this action, leading the troops to their East Village destination. On arrival, they found 70 East 10th Street crawling with cops who did not hesitate to crack their clubs against protesters' "heads, necks, crotches, backs." Some of the night's action, however, was prearranged for the mutual benefit of GAA and the media. According to participant Charles Silverstein, when a "Suicide Squad" of activists vaulted police barriers, "the police 'arrested' them; the pictures were taken, and everybody went home. It made a hell of a story in the papers the next day." Nearing its second anniversary, GAA had sharpened its media savvy. Eager to avoid further embarrassment, Sharison scheduled hearings for Intro 475 in City Hall's council chamber.

From the start, Intro 475 enjoyed support from many prominent figures, including Bella Abzug, Bronx borough president Bob Abrams, Shirley Chisholm, Ed Koch, Kate Millett, Eleanor Holmes Norton (chair of New York's Commission on Human Rights), Gloria Steinem, and Dr. George Weinberg (a straight psychologist who had just published the pioneering *Society and the Healthy Homosexual* [1972]). Nonetheless, the bill also attracted undiluted venom from Bible-toting citizens who, at one hearing, denounced homosexuals for "burning in their lust" and insisted that "God is love, but He has certain standards." Bronx councilman Michael DeMarco inquired of a priest supporting Intro 475, "You're against sin, aren't you?. . . . And isn't, aren't, acts of sodomy sins?" Throughout the hearings, Jim Owles "fumed" and Vito "wept" in response to the bigotry hammering them. They also cheered the eloquent defenses of gay rights mounted by Arthur Evans, Arthur Bell, Jim Fouratt, and Pete Fisher, who read from the Declaration of Independence. A moment of tense levity arose when DeMarco remarked with horror that he'd just spotted "two people in dresses trying to get into the men's room." From the balcony came the screams of Rey "Sylvia" Rivera and another drag queen that they had *tried* to use the ladies' but were barred.

GAA reserved the lion's share of its anger for the mayor. Though Lindsay professed lukewarm support for Intro 475, neither he nor his police and fire commissioners testified on its behalf at any of the General Welfare hearings. On the evening of January 25, 1972, Vito joined three hundred activists at the Ziegfeld Theatre for a march in sixty-miles-per-hour winds to Radio City Music Hall. Supported by other Lindsay critics, including the Jewish Defense League and citizens opposing a public housing project in Queens, GAA set out to disrupt a $300,000 fundraiser for Lindsay's U.S. presidential campaign. "In their best Sunday drag," Vito and a dozen other protesters entered the hall with tickets obtained by a GAA member boasting *Variety* credentials.

The well-heeled audience of six thousand had paid fifty or one hundred dollars per ticket to hear the mayor's campaign promises, followed by a screening of the new Robert Redford heist caper *The Hot Rock*. The show they got, however, was quite different. The second that emcee Alan King introduced the mayor, activist Morty Manford gave a basso roar from the balcony: "Lindsay lies to homosexuals. He's an actor. Gays demand action for civil rights." He and Cora Perotta handcuffed themselves to the balcony railing as Steve Ashkinazy and several other GAA members set off air horns whose wails ripped the hall's ornate politesse. Ernie Cohen sent showers of "Lindsay Lies to Gays" leaflets spiraling down to the orchestra seats. From the stage, Lindsay unwisely tried to chide the demonstrators into silence: "If I may remind the gentlemen [*sic*] of the Gay Liberation Front [*sic*] . . . you are in the wrong forum. All you're doing is damaging your chances of getting the bill I'm supporting through the City Council." From behind his fake Abraham Lincoln beard, Rich Wandel screamed, "Lies, lies!" at the mayor, who then took shelter in the wings. As police extracted Morty and Cora from their cuffs and dragged them from the hall, those GAA members still able to exit on their own steam did so. When Vito swept proudly up the aisle on the arms of male friends, a piercing jeer stopped them: "Goodbye, girls!" Vito pivoted in the heckler's direction and barked back, in rhetoric twenty years ahead of its time, "We aren't girls. We're men who like to fuck men—and you'd better get used to it!"

Two days later, the General Welfare Committee held its vote on Intro 475. The final tally revealed a narrow defeat (7-5, 1 abstention, 2 absences). After all the emotionalism of the hearings and the zaps, the bill's fate surprised no one. In

1972, it was victory enough to have forced the city council to consider seriously gay people's civil rights. But Vito was no longer convinced that high-octane zaps were the best way to attract the great silent majority of New York's closeted, frightened gays. His emerging ideas about community outreach would change the tenor of GAA and give the rest of his life its professional focus.

Within GAA, Vito was becoming a force. A vocal presence at the zaps, he was even more conspicuous at Thursday-night meetings. After thirty-five years, play-wright and screenwriter Victor Bumbalo still has vivid memories of Vito jump-ing up to yell out his ideas: "He would get very passionate about what we *weren't* doing—'We could be doing *more*; we could be doing *this*. . . . Why aren't we chaining ourselves up *here*; why aren't we drawing attention to *this* fact?'" When historian Jonathan Ned Katz joined GAA in 1972, Vito and Arnie often "got up and gave very emotional and irate and angry and militant activist speeches, just spontaneously." Inspired by their eloquent outrage, the partially closeted Katz began going on zaps, stopped writing under the pseudonym "John Swift," and began preparing the masterpiece that he would publish four years later, under his own name, as *Gay American History*.

Vito made a particular effort to reach out to minorities who felt excluded from GAA's predominantly white, male, middle-class membership. Frank Arango, one of the group's few Latinos, wanted to run for delegate-at-large but thought that many members scorned his ethnicity and his Cuban accent. He turned to Vito for advice. Vito reassured Frank that he was a worthy person who should feel sufficiently proud of himself and his English to tell racist detractors "to go and fuck themsel[ve]s." Frank later wrote to Arnie, "Still after 20 years I remember that night, no one before had open[ed] my eyes and mind like [Vito] did, gave me some kind of respect for my self and [for] that I will always be grateful to him." Armed with Vito's encouragement, he went on to win the election in a landslide.

The question remained of how to engage timid people like Frank Arango in gay liberation. Vito was reminded of Arthur C. Clarke's novel *Childhood's End* (1953), one of his early favorites, in which alien colonizers prepare human in-feriors for the end of civilization. After joining GAA, Vito recognized the book's political resonance. Clarke's picture of a passive humanity, willing to accept as law the dicta of inscrutable, infinitely wiser "Overlords," was a parable of any oppressed population allowing itself to be arbitrarily governed. GAA members had overcome their passivity, but what about the hundreds of thousands of gay New Yorkers who wouldn't come near a zap for fear of losing job and family in one fell swoop? The movement needed them as badly as they needed the movement.

GAA tried to reach frightened or indifferent gays through its cultivation of "gay space." In May 1971, the organization set up headquarters in an abandoned four-story firehouse on Wooster Street, in the desolate heart of a SoHo decades from becoming boutique-and-gallery central. For $1,100 per month, the GAA Firehouse offered organization members ten thousand square feet, more than five times the space available at Holy Apostles. It fast became "a home in which [they] could be gay and proud. A home for love, peace, and homosexuality." Along the main floor's wall sprawled a forty-foot mural that Arnie labeled a gay "family portrait" featuring Walt Whitman, Gertrude Stein, the Black Panthers' Huey Newton (after he endorsed gay liberation), Jim Owles protesting at City Hall, and Vito marching on Albany.

From the massive mural, Vito's face looked down over revelers at the popular dances that GAA hosted on Saturday nights. A voluntary cover charge of $1.50 bought dancers all the beer they could drink (sodas cost an extra quarter each). Flanked by white tile, the Firehouse's main hall featured superb acoustics for "a sound system the Fillmore [East concert hall] might envy." Amid pulsating lights, the mostly male crowd boogied to the sounds of the Stones, Aretha Franklin, and the Doobie Brothers. A year earlier, Arnie had never seen two men dancing together. Now observing the crowd from his perch on a spiral staircase, he saw up to fifteen hundred male dancers and felt that he was "part of something powerful." The men weren't just dancers but "our people, our troops!"

The dances didn't thrill everyone. For one thing, though drugs were prohibited at the Firehouse, mescaline was fairly common on the main floor. Some dancers indulged to the point of getting "scary sick" and having to be carried out of the hall. Also, many lesbians felt uncomfortable in such a testosterone-fueled milieu. While Cora Perotta found it easy to meet women at the Firehouse because they were so conspicuous among the men, Karla Jay missed the separate room offered to women at GLF's dances. And at least a few women were unsettled by one male regular who attended dances completely nude. Two lesbians took it upon themselves to knit him a wool penis-cozy, which he dropped into his transparent plastic purse before waltzing off, still starkers. Then there was the ear-splitting noise level. Policemen showed up at the first Firehouse dance bearing three citations: excessive noise, no certificate of occupancy, no permit to assemble. When one cop threatened a raid, Jim Owles replied, with Vito at his side, "You go in there swinging that billy club and you'll have a riot on your hands." The police beat a retreat as Jim, strolling back into the hall, brandished the citations over his head. "Three more pieces of paper to plaster on the wall," he crowed to onlookers.

Vito took a stab at screening zap footage up on the third floor, but few dancers abandoned the main floor's pounding beat in favor of political enlightenment. At any rate, Vito resisted the notion of himself as overtly political. In later years, he insisted, "I always said that [liberation] would happen in social ways. That I didn't give a shit [about] changing the laws, although I knew it had to be done, but that you don't change people by changing laws, and that the way you reach people was through media." One of GAA's chief politicos, Marty Robinson, had little patience for "media" beyond the video equipment used to record zaps. "You're not gonna dance your way to gay liberation!" became his refrain, to which Vito retorted, "I'm not talking about dancing. I'm talking about teaching gay people how to have fun with one another." Among the leadership, Vito was developing a prickly reputation, that of a "perennial hairshirt on behalf of GAA's oftentimes minimized social/cultural program." If this new image meant engaging apoliticals in gay culture, he didn't mind at all.

To realize his goal, Vito became chair of GAA's Culture (Arts) Committee, signing Executive Committee attendance sheets with a camp flourish ("Vito Sophia Russo"). One of his pet projects was the Cabaret Night, offered on alternate Friday nights at the Firehouse. According to Steve Krotz, the Cabaret arose from architectural strain. When too many tired dancers lounged upstairs, they were in danger of crashing through the flimsy Victorian floor. GAA embraced Vito's idea of Cabaret Nights as a safer money-making alternative.

To Vito, the Cabaret was a place where gay performers could relax and be themselves. Actor/singer John Paul Hudson knew well actors' terror of appearing gay to closeted "asshole agents." Before Stonewall, he recalled, "there was no place where you could learn your craft as a performer without doing straight material, singing love songs with the feminine pronoun as if you meant it, hiding hiding hiding." Vito designed the Cabaret to provide artists a rare opportunity for honesty. "For some men," he proudly remarked, "this is the first time they can be in front of an audience and sing a love song to a man." Determined to showcase uncloseted performers with maximum gloss, Vito engaged two Broadway designers, George James and John Dinsmore, who doused the stage with red and gold glitter. Installed as light man, Steve rigged up donated globe footlights and flashing marquee bulbs to illuminate the sparking silver Lambda over the stage. The whole effect reminded Vito of Debbie Reynolds in the ornate home of her most famous film character: it was, he proclaimed, "Molly Brown's drawing room in Denver—and I love it."

The glitzy set did not put all performers at ease. Steve, for example, had never sung as an openly gay man. "I just kind of froze and totally screwed it up the first time." His experience was not unique. At an early Cabaret night, John Paul despaired to hear male singers inserting, out of habit, female pronouns into their repertoire. Vito and Arnie begged that he reserve judgment for future shows.

It didn't take long for things to loosen up. Free beer flowed along with "open affection" from grateful audiences. John Paul found gay audiences "more gentle, more encouraging, more compassionate" than their straight counterparts. Gays, "know[ing] what it is like to be on display and to be unwanted, turned down," were willing to give nervous performers like Steve second chances. Emcee Rusty

Blitz, who had appeared in Mel Brooks's film *The Producers* (1968) and would go on to *Young Frankenstein* (1974) as well as *Sid & Nancy* (1986), was happy to throw struggling performers a lifeline. As a result, the quality of the acts improved and became more diverse. Vito was especially taken by one fellow, "a knockout in his boa, singing Bessie Smith's blues with gay abandon." Blues and folk predominated, but the Cabaret offered considerable comedy as well. Most popular was teenaged Nancy Jo Parker, who recited the entire *Wizard of Oz* script, complete with fluty Billie Burke ("Come out, come out, wherever you are!") and raging Margaret Hamilton (" . . . my little pretty!") imitations. When she warbled "Over the Rainbow" à la Liza Minnelli, Vito quipped, "there wasn't a dry seat in the house."

While laboring to get the Cabaret off the ground, Vito was even busier with his primary contribution to GAA: the Firehouse Flicks, shown on Friday nights and Sunday afternoons. He had not forgotten the excitement of the *Gold Diggers* screening during Pride Week 1970. Almost a year later, he proposed that a film subcommittee be appointed to kick off the Flicks. He decided to start things off light and sexy: Roman Polanski's *The Fearless Vampire Killers* (1967) featured a baroquely queeny vampire (Iain Quarrier) in lust with Polanski himself. The Firehouse audience loved it. Noting their shared laughter, Vito announced, "You've heard people argue about whether there's a gay sensibility. Well, you just experienced it."

Vito built a repertoire around films that he had seen with straight audiences but wanted to watch again in an all-gay setting. As he quickly realized, gays "pick up on things that straight audiences miss—an innuendo, the direction, the way a scene is played. It also seems like gay audiences are always pulling for the underdog." He wanted to use the films as springboards for discussion of machismo, sexism, gender role-playing, romance, violence, and the denigration of gays and lesbians in Hollywood films.

To this end, he planned a wide-ranging roster of films that bridged all major genres and attracted the widest possible audience: comedy (*Twentieth Century* [1934], *My Little Chickadee* [1940], *The Prince and the Showgirl* [1960], *The Loved One* [1965], *Bedazzled* [1967]); animation (Betty Boop, *Animal Farm* [1955]); drama (*Of Human Bondage* [1934], *All About Eve* [1950], *Long Day's Journey into Night* [in a little-seen unabridged print], *The Shop on Main Street* [1965], *Who's Afraid of Virginia Woolf?* [1966], *They Shoot Horses, Don't They?* [1969]); musicals (*The Unsinkable Molly Brown* [1964], the unlikely 3 a.m. double feature of *Thoroughly Modern Millie* [1967] and a Grateful Dead short [1967]); fantasy/horror (*The Man Who Could Work Miracles* [1936], *The Incredible Shrinking Man* [1957], *The Blob* [1958], *Lady in a Cage* [1964]); shorts (*It's a Camp*; *Kiss My Lips, Artchie* [with Jackie Curtis and David Susskind]; *Confessions of a Black Mother Succuba* [1965; billed with Vito's tag "Hmmmm, *sounds* interesting"]; *Report* [1967; dealing with JFK's assassination]);

gay-themed films (Kenneth Anger's *Fireworks* [1947] and *Scorpio Rising, Advise & Consent, Billy Budd* [1962], *The Servant* [1963], *This Special Friendship* [1964; "Bring Kleenex," Vito advised], *Rachel, Rachel* [1968], *The Killing of Sister George* [1968]), and sixties erotica ("which can't be advertised—ask Vito").

Vito also invited directors to Firehouse screenings. Shirley Clarke appeared when Vito screened her landmark documentary *Portrait of Jason* (1967), the story of a black gay hustler. Not only did Clarke participate in a lively question-and-answer session, she also taught the Video Committee how to edit zap tapes. Far more controversial was the visit of Rosa von Praunheim, the German director whose film *It Is Not the Homosexual Who Is Perverse, But the Situation in Which He Lives* (1971) Vito helped bring to New York. Finding gays in toto to be "moody, hectic and vain," Praunheim sought to "activate homosexuals, challenge them to overcome their excessive fear and fight for their rights themselves." This goal resonated perfectly with GAA philosophies, and Vito was delighted to screen a film whose own government had banned it from television. But *Homosexual*'s harsh Brechtian aesthetic, combined with its attack on bourgeois gay-male conformity, enraged many Firehouse spectators. At the question-and-answer session, activists screamed their outrage at Praunheim, who was not surprised to receive a more welcoming reception from the more radical, but now depleted, GLF.

To draw bigger audiences, Vito became a master of the one-liner, many of which appeared in the *Village Voice* as well as in GAA's promotional material. He sold *The Wizard of Oz* with psychedelic irony ("What can one say about a girl who trips on a Yellow Brick road?"), graced *The Blue Angel* (1930) with early seventies currency ("the definitive sado-masochistic *Love Story*"), and exhorted audiences of *The Women* (1939) to "bring your notebook to take down the lines!" Once Vito lured viewers to the Flicks, he intended to keep them coming back for more. He insisted that films be seen properly, which meant the purchase of a twenty-foot-long CinemaScope screen that could be lowered from the ceiling of the Firehouse's main floor. Said screen cost a hefty three hundred dollars and caused some debate in the Finance Committee—what was wrong with the sheet Vito had been using?—but Vito got what he wanted by arguing for "the value of film to gay liberation."

Audiences were electrified. During Gay Pride Week 1971, Vito showed *The Battle of Algiers* (1965), which sent his troops back up 6th Avenue, screaming for their own freedom. In honor of the following year's Pride, he hosted an all-night screening that participant Dan Allen proclaimed "Wall-to-Wall Groovy!" Hundreds of spectators sprawled across the floor in sleeping bags or over one another in cuddly couples. Beginning at 8 p.m. on Friday and continuing well into Saturday morning, Vito's program was aimed squarely at male spectators: *The Women*; *Funny Girl* (1968), paired with Vito's own copy of the television special *My Name Is Barbra* (1965); a Garland special "from one of her worst years";

Wait until Dark (1967); *Rock around the Clock* (1956), which prompted a 4 a.m. dance riot; a trailer for *Cabaret* (1972), only recently released to theaters); and the 8 a.m. finale of *Gypsy* (1962), for which only a hundred stalwart souls remained awake. Dan Allen crowed over the marathon's "celebration of Gay Unity," commenting, "the mood of the audience moved me because the atmosphere pulsated with enthusiasm, sending good vibrations bouncing around and all through the place. Since the 1940s, I've seldom seen a movie audience so vibrant." The crowd screamed for Judy (gratifying Vito with partisan bellows of "Fuck Streisand!") and cackled over Marjorie Main's sarcastic, sexist dialogue in *The Women*. And they had the unprecedented chance to salivate, without fear of assault, over the beefcake images of Alan Arkin, Omar Sharif, and Bill Haley.

To a certain degree, Vito was not above programming his audience's responses. Jeffrey Karaban recalls several Thursday-night "advance" screenings on 24th Street, where Vito would invite a small group to gauge a film's strongest laugh lines and to learn what questions or opinions he might expect the next night. On occasion he also planted comments, directing his buddies to defuse a serious moment with camp or to raise certain discussion topics that he could amplify after a film had ended.

But the audience response he craved most required no scheming. The Flicks were designed for people like Fred Goldhaber, a closeted twenty-four-year-old teacher who attended Vito's Halloween 1971 double feature, *Village of the Damned* (1960) and *Night of the Living Dead* (1968). Fred was dragged to the Firehouse by GAA member Steve Ashkinazy, who wanted to give his friend a sink-or-swim introduction to gay culture. As *Village* began, the audience responded with happy fright: they would, Fred recalled, "shriek and turn to the person on the left or the right and they would hug and hide their eyes in the other person's armpits, and it was simply wonderful. It was so much fun, and I found myself doing it, too. I lost all my inhibitions. It was hypnotic, intoxicating, just glorious. I had never in my life experienced such freedom." Fred laughed along with everyone else when a lesbian yelled at *Night*'s flesh-eating zombies, "Save me a breast!"

Amid the chills and giggles, Fred found himself in the arms of his seatmate. The next morning, the pair shared what Fred calls "a Vito Russo moment" on the platform at Grand Central Station: "Wayne took me in his arms and he gave me the most glorious kiss—I mean, one of those Jennifer Jones/Claudette Colbert *kisses*, you know, where you're going off to war. Actually, I guess I was because at that moment I became a soldier in the army of the gay rights movement." Fred attributes his coming out to "Vito's magic," a softer, more welcoming version of GAA not available at the zaps. Fourteen years later, he joined the faculty of New York's Harvey Milk High School, thus becoming the world's first teacher in a gay high school—an accomplishment, he remarks, that had much "to do with GAA and Vito, the pride that he had in being who he was and finding all these things in the movies and celebrating the gay image."

Like the dances, the film series had its critics, whose comments reveal widening ideological rifts within GAA. When Vito screened one of his personal favorites, the glossy marital breakdown of Albert Finney and Audrey Hepburn in *Two for the Road* (1967), Arthur Evans screamed at him, "How can you show a study of a heterosexual marriage at a gay liberation group?" Vito defended his choice by noting, "We have to look at these people, these are the people who we're being measured against." To the extent that Hollywood "owned" the narratives of romance and marriage, Vito wanted to gauge whether gays and lesbians found any reflection of their own relationships onscreen. Arthur was won over. Though he, like Marty Robinson, had at first resisted any diversion from GAA's political activities, he later acknowledged that the organization's "cultural activities probably influenced people more directly."

Male people, anyway; the handful of women present at Vito's all-night Pride marathon were horrified by *The Women*, calling its roster of cats, simps, and featherbrains a "catalogue of every stereotypic woman ever presented." Vito readily conceded the point but suggested that lesbian spectators use the film as a departure point for discussing women's representation on screen. When he recommended a forum on women in Hollywood films, he was informed that it was not the women's job "to explain their oppression to men because they [would be] forced into a maternal role by such encounters." The result was a stalemate that stymied Vito's planned festival Great Love Goddesses of the Screen (to include *Gilda* and his cherished *Roxie Hart*), "pending reaction of the women in the community." To Vito, this smacked of censorship, which he was also receiving from male activists in response to his Garland and Streisand repertoire. To claims that he was "reinforc[ing] the stereotype" of the diva-crazed "old faggot," Vito suggested that critics consider the hysterical cheers that these singers received at the Firehouse.

Recurring fights indicated the deeper chasms in communication between GAA's men and women. Men had little interest in abortion or child care, while women resented organizational time spent on police harassment in public-sex forums like the piers and trucks along the Hudson. Many women also took offense at the overtly sexual and frequently awful poetry ("My dick is this; my dick is that") that men read at Firehouse performances. Arnie Kantrowitz contends that GAA contained "many men of good will" who genuinely tried to understand women's needs and "give them their piece of the action," but even with the protections of *Robert's Rules* and GAA's second female vice president (Nath Rockhill), many women felt completely overshadowed at meetings. In the spring of 1973, a group of lesbians split off from GAA to form Lesbian Feminist Liberation (LFL). Transvestites, meanwhile, protested their own treatment at GAA.

Despite an early resolution to "reaffirm GAA's support and affection for its transvestite members," Sylvia Rivera and Marsha Johnson felt ignored when they tried to wrest attention at meetings from mainstream gays.

By early 1973, Vito was looking at an organization in chaos. Visibly deranged people had begun showing up and prolonging already lengthy meetings with incomprehensible babble; one mentally ill man offered himself as a candidate for president. And the organization was attracting widespread criticism. GLF had always denounced GAA as too narrow in focus, too conservative, but apolitical gays also declared GAA unnecessary. Why all the fuss? As one man remarked, "Most of us don't consider ourselves oppressed." When activist Marc Rubin tried campaigning for Councilman Clingan in an East Side gay bar, he was told, "Oh, get out of here with all your sanctimonious political bullshit." Playwright Arthur Laurents expressed a popular outsiders' view of GAA by equating its members with grim leftists he had known in the 1930s: "There was no difference. The beards and the leather jackets and the point of order and the furious lesbians and parliamentary procedure. And humorless." Even Pete Fisher, who would become one of GAA's staunchest soldiers, felt "embarrassed" by the open emotionalism he witnessed on his first visit. "I felt as though I were dropping in on a revival meeting of some sort."

With near-religious passion came vitriol. Despite a rule that banned "character assassinations" and "personal attacks" at meetings, tempers frequently flared. Vito was caught in the middle when Jim Owles, who had reneged on a promise to lend sound equipment to GLF, fell under an officers' vote of censure. It was excruciating to hear Steve and their good friend John Paul publicly condemn Jim for misleading the membership. A year later, shortly after Jim lost the presidency, he was physically assaulted during a zap at the Hilton Hotel, where Firemen's Union chief Michael Maye threw him down an escalator and inflicted facial wounds requiring six stitches. Squeamish about blood, Vito gasped to see Jim "looking terrifying, his eyes swollen green and purple." Jim's wounds reminded Vito of the death threats that Steve had had to field as secretary. They had invested so much effort to raise society's awareness of gays, and these were the results?

At his trial, Maye entered the courtroom with hands raised in the style of the Golden Gloves champ that he was. Vito leapt to his feet and screamed at him, "A man is known by the company he keeps!" Fellow activists chorused their agreement, but it didn't matter. Maye was acquitted of all charges.

Vito was losing faith in the efficacy of gay politics.

As usual, film took his mind off his troubles. In 1971, Vito landed a job in the film circulation department at the Museum of Modern Art (MoMA). The salary was "coolie wages," almost certainly under five hundred dollars per month—but

Vito considered his two years at the museum a "spell of perfect weather." As he later reflected, "You couldn't ask for a better job because all you did was look at movies all day and work with very famous people." The position was so tailor-made that he forgave colleagues for referring to movies as "cinema."

In the days before VHS, MoMA's circulating film library provided many titles that were otherwise very difficult to obtain. Vito's duties consisted chiefly of processing requests made by universities, film societies, and other not-for-profit organizations. He also had the chance to contribute suggestions for the Wednesdays at Noon film series run by his immediate supervisor, Margareta Akermark. As he became more familiar with MoMA's vast holdings, he broadened the film vocabulary that he had been developing at NYU. When a client requested material for a class on German Expressionism or silent horror films, it was part of Vito's job to be conversant with *The Cabinet of Dr. Caligari* (1919) and *Nosferatu* (1922).

For a young film fanatic, the office's star wattage was blinding. Getting to keep Orson Welles's Oscar for *Citizen Kane* on his desk, spotting director Elia Kazan (*A Streetcar Named Desire* [1951], *On the Waterfront* [1954]) in a hallway, and recognizing the British screenwriter/director team of Emeric Pressburger and Michael Powell (*The Red Shoes* [1948], *I Know Where I'm Going* [1945]) were impressive enough. But seeing intergenerational heartthrobs Michael York and Gregory Peck pass by en route to screening rooms knocked Vito flat. Another star-sighting occurred when he got to take his mother and Steve to the premiere of John Huston's *Fat City* (1972). Sipping champagne in MoMA's Sculpture Garden, Vito gabbed with coworker Christine Vouriotis and her mother over their luck at being able to rub elbows with so many celebrities. "As we were saying that," Christine recalls, "Paul Newman came through the door, and I remember our mothers just let out a squeal at the same time." Steve, unfortunately, had wandered off and missed the moment.

MoMA also sizzled with sexual energy. During Vito's tenure, the museum screened both Ralph Bakshi's X-rated *Fritz the Cat* (1972) and Fred Halsted's gay S-and-M staple *L.A. Plays Itself* (1972), during whose notorious fisting scene some patrons "shook their fists at the screen and screamed, 'this is *art?*'" The liberality of the museum's programming was matched by the easy play unfolding in its halls and offices. *GAY* advised readers that MoMA was "a well-known paradise for day cruising. The walls [were] filled with the best in modern painting, the garden with the best in modern sculpture, and the galleries with the best tricks." Rampant flirtation and often more occurred in the Department of Film. On any given morning, coworker Ron Magliozzi might find a Tom of Finland print waiting on his desk or receive a friendly proposition while changing reels in the screening room. Reports of on-the-job sex, homo and hetero, regularly surfaced from the cubicles. Ron is quick to point out that the department "wasn't a bathhouse," but it flaunted a sexual freedom that Vito cherished. He was no doubt amused to learn that one of the volunteers was a student working her way through NYU as a tassel-twirling stripper.

As Intro 475 went down in defeat, MoMA provided a safe working haven for gays and lesbians. Film Study Center director Charles Silver contends that in the early seventies, the museum was far more accepting than mainstream corporations. At the same time, he comments, homosexuality was "not something that people talked about directly. There were several gay department heads, as there are now, but it was not something front and center. It was not taken as a proper focus for people to have any idea what you did privately." When Vito began his tenure at MoMA, Charles was emerging from the closet and quietly seeing a coworker who would become Vito's close friend, future *Variety* critic Stephen Harvey. Vito and Stephen often camped it up in the study center while Charles cringed. Vito was "perhaps a little flamboyant" for Charles's comfort level; he found himself "a little uptight" in Vito's presence.

Laurence Kardish, hired in 1968 as a curatorial assistant in the film department's Exhibition Division, considered Vito a type of "new man" at MoMA. Though he was not, to Laurence's eyes, visibly gay, Vito did not hesitate to discuss GAA or his lover at the office. Most people accepted his candor without blinking, though Vito could unnerve older, less politicized gay colleagues. Christine Vouriotis laughs that curator of film Donald Richie, an internationally renowned expert on Japanese culture and film, probably "wanted to beat the hell out of Vito" for his openness. Twenty-two years Vito's senior, Richie didn't hide his homosexuality, but he didn't attend parades or Firehouse Flicks either. He didn't understand the new generation of activists who based their public personae on a sexual identity that he considered narrowly "tribal" at best.

Vito was too steeped in movies to care. He and Christine covered for each other on long lunch breaks that permitted them to see films outside MoMA. Vito also explored at length the film department archives, searching for early gay images and arcane camp. He was particularly taken with the baroque *Scarlet Empress* (1934) and, of course, *The Women*, both of which he screened for a new friend: Bette Midler. *Empress* she dismissed as "all artifice, no substance"; *The Women*'s catty final fifteen minutes she thought "the greatest thing she ever saw in her life" — and came back for repeat screenings.

Vito had met Bette at the Continental Baths shortly before he started work at MoMA. Opened in 1968 and housed in the basement of the Ansonia Hotel at Broadway and West 74th Street, the Continental buried Vito's memories of the St. Marks just five years earlier. While pre-Stonewall bathhouses fostered filth and guilt, the Continental offered polite attendants, proudly cruising patrons, and "spotless" facilities that included showers, steam rooms, an Olympic-sized pool, a gym, a sauna, massage, a TV room, a library, a restaurant, and a cabaret. Within a year, the Continental became a "full-scale resort" with the added perks of manicures, hairstyling, weight training, waterbeds, a roof deck for seasonal sunbathing and barbecues, and a dance floor whose "colored lights, reflectors, spots, mirrors and ultra-modern furniture . . . [put] one in a never-ending festive wonderland." Arnie Kantrowitz often went for a "24-hour vacation": he could arrive at five on a Saturday afternoon, "drop a little acid [and] take a little stroll"—on which he was very likely to encounter Vito amid a parade of men ranging in type from Adolphe Menjou to Lil Abner to a COLT underwear model. During the early seventies, the Continental served Vito as a second home. It was a place to rest between GAA meetings, to meet new guys (he and Steve enjoyed a happily nonmonogamous relationship), and to check out the cabaret's startling new talent, of whom The Divine Miss M was the undisputed queen.

A veteran of Broadway (three years as Tzeitel in *Fiddler on the Roof*), off-Broadway (Tom Eyen's *Miss Nefertitti Regrets* at La MaMa), and nightclubs, Midler made her Continental debut in July 1970 with an eight-week run. Tricked out in a black lace corset and gold lamé heels, she launched a routine spiced "with touches of Jewish, gay, and female humor" along with a jazzed-up mix of forties ("In the Mood," "Chattanooga Choo Choo") and sixties ("Don't Say Nothin' Bad about My Baby") pop. An institution was born. Continental customers, Vito included, loved this brazen caricature of a woman who addressed them as "my dears," favored fruit-heavy headgear, and seemed quite at ease being identified, in a subway graffito, as "a drag queen from Chicago." (Deadpanned Miss M, "I am not from Chicago.") It can only have increased her audience's loyalty when she distributed poppers between songs.

Midler launched the early seventies cabaret renaissance that came to define Vito's nightlife. A once-indispensable art form in Manhattan, cabaret in the sixties had become nearly moribund as older patrons shied away from escalating prices and younger audiences shunned a genre that they considered hopelessly retro. Miss M's frequently lewd meld of big-band-girl-group-doo-wop changed all that. In the words of famed illustrator Robert W. Richards, "Bette single-handedly brought back this kind of very intimate entertainment that wasn't some remote lady in a beaded gown singing Cole Porter songs in a hotel room on the East Side. Bette brought back cabaret, as it's now called, to the people again. And of course it was gay, gay, gay, gay, gay."

From the start, Midler's close kinship with the audience helped win her wide notice. She was surrounded by gay men, for whom she professed strong empathy: "I understand gay guys, I really do. Half the time I think I am one, and I think gay men understand me, too." She also had no problem speaking up for gay rights, telling her audiences, "Open your mouths, for Christ's sake. Don't you get tired of being stepped on?" Bette's onstage banter catered to a newly and proudly out audience that delighted in hearing its coded references voiced in public performance. She responded in kind, declaring gays "the most marvelous audience I've ever had because they're not ashamed to show how they feel about you. They applaud like hell, they scream and carry on, stamp their feet and laugh. I love it. It's going to be very hard for me when I get back before a straight audience." It's difficult to imagine that a mainstream audience would have responded as passionately to Midler's rendition of "I Shall Be Released," which she turned into a screaming cri de coeur for anyone facing social double standards.

Radioactive with eye shadow, braless in a backless, shimmery scoop top, Miss M dished in exaggerated New Yawkese about how her plans to play Fire Island had been thwarted by alfresco sex: "Mmmm, Cherry Grove. I love it. Health spa for hairdressuhs. I was supposed to work at Cherry Grove, you see; I was sposta sing. But they couldn't find room for me in the bushezzz." The audience screamed with laughter—except for one unamused soul down front who got the brunt of Miss M's camp wrath: "Laugh, you mothuhfuckah! You're sitting in the front row! You didn't have to pay to get in heah! Laugh! Oh, he's fabulous; he'll laugh at anything."

Aware that she was competing for her audience's attention, Midler could get caustic when addressing them. Launching into a sultry rendition of "Superstar," she admitted with a steely edge that this "heavy tune" sometimes cleared the room as guys began focusing on each other—"it only takes a song, right?" She informed audiences that her x-ray vision could detect whether anyone had left during intermission; woe to any escapees, whom she warned, "Your mother is gonna hear from me." Midler discussed with journalists her insecurities over being surrounded by so many adoring, but unavailable, men. Nevertheless, she also asserted her powers of sexual conversion ("I was in love with a gay. I made it with him. He never went back to guys after me") and repeatedly stressed that her appeal stretched beyond the gay community. Later in her career, Midler commented that she "refused to really see a lot of things that went on" at the Continental because, as she explained, "I thought that they would devastate me. And I was unprepared to carry those pictures in my mind for the rest of my life." For this reason, she confined herself to her dressing room and the stage and never ventured to any areas where she might find men making love.

Some gay spectators caught a whiff of homophobia in Miss M's remarks and went on the attack. John Paul Hudson had avoided Midler's shows until he was given a free ticket to her Carnegie Hall concert in June 1972. In the pages of GAY, to Midler's core audience, John Paul blasted her as a "phony" and the concert as a "Gay Pride bummer": "Unmask a fag-hag, and you'll find a fag-hater every time." He was especially incensed by her failure, with an audience that he estimated to be three-quarters gay, to mention either the Pride festivities unfolding throughout the week or her long engagements at the Continental, where she "pathetically attempt[ed] to excite males who [were] there to dig each other primarily, to dig her talent secondarily, and finally only tolerate her sexism." In an over-the-top finale, John Paul likened Midler to Joseph Epstein and Michael Maye.

When he read the article, Vito exploded. In September 1971, Midler had commissioned him to film her performance, using a GAA camera, at the Baths. They formed a fast and campy friendship, during which she and her accompanist, Barry Manilow, frequently finished their set and cabbed down to Vito's apartment well after midnight to watch rare Bessie Smith footage. At her final Continental performance, delivered in a stuffed, stifling room far too small for her legion of fans, Vito and Steve waited backstage as the exhausted diva finished her encore, staggered off, and collapsed into their arms, allowing them to carry her to her dressing room. Vito hated seeing her under such conditions ("like inviting 2,000 people to come listen to Joni Mitchell in a phone booth"), but he was enraptured by his latest diva: "I have heard *no one* sing as she sang that night; not Joplin, not Garland, not Piaf, not Streisand, *no one.*"

John Paul's broadside meant war. Vito wrote a scathing letter to the editors of *GAY*, upbraiding Hudson for his demand that Midler declare her love of gays and asserting, "Bette Midler owes her audience one thing: a good show. She does not have to acknowledge Gay Pride Week; she does not have to *thank* gay people for their support; she does not have to be into the movement to be acceptable." These were surprising sentiments from a man who had devoted himself so completely to gay visibility. But Vito's outrage was fed by a sense that John Paul wanted to straitjacket Midler as a cult "gay entertainer" whom the community would eventually renounce as a Garlandesque embarrassment. Vito also declined to have his tastes dictated by anyone, including fellow gays. He adamantly refused "to be told what oppresses me when I know damn well that *being* told is what oppresses me. I will not bow down to the new gay state which is beginning to decide for me what is liberated and what is not."

Vito's letter created a stir at *GAY*. Along with its militancy, editors Jack Nichols and Lige Clarke detected a "breezy tone that [blew] dust from dark closets. " Vito's was the unapologetic voice of the Stonewall generation, precisely *GAY*'s target audience. As the early seventies "newspaper of record for Gay America," *GAY* holds "priceless value today as a time capsule of the post-Stonewall movement's ferment." From 1969 to 1974, the newspaper provided detailed, often exclusive, coverage of gay liberation's baby steps. News of the earliest GAA actions, discussions of the changing Village, Dr. Leo Louis Martello's Gay Witch column, and such cover headlines as "Make Men: Avoid the Draft!" mixed with a bumper crop of male nudes. *After Dark*'s timidity was nowhere in sight. Vito and *GAY* seemed made for each other.

Nichols and Clarke saw exciting long-range possibilities in Vito's letter. They asked him to expand it into an article, which he happily did by slamming not only John Paul but also those Firehouse Flicks critics who rained on his

Garland/Women parade. The editors then requested that he write a regular entertainment column. He agreed and invented a title that he sprang on the homesick Arnie, then trekking the U.S. on sabbatical: I'll Take Manhattan.

Vito's column, which appeared in nearly every issue of GAY from late October 1972 through November 1973, provided a chatty overview of Manhattan entertainment, much of it suffused with political rumination and dishy personal narrative. In keeping with his new title, Vito championed the view that Manhattan was "still the best place in the world to be alive, well and gay." It was, for instance, the only place to fall in love with Broadway matinee idols like John Rubinstein of *Pippin*, at a performance of which Vito cruised a "fabulous blond guy" whose elderly date, Margaret Hamilton, shot the interloper a look he hadn't seen since an errant farmhouse fell on her sister in *The Wizard of Oz*.

Only in Manhattan could one catch the New York Film Festival or the explosion of gay theater emerging off Broadway. Vito openly acknowledged that his political biases might cloud his critical judgment; "one who has been waiting so long to hear certain things said out loud" did not make the most objective viewer. Pronouncing A. J. Kronengold's *Tubstrip* "the most boring two hours you will ever spend," Vito lambasted opportunistic playwrights who "pretend[ed] to be a part of . . . liberated [gay] culture" while exploiting culturally starved "gay people [who would] pay any price to see an ass" on stage. He walked out of Terrence McNally's *Whiskey* after a "macho cowboy did an enormous paranoid trip about being called a faggot," declaring, "I'm through sitting in an audience and being insulted by words like that, put to no constructive use." He was much happier with Al Carmines's *The Faggot*, "a play that should be seen by every person, gay and straight, who believes in struggle toward freedom of sexual expression." Featuring love duets between Oscar Wilde and Lord Alfred Douglas, Gertrude Stein and Alice B. Toklas, the play provided Vito with his first "genuine love [for] and sense of community with gay people of the past." He broke into tears on hearing one character, a secretary of state from the distant future of 1992, insist on remaining in the closet even as society became more tolerant of gays. Vito soon realized he was alone in his sorrow. Other audience members collapsed in derisive hysterics, which, Vito admitted, made him cry all the harder.

Of course, he spent considerable time in movie theaters as well—to the extent that he complained, "If I see one more film, they'll have to treat me for night blindness." Vito took great glee in introducing his readers to such new schlock masterpieces as *The Poseidon Adventure* (1972) and *Wicked, Wicked* (1973) ("what we used to call a camp and a half . . . [it contains] lines like 'How does it feel to have your throat cut, Miss Jones?' 'It hurts.' You'll love it."). He also reviewed porn, though he preferred "to spend [his] time doing" rather than watching sex. Vito even tackled straight porn, calling the infamous *Devil in Miss Jones* (1973) "great fun" and marveling at leading lady Georgina Spelvin's oral talents with a snake and a bowl of fruit.

Through his reviews, Vito also began practicing political journalism, taking explicit notice of homosexual slurs. *Butterflies Are Free* (1972), for instance, drew his wrath for a crack depicting lesbians as "sad, unsmiling creatures." Vito also began rethinking his own feelings about the portrayal of women on film via Eduardo Corbe's play *The Bitches*, an all-gay updating on *The Women*. While still defending his screening of Cukor's film at GAA, Vito felt in *The Bitches* the sting of caricature when not "everybody is in on the joke." He began to appreciate that GAA's women might be genuinely hurt and angry at Cukor's depictions, much as he was by Corbe's. "I am *tired* of hearing about how all gays are bitchy queens, I *resent* being represented as something I'm not, especially to a public that has enough misinformation already, and I *can't* set my people back a whole generation for the sake of a few laughs. *Enough!*"

As Vito's reviews became more overtly political, so did his writing in general. When President Nixon sailed triumphantly into his second term, Vito braced his readers for "the most oppressive period in human history" and wondered whether the "fight [wouldn't] be for access to the border instead of gay rights." But of course, gay rights were never more than a keystroke from his thoughts. Proudly touting himself as a "professional homosexual," he used his column to promote gay businesses and bars, such as the Roadhouse, a flannel and denim den whose employees had "treated customers like family" during a bomb scare.

With *GAY*'s readership of at least twenty-five thousand, Vito had access to a grassroots groundswell that he made every effort to galvanize. Walking around the Village, Vito professed, "Never have I loved my community so much." It thrilled him to "watch the faces of the people on the street and see smiles and open affection where there [had been] only fear a few years ago." As his affection for the gay community grew, he endeavored to alert his readers to their power as a voting bloc. Two of their own, Jim Owles and Charles Choset, were making history as the New York City Council's first openly gay candidates. Vito also pushed followers to their typewriters with a messianic fever that was coming to typify his public persona: "If somebody says something you don't like this week, write a goddam letter. It works." A blizzard of Vito-inspired missives pelted the mayor's office for ignoring gay murders, actor Richard Crenna for a homophobic comment on the Golden Globes telecast, and Cardinal Cooke for his denunciation of abortion rights just as *Roe v. Wade* was signed into law. When Liberace published a memoir that omitted reference to his homosexuality, Vito urged readers to send the pianist "a 200-word telegram congratulating him on his autobiography. Make every word 'Ha,'" he advised.

In between letter and column writing, Vito was taking ample time to enjoy Manhattan nightlife—including his first and only foray into drag. For a Thanksgiving ball held at the Diplomat Hotel, John Paul tarted both himself and Vito up as "S & M ladies," complete with full makeup, wigs, vinyl jackets, sheer black tights, and fur-lined boots that Vito found murderous on his feet. The pair "rapped as [they] got ready, seriously weighing what it mean[t] to be a 'woman' in [their] society." Vito, in John Paul's view, ended up a dead ringer for Irma La Douce, while John Paul, a friend informed him, "looked like a hybrid of Jane Russell and Tony Curtis, which was not quite what [he] had in mind." For his part, Vito didn't enjoy leaving lipstick prints on his glass or having men light his cigarettes. But he was proud to share with readers a retort that he scored after the ball. Outside the Diplomat, a drunk hailed him and John Paul from a passing car: "Hey, you girls must be cold!" In a basso growl, Vito fired back, "Yeah, we're freezing our balls off!"

By Thanksgiving 1972, Vito and Steve's relationship was unraveling. For two years, they had had some very good times. Vito was an irrepressible romantic who loved to surprise Steve with gestures ranging from homemade pasta sauce to an unannounced visit to Puerto Rico, where Steve was spending two lonely months stage-managing a musical revue. And of course, the pair had the fertile common ground of GAA to nurture their relationship. Unfortunately, GAA also began to tear them apart. Two years' involvement in the organization seemed in retrospect like "two decades" crammed full of activity. As chairman of the Firehouse, election, and other committees, Steve was drowning in nightly meetings. As GAA secretary, he answered hundreds of inquiries, from as far away as India, sent by gay-liberation groups that wanted to start their own chapters. In April 1971, he also inaugurated *Gay Activist*, GAA's monthly newsletter, from the dining-room table on West 24th Street.

Vito maintained a proud public face but wondered when Steve would ever have time for him. At a Jersey dinner party, he looked over a friend's beautifully appointed dining room, complete with silver bread basket and ornate china closet, before turning wistfully to Steve: "This is what I want. This is the kind of life I want to live." It wasn't so much material sparkle or suburban domesticity that Vito craved; it was more the time and space to build a cozy life together, a goal that increasingly seemed more pipe dream than possibility.

Tension grew when GAA's Arts Committee mounted Jonathan Ned Katz's play *Coming Out!* (1972). With skits on colonial American homophobia, Walt Whitman, Willa Cather, Gertrude Stein and Alice B. Toklas, Christopher Isherwood, Allen Ginsberg, and the contemporary events of Stonewall and the Snake Pit, *Coming Out!* provided an unprecedented overview of gay American history. It left Firehouse audiences cheering and inspired, in Vito's wry observation, unity among "factions of the gay community unable, heretofore, to agree on the color of an orange." The only problem was that Katz and director David Roggensack cast Steve and not Vito, whose audition left them cold. The exclusion smarted, particularly as Vito was chair of the committee responsible for the production in the first place. Salt hit the wound when Steve received extravagant praise for his performance as the analyst in Judy Grahn's skit "The Psychoanalysis of Edward the Dyke."

Vito gritted his teeth, reminded himself that he had a newly completed master's degree (as of February 1972), and concentrated on the Firehouse Flicks. He even agreed to help when Steve, with several other GAA members, tried to launch a new gay nightclub, When We Win, inspired by GAA's Cabaret Nights. Vito was tapped to emcee a weekly film series. As opening night neared, he rushed backstage after a matinee of *No, No, Nanette!* and wheedled Martha Raye into introducing her films *Hellzapoppin'* (1941) and *The Boys from Syracuse* (1940) at When We Win's kickoff. Raye's enthusiastic response ("Are you kidding? I'd shit!") thrilled Vito.

But when the Sheridan Square Block Association delayed the opening for months, he lost heart, both with the club and with Steve. As their time together dwindled, Vito reacted by enlisting Arnie to tell Steve that he wanted to break up. The news itself, to say nothing of Vito's method of springing it, floored Steve, who had been trying to ignore the fact that his commitments were driving them apart. After an ugly confrontation, Steve realized that he couldn't give Vito the attention he needed. The relationship was over.

To ease his heartache, Vito took a cue from Steve and tried to keep busy. In addition to his MoMA and GAA duties, he was chosen to be the emcee of the 1973 Gay Pride Gala in Washington Square Park. For its fourth annual celebration of Stonewall, the Christopher Street Liberation Day Committee (CSLDC) decided to reverse the usual parade route. Instead of marching uptown into Central Park, marchers would proceed down 7th Avenue toward the Village, where gay liberation was born. CSLDC representatives expressed no small anger when the city denied them use of 5th Avenue, Manhattan's geographic center, where Irish, Italian, Greek, and Polish groups staged their own celebrations. But many gay marchers felt a certain symmetry in concluding the parade around the corner from the Stonewall before heading over to the gala, due to kick off at 4 p.m. on Sunday, June 24.

The gala promised to be tremendous fun. CSLDC Chair John Paul Hudson had appointed Vito head of a special Celebrities Participation Committee that would bring entertainers to Washington Square. Throughout May, Vito threw himself into benefit concerts at Brothers and Sisters, a new Times Square cabaret, where auditions for gala performers were being held. By mid-June, he announced confirmations from openly bisexual film idol Sal Mineo and closeted (but widely suspected) film and Broadway actress Patsy Kelly. Bette Midler hadn't yet answered his invitation. To *GAY* readers, Vito remarked, "I hope she hasn't decided that she isn't interested. That would make me very sad."

As the CSLDC planned the gala, conflict loomed on the horizon. LFL leader Jean O'Leary, an articulate ex-nun, readied a speech denouncing drag queens, who, LFL alleged, ridiculed women for profit. But the CSLDC was permitting only two political speeches, by veteran Los Angeles activist Morris Kight and by

Barbara Gittings. Not even Jim Owles or Bruce Voeller, GAA's current president, found a spot on the dais. Many lesbians, moreover, had been pondering a boycott of the entire march since a significant portion of its sponsorship came from the bars, which smelled of Mafia involvement. The majority of women who chose to participate would keep to the rear.

On June 24, as the march proceeded down 7th Avenue, sideline heckling was nearly nonexistent; "smiling policemen, wide-eyed tourists, and blasé New Yorkers . . . passed [the parade] off with a live-and-let-live shrug." Most strife came from within. At 19th Street, the volcanic Sylvia Rivera, founder of the newly formed Street Transvestite Action Revolutionaries (STAR), tried to jump ahead of Grand Marshal Mama Jean DeVente and restore drag queens to their Stonewall prominence. Mama Jean summoned two marshals, whose clothing and throats Sylvia tore.

By the time the march arrived in Washington Square, tensions were riding high. Vito warily watched the arrival of a crowd—nearly twenty thousand strong—that had carried its animosities for fifty blocks in the brutal summer sun and now expected to be entertained. In skintight slacks and a wildly printed silk shirt unbuttoned to his breastbone, he introduced Barbara Gittings, who got things off to a rousing start by proclaiming, "We are everywhere!" She informed her ecstatic audience that not only were sodomy laws falling "like autumn leaves in state after state," but the psychiatric establishment was about to legitimize gay mental health as well. Majestic under the arch, Gittings assured the crowd, "Those of us who are out are oiling the closet door hinges as fast as we can." She whipped the park into an evangelical frenzy by directing them to chant after her "Gay is good! Gay is proud! Gay is natural! Gay is normal! Gay is gorgeous! Gay is positive! Gay is healthy! Gay is happy! Gay is *love!*" His voice trembling, Vito pronounced Barbara "beautiful" and read a letter from Bella Abzug, urging the community to keep fighting after the recent defeat of the gay civil-rights bill in the city council.

The good vibes continued as Vito brought out the acts. Sal Mineo and Patsy Kelly had failed to commit, but Vito was determined not to disappoint his biggest audience yet. Continental Baths owner Steve Ostrow received polite applause for a light-opera aria; he was better appreciated for the three hundred dollars and band that he had donated to the gala. Exuberantly received was Alaina Reed, an ebony vision in white sunhat and long white gown, rocking the park with "Love Train." Dawn Hampton and Sally Eaton of *Hair* (1968) maintained the crowd's enthusiasm. But things started to go wrong when Ellen Greene, nearly a decade shy of *Little Shop of Horrors* (1982) fame, took the stage to warble "I Met a Man Today." From the audience, one woman screamed, "All right, get off, you're not a lesbian. We want gay people today. Sing on *The Ed Sullivan Show.*"

Matters went further south when Vito introduced the next act, drag duo Billy "Billie" Blackwell and Michael "Tiffany" Bowers. Deciding that "Christopher Street and the English Ascot Race were on the same footing," Billie and Tiffany had arrayed themselves in broad-brimmed hats, floral dresses, and matronly jewelry that Vito found hilarious. Weighing in at nearly two hundred pounds each, the duo looked "like your Aunt Minnie—like Milton Berle in drag." After distributing mimeographed song lyrics to the audience, they shrieked the title tune of the recent off-Broadway flop *Smile, Smile, Smile.* Tiffany didn't expect any problems. Once they realized that the pair was not attempting to ridicule women, radical lesbians had loved their audition at Brothers and Sisters. Most women at Washington Square, however, did not share this admiration. They began to seethe.

Then all hell broke loose. Barefoot in a ripped purple jumpsuit, her ratted black hair a blond-streaked mess, Sylvia Rivera arrived onstage after various thwarted attempts to climb up. She grabbed the microphone away from Vito and waved the stand at her hostile ("Get the *fuck* off!") audience. Flipping the crowd off, Sylvia advised them to "quiet down." Pacing the stage, she announced, "I've been trying to get up here all day for *your* gay brothers and *your* gay sisters in jail." With a voice like broken glass, Sylvia screamed that transsexual prisoners regularly wrote her letters because, she claimed, "I *have* been to jail. I have been *raped* and *beaten* many times by men." She then assailed the crowd directly: "I have lost my job. I have lost my apartment for Gay Liberation. And you all treat me this way? What the fuck's wrong with you all?!" Sylvia finished with a ragged "gay power" chant ("Gimme a GEEEEEEE . . .") that left many celebrants bewildered.

Shaken but determined to allow a dissenting voice, Vito introduced Jean O'Leary. Armed with LFL's prepared speech on the sexism of transvestite entertainment, Jean began by announcing, "It's times like this that I find it very hard to be gay and proud because there's another side of me that's a woman. And I'm insulted by this mockery and these costumes up here by these people," gesturing at men sharing the stage with her. Sitting on the stage with Vito, Arnie watched the unfolding fracas in horror. "This is what the word 'aghast' was made for."

As boos drowned Jean out, Vito stormed back to the mike and attacked his brothers: "Listen to her! You listened to everyone else! Listen! That's the least we can do for each other! Listen to her!" Remarkably, the audience obeyed and allowed Jean to denounce Sylvia as a "man" permitted to "cause a ruckus." She exhorted women not to let men represent them any longer, insisting, to tremendous cheers, that women "can and do show each other who we are" far better than men.

But the war hadn't ended. In a strapless gown, towering blond wig, and tiara, drag queen Lee Brewster, founder of Queens Liberation Front, took the mike and addressed the crowd in a voice that suggested an enraged Kim Novak. "You go to bars because of what drag queens did for you—and let these bitches [gesturing at lesbians below the stage] tell us we're offensive? We gave you your Pride!" Amid mixed cheers and boos, Lee insisted that she was "not going to oil [closet] doors with tears any longer." Tossing her tiara into the audience, she brayed, "Gay Liberation, screw you!" One lesbian called out, "Who does that drag queen think he is?!" The men were getting equally riled; Karla Jay found herself in an absurdist moment when a drag queen attempted to "prove" to her and her partner that he was "a better woman" than they by freeing his penis from his pantyhose. Vito rushed to Lee's side and whispered in her ear, "Don't start a riot; do me a favor! They're already hitting each other."

Nevertheless, Vito was prepared for chaos. Anticipating that lesbians and drag queens would be at each other's throats, he played his trump card: Bette. In a tied-off blouse and tight jeans, her wild mane flowing, Midler wished the crowd a happy fourth anniversary and then pretended she'd just overheard the commotion on the radio and had come to soothe tensions. The means of The Divine Miss M's arrival didn't matter to the Continental faithful or to the thousands who had bought her debut album the previous year. The park began cheering hysterically from the first two words ("And I . . .") of "Friends," her signature song. As she cooed, "And my problems have all gone," a man from the crowd screamed out, "Yes, they have!"—a sentiment that Midler, grinning with one eyebrow cocked, tossed back at him. Accompanied by Barry Manilow and inviting the audience to "sing if you wanna" (did they ever wanna), she soon had Washington Square vocalizing along with her. Vito beamed and danced behind his diva. Pointing at a throng that had been out for blood minutes earlier, Midler reminded them, "You *got to* have *friends!*"

Some historians today dismiss "Midler's cheer [as coming] way too late" to dress wounds. Vito insisted that his friend offered "a tremendously healing presence. . . . She said later that it was one of the great things she did, that she felt like she was Marilyn Monroe singing in Korea." For Vito's part, in open defiance of many of the gay men present, he had honored a lesbian viewpoint and attempted to unite the community whose unofficial spokesperson he was now becoming.

But he was also exhausted—from MoMA, Steve, and Gay Liberation. After the gala, he crawled out of Washington Square and over to Cornelia Street for a quiet dinner with Arnie at Mona's Royal Roost. The following week, they were leaving for a month on Fire Island. Vito needed a long rest and a chance to ponder his next move.

Angelina (Annie) and Angelo (Charles) Russo's wedding day, January 10, 1943. (courtesy of Charles Russo)

Vito Russo, senior portrait. Lodi High School, 1964. (courtesy of Charles Russo)

Vito Russo and Steve Krotz, GAA's Fidelifacts zap, January 18, 1971. (photo by Richard C. Wandel; courtesy of Lesbian, Gay, Bisexual, and Transgender Community Center National History Archive, New York)

Above: Vito Russo and Bette Midler, Gay Pride Gala, Washington Square, June 24, 1973. (courtesy of Arnie Kantrowitz)

Left: Vito Russo, New Line Presentations star, 1973. (courtesy of Charles Russo)

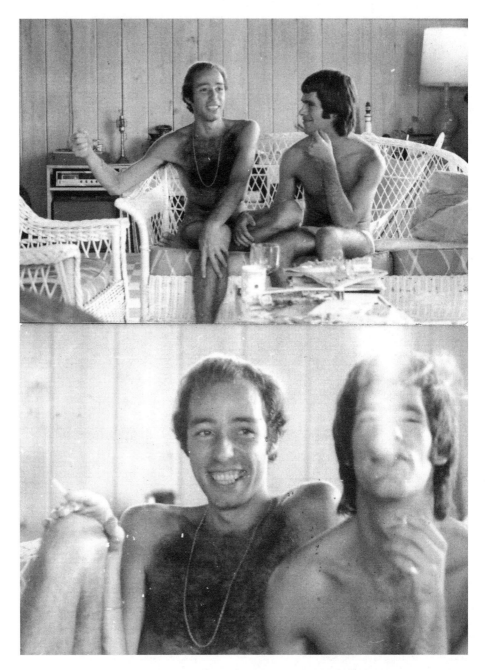

Vito Russo and Bruce Parker, Fire Island, 1974. (courtesy of Charles Russo)

Left: Vito Russo, Los Angeles, summer 1975. (courtesy of Charles Russo)

Below: Valerie Harper and Vito Russo, Los Angeles, summer 1975. (courtesy of Charles Russo)

Above: Bill Johnson and Vito Russo, San Francisco, spring 1977. (courtesy of William R. Johnson)

Right: Vito Russo, ca. 1981. (courtesy of Charles Russo)

THE BILLIE JEAN KING AFFAIR, BY BETTY HICKS
WHY COMING OUT TO STRAIGHT MALE FRIENDS IS SO HARD

Christopher Street

ISSN 0146 7921
CANADA $2.95

JULY 1981 $2.50

YOU OUGHTA B
IN PICTURES!
Vito Russo talks about
gay lives in the movies-
past, present, future

THE SECRET L
HORATIO AL

JOHN PRES
NEW GAY FA

EX
CANO'S
NOVEL

Vito Russo on the cover of *Christopher Street* magazine, July 1981. (courtesy of George Delmerico)

Vito Russo atop the Castro Theatre marquee, San Francisco, June 1981. (courtesy of Charles Russo)

Jeffrey Sevcik, ca. 1981. (courtesy of Charles Russo)

Annie Russo and Vito Russo, Lambda Legal Defense and Education Fund awards dinner, New York, October 18, 1982. (courtesy of Charles Russo)

Vito Russo and Lily Tomlin, Human Rights Campaign Fund awards dinner, New York, October 10, 1984. (courtesy of Charles Russo)

GAA's wiggy elder statesmen: Jim Owles, Vito Russo, Marty Robinson, and Arnie Kantrowitz, ca. 1985. (courtesy of Lawrence D. Mass)

Larry Mass and Vito Russo, celebrating their fortieth birthday, New York, June 27, 1986. (courtesy of Lawrence D. Mass)

Arnie Kantrowitz and emcee Vito Russo, New York City Gay Men's Chorus Concert ("The Movie!"), Lincoln Center, March 22, 1987. (courtesy of Lawrence D. Mass)

Vito Russo and Jed Mattes, New York City Gay Men's Chorus Concert, March 22, 1987. (courtesy of Lawrence D. Mass)

Linda Russo, Charlie Russo Jr., Annie Russo, Vito Russo, Charles Russo, and Vicki Russo, New York City Gay Men's Chorus Concert, March 22, 1987. (courtesy of Charles Russo)

Baby Jane Dexter, Russo family home, Lodi, New Jersey, 1989. (courtesy of Lawrence D. Mass)

Vito Russo and Larry Kramer, first ACT UP demonstration, Wall Street, March 24, 1987. (courtesy of Lee Snider/Photo Images)

One of ACT UP's finest: Vito Russo, Health and Human Services, Washington, DC, October 10, 1988. (courtesy of New Yorker Video)

Elizabeth Taylor and Vito Russo, Museum of Modern Art, World AIDS Day, December 1, 1989. (courtesy of Charles Russo)

Daniel Sotomayor, cartoon, *OutWeek* magazine, December 12, 1990. (courtesy of Gabriel Rotello)

5

"Professional Movement Flash and Trash"

Shortly after the 1973 gala, John Paul Hudson reflected on GAA, the Continental Baths, and the Bette Midler craze. He decided that the scene had the makings of a spicy comedy-thriller. The result, coauthored with playwright Warren Wexler, was *Superstar Murder? A Prose Flick* (1976), a sexy, spoofy roman à clef detailing the apparent murder of "Bess Mittman," principal chanteuse at the "Cosmopolitan Baths." One of the Cosmopolitan regulars is "Guido DiCostanzo," a fierce Mittman loyalist who works for the "Film Museum" and describes himself as "what they used to call a Movie Queen before Stonewall."

Guido is the most sympathetic character in a rogues' gallery of opportunistic crazies. Sporting Lambda T-shirts and jewelry, he is a perennially sunny activist with "bright spaniel eyes" and a "smile so broad it appeared that he had more teeth than came with a standard model." This self-proclaimed "sissy" fills his answering machine with Gay Power sloganeering ("I love you, whoever you are—especially if you're gay") and puts himself in considerable danger to track down his beloved Bess, who—spoiler alert—turns out to be a drag queen. Bucking for a movie sale, John Paul and Warren suggest in the novel's epilogue that Guido be played by *Partridge Family* heartthrob David Cassidy.

Vito loved *Superstar*'s elevation of him and the baths to icon status. In reality, though, he had tired of the Continental, which was imploring patrons to maintain a "positive image" out on West 74th Street, where they should "not impose unbecoming conduct on the public at large." Vito railed to Steve Ostrow that the Continental's patrons were also public citizens whose public behavior was none of Ostrow's business. But the fight almost didn't seem worth the effort.

Vito considered the club's pricey sixteen-dollar cover charge an insult when increasing numbers of heterosexuals were admitted to see Bette as well as Tiny Tim, opera star Eleanor Steber, and Barry Manilow, whose own career was starting to take off independent of Midler's. Realizing that straight audiences often came to ogle gay patrons, Vito resented being treated as an unwitting spectacle, especially when straights attacked gays who dared to dance nude on their own turf. Gyrating alongside Vito, Arnie squirmed to find himself "part of the freaky zoo décor" and mused, "Which side of the bars are the spectators on in the zoo?" Bella Abzug might still campaign for the gay vote at the Continental, where she was shocked to find some of her most passionate supporters wearing Bella buttons and nothing else, but the baths were going irretrievably mainstream.

The bloom was fading from the movement as well. Barbara Gittings attributed the demise to "zap" saturation; observers were becoming progressively "turned off by strident shoutings." Arthur Bell concurred, stating flatly that the "gay lib movement, as we knew it in '69–'72, is dead." Shock tactics no longer tantalized a Watergate-weary audience. The malaise also lay within GAA itself. Too many attended dances or even meetings without incorporating activism into their daily lives. In Arnie's vivid phrasing, "Licking envelopes is useful, but it isn't as liberating as telling your mother you lick the genitals of the same sex."

GAA was permanently supplanted by the newly formed National Gay Task Force (NGTF), an organization whose corporate scope far outreached that of its scrappy predecessor. As Ronald Gold, NGTF's first communications director, put it, "Gay liberation has become a nine-to-five job—there's no other way to do it." Vito never had much interest in a traditional office job, even one dedicated to his favorite cause. He retreated to an oasis fifty miles southeast of Manhattan.

By the early seventies, Vito was no longer a scared kid running to Fire Island in secret flight from New Jersey. He didn't need to escape a closeted work environment or a homophobic family. But he still viewed the island as a netherworld where traditional social rules did not apply. It reminded him of J. R. R. Tolkien's *Lord of the Rings* (1954–55), whose Forest of Lothlórien was an enchanted realm of perfect peace, with total immunity to outside evil. During the midsixties, Vito had witnessed Meat Rack raids in which terrified young men clad only in bathing suits (if that) were herded into police speedboats and locked in Suffolk County jail cells. Shortly before Stonewall, however, mass entrapments came to a permanent end on Fire Island. Its visitors now enjoyed unprecedented safety and freedom.

In the summer of 1971, Vito and Arnie stood on the deck of the newly installed *Fire Island Duchess*, a stately ferry that had replaced the grimy "blood buckets" Vito had taken on his first trips across the bay. As the ferry crested through crisp salt air, Vito reassured his nervous friend, "You're going to love this place. It's magic." Indeed, when Arnie disembarked, noting pastel houses and vibrant flowers running riot at his feet, he pronounced Cherry Grove "cute. If you turned it upside down and back, it would probably snow." Bungalows with the camp names "Pillows of Society," "Wounded Knees," "No Boys in the Attic" (lesbian), and "White Swallows" only added to the sense of living in a gay limbo that had nothing to do with "America," as Vito and Arnie called the mainland on the other side of the bay.

Of course, even in retreat, the pair couldn't remain apolitical, particularly not when rooming with Jim, Steve, and several other GAA companions. Over their Cherry Grove bungalow, they flew a Lambda flag, and the cottage name "Gay and Proud" appeared in bright red lettering on a piece of driftwood next to their front door ("There Goes the Neighborhood" had been rejected as "too subtle"). But the activists soon learned that fun-loving Grovers had little interest in slogans or calls-to-arms. Fire Island was precisely where most gay Manhattanites went to escape such talk. With the Ice Palace only steps away, efforts at political engagement met with dismissal at best.

If Grovers were impervious to GAA entreaties, residents of the Pines, where Vito and Arnie spent July 1973, could be openly hostile. Situated across the Meat Rack from the Grove, upscale Pines houses dwarfed Grove cottages. The Pines attracted a younger, wealthier crowd for whom activism was an annoying distraction from sunbathing, bodybuilding, drugging, and dancing. In Esther Newton's comparison, by the mid-1970s, "the Grove's position was . . . analogous to the dowdy immigrant parents of affluent, scornful, and Americanized Pines offspring." While aging Grovers wanted to retreat into Garland trivia and elaborate drag, most Pines residents wanted the social benefits of liberation without the screaming that made it possible. The Pines' nickname of *"After Darkland"* was well earned. Vito could not relax in an area he labeled the "most apolitical place on earth." He boiled on being informed that Pines men took care not to "flaunt" themselves in front of their few straight neighbors. If one could rub elbows with the glitterati and the world's most beautiful guys, why "muck it up with a lot of animalistic sex in the bushes"?

To Vito, who enjoyed alfresco sex as often as possible, these were fighting words. In the Meat Rack, he found uniquely free, honest communion with other gay men. Everybody knew precisely why he was there; there was "no coercion, there was no exploitation, there was no using people . . . as meat." In the woods, Vito felt, it was possible to "know a person for 15 minutes and be more intimate with that person in 15 minutes than you would be if you had a lover for 15 years." He relished the simplicity of meeting a guy under the stars, making love with him, and then retiring to the dunes for a cigarette and chat if both were so inclined. No pressure, no judgments. Just the kind of unashamed physical rapport that had been one of GAA's founding tenets.

And just the kind of rapport that made Vito, several months after his breakup with Steve, receptive to love again. Strolling the boardwalks that summer, he met Bruce Michael Parker, an elfin free spirit with some superficial resemblance to Steve. While Steve read tarot cards, Bruce practiced astrology; neither had a clear professional direction when Vito met him. A twenty-seven-year-old Alliance, Ohio, native, Bruce held a bachelor's degree in political science from Kent State, with a minor in Spanish, and had served as a Peace Corps volunteer in Ecuador. On his return to the United States, he didn't know what to do with his life. For the time, getting away from Alliance was his main goal. He had grown up in a household where, according to his younger brother, Gregson, the Parkers lived as "five enemies under the same roof." The quiet, studious Bruce suffered physical and emotional abuse from his ex-Marine, "rage-aholic" father, who didn't appreciate that his middle son ran and threw balls like a girl. Despite an engagement to a Kent State coed, Bruce had realized by age thirteen that he was gay; he also realized how little chance he would have to explore his sexuality in a town of thirty thousand. When he finished his Peace Corps stint in 1970, he headed for Manhattan and enrolled at Parsons School of Design. Ensconced in New York's gay life, Bruce worked a series of bill-paying jobs while immersing himself in the career of Maria Callas.

Still smarting over Steve's neglect, Vito craved the ceaseless attention that Bruce poured over him. Bruce, ripe for a guru, was in awe of his new lover. Vito was a force within gay Manhattan culture and politics, he worked for one of the city's most prestigious museums, his byline appeared regularly in the city's gay paper of record—and he was about to make his big-screen debut.

Back in March, on assignment for *GAY*, Vito had screened a twelve-minute excerpt of a film called *For as Long as Possible*. The director was Christopher Larkin, a former monk, building renovator, and speed-reading teacher who had decided that the story of his renouncing traditional religion for homosexuality would make an engaging film. Larkin's ultimate aim was to rectify the negative "'image' of the gay person in our society," which he considered to be "*the* top priority issue [then] for the gay liberation movement." Through the romantic struggles of his protagonist David, an ex-monk and English teacher, Larkin sought to demonstrate the validity of gay relationships. Vito applauded this sentiment and the excerpt itself, which showed a male couple waltzing through the clichés of falling in love. If the plot and its filming were nothing new, the characters' unapologetic homosexuality certainly was. At the screening, Vito also enjoyed meeting Robert McLane, Larkin's openly gay lead, whose honesty Vito found refreshing in a profession renowned for closetedness.

In July, Larkin took McLane and Curt Gareth, the chiseled actor playing David's lover, Mark, on location in the Pines. In the film, Speedo-clad Mark wanders into a living room where two men are discussing the merits of wine enemas. Sitting quietly by are two other young men, one looking like a scrawny high school senior with his Mickey Mouse T-shirt and shy grin, the other a hard-core biker fantasy with his shaved head, huge handlebar mustache, and round red glasses. Vito's acquaintance with Larkin netted him and Arnie these cameos, complete with their own close-ups. Arnie drags on a cigarette and releases what he remembers as the "perfect Bette Davis exhale"; Vito watches with sly amusement as Mark discovers that David, busy with a trick, has locked their bedroom door against him.

The close-ups are far less revelatory than the film, renamed *A Very Natural Thing*, which shows gay men engaged in the revolutionary activities of courting, setting up house, having sex, working, and breaking up. As such, the film was a tough commercial sell. Major Hollywood studios shrank from a story that offered no stars and didn't ridicule or demonize gay people. *Thing* was eventually distributed by the independent New Line Cinema, which lacked the funds to send it into wide release.

Vito was too busy to be disappointed. At MoMA, he had been talking with his boss, film department head Willard Van Dyke, about the possibility of putting together a lecture on homosexuality in film. Van Dyke boasted impeccable credentials: he had codirected the landmark documentary *The City* (1939) and worked, after a brief gray-listing during the McCarthy era, on *The Twentieth Century* with Walter Cronkite. At MoMA, Van Dyke moved easily between the worlds of experimental film and splashy industry promos with Sophia Loren and Carlo Ponti. His versatility earned Vito's respect, and the regard was mutual. Impressed by Vito's passionate office diatribes about gay images in film, Van Dyke invited him to speak on the subject at a Flaherty Seminar summer conference in New Hampshire. The invitation carried considerable weight; one of the other speakers that summer was French experimental filmmaker and New Wave predecessor Agnès Varda. Vito acquitted himself so gracefully that Van Dyke approached him with a second proposal: "You're interested in film and you're active in the gay rights movement. You should be the one to write the book on gay film."

Vito liked the idea but knew that he had just enough material for a presentation, not a book. For the time being, it was better to concentrate on giving more lectures. New Line Presentations, the special events division of New Line Cinema, agreed to publicize his lecture on the college circuit. What had been launched with the lackluster title "Gays in/at the Movies" was soon rechristened, with the help of friend Richard Wall, "The Celluloid Closet: A History of Homosexuality in the Movies." The new title permitted Vito to distill his political thesis: gays' self-imposed invisibility made possible their constant portrayal on screen as villains, victims, or clowns—when they were portrayed at all.

As he began pondering his topic, Vito proclaimed to the *New York Times*, "It is impossible to find *any* film about homosexuality that is *not* oppressive." A few years later, he was equally apocalyptic, if somewhat more specific. Arnie recorded "Vito Russo's final word on film, said with his usual hyperbolic alacrity[:] 'The history of gays in the movies from the Thirties to the Seventies is a trail of blood leading up to *The Boys in the Band!*'" It was inevitable that *Boys* would draw Vito's ire. The film adaptation (1970) of Mart Crowley's smash off-Broadway play (1968) presented a compendium of gay-male stereotypes that clashed mightily against GAA's "gay is good" rhetoric. The majority of Crowley's characters drink themselves blind, rely on psychoanalysts to cope with their homosexuality, savage their so-called friends at every opportunity, and almost never experience anything like love. When the film was released, Vito organized GAA junkets to theaters. His goal was not to censor with pickets or protests, but to invite audience members to join a dialogue on gay stereotyping. (It bears mentioning, however, that Vito celebrated Arnie's thirty-third birthday by hosting a surprise screening of *The Boys in the Band* at his apartment.)

Boys, which Vito blasted as "the ultimate gay cartoon," provided one of his lecture's kickoff images. Juxtaposing the extremely effeminate Emory (Cliff Gorman) against thirties screen sissies Franklin Pangborn and Grady Sutton, he sought to demonstrate how little American cinema had updated its image of gay men in forty years. Vito also reached back to his adolescence and screened clips of *The Children's Hour*, *Advise & Consent*, and *Victim* to illustrate "The Gay Guilt Syndrome" and "Blackmail," subtopics of his lecture. He referenced documentary treatment of gays with CBS's *The Homosexuals* (1967), which featured Jack Nichols, his editor at *GAY*, and tried to offer some hope at the close of his presentation with "Breakthrough" clips of *Sunday Bloody Sunday* (1971) and *A Very Natural Thing*.

During his first year with New Line, Vito brought his lecture to over a dozen colleges and universities in the Northeast. Reviewers praised his careful handling of a "very sensitive issue" and found his delivery "witty and enthusiastic," if "intense." "The Celluloid Closet" was in demand.

To accommodate increased requests, Vito realized that he would have to expand his repertoire. Luckily, one of the world's premiere film archives was within walking distance of his apartment. After quitting his job at MoMA in 1973, Vito remained friendly with many employees in the film department and continued to peruse its holdings. Mary Corliss, wife of his former NYU classmate Richard, was curator of the Film Stills Archive. Vito had few scruples about "borrowing" excerpted or even whole films that suited his needs. In his *GAY* columns, he freely advocated the piracy of unreleased film scores and confessed that he'd taped, with her apparent approval, Bette Midler's Philharmonic concert. He certainly wasn't going to let copyright law stand between him and a fully developed lecture. In the film department's Study Center, he had largely unsupervised access to editing equipment and a vast archive. Eyebrows were raised when a clip from Ken Russell's *Valentino* (1977) vanished—and later turned up in a "Celluloid Closet" presentation that Vito gave at MoMA itself. Co-worker Christine Vouriotis doesn't remember any theft, but she readily acknowledges that Vito could have obtained or written for himself a pass allowing him to remove prints from the building. Following Vito's death nearly two decades later, MoMA colleague Stephen Harvey sneaked back into the museum 16mm prints of *The Wizard of Oz*, *Meet Me in St. Louis* (1944), and *Pick Up on South Street* (1953) that Vito had hoarded over the years. His Garland and Thelma Ritter mania, rather than a desire to expand his "Celluloid Closet" presentation, had prompted him to take these prints—but their long residence in his apartment indicates his conviction that certain films were meant for relaxed public consumption, preferably with his commentary.

As Vito's reputation spread, he received invitations to speak at prestigious universities, including Princeton and Harvard. Conditions at smaller schools were often less than impressive. At one college in Buffalo, Vito stewed over "thoroughly incompetent" students who failed to take care of his hotel bill or provide airport transportation, necessitating a taxi ride that he could ill afford. The promise of three hundred dollars lured him in the middle of February to Amherst, Massachusetts, where he lectured to fifty appreciative Hampshire College students—and then shared a twin bed in a freezing dorm. After a sleepless night, he wasn't even sure if the pot on which he had spent forty-five precious dollars was any good. Arrangements were somewhat better at Rutgers, where he was booked to give the third in a series of lectures titled "The Changing Stereotypes of Women, Blacks and Gays in the Cinema." His predecessors had included the noted film scholars E. Ann Kaplan and Donald Bogle, so Vito was in extremely good company—and his $650 fee (minus New Line's 30 percent commission) made him feel that his work was properly valued. At the same time, he couldn't help but vent some urban outrage over his young Jersey hosts: "I am barely containing my annoyance at the absolute timidity of the students running this show. I haven't the energy to preach to them but I do have a few choice things to say once I begin" the lecture. Whatever "choice things" he expressed went unrecorded. The students cheered his articulate anger over Hollywood's omission of "love" from its portrayals of gays.

One less-enthusiastic audience member was Annie Russo. She had welcomed Bruce into the family as readily as she had Steve, and she even accompanied Vito, however nervously, to Fire Island. But when Vito insisted that his mother and brother attend an early presentation of "Celluloid Closet" for a Hackensack gay and lesbian group, Annie was unprepared. Seeing her son discuss homosexuality with a roomful of gay strangers was too much. When Charlie drove his mother home afterward, she fell into hysterics. Annie needed time to accept the public gay persona that Vito was making national through his lectures and his writing.

Many gay Americans got their news through the *Advocate*, the Los Angeles–based newspaper founded in 1967 to spread the word of the emerging movement. But by the midseventies, the *Advocate* was losing its following. Dense, low-gloss news coverage didn't appeal to an increasingly affluent, Pines-style readership. Enter David B. Goodstein, a Midas-wealthy former Wall Street broker who decided to buy and remake the paper in his own image. In his first issue, Goodstein defined his target audience through pointed apostrophe: "We already know most of you are gay men. What a marvelous and alive person to be! . . . You are employed and a useful, responsible citizen. You have an attractive body, nice clothes and an inviting home." To reach those conspicuous consumers, Goodstein forced a new slogan on his editor, future *Mr. Benson* author John Preston, who blushed, "May I burn in hell for approving [the magazine's] new advertising and promotional theme: 'Touching Your Lifestyle.' It came complete with T-shirts and posters." It seemed fitting that Goodstein had unsuccessfully sought to purchase *After Dark*. A more improbable champion of Vito's writing was scarcely imaginable.

But Vito was hungry to find a broader audience. He had already appeared on national television to champion gay rights. During the summer of 1974, producer Joe De Cola invited him to speak on *ABC Close-Up!* opposite host David Frost and Dr. Evelyn Hooker, the first psychologist to demonstrate scientifically that the emotional health of gay men did not differ from that of straight men. De Cola protested Frost's argument that the panel lacked balance and needed dissenting voices—would Frost push for the same parity on a show about Jews or blacks? Frost remained adamant, however, so Joe engaged notoriously homophobic Los Angeles police chief Ed Davis to tangle with Vito and Dr. Hooker. Vito, who considered Frost "the biggest pig [he had] ever met in [his] life," felt that the host directed the brunt of his on-air bigotry against Vito personally. But he treasured the opportunity to illustrate for a national audience the stereotypes sustained in *The Children's Hour*, *The Boys in the Band*, *The Killing of Sister George*, and his women-in-prison favorite, *Caged*. During the show, Vito projected the kind of authority that would interest a national publication.

Arnie's Christopher Street column, detailing his experiences as a West Village resident and openly gay professor, became a regular *Advocate* feature in early 1975. With his best friend on the staff, Vito wondered how he could get his own foot in the door. The answer arrived when Patrick Merla, personal assistant to Bette Midler, convinced the diva to let Vito interview her for the magazine. As John Paul Hudson had demonstrated three years earlier, Midler had several gay detractors who felt that she had abandoned them as her career soared beyond the Continental. Thinking that Midler could use more-sympathetic gay coverage, Patrick endorsed Vito for the job.

Vito's story put Midler on the *Advocate*'s cover—the first woman to appear there in the paper's eight-year history. It also gave Vito his first shot at a celebrity profile. Preparing her Broadway show *Bette Midler's Clams on the Half Shell Revue*, Midler was frantically busy and granting interviews to very few publications, of which the *Advocate* was the sole gay representative. Clad in a bathrobe and cooking scrambled eggs during the interview, she chatted with Vito in her West Village home. The informality belied an obvious change in their relationship: both realized that Midler was doing Vito a special favor. She sniped at his smoking and asked about the significance of the small stud he sported in his right ear. When he protested that "it mean[t] absolutely nothing," certainly "not an S&M thing," she parried, "Yeah, Vito, that's what they all say."

Oddly, Vito felt the need to tell his former friend that he was "sort of involved in the gay issue," which she declared "nice." On the issue of gay rights, Midler offered, "Oh, hell, Vito, listen. It's all right for *anybody* to be who they are. Just as long as they don't let their dogs shit on the street." As Vito concluded, Midler sent "love to Bruce," and the interview wrapped with a sense that the days when she and Vito shared Bessie Smith on West 24th Street were permanently over. They were now amiable subject and interviewer pursuing very different lives.

Preston liked what he read and promptly assigned Vito a series of profiles. Vito began on familiar turf by courting Bella Abzug, who was sponsoring a congressional gay-rights bill for the second consecutive year. Admitting her pessimism over the bill's chances without "education" of homophobic legislators, she wondered, eight years before Rep. Gerry Studds publicly acknowledged his homosexuality, whether an elected member of Congress could come out and still retain office. At the same time, she situated herself some thirty years ahead of the political curve by offering her wholehearted blessing to gay marriage.

Vito was also taken with Yippie cofounder Jerry Rubin. Wary of an author who had declared homosexuality a sickness, Vito spotlighted potential homophobia from the start: "Why do you think straight men don't like gay men?" he asked. Rubin responded thoughtfully about straight-male fears and declared gay liberation, in its implicit attack on institutionalized masculinity, "the most subversive movement in America." Vito was so stunned by Rubin's endorsement that he abandoned journalistic objectivity and announced that he still believed in dying for his principles—an unfashionable fervor lacking in post-GAA politics. Rubin's admission that his never having had sex with another man limited his potential for personal growth left the interviewer stunned and numbly praising Rubin as "an explorer" and "a nice guy." This is hardly Vito at full rhetorical throttle, but he can perhaps be excused his less-than-deft depiction of a straight man who so completely departed from his expectations of a Neanderthal.

Not all of Vito's interviewees were this cooperative or even coherent. He cautiously accepted an assignment to speak with Tennessee Williams, whose new play, *Vieux Carré*, was shortly to die on Broadway after six performances. It didn't boost Vito's confidence that he was granted only forty-five minutes with the harried playwright, who was preparing to depart for Palm Beach and obviously dodging questions about his latest work. Why Williams agreed to be interviewed for the *Advocate* is a mystery; he told Vito that he "really [didn't] like to talk much about sexual deviation," which he considered "rather peripheral" to his work. He also expressed regret over publishing his sexually frank *Memoirs* (1975), which, to Vito's bafflement, Williams considered "suppressed" in the marketplace. Trying to shape his "dismal" transcript, Vito turned snarky. He depicted the playwright as living in "controlled bedlam," quoted him as having to "piss every hour" for diabetes testing, and closed the interview with an assurance that, Williams's complaint notwithstanding, *Memoirs* was available in airport bookstores.

Vito left Williams in a foul mood. Trying to salvage the interview, *Carré* director Arthur Seidelman made matters worse. Williams, Seidelman assured Vito, "writes all the time. . . . It's an obsession, he's really amazing. He just can't stop writing." Besieged by well-intentioned friends like Jim Owles, who called Vito daily to inquire, "Getting any writing done?" Vito had little use for a workaholic author who had already made his name and fortune. Far more comforting were the words of Christopher Isherwood, whom Vito had met the previous fall at a Gay Academic Union (GAU) Conference in Long Beach, California. When Vito asked if he wrote every day, Isherwood "said he *thinks* about writing everyday. That made me feel better."

Keeping up a steady literary output was no mean feat in a city with new cabaret opportunities on every block. Bette Midler's success at the Continental was partially responsible for the boom, as was, according to historian James Gavin, an early seventies "nostalgia craze." Clubs began springing up around Manhattan to satisfy patrons' thirst for a lone, preferably louche, girl in a pinspot. Their predominantly gay clientele earned them Arthur Bell's sobriquet "The KY Circuit." Readily available drugs made them even more alluring. At Brothers and Sisters, Vito once locked himself in the ladies' restroom to share a joint with several other men. All was bliss until "someone obviously smelled [their] smoke and pounded on the door yelling 'Five minutes, Miss Joplin.' That gives you an idea of what kind of club it [was]."

During 1974 and 1975, Vito worked fulltime at Cinema 5, the distributor of such politically charged films as *Z* (1969), *Gimme Shelter* (1970), and *State of Siege* (1973). It is telling that he barely mentioned this job in later years. With Bruce in tow, he spent far more time watching and writing about the KY Circuit's rising stars. The one-time impresario of East 120th Street was thrilled to join the "little knots of showcase groupies who frantically rush[ed] from Reno Sweeney to The Grand Finale to Brothers and Sisters. 'Can't stop to talk, gotta get a cab. Reno's. Second show. New act. Bye-bye.'" One of Vito's favorite new acts was Alaina

Reed, whom he had coaxed into a volcanic performance at the 1973 Gay Pride Gala. He also championed Laura Kenyon, another gala veteran, whose rehearsal rendition of Cole Porter at the Continental made Vito feel like "James Mason at the Downbeat Club on Sunset Boulevard," about to discover Judy Garland in *A Star Is Born* (1954). Kenyon guaranteed Vito's affection by performing "Where the Boys Are" to a predictably receptive audience and by confessing to him that she owned one of Garland's *Oz* pinafores.

Vito's preferred stop on the KY Circuit was Reno Sweeney. The "mother of '70s cabarets," the club was a West 13th Street "Art Deco wonderland" named for the character played by Ethel Merman in *Anything Goes* (1936). As if that weren't gay enough, the club's performance space combined a black-and-white tile floor "that Fred Astaire might have danced on" with actual palm trees and a neon sign sporting an illuminated palm tree alongside the space's kitsch name, shrieked in electric pink: The Paradise Room. The list of talent that played this room could be a primer of the seventies famous and infamous: Melissa Manchester, Diane Keaton, Marilyn Sokol, Barbara Cook, Peter Allen, Barry Manilow, Nell Carter, The Manhattan Transfer, Holly Woodlawn—even "Little Edie" Beale (of *Grey Gardens* [1976] fame). The clientele was even more celebrity studded; patrons included Bette Midler, the recent Oscar recipient Liza Minnelli, David Bowie, and Diana Ross. According to frequent visitor Robert W. Richards, the audience also included high-society "faghags": "Is that a proper term? I don't care. That's what they are—lovely faghags, really done up with hats and veils. It had a kind of throwback quality to it." For a time, gays and straights mixed comfortably, though gay fans slopped their martinis when chanteuse Ellen Greene addressed them from the stage: "You know, these are the most wonderful moments of my life, and sometimes when I'm home alone masturbating, I think about you guys."

Reno Sweeney introduced Vito to a performer who became one of his closest friends. Baby Jane Dexter (née Jane Nesbitt Dexter) was an explosive blues-jazz-and-rock belter with an outsized voice to match her frame. A Long Island native, Baby Jane had worked as both a cabbie and a door-to-door birth-control instructor (plastic uterus in tow) before finding her way to Reno Sweeney. The club struck her as a "dream come true," a vision from countless weekend Million Dollar Movies in which "singers would have on a fancy dress and they'd come out and they'd only sing one song because that was their job and they were in love with the bandleader or something." But Baby Jane's stage persona could not have been less Alice Faye. Tossing long, two-tone hair along with raunchy patter, she seemed a hippie earth mother heaven sent for Reno's adoring boys. Baby Jane, Vito exclaimed, "had me from the minute she opened her mouth." After mesmerizing him with Bessie Smith's "Do Your Duty," she growled her way through "Don't Get Around Much Anymore" "like an off-duty B-girl." "If you like Red Hot Mamas," Vito advised readers, "she's your girl." He worshipped such Mamas, and Baby Jane instantly became one of his favorite girls, onstage and off.

Steeped in its nightlife explosion, Vito came to think of Manhattan as a movie set where, as he put it, "everytime you head out the door, it feels like something's gonna break out in headlines!" His enthusiasm was contagious. John Preston asked him to record New York's dish and dirt in the *Advocate*'s bi-weekly Entertainment column. Don McLean (aka "Lori Shannon"), Vito's former customer at Mama's Chick'N'Rib, was penning the San Francisco version, so Vito was in friendly company. Late in 1975, when President Ford refused federal money to lift New York from its sinkhole of debt ("Ford to City: Drop Dead," screamed the infamous *Daily News* headline in all caps), Vito did his part for Manhattan tourism, promising skeptical readers that there was "still a miracle on 34th Street . . . in spite of changing values and hard times." When director Paul Mazursky arrived in town to film *Next Stop, Greenwich Village* (1976), Vito wallowed in a downtown scene that straddled the story's 1953 setting and a hardcore, midseventies Village vibe: "It's not every day that you get to see a man in knickers and a newsboy cap cruising a man in leather and chains, holding a 200 lb. German shepherd on a leash. New York, New York." He was also happy to give Fire Island a plug when the Ice Palace featured such cabaret goddesses as Della Reese, Carmen MacRae, and Morgana King, better known to moviegoers as Mama Corleone in the first two *Godfather* films (1972, 1974).

The Ice Palace had changed considerably from Vito's first visit in 1966. By 1975, disco beats were thumping throughout New York, and Vito was obliged to cover a trend he loathed. Not quite thirty, he was even more curmudgeonly about pop music than he'd been in high school. Reporting on a Rolling Stones concert at Madison Square Garden, he kvetched that "it was impossible to hear one word or lyric of the show." But Mick Jagger at least knew from spectacle, so Vito closed his ears and opened his eyes. He did the same at the Manhattan disco 12 West, where he offered backhanded praise for the lighting design. Above all, he deplored disco's lack of romance, the pounding bass and squealing treble that drowned conversation and rendered the dance floor a single throbbing mass. Vito reminded readers, "Hey gang . . . we are *not* one person. We are many and we are all different." He preferred to return to his old Village standby, Peter Rabbit, where someone might ask him to dance while looking directly into his eyes.

Vito was coming to realize that since Stonewall, he had "had a foot in both worlds" of pre- and post-gay liberation. While he fought fiercely for gay civil rights, he clung to the aesthetics of an older generation that would have found his agitating unthinkable. In his twenties, Vito already identified with Harry Stoner, the male-menopause victim played with Oscar-winning malaise by Jack Lemmon in *Save the Tiger* (1973). Like Harry, Vito longed for a Manhattan era "when you could go to the Cotton Club and see Lena Horne, when you could listen to Billie Holiday singing 'Fine and Mellow.'" But such nostalgia exacted an emotional toll. His fanatical devotion to "Judyism," as he and friend Lenny Bloom labeled their Garland fandom, prompted smirks and dismissals from gay friends: "Dead, you know."

It also hurt Vito to realize that the icons of his youth, despite their fan base, often had no interest in gay rights. In February 1973, he accompanied Arnie to Bette Davis's "Legendary Ladies of the Movies" appearance at Town Hall. During the program's second half, Davis took questions from a raucous crowd drunk with camp glee. One spectator asked, "Is there any truth to the rumor that you support the Gay Liberation Movement?" Many gays in the audience hissed at the speaker, a reaction that Vito interpreted to mean, "How dare he ask [Davis] a question connected with that filthy thing called our lives and how we live them?" Davis replied, "No. I'm not agin' it but I don't feel there's a place for me in it." Given the preponderance of gay men at her feet, Vito was miffed by Davis's answer, but the audience's response made him apoplectic. "On the word 'no,' those homosexuals cheered and applauded. Does anybody realize the implications of that? They were *applauding* someone who had just copped out of dealing with their existence. . . . People like Bette Davis *know* that gay people are sniveling little invisibilities that they can deny publicly and get away with it." In his *Advocate* columns, Vito made sure that celebrities couldn't get away with it quietly.

As the Continental had, Reno Sweeney began attracting mainstream audiences who weren't always comfortable surrounded by gays. Vito went on the offensive, determining to be "as openly and visibly gay as possible while on the premises, just to remind [the owners] where they came from." At the etched-glass door, he confronted veteran columnist Radie Harris about homophobia in her writing. She favored him with an unnerved and eminently quotable reply: "Oh, darling, that's impossible! Some of my best friends are gay. . . . The thing I don't like is all the screamers. It's unnecessary and unattractive." Sometimes bigotry came from the cabaret stage itself. Introducing "A Man Could Be a Wonderful, Wonderful Thing," Julie Wilson dedicated the number to "all the ladies . . . uh . . . *women* in the room." The line drew a laugh, but Vito, bristling at the pre-Stonewall "lady" reference, saw "no reason why that song couldn't have been dedicated to *everyone* in that room, especially considering the number of gay men present."

At least Wilson acknowledged her gay audience. When Vito pursued bigger names, he often found them terrified of the gay press. As "Mandy" climbed the charts, Vito tried to score an *Advocate* interview with Barry Manilow, whose manager insisted that the singer didn't "appeal to blacks or gays and [had] no audience in either group." To appear in a gay magazine, he argued, "would damage [Manilow's] career." Vito encountered similar resistance from Broadway star

Gwen Verdon, whose agent informed Vito that Verdon would be "insulted" to be approached by the *Advocate*. Trying to get himself on a screening list at Universal Pictures, he identified himself as an *Advocate* writer and received the brush-off, "What is that, a fag paper?" The studio became friendlier after Vito put in phone calls to *Variety*, Arthur Bell, Warner Bros., Paramount Pictures, and Rex Reed.

He often encountered suspicious stubbornness even when not representing the *Advocate*. By the mid-1970s, the literary powers-that-were had pegged Vito as a troublemaking "Boy in the Band." Choice assignments often eluded him. When *Rocky* (1976) became a monster hit, Vito tried to interview leading lady Talia Shire. Her publicist begged off, pleading Shire's interview overload, but Vito smelled a rat. Though his article was to be for *Italian American Magazine* (*IAM*), not the *Advocate*, he suspected that the publicist was dismissing him out of hand as "just a gay writer." A closeted lesbian performer whom Vito did interview for *IAM* told him horror stories about her male colleagues' torment of her over the years—"they say filthy, disgusting things to her, like . . . if she sucks [their] cock[s], she'll be straight"—but authorized none of this material for publication. She later called Vito in a rage when he printed that she had refused an interview for the *Advocate*, an announcement that she took as tacit indication of her lesbianism.

The frustration that Vito felt over such denial became "the dominant force in [his] life." He bemoaned that closeted performers had "bought all the lies, [had] bought all the dreams" that public figures are necessarily heterosexual. Vito's impatience led him onto rocky moral terrain. On one hand, he staunchly advocated personal freedom and argued that "nobody has a right to force a person out of his closet. Or to tell him how to lead his life." On the other hand, he didn't hesitate to publish heavy, often repeated hints about Liberace, Anthony Perkins, Rock Hudson, and Stephen Sondheim long before they came out or were outed publicly. Vito was also happy to dish with students after "Celluloid Closet" talks about who in Hollywood was gay and sleeping with whom. And he thoroughly enjoyed harassing those who bragged about newfound heterosexuality, as when, at the 1976 Theatre World Awards party, actor "William Atherton was telling everyone in the room who would listen how Aesthetic Realism cured him of his homosexuality so [Vito] kissed six press agents right under his nose and he cleared out."

At the *Advocate*, faced with Goodstein's conservatism, Vito was more circumspect. When reviewing Craig Zadan's book *Sondheim & Co.* (1975), he praised Sondheim for composing songs with an honesty that might inspire future authors to "write gay characters into their plays without having to worry about changing pronouns." Vito gallantly failed to mention either Sondheim's homosexuality or that the composer had never written lyrics for a gay character.

Vito's caution in this review may also have stemmed from his friendship with the author. The two had become close several years earlier in the closet shadows of *After Dark*. Craig took Vito to see "Liza with a Z," Liza Minnelli's fabled 1972 concert at the Lyceum Theatre; Vito, in turn, introduced Craig to Bette Midler—who would later star in his television production of *Gypsy* (1993)—and demonstrated to his young friend "that [gay] people actually could be that out of the closet, that people could be that public, that people could be that political." When Craig moved to Hollywood a few years later, he took Vito to starry soirees where, Vito claimed, Craig would begin the evening by warning him, "Okay, don't start any fights with [closeted] people tonight!"

Craig insists that he never issued Vito any such warnings. In the first place, he points out, Vito understood the degree to which working actors had to stay closeted in order to stay employed. Moreover, Vito never pressured Craig to come out or to champion gay rights publicly, not even when his career as a film producer (who eventually numbered *Chicago* [2002] and *Hairspray* [2006] among his credits) took off. Vito was equally gentle with Dean Pitchford, Craig's then-lover, who went on to write the screenplay for *Footloose* (1984) and to win an Oscar for his lyrics to "Fame" (1980). While living with Craig in New York, Dean was a rising young actor who played Broadway's "Pippin" and costarred on the soap operas *One Life to Live* and *Search for Tomorrow*. Amid his successes, he was "terrified that if casting directors got confirmation of who [he] was, what [his] sexual orientation was, [he] wouldn't work anymore." Recognizing his friend's fear, Vito did not make Dean's "coming out [or] anyone's coming out a badge of honor. . . . Vito was very sensitive to the fact that he was out and proud, and he was comfortable in his skin, but he also understood that it wasn't so easy for other people in other walks of life." For all his anger at the homophobia that kept Broadway and Hollywood closets locked tight, Vito was too starstruck to push militancy on his successful friends.

His reticence was particularly noticeable with Lily Tomlin. Vito met Lily through John Paul Hudson, who had performed the 1967 cabaret act *Two Much!!* with her at the Madeira Club in Provincetown, Massachusetts. When John Paul introduced Lily to Vito, she was amused by his name. Her most famous character, the smarmy, snorting telephone operator Ernestine Tomlin, occasionally contacted an unseen repairman named Vito. Lily had never met an actual Vito, but the coincidence made it simple for her to remember him. Their friendship gelled after Lily's run-in with Chita Rivera at a Sunset Strip club, where Rivera rattled on about her "boy dancers," a potentially homophobic term that raised Lily's hackles. "I didn't like that. I didn't say anything, but I kind of zoned out. And then a few minutes later, I heard her say 'purse nelly.' And I kind of woke up and I said, '*What* did you say?' And she said [in a Bronx slur], 'Whaaa, I dunno, whadisay?' And I said, 'You just said something a few minutes ago; I want to know what it was. What did you mean by that?' This went on for like two or three minutes, just unbearable and unforgivable on my part. . . . I said, 'You said *purse nelly*. And I want to know what you meant by that.' And she said, 'Purse nelly. You know, pursenelly, purson'ly, personally.' When I got that she meant 'personally,' I laughed till I was sick. And I didn't even have the good grace to admit to her that I was a schnook." As soon as Lily got home that night, she called Vito to share the story. He so loved the misunderstanding that he occasionally used it to sign off his letters, for example, "Purse nelly, I think this country is going to the dogs."

When John Paul asked Lily to appear at the 1973 Gay Pride Gala, she broke contact with him for several years. However, she remained in touch with Vito, who did not pressure her to come out. In 1971, when Lily met Jane Wagner, her longtime partner and collaborator, she received a phone call from Jill Johnston, *Village Voice* dance critic and author of the newly published *Lesbian Nation*. "[Johnston] pretty much threatened me," Lily recalls. "She said, 'If you don't come out, I'm going to do such-and-such.'" Lily doesn't remember the exact message, but it was sufficiently threatening that she likened the experience to "the Secret Service coming to [her] door and planting a chip in [her] shoulder." After firing back a snappy retort, she never heard from Johnston again. As a prominent TV star soon to tackle movies and Broadway, Lily appreciated a friend like Vito who could respect her reserve. A decade later, in fact, she and Jane based a sympathetic character in their play *The Search for Intelligent Signs of Life in the Universe* (1985) on him: Lyn's lover Bob "*listens* with an intensity that most other people have only when *talking*." Lily loved Vito's ability to listen without judging.

He demonstrated as much when he introduced her to Massachusetts state representative Elaine Noble, the first openly lesbian political official in America, and Noble's lover, *Rubyfruit Jungle* (1973) author Rita Mae Brown. In an all-night Boston gab session, Lily was able to discuss her feelings about gay politics and coming out. She was gratified to hear that Noble and Brown would support her no matter what. Vito's support was a given. Even if privately he tired of her "double edged playing around with the truth," he honored Lily for never pretending to be straight. "At least you never have a beard."

Looking back, Lily wishes that Vito had pushed her a bit harder to come out. "Maybe it would have motivated me in a way," she remarks, and given her the courage to stand up to a religious mother who, before her daughter's shows, would beg, "Please don't mention any body parts!" Vito did prod Lily toward astonishing frankness on her album *Modern Scream*. While she was working on the recording in July 1975, *Time* magazine promised her a cover story if she would acknowledge her lesbianism. Thinking the offer a "bribe" and a "buy-out," Lily refused, but she called Vito for his reaction. He suggested incorporating the scenario into a *Modern Scream* routine in which an interviewer asks Lily, fresh off filming a bedroom scene with Keith Carradine in *Nashville*, "what it was like seeing [her]self making love to a man on the big screen." Playing herself on the album, Lily asserts, "I've seen [heterosexual] women all my life, so I know how they walk, I know how they talk. . . . People just don't understand; you don't have to be one to play one." The interviewer (also voiced by Lily) replies, "I guess people are pretty amazed that a woman who looks like you do can play a heterosexual realistically and still be perfectly normal." Recalling the routine now, Lily comments, "I was *thrilled* to have that inspiration from Vito, and I thought it sort of took care of *Time* magazine in a way that was more acceptable to me." Openly gay U.S. Air Force technical sergeant Leonard Matlovich ended up on the September 8 cover.

Helping Lily with *Modern Scream* gave Vito an idea. Perhaps she could help him, too. He was planning a trip to LA to interview a number of celebrities, including Lily's *Nashville* costar Ronee Blakley, for various publications. What a coup to land an *Advocate* interview with the country's hottest comedienne immediately after her big-screen debut! But Lily resisted. Not only had she stopped giving interviews, but more importantly, she told Vito, "I don't want to be interviewed for a gay newspaper and not come out. I really feel that would be dishonest. . . . Please don't talk me into it unless I make the decision to come out." This was far more encouragement than Vito expected. Two years earlier, Lily had gone so far as to tell a *New York Times* reporter that her lovers included "50 women and 20 men." But in 1975, when Don Shewey of Boston's *Gay Community News* asked her whether she was lesbian, she briskly sidestepped: "I don't think it's my business to discuss my sexuality . . . or *your* sexuality." Now she might be willing to come out, with Vito at the typewriter. It seemed too good to be true.

Vito was an ardent fan of Edith Ann, the self-satisfied, rocking-chair brat ("And that's the truth, *pbbbbllllllbbbttt*") whose popularity stood second only to Ernestine's. He and Lily liked to crack each other up with Edith Ann impersonations, some of which, she believes, he invented. Vito decided to defuse the potentially tense interview by coaxing Edith Ann and Ernestine into the conversation, soliciting their opinions on Lily's career as they visited the upscale restaurant Ma Maison, whose decorum they did their utmost to shred. Although occasional efforts at seriousness did surface, as when Vito referenced Dick Cavett's sexism or John Wayne's pro-Vietnam swagger, for the most part the piece is as camp as the Dynel-wigged statues flanking Lily's pool.

Then, near the end, she dropped a bombshell: "Listen, Vito, this is for The ADVOCATE. It's going to look funny if we don't discuss the gay issue." Vito didn't take the bait but instead asked Edith Ann to play a word-association game. Lily muscled back in to offer another hair-raiser: "Vito, do you think that there's a good reason why gay performers don't come out of the closet?" He spluttered a response about family peace-of-mind, which she dismissed with a dollop of rationalization: "Yeah, but that doesn't mean that any of that is justified or right even though on a professional level [coming out] is still not safe to do." Vito euphemistically encapsulated his friend as working "at change, always with an eye toward being a little gentle with those who don't understand."

Today, Lily claims that she did not ask Vito to avoid her sexuality in the article. His deflection of her direct questions may reveal simple protectiveness of a friend with a great deal to lose. Privately, Vito felt sorry for Lily and Jane, arguing that "if only they were out there wouldn't be such a vicious reaction from the fag and lezzie baiters." But he felt compelled to maintain Lily's privacy until the end of his life. In his will, Vito directed that his twelve hours of interview tape with Lily, on which she openly discusses her lesbianism, be returned to her after his death. The bequest is unique; all other interview tapes he willed "to a reputable gay archive."

Vito was equally careful when interviewing Peter Allen, the flamboyant Australian singer-composer who had been the first Mr. Liza Minnelli. In Manhattan, Allen found fame at Reno Sweeney as "the first male performer to have a cult following on New York's notoriously female cabaret circuit." In part, Allen's appeal stemmed from broad hints at the sexuality he never quite revealed. "As he shimmied in a sequined T-shirt, shook a maraca, and threw his leg up on the piano," cooing such lines as "You all know I'm bi-*coastal*, right?" Allen hardly attempted to deny his homosexuality, but he also didn't mention it overtly.

In their talk, Vito allowed the performer a latitude that seems almost parodic—the price he had to pay for firsthand dish about Allen's former mother-in-law, Judy Garland. Throughout the resulting article, the singer receives Vito's curdled praise for exuding "total self-acceptance onstage." Salivating for a confession, Vito noted to Allen that because "so many performers actively hide who they really are . . . it's refreshing when someone is real." Allen called his bluff and retorted, "Yeah, but to do a good job of hiding your real self you have to be fabulous-looking and have a fabulous voice etc." Charming but evasive chatter ensues.

Spending time with stars like Allen and Tomlin was a highlight of Vito's occasional trips to Los Angeles, a city he otherwise detested. Sounding like a gay Woody Allen, Vito remarked of LA, "[Its fans can] really and truly have it, and I mean *all* of it (the mellowness, the sunshine, Taco Bells, and the police)." He was, nevertheless, thrilled to be moving in ever more stellar circles. His principal conduit to this world was Richard Amsel, the renowned illustrator whose poster art for *The Sting* (1973), *Murder on the Orient Express* (1974), and *Chinatown* (1974)—to say nothing of Bette Midler's first two album covers—evoked the kind of lush Hollywood nostalgia that fed Vito's dreams. Richard and Vito clicked instantly at the artist's Upper East Side apartment, where he hosted screenings of his many 35mm movies on a ten-foot screen. When the FBI caught wind of Richard's collection, Vito and Bruce helped him, Baby Jane Dexter, and their friend Dori Hannaway stash away hefty reels of *Gone with the Wind*, *The Wizard of Oz*, and *The Ten Commandments* (1956), along with a trove of Vito's favorite Disney films (*Snow White* [1937], *Dumbo* [1941], *Bambi* [1942], *Cinderella* [1950]).

To Vito's chagrin, Richard was not completely open about his homosexuality. But he was well connected in Hollywood's highest gay circles. His friends included entertainment manager Stuart Cohen and Stuart's professional and personal partner, Rudi Altobelli. Among his clients, Stuart numbered Valerie Harper, Sally Kellerman, and Martin Sheen, all of whom he offered to Vito for interviews. Rudi claimed Katharine Hepburn and Henry Fonda on his own roster, but he became better known as the owner of the mansion at 10050 Cielo Drive, where Charles Manson's followers murdered Sharon Tate and four others in 1969. During the summer of 1975, Vito spent two weeks at 10050 with Dori, Richard, and their friend Bob Esty, the musical director who was renting the house. If its past bothered him, Vito didn't mention it. Instead, he concentrated on making the interview rounds with Richard in tow as his photographer.

Having just won an Emmy for the first season of *Rhoda*, Valerie Harper was one of the biggest names in television. She certainly didn't need an *Advocate* interview, but Stuart urged her to accept, claiming, "You know the gays love you! We love you!" She consented. Vito couldn't have been happier. On *The Mary Tyler Moore Show*, Valerie had voiced one of prime-time television's first, and certainly most positive, references to homosexuality by informing snooty Phyllis Lindstrom (Cloris Leachman) that her brother Ben (Robert Moore) was gay. What had been conceived as a scandalized whisper Valerie insisted on speaking aloud, without judgment. Being gay, she reasoned, simply meant that Ben was "unavailable as a marriage partner; not that there [was] anything wrong with" his sexuality. Her bright delivery of the line prompted "the longest laugh in the history of *The Mary Tyler Moore Show*." It dazzled Vito. This was exactly the kind of nonchalant visibility he was fighting to obtain for gays and lesbians.

With more than a decade of New York dance experience to her credit, Valerie was comfortable with the subject of homosexuality. During the interview, however, she seemed sincerely surprised when Vito informed her that ten years earlier, their conversation would probably not have been possible. When he mentioned that many closeted performers were ashamed of themselves and their lovers, Valerie protested, "Oh, don't say that, darling. That hurts my heart." For her sympathetic stand, Vito pronounced her "living proof that the world [was] changing for the better." And the interview brought Valerie a poignant moment years later. While performing as Edna St. Vincent Millay for PBS in Lincoln, Nebraska, she was approached at her hotel by a nervous young employee. After shyly asking to speak to her, he confessed, "I read your article in the

Advocate and it meant so much to me that you don't look down on people like me." Valerie was heartsick over the boy's isolation but wanted to shout, "Yay, Vito!" for his helping at least one gay reader to realize that he wasn't alone.

Back in New York, Vito got the chance to interview old Hollywood for a new gay literary magazine, *Christopher Street*. The resulting article is a crazed taffy-pull in which Vito solicits Debbie Reynolds's views of homosexuality, which were delicately tolerant at best. She confessed to Vito that she was "still a little startled at seeing [lesbians] together," was aghast to hear rumors surrounding the late Agnes Moorehead's lesbianism, and acknowledged instructing the chorus boys in her show, "*I'm* the girl onstage. I don't care if you're the girl offstage, but on-stage you have to come across as a very strong guy." Vito ignored much of this but informed Reynolds that many gay people felt ignored by mainstream Holly-wood movies. With startling chutzpah, given the readership she was addressing, Reynolds replied, "Yes, but I think you have to realize, really now, that the majority of people are *not* gay and that mass audience is out there." Though she loved her gay friends, thought Vito's earring "cute," and was heartened by the country's increasing tolerance, she was still a self-professed "square when it came to moral issues." One can practically feel the breeze of Vito's sprint to the door as he promises Reynolds, "I will never have a ring put through my nose."

As always, Vito balked at being instructed to behave decorously. Directives were particularly galling from other gays, especially a colossus like David Good-stein. Vito worked contentedly at the *Advocate* as long as he ignored his boss's conservatism. He was certainly grateful for his wide new readership. Under Goodstein's guidance, the *Advocate*'s exploding circulation became an industry success story that earned the front-page attention of the *Wall Street Journal* and the *Los Angeles Times*. But Vito remained uneasy over the magazine's lack of rad-ical vision and its evident concern with "teaching gay people to be respectable" rather than "re-structuring the society that we live in to accommodate differ-ence." Vito had no interest in "saying to the world, 'We're just like you, so you should accept us.'" Rather, he asserted, "What we really should be saying is, 'We are *not* like you *at all*, which is why you should accept us.'"

Goodstein didn't believe in teaching straight society about gay life. He also had no use for "self-appointed gay leaders," the "jackals" and "media freaks" who, "unemployable, unkempt, and neurotic to the point of megalomania," participated in "leftist and 'Third World' demonstrations" that had nothing, Goodstein alleged, to do with gay rights. Rather than encourage reticent gays to come out and contribute to the cause, he argued, the movement should "find ways to encourage them to do what they can from the safety of their closets." A more flaming red flag Goodstein could not have thrown in Vito's face. Along with Arnie Kantrowitz, George Whitmore, Allen Young, and two other *Advocate* writers, Vito denounced Goodstein's racist, classist views as well as his apparent call "for a return to the closet—a new kind of 'expensively-decorated' closet to be sure." His days of heavy *Advocate* output were dwindling.

Which was just as well, for he was now turning his attention to the gay conferences springing up around the country. Presenting "Celluloid Closet" at Indiana University's Gay Awareness Conference, University of Massachusetts at Amherst's "Gay Rites of Spring," and at GAU's "Gaythink" at Long Beach State University (LBSU) (now California State University, Long Beach) brought Vito's ideas to a far broader audience of students, professors, and journalists. Meeting such icons as Christopher Isherwood and Rita Mae Brown, and seeing gay people come together from across the United States to share their ideas, experiences, and politics, inspired Vito in his own work.

The conferences also provided a spark that he was missing at home. After three years of quiet domesticity, Vito had grown itchy. He still loved Bruce but had to face a difficult truth: he had settled for a lover who, lacking his own ambitions, had devoted himself entirely to being Mrs. Russo. As Vito's star rose, Bruce's remained earthbound. Longing for an equal, Vito began looking elsewhere.

Through the conference circuit, Vito plotted to meet a man who'd been fueling his fantasies for years. In 1973, he had seen the short film *A Position of Faith*, which relates the story of William Reagan Johnson, a United Church of Christ minister who became the first openly gay person in the history of Christianity to be ordained. In the film, the clean-cut, bespectacled twenty-five-year-old speaks articulately about sexuality as a "question of *re*pression or *ex*pression." Buffeted by bigots who pronounce homosexuality an "abnormality," a "sinful act," and a sexual "*dis*orientation," Johnson felt that his ordination represented Christianity's first step toward openness and understanding for gays. The story landed in the *New York Times*, which reported Johnson's hope "some day to share a deep love relationship with another man." Vito added *A Position of Faith* clips to his "Celluloid Closet" presentation while falling quietly in love with the film's courageous, handsome hero.

How to meet him? Bill Johnson had left his hometown of Houston for San Francisco, where he was finishing a doctorate at the Institute for Advanced Study of Human Sexuality. In October 1976, both Bill and Vito were scheduled to speak at "Gaythink" in Long Beach. As soon as Vito realized this, he prevailed upon his host, LBSU student Giovanni DeLuzio, to offer Bill housing as well. Gio agreed, and Vito met Bill at Gio's apartment over Halloween weekend. Easy conversation led to kissing and lovemaking—until the pair realized that they were an hour and a half late for the conference's opening reception, where the speakers were being honored.

At the time of their meeting, Bill knew of Vito's *Advocate* writing and was "excited to meet another gay activist who shared [his] passion for being openly gay and for the welfare of the community." Vito's "Closet" presentation impressed him, as did his status as a fellow gay celebrity who didn't seem threatened by Bill's own prominence. Vito, though afraid to let himself seem "vulnerable" to Bill, was powerfully smitten. Here was a man with his own rock-solid identity, a man who didn't want to run Vito's projector during the "Closet" lecture. Vito couldn't resist Bill's seductive self-possession. In short order, he informed his new flame that his relationship with Bruce was over. This was news to Bruce, who gamely told Vito that he "would be disappointed in [Vito] if [he] stifled [his] feelings out of concern for [Bruce's]." As with Steve, Vito's relationship with Bruce was not monogamous. At least verbally, they espoused an open philoso- phy: "We *have* to do what we *know* we want or we're not people—we're your basic 'couple' with all the right 'effects.'" Now enamored of Bill, Vito sought to bring his foundering relationship with Bruce to a "painless" conclusion even as he mused, "I wonder if that's possible."

Bill, who still considers Vito one of the most honest people he's ever met, does not think Vito was lying when he told Bill that his relationship with Bruce had ended. "I think in his own mind, he thought it *was* over," Bill explains. "But it wasn't clean. It wasn't mutually over. It was over so far as *he* was concerned. And so far as he was concerned, it gave him the freedom to do whatever he wanted to do in terms of a new relationship."

Bruce, meanwhile, was falling apart. The man who had been the center of his world for three years wanted out. He struggled to be breezy about it all, read- ing Kahlil Gibran's writings on love and freedom in *The Prophet*, even asking Vito for Bill's birth date so he could do his astrological chart. He initially maintained composure when Bill flew to New York in December for a visit. But after some polite conversation, Bruce lost control and screamed at Bill, "Who do you think you are, stealing my lover?" Vito was horrified. It was his first realization that Bruce didn't share his view of their neatly concluded relationship. Terrified of a life without Vito, Bruce blasted him as "cruel and selfish," at which Vito "crumbled and curled up in a ball and cried for hours." How could Bruce say that? Vito had told him long ago that he thought his life would take a different direction than Bruce's. As he withdrew from Bruce and gave his love to Bill, Vito acknowledged his former lover's pain but dismissed the charge that he had destroyed his dreams: "I know a dream when I step on one, honey, and I don't feel I've stepped on any. Maybe I have but it wasn't my dream so I didn't recognize it." Bruce, Vito shrugged, would survive. Their breakup was "not some kind of a catastrophe. . . . It's a process, not an 'event.'"

Vito threw himself into the bittersweet headiness of an extremely long- distance relationship. At the Omnibus, where he was working evenings while trying to keep days free for *Closet* research and writing, Vito wrote such frequent letters to Bill that Ed McDonald repeatedly threatened to fire him. His monthly phone bill soared to $140, $16 higher than his rent. He mooned about favorite films he wanted to share with Bill, who estimated that he'd seen a total of five movies while growing up. Flush with the $450 he had cleared for his Rutgers lecture, Vito considered blowing $150 on a new Technicolor 16mm print of *Summertime*, which he longed to show Bill. He barely kept his wits through the end of January, when he escaped to San Francisco for three weeks. During the trip, the pair took a romantic ride down the Pacific Coast Highway. Vito ran like a child amok through Disneyland and glowed at dinner in a Big Sur tree-house restaurant "lit with candles and [the lovers'] eyes." He also accompanied his new lover to church, where he experienced "a true communion for the first time since childhood."

Returning to New York, where Bruce had yet to vacate their apartment, was an ordeal. But for the moment, Vito had plenty of other obligations. Islanders Club director Blue Flettrich offered Vito his first trip across the Atlantic if he would preside as movie host on a gay cruise to Corfu, Sicily, Tunis, and Dubrovnik. Though the Islanders was a defiantly apolitical organization, Vito was desperate to think about something other than Bill. Distraction occurred at Dubrovnik customs, where officials "*freaked* when they opened a cardboard box full of *Advocate*s, [and began] yelling something about pornografia for men." Vito tried to stay calm, reassuring himself, "The whole customs dept. looks gay to me, especially two honchos loading the bus who can't take their eyes off of me." Out on the water, he grumbled about 4 a.m. screenings and a wave-sensitive projector that was forever in danger of toppling during *Queen Christina* (1933), *King Kong* (1933), *Born Yesterday* (1950), and *Cabaret*. Complaints aside, he loved showing these films to an audience that included chanteuse Barbara Cook (the cruise's musical entertainment) and poet Rod McKuen. The trip was a welcome, if too brief, respite.

On 24th Street, Bruce was trying to steel himself for the inevitable rupture, which finally arrived on March 13, 1977. At 2:30 a.m., he packed quietly in the bedroom while Vito watched Hitchcock's *Strangers on a Train* (1951) in the living room. For a short time, Bruce relocated to a friend's apartment on West 13th Street. A few months later, he left the United States to join the Bhagwan Shree Rajneesh's ashram in Pune, India. Vito said good-bye in a scene that continued to haunt him: "I keep seeing Bruce through the rear window of a taxi, his head framed by the lights of Seventh Avenue at dusk. He looked so small and vulnerable. 'Want to come to [the] airport?' And I said no. What is it makes me so adamant about not seeing people off at trains and airports? If I couldn't go with Bruce I'll never go for anyone else." Despite his nonchalance, Vito realized that he had hurt Bruce deeply and was frightened of facing the same unceremonious termination with Bill, to whom he confided: "It scares the hell out of me that you'll just run one day without checking with me first." But when Bill, proudly sporting a Mickey Mouse button, confessed to the *San Francisco Chronicle* that Vito was "the man I love," he was heartily reassured.

Bill was much less placid. During his December visit to New York, he had been thoroughly unnerved to learn of Vito's longtime obsession with him. At his apartment, Vito, adopting an artificially casual manner, set up his projector and announced, "Let's watch a movie." To Bill's astonishment, his own image suddenly filled the wall. Vito had failed to mention that he owned *A Position of Faith*, much less that he'd fallen in love with Bill long before actually meeting him. What Vito intended as a romantic gesture Bill found "very creepy." Yet Bill had also grown bored with San Francisco, where he had failed to find Mr. Right. Cautiously, he decided to take the plunge with Vito. They enjoyed each other's company, and the thought of living in New York seemed an exciting adventure. Certainly Vito never entertained the idea of relocating to San Francisco. His perspective, according to Bill, "was that everyone in the world should want to live in NYC and I was among the lucky ones who could live there." When Vito returned west in the spring, he attended Bill's graduation on May 26, helped him pack up his Hyde Street apartment, and then began their long drive together back across the United States.

The trip was a disaster almost from the start. Anxious over leaving his friends and having no New York job prospects, Bill had no interest in sex. He also was beginning to realize that his physical attraction to Vito was minor at best. Feeling neglected, Vito grew "understandably upset," while Bill "was upset at being unable to give him what he wanted." It was dawning on Bill that despite Vito's supercharged public persona, he was "a very insecure person. It's not uncommon for insecure people to be highly visible people; you push the performance button and perform and write and speak and do all those things in the public eye. Privately," Bill feels, "[Vito] had a lot of insecurities. I think he led with his need to be sexually attractive and attracted, and I didn't lead that way. . . . I had already learned that loving someone is about a lot more than being sexually attracted." Bill and Vito tried to dismiss the tension as travel stress. But matters continued to deteriorate as they made their way across the South.

The new couple stopped in Houston so that Vito could meet the Johnsons and Bill could celebrate his upcoming birthday with his twin brother. Bill's mother, his brother, and his brother's male lover were incensed that Bill put his arm around Vito on the living-room sofa. When Bill wandered into the kitchen, he discovered the trio "all talking about how terrible it was that we were having these public displays of affection and how wrong they felt that was. I was *livid*." So much so, in fact, that Bill insisted on leaving Houston the day before his birthday. He and Vito drove on to Chapel Hill, North Carolina, to visit a college friend of Bill's—but by this point, Vito, outside Manhattan for almost two months, was "desperately homesick. [He] desperately wanted to get back to

New York. He was miserable." They arrived in Manhattan on June 15 with Bill feeling "clinically depressed" and "trapped."

Unfortunately, there was no Plan B. Bill's boxes began arriving from San Francisco and filling Vito's tiny apartment. While he and Vito crammed his possessions into overflowing drawers, Vito's "stuff was out [on display], and [Vito's] stuff *stayed* out." It was extremely difficult for Bill to assert his identity in Vito's apartment or in a city where he remained unemployed for several months. In the five years since his ordination, Bill had been offered no church positions; he was still too controversial as The Homosexual Minister. In early 1977, he told a *New York Times* reporter that he no longer wanted his own parish. What exactly he did want was unclear.

Bill also felt insecure about fitting in with Vito's sophisticated New York friends. In part, his fear was borne out by jokes that Jim Owles and Arnie Kantrowitz made about how Vito had driven Bruce (now renamed "Bhavo," or "student," by the Bhagwan) to "take the veil." In Vito's intensely secular crowd, religious conviction was a source of amusement or derision. He informed Bill point-blank, "Look, I respect what you do, but I don't really want any part of it." Bill wondered how Vito would have felt had he said the same to him about movies.

In any case, Vito was too busy cultivating his profile to pay much attention to the relationship he had wanted so badly just a few months earlier. Weeks before he and Bill returned to New York, Vito figured prominently in Arnie's newly published memoir, *Under the Rainbow: Growing Up Gay*, the first book to trace a gay individual's full coming-out, from childhood through activism. Arnie dedicated *Rainbow* to Jim and Vito, who loved the book but privately complained to Arnie about his overwrought portrayal: "Every time I show up, I'm crying!"

Vito also began appearing as a guest interviewer on cable Channel J's *Emerald City*, which executive producer Gene Stavis calls "the first gay television show of any kind." Billed as "gay on j," *Emerald City* was an attempt, in associate producer Steven Bie's words, "to create *After Dark* magazine on television; [it was] a magazine-format show, like a *60 Minutes* thing." More specifically, it was *60 Minutes* with gay-friendly entertainment (Wayland Flowers and Madame; Barbara Cook and Geraldine Fitzgerald singing at Reno Sweeney), gay news segments, and gay and camp interviews (Holly Woodlawn, the Village People, Eartha Kitt). In his interviews, Vito asked Bella Abzug if she received obscene phone calls and chatted with John Waters, the mandarin trashmeister behind *Pink Flamingos* (1972) and *Female Trouble* (1974). Though at first broadcast only to Manhattan viewers, *Emerald City* soon received airtime in San Francisco as well, giving Vito bicoastal exposure.

Vito's new visibility did nothing to ease his financial woes. Bill drained his meager savings before securing a job in December as a secretary for the Lutheran

Church of America. He was grossly overqualified for the position, but it was the only church-related work he could find after the United Church of Christ turned him down flat. And the job lasted only six months. In May 1978, Bill announced to his closeted boss that he could not in good conscience work for a church that refused to ordain gay people. Once more, he found himself unemployed.

Vito's erratic work schedule also didn't help the couple. On the electric typewriter he had inherited from Bhavo, he pounded away on articles and "Closet"-related materials until 3 or 4 a.m. After a few hours' sleep, he sprang out of bed and raced off to the day's many appointments and interviews, followed by evening shifts at the Omnibus. When Vito left the apartment, he offered a vibrancy for public view that he could not sustain at home. Overwhelmed by money pressures and a relationship that seemed ever less viable, he often suffered depression that made him withdraw into long silences or naps. Fighting his own mood swings, Bill sometimes found it difficult to be supportive, especially as he realized that anything he knew about Vito's life came from hearing Vito's end of phone conversations with Arnie, Jim, Arthur Bell, Baby Jane Dexter, or Lily Tomlin. As their emotional intimacy waned, Bill grew even less interested in sex, sending Vito into deeper depression. The pair frequently got stoned on grass as a means of escaping their irreconcilable problems.

The bottom finally fell out in June 1978, a year after Bill had moved in with Vito. One evening at home, Vito was holding forth about a topic that did not inspire Bill to set aside the book he was reading. Vito exploded. "He grabbed my book, threw it down, and slapped me hard. Later, I realized that his frustration at the non-sexual nature of our relationship had reached the point of eruption, but that did not assuage the fact that I was horrified," particularly since Vito knew that Bill had suffered physical abuse as a child and sexual assault from a former boyfriend. Vito apologized profusely, but Bill "no longer felt safe." He moved out immediately.

Following Bill's departure, Vito entered a dark period. After a year of unrequited love, he was experiencing his second ugly break-up in fifteen months. His financial situation was a nightmare. And he despaired over the homophobia that was engulfing the country.

In June 1977, Anita Bryant's "Save Our Children" campaign had succeeded in overturning Dade County, Florida's gay-rights ordinance. The former Oklahoma beauty queen and orange-juice spokesperson had attracted little serious attention when she began sloganeering ("If homosexuality were normal, God would have created Adam and Bruce") the previous January. But her victory in Dade County revealed a deep wellspring of antigay hatred that the moribund movement could not hope to drain. Stonewall-era agitation was dead in 1978. All of Vito's former GAA cronies had left politicking: Arnie was struggling to earn tenure at Staten Island Community College; Jim was working for the city-planning commission in Queens; Marty Robinson had returned to fulltime carpentry; Arthur Bell was advising *Voice* readers to forget about gay rights; Arthur Evans was in San Francisco running the Buggery, his Volkswagen repair business, with fellow GAA vet Hal Offen; even Sylvia Rivera had retired to Tarrytown, where she worked in food concession. The scrappers were gone. Those who remained were exhausted by infighting. Emceeing the 1978 Gay Pride Rally in Central Park, Vito remarked to Lily, "Grace Jones showed her tits to a few thousand lesbians and sang 'I Need A Man' and all hell broke loose. The usual routine. . . . I'm grateful I didn't get punched out for being a man."

In the place of gay unity and purpose was a rising tide of homophobia, inspired by the institutional blessing that bigotry was receiving around the country. Following Dade County, voters revoked gay civil rights in St. Paul, Wichita, and Eugene. Driving across Mississippi in the summer of 1978, Vito heard a disc jockey announce the defeat of a gay-rights bill with the benediction, "Go get 'em, Anita!" That fall, as he was strolling in San Francisco with Arnie and Hal, several teenage boys began heckling them with taunts of "Anita Bryant rules!" and, in a reference to the jailed killer of gay San Francisco city supervisor Harvey Milk, "Free Dan White!" Hal lunged to punch one boy in the face. But physical retaliation wasn't Vito's style, and homophobia wasn't always so easily dispatched. Out touring with the "Closet," he came across a flyer posted in response to an upcoming gay gathering: "Any person acting in a very strange manner / Will proceed to be dismembered by the famous HOMO HAMMER. / And anyone that looks to us in any way queer / Will undoubtedly be punctured by the deadly QUEER SPEAR."

This kind of violence was already erupting in Manhattan. Bill and Vito often avoided walking on 9th Avenue near their apartment; 19th and 20th streets were hangouts for teenagers who liked to harass and occasionally attack gays. In July 1978, Vito covered the story of six gay men, including a former Olympic figure skater, who were bashed in Central Park by a gang of bat-wielding teenage boys, one of whom described his victims as "queers, faggots, homos," and declared, "We hate them." That fall, New York's gay civil-rights bill went down in flames for the seventh time. Considering these developments, Vito perceived "a larger and more threatening movement against people who [were] different in any way." As gay ordinances and protections fell in succession, Vito pondered a move to Amsterdam, but his love of New York and outraged gay pride kept him home. The bashings and bigotry, he insisted, only made him "angry and more determined to allow [homophobes] to see who [he] really [was] wherever [he] went], not willing to be swallowed up." If he could combine visibility with fun, so much the better. An opportunity arose when Vito, Barbara Gittings, and the Reverend Malcolm Boyd (author of *Take off the Masks* [1978] and *Gay Priest*

[1987]) decided with several other gay activists to invade Disneyland and leave a "deliberately outrageous" impression on disapproving parents.

The country's increasing antipathy toward gays did not prevent Vito from receiving invitations to lecture at prestigious nonacademic venues, where a more diverse and influential audience was becoming aware of his work. His former NYU classmate Adam Reilly invited him to present the "Closet" as the kickoff to a Gay Pride series at the American Film Institute (AFI) Theater in Washington's John F. Kennedy Center for the Performing Arts. Adam had been handpicked by AFI head George Stevens Jr. (son of the film director who had helmed *A Place in the Sun* [1951], *Giant* [1956], and *The Diary of Anne Frank* [1959]) as director of the AFI Theater. During his AFI tenure, Adam brought in Deborah Kerr, Franco Zeffirelli, and Elizabeth Taylor to discuss their work. Vito was now standing on boards commandeered by idols.

His success at AFI made it possible for him to lecture at the Fox Venice Theatre in Los Angeles. Cautiously out film actor Dale Reynolds was so impressed by the presentation that he founded Gay Actors' Rap at the Los Angeles Gay Community Center. Within a few years, this informal consciousness-raising group blossomed into the Alliance for Gay Artists in the Entertainment Industry (AGA), which dedicated itself "to the encouragement of positive and realistic portrayals of homosexual people in the media." Vito was very proud of his part in this organization's birth.

By the time he brought the "Closet" to San Francisco's Roxie Theatre in December 1978, just a few weeks after the assassination of Harvey Milk and Mayor George Moscone, Vito was an established star of the gay communities on both coasts. Next to the American premiere of the Buñuel-Dalí film *L'Age d'Or* (1930), Vito's sold-out Roxie appearances inspired the theater's largest-ever draw. By this point, the "Closet" presentation had ballooned to two-and-a-half hours, followed by a thirty-minute question-and-answer session. Though Roxie co-owner Tom Mayer and his associates were delighted by the business that Vito attracted to their theater, they were also uneasy that Vito had not obtained studio permissions for his dozens of clips. They chewed their nails as Vito spoke, realizing that if a studio representative showed up, the Roxie would be legally liable for charging audiences to see unauthorized material. Mayer might have refused to book Vito at all had he known that United Artists (distributor of *Valentino* and *Sunday Bloody Sunday*) was aware of clips that he had pirated from MoMA. At the height of his lecture's popularity, Vito was facing the possibility of a five-thousand-dollar fine or a year in prison.

At the same time, he was enjoying an audience rapport that he often didn't find among undergraduates, who were largely unfamiliar with his repertoire. At the Roxie, Vito happily noted, "audiences were right there understanding even what I didn't say." He also realized, with mixed feelings, that celebrity was now a part of his life. As his professional reputation grew, guys often ascribed to him a "boring and respectable" veneer that he was eager to avoid. San Francisco seemed to be filled with "star fuckers" after his time, conversation, and, sometimes, his body. He began withdrawing into himself, preferring the baths or anonymous encounters for a sexual release that entailed no personal obligation. His growing cynicism made him appreciate all the more a new friend like therapist Joe Brewer, whom he had met through Bill and who offered him a "sense of caring apart from wanting to 'know' Vito Russo, professional movement flash and trash."

Not that he refrained from carousing at the corner of Castro and Market streets, "the crossroads of the gay world," where there were "really too many sexy men to allow for the possibility of justice in the world." Unfortunately, too many of these hunks seemed to Vito sexually repressed, unable to voice their fantasies with the honesty that he found especially arousing. "Everybody's afraid of sex," he moaned. But perhaps he should have been as well. On his return to New York, he tested positive for syphilis (again) and was grounded for three weeks. Merry Christmas! In a ripe snit, he pondered a few men he would "like to infect just for the settling of scores." If only he weren't "too moral" to use sex or an STD as a weapon.

While battling illness, Vito was also mired in yet another round of financial distress. He tried to make light of the situation—"You're poor when your trick loses a quarter from his trouser pocket while getting dressed and you don't tell him cause you need the quarter"—but his financial state at the beginning of 1979 was at its lowest ebb in years. His mother had given him fifty dollars for Christmas; Bhavo, in a forgiving mood, had sent one hundred dollars from India, where he was very content. These gifts meant that Vito could pay his January rent, but he couldn't take care of the bills accumulating in his desk drawer. He couldn't even buy food. At least once, Arnie showed up at Vito's front door with an armload of groceries to tide him over for a few days. Omnibus stints simply couldn't keep him afloat.

In the acknowledgments of *The Celluloid Closet*'s first edition, Vito gushes, "As usual, thank God for the ghetto." The gay Village ghetto that he'd been so eager to escape after college made it possible for him to survive into his early thirties. In April 1979, he began working the counter at the St. Marks Baths restaurant, thereby fulfilling his lifelong ambition to enter, however indirectly, Polly Adler's line of work. Men in towels were far more generous than their dressed counterparts. To Vito's astonishment, he could make up to $200 in an eight-hour shift. (His monthly rent was still under $150.) From midnight to 8 a.m., six days a week for months, he stood behind the snack bar, a cigarette perpetually dangling from his lips, serving up free carrot cake to his friends and taking in the action from "the best seat in the house."

The St. Marks itself was no longer the cesspit it had been during Vito's undergraduate days. The dark, moldy corridors of the midsixties now sported black tile and stainless-steel trim. A Jacuzzi, a full-time masseur, a swimming pool, and a sundeck completed the postliberation picture. Owner Bruce Mailman never locked the front door and forbade clocks on the walls. He wanted customers to have a sense of timelessness, complete remove from the stress of the outside world. This prompted occasional hysteria. When patrons asked Vito if it was still the weekend, "more often than not, it was Tuesday." As Vito chuckled, "You must take care how you tell such news to a person who should have been at the office yesterday." In calmer moments, he loved watching businessmen arrive in three-piece suits only to reemerge at his counter wearing slave collars and chains. The refreshing lack of disco music made it possible to hear sexual activity taking place in cubicles whose partitions did not quite meet the ceiling. Vito, along with everyone else in the building, laughed uproariously on overhearing a role-play gone awry: "On your knees!" "Yes, sir!" "Kiss my boot!" "Yes, sir!" "Touch the head of my cock!" "Yes . . ." "Yes, *what?*" "Yes, *Mary!*"

When Vito started working at the St. Marks, he was in carnal heaven. In line with their generation of sexual liberators, he shared Arnie's conviction that anonymous sex "is a kind of promiscuous giving. . . . When a strange man in need whispers in the dark, 'Please hold me, just hold me,' and you hold him, it is a loving of all humanity, not of a specific individual." But Vito also realized that such generosity, given or received, could exhaust him. He reminded himself to think of the St. Marks "as a job and not as a candy store." Recognizing boredom in the eyes of some regulars, Vito was beginning to realize that "intimacy with concentrated doses of sexuality can breed impotence, contempt for sex partners and even intolerance."

During a conversation with *Christopher Street* editor and St. Marks habitué Michael Denneny, Vito discovered a drawback of the ultra-liberated gay lifestyle. By the late 1970s, Denneny remarks, many urban gay men "had actualized our fantasies to an extraordinary degree. . . . We had sort of stepped through the looking glass. The sex we were having—it had taken about a decade—but the sex we were having was as good as the fantasies we could come up with." But at a psychic cost. One night at the St. Marks, Michael complained to Vito that he hadn't scored a single time all evening. Vito regarded him strangely and remarked that he had seen him having sex with at least four different men. The pair discussed at length the paradox of achieving one's lifelong fantasies only to find oneself mentally detached from them.

It was one thing when two gay men in a bathhouse discussed possible fallout from promiscuity. It was quite another when Hollywood took on the subject, particularly under the direction of William Friedkin, who had infuriated gay activists a decade earlier with *The Boys in the Band*. In the spring of 1979, Friedkin was preparing to film *Cruising*, an adaptation of Gerald Walker's novel (1970) about serial killings of gay Manhattan men. Vito's antennae sprang to full alert. He deplored the book for presenting "self-hatred and psychosis as products of homosexuality, asserting that all homosexuals are recruited by the first men with whom they have sex." Enraged by the imminent filming, Vito met with Arthur Bell, *Christopher Street* publisher Chuck Ortleb and editor Tom Steele, and political strategist Ethan Geto at the West Village apartment of NGTF's Ron Gold, who had, through Hollywood connections, obtained a copy of *Cruising*'s shooting script. The men were revolted. According to Tom, "The original script was full of really sick stuff about gay people; it was really upsetting. Gay people are fistfucking each other all the time and putting chains in their mouths and making each other, killing each other." The group determined to prevent the movie from being made.

To be fair, Walker's novel is not quite the horror show that Vito remembered. It is told largely through the perspective of two closeted characters who loathe gays with an intensity that even Anita Bryant might have found extreme. Walker takes crude care to show that their homophobia stems from squelched homosexuality and professional stagnation. The character of Alfred, a sympathetic gay professor dropped from Friedkin's drastically different screenplay, counsels the murderer Stuart, "Sucking some guy's prick or letting him fuck you in the ass can be less damaging than living out your days *wanting* it. As they say—try it, don't deny it." Though hardly a GAA banner, Alfred's comment is a relatively progressive warning on the consequences of sexual repression.

But in the summer of 1979, the novel's effort at subtlety eluded activists who had seen far too much real-life bashing and had no reason to trust Friedkin with their portrayal on screen. As the director scouted locations among West Village leather bars, Arthur Bell mounted a frantic attack in his *Voice* column. Having seen Friedkin perform a "hand-on-the-hip, lisping routine" while discussing *Boys* at a 1975 lecture, Arthur feared that *Cruising* "promise[d] to be the most oppressive, ugly, bigoted look at homosexuality ever presented on the screen, the worst possible nightmare of the most uptight straight and a validation of Anita Bryant's hate campaign." Arthur issued a call to arms: "I implore readers . . . to give Friedkin and his production crew a terrible time."

Vito shared Arthur's blood thirst. He tried to enlist family support at one of his mother's Sunday dinners, where he railed over pasta against Al Pacino, whom the Russos had adored in *The Godfather*, for appearing in such homophobic trash. Then he recommended a massive whistle-blowing campaign in the West Village to disrupt filming. Vito wielded one of the whistles himself—but he did so with torn emotions. When Arnie and Vito attended an anti-*Cruising* demo, they watched from the sidelines and did not participate directly. As with *The Boys in the Band*, they did not want to seem in any way supportive of censorship. It was better, they held, to let Friedkin make whatever movie he chose and then to picket or leaflet afterward if they deemed it objectionable. Vito described himself as an "observer," not a participant, while protesters' whistles and wire cutters impeded the sound crew and racked up costly reshoots.

In part, his detachment was journalistic. Assigned to cover the shoot and interview Friedkin for *New York* magazine, Vito was present for filming at the Cockpit, an underground sex club doubling for the more notorious Mineshaft. He also traveled uptown with the director on a location hunt at the West Seventies Candle Bar and in Harlem. To Vito, Friedkin furiously denied that *Cruising* could inspire homophobic spectators to commit violence against gays. But then he doubled back, remarking, "Can I tell you honestly that my film will not hurt gays? No." He further asserted that *Cruising* "might very well provoke more men into this kind of life. It's there. It exists. It's the truth." Whether "this kind of life" refers to homosexuality, leather sex, or homicide—or all three—remains unclear. Vito finished the assignment with a mixture of frustration and dread.

The following February, he attended a press screening of *Cruising* with Arthur Bell and Tom Steele. Vito "watched in horror" as the Cockpit scene unfolded onscreen. It was clear that Friedkin intended to exploit the club's seaminess, not to humanize the men appearing in the scene. The voyeuristic camera lingers on leather hoods, aggressive kissing, and fistfucking in a manner that courts only mainstream shock, not eroticism or understanding. Friedkin's attention to the carnival diverted him from his own script, plot points of which seemed to confuse him. After pronouncing the killer heterosexual, he was asked by a reporter how one of the victims ended up with semen in his rectum. Friedkin replied, "That's interesting. I didn't notice that." In a rage, Arthur leapt up and stormed down the aisle, brandishing his cane and screaming at the director, "You fucking piece of shit! You trash! You scumbag!"

Tom thought the whole scene "great theatre." But Vito was unamused, both by the film and by having to scream, yet again, at someone in power who couldn't understand gays' desperation to be represented fairly.

He needed time away. It was fitting that he would receive it from the world's only living convicted blasphemer.

In early 1976, through mutual *Advocate* connections, Vito met Denis Lemon, a "tall, pale, slightly Dickensian figure" and cofounder of London's *Gay News*. That June, Lemon published James Kirkup's poem "The Love That Dares to Speak Its Name," in which the speaker, a Roman centurion, removes Christ's body from the cross and makes ecstatic love to it, proclaiming, "This is the passionate and blissful crucifixion / same-sex lovers suffer, patiently and gladly." Mary Whitehouse, the grandmotherly founder of Britain's archconservative National Viewers' and Listeners' Association, promptly sued Lemon and *Gay News*.

Despite the support of such celebrities as film director Lindsay Anderson, playwright Harold Pinter, and actors Glenda Jackson, Derek Jacobi, and Ian McKellen, Lemon was found guilty of "blasphemous libel" in July 1977. He received a nine-month suspended prison sentence and a fine of $870 (the paper itself was fined an additional $1,740).

Two years later, when Lemon asked Vito whether he'd like to join *Gay News*'s sixteen-member staff, Vito jumped at the chance to work with this real-life martyr. Two weeks after the *Cruising* debacle, he took off for London with $350 to his name.

Culture shock awaited him across the Atlantic. London society was far more conservative than Vito had anticipated, particularly with regard to homosexuality. Shortly before his arrival in February 1980, the customs office had impounded and burned five hundred copies of *The Joy of Gay Sex* (1977). *Gay News*, England's principal forum for gay writers, struggled mightily for newsstand display and distribution, while the paper's cramped, dingy offices, located in the gay ghetto of Earl's Court, hid behind barred windows that could not always keep out burglars or hurled bricks.

Vito didn't care. The escape from New York mitigated a certain amount of danger and repression. He settled into the three-story Islington row house that Denis shared with his lover, Anthony. Vito tried to ignore the fact that Anthony, like entirely too many San Francisco friends, was a vegetarian. Luckily, he could distract himself with Denis's five thousand record albums and—a very welcome addition to Vito's life—VCR. For his first several days, Vito barely slept or saw London. He was far too busy inhaling *Marked Woman* (1937), *Now, Voyager* (1942), *Cabaret*, and *The Stepford Wives* (1975). When he finally tore himself away from telly, he made a pilgrimage to the Cadogan Lane cottage where Judy Garland had died eleven years earlier. Studying the Crown jewels, he was taken by the Star of Africa diamond in Edward VII's scepter—"Would love to have it for wearing while cruising the [New York sex club] Glory Hole," he scribbled to Arnie.

In retrospect, Vito would claim that he "fell in love with London" and its people. Certainly he was charmed to be in a city whose citizens massaged "thank you" into "thank you so very much" and referred to Yanks as "their American cousins." And he got a decided kick out of being told by one new acquaintance, "America has given us 3 great things—*Gone With the Wind*, jazz and fist fucking." But he was also frustrated by a frightfully polite culture in which he couldn't scare up a good argument on the economy or the U.S. conflict with Iran. On British gay politics, he waxed more sour still. "They hate me here," he groaned to Arnie, "because I'm not a political purist. I love it. They're such fuddy duddy schmucks to think that anyone cares about all the things we were arguing about ten years ago," particularly lesbian separatism. In discussions of community organizing, he heard unwelcome echoes of GAA debates from the early seventies: "It's the old where are your women? Where are your blacks? routine. I just laugh like hell in their faces and they see me as non-committed. I told them I wasn't interested in boring people to death for the rest of my life." If Denis had wanted a contentious Yank on his staff, he hit pay dirt with Vito.

At the same time, Vito's role on the paper wasn't immediately clear. His New York acquaintance David Rothenberg already contributed the frequent column Letter from America, while fellow Gothamite and film critic Jack Babuscio wrote the majority of *Gay News*'s movie reviews. That left Vito rather little to do for his weekly salary of fifty pounds. At a loss, he tried his hand at a new form, travel writing. The *Gay News* stint afforded Vito his first extended opportunity to journey outside the United States. He regarded his new surroundings with boundless curiosity, though he was, as ever, incapable of impartial observation. Inevitably, he zeroed in on a culture's gay politics, second only to its male population. Luxuriating in Stockholm, the blond-obsessed journalist squealed to Arnie (forever "Cher" to Vito's "Sunny"), "Oh Cher! The men! I was sure the phone would ring and I'd wake up on 24th Street. I kept pinching myself."

He was even more impressed by Stockholm's tolerance for public displays of affection. It was possible, he exclaimed to his parents, to "walk down the street in Stockholm holding another guy's hand and the straight teenagers and their girlfriends say good evening to you. . . . When I told them you could get beaten up for that in New York they said 'why?' and I couldn't explain it—I still don't know why myself." While in Stockholm, Vito demonstrated against foreign secretary Lord Carrington, visiting symbol of British homophobia. Joan Baez serenaded the protesters from her hotel window with an a cappella rendition of "We Shall Overcome" before joining them on the street to sing "Gays and Lesbians Together" to the tune of "The Battle Hymn of the Republic."

Vito didn't find such political commitment on his other *Gay News* junkets. He arrived in sun-soaked Mykonos fed up with the closet cases of Uranian Tours and feeling like "the [Baby] Jane Hudson" of the isle. His spirits rallied as he strolled arm-in-arm with a German tourist and chatted with a straight couple who didn't blink over the men's open affection. But that was before he was asked not to kiss a male friend in a bar where straights were unself-consciously smooching. It was also before he interviewed Mykonos's mayor, who acknowledged the island's dependence on gay tourism but declared that, as a Greek man, he could not "ever accept that [homosexuality] is natural." Trying to cheer himself up, Vito attended a *Satyricon* theme party thrown by a drag queen acquaintance from New York. Much as he liked his own improvised costume of black jockstrap and flowers, he was outshone by zaftig film producer Allan Carr (*Grease* [1978], *Can't Stop the Music* [1980]), who came as Caligula, "all decked out in a black tent and gold jewelry [with a] laurel wreath." Carr "did a Garbo at first when he spotted [Vito's] camera, screaming 'What are they [*sic*] for?'" Vito rolled his eyes. By now closetedness in a gay resort was irritating second nature to him.

At least Mykonos gave him a chance to experience a new culture. When *Gay News* sent him to Fort Lauderdale and Key West, neither of which he had ever visited, he found little besides insanely expensive meals, noisy disco, and marauding straight teenagers. In Lauderdale, where armed guards stood watch at his hotel and at most of the gay clubs, Vito was advised to make a show of checking out women to avoid attack. "This," he instructed readers, "is no way to live." The residents of Key West he found marginally more open, if amused by the sight of a frantic New Yorker desperate to do his laundry the second he arrived. Adolescent thugs were grudgingly respectful of gay visitors: "Yeah, there are a lot of fags in town. But you gotta be careful. Some of 'em can beat the shit out of ya." Vito was disgusted by the naïveté of a Key West brochure proclaiming: "Gay Rights will never be an active cause in Key West. There is present here today what gays are fighting for the world over." Not as far as Vito could see. The island cut itself off from news of homophobic killings at the Ramrod, a West Village bar. Far more attention was accorded the concurrent death of a film legend, as announced in bright pink chalk at two gay watering holes: "'God Bless Mae West.' And that," Vito sniffed, is "as real as it ever gets in Key West."

He traveled to Florida with two British men who had won the trip at a costume contest in London. The couple proved perfectly friendly, but Vito had had more than enough of gay domesticity. Though Bill was now nearly two years in the past, the wounds still stung. Within days of his arrival in London, he sneered at Denis and Anthony's "great show of endearing little squabbles and mock battles about 'tricks' and things, all the bantering and harmless game playing of lovers." He found his hosts "charming and lovely together," but marriage "sure isn't for [him]." In his journal, he asserted, "The last thing I want is 'security' in knowing that one person is 'mine.' Perhaps because I would then have to be someone else's 'mine' and I have no intention of letting anyone get that close to me." This conviction became the leitmotif of his *Gay News* writing.

Into an interview of his old *Advocate* nemesis David Goodstein, Vito dropped a lengthy non sequitur about "alternatives to rigid fidelity" and his own refusal to be cowed into monogamy by politically correct gays. In an otherwise flattering interview of Italian film director Franco Brusati (*To Forget Venice* [1980]), Vito clucked that the older (and closeted) man seemed "not to have thought about the possibility of complete, adult people, straight or gay, for whom marriage is simply not an option." In a rave review of Edmund White's book *States of Desire* (1980), Vito praises White's vivid description of a Mineshaft master/slave routine between middle-aged lovers, whom Vito finds far more interesting than "a nice, acceptable couple who live in the suburbs and cook dinner each night, retiring with a good book."

Shortly before Vito went to London, future gay historian Stuart Timmons invited him to give a "Closet" lecture at UCLA. The undergraduate Timmons felt deeply drawn to the sophisticated easterner, whom he remembers fondly as a "swashbuckling clone." Following their brief fling, Stuart "got a bit infatuated and was kind of astonished when after a night or two [Vito] was off in someone else's bed. But that was 1979, and that was Vito Russo from New York." With "clone," Stuart references the generally derisive late-seventies slang term for a gay type that Vito epitomized: tight button jeans and boots, flannel shirt, close-cropped hair, wide (but neatly trimmed) mustache, countless sexual conquests. It was the urban, post-Stonewall look of macho liberation for thousands of gay men who'd grown up tormented sissies. From the late 1970s until the end of his life, "clone" was Vito's permanent affect, and he defended it passionately.

In London, as in New York and San Francisco, many gay men ridiculed the clone look as a silly sham, an offensive "putting on" of faux-masculine trappings that were inherently sexist and conformist. Vito lashed back at critics for promoting dress codes that desexualized gay men. In Vito's eyes, clones, himself included, were "a walking advertisement for sex." He saw nothing wrong with conveying through clothing his interest in connecting with other men in very specific ways. Through his look and manner, he hoped to achieve what he acknowledged as seemingly contradictory goals: "I want society to cease viewing gays as defined solely by our sexuality and at the same time I want the freedom to be as unabashedly sexual as I wish."

Many readers were livid. At the popular London disco Heaven, some gay men spat in Vito's face. Others approached him to demand, "Why is there no love or friendship in your life?" or to scream, "How *dare* you champion sex for the sake of sex!" *Gay News* received letters arguing that Vito, suffering "from the classic U.S. masculinity complex," could not understand the subtle cross-class erotics that drew many upper- and middle-class British gay men to clone aesthetics. Vito threw up his hands. "After 15 years of working in greasy kitchens and having no money I'm accused of exploiting the working classes."

His resignation didn't last. He was tired of conservative, husband-hunting British gays who "spend two hours with a stranger and are in love." He grimaced to receive from one admirer a four-page love letter remarkable only for its "constant misspellings. A shitty thing to notice in such a nice letter but that in itself tells me something about my reaction to" the author—and to romance in general. As Vito sternly warned Arnie, lovesick on a San Francisco sabbatical, "we're taught to want fireworks. Fireworks are for the Fourth of July." His own dream man would be "someone who's so busy leading his own life that when [they saw] each other [it would be] like a vacation. . . . He should also be absolutely brilliant but hardly ever say anything and live across town."

Of course, talk like this fairly begs Fate to stick out a foot. In the middle of his antiromance rants, Vito fell hard for Graham McKerrow, a twenty-five-year-old Oxford native who joined the *Gay News* staff shortly after Vito. With his trim black beard, bright green eyes, and articulate wit, Graham dazzled the brash American who'd just written himself off the market. Unfortunately, the dazzle wasn't mutual. Though "enchanted" by Vito, Graham had recently broken up with a man ten years his senior and wasn't looking for another lover, particularly not one who pushed romance so relentlessly. By his own admission, Vito went "crazy" in his pursuit of Graham, "acting like a fool, calling him 4 times a day, getting angry when he had to work late, being 'hurt' a lot. . . . [Vito] *hated* waiting around for Graham two or three nights in a row. Hated not being [his] own person, depending on someone else showing up to make [him] happy, etc." As Vito recognized Graham's lack of interest, he indulged in epic self-pity: "Too bad, Vito. Another brilliant stroke of luck. No roses, no romance, no heaven. Just the shell game. Again. And it's fixed. He should really love me. We'd be great."

Vito's frustration did not prevent him from scheming mightily to meet Graham in Paris after his trip to Mykonos. The goal, he glumly confessed to Arnie, was a Sunday 8 a.m. reunion atop the Eiffel Tower. "With my luck," he snarled, "it won't open till 10." Declaring himself "too old for this sort of thing," Vito purchased a train ticket that would take him, standing, across four countries in three days. Graham arrived in Paris ahead of Vito, and the pair took off to explore a city that only Graham had seen, once during childhood. Rounding a corner, they discovered the Paris Opera. "We both just fell into each other's arms with the shock of how beautiful Paris was."

Though he enjoyed the trip, Vito knew that the romance was doomed. And he was not visiting Paris entirely for pleasure. The previous August, a dear friend, twenty-eight-year-old Marc Sutton, had been murdered while working the coat check of a Parisian nightclub. The crime had gone unsolved, and Vito determined to gather whatever clues he could in Paris. With his college-level French and total ignorance of Parisian culture and geography, the search turned up nothing, but Vito felt somewhat mollified for having tried. He felt the same about Graham and romance.

Vito returned to New York in October 1980, flying on adrenaline. Since February, he had seen much of Europe on an employer's dime, had presented the "Closet" in London, Stockholm, Amsterdam, and Dublin, and had railed against love only to fall its foolish victim. It was time to go home, where he was determined to write himself into gay history.

6

Building the *Closet*

Vito came back to New York a hot commodity. He had brought the "Closet" to the capitals of Europe, and *Gay News* gave his wisecracks transatlantic snap. Professionally, he was on fire.

Politically he was in despair. He returned to a country pitching itself into right-wing freefall. On November 4, 1980, Vito, Arnie, and Jim huddled around Vito's ten-inch television screen and watched numbly as Ronald Reagan trounced rivals Jimmy Carter and John Anderson. Republicans swept the Senate races and racked up thirty-three seats in the House of Representatives. Alphonse D'Amato, a vocal opponent of gay rights, ascended to the New York State Senate. The three GAA veterans, in Arnie's understatement, were "depressed" over the evening's returns.

In step with the more conservative times, gay American men settled into quiet, more affluent lives than they'd ever known. As Vito reported in one of his final articles for *Gay News*, the average annual gay household income spiked to twenty-three thousand dollars, 50 percent higher than the national average. Was it inevitable, he asked, that ready cash incurred a sense of "privilege which saps not only the will to fight against certain injustices, but eliminates the *need* to do so?" As gay yuppies flourished, Vito lacked both the will and the funds to join their apolitical numbers.

Not that he was opposed to gay professionalization. In January 1981, Vito covered the first meeting of the Gay Press Association (GPA), a three-day extravaganza held at Manhattan's Roosevelt Hotel and attended by over eighty writers, editors, photographers, and sales reps from gay publications nationwide. If organizer Joseph DiSabato sounded alarmingly like David Goodstein in his preoccupation with "such countercultural issues as circulation, advertising, distribution, and effective business management," he also caught Vito's attention for placing "pay staff" high on his list of priorities. After years of freelancing and struggling to wrest paychecks from practically every paper carrying his byline (the *Advocate*, under Goodstein's business savvy, being a notable exception), Vito applauded DiSabato's commitment. Banding together with several other writers at the conference, Vito helped form a committee "to investigate the status of gay journalists in areas like syndication, health benefits and just plain old payment for work delivered." These goals would have sounded hopelessly Establishment to Vito in his Firehouse days, but now, in his midthirties, he had come to appreciate the value of a certain material security.

Such security was nowhere to be found with his latest employer. Sinking in a sea of red ink, *Christopher Street* publisher Chuck Ortleb had founded the *New York Native* as "a gay *Village Voice* that would pander . . . to the gay male desire for smooth flesh and bulging sex organs" sufficiently for him to turn a profit and save his foundering magazine. The *Native* quickly became the most substantial and longest-running gay newspaper in New York. Its first cover story focused on the recent Ramrod killings, which, coincidentally, prompted Annie Russo to fire off a mini-manifesto to the *Daily News*: "As parents and family of a gay human being, we are furious and saddened at what happened at the Ramrod. . . . Gays should get out of the closet and stand up for their rights. Don't lose hope. We are with you all the way." Noting his mother's zeal on behalf of gay rights, Vito redoubled his own commitment to the gay press.

Unfortunately, the *Native* suffered the same financial woes as most gay publications. During the paper's infancy, editor Tom Steele grimly recalls, "no one was paid anything." He showed potential writers his own pathetic income tax return to prove that he wasn't hoarding funds. According to advertising manager Tom Duane—later a New York state senator—*Native* writers often left the office without their expected checks. But Tom Steele realized that the new paper filled a yawning void in gay communication. He rallied his contributors with the grassroots vigor that Vito had found irresistible since his first days at *GAY*: "I don't think any of this stuff could appear anywhere else. We need to build this up. New York needs a gay newspaper!" Vito fully conceded Tom's point. Besides, he had a brilliant idea for his own contribution.

Nearly every day throughout the seventies, Vito found time for phone gab with Arthur Bell. At decade's end, Arthur's *Voice* gossip column, Bell Tells, was an institution, the forerunner to Michael Musto's La Dolce Musto. By his own estimation, Arthur was "really *feared*" in New York. He exulted in sensing that people were "scared shitless" over what might pour out of his typewriter from week to week. Vito, tired of being offered Arthur's sloppy seconds, was jealous. "I always say that if the phone rings and it's the *Voice* then a gay person must have gotten killed the night before and Arthur Bell is out of town." At the same time, Vito lived for the dirt that Arthur dumped into their daily chats. Nobody in town had better access to the glitterati or knew more of their secrets. What if Vito and Arthur combined forces? Gay Manhattan might never recover.

As soon as the first *Native* hit the stands, Vito rushed to Tom Steele's office with a breathless proposal. "Would you be interested if Arthur and I just talked about whatever is on at the moment and we transcribed it and gave it to you?" Tom pounced on the idea. "Well, who wouldn't? These two guys were hilarious. The paper, God knows, needed levity, and they just knew so much." Tom may not have realized that Vito and Arthur had no intention of confining themselves to film gossip. They set about writing a column that "should end some friendships once and for all." The Russo/Bell Connection was born.

Vito and Arthur's first entry, published in the *Native*'s third issue, promised an "unexpurgated" account of their phone conversation on December 23, 1980. (The two friends supposedly shared transcription duties, though it's likely that Vito did most of the grunt work. In one conversation, he directs Arthur not to withhold any gossip in the event that "maybe [he's] not taping.") In early Connection columns, the authors dish themselves as much as others. Arthur confesses his latest case of amebiasis, which he fears he may inadvertently have passed to Queen Elizabeth by shaking Kim Novak's hand. Vito, down all week with a cold, relates that Aunt Jean has asked him to schlep up to the Bronx to collect a medicinal meal. "Mine is the only family where they ask you to get on a train and come to University Avenue so they can get you well with chicken soup."

Friends and foes alike crowded the Connection. Both men lavishly praised their pals. Arthur allowed that Larry Bush was "quite a good writer" and pronounced *New York Post* gossip columnist Liz Smith "the loveliest person." Vito dubbed Arnie "lovely" and novelist Felice Picano a "doll." But Vito and Arthur knew that people weren't following their chats simply to learn whom they adored. Thus the venom flowed, even against friends. Arthur expressed open distaste for *San Francisco Sentinel* (and later, *Chronicle*) critic Edward Guthmann— whom Vito liked. Vito taunted Arthur about his age, and they took every opportunity to slam Stuart Byron, a difficult *Voice* writer who could name Vito as one of his few friends. Vito identified his own tricks by full name and gleefully joined Arthur in slamming—twice—William Atherton. On the occasion of the actor's wedding, Vito scoffed, "Now they can name their first child 'Living Proof.'"

The columnists' targets didn't always live across the country or above the barbs of the gay press. Not for nothing did they warn in one entry that names had been "only slightly edited to avoid three local suicides." When Vito quoted novelist Andrew Holleran as canonizing himself and Felice Picano as "the status of gay literature," Arthur replied, "Hahahahahahaha. Constant writer throws up." Vito fired his own share of buckshot, which drew screams from the wounded. He tried to mitigate one attack on the inflated prices at a new nightclub, s.n.a.f.u., by calling the owner, Lewis Friedman, "nice and little." Friedman, who wore platform sneakers to disguise his height of five feet two, didn't appreciate the epithet "little." As the previous owner of Reno Sweeney, he had comped Vito into countless concerts and couldn't understand the betrayal. He called Tom Steele in a rage.

In another ill-advised move, Vito used the Connection to document a fight with a friend. In an article for the *Soho News*, he had announced the city council's anticipated killing—for the tenth year—of the gay civil-rights bill. He quoted an old GAA buddy, politico Allen Roskoff, on the responsibility of Mayor Ed Koch for the bill's likely failure: "The bottom line is crazy Eddie. He has to get off his ass and do what he did for the tenants' bill and the unions' bill and the pothole bill." Allen went berserk at seeing his words in print and buttonholed Vito at the Eagle, demanding, "Vito, how could you do that to me?" He then tried to soften his tone by advising, "You don't call the mayor Crazy Eddie in print without referring to him as the mayor or Ed Koch." Defensive, Vito compounded his felony by recording the whole contretemps in the Connection. Having been Jim Owles's lover, Allen had repeatedly witnessed what he considered Vito's "bitchy" sense of humor. He was furious to find it directed against himself for gay New York's amusement.

For the most part, readers found the column hilarious. Tom Steele and *Native* coeditor Michael Denneny were thrilled by the responses. After several Russo/Bell entries, Vito raved in his journal, "Column with Arthur in N.Y. Native a smash—everyone is talking about it and it may even be a book someday." Michael had already hinted in that direction, and though Vito and Arthur chortled over whether the column was more "social history" or "social disease," they realized that they were indeed recording a vibrant cross-section of gay New York history.

Accordingly, they didn't limit the column to gossip. Vito championed self-defense classes offered to gay men at Greenwich House. He also gave enthusiastic nods to the experimental gay performers in San Francisco's Sisters of Perpetual Indulgence, a kamikaze drag troupe, and Bloolips, a British group whose expert mixture of clowning, impromptu drag, music-hall send-up, and political commentary intoxicated Vito. It surely didn't hurt that he was having a fling with "Naughty Nickers" (Nicholas Phillips), a twenty-one-year-old Bloolips neophyte, or that he had shepherded the group, who had never experienced anything like the bacchanal of Manhattan nightlife, to Hellfire, a straight/gay S and M club. Bloolips leader Bette Bourne declined to accompany them, but his lover, "Precious Pearl" (Paul Shaw), went happily and was stunned to check his clothes at the door and see "dungeon stuff, people tied up in slings and getting pissed on." This was not Vito's scene, but he relished playing tour guide and promoting his friends as they made their American debut on the Lower East Side.

The Connection appeared in sixteen *Native* issues throughout the better part of 1981. Despite the column's popularity, it eventually petered out in late October and never did become a book. Part of the problem was Arthur's health. In early March, he was hospitalized with retina damage caused by advancing diabetes, which he tried to keep secret. In the column, Arthur treated his failing eyesight as a joke, but it made writing difficult.

Vito's writing, meanwhile, was on an upswing that lifted him permanently above the Connection and local journalism. The day after Gay Pride 1981, he announced that he had just experienced the best weekend of his life. After eight years of labor, *The Celluloid Closet: Homosexuality in the Movies*, his lecture-turned-book, hit stores nationwide. Vito beamed from the cover of *Christopher Street* magazine and embarked on a seven-city autograph-and-lecture tour. Countless lonely hours spent trawling film archives across America and Europe had paid off. Vito couldn't help but crow to Arthur and their readers that the recent weeks had been "glorious. . . . A book is born," he exulted. For several years, he hadn't thought "it would ever happen."

Neither had the majority of Vito's nearest and dearest, most of whom held "responsible jobs during daylight hours and [had] no call to be awake at four in the morning, listening to stories about sissies in the 1930s." One of those friends was Jim Owles, who had prodded Vito with the same irritating question for three years: "Well, is it done yet?" Another was Arnie, who had been jolted out of more than one sound sleep to soothe Vito's anxieties over money, writer's block, and the prospect of never being able to finish the book. But Arnie was used to this hysteria. He had been present since Vito's earliest *Closet* efforts.

In the summer of 1974, Vito, Bruce, and Arnie had rented a Cherry Grove cottage that Bruce dubbed "The Way We Are." It was meant to be a writing haven away from the diversions of Manhattan. At the time Arnie was hard at work on *Under the Rainbow*, while Vito, with a year's worth of "Closet" lectures to his credit, was trying to begin the book that he was still calling "Gays in/at the Movies." As the pages of Arnie's memoir piled up, Vito sat flummoxed. Swathed in white silk pajama bottoms or a roomy black-and-white striped caftan, he listened to the clackety-clack of Arnie's typewriter while staring idly at his own. The raw material just wasn't there. There was no way to parlay a twenty-minute presentation on *The Children's Hour*, *The Boys in the Band*, and *Victim* into a book-length discussion of homosexuality in film. The specter of all the research yet to be done sent him straight to the beach, the Meat Rack, or Manhattan. Arnie laughed to see his friend taking pricey water planes back to the city to collect unemployment checks or to pick up groceries cheaper than those available on Fire Island. Such a move showed "a marvelous style," if not also the chutzpah that Vito wore like a second skin.

No amount of chutzpah could help Vito brazen past one unavoidable fact about his book: he wasn't the first to discuss gays and film. While still in college, he'd discovered Winston Reynolds's ten-page "History of Homosexuality in the Movies" (*Drum*, October 1967). More recently, and far more chillingly, a book-length discussion of the topic had found its way into print.

In 1972, Holt, Rinehart and Winston published Parker Tyler's *Screening the Sexes: Homosexuality in the Movies*. Tyler was an empress dowager of criticism who had already published books on Charles Chaplin and underground film along with studies of Van Gogh, Renoir, Degas, Cezanne, and Gauguin. He was also the author, with Charles Henri Ford, of the explicitly gay (and widely banned) experimental novel *The Young and the Evil* (1933), as well as a biography of Ford's painter-lover, *The Divine Comedy of Pavel Tchelitchev* (1967). But Tyler had no political investment in gay subject matter. Born in 1904, he had reached his midsixties when Stonewall exploded and did not participate in gay liberation. In *Screening the Sexes*, he gives token nods to GAA, GLF, and the Mattachine Society, but he seems to miss the deep philosophical cleavages dividing them. He interprets gay imagery through the aesthetic lens he had employed for nearly thirty years. One year before the publication of *Screening the Sexes*, Andrew Sarris attacked Tyler for his "pose as the high priest of high art in the temples of the philistines." The fact that Tyler had "never come out into the open on the real-life basis of his [critical] bias"—his homosexuality—made his criticism seem precious and evasive to many post-Stonewall readers.

Screening the Sexes proclaims its focus in its subtitle, but the book's baroque prose style reveals Tyler's insecurity about analyzing a subject that had brought condemnation to his early writing. Eager to secure the "seriousness" of his topic, he invents a "god of homosexuality, Homeros," whose playful, androgynous spirit infuses all filmed representation of gayness. Unfortunately, Homeros cannot rescue Tyler from fatal defensiveness. Introducing a homoerotic reading of *The Great Escape* (1965), Tyler announces, "I was prepared to hear the worst charges against me that could possibly assault a critic's integrity. People may go so far as to say that I'm not only homosexual myself, but a systematic fantasizer determined to use the movies as propaganda to slander normal sex and completely innocent motives." This was, in fact, Sarris's snide implication, so Tyler was not imagining potential hostility to his work. Afraid to analyze homosexual desire literally, he retreated into the safety of mythology. Of Visconti's *Death in Venice* (1971), adapted from Thomas Mann's novella of thwarted yearning, Tyler asks, "Is Tadzio, whose arm finally points toward the infinite while Aschenbach tries to rise and instead falls dead, an Angel of the Resurrection?" He is equally indirect when analyzing the fatal desire of Claggart for Billy Budd in Peter Ustinov's film (1962): "Billy's innocence, combined with his youth and beauty, and especially his death as a symbol of resurrection, qualify him as an incarnation of Homeros."

When Tyler edges closer to contemporary subject matter, he betrays biases that put him squarely at odds with post-Stonewall rhetoric. By 1971, he was well aware that activists were attacking associations of gayness with impropriety or unhappiness. This realization didn't prevent him, clearly uncomfortable with "the new homosexual militance," from putting his geriatric foot in it time and again. In the book, he is all too eager to sympathize with the "therapeutic" police raids that had just lost their grip on the Meat Rack and to declare that while homophobia still exists, modern society no longer expresses "outrage" at the "private and public misfortunes" of gays and lesbians. Even as these words reached print, GAA was shouting its own outrage in the streets. When he died in 1974, Tyler left behind gay successors who relegated his work to Victoriana.

Still, *Screening the Sexes* gave Vito a necessary starting point, far more so than he acknowledged in later years. When interviewers asked him about the genesis of *Celluloid Closet*, Vito invoked Tyler with Oedipal annihilation. He found *Sexes* "inadequate," "esoteric," and "elitist"; it was an annoyingly apolitical book that refused to tackle homophobia; it was "difficult to read"; Vito could not name even "a dozen people who [would] admit to having gotten through" it. In fairness to Tyler, it should be noted that *Sexes* did receive strong notices in *Film Quarterly*, *Publishers Weekly*, and the *Kirkus Review*. However, it is unquestionably better known today as the book whose shortcomings showed Vito Russo how to shape *The Celluloid Closet*.

Where Tyler's focus had been heavily European (Visconti, Fellini, Bergman, Losey, Pasolini) and experimental (Warhol, Morrissey, Smith, Anger), Vito determined to write a "plain spoken history of the various ways in which gay characters have been portrayed by commercial American film." In contrast with the remote, apolitical *Sexes*, Vito was determined to examine how homophobia on- and offscreen informed Hollywood's more mainstream portrayal of gays. He also aimed to capture a "wider and less specialized audience" than Tyler's. He hoped to write a book that his mother "could read and understand. [She didn't] know shit from shinola about Kenneth Anger or The Film Forum, but she sure as hell [knew] that Roddy McDowall got called a pansy by James Caan in *Funny Lady* [1975]." Vito targeted "the average mainstream moviegoer, so these people could be made to understand how they were being manipulated" by Hollywood bigotry.

His first step, Vito realized, was to unearth all gay images in commercial American film. He was already conversant with many postwar examples, and it was obvious that he should revisit any film bearing the names Tennessee Williams, Gore Vidal, or Truman Capote. Beyond these instances lay a brick wall. In an era before Betamax/VHS, Vito began scouring musty shelves and 16mm archives without the benefit of a Library of Congress "Homosexuality in Motion Pictures" subject heading. He put out a desperate call to friends, film critics, and movie queens of all genders and orientations: if they came across any gay character or plotline, no matter how obscure, could they write it down and send it to him? Responses began pouring in. Some contained wishful thinking, allegations of gayness where none existed. Some referred him to gay allegory, as per Andrew Sarris's suggestion that Vito check out *My Son John* (1952), in which Robert Walker's parents gradually learn that their son is a . . . Communist. (Sarris's reference made Vito chuckle, but *John* ended up in the *Closet* just the same.) Other people stopped Vito at parties or on the street to remind him of films that he knew but had never considered for the book: "'Oh, *God*, have you seen *The Black Cat* [1934] with Boris Karloff and Bela Lugosi?' And I'd say, 'What's gay about that?' And they'd say, 'Take a look at it and you'll see.' And they were right!" After years of surprising audiences with gay content in films they thought they knew inside out, Vito was getting a taste of his own medicine.

Flooded with references, he needed some kind of organizing principle. He found his hook upon meeting Bill Johnson at GAU. During the fall 1976 semester, Bill was teaching men's liberation classes at San Francisco State College (later University). Inspired by talks with his new lover, Vito began thinking about how men saw themselves and their prescribed roles in society. The "phony masculinity" of men terrified of being branded gay began to anger him. That anger manifested itself in his "Closet" lectures, the openings of which now took on an aggressively feminist tone: "The first thing I say to audiences when I lecture on film is the reason why it's supposed to be an insult to call a man effeminate is because it means he's like a woman and so he's not as good as a man." The topic also inspired one of Vito's rare early forays into the straight press when he analyzed the "death of machismo" for the unlikely source of *Bell Telephone Magazine*—which was so nervous about its freelance author that he received vague billing as a "lecturer on stereotyped roles." As straight men took baby steps toward acknowledging their sensitivity, Vito was distressed to find a reactionary "hatred of women" among gay men, especially those who advocated all-male discos or decried drag queens in Pride marches. Even the self-proclaimed "effeminists," who promoted nonmacho behavior among gay men, seemed to Vito "to advocate a return to the Fifties idea of gay men as being 'like women' inherently. This ignore[d] that the female role is just as full of shit as the macho man role they [were] all attacking." To Vito, true gender liberation meant "re-defining and creating an identity free from the necessity of choosing male or female roles."

Experimenting with his own gender identity, Vito began wearing what friend Joe Brewer labeled "some of the strangest clothes ever assembled." Sometimes he accessorized the clone's flannel and denim boots look with a flash of his favorite color: a pink belt or socks. Or he might abandon clone drag altogether and parade down Castro Street sporting a pink chemise Lacoste shirt and short shorts that Edward Guthmann remembers with a fond laugh: "I don't know how to describe [Vito's outfit]. It looked very fruity. Vito with his hairy legs and probably some sneakers. . . . If Vito was wearing something that would scream 'gay,' it didn't matter to him. So many gay men are trying to play it down and be acceptable. So many work really hard to be 'butch' and Vito was not like that at all."

Writing, lecturing, and toying with his own masculinity helped Vito discover one of *The Celluloid Closet*'s central arguments: Hollywood's representations of homosexuality proceeded from ossified American notions of (im)proper male behavior. From the silents through the films of the seventies, men who didn't "act like men" were coded gay; women who acted "too much like men" faced the same stigma. This revelation was vital for tracking homosexuality in films released before 1964, the year that *The Best Man* and *Lady in a Cage* belatedly introduced the terms "homosexual" and "gay" into mainstream American movies. Vito set about finding filmed sissies who predated the language that named them.

He had an invaluable resource in his friend Adam Reilly at AFI. The author of a book on Harold Lloyd, Adam was an expert on American silent film. He pointed out to Vito that Lloyd comedies, as well as Laurel and Hardy features, were rife with gay overtones predicated on sissy behavior. From his vast 16mm collection, Adam was able to copy numerous sequences for Vito's use in both his lecture and his book manuscript. Chaplin's *A Woman* (1915), Stan Laurel's *The Soilers* (1923), and Lloyd's *Sailor Made Man* (1921), *Grandma's Boy* (1922), and *The Kid Brother* (1927) came to anchor Vito's illustrations of early American effeminacy. Adam also expanded Vito's sound repertoire by dubbing for him sequences from *Red River*, in which John Ireland and Montgomery Clift fondle and fire each other's guns to considerable homoerotic effect.

While staying with Adam and his partner Everett Engstrom in May 1978, Vito spent two weeks gorging on films at the Library of Congress (LOC). Sixteen and thirty-five millimeter prints of extremely rare movies, such as Hitchcock's thriller *Rope* (1948), abounded. Any U.S. citizen was entitled to see any film in the library's vast holdings for free. Vito devoured three titles per day, though many of them—*Boom!* (1968), *Performance* (1970), *Busting* (1974)—sickened him with their queasy dread of gay men.

Several archives proved less accessible than the LOC's. In August 1978, Vito traveled to Los Angeles for three weeks of research at UCLA, the Motion Picture Association of America (MPAA), and the Academy of Motion Picture Arts and Sciences (AMPAS). The MPAA didn't pan out. As Vito wrote to Lily Tomlin before his trip, if he did manage to gain entry, it would be "the first time they've let someone in." AMPAS's Margaret Herrick Library opened its doors to Vito, but getting what he needed required careful strategizing. Stuart Timmons, who worked in the Herrick Library during the late seventies, claims that a certain protocol was required for talking with closeted Academy officials about gay matters. That a gay activist would have to play "diplomat" to get his materials was simply part of the game. Vito swallowed his pride and jumped in.

While in LA, Vito also hoped to interview several actors, writers, and directors who were gay or who had contributed to gay imagery in American film. But in the late 1970s, he discovered, there were no influential "gays in the industry . . . who want[ed] positive gay films made." He lamented, "It's the difference between being proud of your heritage and being ashamed of who you are." Of the gays he approached in Hollywood, "not a single one would speak *for* the record; some would speak *off* the record, but nothing any of them said was useful."

Ironically, Vito had his best luck with straight actors who had played gay. Don Murray invited Vito to his Broadway dressing room after a performance of *Same Time, Next Year* to discuss his participation in *Advise & Consent*. In LA, Perry King, fresh from playing a gay man turned straight in *A Different Story* (1978), shared Sylvester Stallone's preproduction advice, "Don't play no faggots." Robert La Tourneaux, the gay actor who appeared as the hustler in *The Boys in the Band*, couldn't land a film role afterward and bitterly insisted that playing Cowboy cost him the lead in *Love Story* (1970).

These chatty actors were the exception. Vito received "some very polite personal 'no's'" to interview requests from Al Pacino, star of *Dog Day Afternoon* and *Cruising*, and Paul Newman, who played the quasi-gay Brick in *Cat on a Hot Tin Roof* (1958) and had, more recently, purchased the film rights to Patricia Nell Warren's pulp gay love story *The Front Runner* (1974). Sixteen years after starring as the tortured Martha in *The Children's Hour*, Shirley MacLaine consented to an interview but then drove Vito insane with repeated cancellations. Barbara Stanwyck, about whom rumors of lesbianism had circulated for years, refused to discuss her lesbian madam in *Walk on the Wild Side*.

Director Edward Dmytryk (*Crossfire* [1947], *Walk on the Wild Side*) expected payment for an interview, prompting Vito's poverty-stricken wail to Lily, "What goes on with these people? Don't they know art when they see it?" But directors were generally more receptive than actors and often provided invaluable production history. Bryan Forbes told Vito that Columbia Pictures cut from his *King Rat* (1965) a sequence involving one character's sex change and subsequent suicide. Richard Brooks agreed to meet with Vito, though curiously, whatever he said about his novel *The Brick Foxhole* (1945) (which Hollywood de-gayed as *Crossfire*) or his films *Cat on a Hot Tin Roof* and *Looking for Mr. Goodbar* (1977) went unrecorded in *The Celluloid Closet*. Robert Aldrich gave Vito considerable backstory on his filming of the landmark lesbian drama *The Killing of Sister George*, particularly Angela Lansbury's revulsion over being offered the title lead and Susannah York's inability to film a convincing love scene with Coral Browne (211, 212). Unfortunately, Vito leaves us guessing as to what Aldrich felt about the squeamish homophobia in two of his other films, *The Legend of Lylah Clare* (1968) and *The*

Choirboys (1977). But he does quote Aldrich's provocative assertion that director James Whale (*Frankenstein* [1931] and *Bride of Frankenstein* [1935]) threw away his Hollywood career by refusing to hide his homosexuality (50). Novelist Christopher Bram questions this interpretation of Whale's professional demise, but he names *The Celluloid Closet* as the first source to inform him about Whale's homosexuality. Bram eventually fictionalized Whale's life in his novel *Father of Frankenstein* (1995), which was adapted into the Oscar-winning film *Gods and Monsters* (1998).

Vito had excellent luck with several prominent screenwriters. Stewart Stern confirmed that Vito wasn't just imagining romantic longing between Sal Mineo and James Dean in *Rebel Without a Cause* (1955); Arthur Laurents kept him in stitches with accounts of censors' hysteria over the "homosexual dialogue"—for example, "My dear boy"—in his original screenplay of *Rope* (92). Gore Vidal provided Vito with an uproarious tale, which he later re-created in perfect deadpan for the screen version of *Celluloid Closet* (1995), about his worming homoerotic subtext into *Ben-Hur* (1959) past oblivious (and homophobic) star Charlton Heston (77).

With Mart Crowley, author of *The Boys in the Band*, Vito had a rockier rapport. Well aware of what gay activists thought of his play, Crowley met warily with Vito. Aiming for politeness, he conceded of his self-loathing main character, "Nobody would try to pass Michael off as having today's [1978] consciousness" (177). Vito kept things friendly by telling Crowley that he admired his play. On the whole, Crowley thought their interview was "quite civil."

He was, therefore, horrified to read the *Closet*'s attack on his film for presenting "a perfunctory compendium of easily acceptable [gay] stereotypes" whose "zippy fag humor . . . posed as philosophy." Though *Boys* offers some "attractive and functional gay men" in the characters of Larry and Hank, a couple trying to work through difficulties and stay together, Vito dismisses the film as an instant "period piece" (177).

Though allowing that Vito scores some "good and valid points" in his critique of the film, Crowley emphatically disputes Vito's claim that *Boys* occasioned "the first time gay people protested against a Hollywood movie." In the first place, Crowley notes, *Boys* was definitely not a "Hollywood movie." In fact, as the film's producer, he turned down offers from Paramount Pictures and überproducer Ray Stark specifically so that he could keep control over the casting, retaining all nine of the original stage actors and shooting the film in Manhattan. Crowley is, moreover, hard pressed to recall any protests at the film's New York or Los Angeles premieres. In fact, he claims, "the real backlash against the film began with [*The Celluloid Closet*] and [Vito's] promotion of it. Frankly, I got the idea that Russo saw 'this one' as his MAIN CHANCE—and worked it. . . . One could feel the reverse of 'flop sweat' coming out of his pores: a HUNGER to *use* the play to make his mark—i.e. grab attention at any price."

Vito generally didn't let personal relationships come between him and film. As he worked on the book, one sexy guy approached him with the offer of a "tumble," provided that Vito "could stop talking about film for an evening." Vito shrugged. Deep into his writing, he was "not interested in non-film talk or tumbling." Many other men found Vito's passion for movies deeply engaging. As soon as he unearthed a new film or a fleeting gay reference, he rushed to friends to gauge their reactions. Listening to Vito, art historian Jim Saslow recalls,

> You just knew he was going to tell you things that no one else had ever looked at or faced openly, and then it would be very funny because he'd show you a clip from a film where the two guys are obviously eyeing one another with some kind of suggestive *leer* and no one had ever talked about it because it was something that the editor had sneaked in or the actors had sneaked in and there was that terrible conspiracy of silence all through the forties, fifties, sixties about things that were right out there. . . . Vito just had this sort of infectious *glee* like [Saslow imitates Vito's animated tone] "I found another one! Here's another one!" That was the attitude . . . the idea was that he was gathering up example after example of gay content in movies and basically saying, "I'm going to document this so well and so extensively that no one will be able to deny it anymore."

Vito was especially gleeful when he had something to show audiences. He leapt at the image that would become the *Closet*'s first: a still from a Thomas Edison experimental film (1895) that depicts two men waltzing before a violinist. While traveling through Amsterdam, Vito discovered a 1901 Berlin catalog that listed the film's title as *The Gay Brothers*. Vito rushed this provocative title into print, prompting later allegations against both the title and Edison's supposed suggestion of homosexuality. At Amsterdam's Gay Arts Festival, Vito also ran across "the very first gay liberation statement ever made on film." *Anders als die Anderen* [*Different from the Others*] (1919) stars Conrad Veidt (later a memorable villain in *Casablanca* [1943]) as a homosexual violinist ruined by blackmail. Dr. Magnus Hirschfeld, whose progay Institute for Sexual Science predated Stonewall by more than half a century, appears as himself to plead tolerance for homosexuals criminalized under Paragraph 175 of the German Penal Code. Christopher Isherwood recalls that during the 1930s, Nazis opened fire at an audience watching *Anders* (20–21). They subsequently destroyed what they presumed to be all copies of the film, which retreated to mythical status until one print was discovered in the Ukraine, restored in Berlin, and then screened in Amsterdam in 1980. Vito saw the film dubbed in Russian and subtitled in Dutch—but he "got the drift," especially when the festival organizer translated it into English for him. Seeing *Anders* in any language was like looking back through time at ancestors he hadn't known existed. It became one of the centerpieces of his lecture and his book.

Europe also yielded a bumper crop of rare illustrations that Vito had despaired of finding in the United States. Within a week of arriving at the *Gay News* office, he located forty-two photos, which a staff photographer offered to duplicate for the low price of two pounds apiece. A few weeks later, he turned up thirteen more images at the British Film Institute, which seemed to specialize in American photos featuring the homoerotic male gaze. Sizzling stills from *Flesh and the Devil* (1927), *Wings* (1927), *The Big Sky* (1952), and *Rebel Without a Cause* promptly went into the manuscript. But Vito quickly realized that no archive in the world contained the images of gay and lesbian romance that he hoped to include in the book. This lacuna meant running films with painful slowness to photograph individual frames: "I mean, that's how you get Peter Finch kissing Murray Head in *Sunday Bloody Sunday* or Garbo kissing Elizabeth Young in *Queen Christina*. They don't make stills of the things I was looking for." Processing these photographs for publication was expensive—fifty dollars each—but they were indispensable for Vito's documentation of homosexual desire.

As interviews and photographs fell into place, Vito continued screening films in archives throughout Europe and America. Before he began the major drafting of *Celluloid Closet*, he scrutinized roughly four hundred movies for homosexual content or innuendo. Only when the bulk of his viewing was completed did he turn his full attention to writing.

Thanks to the New Line lectures, Vito came to the notice of a wunderkind at International Creative Management (ICM). Joseph Edward ("Jed") Mattes had moved to New York from Dubuque, Iowa, in 1970 as a teenager desperate to find gay community. While still in his early twenties, he landed a job in the ICM mailroom and quickly worked his way up to agenting, representing such prominent figures as children's author Theodore Geisel (Dr. Seuss) and actor Leonard Nimoy. But Mattes was also passionately committed to the burgeoning field of gay literature. Armistead Maupin, winning national attention with his *Tales of the City* series, signed on as a client, and Mattes's roster eventually included Urvashi Vaid, Greg Louganis, Michelangelo Signorile, Eric Marcus, Betty Berzon, and Gabriel Rotello. It is no exaggeration to say that Mattes shepherded into existence a significant cross-section of modern gay American writing.

Besides all that, he was a looker. With a shock of thick blond hair tumbling over his forehead, the boyish, corn-fed Iowan caught Vito's eye at once. The two enjoyed a brief fling just as Vito was leaving Bruce for Bill. The romance didn't last but the friendship did, as did Jed's unerring advocacy of Vito's work. Jed's first advice to Vito was to concentrate exclusively on the book and stop writing all those time-consuming articles for the *Advocate*. Knowing that Jed was capable of getting results, Vito obeyed. When Prentice-Hall expressed interest in, then declined *The Celluloid Closet*, Jed shopped the book to seventeen other publishers, most of whom responded, "Who cares? There's not a market for this book," or pointed out that if such a market did exist, Parker Tyler had already cornered it. Vito was astonished. Didn't publishers recognize gay men's endless affinity for movies? And what about the book's crossover appeal to "film freaks" of all sexualities? More broadly, the field of gay publishing was beginning to boom. Jonathan Ned Katz's *Gay American History* appeared in 1976, followed by Jeffrey Weeks's *Coming Out* (1977), and Michel Foucault's groundbreaking *History of Sexuality* (1978). The year 1978 saw the publication of three important, and widely divergent, gay novels: Edmund White's *Nocturnes for the King of Naples*, Andrew Holleran's elegiac *Dancer from the Dance*, and Larry Kramer's scathing satire *Faggots*. Vito wanted to take his place among these sudden giants.

Fortunately, he had a friend in the industry. Homer Dickens, a Harper & Row editor and Omnibus regular, recognized the *Closet*'s market appeal and helped Vito pitch it. The Harper & Row board assigned Homer to the book and offered Vito a contract on March 11, 1978. When he received half of his five-thousand-dollar payment on signing, he and Arnie celebrated with a bottle of Korbel champagne. But the party was short lived. Vito's contractual deadline was October 1. He had just over six months to write a book that he'd barely begun.

In a sense, Vito had been writing *The Celluloid Closet* for five years. The book's central arguments sprang from his lectures, and in the *Advocate* he had been rehearsing specific film analyses (*Reflections in a Golden Eye* [1967], *The Sergeant* [1968], *The Boys in the Band, Norman, Is That You?* [1976]) that he recycled nearly verbatim in the manuscript. That left him with several hundred films yet to categorize.

He proceeded with a few guiding principles. Harper & Row was terrified that Vito intended to use the book to "name names," that is, to stage a mass outing of Hollywood stars. Vito took a higher ground, arguing that while any actor's sexuality, regardless of orientation, should be known, it would be "immoral" and "valueless" to drag the reluctant from their closets (xi). Which left the question of what exactly the book *would* cover. Neither Vito nor Harper & Row wanted a coffee-table tome with glossy pictures of Hollywood's deviants. But the publisher did insist that the book should be "lively and funny and narrative and interesting and *not* a political book." Vito blinked over this last clause. The movement's current malaise notwithstanding, he still considered himself a "militant gay activist," and his first impulse was to pen a diatribe against Hollywood's generally vicious portrayal of gays and lesbians. A cooler head prevailed when he realized, rightly, that "nobody would want to read a yell." He also relaxed when a few straight editors at Harper & Row took up his cause, agreeing with him that a post-Stonewall book on gay imagery couldn't help but be political. Now he had the task of writing an edgy but funny book—in other words, putting his personality on paper.

He began from inside the closet. Though Vito had no interest in outing any one individual, he was determined to expose Hollywood's conspiracy to keep homosexuality hidden or demonized. The book's central tenet drew on GAA's commitment to visibility at any cost: "The big lie about lesbians and gay men is that we do not exist." In part, Vito blamed would-be Hollywood moralists for perpetuating this lie throughout most of the twentieth century. And he certainly denounced closeted industry gays who, fearful of their own exposure, permitted only silence and stereotyping to reach the screen. But Vito reserved most of his rage for the closet itself. "To see homosexuality as a dirty secret," he argued, "is something we all learned as children, both gays and straights." He demanded that gays and lesbians abandon this mind-set and recognize how deliberately the media had cheated them of fair representation. It was high time they politicized their thinking. "We have cooperated for a very long time in the maintenance of our own invisibility. And now the party is over" (xii).

With the closet as his book's central conceit, Vito plotted a roughly chronological discussion of how Hollywood applied various forms of silence in its treatment of gay characters. He had his chapter outline and titles set in stone from the first draft. Chapter 1, "Who's a Sissy?," would focus primarily on films spanning 1895 through the late 1930s, a time during which homosexuality was communicated via a character's departure from gender convention. "The Way We Weren't," chapter 2, brought the discussion into the 1940s and 1950s, when gay characters "were routinely laundered off the screen" (63), even in films adapted from novels and plays about homosexuality. Chapter 3's title, "Frightening the Horses," Vito borrowed from Mrs. Patrick Campbell and, more directly, from Pauline Kael's review of *The Killing of Sister George*. In the 1960s, homosexuality became more visible onscreen as the Motion Picture Production Code, established in 1934 to safeguard American film audiences from morally questionable material, lost its bite. Nevertheless, as Vito contended, the freer post-code atmosphere only meant that gay and lesbian characters moved "out of the closets and into the shadows" (127). Far from receiving thoughtful treatment, homosexuality in the 1960s became "the dirty secret exposed at the end of the last reel" (123). Finally, chapter 4, "Struggle," detailed the efforts of Hollywood in the 1970s to come to terms with the increased visibility of the post-Stonewall gay movement while still chafing at the possibility of a gay hero onscreen. The general result was a dizzying panoply of cartoonish victims and villains who, Vito felt, bore little resemblance to anyone he knew. As stated in his concluding remarks, "There have never been lesbians or gay men in Hollywood films. Only homosexuals" (246).

Before he started writing, Vito dug in his heels about the parameters of the films he would be analyzing. Though guessing (correctly) that he would face criticism for omitting such gay staples as *Death in Venice*, Bertolucci's *The Conformist* (1971), and Pasolini's *Salo* (1975), he realized that these films would clutter his arguments about American masculinity and femininity. Discussions of Eisenstein's *Qué Viva México!* (1930) and Murnau's *Tabu* (1931) did not survive the first edit. Also, though acknowledging the experimental directors Kenneth Anger, James Watson, Melville Weber, Gregory Markopoulos, and Maya Deren, Vito generally omitted experimental film from his roster. In part, this was a personal choice for a critic who ran screaming from alternative cinema: "I've had enough real Warhol to last several lifetimes and I don't need any imitators to remind me what it was like to be bored to death for two hours. And yes, I know all about the value of experimental film, but as far as I'm concerned they can experiment somewhere else." Beyond his personal tastes, he believed that experimental film was "just another way of dismissing homosexuality—by making it so precious and poetic that it becomes strange and beyond the reach of most people." Vito targeted films that he knew reached "huge numbers of people" and thus had a marked effect on how gays were viewed in society.

With his original deadline of October 1 now three months past, Vito began writing in earnest after New Year's 1979. He sat down with high hopes, imagining himself and his yet unwritten tome plastered across the coveted billboard over Sheridan Square. But how to jumpstart chapter 1? He snickered over Dorothy Parker's definition of a writer as "someone sitting at his desk with a fresh piece of paper in his typewriter waiting for the phone to ring." Daydreaming was understandable; he wasn't off to a promising start. He began "Who's a Sissy?" with an academic dryness that made him itch: "The reason that this section is concerned primarily with the genesis of the sissy and not that of the tomboy . . ." Yawn. The second draft he opened with a knockout punch: "Nobody likes a sissy. That includes dykes, faggots, and feminists of both sexes." There. That ought to keep 'em reading.

Who exactly was a "sissy," and why was he so central to early screen portrayals of homosexuality? In keeping with his American focus, Vito read the sissy, a stock comedy figure in films of the teens through the thirties, as fallout from the young nation's "pioneer spirit." To the extent that a "real man" existed, "the creation of the sissy [was] inevitable" in order to show what a "real man" was not. Even detached from explicit homosexual connotations, the sissy obliquely introduced the concept of homosexuality onscreen "as an unseen danger, a reflection of our fears about the perils of tampering with male and female roles" (5, 6). Vito set about demonstrating the ways in which effeminate characters played by Harold Lloyd, Edward Everett Horton, Eric Blore, and Franklin Pangborn provided "yardsticks for measuring the virility of the men around them" (16).

Charting the sissy's evolution against changing Hollywood standards proved tricky. Cinema's need of the sissy as homosexual shorthand became more urgent and, ironically, more indirect after the introduction of the production code, which banished "sexual perversion" (along with rape, incest, abortion, open-mouthed kissing, and white slavery) from the screen. But how much code history could Vito expect his readers to know? He had to force himself to remember that he was not writing for an audience of film historians. What began as the most fleeting reference to "pre-Code years" (D1, 42) ultimately expanded into detailed coverage of the code's genesis under former postmaster general Will Hays and its subsequent name changes (31). Vito wanted to take no chances on losing readers' comprehension or interest.

More than in later chapters, Vito struggled with the argument of "Who's A Sissy?" He knew that he didn't have enough "sissy" material to fill an entire chapter. He also knew that "sissy" portrayals were mounted contemporaneously with a variety of lesbian characters who often weren't used for comedic purposes. Moreover, despite his determination to focus primarily on American films, Vito realized that early German representations of homosexuality, such as in *Anders* and *Pandora's Box* (1928), were often more explicit than their American counterparts and demanded analysis. Finally, ever mindful of his lay readership, Vito feared basing an entire chapter on obscure silents and early talkies that no nonspecialist could be expected to recognize.

Trying to address these problems, Vito turned the "Sissy" chapter into a fascinating but chaotic catchall that strains to link extremely different films through the accident of having been made during the same era. He carefully records the lesbian erotics of *Pandora's Box, Morocco* (1930), *Queen Christina, Dracula's Daughter* (1936), and *Mädchen in Uniform* (1931)—but these films lack connection to male effeminacy and seem to need their own chapter, one dealing at length with lesbian sexuality. *Mädchen*, moreover, is a German film; while Vito contrasts it with *The Children's Hour* and provides a detailed overview of its censorship in America, he does not indicate what, if anything, the film illustrates about American attitudes toward gender. The discussion of *Anders* creates similar confusion. While in Amsterdam after finishing the *Closet*'s second draft, Vito picked up the program that accompanied *Anders*'s original screening in 1919. He raced to include this invaluable source material in the manuscript, noting that the suicide of *Anders*'s protagonist anticipates suicides that would befall gay American characters of the 1960s and 1970s in epidemic proportions (21). The first American character to follow this path is the unseen Skipper in *Cat on a Hot Tin Roof* nearly forty years after *Anders*'s debut and more than twenty years prior to its rediscovery. How likely is thematic influence?

Efforts to make the chapter's older films more relevant for modern readers also ran aground. In his first draft of "Sissy," Vito aims for historic coherence and focuses almost entirely on films immediately preceding and following the production code. In subsequent drafts, including the published version, he takes pains to link older representations of male homosexuality with later, more familiar examples, such as *Tea and Sympathy* (1956), *Some Like It Hot* (1959), *The Sergeant*, *The Rocky Horror Picture Show* (1975), and *La Cage aux Folles* (1978). The presence of these titles in "Sissy" is obviously a bone tossed to readers who, Vito fears, may tire of plowing through dozens of films that predate their birth. To justify the later films' anachronistic presence, he argues that representations of men in drag and/or men attracted to other men changed very little throughout the twentieth century. Across the decades, such characters figured disproportionately in comedy and horror, incited hostility from straight society, and seldom met with happy endings. It's hard to deny these claims, but it's also disingenuous to pretend that filmmakers or audiences of the twentieth century's second half approached gay-themed material with the same preconceptions as their predecessors. While *Rocky Horror* and *La Cage* may borrow earlier sissy trappings and plotting, their defiant post-Stonewall sensibility frames, even promotes, homosexuality with an explicitness that would have been unthinkable under the production code.

Vito made far more successful efforts to draw readers in by borrowing from Richard Dyer, whose short anthology *Gays & Film* (1977) predated *The Celluloid Closet* by four years. In Dyer's work, Vito was particularly drawn to the concept of "bricolage," a term adapted from Claude Lévi-Strauss to indicate gay spectators' "playing around with [filmed] elements available to [them] in such a way as to bend their meanings to [their] own purposes." Dyer's adaptation of bricolage signaled exciting possibilities for gay audiences who were used to tolerating heterosexual movies that either denied their existence or turned them into a joke. Now it was possible to reverse the joke and read ostensibly straight imagery through a gay lens, thereby inviting gay audiences to participate in interpretation and make spectatorship their own. Vito eagerly acknowledges the presence of "covert" gay audiences as far back as 1936, when *Sylvia Scarlett* allowed them to feast on the image of Cary Grant sleeping with a cute boy—even if "he" is actually Katharine Hepburn in disguise (14). Though skipping too quickly over *Rocky Horror*'s enduring cult popularity, Vito does reference the baroque Freudian excesses "that keep present-day gay audiences howling" through *Johnny Guitar* (1954) (53, 103). He also notes the inadvertent political expediency of *The Boys in the Band*, which, he claims, "moved homosexuals throughout the country" to protest their image on screen and to examine their own degree of self-acceptance (176, 177).

Vito knew from the Firehouse Flicks that apolitical spectators could be radicalized once they began participating actively in interpretation. Though still mindful that the book should not seem an off-putting "yell," Vito attempted between drafts to embolden its political messages such that readers would recognize their own stake in spotting homophobia onscreen. The finished *Closet* thus contains a number of overtly political observations that help unify its cross-generational survey: effeminate men, onscreen and off, are subject to terrifying violence (54); gays may be bashed onscreen, but seldom with an examination of homophobia's causes (70); gay men too often replicate the macho imagery on which the empty signifier of a "real man" depends (83); American films almost never depict a "gentle man" who happens to love other men (72); American films almost never show the possibility of parents accepting children's homosexuality (149); American films, well after Stonewall, made virtually no acknowledgment of gays' political evolution (164). While drafting, Vito also realized that the book required detailed analysis of the lesbophobia souring portrayals of female friendships in the 1970s. Discussions of *Sheila Levine Is Dead and Living in New York* (1975), *Julia* (1977), and *Girlfriends* (1978) were added to the final manuscript (88–89). The addition of these central points to later drafts indicates Vito's rising urgency to show readers their own investment in reading film alongside him.

Writing steadily through the first half of 1979, Vito neared the completion of his first rough draft in summer. Dissatisfied with the manuscript, however, he let his apartment slide into a grimy mess, stopped returning calls, and gave up on "being particularly polite to people." He tried to convince himself that personal distress was the inevitable result of artistic labor: "I've become convinced that I work best when the rest of my life is in a chaotic state—or perhaps the chaos is caused by the fact that I'm working so hard and haven't allowed anything else to get at me." In July, friend Mark Pinney recognized Vito's angst and invited him to spend a month at his house in Garrison, New York, where he could work far from Manhattan's many distractions.

While in Garrison, Vito slogged away at problems still slowing his argument. For days he agonized over the linked analyses of *The Killing of Sister George* and *The Boys in the Band*. Based on popular plays and premiering, respectively, one year before and one year after Stonewall, the two films made the perfect "liberation" coda for a decade in which homosexuality was exploited as a seamy "gotcha" plot point. With lesbian and gay protagonists, *George* and *Boys* communicate their characters' homosexuality immediately—problematizing Vito's contention that in the 1970s, a "hero still could not be queer" (179)—and underscore the exorbitant psychic price that characters pay for any degree of self-acceptance. In his wrap-up to "Frightening the Horses," Vito wanted to present the two films as a twinned pivot between sixties shadows and seventies openness. Unfortunately, pairing them proved more difficult than he'd anticipated. While none of Mart Crowley's *Boys* celebrates being gay, *Sister George*'s June Buckridge has great fun as a snorting, stomping butch. Her outrageous persona may cost her both her lover and her television soap role, but she barrels through the film with little of the misery that hampers the *Boys*.

Vito broke his block by recognizing that the reception of the two films was nearly identical. America took *George* and *Boys* as "definitive portraits of gay life" (170). George's rollicking butchness and, in *Boys*, Emory's electric effeminacy comforted audiences who "had never met a live homosexual in their entire lives" but thought they could easily recognize the signs of gayness (175). Both films also confirmed the notion that being gay or lesbian, no matter how well one accepts it, does not lead to peace. Sister George ends up alone and demoted, literally mooing in the voice of the cow character she must now play for a children's show; in *Boys*, Emory is beaten to a pulp, Harold's sole romantic consolation is a hustler who doesn't want to spend the night with him, and Michael, easily the band's most self-loathing member, ends the film by departing to midnight Mass in apparent atonement for his sexual "sins." Together, *Boys* and *Sister George* helped Vito demonstrate that although the gay sixties may have ended more forthrightly than they began, they certainly didn't portend gay joy in the next decade.

While enjoying Garrison's pastoral peace, Vito began torturing himself over his final chapter, "Struggle." Fifty pages into the drafting, he confessed, "[I feel] no excitement because I hate it. Don't know how to pull it into shape—want to run away but have to get it all down and try to make it sing in a second draft. . . . The book is full of information but except for certain sections it's not exciting and it has to be." In part, the problem was one of relentlessly grim source material. For every psychologically believable treatment of homosexuality in 1970s films like *Sunday Bloody Sunday* or *Cabaret,* there were a dozen others in which gays were savagely lampooned, "cured" of their homosexuality, or murdered. Even an allegedly progressive movie like *The Ritz* (1976), an adaptation Terrence McNally's Broadway comedy, Vito found filled with "looney tunes" rather than realized characters. It irked him that *The Ritz*'s bathhouse denizens were presented "as though the existence of gays in such a place were joke enough" (219). He tried to smile at a press screening where Pauline Kael—a critic whose homophobia Vito frequently flags in the *Closet*—remarked to him and Arthur Bell, "It's a sad day for you people." But *The Ritz* so offended him that he stalked leading lady Rita Moreno at a premiere party, demanding whether she felt her film would "reinforce Middle America's stereotypes" of gays. Affronted, Moreno shot back, "Don't give me stereotypes! We're a *farce,* darling." She was, however, sufficiently angered by stereotypes to confront Vito two days later at a Fire Island fashion show, where she spotted him in a "faggot"-emblazoned T-shirt. "I hate that word," Moreno spat. "It's like spic."

Doggedly chronicling miserable 1970s portrayals, up to the grisly attacks of *Cruising,* left Vito as limp as his prose. In his second draft, he still had no idea how to lift himself or his manuscript out of the dumps. He made the problem worse by attacking his readers along with Hollywood in the book's new downer of an ending: "The movies have 'done' nothing to homosexuals. We've done it to ourselves. We didn't recognize each other nor did we recognize ourselves. We tried to fit into society on its terms, always failing, always filling the stereotype because we believed it and wanted to belong on any terms" (D2, 393).

This was not the proper reward for readers who had just waded through 250 pages of oppression. Vito's anger was spoiling a book that needed to yield equal portions of outrage and affection. The new ending, he despaired to Arnie, is "not just faulty but genuine shit. I'm not stupid or blind and the book isn't very good." In his frustration, Vito took to lashing out at friends like Howard Rosenman, an openly gay producer about to premiere the Barbra Streisand vehicle *The Main Event* (1979). Over dinner, Vito excoriated Howard for "selling out to the Establishment" rather than making "radical movies." Having worked furiously to establish himself in Hollywood, Howard felt betrayed by Vito's attack and was tempted to dismiss his friend as "a kind of loser" who enmeshed himself in esoteric "bullshit" rather than a viable cause. Howard gently declined to point out that Vito lived for Hollywood, no matter his criticisms of it.

Vito later apologized to Howard for his outburst. He realized that his anger stemmed more from literary helplessness than genuine disapproval. Unfortunately, he wasn't getting much support at Harper & Row from Homer Dickens, whom Vito was coming to consider "the biggest idiot [he had] ever met." Their relationship began well; Homer was a renowned film connoisseur who had published books (*The Films of . . .*) on Katharine Hepburn, Ginger Rogers, Marlene Dietrich, Barbara Stanwyck, and Gary Cooper. He had also assembled a huge assortment of obscure stills, including images from the original *Ben-Hur* (1925), *Irene* (1926), *Caged, Caprice* (1967), and *They Only Kill Their Masters* (1972), which he offered to Vito for the book. However, the man who lived by Constance Bennett's dictum to "keep it light!" was not ideally suited to oversee Vito's work. Vito privately attacked Homer for his "lack of interest, insight, involvement in [the] project," charging, "He hasn't the slightest idea what the book is all about, how to present it, what to say about it or how to promote it." Homer was also not disposed to do the sort of hand-holding that Vito had come to expect from friends like Arnie. One day, hoping to elicit a compliment from his editor, Vito told Homer that Jed Mattes had just sent him a congratulatory telegram on the book's latest draft. Homer airily replied, "He's your agent, darling, he has to say things like that" before switching the subject to Dietrich.

Vito did recognize a grain of wisdom in Homer's "keep it light" mantra. His anger at friends and at Hollywood was beginning to sabotage the book. To soften its tone, he had to infuse it with the humor and "offhand, breezy writing" he had originally planned. Unable to muster necessary cheer in his grungy apartment, Vito turned to wealthy friends with idle real estate at their disposal.

As soon as he returned to Manhattan from Garrison, Bruce Mailman, owner of the St. Marks Baths and soon-to-be owner of the legendary Saint disco, offered Vito use of his empty Pines house during the fall. The frustrated author spent several tranquil stretches in September and October on the island, tinkering with his manuscript and letting the crash of the waves soothe his jangled nerves.

In late November, he packed up several hundred ragged pages and headed for Los Angeles, which, he stewed, was filled with "lots of rich people—younger than [he] and less talented—not a good place to be poor." On the other hand, it also contained the vacant Los Feliz mansion that Lily Tomlin had bought a year earlier and was thoroughly overhauling before she and Jane took occupancy. There on DeMille Drive, Vito found an expansive nest saturated with Hollywood lore. The house, which sat directly opposite the former residences of Cecil B. DeMille and Charlie Chaplin, had been owned by W. C. Fields, who lived there with his lover, Carlotta Monti. Down a slope was the home of soprano Deanna Durbin, at whose swans Fields fired BB's whenever the diva flexed her vocal cords. A pond on Lily's property had its own fatal history: DeMille's toddler grandson, the son of actor Anthony Quinn, had drowned there.

What better place to invoke Hollywood horrors and filter them through a camp lens? For weeks, Vito slept on a pullout couch in Lily's basement, which he had turned into an impromptu office with stacks of film books that served double duty as reference material and dining-table legs under a rickety board. During the days, he escaped contractors' deafening hammering and choking dust clouds by haunting the UCLA and AMPAS archives for last-minute research. At night, he visited with Lily's assistant, Cheryl Swannack, and pounded away on his revisions while standing up at a kitchen counter with stove burners as his sole source of heat. When the mansion's cold became too oppressive, Vito moved to a Santa Monica beachfront bungalow belonging to John Morgan Wilson, a new friend and mystery writer backpacking his way through Wyoming and Utah. With John's cat for company, Vito continued to lighten the *Closet*'s tone. John returned to find Vito freshly departed and his home altered, not necessarily for the better: "The cat was fat and happy but all the windows were closed tight and Vito's tobacco smoke permeated every inch of the house." Vito, meanwhile, was on his way back to New York with a fully revised, significantly sunnier manuscript.

In his revisions, Vito took pains to remind readers that Hollywood's early sissies were "fun," a "refuge for nonconformity," not simply examples of masculine failure (D2, 38). If Franklin Pangborn fought to defend his masculinity offscreen with "five hard knuckles," onscreen he was, Vito now grinned, "one of the girls" (34; D1, 50 [handwritten addition]). He allowed himself to laugh about the homoeroticism of silent films that made later audiences uneasy: "If only people wouldn't assume that all those loving brothers were as queer as three-dollar bills, men could hug without having nightmares" (D2, 94). Referencing the sexy vibe between costars Robert Redford and Paul Newman, Vito jested of their leading lady, "After all, who remembers Katharine Ross from *Butch Cassidy and the Sundance Kid* [1969]?" (81). He recommended that the prehistoric transsexual howlers *Children of Loneliness* (1939) and Ed Wood's *Glen or Glenda?* (1953) be scheduled on midnight double bills with *Pink Flamingos* (1972) (D2, 146). Of the dimwitted sexual politics in *M*A*S*H* and *Tell Me That You Love Me, Junie Moon* (both 1970), Vito chortled, "People really thought that a good [heterosexual] lay cured homosexuals" (D2, 246). In revisions, he also took care to rein in humor that might offend readers, as when he redlined a reference to Erik Rhodes's effeminate Italian gigolo in *The Gay Divorcee* (1934) as "the oiliest spaghetti sucker of the 30's" (D2, 45).

The manuscript now reflected Vito's irreverent personality. Richard Dyer rightly points out that despite the *Closet*'s catalog of sins against homosexuals, "[Vito] *loved* Hollywood . . . he loved Clifton Webb and a whole lot of the images that perhaps from a certain kind of politically correct gay liberation viewpoint one shouldn't love." Clifton Webb may have provided the "ultimate sissy portrait" via the viper-tongued, homicidal Waldo Lydecker in *Laura* (1944), but what thoughtful gay viewer could fail to admire Webb's "classic portrayal of a homosexual," the fussy Elliot Templeton in *The Razor's Edge* (1946) (45)? For all his raving about the murderous lesbian stereotypes of *Caged* (101–2), Vito planned a *Caged* theme party at which all attendees would come dressed as their favorite character. (For himself, Vito chose the prim prison reformer essayed by Agnes Moorehead, though he also loved leaving New Year's Eve phone messages for Tom Steele in the persona of sadistic matron Hope Emerson.) If Paul Mazursky's *Next Stop, Greenwich Village* (1976) was "depressing as hell" for Antonio Fargas's performance as "Bernstein the depressed faggot" (228, 338), this didn't stop Vito from showing the film constantly to friends and family right up to his final day at home in 1990. While packing for New York University Medical Center, Vito ignored his spiking fever and racking cough long enough to screen, with commentary, *Next Stop*'s first scene for his brother. Charlie had never seen the film, and Vito had to share the love.

He attempted to give the same joy to his readers. Early lectures had taught him not to end on a tragic note. Arnie once suggested that Vito conclude the "Closet" with a necrology summarizing the dozens of murders and suicides that had befallen gay characters throughout film history. It was an inspired idea, but not for a lecture. Audiences left dispirited. When Vito moved the necrology to an earlier slot, it scored strong thematic points but left room for hope. The book's necrology traces the violent deaths of over thirty gay characters from *Anders* through *Cruising*. Vito placed it immediately before the index, visible only to readers who sought it out. As a buffer, he preceded it with a filmography consisting of flippant capsule summaries of nearly four hundred gay-themed films. A few samples: *Cinderella*'s mice "Jock and Gus-Gus aren't just good friends" (249); in *Fame* (1980), Paul McCrane is "the only gay student at Performing Arts High School (if you can believe that one)" (250); in *Myra Breckenridge* (1970), "Rex Reed wakes up in a hospital bed and screams, 'My tits! Where are my tits?'" (255).

So much for the supplementary material. There was still the problem of how to buoy the final chapter's leaden finish. By the time he was wrapping up the draft, Vito had despaired that even he had no idea of "how Hollywood might make a film that would portray [gays and lesbians] properly." He belatedly recognized the "enormous naivete" that had permitted him to expect fair treatment from an industry whose economic interests limited its politics. At the same time, he knew that he couldn't send readers off feeling depressed or defensive. Once more he turned to Professor Kantrowitz for advice. For the book's end, Arnie recommended "something optimistic, perhaps a view of the ways things would, should and could be in a better world of filmdom."

For Vito, that "better world" was best represented by gays and lesbians making films about their own lives and not waiting for Hollywood to do it "fairly." In the mid-1970s, he became friendly with members of San Francisco's Mariposa Film Group, which was compiling a documentary called *Who Are We?* from interviews of over two hundred gay men and lesbians. Vito enjoyed a brief fling and then a lifelong friendship with one Mariposan, Rob Epstein, a handsome blond New Jersey native who had gotten involved in the documentary upon moving to San Francisco. Soon after meeting Rob, Vito introduced him to his Garrison host, Mark Pinney, who appears in the film as a suited, straitlaced gay executive. Eventually, the film's scope was whittled down to twenty-six interviews of subjects ranging in age from eighteen to seventy-seven, including women and men from a wide sampling of professions, races, and gender manifestation. The speakers sat before cameras and talked openly about their struggles toward self-acceptance, their sense of themselves as gay or lesbian. The finished film was titled *Word Is Out: Stories of Some of Our Lives* (1978).

Producer Peter Adair described himself as "quite frankly, a propagandist" who felt, along with the other Mariposa members, "tremendously concerned *not* to put across a political point of view *other than* 'gay is good.'" That suited Vito, exhausted by endless media messages that gay was far less than "good," just fine. Pronouncing the film "an electric piece of history," Vito was enthralled by *Word Is Out*, which, he argued, provided rare confirmation of "the remarkably common experience of growing up gay in America, a straight world" (244, 245). The subjects' battles with family, the medical establishment, and the law seemed to Vito a *tableau vivant*, a "future volume of Jonathan Katz's *Gay American History* come to life while still being written."

Word Is Out provided precisely the conclusion that Vito had been seeking for his book. The film gave many viewers their first glimpse of a gay community and thus vanquished the "great enemy" of invisibility (246). It also refused to present homosexuality as a tawdry plot device or a tragic aberration. Mariposa's subjects were not victims, villains, or ciphers. To the extent that they were stereotypical—a preening drag queen, a stone-butch "husband"—they, not a smirking straight director, were in full control of their own stereotypes. Finally audiences had a chance to see actual gays and lesbians, not the minutely defined "homosexuals" whom Hollywood had been filming for decades (246).

Finishing *The Celluloid Closet* was no easier for Vito than writing it had been. Watching Vito work, Bill Johnson considered him a "perfectionist" who undermined his own efforts: "It was, ironically, a fear of success, of not being able to meet his own high expectations, that was holding him back" from completing the book. After typing out the nearly four-hundred-page manuscript twice and incorporating hundreds of changes, Vito still felt that he hadn't quite nailed it. While in London he howled across the Atlantic to Arnie: "I know it needs a lot of work and intend to give it a lot of work even if it means starving and dragging out the 'when will it be finished?' all over again. Cher, it can't just be OK, it has to be terrific."

During the months of travel for *Gay News*, his heartbreak over Graham, and his return home, Vito finally got the manuscript where he wanted it. Submitted to Harper & Row during the fall of 1980, it arrived two years late with a dedication to his parents and to the memory of Marc Sutton, the friend who had been murdered in Paris the previous summer.

In January 1981, Vito studied the galleys with muted satisfaction—he "liked [the book] better this reading."

For Vito on Vito, that was high praise.

For a book of such long-lasting appeal, *The Celluloid Closet* received decidedly mixed notices. To Vito's relief, some reviews were unqualified raves. Both *Booklist* and *Christian Century* offered emphatic, if compact, endorsement. Vito was also pleased by squibs in *Library Journal*, *Kirkus Review*, and *Publishers Weekly*. More substantive praise came from Arthur Bell, who extolled in *The Hollywood Reporter*, "This is the book I've been yelling for since the gay liberation movement began in 1969. . . . [*The Celluloid Closet*] is militant and marvelous and must be read by anyone who goes to the movies, and isn't that just about everyone?" The book was also cheered in London. The *Observer* hailed *Closet* as a "witty, good-tempered survey," while *Gay News* marveled at Vito's "remarkable ability to stay sensible and dispassionate about films and characters that make many of us lose our cool." Who had expected such sangfroid from the bigmouthed New York activist?

Not all reviewers sensed serenity in Vito's writing. Though critics generally admired the "scrupulous research" that yielded "a wealth of fascinating material" and an abundance of "marvelously bizarre facts," they also grew impatient with Vito's exhaustively expressed anger. Stephen Harvey, Vito's MoMA crony, didn't feel that Vito had sufficiently animated his last chapter; "example after lugubrious example" of depressing gay fates weigh down the argument. In *The New Republic*, Rhoda Koenig groaned over Vito's insistence on including "every one- and two-line fag gag he's ever heard." Stephen Farber echoed Koenig in his *American Film* critique, which faulted Vito for being "so determined to mention every film ever made on [his] subject that larger themes are frequently sacrificed to a slavish chronicle of specific movies." Discomfort over the *Closet's* onslaught of homophobic examples sometimes bled into discomfort over gay politics. David Chute of *Film Comment* excused Vito for allowing his "activist feathers [to] get ruffled," but he also chided him for uncertainty over his book's true purpose: "Again and again, you can feel his critical and his activist muscles pulling in opposite directions." Chute's colleagues were often less tolerant of the activist-author. Koenig tired of Vito's "too-insistent ideology," while Farber resented Vito's "grating tone," his "preaching" of "an irrelevant sermon on society's mistreatment of gays."

Was Vito an activist or a critic? Some reviewers seemed to feel that he couldn't be both; as Koenig argued, "Humanitarianism and art don't proceed from the same impulse or have the same goal." Others dismissed Vito's critical faculties altogether. In the *Times Literary Supplement*, Peter Conrad slammed the *Closet* as a "compendious gabble," a book "lacking critical subtlety and parlously ignorant of any culture outside the companionable dark of those art cinemas in London, New York, Los Angeles, San Francisco, Washington, and Amsterdam." Lest Conrad be branded homophobic for such innuendo, he rushed to assure readers that he admired "good" gay criticism—*Screening the Sexes*. In his zeal to tear down closet walls, Vito seemed to spot homosexuality in unlikely sources, trumpeting his "jubilant conscription of new and hitherto unsuspected recruits." Intentionally or not, the word "recruits" cast Vito in the unfortunate light of an alley-lurking pedophile, waiting patiently to lure "innocent" films into his net.

Other critics took the same tack: how dare Vito infer homosexuality from any film not expressly about homosexuals? As an "avowed gay," *Choice's* anonymous reviewer boomed, Vito "lacks objectivity." Why, he even brands *Frankenstein* "a homosexual film without offering substantiation or even indicating who is supposedly homosexual." This critique is curious on two counts. Nowhere in *Celluloid Closet* does Vito refer to *Frankenstein* as a "homosexual film." Instead, he notes the "homosexual parallels" in *Frankenstein* and *Bride of Frankenstein*; both films present the Creature as an aberration of nature hunted by a murderous society wishing to stamp out difference (49–52). Also, while Vito does reference James Whale's gayness, between drafts he considerably muted its prominence. His analysis moves from the bald statement, "Director James Whale's homosexuality certainly influenced the overall vision of the Frankenstein monster as the 'aberration' which eventually destroys his creator" (D1, 68A, 8) to the much more temperate assertion, "In both films the homosexuality of James Whale may have been a force in the vision" of the loathed Creature (50). These are not the words of a recruiter. They are the words of an author who senses bigoted critics on the horizon.

Openly gay critics sometimes joined the attack. In the *Los Angeles Times*, John Rechy, author of the landmark autobiographical novel *City of Night* (1963), dismissed Vito's arguments as "long recitations of plots" that "reach simplistic conclusions." Bizarrely, Rechy went on to fault Vito for missing the homoerotic subtext of Hollywood westerns and "buddy films"—a motif that Vito discusses at length in *Red River*, *Midnight Cowboy* (1969), and *Thunderbolt and Lightfoot* (1974) (78, 80–81, 84–86). Rechy also took Vito to task for exalting the "blown-up home-movie 'documentaries'" of a posturing 'Socialist' German film maker"—i.e., Rosa von Praunheim—whose work Vito actually labels "highly dogmatic, almost dictatorial" and "distinctly nonfeminist" (204, 205).

Vito expected critics to fault him for leaving Fassbinder, Eisenstein, and even John Waters out of his discussion. He made no effort to defend these omissions, but he did try to stave off certain philosophical objections that critics might take to his work. To an *Advocate* interviewer he insisted, "Because I talk so much about changing concepts of masculinity, I consider [*The Celluloid Closet*] a feminist book. It's not a coffee-table book." Some reviewers begged to differ. In the socialist journal *Jump Cut*, Martha Fleming contended that the *Closet* was "not a materialist feminist book about sexual representation and ideology by a sexual liberation activist." It was, rather, "a book about straight images of homosexual people by a liberal gay man." Fleming took strong issue with Vito's "fundamentally gay male analysis," as evidenced when he identifies a "gay sensibility" in the lesbian-themed *Mädchen in Uniform* (56). In Fleming's view, "saying gay and intending to include lesbians under the umbrella roughly parallels saying mankind and presuming to include women." She finds Vito similarly naïve for disregarding the depiction of gay and lesbian characters' social class.

Other critics also faulted Vito for theoretical naïveté. Robin Wood consigned *The Celluloid Closet*, which "gives us much information and little theory," to the "coffee tables" of "friendly liberals." He vastly preferred the criticism of such theoreticians as Richard Dyer and Eisenstein scholar Andrew Britton, who are "able to go much further and say much more [than *The Celluloid Closet*] because they are equipped to assault the major social/ideological institutions of our culture instead of being partially ensnared by them." In the *Soho News*, Jonathan

Rosenbaum took a similar swipe by noting that Vito's faux "leftist stance and an overall piety in relation to capitalism of the film industry make for strangely compatible bedfellows." In other words, Vito's exclusive focus on mainstream commercial fare belies his rage at its homophobia. His avoidance of sexual, social, and economic theory proves that he had no serious interest in deconstructing Hollywood's homophobia.

In his generally positive review of *Celluloid Closet*, Richard Dyer reproached Vito for falling on the wrong end of a "gay liberationist versus a social materialist theory/politics" continuum. The former philosophy, Dyer explained, holds that homosexuality is an historically repressed "essence" within certain individuals that only recently exploded in a "Gay Is Good!" release. The latter considers homosexuality a linguistically constructed category designed by oppressors to keep deviants in their social place. In fact, Vito tried not to read films in a social vacuum; he references homophobic attitudes in contemporary journalism (e.g., *Coronet*, *Commonweal*, *Time*, *Newsweek*) and film reviews (particularly in the writing of Richard Schickel and Pauline Kael) in order to explore how they both reflected and helped determine the treatment of gays onscreen. But it is also true that he had no interest in interrogating the social or material foundations of homosexuality. His own experience of desiring other men and encountering homophobia both onscreen and off convinced him of the political efficacy of his arguments.

Reminded of his critique today, Dyer shudders, "Embarrassing, all that jargon." He notes that Vito was writing about film during an era when sexuality was undergoing formidable theorization. "If you were an academic," Dyer remarks, "you had to think" in such abstruse terms in order to gain professional acceptance. "You had to think the basically Foucault-influenced idea that [sexuality] was all a social construction, so [in my review] it's almost like I was going through that in order to show that I knew that argument." Rethinking his position today, Dyer believes that social constructionism is more useful in discussing pre–nineteenth century representations of homosexuality. "When you're talking about film," Dyer concedes, "I'm not sure how much difference [social constructionism] makes since films were all made very much within the period of a quite fixed idea of what it means to be gay."

More to the current point, Dyer emphasizes that nearly thirty years after its initial publication, *The Celluloid Closet* "hasn't been surpassed, really." Though the canon of gay films has exploded since 1981, Dyer argues, "I don't think anyone's changed the overall story. I think [Vito] laid down . . . the basic line of development and sets of concerns of Hollywood cinema: what are we to think about camp figures, and sissy figures, and so on? What do we think about stereotypes? What do we think about all these deaths of lesbians and gay men in movies?" Subsequent critics have answered Vito's questions in their own ways, but the questions themselves remain integral to film criticism.

Vito paid little heed to critics. When Stuart Byron (inaccurately) warned him that Stephen Harvey's *Voice* review would be a pan, Vito shrugged off his concern: "Maybe [Stuart's] right but so what—everybody has to do what they have to do." The one review that prompted his written response was Rosenbaum's in the *Soho News*. Vito described it in his journal as "a sort of condescending piece by a straight leftist sympathizer who admires Robin [Wood] and Richard [Dyer] and Parker [Tyler] and cries out for trenchant analyses of Eisenstein and Fassbinder—dull as dishwater but current as hell." This simply wasn't Vito's critical style. And his currency, he gloated, didn't suffer for it. After the *Closet* had enjoyed several years of prominence, Vito confessed to an interviewer that he relished his success specifically "because it pisses off Marxist-feminists. They hate me because my book is so popular, because they think my work isn't serious enough. It just makes them *so* angry that so many people listen to me and read me. That couldn't make me happier because it shows them that they're wasting their time on dry, stupid politics when they could be reaching people with more accessible language."

Vito wasn't exaggerating his own or his book's popularity. When the *Closet* officially appeared on July 1, 1981, he was in the middle of a whirlwind promotional tour that few academic critics ever experience. He took his first trip to Chicago, where he so wowed audiences that he was invited back twice that fall: in October to give GAU's keynote address and in November to present his lecture at the Chicago International Film Festival. The tour continued smoothly in Boston, Washington, and Los Angeles.

In less cosmopolitan cities, Vito slammed headfirst into the kind of bigotry he generally avoided in Manhattan. Giving a radio interview in Tucson, he was at the mercy of a hostile crew incensed "by the fact that they had a fag on the show and that the interviewer was going to have to talk with me for fifteen minutes." Another interviewer, an African American woman, blindsided him by beginning their on-air chat, "Mr. Russo, I confess I find homosexuality disgusting. . . . Why is it necessary to write a book *at all* on such a subject?" When Vito retorted that her question was the equivalent of asking "my brother and his wife not to wear a wedding ring or show their children in public," the interviewer replied, "Now, Mr. Russo, one must recognize that we live in a heterosexual world." To which Vito, neck veins bulging, shrieked, "*NO WE DON'T!* That's like saying that we live in a *white* world." The conversation devolved from there. But at least the interviewer didn't hold Vito responsible for natural disasters. In Denver, where his appearance coincided with three tornadoes, homophobic sky-watchers "called in to the radio station and blamed [him] for being in town."

Denver also yielded unexpected sweetness. Adam Reilly, now director of Denver Center Cinema, devoted the Gay Pride month of June to screenings of over twenty films analyzed in the *Closet*. Vito kicked off the festival with a rousing lecture on June 5, one day after he received his first paperback copies of the

Closet via Federal Express from Harper & Row. He fell in love with the cover design, a silver, black, and white suggestion of a film reel with miniature stills from the book filling the reel's sprockets.

Vito dedicated one of the first copies to the other houseguest staying with Adam Reilly and Everett Engstrom: cherubic politico Sean Strub, who had tried to pick Vito up at New York's GPA conference the previous January. At the time, Vito had been too engrossed to notice the twenty-three-year-old Iowan's attentions, but in Denver, the pair clicked. Despite his youth, Sean was highly accomplished. At seventeen, he had worked as an elevator operator at the Capitol, where he chatted with Senators Gary Hart, Ted Kennedy, John Glenn, and Edmund Muskie. Within a few years, as executive director of the Kentucky Democratic Party, he secured from Tennessee Williams the first celebrity endorsement of the fledgling Human Rights Campaign Fund. Even without knowing that Sean would go on to run for Congress and to found *POZ*, a key magazine for people with HIV and AIDS, Vito was duly impressed.

Eight months after his turmoil over Graham McKerrow, Vito considered Sean "a patch of perfect weather." A torrid fling resulted. One evening, as they shared a joint on Adam and Everett's porch, Sean began hallucinating that a parked Volkswagen bug had "turned into a frog before [his] very eyes and was hopping up the street, leap-frogging over the other cars." Sean described this vision to Vito, who requested "every detail imaginable (what color was the frog, did it see [them], how large was it in relation to the cars, etc.)." The next morning, Vito presented Sean with a copy of the *Closet*, in which he had inscribed: "I didn't see any frogs, but I know a prince when I meet one. Love, Xxx Vito." Lying in Vito's arms that night, Sean whispered, "If I had to die when I was young I would want it to be at the end of a day like this."

Vito returned to New York in a romantic tizzy. On the plane from Denver, he counseled himself to learn "to accept the joy of the moment and let it go gracefully when it's finished." Then, abruptly skeptical, he wondered "if we ever really learn anything at all." He mused, "We think we're so safe and protected from our emotions and then someone like Sean comes along and forces us to redefine feelings about everything—relationships, priorities, the meaning of life, everything. Yet another example of how I'm torn by the life I choose to lead, one of impermanence, constant travel, solitude for my writing always at war with a deep desire to find someone like [Sean] and discover a free, loving way to commit to another person without the restrictions which usually come with falling in love." Vito didn't see long-term prospects with Sean, who had returned to Lexington, but he felt certain that the young man would "stay in [his] heart for a long while to come."

For several days, anyway. Vito was poised to enter "probably the best[,] most exciting two weeks in [his] life so far." On June 19, just as the *Closet* began appearing in bookstores all over Manhattan, Vito flew to San Francisco, where he was scheduled to present his lecture and *Mädchen in Uniform* at the palatial Castro Theatre for the International Lesbian and Gay Film Festival. He spent the week racing about town, swilling champagne, being showered with gardenias, and overseeing a private Castro screening of Midler at the Continental plus Garland and Streisand's soaring 1963 duet, "Get Happy/Happy Days Are Here Again," on Garland's TV show. In the middle of all this hubbub, the San Francisco Gay Men's Chorus returned home from a concert tour. Vito joined the thousands who serenaded them on Castro Street with "San Francisco," the adopted anthem that honored their exquisitely gay hometown.

On the afternoon of the festival's opening, Vito strolled down Castro Street with Rob Epstein. Rob glanced up at the Castro Theatre marquee, where a very tall, blond young man on a ladder was dropping into place the title letters of Rob's latest film, *Greetings from Washington, D.C.* Vito followed Rob's gaze but missed the marquee altogether. He had just made eye contact with Jeffrey Allan Sevcik.

Within a week of the *Closet*'s publication, Vito had spotted the love of his life.

7

"A Time of Major Change"

Electricity crackled beneath the Castro marquee. Six feet four inches tall and perched atop his ladder, Jeffrey Sevcik towered over Vito—indeed, over the entire street. His golden hair glinted in the afternoon light as he struggled, his hands full of slippery plastic letters, to maintain balance ten feet off the ground. He flashed Vito a grin before turning back to his work.

Heart hammering, Vito entered the theater. For the first time in weeks, his mind was not on tomorrow night's lecture. Like the lovestruck Judy Garland flying over the trolley tracks in *Meet Me in St. Louis*, he remembered "how it feels when the universe reels." Who could introduce him to that beautiful man?

Schmoozing in the Castro lobby after his lecture, Vito looked around for his new *objet*. No luck. He sought distraction by flirting with a buddy, photographer Rink Foto. Already taken, Rink disentangled himself from Vito's grasp. Then as they stepped out into the street, Rink spotted the perfect diversion for his amorous friend. Still clad in the maroon and gold vest that served as his work uniform, Jeffrey was emerging from the theater. Rink turned Vito in Jeff's direction, informed him that the "CT" embossed on his vest did not stand for "Cock Tease," and introduced the two men.

Vito didn't mind craning his neck to gaze into Jeff's eyes. He rarely encountered this kind of lanky, towheaded beauty on Manhattan's streets. Jeff seemed exotic to Vito, all the more so when he opened his mouth.

With no date for the festival's opening-night party, Vito asked Jeff whether he was planning to attend, "hoping he would go just because [Vito] asked. 'I don't socialize[,]' he said," leaving Vito "crestfallen and fascinated." Nevertheless, Jeff "shyly stayed near [him] afterward and came to the party[,] then to the hotel where they held each other until morning and [Vito's] flight to L.A," where Vito was to continue the *Closet* junket. Jeffrey accompanied him to the airport and left a romantic message for him at the Beverly Hills Hotel: "Been with you all day; just wanted to call and say hello." Less than a week later, Vito was preening that this "*very* lovely, quiet, special" guy was Manhattan bound.

Born April 10, 1955, Jeff was nearly nine years Vito's junior. In a single year, he was the third significantly younger man who had made Vito reconsider romance. Now thirty-five, Vito paid no attention to men his own age.

Jeff hailed from a Pittsburgh family, the fourth of five children and the only boy. His father worked in a dairy in the suburb of McKees Rocks, while his mother stayed home with the kids until her youngest, Jeff's sister Adele, started school. When their three older sisters grew up and relocated to Arizona, Colorado, and Delaware, Jeff and Adele were left alone with their parents.

Jeff got along beautifully with his mother, who, like Adele, shared his tastes in music and happily memorized Barbra Streisand albums with him. Mr. Sevcik was somewhat reserved with Jeff, disappointed that his extremely tall son had no interest in basketball—or any other sport, for that matter. Jeff was a strong student who excelled in French and English and, despite his shyness, loved acting in high school plays. Few McKees Rocks kids shared his love of Broadway musicals or old movies, so Jeff's social circle remained small.

Jeffrey longed to leave Pittsburgh and follow the wandering example of his older sisters. But where to go and how to get there? Lacking his sisters' sense of purpose and direction, he expressed his vague yearning in poetry:

> Somebody come
> And take me away from here
> I can't seem to do it by myself
> Take me somewhere
> I don't care where
> Just so it's far from here
> Let's go west and take a rest. . . .
> I won't imagine what it'll be like
> How we'll do it
> Or anything like that
> I'm ready

Jeff's unnamed western destination materialized at the continent's far edge. In September 1973, he enrolled as a freshman at San Francisco State College (SFSC). At that point, he probably had not heard the nicknames ("Baghdad by the Bay," "Sodom by the Sea") assigned his new hometown during its early days. But it's also unlikely that he would have moved over two thousand miles from home without some awareness of the booming gay population that had begun, through the colorful campaigns of Harvey Milk, to assert its political voice.

At eighteen, Jeffrey was no more political than he would become in adulthood. It was romantic connection that San Francisco promised the isolated aesthete,

> A loner full of dreams   bitter hopes
> And wanderlust. . . .
> Perhaps I'll find
> a loving heart there for me
> Leftover love renewed

His new city also meant artistic and personal exploration. At SFSC, he took courses in acting, directing, film, dance, drawing, painting, rock and roll, and gay literature, a subject he could not have studied in the Pittsburgh of his adolescence. He also began penning volumes of poetry toward an interdisciplinary degree in Creative Arts. After thirteen rocky semesters, Jeff earned his bachelor's degree in January 1980.

After graduation, Jeff had no particular goals save laboring over "an unfinished pyramid of poetry" that would eventually "become [his] tomb." He was distracted by two film characters who reminded him, to a paralyzing degree, of himself: Geraldine Page's immaculate, detached decorator in *Interiors* (1978) and Mary Tyler Moore's immaculate, detached mother in *Ordinary People* (1980). Jeff related all too well to the perfectionism that blocked these women from closeness to others or from completing professional tasks that might bear telltale flaws. He agonized over finding *just* the right size basket for his mail slot and *just* the right color drain board for his dishes. Certainly he couldn't send out poems that an editor might declare unpolished. And certainly he couldn't take a demanding job that might expose him as a less-than-perfect worker. Instead, he nestled behind the Castro Theatre's candy counter. The salary was negligible, but Jeff had already moved to elegant Upper Terrace with an older lover, Rick, who paid for their breathtaking view of the Bay Bridge. Working at the Castro gave Jeff endless access to free movies as well as the chance to exercise his creativity by hand lettering banners for upcoming features.

Jeff had plenty of fans in San Francisco. According to Rink Foto, the city's myriad gay clerks and waiters deemed Jeff "the light of their lives." To his Castro coworker Mary Rose Kent, being with Jeff "was like stepping into the sunlight." She was charmed by his gentle sweetness and touched when, after having known her for some time, he bashfully announced, "I really like you. Can we be friends?" She thought they already were but accepted eagerly, happy to discuss the poetry of Denise Levertov and Diane Wakoski with him. Jeff's Castro boss and former SFSC classmate, Allen Sawyer, was enchanted by his otherworldliness, which reminded him in equal measure of Peter Pan and Eliza Doolittle.

Allen, like many gay men, was strangely attracted to a guy who "didn't emanate a sexuality." To Allen, Jeff "was not a sexual person, but there was something very innocent—you almost wanted to mother him, really. Everyone who met him fell in love with him." Laughing, Allen remarks, "I think all of us tried to be his boyfriend, but none of us succeeded." Except Rick. And then Vito.

Three weeks after their introduction, Jeff arrived in New York just in time for Vito's birthday. When Jeff pronounced himself "good for" Vito, Vito took notice. A couple weeks later, back from raucous book signings in Washington, Boston, and Chicago, Vito retreated with Jeff to Fire Island, where they spent delirious nights making love on the beach. Vito melted over this young man whose long, tanned body was as delicious as his encyclopedic knowledge of all Academy Award winners and his ability to recite with Vito, verbatim, the final scene from *Two for the Road*. Affectionate nicknames quickly sprang up. Vito became "V" or Jeff's "Marlboro Man"; the tall, skinny Jeff was "Asparagus" or "Choppers" for his beautiful teeth. On the sand, Jeffrey told Vito that he loved him and wanted to be his man.

In San Francisco, Jeff's friends began to realize that his feelings for Vito would be luring him away to a hyper city that seemed so inappropriate for someone of his sweet reserve. Misgivings were inevitable. Mary Rose, for instance, wondered how someone so ingenuous could survive in New York. But everyone donned smiles for Jeff's sake. Allen even donated his apartment so that the new couple could experience Jeff's favorite movie, *The Member of the Wedding* (1952), in honeymoon hush. For Vito, the highlight of this Carson McCullers adaptation was Ethel Waters's haunting a cappella rendition of "His Eye Is on the Sparrow." Jeff was transfixed by Julie Harris's performance as restless, lonely tomboy Frankie Addams, who shared his sense of not fitting in anywhere.

Vito recognized Jeffrey's aimlessness but tried to ignore it. That summer, with the entire world celebrating Prince Charles and Lady Di, improbable love was in the air. So what if Jeff, at twenty-six, seemed like "a kid in a lot of ways" and had no idea how to jumpstart his life? So what if he confessed that while he enjoyed visiting Vito in New York, he wasn't sure he ever wanted to live there? Such obstacles were made to surmount, and Vito made sure that Jeff saw Manhattan at its most glamorous. Jeff swooned on spotting Geraldine Page, who lived two blocks south of Vito, in a local vegetable store, and Jeff and Vito both screamed in a club upon meeting, through one of Vito's many cabaret connections, Lena Horne and Hedy Lamarr. Vito took Jeff to a press screening of *Ragtime* (1981), adapted from E. L. Doctorow's best seller and featuring the breakout performance of Elizabeth McGovern as Evelyn Nesbit. A few days later, they were chatting up the new star on a Village street.

Jeff realized that these moments were impossible in San Francisco. They, like Vito, could be found only in New York. He prepared to tell Rick that their relationship was over. Vito, meanwhile, squelched all hesitation: "Jeffrey Sevcik is the man I love. No adjectives to describe the time we've had—thrown away the world and fallen in love with each other. A new feeling hardly describes what this is—he's everything I ever wanted—told him so and he loves me loves me loves me loves me. . . . [It's] hardly possible to believe I'm this gone but I am." On August 31, two months after their meeting, Jeffrey moved to New York and in with Vito.

Everything began smoothly as Jeff jumped into Russo family doings. For Halloween he and Vito painted themselves in elaborate clown makeup and invited Vito's young nieces, Vicki and Leslie, to join them for the annual Greenwich Village parade. The girls, who loved spending time in the city with Uncle Vito, got to meet a celebrity. The famous price tag dangling from her hat, *Hee Haw*'s Minnie Pearl had the drag queens abuzz. Vito yanked his charges up to the yahoo diva and commenced introductions. Pearl was no Page, but she was still a star, and Jeff shared his new nieces' excitement.

At thirteen, Vicki realized that her uncle's attraction to Jeff stemmed from Jeff's seeming "like a big kid." Lacking his lover's years of activism and authorial struggle, Jeff provided Vito with a welcome retreat from adult cares. Vicki felt that, buried under his glib Manhattan cynicism, Vito had a "great childlike outlook on life—[a belief] that everything would be OK and there were no boogeymen in the closet and everyone loved each other. Jeff was still very much that way." Vito echoed Vicki's opinion, perceiving in Jeff "the kind of person [he] was when [he] was a teenager, but [Jeff] still had that childlike teenage innocence."

For a time, Vito found Jeff's innocence winning. But insecurities soon flared. After a month of cohabitation, Vito fretted that he was making things "almost impossible for [Jeff] by seeming to want him too much, to know his thoughts." He reflected in his journal, "[I seem to] always be afraid he isn't liking it here, liking *me*—afraid that it isn't 'working' and afraid of outside things. I want to let him go—to let him be Jeffrey—and still be his partner in life. I hope that is possible. I love him so much." Vito didn't specify the "outside things" worrying him, but Jeff's lack of professional drive surely numbered high among them. Six weeks into their shared life, Vito admitted that his new lover had "little or no ambition to do anything but work part time and get by." He gingerly qualified his misgivings: "That's not a situation I can live with but I'm willing to give it time to change. How much time I'm not sure."

Vito felt momentarily reassured when Jeff, through the help of Vito's journalist friend Brandon Judell, took a job at Rockshots, a gay greeting-card warehouse in Chelsea. But from day one, Jeff felt grossly misplaced amid the company's near-pornographic inventory. When Rockshots' owners threw a party at Studio 54, he showed up in a nerdy bowtie. And he hated the work itself. Colleague Natalie Lessinger shudders over the "huge, filthy, and non-ventilated" room where they packed boxes with merchandise. Jeff was driven mad by regular radio announcements of the time, which seemed to pass all the more slowly for being so relentlessly tolled. He rebounded when Natalie brought in tapes of Aretha Franklin and his beloved Van Morrison, but his cheer didn't last.

Matters at home weren't helping. Friend Wesley Greenbaum was distressed to see the transplanted San Franciscan frequently arrive at work in tears. Jeff tried to write off his crying as "just one of these things" he did, but he was in obvious pain. Despite Vito's resolve to give Jeff copious space, by December he couldn't refrain from lashing out. He didn't know what to do with a lover who didn't "make or see friends, [didn't] go out much, [wouldn't] get involved in the apartment except to keep it clean, [didn't] like his job at Rockshots and [didn't] seem interested in getting anything else although neither of [them had] any money." Vito reluctantly admitted, "I don't see how such a situation can continue." For his part, Jeff couldn't understand why Vito didn't appreciate what he had: the perfect househusband. To say that Jeff kept their home "clean" was a sorry understatement. The boxes underneath the kitchen sink were perfectly aligned; the sink itself contained not a drop of excess water. Vito became a somewhat unwelcome intruder in his own apartment. One evening after Jeff had scoured the kitchen from floor to ceiling, Vito tried to get a late-night snack. Jeff blocked the doorway, intoning, "The kitchen is closed." Exasperated, Vito barked back, "A clean house is nice, but it's not the meaning of life!" He was relieved when Rick called, offering Jeff a trip to Hawaii over Christmas. Vito urged him to accept and return temporarily to San Francisco, where he could ponder his next move. They needed time apart.

Vito didn't have time to babysit an insecure lover. The publication of his book marked a "time of major change" in his life. On a flight to Dallas, Vito was tickled to turn in his seat and discover a fellow passenger deep in the *Closet*. Friends reported that bookstores were regularly selling out their stock. After listing the book as its top seller in mid-July, Harper & Row ordered a second printing for October. *US* magazine published a lengthy excerpt from the last chapter, "Struggle." But Vito noted with some irritation that the major New York papers were ignoring his work. The *Times* wouldn't print the word "gay" outside quotation marks until 1987; certainly it wouldn't deign to review a book based so squarely on progay politics. Vito ended up in its august pages by accident.

In celebration of Gay Pride 1981, Armistead Maupin wrote a whimsical op-ed piece that cited Vito as a gay expert on Stonewall and Judy Garland. Stop the presses! *Times* editors informed Maupin "in no uncertain terms that [he] couldn't call [Vito] 'gay.'" He recounts, "I pointed out that he was a well-known activist, that he was openly gay, that he'd actually written a book that was written from that standpoint. They said that didn't matter; they had libel laws to consider and I would have to get an affidavit from Vito to claim himself queer." Maupin called Vito, who raced up to the *Times* offices and gleefully proclaimed his homosexuality for his hometown's paper of record.

With his sudden visibility, Vito was amused to become "something of a catch" and reminded himself to "enjoy it while it last[ed]." But his new fame also robbed him of privacy and put him on an unwanted pedestal. Prior to the book's publication, Vito had prized the anonymity of being a writer. Now he found himself "whispered about in bars and at the baths." Men pointed him out on the streets and, as Lily had warned him from her own experience, approached him seeking wisdom he didn't have. For the first time, he got an unlisted telephone number.

Of course, fame also had its perks, not the least of which were financial. In a single week at the end of June 1981, Vito earned five thousand dollars, by far the most money he had ever received at one time. With new fortune came a desire to upgrade his image. He was tired of the dirt-poor "radical chic" look he had sported in furnishings and clothes since college. His apartment underwent months of noisy renovations. Vito's father dutifully shuttled in from Lodi to build Vito his first closet for his ever-expanding film library. Contractors began demolishing the kitchen and bathroom, leaving Vito with a bathtub in the living room and no shower. But the end result justified the chaos. Vito loved the spotless white, gray, and sky blue apartment that he alternately likened to "a Dior perfume box" and "the animation sequences from *Mary Poppins*." To keep things a bit off-kilter, he splattered Pollock-style paint splotches across his newly finished floors.

The man responsible for all this upheaval was celebrated fashion designer Clovis Ruffin. In the summer of 1979, Vito had enjoyed a quick affair with Clovis that sent his self-esteem into a tailspin. With his dark blond hair, cool blue eyes, and lean physique, Clovis had beauty to burn. He also had two other attributes that Vito found perversely fascinating: wealth and fame. While still in his twenties, Clovis had begun designing casual, T-shirt-style dresses for young professional women. The look took off and netted him enough money for a tower apartment in the magnificent Ansonia Hotel. Soon afterward, he moved to a penthouse in Abingdon Square, much closer to the gay action.

Clovis traveled in exalted, A-list circles that Vito glimpsed only through Lily Tomlin or Craig Zadan, both of whom had long since decamped to LA. Despite his scorn for the Pines/Studio 54 circuit, Vito wasn't averse to exploring this world on Clovis's splendidly attired arm. As he confessed in his journal, "I never wanted to be rich in my life until I met Clovis Ruffin." Attracted to Clovis's looks, prodigious knowledge of film, and artistic "genius," Vito lamented not fitting the image of Clovis's ideal lover, some gorgeous "extra from Hollywood Blvd" who wouldn't challenge Clovis's own sense of superiority. While agreeing with Bill Johnson that he and Clovis were "the mismatch of the century," Vito couldn't deny that the designer had much to teach him about fashion. "I'd let him change my wardrobe," Vito resolved, "but not my values."

Clovis went to work on Vito's wardrobe. After spending much of the seventies in jeans, T-shirts, sneakers, and an awful rabbit-skin coat, Vito learned from

Clovis "how to dress with a kind of elegant touch, simple but smart, like a grown up." A camel coat, slacks, button-down shirts, and loafers came to typify his eighties style. Vito was delighted with his new look, but it didn't take him long to recognize Clovis's shortcomings. In Andrew Holleran's story "The Penthouse," Clovis's alter ego, Ashley, is a bullying host with a voice "as hard and flat as a frying pan he had just used to hit you over the head. ('Next to Ashley,' someone said, 'Thelma Ritter sang bel canto.')" Ashley endears himself with such pronouncements as "I've got money, looks, fame, and a big cock. Who can have sex with me?" But he earns partial redemption by deferring to Victor, "the author of a book on Hollywood's treatment of homosexuals," on the subject of film.

Vito's friends were less than taken by Clovis. Baby Jane Dexter appreciated his fondness for Vito but found him "snobby and cruel," given to ridiculing others "in a queeny, nasty way." Felice Picano, who considered Clovis "a monster hidden inside the body and face of a beautiful man," agrees. He was present one afternoon in the Pines when Clovis greeted a friend who'd recently put on a few pounds with "I see you're modeling clothes for the larger woman these days." Arnie, whose opinion Vito valued above all others, thought Clovis repulsive. Despite his close friendship with Vito's Islanders Club colleague Eddie Rosenberg, Clovis never missed an opportunity to crack Jewish jokes. For Vito's sake, Arnie let them pass as long as he could. Finally he exploded, telling Clovis he'd prefer not to see him rather than suffer any more of his "anti-Semitic shit." Though Clovis and Arnie never spoke again, Vito maintained a tenuous friendship with the designer.

Yet he tired of Clovis's constant pushing him to "do something" with his life. As the *Closet* neared publication, Clovis berated Vito for publishing his first book at thirty-four. To Vito's protests that some people achieved fame only after death, if at all, Clovis retorted, "Don't hand me that bullshit. I don't want to hear anything about great people who get famous after they're dead. . . . It's better for you to have a column like Liz Smith for ten years than to be famous twenty years after you're dead." The remark stung, but Vito also realized that Clovis was jealous of his new stature in the gay community.

While still lecturing on the college circuit, Vito had started speaking in some impressive Manhattan venues. He was flattered when the Violet Quill Club, whose members included Edmund White, Andrew Holleran, Felice Picano, and Robert Ferro, invited him to read two chapters of the *Closet* at their final meeting. On that evening, White read from his forthcoming novel *A Boy's Own Story* (1982), placing Vito's work in very distinguished company. According to Felice, Quill members didn't open their meetings to guests; when they decided to do so, Vito was the only candidate on whom they all agreed.

The following year, Vito joined White, Arthur Bell, Kate Millett, Jim Fouratt, journalist Jeff Weinstein, and novelist Bertha Harris on a panel at 5th Avenue's

New Museum, where speakers were asked to address the question, "What is the impact of homosexual sensibility on contemporary culture?" Weinstein dropped a zinger that Vito would quote for the rest of his life—"No, there is no such thing as a gay sensibility and yes, it has an enormous impact on our culture"— but Vito earned the evening's biggest laugh when he referenced Arthur's recent cocktails with Elizabeth Taylor and Richard Burton ("Now *that's* gay sensibility."). Turning serious, he defined "gay sensibility" as gay spectators' "nostalgia for something they have never seen before—themselves on screen." At the evening's close, a young woman from New Zealand rose to address the panelists: "I just want to say that as a young gay person—I was born in 1960—I owe a lot to you lot, and when Vito Russo [asked] why did you all come here tonight, part of the reason is you—because when I was growing up sexually, I had Kate Millett, and I had Vito Russo, and I had Bertha Harris, and I'd just like to acknowledge that, and say—thank you. I think there has been a lot of progress in the development of gay sensibility, and I think it has a lot to do with you here."

Vito was also courted by major Manhattan theaters. In October 1981, he delivered the "Closet" at the Upper West Side's Beacon Theater—one of the grand old movie palaces he had haunted as a kid with Perky. The following spring, the 8th Street Playhouse, a popular West Village revival house, invited Vito to kick off a six-week gay pride festival for which his opening-night lecture introduced the screenings of over sixty films discussed in the *Closet*.

Vito donated the Beacon lecture as a well-received benefit for the Gay Press Association. Not all his efforts at fund-raising were so successful. In 1982, Rob Epstein was seeking support for his film on Senator John Briggs's Proposition 6 (which sought to ban gay teachers from California public schools) and on Harvey Milk. Since Vito had proven so helpful with *Word Is Out*, Rob asked him to assist with this latest project. Vito had the perfect idea, one he'd mulled over during times of financial trouble for the past two years: why not charge to screen his film of Bette Midler at the baths? He told Rob he'd be glad to help out.

When Midler got wind of the benefit, she was furious. Not only had she not given Vito permission to exploit her image, but the Continental footage showed her mooning her audience. Now a major star with a Grammy, a Tony, and an Oscar nomination to her credit, she wanted to divorce herself from those long-ago high jinks. Midler's lawyer informed Vito that she would sue him if he went ahead with the screening. Though determined not to relinquish the film, Vito agreed not to show it in public. He also tried to put a positive spin on the situation for disappointed fans. "I don't want anyone to get the idea that [Midler]'s being nasty to the gay community," Vito insisted. She had every right to determine where and how her image was shown.

This stab at diplomacy barely masked his outrage. *Why* couldn't Midler authorize a benefit screening for gay fans who remained loyal to her long after she had abandoned them? And this wasn't Vito's first run-in with the diva. In 1975, they engaged in a screaming match that nearly brought the police. At a party, Vito criticized one of Midler's friends, a "famous male singer," for staying in the closet. Bette bellowed back, "After singing in shithole towns all across the country and busting his ass to be a success, why should he come out and throw it all away for *your* cause?" Vito "quietly reminded her that [gay pride] was [the singer's] cause too, even if he didn't know it, and dropped the subject." Thereafter, Midler and Vito lost touch. Her threat of legal action was their first communication in nearly seven years.

In contrast, Vito's friendship with Lily Tomlin thrived. In 1979, she offered to pay him for a treatment of *Wicked Woman* (1953), a remake she was planning of the B noir classic. Nothing came of this plan. He was buried in *Closet* drafting, while she was busy making *9 to 5* (1980) and *The Incredible Shrinking Woman* (1981). But when *Esquire Film Quarterly* commissioned him to write a story on the filming of *Making Love* (1982), Lily once again invited him to stay in her Los Feliz mansion.

Vito arrived in Los Angeles the night before the 1981 Academy Awards. This year's ceremony held strong personal interest for him beyond the usual hoopla. Lily was scheduled to present an award, and Vito's friend Dean Pitchford was nominated in the Best Original Song category for his lyrics to "Fame." On the morning of the show, Lily served Vito breakfast in her solarium while they watched trashy late-morning TV. Suddenly a special news bulletin burst on the screen: Ronald Reagan had just been shot in Washington, DC. Though no fan of the president, Vito was horrified over his "poor, sick, battered country" and its ceaseless insistence on "killing and killing." The Oscar telecast was postponed one day.

As usual, Hollywood lifted Vito's spirits. Dean won the Oscar, and the morning after the show, Vito reported to The CowBoy, a country and western bar where *Love* director Arthur Hiller was readying an early scene. Vito had mixed feelings about this project. On one hand, the story of a successful doctor (Michael Ontkean) who leaves his wife (Kate Jackson) for another man (Harry Hamlin) was a Hollywood first—as was the sight of two sexy, shirtless leading men enjoying an open-mouthed kiss in close-up. On the other hand, Arthur Bell had already read the script and pronounced it "so inoffensive that it's offensive." The characters were all extremely attractive, understanding, and liberal to a fault. Claire, the abandoned wife, has a sun-washed reunion with her ex before he returns to the drop-dead 5th Avenue aerie that he shares with his handsome lover. Vito snickered, "If everything goes as planned, *Making Love* may well become the *Guess Who's Coming to Dinner* [1967] of gay rights." That wasn't necessarily a good thing. *Dinner* had attracted plenty of criticism for offering an impossibly placid look at interracial marriage. Fifteen years later, would *Making Love* prove more daring for gays?

Skepticism aside, Vito was very impressed by the courage of *Love*'s screen-writer, Barry Sandler, who was using this film as his professional coming out after penning one critically savaged biopic (*Gable and Lombard* [1976]) and one medium Agatha Christie adaptation (*The Mirror Crack'd* [1980]). As the only openly gay member of *Love*'s production team, Barry had considerable invest-ment in the project. He confessed to Vito that he had been "very afraid for a long time to write this movie. . . . It meant exposing a lot of nerves." His was the kind of all-for-honesty ethic that Vito treasured.

Well aware of Vito's reputation, Sandler was thrilled to introduce him on the set, where cast and crew "had a sense that this film was a breakthrough, that there was historic significance to the film, that it was the first film made that dealt positively with the subject. So [Sandler thought] everybody felt that they were doing something more than just making a movie." Vito got this impression from the actors and director. At the Mother Lode, a Hollywood gay bar used for a crucial scene in the film, extras were overjoyed to be appearing in a gay movie with a happy ending. Director Hiller, Vito reported, was "very sweet," as was Kate Jackson. Playing the beefcake novelist who leads Michael Ontkean astray, Harry Hamlin dazzled Vito with his beauty ("bigger tits than Jane Russell," Vito panted) and his no-nonsense professionalism. The straight actor had been jittery over his love scene with Ontkean until declaring, "Oh, fuck, this is what I've got to do, and if audiences don't like it, screw them." He attacked the scene with both lips and gave Vito great copy.

The *Esquire* feature also gave Vito visibility in mainstream journalism. *Movie-goer* magazine, distributed free in theaters nationwide, took notice and assigned him to an array of celebrity interviews. Offered one thousand dollars to profile British newcomer Rachel Ward, Vito bit hard. The money, he enthused, would mean "900 more than I have at the moment." He settled in to *Moviegoer*-style gush, an updating of the *Modern Screen* prose rampant during his youth. Of the starlet, he burbled, "Some people are born with a personal letter from the Great Casting Agent in the Sky, and Rachel Ward's one of them. She tried on the glass slipper and it fit the very first time around." Intellectually he was on autopilot, but the pay was irresistible. Plus he got to meet some fascinating people.

David Bowie impressed Vito by breaking appointments to speak with him and by seeming "not at all as I expected—handsome, quiet, charming, British, well read and sincere." Jessica Lange, achieving major stardom with her perform-ances in *Frances* and *Tootsie* (both 1982), jolted Vito with her total nonchalance over being the unwed mother of Mikhail Baryshnikov's daughter. *Moviegoer* allowed him a brief underground foray with a profile of Anne Carlisle, star of the indie smash *Liquid Sky* (1983)—a heavily lesbian- and gay-themed sci-fi romp that Vito inexplicably omitted from the revised *Celluloid Closet*—but for the most part, his assignments reflected the vanilla tastes of *Moviegoer*'s readership.

After a lifetime of Hollywood worship, Vito was distinctly unimpressed by celebrity histrionics. Thinking Nastassja Kinski an "asshole" for "fucking up [their] follow-up interview," he took great glee in painting her as a pretentious ditz, ostentatiously flaunting a copy of Rimbaud at their breakfast interview while sloshing orange juice over her oatmeal. He also used an occasional interview to settle old scores, as when he goaded Angela Lansbury into defending her long-ago refusal of the lesbian lead in *The Killing of Sister George*.

Vito's toughest interviews were of closeted celebrities. At the New Museum, he had gone out of his way to protect Lily when Jim Fouratt disingenuously asked, "Why doesn't Lily Tomlin come out—*if* she's gay?" A year later, profiling Lily for *Moviegoer*, Vito omitted any reference to her sexuality. In 1986, recycling substantial chunks of this interview in an *Advocate* profile, he maintained an uneasy distance from the truth. He quotes Lily on living with Jane Wagner, her partner of fifteen years, but the piece's most significant references to gayness are to Hollywood AIDS panic and characters in Lily's new Broadway show, *The Search for Intelligent Signs of Life in the Universe*. In limp self-justification, Vito hazards, "I *hate* it when a writer gets too cozy with a subject."

This was a case of the lady protesting too much. Vito's livelihood depended on his ability to cozy up to celebrities, though they often didn't grant him the chance. Film mogul Allan Carr, four years after shrieking over Vito's camera at a gay Mykonos club, kept his interviewer at arm's length. Though using the *Advocate* to publicize his new Broadway show, *La Cage aux Folles* (1984), Carr remained resolutely mum on his sexuality, demurring, "People can think whatever they like about me." Vito was forced into some riotous indirection, noting the extreme B-movie decor of Carr's Hollywood mansion (featuring rooms named, in pink neon, after stars of obscure Egyptian epics) and quoting his insistence on "maintaining the illusion" of celebrities' private lives.

As usual, Vito writhed when faced with "the LA mentality" on "success, people, appointments, living style, friendship, etc." But in the fall of 1982, as *Closet* sales reached thirty-five thousand and the book went into its fourth printing, Vito was happy to head west and collect the first of the many awards coming his way. On October 4, the Alliance for Gay Artists in the Entertainment Industry (AGA) honored him with a special prize at its second annual Media Awards ceremony. One of his fellow honorees was Robert Preston, who told Vito that *The Celluloid Closet* had been indispensable as he prepared his role of Toddy, Julie Andrews's gay mentor, in *Victor/Victoria* (1982). Before a starry gathering that included presenters Patty Duke Astin, Ned Beatty, Linda Lavin, Bernadette Peters, Lynn Redgrave, and Barry Sandler, Vito accepted his award from Zelda Rubinstein, the pint-sized psychic from *Poltergeist* (1982). He scored a laugh when he thanked the crowd for delivering him from his more typical speaking engagements: "Usually I'm sitting in New York and the phone rings and someone wants me to take a Greyhound bus to Schenectady in February to be on a talk show where the host hasn't read my book but would love to know what two men do in bed." He then praised AGA for foregrounding the word "gay" in its title and named as one of his pet peeves seeing "some person on a TV talk show saying to the majority, moral or otherwise, 'Please accept us because, after all, we're just like you.'" Vito continued, "I think what needs to be said is *'Grow up!'*. . . . We're not all the same, and we should teach people to see the beauty in difference, to appreciate it without trying to change everyone into an acceptable norm." He concluded with a power jab at closeted actors: "In the words of Rita Mae Brown, 'I've heard all the excuses, honey, and they're all shit.'" The applause was thunderous.

Two weeks later, Vito brought the same brashness to the Lambda Legal Defense and Education Fund's seventh annual awards dinner at New York's Sheraton Centre. Honored alongside Washington mayor Marion Barry, Vito glowed to receive his award from Arnie. But the upscale, sixty-five-dollars-per-plate audience didn't care for Vito's insistence that gay people were *not* just like everyone else. Lambda's gay lawyers and politicos prided themselves on their hard-won mainstream respect. So when Vito remarked, "If there were no difference [between gays and straights], there wouldn't be a problem," much of the room glared back in steely silence.

This wasn't a reaction that Vito often encountered from audiences. He was far more used to the ovation that greeted him in June 1983 at the Stonewall Awards. Nominated in the category of Best Male Writer, Vito had formidable competition from Dennis Altman, Jonathan Katz, and Edmund White. When he was named the winner, he bolted to the Beacon stage, a white carnation tucked behind one ear, and exclaimed, "Shit! I didn't think I'd win; I would have worn a dress."

Offstage Vito was feeling much less jocular. He chastised himself for "basking in old glory" when he should be moving on to some new project. Since finishing the *Closet*, his most significant noncelebrity journalism had been an outrageous *Village Voice* spoof asking, "Why Is Leather Like Ethel Merman?" and a cranky diatribe for the *Native* explaining "Why I'm Not Marching" in the 1983 Pride festivities. (He wanted nothing to do with Christopher Street's "dreadful street festival," where bigoted merchants sold calzones and pastries "to a bunch of people out of whom under any other circumstances they would like to beat the living shit.")

More-substantial writing ventures weren't panning out. Given the popularity of his *Moviegoer* profiles and the *Closet*'s brisk sales, Vito considered himself an ideal celebrity biographer. But Gary Carey beat him to Judy Holliday, and he couldn't interest anyone in a book on James Whale. He then tried to scare up interest in an unauthorized biography of Paulette Goddard. To Jed Mattes he promised a book "which would move easily beyond 'star talk'"; Goddard was, he argued, "one of the few living movie stars whose personal life is surrounded almost completely by mystery and glamour." To Felice Picano, he raved about Goddard as a Queens scrapper who overcame poverty by cheerfully sleeping her way to the top. Harper & Row agreed that Goddard's life was marketable but only in the hands of a different author. Vito groaned that he was tired of "auditioning again—now [he knew] why it was such a big deal when Crawford had to test for Mildred Pierce after all those years."

He did nail one audition that mattered to him deeply. His old GAA buddy Doric Wilson had dramatized the Stonewall riots in a new play for The Other Side of Silence (TOSOS), the gay theater company that he had founded in 1974. Set on the eve of Stonewall, *Street Theater* assembled a group of drag queens, tough dykes, leathermen, closet cases, and the characters of Michael and Donald, Freudian casualties from *The Boys in the Band*. Vito landed the part of Jordan, an initially closeted student radical who flaunts "a spectrum of buttons advocating every political cause except his own." The fact that Clovis Ruffin, confidently "trying on berets and carrying Stanislavsky around," went uncast was icing on the cake. Vito was surrounded by actors who had, in Doric's phrasing, "Gay Lib or underground theater credentials up the bunghole." Other cast members included Harvey Perr, who had written the highly lauded lesbian teleplay *The War Widow* (1976), and Billy Blackwell and Michael Bowers, the "Billie and Tiffany" drag duo who prompted inadvertent rioting at the 1973 Pride Gala. *Street Theater*'s wigs were the creation of drag legend Ethyl Eichelberger. Vito was in vivid company.

He took the venture entirely tongue-in-cheek. For his program bio, he identified himself as a "native New Yorker who was kidnapped from a cabbage patch as an infant by loving heterosexuals. After being raised in an alien environment for eighteen years, he managed to escape and was found, washed ashore in Cherry Grove, by two radicalesbians who raised him as their own. . . . He likes Tom Waits and Checker Cabs. He hates soft boiled eggs, disco music, and organized religion." When *Street Theater* opened in November 1982 at the Basement Theatre, Vito received good notices (the *Native* dubbed his performance "charming") and enjoyed himself during the five-week run. Artistically, however, he deemed the play a "disaster"—an assessment seconded by Doric. Director J. Kevin Hanlon, who had wanted to cast Taylor Mead and other Warhol regulars, resented the Stonewall-savvy actors on whom the playwright insisted. Anarchy ensued. The *Native* carped that even "the most basic amenities of blocking and interpretation were in woefully short supply" in a production with "no coherent performance style or directorial vision." Though the play received a successful extension at the Mineshaft, Vito had had his fill of theater. Plenty of other interests were competing for his attention.

On Friday, July 3, 1981, Vito scribbled a randy *Closet* inscription to Doric: "Since you bought a copy you can take my clothes off—Love you xx Vito." That morning, he failed to notice an article that appeared on page 20 of the *New York Times*. Even if he had read "Rare Cancer Seen in 41 Homosexuals," the piece gave gay men two reasons to dismiss it out of hand: (1) the author, Dr. Lawrence K. Altman, proclaimed that although eight men had already died, the "cause of the outbreak [was] unknown" and presented as yet "no evidence of contagion"; (2) Altman quoted Dr. James Curran of the Centers for Disease Control as reassuring nervous straights that there was "no apparent danger to nonhomosexuals from contagion." Many gay readers smirked. Ah, yes. So long as the hets were safe. The article was just pseudo-scientific nonsense from a paper that blushed blue where gay news was concerned. The *Times* didn't mention this strange new cancer again for nearly two months, by which time the number of those afflicted had more than doubled.

Overwhelmed by the publication of the *Closet* and his romance with Jeffrey, Vito barely noticed these developments. But central as he was to gay political and social circles, he began receiving disquieting bulletins far earlier than most people. The first casualty was Nick Rock, a sweet, sexy bartender from Vito's Islanders Club days. When he returned from Europe in October 1980, he heard the wrenching story of Nick's lover, Enno Poersch, carrying the emaciated Nick in his arms from house to house in the Pines, begging, "Does *anyone* know what's wrong with Nick?" No one did until, bafflingly, he was diagnosed with toxoplasmosis in November. By January he was dead. Altman's article was still six months off.

In the summer of 1981, Stephen Harvey of MoMA began suffering a "weird siege of immobilizing complaints . . . agonizing stomach viruses, flus and fevers, an eye infection that made [him] look and feel like Quasimodo." At the same time, Jed Mattes told Vito about the sudden illness of his Fire Island housemate, Joffrey Ballet fundraiser Donald Krintzman. Over the July 4 weekend, Krintzman distributed photocopies of Altman's article among his friends in the Pines. Within two weeks, he was diagnosed with Kaposi's sarcoma (KS), the cancer that was starting to explode in purple blotches all over the bodies of gay men, the majority of whom died within months. In his doctor's office, Krintzman bumped into fellow patient Larry Kramer, who was beginning to think that these inexplicable illnesses weren't isolated cases. On August 11, Kramer invited Krintzman and some eighty other men—the "crème de la crème of New York's A-list gay nightlife"—to his 5th Avenue apartment, where the NYU Medical Center's Dr. Alvin Friedman-Kien implored his affluent audience for research funds.

Vito, who was spending that week in San Francisco with Jeff, wasn't present. Even if he had been in town, he probably wouldn't have made Kramer's guest list. At the time generally unsure where he would find next month's rent, Vito had nothing to spare for medical research. Still, he gave the new disease a nod that fall by blasting the National Gay Rodeo for naming muscular dystrophy as its charitable beneficiary even as "gay men [were] dying from a rare form of cancer [that] desperately need[ed] research and funding." The following spring, in April 1982, he swallowed his hatred of disco and dutifully attended "Showers," a benefit for the newly formed Gay Men's Health Crisis (GMHC), at the once legendary, now declining, Paradise Garage. Slathered in lurid red for the festivities, the Garage housed hundreds of disco divas gyrating to the stylings of the Ritchie Family and Evelyn "Champagne" King, debuting "Love Come Down." Vito winced. It was all for a good cause, but this cacophony was precisely why he preferred to hole up at home with Billie Holiday. About the disease they were all there to fight, this recently named "Gay-Related Immune Deficiency" (GRID), he had already determined that it simply was "not gonna happen" to him.

But as a regular reader of the *Native*, Vito couldn't ignore the illness's mounting press. In May 1981, the paper scooped the *Times* by six weeks when it published the world's first journalistic article on AIDS: Dr. Lawrence Mass's "Disease Rumors Largely Unfounded." Over the next two years, Mass's pieces on the new cancer appeared regularly in the *Native*. A cofounder of GMHC, the physician steeped himself in the few available facts and the hurricane of rumors surrounding the disease. His writing of the period shows a clear-eyed attempt to process bewildering medical information for lay readers. In "Cancer in the Gay Community," Mass quotes Friedman-Kien's assertion that "most (but not all) of the homosexuals in [their] study admitted to having had multiple sexual encounters with different partners, and to having had a variety of past infections." For someone who frequented the baths and the Glory Hole as regularly as Vito, and for someone who had suffered syphilis along with other sexually transmitted diseases (STDs), these were terrifying words. Even more frightening was Mass's declaration that "as many as 80 to 85 percent of sexually active gay men in some major cities [might] already be immune-deficient" without knowing it. A "time bomb," he warned, might be lurking in their systems.

Despite his fear, Vito couldn't help but admire Mass's efforts to counter the rising hysteria. Bracketing the doctor's meticulous reportage were some welcome jests, as when, enumerating the disease's possible cofactors (poppers, rimming, collateral STDs), he cracked, "On the superficial basis of numbers alone . . . wearing handkerchiefed Levi's and having Judy Garland records in one's collection might also seem risky." Mass also tried to avoid indicting sexual activity amid growing suspicion that sex and compromised immunity were somehow related. Well before the identification of a blood-borne virus, many gay men were voicing the panic that Larry Kramer articulated in the *Native*: "All it seems to take is the one wrong fuck. That's not promiscuity—that's bad luck."

Mass advocated calm and self-regard, flatly denying that "immorality" could cause illness. He advised his gay readers not to "waste valuable energies on negative reactions to sex. Now more than ever, ignorance, arrogance, and hypocrisy about sex [were] to be repudiated. If anything, [gay men should] be even more genuinely affirmative about [their] sexuality."

A few days before Christmas 1981, Vito invited Mass to a cocktail party at his apartment. Several of New York's gay literati were already milling about his redecorated two rooms: Larry Kramer, Andrew Holleran, Felice Picano, *Native* and *Christopher Street* publisher Chuck Ortleb. Amid the crowd, Mass spotted a sharp English professor he'd met over a year earlier at the Everard Baths. He wandered over to reintroduce himself to Arnie, who drew a blank. The din of the party didn't allow much chance for reconnection, and on departure, Arnie forgot Larry anew. When they met again at Vito's in March, Larry had to identify himself and explain once more how they had met. The following August, when they bumped into each other at the Everard, Arnie finally remembered the handsome, bearish doctor with the thick black beard and warm dark eyes. A month later, he moved his toiletries from his Upper West Side flat to Larry's Chelsea loft.

Vito was delighted to play a part in Arnie and Larry's romance just as his own love life got cooking again. In January 1982, Jeff returned to San Francisco at Vito's suggestion. Within weeks, Vito was miserably lonely. At the end of February, he interviewed Jessica Lange and Jessica Harper in Los Angeles, where Jeff joined him before they flew north together for ten blissful days in San Francisco. Though Jeff still had no idea what to do with his life, he and Vito agreed to work on their problems. At the end of May, Jeff moved back to New York.

Vito's New York friends were less charmed by Jeff than his San Francisco circle. Theater critic Don Shewey thought him a "tall blond cutie-pie," decidedly "not the brightest light on the dashboard." In Don's view, Vito and Jeff seemed more like "playmates" than a well-matched couple. Bill Johnson agreed. Between Vito and Jeff, Bill noticed no serious moments; everything seemed to be smiles and silliness. But Bill also felt that in some way Jeff made Vito feel "safe"—that his rangy frame was literally big enough to envelop Vito and shield him from unnamed fears.

Arnie and Larry did their best to accept Jeff, but Larry guessed him to be clinically depressed while Arnie found it frustrating trying to relate to someone who seemed a veritable "non-presence." For his definitive portrait of Jeff, Arnie offers a tableau that he accidentally witnessed during a weekend visit to East Hampton. Entering a room, Arnie came upon Jeff gazing at himself in a closet mirror: "He was sitting in front of it in the pose of The Little Mermaid, with one leg on top of the other, and just [Arnie adopts a wispy tone]—brushing—his hair—and doing it totally sensually—[he was] completely involved in the process—'I love . . . my hair . . .'" Asked whether they considered Jeff to be self-absorbed, Arnie and Larry both laugh and reply, "Totally." Despite his love of film and of Vito, they believe that Jeff never bothered to read *The Celluloid Closet*.

Vito realized that the problems plaguing their relationship were still with them. Unable or unwilling to hold a job, Jeff defaulted on his half of two months' rent. While insisting that he still felt "good" about his lover, Vito had to admit that Jeff was more a "dependent" than an equal. Vito upbraided himself for getting caught in a familiar trap, expecting equal measures of "closeness and independence" in a relationship. In gross underestimation of Steve and Bill, he mused, "None of the men in my life have ever been go-getters of any kind. Perhaps that's a mistake or perhaps the mistake is thinking that I can live with another person on a regular basis. It's taken me 36 years to even consider that I belong by myself." As a writer, he needed privacy and space. In their tiny apartment, he could never escape his lover's fastidiousness. Vito complained in his journal: "[Jeff] does his nails for hours at a time, can make a bed for 30 minutes until it's right. Drives me nuts." As did Jeff's stony silence when they went out. As did his sexual conservatism. Knowing Jeff's distaste for extracurricular play, Vito agreed to his first monogamous relationship. A year later, he was feeling the strain. Exclusivity didn't come naturally to him.

By 1982, the sexual landscape was beginning to change. As more gay men fell sick, Vito was questioning the safety of what went on at his favorite sex clubs. Although "GRID" was renamed "AIDS" (Acquired Immune Deficiency Syndrome) in July 1982, there was still very little information available about what caused it. By March 1983, San Francisco doctor Marcus Conant was advocating the very unpopular suggestion that gay men use condoms during sex. This idea wasn't new back East, where Vito's long-time physician, Ron Grossman, had spent years begging gay patients to wear their rubbers. On "bended *knee*," he would implore, "Blank, this is your fifth case of gonorrhea this year! What does it take?!" But condoms were thought the province of horny heterosexual teenagers, not sophisticated gay men. The box of Trojans sitting in Dr. Grossman's desk drawer remained undistributed.

When Vito was treated for syphilis in 1979, his view of condoms was exactly the same as that of the hundreds of other gay men parading through Dr. Grossman's office. But three months ahead of Dr. Conant's warnings, Vito began to push condom use among his friends. In December 1982, upon meeting twenty-two-year-old politico David Kirby, he "turned the Serious Volume up and said, 'You know you have to wear condoms when you have sex.'" This was news to David, who "didn't even know that it would be possible to prevent [AIDS]; it didn't even *occur* to [him] that it would be transmitted [sexually]." He comments, "[Vito's message] just stuck with me, and boy, I—it stuck with me."

Instructional moments notwithstanding, AIDS wasn't foremost in Vito's mind. Arnie and Larry, he snorted, were "obsessed" with the topic. When Jim Owles dismissed AIDS as a media distortion and argued, "It's not as if all of us are going to die," Arnie soberly replied, "Our world is going to crumble around us." Vito agreed with Jim; "[Larry was] super paranoid about everything— they'll blame the gays for diseases, they'll come to get us etc etc." Vito determined to focus on other matters. "I'll stick to worrying about my TV show," he vowed, "and make my contribution that way."

Ironically, the show in question came about through Larry's commitment to fighting AIDS. In June 1982, he had appeared on the first television program about the syndrome, a thirty-minute WNYC-TV broadcast titled *The Lavender Connection*. Producers Rick Siggelkow, Silvana Moscato, and WNYC director John Beck noted the passionate audience response and began to consider a weekly program on gay and lesbian issues. Chuck Ortleb strongly supported the idea, arguing to Siggelkow and Beck that through television, they could reach a much wider audience about AIDS than he could through the *Native* or *Christopher Street*. In late September, the production team approached Vito to cohost the show with Moscato. With his writing at a standstill, he jumped at the opportunity. Vito christened the program *Our Time*, a title he borrowed from an anthem in the recent Stephen Sondheim Broadway flop *Merrily We Roll Along* (1981).

Our Time's sole predecessor was *Emerald City*, the late seventies gay-themed magazine show for which Vito had served as an occasional interviewer. This new show, its creators decided, would also focus on the gay arts community. Vito arranged interviews with the founders of the lesbian performance troupe Split Britches, with the codirectors of the newly formed Meridian Gay Theatre Company, and in the dressing room of Harvey Fierstein, whose epic *Torch Song Trilogy* (1983) would shortly win Tony Awards for Best Play and Best Actor. When Tennessee Williams died in February 1983, Vito and coproducer George DeStefano assembled a tribute that included an interview with one of Williams's frequent stage and screen interpreters, Madeleine Sherwood.

But *Our Time* went far beyond entertainment. It also featured interviews with gay activists and politicians. It explored AIDS, drag, racism, ageism, substance abuse within the gay community, gay history, strategies for coming out, and the plight of gay teachers. Weekly street interviews solicited popular opinion on these and other topics. Vito, determined that the show reach a broader audience than white, wealthy, middle-aged gay men, planned segments on Latino and black gays and lesbians, as well as gay youth of all races. Months before Manhattan opened its first LGBT community center, Vito filled each broadcast with calendar listings of events and meetings of interest to the gay community. In its efforts to inform and entertain, *Our Time* became television's first news show for the lesbian and gay community.

The WNYC brass, however, didn't appreciate *Our Time*'s historic importance. In the days of high Reaganism, New York City was under the stewardship of bachelor Mayor Ed Koch, who had previously championed gay civil rights but now, with AIDS on the rise, didn't want to associate himself closely with gay causes. Owned by city government, WNYC was an improbable home for *Our Time*. Station bureaucrats demanded to know why the show wasn't airing on PBS, if it had to air at all. Only John Beck and Rick Siggelkow's iron determination saw their baby to the screen.

Before filming began in January 1983, the production team convened an advisory panel to brainstorm topics and guests. The staid Municipal Building had seldom seen such an outré grab bag of visitors. City officials gaped at the sight of seventy-three-year old *Naked Civil Servant* (1968) author Quentin Crisp, resplendent in eye shadow and silk scarf, wandering the halls lost. Another advisor arrived after witnessing a police raid on Blues Bar, a gay African American Times Square hangout where one officer capped off thirty thousand dollars' worth of damage by slamming bullets to the floor and shouting, "These are faggot suppositories!" The *Our Time* visitor scooped the bullets up, the better to slap them the next morning on a Municipal Building conference table. "*That's* what this show should be dealing with."

Alas, homophobia was one of the few major issues that *Our Time* did *not* tackle in its thirteen-week run. The producers adopted a far lighter tone for their premiere episode. In a pale blue shirt unbuttoned to reveal copious chest hair, Vito addresses viewers with a grin: "Hey, are you sick and tired of watching the gay son on *Dynasty* pop in and out of the closet like a jack-in-the-box? Is he gay or straight this week, or what? Also, did you stop watching *Hollywood Squares* when Paul Lynde died—and even Richard Simmons can't cheer you up?" From its debut, *Our Time* offered itself as a cure for gay and lesbian viewers sick of seeing their lives laundered off the small screen.

The production team realized the gold mine they had in Vito's Rolodex, brimming with the names of everyone who was anyone in the gay community. The first guests included historian John D'Emilio (author of the newly published *Sexual Politics, Sexual Communities*), Harry Hay (founder of the Mattachine Society), and Vito's friend, veteran lesbian activist Barbara Gittings. Hay, who appeared on camera in red velvet pants, a glittery black scarf, and one ornate earring, delighted Vito with tales of his activism dating back to the twenties, when gay men were referred to as "temperamental."

Vito couldn't have been happier with the episode's content. Production circumstances were another story. *Our Time* was assigned a minuscule budget: $30,000 for all salaries. Associate producer Jay Blotcher, earning $45 every other week, took to skipping meals and hopping over subway turnstiles. When the young man pleaded extreme poverty, Siggelkow raised his salary to $125 per week—a veritable fortune to the recent college grad and *Native* journalist. The *Our Time* set was equally humble, a tableau of early cable-access penury. For the first few episodes, hosts and guests sat on wicker-back dining-room chairs with a plastic cube "table" as the only other furniture. In later weeks a plum loveseat, glass coffee table, and flowers softened the show's look, but producer Barbara Kerr chuckles that the loveseat was lifted from another WNYC office. She was less amused by having to beg the station for three-quarter-inch videotape.

Used to indigence, Vito ignored the set and the dismal salaries. But lapses in professionalism made him burn. *Our Time*'s first broadcast on February 27, 1983, was riddled with glitches—whether through "political sabotage or technological ineptitude," Blotcher wasn't sure, but it gave the show an inauspicious debut. Vito, meanwhile, was seething over coproducer Silvana Moscato, who, he declared, "really has to go." Deeply uncomfortable on camera, Moscato cried before the taping of her segments. Her reading of cue cards is painfully obvious, and several flubbed lines remain in finished takes. Recognizing her fragility, Vito tried to be patient and helpful. Jay Blotcher thought his mentor "lesbian underneath" the skin; Vito did whatever he could to secure maximum exposure for women. But after watching Moscato's deadly interviews of lesbian-music pioneers Alix Dobkin and Meg Christian in episode 3, he had to pull the plug.

For Moscato's replacement, Vito approached film and dance critic Marcia Pally, whom he had been considering for months. Pally had published for several years in *Christopher Street*, the *Advocate*, and the *Native*, in whose offices Vito popped the question. When she protested her inexperience in television, Vito reassured her that the show was "experimental," insisting, "We'll work it out, let's do it!" Emboldened by his confidence, Pally swallowed her hesitation.

She needn't have worried. The camera adored her clear blue eyes, high forehead, and the glossy dark hair that she wore swept up in combs. Like Vito, Marcia was wholly at ease on camera, addressing her interview subjects warmly and her home viewers as if they were physically present. And her sensibilities complemented Vito's beautifully. For their episode on drag, Marcia donned a fedora and tux to croon, à la Dietrich, "Falling in Love Again" to the camera. From under a beribboned, broad-brimmed hat, Vito revealed his mustachioed face and inquired of viewers, "Does drag make you nervous? Why do you suppose it is that it's acceptable for women to wear pants but not for men to wear a dress?" After the cohosts switched hats, Marcia sniffed a rosebud at Vito's left nipple while he reminded viewers of drag queens' role in Stonewall. He then interviewed Michael ("Tiffany") Bowers and showed him a clip of the 1973 Pride Gala fracas that reduced Bowers to tears. (Bowers may also have been crying for the failing health of his longtime performing partner "Billie" Blackwell, who would die of AIDS complications before the month was out.)

Vito held Bowers's hand and tried to comfort him—but the real drama that day was behind the scenes. One of the episode's other interviewees was "Little John Basso," Vito's former GAA crony, recently released from jail after serving several years for a Brooklyn bank robbery. When Vito asked his opinion of *Dog Day Afternoon*, the film made about his experience, Basso declared it "about 70% garbage" and argued that although leading man Al Pacino was "cuter" than he was, he was "not as nutty and . . . not as comical." Vito breezed past this self-aggrandizement, possibly because he could see what was unfolding just beyond the camera's view. Basso's former lover, transsexual Liz Eden (née Ernest Aron), had just finished her interview with Marcia. Eden stood in the shadows, fuming over Basso's repeated references to her as "Ernie." Her parents didn't yet realize that their son had become their daughter. The second Basso left the set, Eden tore after him, shrieking, "You *fucker*! I'm gonna make sure you go back to prison!" Out of the building Basso raced, with Eden in hot pursuit.

Through her own connections, Marcia secured some significant interviews, including one of director John Sayles, promoting his acclaimed lesbian drama *Lianna* (1983). She also got her share of on-set drama through Brad Davis, the volatile star of *Midnight Express* (1978) and, more recently, Fassbinder's homo-erotic *Querelle* (1983). Having previously interviewed Davis, Marcia knew to expect the unexpected. At one of their meetings, he emerged from his hotel bedroom and announced, "Sorry I'm late—I was just jerking off." On the *Our Time* set, Jay Blotcher watched warily as Davis and his *Querelle* producer, Dieter Schidor, returned from a bathroom visit "extremely elevated in mood" and racing about the room.

Given occasional tension on the set, it's no wonder that Vito and Jay got blissfully stoned at the end of most shoots. Doing so can only have helped Jay the day that Vito asked him whether he'd come out to his parents. When Jay said that he had, Vito replied, "You're on in five minutes." Their scheduled guest from Parents and Friends of Lesbians and Gays had canceled at the last minute. Jay was his startled, last-minute replacement.

It's also no wonder that Vito booked friends on the show to soothe his anxieties. He coaxed Jed Mattes into discussing his struggles with alcoholism and historian Martin Duberman into participating on a panel reviewing racism in the gay community. Arthur Bell, who told Jay that he thought Vito was wasting his time on television and should return to writing, accepted an invitation as well. Arnie, discussing his nostalgia for GAA and his insistence that gay men, in the face of AIDS, must "care for [themselves] and each other," made a much less acidulous guest than Arthur. He did, however, get in one sally at a bigot's expense. When Vito announced that upcoming guests would include drag queens Sylvia Rivera (who ultimately did not appear) and Sister Missionary Position (from San Francisco's Sisters of Perpetual Indulgence), Arnie hooted, "Great!

All of Jerry Falwell's favorite people!" The joke was well timed, as Vito found Falwellesque sentiments in *Our Time*'s mailbag. One, written two days before the show's debut, he read on the air: "It comes from Queens, New York, as if you couldn't figure that out. 'Dear Sir: I deeply resent the new homo [Vito grins] cable TV show. . . . The world is in [*sic*] bad enough without having this evil in our home. Needless to say, this is going to be stopped. It is a sick show for sick pepel,' P-E-P-E-L . . . and it's signed, 'A Disgusted Mother.'" Vito urged viewers to send in more letters and pledged that *Our Time* would not be stopped, especially not by anonymous doomsayers.

He recaptured the show's humor by bringing on his friend, activist and author Karla Jay, as wacky lesbian advice columnist Gabby Tidbit. In her segment, "Gabby" ribbed the episode's other guest, Rita Mae Brown, who had recently broken up with Martina Navratilova. Spoofing Brown's southern persona, Gabby read a letter dripping in Spanish moss from "RMB" ("that stands for Really Mad Bachelorette"), seeking advice on how to cope with being left all alone on her Virginia plantation with five cats, three cars, a labia-shaped swimming pool, and "a dumb old tennis court." To Karla's shock, Brown, whom she'd known since their Lavender Menace days of 1970, didn't recognize her. She only learned Gabby's identity when Vito spilled the beans.

Our Time's most prominent guest was Lily Tomlin. In late January 1983, when she flew to New York to host *Saturday Night Live*, Vito pounced. The following Tuesday, he and several crew members picked her up at her Midtown hotel and drove, with Lily poised on Vito's lap, to frigid Central Park to film a few skits. Seated on the ornate stone balustrade above Bethesda Fountain, Lily played an airhead poet who performs her progay verse creations (written by Jay as an *Our Time* promo) for the camera.

Vito was overjoyed. Lily, when she saw the footage, was not. Deciding that she didn't like the material or her performance of it, she wouldn't allow the segment to be aired. When Vito moaned that the show needed her star power, she allowed him to film her in a different sequence—but it would have to be several months later in Cleveland, where she was touring. He and a small crew scraped together funds and flew west to meet Lily in character as earnest Mrs. Judith Beasley, self-appointed emissary of "the heterosexual community" to gays and lesbians.

Sitting in a lesbian bar and screaming over the din of Bowie's "Let's Dance," Mrs. Beasley winks at her closeted creator when she laments that many of the patrons will not show their faces to the camera. Later, at the entrance to a gay-male bar, Mrs. Beasley offers up a "Quiche of Peace" to the doorman. Asked by interviewer Vito if her husband likes the dish, Mrs. B shakes her head and sends up Bruce Feirstein's then-bestselling book: "You know, real men don't eat quiche. I know they can't spell it." The episode went on to be *Our Time*'s best loved.

The series' most important episode focused on AIDS. Just as the show was filmed in early March 1983, Larry Kramer published a *Native* article whose title, "1,112 and Counting," referenced the number of known AIDS sufferers, nearly half of whom were gay or bisexual men in New York City. Like most readers, Vito was floored, and then inspired, by Kramer's first two sentences: "If this article doesn't scare the shit out of you, we're in real trouble. If this article doesn't rouse you to anger, fury, rage, and action, gay men may have no future on this earth." Kramer went on to blast overflowing hospitals, the indifference of the National Institutes of Health to a "gay" disease, the relative silence of the *Advocate* and the *Village Voice* about so many gay deaths, and a New York City mayor who refused to meet with the gay community to discuss AIDS or to speak publicly about the escalating health crisis. His rhetoric amped up GAA-style anger a thousandfold. The community was trying to salvage not jobs or housing but gay lives.

At the start of the show, Marcia calmly defined AIDS and specified its mortality rates. Vito, by contrast, was a nervous wreck. He stumbled over his notes while announcing that more than two hundred AIDS cases had appeared in the previous week alone. He stabbed an index finger at the camera to underscore that in November 1982, New York saw forty-seven new AIDS cases, the total number of which worldwide was expected to double by the end of 1983. A cut to Vito's street interviews found one gay man remarking that although he practiced monogamy, one of his acquaintances was "still as active as possible." His circle of friends, the man reported, called him "The Carrier." The man chuckled, but Vito's off-camera chill was palpable.

Later in the episode, Vito interviewed Virginia Apuzzo, executive director of the National Gay Task Force (and eventually, President Clinton's associate deputy secretary of labor), who told him that New York City spent more money in the winter of 1983 shoveling street snow than it did on AIDS care or research. In the same segment, Larry Kramer reached an apocalyptic pitch: "We have never been in such a terribly threatening position. The whole history of being gay, the whole history of homosexuality—this is life and death; we are *dying*." As he would for the rest of his activist career, Kramer attempted to kick-start gays to political action: "We are going to have to *unite*; we are going to have to be *angry*; we are going to have to be perceived as a *threat*." Vito echoed these sentiments, commenting, "I don't blame you for being angry; I'd like a lot of people in this community angry."

Nothing seemed to stir more anger in the gay community than the debate over gay-male promiscuity, a topic that hit Vito squarely in the heart. While he was readying *Our Time* during the late fall of 1982, two *Native* articles set the debate's terms at full volume. The first was cowritten by Richard Berkowitz, whom Vito had met in 1976 when the Rutgers journalism major interviewed him for his school newspaper. Six years later, while working in Manhattan as an

S and M hustler, Berkowitz discovered that he had AIDS. With fellow patient Michael Callen (later lead singer of the Flirtations) and their doctor, Joseph Sonnabend, Berkowitz began canvassing his support group to find common denominators among gay men who were falling ill. Listening to the group's stories, he concluded that "everyone was a huge *slut!*" Speculation about a single AIDS-causing virus had begun to spread, but Berkowitz and Callen didn't buy it. In their *Native* article, they identified themselves as practitioners of "excessive promiscuity," insisting, "We know who we are and we know why we're sick." By visiting countless "bathhouses, backrooms, balconies, sex clubs, meat racks, and tearooms," they theorized, they had flooded their bodies with "*common* viruses and other sexually transmitted infections." For Berkowitz and Callen, AIDS wasn't a matter of "good luck/bad luck" with regard to some as-yet unidentified virus; the operative question was "Did you live like a sex pig, or didn't you?"

From the outset, the "promiscuity" hypothesis seemed flawed. How could it account for the intravenous drug users, Haitian immigrants, and blood-product recipients who were also falling ill? It also raised a storm of protest among gay men who felt that the "war on promiscuity" attacked their very identities. Dance critic Charles Jurrist lashed back at Berkowitz and Callen in the *Native* the following month, arguing that since the cause of AIDS remained unknown, it was surely "premature" to halt the sexual freedom that had been the heart of gay liberation. In any event, Jurrist snapped, male sex drives didn't lend themselves to monogamy.

Vito empathized with elements of both arguments. Over the years he'd paid too many tiresome visits to Ron Grossman's office not to realize that his very active sex life carried consequences. But he also reveled in his sexuality and the deep connection that he received from making love with other men. Knowing that many gay men were torn between these conflicting impulses, he invited Callen and Jurrist to air their views on *Our Time*. Backstage, the discussion became so heated that Vito had to flip a coin to decide which speaker would go first. Jurrist won the toss and added to his *Native* arguments the observation that one of his opponents was a former hustler "who provided pain for a price." When he heard this, Berkowitz considered legal action. Having been very discreet about his work, he surmised that Vito, whom he perceived as disapproving of his stance on promiscuity, had shared the information with Jurrist in an effort to smear Berkowitz on the air. Following Jurrist, Callen advanced a message of positive sexuality. Sex was far from "over," he insisted; AIDS simply meant that gay men had to begin practicing "safe sex" with condoms, jerk-off clubs, and closed circles of sex partners. Anything else represented a dismissal of life or an ignorance of death.

Gay Manhattan loved *Our Time*, a fact that producers realized not just from positive word of mouth but also from the unsolicited contributions that poured in from the community. To Rick Siggelkow's amazement, viewers volunteered checks of varying sizes, which he took as "a great testament to the fact that the show was really touching people's lives." The powers at WNYC told Rick they would authorize a second season if he personally could raise funds to meet increased overhead the following year. That much love the show did not receive. After thirteen episodes, WNYC took *Our Time* off the air in early May 1983.

As the show came to an end, Vito enjoyed one perfect evening at Madison Square Garden, where Ringling Bros. Barnum and Bailey Circus mounted a fundraiser for GMHC. Having promoted the event for weeks to his viewers, Vito was extremely gratified on the night of April 30 to see the Garden's nearly eighteen thousand seats sold out. To no one's great surprise, the mainstream media didn't show up. But celebrities did. Leonard Bernstein conducted the national anthem. Grande dame Hermione Gingold was seated alone a few rows away from Vito, who raced over and asked her to join him. Even Mayor Koch appeared and uttered, according to Andrew Holleran, "all the right things." The event was a spectacular success.

It was the best evening Vito had for a long time. Two days later, he learned that Larry Mass had fallen into a suicidal depression. While battling addictions to alcohol and marijuana, Larry was paralyzed with despair over ferocious GMHC infighting and his own powerlessness as a physician forced to watch gay men die at escalating rates. He checked himself into St. Vincent's Hospital for treatment. A long road to recovery lay ahead.

Vito's life was spiraling out of control as well. For one thing, his mother was losing mental and physical ground. A hypochondriac, Annie was in and out of hospitals with a variety of ailments that were destroying her peace of mind. A benign spot on her colon sent her into hysterics. Vito ran telephone interference but left Charlie to deal with their mother's many visits to doctors' offices and emergency rooms.

More pressingly, Vito was reaching another impasse with Jeff, whose reclusiveness, aimlessness, and mood swings had become unmanageable. Vito longed to "fix" everything, but he was also convinced that the relationship's main problems stemmed from Jeff's refusal to take on adult responsibilities. In the middle of July, Vito asked him to leave the apartment. Jeff took the request badly and told Vito that he felt he was being tossed "out in the snow" with nowhere to go. Groaning over this unseasonable turn of phrase, Vito borrowed a line from Thelma Ritter to record it in his journal. Jeff's melodramatic exit, he giggled, had "everything but the bloodhounds snapping at her rear end." Sarcasm aside, Vito mourned that he could neither help Jeff nor live with him any longer. He struggled to convince himself he'd done the right thing. For future relationships, he resolved, "no more wives"—only men "so rich it's ridiculous or so motivated they're never home."

His own motivation was nil. Without a compelling project, Vito wasn't trying to make his own opportunities. It was all too easy to lie about the apartment watching cable, working crossword puzzles, and savaging himself as "a fraud or lazy or a lazy fraud." Throughout the blazing summer of 1983, he couldn't rouse himself to any effort. A trip to Fire Island, where the mood was sepulchral, offered no relief. According to one regular, many gay men were terrified of catching AIDS from Meat Rack mosquitoes. During his uncharacteristically sexless week, Vito found the population sparse and subdued. Those present made him feel small. It wasn't easy, he remarked, "[being] surrounded constantly by people my age making it big. Feeling more and more limited by my own ideas of life, having money, succeeding, doing what one does. Everyone seems to take care of their future and themselves. I seem to drift along trying to be likeable and in the end you're a loser and they don't like you."

In August, with $185 to his name, he took the drastic measure of selling his 16mm copies of *Victim* and *The Gay Deceivers* (1969) to Adam Reilly. The loss cut deeply, but he couldn't turn down $350. He also couldn't turn down a job as manager of the 8th Street Playhouse, where *Closet* features had been such a hit the previous summer. The stint lasted ten days. The hours and pay ($225 per week) were atrocious, but what most upset Vito was the behavior of his boss, a man with AIDS who continued to sleep around because, he claimed, "'I can't stop living.'" Vito retorted in his diary, "Wanna bet, Steve? Shocking." Vito began monitoring his own body for signs of illness. He started on vitamins, added ten pounds to his rail-thin frame, and convinced himself that he didn't have AIDS.

He had to admit that a poor diet and nicotine addiction—which even hypnotism couldn't cure—were adding to his troubles. With "no boyfriend and a crazy mother," he also knew that being alone made it harder for him to cope with stress. Over the next several months, Vito and Jeff paid each other a couple of lengthy visits in San Francisco and New York. After a painful week in San Francisco, he confessed to Jeff, "I have never really loved anyone as much as I love you and it's been very hard for me to accept that it hasn't worked out the way I know we both wanted it to." Fearing that he might be doomed to a life of solitude, Vito felt that he should do anything necessary to win Jeff back.

For the time being, however, they were a continent apart, and Vito needed companionship. Back in New York, he was trying to avoid the bar scene, where AIDS panic seemed to be driving all of gay Manhattan toward instant marriage. One would-be bridegroom was John Bovée, a twenty-five-year-old store manager whose professional ambition, trim build, and dark blond looks Vito found appealing. John fell hard for Vito, but the feeling wasn't quite mutual. His "upwardly mobile values" Vito deemed a little too Clovis for comfort. Not returning John's affection filled him with regret, which was becoming an unwelcome pattern in his love life. "I seem to be developing a great capacity for guilt—guilty because I can't please John, guilty because I hurt Jeff." He decided to put romance on indefinite hold.

Work, thankfully, started offering some exciting opportunities. Rob Epstein and codirector Richard Schmiechen had just finished *Out of Order*, the film that they had begun as a study of the Briggs Initiative (California's Proposition 6) and Harvey Milk. While working on the project, they realized that Milk's story was far more compelling than Briggs's. After considerable refocusing and a title change, *The Times of Harvey Milk* was ready for exhibition. Unfortunately, it had no distributor. Facing a PBS airdate along with bookings at the Telluride and New York Film Festivals, Rob and Richard signed with a New York start-up company, Teleculture, and requested that Vito be hired to oversee the film's national publicity. Rob was convinced that Vito's connections in media and the gay community could work word-of-mouth miracles for *Harvey Milk*. Vito didn't let him down. Though he considered Teleculture's director "the asshole of the eighties" and the splintering company a "fucking mess"—"just like the last days of Cambodia"—he gave his all to promoting the film.

The story of Milk's rise to political power, and his insistence that gay rights demanded gay visibility, inspired Vito. In early November 1984, at *Harvey Milk*'s San Francisco premiere, Vito's political anger came roaring back to life. Before a Castro Theatre audience, he attacked gay men for even considering a vote for Ronald Reagan, then running for his second presidential term. Only gay fools, Vito railed, would look to Reagan to protect their financial assets while his Supreme Court stripped away their civil rights. On a lighter note, he predicted that *Harvey Milk* would go on to win the Oscar for Best Documentary Feature— which it did the following March, the first gay-themed film to do so. Vito was elated to see a film on which he had worked reap Hollywood's highest honor.

Vito was racking up more honors of his own. As *Closet* sales continued to ring, more organizations showered its author with accolades. In October 1984, he received a community service award from the *Washington Blade* and from Washington's first International Gay and Lesbian Film Festival. That same month, at the Waldorf-Astoria Hotel in New York, Lily Tomlin presented him with the Human Rights Campaign Fund's first Arthur Bell Arts and Humanitarian Award.

Vito was extremely proud to be honored in his friend's name, but the moment was bittersweet. Arthur had died the previous June of complications from diabetes. Two days before his death, Vito visited him at St. Vincent's Hospital, where he found the fifty-one-year-old reduced to "a shrunken old man." With flagging concentration, Arthur stayed awake long enough for the two old friends to acknowledge their love. Speaking at Arthur's memorial a few weeks later, Vito thanked him for his earliest activist lessons: "He taught me that following the rules doesn't really guarantee you respect. . . . And he taught me that it is not tasteless to stand up and have the courage to be who you are."

Death was asserting terrible omnipresence in gay Manhattan. In July 1983, Eddie Rosenberg was diagnosed with KS and *Pneumocystis carinii* pneumonia (PCP). When he died in December, Vito froze. Just a week earlier Jeff had called from San Francisco, where his dentist had found suspicious spots in his mouth and referred him to an oral surgeon. Vito held his breath.

Two months later the walls crashed in. Vito's friend, thirty-one-year-old singer David Summers, received a KS diagnosis. Vito had met David over ten years earlier when he costarred as New Boy in Town in Al Carmines's play *The Faggot*. Since then, David had garnered an impressive reputation on the cabaret circuit, where his campy, smart-alecky sense of humor matched Vito's. David's illness devastated Vito, who could no longer close his eyes to the "medieval horror story" unfolding around him. In his journal, he gasped, "I can't accept David's illness as fatal, can't believe he may die. Or that it could happen to me tomorrow." Acutely aware that David had done nothing he himself hadn't done ten times over, Vito tried to ignore the noose tightening around his own neck.

On April 23, he took only minor comfort in Health and Human Services' announcement of the discovery of HTLV-III (later renamed HIV), the virus that causes AIDS. A foolproof blood test and vaccine were allegedly in the works. What did these developments matter, Vito wondered, when life had "changed for all those [he knew] and for [himself] for all time"? Already an impenetrable curtain hung between past and present; already people talked "about 'the old days' with new meaning—they refer[ed] to a time when danger was not a part of everyday existence, when sex and death were strangers and when the future existed." Vito couldn't help but ask why he personally knew so many of the afflicted. True, half of the AIDS cases were in New York and he was extremely well connected, but it seemed to him that he knew a disproportionate number of dying young men. As he would later describe these days, "I mean, suddenly I was knowing a dozen people who were sick instead of two. Suddenly there were thirty people who were sick instead of four. And it hit you like an overwhelming wave of water. Suddenly cold water was thrown in your face. Everybody was dying."

Vito's reserve cracked further as public reaction to AIDS—and more broadly, to gay men—snapped into focus. Less than a year before his death, Arthur Bell had been accosted in a diner by a young woman who told him, "You gay pricks who deserve to die are dying." He responded by spitting in her face and remarking, "If I've got AIDS, you've got it." One random bigot in an East Side restaurant was an irritation; bigots who commanded the eyes and ears of millions were terrifying. In November 1984, before being barred by the American Psychological Association, Dr. Paul Cameron got significant media coverage by attacking gay men as "worse than murderers." Jerry Falwell called for quarantining people with AIDS. In Vito's own backyard, *New York* magazine critic John Simon trumpeted in a lobby, "Homosexuals in the theater! My God, I can't wait until AIDS gets all of them!" Mortified by these developments, Vito attended the first preview of Larry Kramer's new play, *The Normal Heart*, which detailed the early years of the AIDS crisis in New York. Its depiction of gay men's battles with each other, city bureaucracy, and their own bodies devastated him.

In this depleted state, he received the phone call that he'd been dreading for nearly eighteen months. Jeff lay in a San Francisco hospital with PCP.

Jeff had been terrified of AIDS. He shared his fear with Vito, who tried to brush it aside. When he insisted, "This is inside my body, I know it—I'm so scared," Vito refused to listen. Jeff had so many complaints, and this was one that Vito, gripped by his own fears, simply wouldn't entertain. When Jeff returned to San Francisco in July 1983, his friends, partners Allen Sawyer and Tom Harding, got him a job at Captain Video. Processing greasy porn tapes, Jeff fled to the bathroom several times a day to scrub his arms up to the elbows. Germ-phobic under the least threatening circumstances, he now perceived himself under constant attack. When he received his diagnosis in April 1985, he burst into tears and confessed to Tom, "What I feared most has happened."

Within hours of learning the news, Vito was on a plane from Newark bound for San Francisco. In his journal, he released the panic that he wanted to conquer before entering Jeff's hospital room. "My love my love Jeffrey my golden boy, my man. My heart is breaking tonight. This night should never have come to me. . . . Oh he is sick and I feel that I am dying of it. This disease has my honey. . . . My darling my love my heart hurts so much. . . . This endless flight and Jeffrey terrified in a hospital my god my god my god oh no no." Vito longed to heal Jeffrey with his touch, "to hold him in my arms and kiss his eyes I want to feel him next to me in the sun and hold his hand I want to give him life I don't want him to die. He can't just die this way." At the same time, unspeakable guilt was tearing at him. As he approached San Francisco, Vito couldn't help wondering, "Did I give him this? Have I killed Jeff with something inside of myself?"

Jeff's sister Theresa collected Vito at the airport and drove him directly to Children's Hospital. At the door to Jeff's room was a nurse taping up warnings against contact with bodily fluids. Vito burst into the room and found Jeff sitting up in bed. Absurdly, Jeff asked, "Honey, did you hear?" Vito drew a breath and sat down on the bed. "I told him that we were gonna do this together. That it was gonna be all right. I wanted so much to convince him that—I knew immediately, just from what I knew of in the community, that if he didn't fight, he would die." For his part, Jeff jockeyed between acceptance and denial of his illness. In braver moments, he told Vito what he wanted to hear, that he was "committed to fight" the disease. Vito, meanwhile, tried to swallow his anxiety over the heterosexuality of Jeff's doctor and his fear that the illness would claim him as well. He strove to be stoic while facing "the most serious thing [he had] ever had to deal with in [his] life." At the very least, the crisis would give him "a chance to change [his] life." He told himself, "I have to seize this and make it a life thing and not an ending."

When Vito flew back to New York a week later, one thing was clear: he would move to San Francisco as soon as possible. Jeff was wary. "Do you realize the commitment you're making?" he asked. Not only had their relationship repeatedly proved unworkable, but Jeff couldn't imagine his lover, the quintessential New Yorker, relaxing into San Francisco's Zen vibe. Vito accepted these challenges. For the first time in his adult life, he tried to perceive some benign "higher power" whose good intentions he could trust.

Vito certainly discerned goodness in the friends who rushed to his aid. Jeff's sister Chris drove her 1977 Saab from Vail, Colorado, to San Francisco so that Vito and Jeff wouldn't have to rely on cable cars for transportation. Money poured in from far-flung locations: Allen Sawyer and Captain Video contributed $350 toward Vito's return airfare on April 30, Mark Pinney mailed Vito $500, and Arnie and Larry paid $900 of Vito's soaring American Express bill. Of greatest help was Larry Bush, who found Vito work as a media consultant with the San Francisco AIDS Foundation (SFAF). The job's inconsequential $440 per week left Vito unable to afford decent housing, so Larry offered, rent-free, his spacious three-bedroom apartment in the Mission District.

On May 6, 1985, Vito began work at SFAF. The sex-positive organization seemed an excellent fit for him. Its colorful posters, featuring two taut male rears and the slogan "You Can Have Fun (and Be Safe, Too)," had decorated the city for over a year. But when Vito arrived in San Francisco, health officials and community activists were in an uproar over the first blood tests to detect antibodies to HTLV-III. The results of a positive reading were distressingly unclear: Would people with the antibodies necessarily develop AIDS? Would the results be made public? Would patients be required to submit lists of all previous sex partners? Would they lose jobs and housing based on test results? Were quarantines out of the question? SFAF shared these concerns until the San Francisco Health Department established free, anonymous Alternative Test Sites (ATS). In May 1985, although 78 percent of San Francisco's gay men indicated that they would not take the test, SFAF began producing literature to inform people about where it was available and what facts it could, or could not, reveal. This was where Vito's position at SFAF came in.

Working for SFAF's education and prevention department, Vito collaborated with Adair Films on a ten-minute video to be screened for visitors at the city's ATS before they had their blood drawn. Outlining the legal risks of the test's disclosure, the video underscored that a positive reading of HTLV-III antibodies could not definitively indicate that a person had or would get AIDS. With coworker Nancy Stoller, Vito helped develop brochures, distributed both at SFAF and the ATS, reviewing these issues at length. The SFAF writers struggled to make complex issues comprehensible for the least literate client while informing better educated readers about the latest scientific findings.

Vito's time at SFAF was taxing. The organization's twenty employees shared a powerful sense of purpose and felt that they were doing "really, really important work." At the same time, with very limited funds, departmental turf wars were frequent and bitter. Individual divisions often didn't care what happened to their counterparts as long as their own projects got approved. And death was a daily reality at SFAF. Many of its own employees were ill, and everyone was grieving the loss of loved ones. Depression at the office was unavoidable.

It was especially hard for Vito to concentrate on work while Jeff deteriorated. His determination to fight the illness was destroyed by a new doctor who, when Jeff protested that he didn't want to go on a high-fat diet and gain weight, replied, "You're not worried about heart disease. You'll be dead in a year." Vito shouted his anger and confusion in letters to Arnie. How was Jeff supposed to react to a death sentence? Keeping the faith wasn't easy when his recovery depended on such a range of variables: "*If* he gets experimental drugs, *if* he doesn't get placebos, *if* [the drugs work] anyway." These uncertainties came on top of constant assault from bigots to whom "the Jeffs of the world [were] those awful homosexuals who are spreading their AIDS to our children through their sick lifestyle. It makes you want to kill. It makes you want to die. What an awful place to live and what an awful time to be alive." In the final analysis, Vito concluded, "nobody knows shit, Cher, and they're just as scared as I am." Arnie pledged his support and urged Vito to hold tight by tossing back at him one of his pet phrases: "I only dread one day at a time."

Vito boiled when Jeff's doctor dismissed vitamins and good nutrition as possible immune-system boosters. At the same time, better counsel seemed impossible to find. "Every quack in town," Vito snapped, "has given us advice—they have everything here from holistic hypnosis to vegetarian banking. A woman at Au Natural Health food store on Market [Street] put Jeff on to a no yeast diet which is hogwash as far as I'm concerned." Unfortunately, Jeff had no interest in other treatments. Vito tried desperately to get him into trials for the new drugs ribavirin and Foscarnet, but Jeff, clinging to his macrobiotic diet, refused.

Vito and Jeff's rapport was again deteriorating. At home, Vito found his behavior intolerable. An inveterate neatnik to Larry Bush's "slob," Jeff turned moody and difficult whenever his host left an errant cigarette pack lying about the house. Exploring New Age philosophies, Jeff became imperious about the colors he wanted around him. Blue he considered "healing"; yellow was toxic. For Vito's sake, Larry tried to be a good sport about the color wars, quipping, "Well, I never looked good in yellow."

Beyond his problems with Jeff, Vito was miserable in San Francisco. In late May, three weeks after his arrival, he bemoaned the city's lack of summer and spark: "It's never quite hot here, just pleasant, like their people. This is basically a small town." Living in San Francisco convinced Vito more than ever that he was a New Yorker at heart. Unlike London, San Francisco was "not a world-class city." It frustrated him to live in a town where people didn't "enjoy a good *scrap*." His efforts to start a political wrangle at Café Flore always ended with the same anticlimax: "You say something volatile to somebody and they just sort of smile . . . nothing upsets anyone!" And California cuisine was simply unacceptable. Reviewing the menu at a vegetarian restaurant, he announced, "If I see any tofu on my plate, I'm going to start shrieking." Plus the *looks* he got from friends when he lit up a cigarette at Orphan Andy's on Market Street! Fuhgeddaboutit.

Accompanied by Jeff, Vito ran back to New York at the end of July for a quick reality check. The week before, Rock Hudson had announced that he had AIDS; suddenly everybody was paying attention to an epidemic that had begun four years earlier. On Friday, August 2, Vito was visiting with Arnie when he glanced down at his leg. Tucked in the hollow behind his knee was a dark spot he'd never seen. Vito refused to delude himself. He knew perfectly well what it was. So did Arnie, who rushed Vito to Dr. Grossman for a biopsy.

Five days later, Vito was back in San Francisco with Arnie and Jim Owles at his side. On August 8, Ron Grossman called him at SFAF. To their mutual astonishment, the biopsy had come back negative. The spot on Vito's leg was a mole, nothing more.

Vito returned to work feeling much better about his health, his job, and his temporary home. On Tuesday, August 13, his phone rang at SFAF. It was Ron again, this time sounding ragged. "I will never, *ever* be able to make this up to you," he began. Vito froze. "I don't know how to tell you this, but the lab switched your slide with the slide of an 86-year-old heterosexual woman who has gotten a KS diagnosis, which is not possible. So I'm sorry to tell you this, but it turns out it's positive after all and you do have KS." Vito hung up the phone and burst into tears. He told Nancy what had happened and asked her not to tell anyone. Arnie, whom Ron had already alerted, raced to SFAF with Jim. As he awaited their arrival, Vito sat in a stupor at his desk. His reaction to Ron's call took on cinematic coloring: "At that point I sort of felt like Susan Hayward in *I Want to Live!* [1958], you know, with the governor giving her a pardon every five minutes and then the phone ringing. It just drives you *nuts*. The *stress* was enormous. I was at the end of my emotional rope—and this was the final verdict. The final verdict was that I had AIDS." His life expectancy, Ron estimated, was one year.

Arnie and Jim swung into immediate action. They picked Vito up at SFAF and took him and Jeff out to lunch. Several days later, they tried to cheer Vito with a trip to the Great American Amusement Park. The following week, they arranged a trip to Lake Tahoe, where Jeff's depression made everyone miserable.

Arnie sensed that Jeff was jealous to see Vito, as a newly sick person, receiving the attention that had been reserved for him. Utterly despondent, Jeff "became this thing we were pulling along on wheels." After two days, when Arnie intervened and told Jeff that he needed psychological help, Jeff shut down completely and put himself on a bus back to San Francisco. Once more, Vito could see their relationship heading for the rocks.

Upon learning of his illness, Vito adopted a staunch resolve to "think clearly, have hope, be strong, not give in, not despair for [himself] and for all the fine loving people around [him]." He refused to be "a sick person if [he could] help it." The example of David Summers, thriving eighteen months after his diagnosis, inspired him. He determined to get himself and Jeff to Montreal for an upcoming Foscarnet trial. "I am not yet ready to prepare to die," Vito declared. "I am ready to prepare instead to dine—preferably in Europe or on a cruise to the Caribbean."

Before heading abroad, Vito knew that he had to return to New York. His closest friends were there, and for the sake of his own health, he had to be where he felt most comfortable. He also had the prospect of being hired as GMHC's public information officer at an annual salary of twenty-eight thousand dollars—far more money than he had ever earned in a year. The unsolved dilemma was Jeff, who wanted him to remain in San Francisco. While that was out of the question, so was leaving Jeff alone. The need to take care of his childlike lover still ruled him.

Vito and Jeff returned to New York on October 10, 1985, one week after Rock Hudson's death made headlines worldwide. Two days later, Arnie and Larry threw their friends a "welcome back" brunch that ended in emotional disaster. One of the guests was Richie Brandys, a significantly younger friend with AIDS. Richie had recently lost his hair to chemotherapy and was struggling with a paralyzed arm that left him unable to tie his shoes or zip his fly unassisted. Appalled by this sight, Vito retreated to a corner of the loft, "musing on subjects like whether it's worth saving receipts if one isn't sure that he will live to file another income tax return. 'They've taken my future away,'" he told Arnie. Within days, Vito fell into deeper depression when he learned that John Bovée's brother Gene had died of AIDS complications. At the memorial, Arnie and Vito held hands and sobbed, realizing that they were "crying as much for the death that threatens to end [their] 15 years of love as [they] were mourning for those already gone." Vito asked Arnie to help him die if his suffering became intolerable.

Fighting off despair, Vito threw himself into medical research. From the earliest days of his diagnosis, he impressed doctors with his knowledge of AIDS. Dr. Marcus Conant, one of the first doctors to treat AIDS patients and a cofounder of the organization that would become SFAF, saw Vito in San Francisco and found him extremely upbeat. His familiarity with experimental drugs clearly came from informed reading, not rumor or speculation. In New York, Ron Grossman was stunned by the meticulous letters he received from Vito. By the end of August, Vito was already assessing antiviral drugs and immune modulators. From Ron he sought advice on whether his instinct to "kill the virus and keep it from replicating" while he still enjoyed a high T-cell count was sound. Reviewing Vito's questions today, Ron remarks, "Here is Vito Russo who, to my knowledge, does not have an MD after his name, getting it *exactly right* in 1985, when most doctors [hadn't] a clue."

Vito's questions grew dauntingly specific as he ran up against contradictory medical information. Noting ribavirin's low toxicity and apparent efficacy at blocking the virus, he asked his friends in Bloolips to bring him a supply from Mexico, which, unlike the United States, sold the drug legally. ("Very heavy, wasn't it," Bette Bourne sighed over the six-month supply that he kindly hauled across the border.) But before Vito began taking it, he consulted Dr. Linda Laubenstein at NYU Medical Center. Dr. Laubenstein warned him that the drug could only block the virus at the daily dosage of 1800 mg, which caused dreadful side effects. Other doctors informed Vito that they had seen wonderful improvements in AIDS patients taking ribavirin at precisely that dosage. He turned to Ron in frustration. "Why all the apparent disparity of belief? Please understand that I'm not being belligerent here. To me and thousands like me this isn't a research game, it's a daily emotional battle." Ron, of course, had no definitive answer to Vito's questions. He could only offer words of comfort and admiration to a self-taught patient who realized that "sitting around and doing nothing was not an option."

As Vito bombarded doctors with letters and phone calls, Jeff continued to ignore medical reality. He found hope in the New Age teachings of Louise Hay, who preached that individuals create their own illnesses and find cures through self-love. After a Catskills retreat, Jeff returned to New York and threw away all his medicines. Hefting a trash bag clattering with prescription bottles, he announced, "I don't need any of this anymore. I'm cured." In January 1986, he accepted GMHC's referral to a nutritionist who decided what was "right for his clients [to eat] by holding the item over their stomach and if the client's arm raise[d], he prescribe[d] the item." Vito couldn't toss his eyebrows high enough. "Give me a break here" was his sole reply. To appease Vito, Jeff consulted with Ron once or twice, dutifully recording the carb-, cream-, and vegetable-heavy diet that became his sole weapon against AIDS.

Hoping that Jeff's beliefs might give him strength, Vito tried to encourage the dietary regimen for as long as he could. But it was becoming harder to reach his lover. Upon discovering his own first KS lesion, Jeff retreated permanently into a fantasy world where he could block out any unpleasant messages. Vito began finding it impossible to spend any time with him. His sense of hopelessness grew as Jeff spent "most days lying in a dark room staring at the ceiling and generally spout[ing] all sorts of nonsense." The breaking point had finally come.

Racked with guilt, Vito asked Jeff to leave the apartment on February 1. As Jeff retreated to his parents' home in Pittsburgh, Vito began seeing a psychotherapist. Two weeks later, he took off for Sydney and Melbourne, where he was presenting the "Closet," and Honolulu, where he was taking a badly needed vacation. At the same time, Jeff left Pittsburgh for San Francisco. With his health failing, he wanted to return to the city he considered home.

In San Francisco, Jeff went to see Nancy Stoller at SFAF. Startled by his dramatic weight loss, she drove him back to Mary Rose Kent's apartment, where he was staying. Nancy marveled that in his condition, Jeff could still climb stairs. In fact, he couldn't. One night, on his way downstairs for a drink of water, he fell. Mary Rose realized that a crisis had been reached and told him he needed a doctor. Jeff replied, "I'm just so afraid that if I go into a hospital, I'll never come out again." It was the likeliest scenario, but as his mother and sisters noted, he had surpassed their power to help him. They bundled him up and took him to San Francisco General.

On March 5, knowing that Vito was traveling, Larry Bush left word for Arnie that Jeff was dying of lymphoma. When Arnie called the hospital the next morning, he reached Jeff's mother, who told him that Jeff was "breathing his last." When her son's chest fell for the last time, Mrs. Sevcik turned to Larry and commented, simply, "I guess that's all there is." One month shy of his thirty-first birthday, Jeff was gone.

At the moment of Jeff's death, Vito was high over the Pacific Ocean, flying from Melbourne to Honolulu. Asleep in the cabin, he awoke with a violent start. "V!" Was Jeff calling him? The next morning he arrived in Honolulu, where he met Joe Brewer for lunch. After the meal, they returned to Vito's room for a nap. Their rest was interrupted by a sharp knock. Bizarrely, the desk clerk was trying to reach Joe for a call. When he picked up the phone, Joe heard the voice of Allen Sawyer asking him to tell Vito that Jeff had just died. Joe crept back to Vito's room and shared the news. As he did, Joe related, Vito "just *came apart*. I was holding him, sort of from behind, on top of the bed, and he just sort of leaned forward like a doll—forward—and he just shattered."

Hours later, Vito was on a flight to San Francisco. Tom Harding picked him up at the airport and drove him directly to San Francisco General, where he was taken to the morgue. An attendant slid out a drawer, and there was Jeff—but to Vito, "it wasn't. No way was it Jeff. He had that little bump on his nose [laughing] that told me it was Jeff. And I remember that I combed his hair—because he was always doing that. . . . I took a comb out of my pocket and I combed his hair and I talked to him for a little while."

To Vito's surprise, the Sevciks had left the cremation and disposition of the ashes to him. Jeff's sisters and elderly parents had no friends or family in San Francisco and nowhere to stay for any length of time. Figuring that Vito and Jeff's friends would see to a ceremony, they returned home shortly after his death.

With Rob Epstein, his partner Jeffrey Friedman, Allen and Tom, and Larry Bush, Vito climbed a hill high above Jeff's beloved Castro to strew a portion of his ashes. As he bade good-bye to his golden boy, a strong breeze whipped up out of nowhere and blew some of the ashes back in the mourners' faces. Larry remembers someone remarking, "That's the one way you know you're gonna cry for Jeffrey." The comment wasn't intended maliciously, Larry insists; it was merely emotional fallout among a group of friends, mostly under forty, who had already seen an impossible number of deaths.

When Vito returned to New York on March 11, Arnie met him at his apartment. From his suitcase, Vito drew a small canister with the balance of Jeff's ashes. As Arnie took a respectful glance inside, Vito began picking at his scalp. "'It's [Jeff's] ashes,' he said. 'It was very windy while we were strewing them and I didn't have a chance to take a shower'" before leaving San Francisco.

Arnie could only hold his friend and let him cry. Death had followed Vito back to New York, which itself was becoming a citywide graveyard.

8

The Activist in Wartime

After Jeff's death, Vito collapsed in grief and self-blame. The lover he had three times turned out of his home was gone forever. For the first time, Vito confessed, "I understand real guilt, regret, recrimination." While mourning, he panicked to see a second KS lesion appear on his skin. Time was no longer his friend. A few months from his fortieth birthday, he determined to make every second count.

Trust Manhattan to send his spirits soaring. One week after Vito's return, the city council passed Intro 2, the gay civil-rights bill. After fifteen years of disappointment, New York's gay population would finally enjoy protection from discrimination in housing, employment, and public accommodation. Arnie and Larry heard the news on the radio and raced down to Sheridan Square. There stood Vito, mere feet from the Stonewall, while Jim Owles, though long retired from gay politics, addressed a rapturous crowd from atop a flatbed truck. Choked with emotion, GAA's first president proclaimed March 20, 1986, "the best day of [his] life." That night Arnie and Vito attended a celebratory dance at the Lesbian and Gay Community Center on West 13th Street. For a few hours, GAA's Firehouse seemed risen from the ashes.

A few weeks later, eager to distract Vito from grief, Arnie, Larry, Jim, and Brandon Judell accompanied him on a gay Caribbean cruise for a look at Halley's comet, unglimpsed since 1910. When the view proved disappointing, Vito focused on the sun and the drag shows. But he felt uncomfortable on a boat where many of the passengers were openly shunning one ill man and his lover. Though Vito's sickness was scarcely visible, he felt a chasm yawning between him and healthy gay men.

Striving to stay upbeat, he announced that he would reopen his home to community film screenings. For younger viewers, these evenings provided an introduction to sacrosanct camp. Tireless GMHC legal counsel Mark Senak, on whom Vito nursed an unrequited crush, discovered *The Women* at Vito's and found his host's dishy commentary as engaging as the film itself. To more-seasoned viewers, Vito eagerly showed off obscure films or those newly released on VHS. For one crew, he presented the Barbara Stanwyck melodrama *The Strange Love of Martha Ivers* (1946) with his own editorial: "This is the craziest movie ever made. All the guys seem like fags, and she seems like a dyke, and yet we're supposed to believe they're in love."

Some of Vito's guests, such as comedy writer Bruce Vilanch and future Oscar-winning director Pedro Almodóvar, were famous for their knowledge of Hollywood arcana. One especially versed visitor was Charles Busch, whose drag turns in his plays *Vampire Lesbians of Sodom* (1984) and *Psycho Beach Party* (1987) were seismic downtown hits. Enamored of Charles's florid stage persona, Vito invited him to a showing of the musical revue *Hellzapoppin'*, where Charles met his partner, writer Eric Myers. Their introduction was classic Vito. When an obscure chanteuse took the screen, Charles heard a voice across the room pipe, "Oh, that's Jane Frazee!" The reference stumped even Charles, whose first thought was "Who the *fuck* is Jane Frazee?" His second was "Whoever knows from Jane Frazee, I gotta meet this one." More than twenty years later, Charles and Eric are still together.

Vito also sought the comfort of old friendships. As they had been for years, Arnie and Jim remained his emotional mainstays. Several times a month, the trio shuttled between one another's apartments for bloodlust matches of Uno, Milles Bornes, and Risk—all games that demanded annihilation of one's opponents while hurling over the table "well-timed darts composed of indelicate reminders about [their] unfulfilled dreams, [their] lost loves, and [their] vices, whose details [they] all shared." During Risk, in which players attempt world takeover, Vito "took on the demeanor of a whimsical Genghis Khan," inhaling Mallomars and grinning as his friends howled over his dastardly moves. Poker games, with nickel-and-dime stakes, were less lethal. Larry often joined in the fun, as did Jim's young protégé, David Kirby. These evenings unfolded under a haze of pot smoke, good-natured gossip, raunchy stories, and the deep-retro offerings of WNEW-AM's *Jukebox Saturday Night*: "Chattanooga Choo Choo," "Little Brown Jug," anything Sinatra, Garland, Bennett, Vaughan.

To Vito these gatherings yielded far more than banter and bitchery. They were a buffer against loneliness. Well after midnight, when his weary guests rose to leave, Vito faced frightening depression. He suffered from acute insomnia and penned innumerable journal entries while waiting for his sleeping pill to kick in. The constellation of iridescent white stars splashed across the ceiling over his bed provided little comfort. In the pitiless predawn hours, he had nothing to do but mourn his golden boy and dread the virus staking implacable claim to his own body.

In an effort to keep his house filled, Vito played constant host. Dean Pitchford had always marveled at his friend's ability to assemble a ripping party from
two bottles of wine and a bag of potato chips. Now ill, Vito took to high-culinary
nesting with a vengeance. Mindful of HIV, he avoided pork and uncooked vegetables. But it was open season on all other foods, and he took special pride in
reprising the lavish holiday dinner parties that he used to throw with Bruce. Even
an accomplished gourmet like Larry Mass salivated over Vito's expert cream of
broccoli soup, his "moist, perfect chicken cordon bleu," and his scrumptious
array of apple, sweet potato, and pumpkin chiffon pies.

One new guest was Joe De Cola, the producer who had booked Vito on *ABC
Close-Up!* in 1974. A twice-married father of four, Joe eventually chose Vito as
the first person to whom he confessed his homosexuality. While still closeted, he
accepted Vito's invitation to an all-male Thanksgiving dinner. During the party,
Vito produced a photo album. Joe was startled to hear the men murmur, "Oh,
he's gone," or "Oh, did you know so-and-so is gone?" of someone on nearly
every page. He probably didn't realize that the pictures were not recent. As
AIDS began to strike his circle, Vito stopped taking photos. Remembering was
too painful.

Work kept grief at bay. In 1986, *New York Newsday* hired Vito to write a series
of celebrity profiles. His tenure at *Moviegoer* had prepared him for puff pieces,
and he was invigorated to tear around the city's swankiest hotels chatting with
Federico Fellini, Alan Alda, Spalding Gray, and Danny DeVito. *Newsday* also
gained him access to the set of *Prick Up Your Ears* (1987), where he visited with director Stephen Frears and costar Vanessa Redgrave. Detailing the rise and murder of openly gay playwright Joe Orton, *Ears* provided Vito with a rare chance
to discuss gay issues for mainstream readers. But he seethed when an editor
snipped his rant against "heterosexuals who don't like gays and gay people who
don't like themselves," that is, those viewers offended by the film's unflinching
depiction of gay sex and violence.

As his first *Newsday* articles went to press, Vito learned that he had won the
San Francisco International Lesbian and Gay Film Festival's first Frameline
Award. He received the honor at the Castro Theatre, where he presented an expanded version of the "Closet" that lifted a sellout audience of over fourteen
hundred patrons to their feet. Afterward he attended a tribute dinner at which
his many San Francisco friends told their favorite Vito stories. Thinking himself
"the richest person on earth," Vito gratefully accepted the praise along with a
raft of roses and cards. The evening reminded Joe Brewer of an episode in *The
Adventures of Tom Sawyer*, in which Tom and Huck, presumed dead, attend their
own funeral and hear the wonderful things their friends say about them. Joe was
moved to see Vito receive such heartfelt compliments while still alive.

Of course, awareness of Vito's precarious health made everyone's comments all the more poignant. Illness was permeating every corner of his life. Just when he was able to forget AIDS for a few minutes, his dentist of seventeen years abruptly severed their relationship. Vito realized that he could no longer assume anyone's good will, much less his own peace of mind. He attempted to process the dueling excitement and anguish of his life:

> I eat in good restaurants, I travel and I lecture and I write and people like my work and send me notes and flowers and come to my table in restaurants and give me their phone numbers and invite me to dinner and fly me to Australia and California and ask me to Paris and Berlin and give me awards in Washington, DC, and San Francisco and ask me to appear on television and radio and quote me and treat me like someone special. On the surface that's my life. But what's my life? I'm hurt so easily, made lonely so easily, feel so strongly that I won't have romance again—that few of us will—yet I survive and will survive all of this. I have a sadness and a joy that are equally indestructible—an anger that has nowhere to go.

The last clause wasn't quite true. His anger had found a new outlet. In September 1985, a group calling itself "The Family Defense Coalition" staged a two-day picket in front of the St. Marks Baths. One protester carried a sign screaming, "The Gay Baths May Spawn an Epidemic of A.I.D.S. That Will Devastate New York!" New York papers poured gasoline on this panic. The muckraking *Post* led the charge with a series of editorials, cartoons, and articles equating gay sex with death. A letter published in the *Daily News* suggested that the noun "gay" be changed to the acronym "sap" for "sodomite-anal-pervert." In the *Times*, William F. Buckley Jr. proposed a policy with unmistakable Nazi parallels: "Everyone detected with AIDS should be tatooed [*sic*] in the upper forearm, to protect common-needle users, and on the buttocks, to prevent the victimization of other homosexuals." Anita Bryant seemed tolerant by comparison.

In response, Vito, Arnie, Jim, and Marty Robinson convened on October 30 at the New York State Council for the Arts to discuss strategy with the gay writers Gregory Kolovakos, Allen Barnett, Darrell Yates Rist, and Barry Adkins. How should they answer the hate-mongering inspired by AIDS? Vito argued that the gay community needed an organization to scrutinize the media's representation of homosexuals. All instances of homophobia should inspire blistering GAA-style zaps. The new organization named itself the Gay and Lesbian Anti-Defamation League (GLADL)—a title that stuck until the Anti-Defamation League of B'nai B'rith, having copyrighted the term "anti-defamation" in 1913, threatened to sue. In response, the group renamed itself the Gay and Lesbian Alliance Against Defamation (GLAAD).

Spurred by AIDS panic, homophobia was leading to the rise of self-appointed sex police. Within a single month, four gay sex clubs—the Mineshaft, the Anvil, Hellfire, and the St. Marks Baths—were padlocked by the city. On the day of the St. Marks's closing, Plato's Retreat, a straight swingers' club operating on the site of the former Continental Baths, reopened its doors. Vito decried not only the city's homophobia but also its official denial that heterosexuals were at risk for AIDS. Now more than ever, he deemed informed, consensual sex—whenever, wherever, with whomever—a civil right. He refused to believe that promiscuity in and of itself was in any way immoral. "I don't regret the '70s for a second," he declared. Even in the wake of AIDS, "I don't want to take it all back." Committed to protecting his partners' health, Vito had long been practicing safe sex, but he could not accept governmental enforcement of such behavior. The inveterate smoker argued that he would not "go into a restaurant and rip a cigarette out of someone's mouth because it might give him cancer." Similarly, he maintained, "[If I saw] one guy fucking another guy in a back room and not using a rubber, it's none of my business. I do not have the right to control someone else's life." Adults had to make their own decisions about their own bodies.

Not all gay men shared Vito's opinion. Many endorsed the sex clubs' closing in the interest of public health. At GLAAD's first town-hall meeting, which packed over seven hundred angry, anxious gays and lesbians into a West Village church, Vito attempted to channel flaring differences of opinion. Whatever their views on the baths, he told the crowd, they must not be blinded to the exploitation of AIDS "by right-wing fanatics and yellow journalists [determined] to create a witchhunt mentality against lesbians and gay men" in New York. With screams of approval echoing around him, he thrust his right arm high over his head and flashed the hall a V-for-victory sign. Dazzled by the electric speeches of Vito and of fellow GLAAD Board members Rist and Jewelle Gomez, a *Native* reporter hailed the evening as a "New Stonewall."

In November, when GLAAD assembled its first slate of officers, Arnie accepted the position of secretary. Vito wasn't interested in assuming a leadership role. To vice chair Marcia Pally, he promised to serve on the board for six months. If the organization survived that long, it would no longer need him. If it didn't, c'est la vie. He did, however, agree to emcee GLAAD's first action, a rally targeting the *New York Post* on Sunday, December 1.

Despite cold, wet weather and a long ride downtown, some eight hundred protesters showed up to hurl invective at the *Post*'s empty building. The timing left something to be desired, and the organization's cooperation with the police prompted the departure of several radical activists. But enough people turned up shouting, "Fight AIDS, not gays," "Close the *Post*, not the baths," and "Don't advertise in the *Post*" to make the paper's owners nervous. Publisher Rupert

Murdoch ordered a meeting between gay activists and the editorial brass. Though no champion of gay rights or AIDS legislation, Murdoch also had no desire to see his major advertisers—including Macy's, Bloomingdale's, Chase Manhattan Bank, and, in brutal irony, the Broadway show *La Cage aux Folles*—inundated with anti-*Post* letters and phone calls. It was bad enough that protesters left hundreds of rags at the paper's doorstep with camera-friendly symbolism.

During GLAAD's early months, Vito was often absent from meetings due to Jeff's advancing illness. But his contributions helped get the group off the ground. Jewelle Gomez felt that Vito performed a "very important function" within the infant organization: soothing people's outrage over homophobia while maintaining the group's focus on media. Marcia Pally concurred. When people arrived at GLAAD, she recalls, they came with urgent needs to tackle homophobia in such far-flung areas as religion, AIDS policy, and news media. Vito recognized that the organization would founder if it didn't adhere to its media-based mandate to "promote and improve public understanding of the history, achievements, and contributions of gay and lesbian people." Marcia appreciated Vito's ability to be "very, very clear about distinguishing GLAAD from other organizations, keeping his eye on the mandate, but in a way that made people feel welcome." He knew well from GAA what could happen to an organization that marginalized sectors of its membership.

He was also eager to help GLAAD attain a national profile. An early opportunity arose in exuberant street-theater protests against Buckley's tattooing proposal. Gathered before the *National Review*'s East Side offices, some GLAAD members impersonated Buckley and Hitler attempting to tattoo arms and buttocks. Others were costumed as "mad doctors trying to give people mandatory blood tests," while less animated demonstrators simply stood behind wire fencing and wore signs marking them as People with AIDS (PWAs). The ploy worked. After meeting with GLAAD and GMHC representatives, Buckley went on ABC's *Nightline* to retract his ghoulish suggestion.

Vito departed from the GLAAD party line when he deemed it too divisive or chickenhearted. Along with the majority of gay America, he erupted over *Bowers v. Hardwick* (1986), the Supreme Court decision that upheld Georgia's sodomy law and authorized states to criminalize the private sexual acts of consenting adults. To add stinging insult to injury, the decision was handed down on June 30, less than a week before New York City celebrated Liberty Weekend, which for Vito had lost all meaning. On July 4, a massive protest was held in Sheridan Square. Permits be damned, demonstrators decided to march their anger down to Battery Park, where Statue of Liberty festivities were in full swing. On behalf of GLAAD, Darrell Yates Rist cautioned the crowd not to ruin tourists' fun and prejudice them against the cause. The twenty-five hundred gay men and lesbians massed before him were in no mood for schoolmarm lectures, particularly not on behalf of straight out-of-towners. After stopping 6th Avenue traffic with a sit-in, the livid crowd surged toward the harbor to "abort the Fourth." At the water's edge, Lady Liberty looming behind him, Vito blasted the Supreme Court's sanction of bigotry and energized exhausted marchers with a stirring defense of gay and lesbian rights.

Darrell's brand of timidity, straight out of Mattachine 1965, infuriated Vito. He also didn't like the direction the organization was taking under Gregory Kolovakos, who seemed to want another NGTF, complete with governing body, mailing list, and notable absence of democracy among the membership. Vito was tired of what he considered "the fatal flaw of every group since the [gay] movement began," namely, GLAAD's insistence that its leaders give 110 percent and "starve to death for the cause." Finally, he was fed up with the infighting of Gregory, Darrell, and Marcia. Vito assailed the GLAAD officers along with the gay community at large for forgetting that "people [were] dying all around [them]." He issued a blistering reminder: "We're grief-stricken. We're politically impotent. We're besieged by bigots, crackpots, and morons."

By the summer of 1986, the six months of service that he had pledged the board had elapsed. Along with half of the organization's founders, Vito stepped down and returned to his own work.

In 1982, one year after the publication of *The Celluloid Closet*, Vito had gnashed his teeth to see Hollywood churn out five gay-themed films: *Partners*, *Deathtrap*, *Making Love*, *Personal Best*, and *Victor/Victoria*. The quality of these films varied widely, but their unprecedented confluence made the *Closet* seem instantly dated. Over the next few years, Vito recorded scads of gay killers, gay simps, and unrelenting fag and dyke jokes that indicated how little Hollywood had reconsidered its primitive view of homosexuals. An updated *Closet* was due.

Vito discovered that actors and directors in 1986 were no more eager than they had been a decade earlier to discuss gay-themed work. In fact, with AIDS paranoia rampaging through Hollywood, closet doors were more firmly locked than ever. The topic of homosexuality itself was still relegated to "the realm of gossip and innuendo," all the more so now that it was linked with a fatal illness. Many requests for interviews were either turned down or ignored, while the majority of those who agreed to speak on the record were straight. Director John Sayles described his problems finding financing for the lesbian indie *Lianna*, while Nora Ephron attempted to justify why she glossed over her protagonist's real-life bisexuality in the screenplay of *Silkwood* (1983) (296, 294). Canadian actress Helen Shaver, who played the closeted lead in *Desert Hearts* (1986), told Vito that she thought the film transcended the limitations of a coming-out story by making audiences indifferent to the characters' lesbianism (315). Don Scardino, a supporting player in *Cruising*, took the belated opportunity to criticize his film for sensationalizing homophobic violence rather than investigating its causes (259). To Vito's amazement, he landed an interview with Christopher Reeve, who professed bewilderment that any straight actor would have a problem playing a gay character (295).

When gays were willing to talk with Vito, it was often at careful remove. Actor James Coco discussed his gay roles in *Only When I Laugh* (1981) and *There Must Be a Pony* (1986) but did not mention his experiences as a closeted actor (288). Screenwriter James Kirkwood attacked the excision of a gay scene from his novel *Some Kind of Hero* when it was adapted into a Richard Pryor vehicle (1982), but made no comment on the far better-known gay characters of his book for *A Chorus Line* (1985), then being sanitized for film (288). By contrast, *Parting Glances* (1986) director Bill Sherwood was gaily effusive, explaining his determination to make films in which characters' homosexuality is "assumed," not underscored (311). Vito lionized Sherwood as much for his openness as for his richly textured, self-assured debut film.

Inspired by his work with GLAAD, Vito focused on the increasing antigay verbal and physical violence of mainstream film. In part, he blamed AIDS phobia, but he argued that the deeper cause was American resistance to increased gay visibility (249). As a result, "use of the word *faggot* ha[d] become almost mandatory" in Hollywood. After declaring examples "almost too numerous to catalogue," he provides a string of them spanning some ten pages (250–59). It also doesn't escape his notice that many films continue to portray homosexuality as a lamentable "choice," that gay bashers are still portrayed as heroes, and that heroes are practically never gay (248, 249, 258). One purveyor of the "choice" thesis was *Time* critic Richard Schickel, whose ongoing homophobia Vito doggedly tracked. He also took renewed aim at Pauline Kael for her snide putdown of the "gay" sensibility in *Rich and Famous* (1981), the directorial swan song of elderly, closeted George Cukor (254, 302, 299).

Actors' insensitivity infuriated Vito. He was particularly offended by Bette Midler's shrill warning, in *Down and Out in Beverly Hills* (1986), that Richard Dreyfuss might contract AIDS by performing mouth-to-mouth resuscitation on homeless Nick Nolte. Screening the film several months after his own diagnosis and within weeks of Jeff's death, Vito empathized with PWAs in Midler's audience who, hearing her line, would feel "even more like outcasts than they ha[d] already become at the hands of a panic-stricken, misinformed society" (256). He bewailed the "woefully limited consciousness" of the onetime Continental goddess, whom he dismissed along with the many actors who were "just willfully stupid about anything that [didn't] pertain to their own careers." Yet he made an effort to reach out to Midler when she told *Vanity Fair* that she felt guilty, in the wake of AIDS, for having helped to make bathhouse culture seem like fun. Vito dashed off a letter reminding his former friend that "it *was* fun and she should feel good about the past, present and future."

Despite Vito's righteous indignation, some friends felt that he had betrayed them in print. Director Rosa von Praunheim was "disappointed" by Vito's savaging of his early films as doctrinaire and antifeminist (204–5). Barry Sandler was bewildered. Given Vito's friendliness on the *Making Love* set, Sandler was stunned to read the *Closet*'s trashing of his film as a "timid rehash of Fifties soap operas" (272). Twenty years later, the screenwriter kindly credits Vito with a "fair assessment" of his film. In reality, the film's daring is far more impressive than Vito allowed. In 1982, no other Hollywood film approached the depiction of tender gay lovemaking, much less a happily domesticated ending for a gay protagonist.

But that was precisely Vito's point. Titling his new chapter "Taking the Game away from Hollywood," he concluded that American cinema would never offer acceptable representations of his life. Desperate not to lose mainstream dollars, Hollywood was "and will always be a chickenshit." It could only produce films "about homosexuality," not films depicting "people who happen to be gay in America and how their lives intersect with the dominant culture" (326). For any ambitious portrayal, Vito argued, one had to look past Hollywood. Contemporary foreign films were far bolder in their portrayal of gay sexuality and relationships. In contrast with *Making Love*, the unapologetic, graphic sexual adventuring of *Taxi zum Klo* (1980) and *Prick Up Your Ears*, alongside the complex exploration of racism and homophobia in *My Beautiful Laundrette* (1986), seemed to Vito the vanguard of a new gay cinema (270). By early 1986, American independent cinema was also growing up. Vito gave special mention to two landmark documentaries (*Harvey Milk*, *Before Stonewall* [1985]) that he had helped promote. *Abuse* (1983), *Buddies* (1985), *Parting Glances*, and *Desert Hearts* were narrative films with gay and lesbian protagonists whose sexuality was not posed as a plot-driving problem but rather taken for granted as part of the larger story (273–74, 314–20). Such films, Vito held, were the future of homosexuality on screen.

During the summer of 1986, while working on the *Closet* update, Vito began thinking of turning his book into a ninety-minute film for PBS. What he had in mind was a gay take on the pastiche *That's Entertainment!* (1974), compiling the most (in)famous depictions of gays and lesbians in cinema.

The logical people to bring on board were Rob Epstein, a recent Oscar recipient for *Harvey Milk*, and Adair Films's Janet Cole, who had worked with Vito on his SFAF videos. *The Celluloid Closet* film, he wrote his collaborators, should be "as show biz as possible without losing the social content which, in most cases, is implicit. If we hope to sell this to people, I think it has to be sold as entertaining first and worthwhile second." He then set to work on a proposal that, "showbiz" intentions notwithstanding, echoed *Closet* rhetoric, structure, and use of examples.

Janet and Rob grimaced. Vito's approach was too academic and angry, "bordering on a diatribe." Nobody watched movies, even on PBS, hoping to "learn." The pair softened the proposal's tone by emphasizing the "humor and hilarity" in early gay portrayals and pointing out the "comic relief" even in 1960s stereotypes. While honoring Vito's critique of homophobia, Rob and Janet attempted to broaden its appeal by likening gays' cinematic representation to that of blacks and women, other groups whom Hollywood had hardly rushed to depict fairly.

Then there were the clip problems: number, length, and cost. For his ninety-minute film, Vito proposed the use of clips from nearly one hundred movies—few lasting longer than thirty seconds each, he insisted. Yes, he knew they didn't come cheap. On average, rights cost two thousand dollars per minute. The actual figure, Vito chortled, varied per studio: "Some charge by the foot and others by the minute. Insert joke here." Major funding was needed. Vito was seasoned at traveling hat-in-hand, but doing so never got any easier. His motivation increased when Ian McKellen, the newly out, Tony Award–winning actor, agreed to narrate the film and offered the use of his name for fund-raising.

While *Closet* revisions went to press and Vito labored over the film adaptation, he received several prestigious speaking engagements. As part of Gay Pride programming in late June, he introduced *Anders als die Anderen* for WNET-TV. That fall, along with poet Manuel Ramos Otero, he was named a writer-in-residence at Columbia University's Center for American Culture Studies, where he gave a series of lectures on gay images in film, television, and journalism. He also convened a panel titled "Independent of Hollywood," in which his friends, filmmakers Artie Bressan (*Abuse, Buddies*), Jan Oxenberg (*A Comedy in Six Unnatural Acts* [1991]), and Richard Schmiechen (*The Times of Harvey Milk*), discussed their struggles to secure funding for gay and lesbian projects.

The gig he enjoyed most came during the winter of 1987. Gary Miller, director of the New York City Gay Men's Chorus (GMC), was planning his spring "Pops" concert at Lincoln Center's Avery Fisher Hall. This year's offering was to focus on the music of Hollywood, and Gary wanted a knowledgeable, charming host to place songs in historical context. His friend Vito, a rabid GMC fan since the group's founding in 1981, was the logical choice. Along with staff arranger Larry Moore, Gary conducted several meetings at Vito's apartment to select repertoire. Chain-smoking, Vito croaked out the lines of less familiar Hollywood fare—leaving the three men to realize that his talents were far better suited to the role of emcee than that of chorus member. He compiled Disney, Garland, and Marilyn Monroe montages and suggested guest artists for solo numbers: Broadway belter Sharon McNight for "Miss Celie's Blues" from *The Color Purple* (1985), Reno Sweeney alum and pal Marilyn Sokol to growl the comical "It's the Animal in Me," Jo Sullivan Loesser to coo her late husband's "Spring Will Be a Little Late This Year," and cabaret dowager Sylvia Syms to bring smoky gravitas to the Gershwins' "They All Laughed" and "How Long Has This Been Going On?" The only moment of contention arose when Vito insisted on making the evening's final guest Baby Jane Dexter. What better way to end the concert than having her crack the Fisher rafters with "Forever Young"? When Gary pointed out that the Dylan tune had not originated in a film, Vito stubbornly insisted, "All these divas we're celebrating remain 'forever young' in our memory." He won the fight. Baby Jane was in.

On the balmy evening of Sunday, March 22, Vito strutted across the Avery Fisher stage in a black tuxedo brightened by lavender bowtie and cummerbund. Out in the audience, Charlie Russo gasped, "Holy shit!" as a roaring ovation greeted his brother. It was his first indication of how beloved Vito had become within the gay community. Vito basked in the applause before announcing, "Hello, everybody. This is Mrs. Norman Maine." The crowd needed no program notes to identify Garland's *Star Is Born* curtain line. For the next three hours, Vito held twenty-five hundred spectators in the palm of his hand.

His original plan, Vito remarked, had been to present "movie songs written or performed on the screen by world-famous heterosexuals. But," he explained, "we only ended up with seventeen minutes' worth of material." The audience howled, and Vito sent the chorus into a medley of tightly arranged Oscar winners reaching back to "The Way You Look Tonight." Arnie beamed to hear the men's wistful take on one of his favorites, "It Might as Well Be Spring."

Seated next to Arnie, Larry judged Vito's presentation "funny, witty, *extremely* informative (you scarcely realized you were taking a mini-course in Hollywood and gay history) and *so* loving!" As the evening progressed, Vito made *Closet*-style pronouncements on the gay content of *Darling* (1965) and *Thunderbolt and Lightfoot* (1974) and provided buckets of backstory on the making of *Snow White*, *The Wizard of Oz*, *Yankee Doodle Dandy*, *Meet Me in St. Louis*, and *On the Town* (1949). He editorialized at length, accusing *From Here to Eternity*'s Donna Reed of stealing the 1953 Best Supporting Actress Oscar from Thelma Ritter in *Pick Up on South Street*, but saving his strongest venom for "that pig" Grace Kelly, who "snatched Judy's [*Star Is Born*] Oscar and ran off to Monaco." He provided a tribute to screen couples that plunged from earnest to campy to lethal: "Gable and Lombard; Tracy and Hepburn; [pause] Redford and Newman [laughter]; Joan Crawford and Bette Davis [laughter]; Cardinal Spellman and Gore Vidal [riotous laughter]; Mayor Koch and that guy who used to work at the Adonis Theater [hysterical laughter, mingled with 'Oooo's] —this is where I've been instructed to stop!" It's unlikely that the mayor was present for this sally.

The evening's encore was John Kander and Fred Ebb's "New York, New York," which Vito introduced by squawking, "A long time ago somebody asked Jimmy Durante to play Hamlet—he said, 'The *hell* with those small towns! I'll take New York!'" The concert ended stratospherically with two hundred male

Liza Minnellis offering a gospel-style Valentine to their city of choice. In closing, Vito saluted his "family" onstage: a "fighting, courageous, caring community" of men "who can wear little hats with veils at a Tupperware party on Fire Island on Sunday and on Monday morning go out and slay a very real dragon. You'll never know how proud I am of the faces I see with me here."

Clustered in the orchestra seats, Vito's biological family was well represented. From the stage, he blew a kiss to his ecstatic mother; sister-in-law Linda and niece Vicki vowed they would attend more gay events, for they'd never seen a shorter line for the ladies' room. The Russos' presence at the concert mattered deeply to Vito, who had long wanted his father and brother to recognize his prominence. At the same time, the "very real dragon" of his speech frayed his confidence. More than eighteen months after his diagnosis, he had only recently told Charlie that he had AIDS. His parents, though suspicious since Jeff's death a year earlier, had yet to be informed. On the night of the concert, Vito was terrified that the merciless stage lights would make him look sick or that a forgetful friend might mention his illness to Annie at intermission.

These fears were fed by ongoing sorrow. Vito had already lost Joey Foglia, the buddy who had introduced him to Fire Island twenty years earlier, as well as Richard Amsel. By late 1986, mortality reports were rolling in relentlessly. Vito's journal during these months reads like a battle scroll: "Chuck Solomon died this week, also Gordon McGregor, Michael Koonsman, Bob White, Diego Lopez. Emotionally overwhelmed. Doug Lambert dying in London. Just so much I can take. Artie Bressan seriously ill with chronic hepatitis." A week later Doug, a friend from the *Gay News* days, died, and GLAAD cofounder Gregory Kolovakos was diagnosed with HIV.

Artie Bressan's illness devastated Vito. He and Vito connected strongly over Artie's films *Abuse* and *Buddies*, but the pair had met far earlier, as gay boys sorely out of place in macho East Harlem. Now AIDS had touched Vito's childhood. It also gripped his NYU days when Adam Reilly came down with shingles. To Everett Engstrom, his mortified partner, Adam's face "looked right out of a B-movie horror film. [The shingles] just exploded—it looked like he'd been beaten with a meat cleaver on one side of his face." Eight months later, Vito spoke to Adam for the last time by phone. His voice was so faint that Vito had to strain to catch even the few words he choked out. Within a week, Adam died in a Denver hospice. In his journal, Vito mentioned only that Adam's obituary had appeared in *Variety*. The pain was becoming impossible to record.

With the exception of Jeff's, the hardest death for Vito to endure was David Summers'. At thirty-four, David had fought KS and PCP for nearly three years. To Vito, he was a model of take-charge advocacy. As his health flagged, David cofounded the People with AIDS Coalition (PWAC), got himself arrested at City Hall when trying to testify on behalf of gay rights, and addressed the Gay and Lesbian Youth of New York about safe sex. At an AIDS vigil, he awed Vito with his own self-respect as a PWA: "The assumption is that we should be ashamed of having AIDS, that we should play the victim. Well, I am not ashamed of having AIDS any more than I am of being gay. And you're looking at *one proud faggot*!"

As David weakened, his partner, Sal Licata, asked Vito to serve as speaker and pallbearer at the funeral. Vito wasn't at all sure he was up to either task. On the day of David's death, Vito developed his third KS lesion; two more followed within two weeks. Gripped with grief and terror over his own health, Vito attended the funeral with Arnie, Larry, and Jim. Arnie wept uncontrollably at the singing of "Amazing Grace" and when Vito intoned of gay men with AIDS, "We are not expendable." Vito kept control until he helped wheel David's coffin out of the church. The finality was too much to bear. He dissolved into tears.

During the mideighties, gay men groped for analogies to convey the randomness of the deaths battering them. The experience reminded some of Agatha Christie's *Ten Little Indians* (1939), in which guests stranded at a remote country house are picked off, one by one, by an unseen killer. Vito felt that he was caught in a "grisly game of musical chairs." "Everyone who's sitting is safe and those who couldn't find a seat when the music stopped are gone and never seen again. They're out of the game. The people sitting are relieved, guilty, smug, sad, all thinking 'Thank God it's not me—this time.' And then the music begins again and the fear grows." As his disease progressed, Vito's AIDS metaphors darkened. He came to feel that he was living through the Holocaust, but with an important difference: Holocaust survivors at least knew they had weathered the worst. For PWAs, "the dying continue[d] and [they didn't] know if anyone [would] survive."

Medical reality did nothing to dispel his fears. Two weeks before his triumph at Lincoln Center, Vito's T cells crashed, leaving him without a functioning immune system. His primary antiviral, ribavirin, was doing a rotten job of warding off HIV. At the hefty daily dose of 2400 mg, it also exacerbated his preexisting anemia and left him listless and irritable. When he didn't call Ron Grossman for the results of his most recent blood work, Arnie and Larry took the initiative. It was urgent that Vito know of his T-cell deficiency and begin aerosol pentamidine right away to prevent PCP. Vito took the news badly but soon reported to Ron's office for "misting." The drug left a bitter gun-metal taste that clung to the throat, tongue, lips, and mustache for a full day. Its unpleasantness aside, Vito believed that pentamidine spared him from pneumonia. The following year, he introduced his nebulizer to Australian doctors who knew of the device but had yet to see one.

In the meantime, Vito resented having to hike to Ron's office for regular misting when it was possible to dose himself at home. And as he expanded his drug regimen to include the alleged immune boosters Naltrexone and DNCB, he also resented that Ron wasn't available for unlimited consultation. From the time of his diagnosis, Vito was willing to try any drug that might help him without seriously endangering his health. In the absence of timely Food and Drug Administration (FDA) approval of AIDS drugs, patients were obliged to take chances on compounds anecdotally endorsed by doctors and other PWAs. Unfortunately, Ron's time and emotional energies were stretched to the limit. Of the first one hundred AIDS casualties in New York City, ten were his patients; of the first ten thousand deaths in the United States, he had personally treated one hundred. Losing a patient a week, Ron and his staff were "hard pressed to sustain [their] enthusiasm and not show [their] grief." He couldn't always sit with Vito to discuss the latest experimental treatment. Vito recognized Ron's burden but growled, "This is my life we're talking about and as far as I'm concerned I'm the most important patient you've got. If I didn't feel that way I'd be an idiot. And if I didn't fight to have my questions addressed in a more leisurely (!) fashion, I'd be a moron."

Desperate, Vito didn't limit his consultations to Ron. He found an invaluable resource in a new friend, Dr. Howard Grossman, who described himself as an old-fashioned "country doctor" tending to countless PWAs in Manhattan and on Fire Island. As Vito's illness progressed, he spent hours each day calling doctors out of the blue for their advice. Power, he felt, was akin to grabbing a dentist's testicles and cooing, "Now, Doc, we're not gonna hurt each other, are we?" Vito was willing to exploit that power if it meant getting informed feedback on possible treatments.

One drug that fueled considerable excitement was AL 721, an Israeli compound derived from egg yolks and thought to render cell membranes resistant to HIV. Unavailable in the United States, the drug was imported and distributed by the PWA Health Group, a new underground network that Vito joined. As a natural food substance, AL 721 posed minimal risk of toxicity. It was easily stored in ice-cube trays and could be spread over bread, like butter. But its production entailed drama, at least with Vito at the helm. During the summer of 1987, when Arnie and Larry rented a Cherry Grove cottage for their ailing friend, Vito awoke his hosts in the middle of the night with a blender's nerve-shredding shriek. Arnie tried not to mind; after all, "how could you be mad at a man when the man was trying to save his life?"

He and Larry did mind, however, when Vito's drug cocktail caused noisy flatulence for which he seldom excused himself. Larry considered such behavior a sign of depression. If so, Vito's mood was in keeping with the tone of the island that summer. The recently widowed Sal Licata reminisced about the days when gay men of the Grove "would talk about Quaaludes, cocaine and ecstasy. Today, they talk about AZT [azidothymidine], AL 721, and doctor's appointments."

The seemingly impossible had happened, Sal noted, when "a hot Uno game is discussed more than the hot muscled number on the beach."

Vito joined Arnie and Larry for some of those Uno matches at Sal's house. But he was growing aggressive toward his hosts, whose relationship and relative affluence he had begun to resent. It was hard enough being sick; it was harder still to be around healthy men with the luxury of focusing on their lovers and their apartments rather than their T cells. "What I wouldn't give," he hissed, "to have a plumbing problem in my co-op." Unable to afford the nine-thousand-dollars rent that his friends donated to raise his spirits, Vito often ignored their generosity and acted out. Trampling on Arnie's writing schedule, he invited over friends and then threatened a stormy walkout when Arnie attempted to protect his workspace. He also resorted to gallows humor ("I can't help with the dishes. I've got AIDS.") to excuse his laziness around the house. His resentment boiled over at "country-house" squires, whose blather on crockery and gardens he found insufferable in the face of the plague. When one beach bum directed him not to discuss disease at his house, Vito flew to his typewriter and slammed Grovers for their insufficient response to AIDS.

Vito's anger stemmed from escalating health concerns. For most of 1987, he fretted over a painful gum fistula, the result of a botched tooth extraction in April. When the abscess failed to heal, Vito worried that bacterial infection would further tax his immune system. He was also agonizing over whether to begin taking AZT, the first and, for years, only AIDS antiviral endorsed by the FDA. Early studies indicated that the drug stabilized the health of those who had suffered at least one bout of PCP. Its approval just six months after Jeff's death made Vito weep as he pondered the extra time his lover might have enjoyed.

At the same time, Vito knew that AZT could exacerbate KS and was not recommended for patients who had avoided PCP. And its initial trials were brutal. Vito was approached to be a guinea pig for a National Institutes of Health (NIH) trial, during which he would have a catheter implanted in his chest and be fed AZT intravenously for twelve weeks. Needle-phobic under the most benign circumstances—nurses had to restrain him bodily so that Ron could perform a simple blood test—Vito approached the prospect with dread. Jeffrey Lawrence, a doctor friend, advised him to skip the trial. With his relatively stable health, Vito could wait until AZT was available in pill form. It was fortunate that he did. Sixteen trial patients who were given a placebo rather than AZT died.

Compounding Vito's depression, the summer of 1987 was a brutal season for AIDS deaths and illness. Ridiculous Theatrical Company founder Charles Ludlam, whose writing and acting Vito much admired, died in late May. Vito's friend, San Francisco filmmaker Curt McDowell, followed in June, and New York mourned the passing of *Chorus Line* impresario Michael Bennett in early July. Three of GMHC's six cofounders—Nathan Fain, Paul Popham, and Paul

Rapoport—died within a span of two months. Soon afterward, Vito received a phone call from Bill Sherwood, who had developed AIDS. "The most promising young gay director in this country," Vito mourned. "There is no such thing as fair." That same day, Larry and Arnie kept from Vito the news that Artie Bressan had shrunk from a six-feet-two, 200-pound hulk to a 120-pound skeleton whom Larry likened to a "concentration camp corpse." Artie died at the end of July, followed four days later by Tom Doerr of GAA. Occurring in such rapid succession, the deaths left no time to grieve properly. Near the end of September, Vito joined Sal Licata, Rob Epstein, Jeffrey Friedman, and several hundred others to scatter rose petals on the chilly Pines beach. Vito clutched Sal as the two men keened over their deceased partners. Where was the meaning in so much loss? "For the first time," Vito admitted, "I considered that I could go nuts."

One man in San Francisco was working on a project that would elevate AIDS grief into art. In his backyard, former Harvey Milk aide Cleve Jones had designed a quilt panel to honor a fallen friend. Eight months later, a collection of 1,920 panels spanning the size of two football fields was unveiled on the Mall during the National March on Washington for Lesbian and Gay Rights. When Vito first heard about The NAMES Project AIDS Memorial Quilt, he smirked with Gothamite condescension. "Oh, that's a nice gesture—so California." A few months later, he finished two quilt panels that he had designed himself—one for Jeff, one for Tom Doerr—and headed for DC.

In 1979, the first national march for lesbian and gay rights had drawn seventy-nine thousand participants, Vito included. In October 1987, galvanized by AIDS grief and anger, the number swelled to somewhere between two hundred thousand (the U.S. Park Police's typically conservative estimate) and half a million (march organizers' typically exuberant estimate). With temperatures below 60 degrees, the weather wasn't ideal for those with compromised immune systems. And Vito steamed when Arnie and Larry announced their intention to join two thousand other couples at the Internal Revenue Services building for a mass "marriage" ceremony protesting antigay taxation and inheritance laws. Boyfriendless, Vito felt left out and asked his friends not to participate. But the March itself stirred him, particularly when Harvey Fierstein, in his trademark croak, congratulated the hundreds of thousands who had poured onto the Mall. "We have come out of the closets, out of the shadows, and we marched into fuckin' history!" Presidential hopeful Jesse Jackson roused the crowd by announcing, "America is a quilt made up of many patches, many pieces, many colors, many sizes, many textures—but everybody fits. Everybody counts. Everybody must have equal protection under the law in the real America!" Deafening cheers ricocheted off austere federal facades.

Jackson's "quilt" analogy tragically complemented the many memorial panels within easy view from where he stood. Over a sea of silk, sequins, ribbons, lamé, and leather floated the voices of Whoopi Goldberg, Lily Tomlin, Congresswoman Nancy Pelosi, and San Francisco's imminent mayor-elect Art Agnos, somberly tolling the names of those lost. Vito laid his two panels on the grass. Jeff's, which Baby Jane had hemmed, was topped by a sleeveless red-and-white striped shirt and contained the block-stenciled caption, "Jeff Sevcik, His Eye Is on the Sparrow, 1955–1986." Underneath Jeff's name, Vito tacked a lurching line of sparkly pink sequins that he later regretted. "Jeffrey was a perfectionist," he commented with a grin, "and I'm sure he would hate this panel."

Vito took in the vast network of panels that blanketed the Mall. As he and Arnie walked among them, Arnie reflected that it was like strolling through a graveyard where he knew all the dead. Every turn seemed to bring a new stab of pain: here was an old activist crony or an admired leader, there a former lover or Ice Palace dance partner. The two friends took copious advantage of the tissue boxes distributed over the Quilt's walking paths.

Vito left Washington determined to take better care of his physical and mental health. Five days after returning to New York, he started AZT and experienced a surge of energy—too much, in fact, as the drug turned him into a "babbling storm trooper, writing letters to everyone who [made] a false move." Still, he rejoiced to see a quick and significant drop in his viral load. For extra measure, he added Imuthiol, thought to stimulate T-cell development, to the cocktail.

Shortly after Jeff's death, Vito began supplementing occasional therapy with bereavement-group counseling. Now fighting insomnia and free-floating anxiety, he began seeing Dr. Stuart Nichols, who had written about mental-health care for PWAs during the dark days of 1982 and organized the first extra-institutional AIDS support group. Vito thought his new psychotherapist a "great man," in no small part because he prescribed Ritalin, Dalmane, Xanax, and Naprosyn to help his patient manage mood swings.

On these meds, Vito began feeling physically and mentally stronger than he had since before Jeff's death nineteen months earlier. Riding the wave, he decided that it was time to tell his parents of his illness. For one thing, he reasoned, the recent improvements in his health could be used to buffer the revelation. More urgently, two years after his diagnosis, he could not keep lying to Annie and Charles about why he couldn't come to Jersey whenever they called. He especially didn't want his mother to guess the truth by seeing the visible signs of his illness. To cushion the blow, he enlisted Charlie and Linda, cousin Perky and her husband Joey, and niece Vicki, now a college sophomore and old enough to help contain some of her grandmother's anxiety. One week before Thanksgiving, Vito collected Perky in Queens and drove her to Lodi to share the announcement.

Annie got suspicious from the moment her usually chatty son and niece entered the house silently. Eventually she asked Vito point blank, "Did you come here to tell me that you're sick?" He admitted as much and tried to tell her about his diagnosis, but she could only blurt "I don't want to hear it!" over and over. To her repeated questions as to whether he was going to die, he refused to sugarcoat the answer: "I hope not." Yet to Vito's surprise, there was little ranting and raving. Both Annie and Charles cried a bit, but that was the extent of their emotion. Charles held his son's hands and told him they would get through the crisis together. After her initial refusal to hear the truth, Annie quietly asked, "Do you know why I'm not hysterical? I suspected this all along and I was just wondering when you were going to decide to tell us." Charlie slipped his brother a twenty and turned back to the football game on television. And the evening carried on like any other on Blueridge Road: family gossip, raucous laughter, and bottom-less bowls of pasta. Vito left nonplussed. His mother's nonreaction stunned him. On their way back to Queens, he asked Perky, "Do you think she didn't care?"

The question was disingenuous. If anything, Annie cared too much. The news dealt her an emotional blow from which she never recovered. The next day she ran to Charlie and Linda's house, where she fell to pieces, insisting, "He doesn't have a chance! He's gonna die!" Vito was often less than patient with his mother's tendency to panic. When she attacked family members whom she deemed insufficiently supportive of her son, he privately accused her of turning his illness "into a forum for her mean-spirited sarcasm." His tolerance waned with his illness, particularly around holidays, when he felt that his "crazy hyster-ical mother" should "really be in a straight jacket, preferably in a nice institution far away from *me*." Certainly there was no way he'd be fulfilling her dearest wish, that he move back to Lodi so she could take care of him. Vito's acid response: "I'd rather die in New York than live in New Jersey." That Annie was losing not only her son but her best friend, her window on the world of travel, art, and all things glamorous, seemed not to occur to Vito. He was already too absorbed in the activism that would occupy the rest of his life.

Vito and Larry Kramer had never been friends. Eleven years older than Vito, Larry traveled in far more affluent, far less political circles. In the early 1970s, as GAA was gathering steam, Larry returned to America from a decade in Lon-don, where he had worked for Columbia Pictures and earned an Oscar nomina-tion for his screenplay of *Women in Love* (1970). He summered with the Fire Island A-list and looked down his nose at gay activists, whom he considered "loud-mouths, the unkempt, the dirty and unwashed, men in leather or dresses, fat women with greasy, slicked-back ducktail hairdos. Another world." The closest he came to GAA was an occasional Firehouse dance.

Larry met Vito in 1978 on the set of *Emerald City*, where Vito interviewed him about his novel *Faggots*. The book's portrayal of New York gay men as shallow sex fanatics incapable of emotional commitment enraged many readers. Craig Rodwell refused to sell the novel at the Oscar Wilde Memorial Bookshop. In

Manhattan and on Fire Island, friends cut Larry dead. Vito was baffled by these reactions. While he disagreed with the book's condemnation of promiscuity, he admired its attack on a community that took beau monde revelry entirely too seriously. If Andrew Holleran's *Dancer from the Dance* lent gays all the doomed grandeur of the Fitzgeralds, *Faggots* painted them as the waterfront brawlers of *Min and Bill* (1930).

Vito and Larry did not connect over their considerable knowledge of film. Unimpressed by old Hollywood, Larry seldom attended Vito's film nights. They came together instead over their hair-trigger outrage at homophobia and AIDS injustice. As Vito joked, "Lar, we're both cranky and angry. Nobody understands that cranky and angry for us is the same as big tits for Jane Russell, or Judy singing 'Over the Rainbow.'" The anger that cemented their friendship was inspired by GMHC, the organization begun in Larry's living room in 1982 and from which he resigned in disgust in 1983.

Larry had long criticized GMHC as hopelessly bureaucratized and overrun by social workers trained to deal with daily crises, not political strategy. In early 1987, he declared war on executive director Richard Dunne for allowing GMHC to lapse into a "funeral home" that cared for the dying but did nothing to help the living. When would it start agitating for citywide safe-sex education or the release of affordable AIDS drugs? Larry insisted that GMHC stop sweating over its tax-exempt status and establish a department dedicated exclusively to advocacy, protests, and civil disobedience.

When GMHC failed to respond to these suggestions, Vito sent a long letter to the *Native*, arguing, "[I don't need GMHC to] make out my will, teach me how to die with dignity, or tell me where I can buy a shade of Max Factor that will hide lesions if they develop." Vito honored the heroism of volunteers who tended the dying, but he screamed for GMHC to find its anger. By 1987, a decade of respectable, bureaucratic gay politicking had allowed thirty-two thousand people— ten thousand of them in New York City—to develop a fatal illness. Vito urged GMHC to "take a chance on offending someone, somewhere, sometime" by raising its voice to governmental institutions that were allowing thousands to die by not facilitating drug research. To remain silent in the face of such negligence was unconscionable. In parting shot, Vito raged, "We're exhausted and we're threatened with death, darlings. Where the hell are you? Waiting on line to get into the new Bette Midler movie? Get your asses into the streets."

Hundreds were ready to join him there. On Tuesday, March 10, 1987, Larry phoned dozens of gay politicos and media mavens. Andy Humm of the Coalition for Lesbian and Gay Rights received one of the calls. Nora Ephron, Larry informed him, had just canceled her speaking engagement at the Lesbian and Gay Community Center. Larry was taking her place and instructed Andy to appear. When Andy protested that he'd heard Larry speak the previous week,

Larry bellowed back, "You just fucking *be* there!" before slamming down the receiver. Andy obeyed. So did some 250 others, including Vito, Arnie, and Larry Mass.

After announcing the current number of AIDS cases, Larry Kramer directed two-thirds of the audience to rise. "At the rate we are going, you could be dead in less than five years," he told those standing. In Arnie's comparison, Larry was turning himself into Puritan minister Jonathan Edwards, who terrorized congregants by comparing them to spiders dangling by the frailest threads over perdition. When, Larry demanded, would the gay and lesbian community flex its political muscle and *force* the NIH to stop giving placebos to so many drug-trial patients, *force* the FDA to approve such possibly helpful drugs as ribavirin and AL 721? When would the government get the message that gays were "willing to be guinea pigs" and test promising medications? "Give us the fucking drugs!" Larry shouted.

Community outrage had finally found a voice. Two nights later, Vito returned to the center with 350 people calling themselves the "AIDS Coalition." Over several passionate hours, they debated how to gain maximum media attention. Some suggested stopping newspaper delivery trucks or blockading television network offices. Others advocated cutting off Manhattan altogether from the boroughs and New Jersey. Vito recommended that demonstrators buy a bunch of old wrecks, drive them to the bridges and tunnels, and abandon them. Traffic snarl for days. Priceless publicity.

The group wasn't ready for such ambitious insurrection, but it did endorse the possibility of shutting down Wall Street. At the world's financial nerve center, the demo would rivet the media while publicizing the dizzying price tag (ten thousand dollars) that pharmaceutical company Burroughs Wellcome had slapped on a yearly supply of AZT. Plans were made to disrupt business-as-usual on the morning of Tuesday, March 24, 1987. In the meantime, the group received its official name from social worker Steve Bohrer: AIDS Coalition to Unleash Power (ACT UP). The new, nongay name was in keeping with an organization that, though heavily populated by gay white men, determined to reach other communities affected by AIDS: blacks, Hispanics, Haitians, prostitutes. The name also emphasized the group's commitment to challenge authority with theatrical flair.

Less than a week before ACT UP's first demo, Vito wasn't sure he could trek down to Wall Street. With his T cells evaporating, crowds presented a risk, as did sitting on the cold concrete of lower Broadway. The GMC concert two days earlier provided him with inadvertent inspiration. Larry Kramer had asked Vito to promote the demo and ACT UP from the stage. When Gary Miller, feeling that a concert was an unseemly occasion for politicking, refused to allow any announcement or the distribution of flyers in the theater, Vito tried to change his mind.

Gary stood firm. On the afternoon of the concert, Larry called him to make a final entreaty. When Gary tried to explain his refusal, Larry barked, "Then you'll just have to take responsibility for all the members of your chorus who are going to die" and hung up. Though Vito wouldn't have phrased it so harshly, he understood Larry's urgency. He attended the Wall Street demo in full voice.

At a bitter 7:55 a.m. on March 24, Vito sat in the middle of Broadway with Arnie, who was busy "cursing the earliness of it all." Around them swarmed signs proclaiming AZT "The Great Pacifier" and querying President Reagan, who had yet to mention AIDS publicly, "Your Son Is Gay: Aren't You Worried about Him?" Others carried oversized dollar bills stamped with George Washington's likeness on one side and the slogan "Fuck Your Profiteering" on the other. Reams of AIDS facts sheets and copies of Larry's recent *New York Times* op-ed piece, "The FDA's Callous Response to AIDS," were distributed to spectators. Before the gates of Trinity Church, ACT UP hung an effigy of FDA commissioner Frank Young, donated by Joseph Papp of the Public Theater, where *The Normal Heart* had debuted two years earlier.

When the demo wrapped, protesters chorused to onlookers, "This is just the beginning!" They were right. ACT UP had just begun a decade of the world's most visible, imaginative, and controversial AIDS activism. In May, the group selected a slogan that perfectly epitomized its philosophy: "Silence=Death." The Gran Fury art collective poised these iconic words in white capital letters against a black background and under a pink triangle, the symbol that Nazis forced homosexual men to wear in concentration camps. This stark image began appearing on shirts and signs around the country.

Vito found the merchandising of ACT UP grimly hilarious. What was next, "Silence=Death" coffee mugs? But he admired the group's ability to convey its message so economically. Plus anyone paying the slightest attention knew that ACT UP's Monday night meetings at the Lesbian and Gay Community Center were the principal source for updates on AIDS drugs and policies. Vito attributed his survival to the Treatment and Data Committee's weekend "Teach-Ins," which anyone could attend for tutorials on drug developments.

ACT UP's core membership, in David B. Feinberg's pungent summation, was comprised of "three hundred rabid activists, politically correct lesbos, muscle-bound homos, demented radicals, fervent idealists, commie symps, pinko fags, concerned straights, and cynical queers both male and female." This spirited crew spearheaded a return to the in-your-face, zap-happy activism that GAA had launched some seventeen years earlier. ACT UP meetings reminded Vito of GAA's—often to a wearying degree. While GAA had relied on *Robert's Rules of Order* to prevent showboating, ACT UP declared such procedure too bureaucratic. It adopted a modified set of guidelines by which a pair of rotating moderators presided over each week's meeting. Frequent moderator Ann

Northrup recalls "some very minor, basic rules" about the length and quality of contributions from the floor, but generally, moderators tried to refrain from "actually controlling [the conversation] or trying to be too intrusive." This free-form process, she asserts, "seemed always to produce brilliant results. I always felt that we came to the right decision through the process of completely open, uncensored discussion. True democracy in action."

Vito didn't always agree with this assessment. At forty-one, he was nearly twenty years older than many ACT UP members who considered him an "*éminence grise*" from a prehistoric era of activism. Furious and terrified about their own serostatus, these youngsters often expressed their opinions with a shrillness that Vito found difficult to endure. Before ACT UP was a year old, he cautioned himself to "pay more attention to the toll [the group took] on [him] in mental and physical stress." Angry kids weren't the sole contributors to his elevated heart rate. In the wake of GLAAD, Vito felt "disheartened when [he saw] messianic frauds like [Darrell Yates] Rist making all sorts of grandstand speeches with no humanity or true compassion to back it up." If Rist was an example of new gay leaders, Vito wrote in his journal, then "[s]ave me from leaders and save me from ever being seen as one."

Though younger activists often looked to Vito as a mentor, it wasn't a role he actively sought at meetings. Sometimes arguments reached a crazed pitch, as when members debated the pros and cons of splattering Santa Claus with blood on national television during the Macy's Thanksgiving Day Parade. Swamped by such rhetoric, Vito often remained silent. He stood in the back of the packed room listening, his arms filled with demo and drug literature spilling from tables near the entrance. When he did speak up, it was to insist that ACT UP focus on its original goal: getting drugs into bodies as quickly as possible. Competing agendas invited his wrath. When some members castigated the room for not supporting the homeless PWAs of Tompkins Square Park, Vito exploded. "I'm into saving my friends' lives. I don't want every moron who ever lived rushing into an ACT UP meeting and saying, 'The issues today *are*—and if you don't follow us, you are betraying your brothers and sisters.' This is crap; I've heard this for 25 years."

Vito began saving his energies for the Media Committee (MC), whose meetings he often hosted at his apartment. Like Vito, MC members came with extensive media experience. David Corkery had been a producer of *Good Morning America*; Scott Robbe had worked for Lifetime; Michelangelo Signorile was a rising star on the Manhattan gossip circuit; Bob Rafsky was a whiz at Howard J. Rubenstein Associates (Donald Trump's PR agency); and Jay Blotcher had cut his teeth on *Our Time* and the *Native*. Not only were these guys media savvy, they were also great fun, the sort who lingered at Vito's for a screening of *All about Eve* or who squired him on all-night tours of the Rawhide and the Spike.

Though the MC was born with the goal of ensuring "consistent and accurate coverage" of ACT UP actions, it quickly expanded its horizons. For its first major action, the group targeted the *New York Times*, whose AIDS journalism MC members attacked as spotty, belated, and unnecessarily apocalyptic. In a manifesto summarizing principal criticisms, Vito faulted the *Times* for relying on FDA information and ignoring the grassroots story of PWAs tracking down drugs that were years away from governmental blessing. Reporters' responsibility, he argued, was not to verify experimental drugs' efficacy, but to inform the public about drugs that were circulating widely without FDA approval. He also demanded that the *Times* cease its "doom and gloom" reporting on AIDS, which was not as "invariably fatal" as the reportage led readers to believe. Where were stories of survivors?

To help publicize the cause, Vito turned to a new friend, GMHC volunteer Judy Peabody. A 5th Avenue philanthropist, Peabody had been involved in social causes since the late sixties, when she and her husband Samuel (brother to former Massachusetts governor Endicott Peabody) helped found Reality House, a Harlem drug rehabilitation center. Peabody adored Vito, whom she bundled in expensive scarves and whisked off to tony lunches complete with limo service. She also got the MC audience with Dr. Mathilde Krim, cofounder of the American Foundation for AIDS Research (AmFAR) and the widow of Arthur Krim, former chair of Orion Pictures. Dr. Krim had the ear of *Times* publisher Max Frankel, who declined to meet with the MC but referred the group to his science reporters about the focus of their AIDS coverage. This wasn't nearly enough for Vito, who felt that Frankel, like his reporters, simply didn't care about the suffering of PWAs. In a fury of indignation, he turned to his journal: "We are passing through the worst kind of human misery and everyone else isn't noticing. They just smile and talk about the weather while the body count mounts. It isn't happening to 'them.'"

Vito's growing sense of AIDS activists as a beleaguered "us" and everyone else as an indifferent "them" informed his most famous speech, which he delivered in Albany on the last day of ACT UP's "Nine Days of Rage" (later dubbed "Nine Days of Rain," owing to miserable weather). On May 7, 1988, still frantically drafting, he took a bus to the state capital, where the AIDS Memorial Quilt lay on display. On arrival, he nearly forgot the seriousness of his mission. ACT UP pulled in simultaneously with the Pinkster Fest, an annual spring celebration complete with Miss Tulip contestants, which made for hilarious contrast with the activists. Activist Ron Goldberg paints a vivid picture: "Out we come—leather jackets, black jeans, silence=death, and all of a sudden we're in, like, the land of gingham. There were arts and crafts booths and funnel cake. And, we're just kind of, like, walking around, like—'you know where the Quilt is?' You know. And then we get to—there was a street right before the

Quilt, and there were all these beauty queens in open convertibles . . . waving. So, our queens saw their queens." The two cultures eyed each other with wary amusement.

The laughs ended when Vito took the mike at the Capitol plaza. Because May 7 was a Saturday, he was screaming himself hoarse at an empty governmental structure—which quickly seemed a touch of poetic genius. "If I'm dying from anything," he announced to the crowd, "I'm dying from the fact that not enough rich, white, heterosexual men have gotten AIDS for anybody to give a shit." As if in answer to newspaper editors, he yelled, "Living with AIDS in this country is like living in the Twilight Zone. Living with AIDS is living through a war which is happening only to those people who are in the trenches. Every time a shell explodes, you look around and discover you've lost more of your friends. But nobody else notices. It isn't happening to them." Vito contrasted his life with those of people who needn't spend "days and nights and months and years trying to figure out how to get ahold of the latest experimental drug and which dose to take and in what combination with other drugs and where do you get it and for how much money because it isn't happening to them, so they don't give a shit." Why, he demanded, did public service announcements about AIDS target exclusively straight audiences who were forever reassured that AIDS wasn't their problem? And how could activists possibly fight for research and drugs when they were exhausted from fighting hatred and ignorance?

Suddenly a car filled with young men rounded the corner. From the windows erupted lusty screams of *"Faggots!"* Vito paused, waiting for the vehicle to speed away. "If there were more of us and less of them, AIDS wouldn't be what it is in this moment of history," he remarked before concluding his speech.

"AIDS is a test of who we are as a people. When future generations ask what we did in the war we have to be able to tell them that we were out here fighting." One day, he vowed, the crisis would be over. On that day, he intended to be standing tall and healthy, ready to "kick the shit out of this system so that this will never happen again."

The crowd went wild. What they had just witnessed was Vito at his seductive peak, the reason why, despite his anger, he was becoming known as "the kinder, gentler voice of ACT UP." The implicit comparison was to Larry Kramer, whose rage often alienated the rank and file. Vito's MC colleague Scott Robbe thought of Larry's "bad cop" as the polar opposite of Vito's "good cop." Of the two, Scott avers, "Vito was the one who was adored" by the membership. To be fair, ACT UP "mother" Maxine Wolfe remembers Larry as "really approachable" beneath his prickly exterior; he kept a listed number in the Manhattan telephone directory and quietly provided financial and emotional support to several ACT UP members. Larry himself recalls that he couldn't go to a meeting without being buttonholed by panicky members begging him for new drug information. But Larry also acknowledges that Vito "was just more beloved than [he was] and was probably able to [communicate anger] with an ability of not making other people as angry as [Larry did]." Vito tried to help him with this problem. After listening to a rough draft of a speech that Larry intended to deliver to a Human Rights Campaign Fund audience, Vito asked him, "Do you love them?" Larry answered yes. "Then you have to tell them so!"

Despite his frequent misgivings about meetings, Vito's campy personality jibed well with the ACT UP membership, which tended to be smart and show-biz obsessed. The younger men were often surprised to learn that Vito, eager for seatmates on a long bus ride, would talk with them about anything from politics to movies. Vito became Maxine's eternal fan when he heard that she'd attended Judy Garland's 1961 concert at Carnegie Hall—and when he heard her explaining to the younger guys that, yes, some lesbians loved Garland, too. Maxine shared Vito's passion for show tunes, as did Ron Goldberg, a musical-theater devotee who became known as the ACT UP "chanteuse" by setting the group's chants to melodies from *Guys and Dolls* (1951) and *Camelot* (1961). Vito, Ron, and Maxine proposed the formation of an affinity group called "Ada, Stop!" named in honor of firebrand Communist Comrade Ada, a character in Kander and Ebb's musical *Flora the Red Menace* (1965) who won't cease agitating even when court-ordered to do so.

ACT UP adopted Vito as its most charismatic Ada and asked him to repeat his Albany speech for a takeover of the FDA in October 1988. As fate would have it, Larry spent the weekend of the demo in a hospital. Vito emerged its undisputed star.

On the afternoon of Monday, October 10, Vito stood on the steps of the Health and Human Services (HHS) building in Washington, waiting to be introduced by San Francisco prostitute and AIDS activist Carol Leigh, also known as the "Scarlet Harlot" and the "Safe-Sex Slut." Radioactive in red sequined gloves, a red-feather headdress, and a star-spangled flag spanning her mighty bosom, Leigh declared herself the presiding judge for the *People's Tribunal vs. Ronald Reagan, the Administration, and Congress*. She then invited Vito to "read the charges" against the government. He stepped up to a microphone surrounded by huge black-and-white stencils of Reagan, George Bush, Jerry Falwell, Dan Quayle, and Jesse Helms, all stamped across the forehead with the verdict "Guilty" in red capital letters. Painfully thin in his Silence=Death T-shirt, Vito launched into the Albany speech with a few significant changes. "Ronald Reagan" was now "that moron who calls himself president of the United States." (He paused as chants of "Guilty, guilty!" issued from the crowd.) Vito was now besieged not only by "opportunistic infections" but also by "opportunistic politicians and crazies on the Right *and* the Left who are using AIDS to push their bullshit ideology by exploiting [*his*] *movement*!" Given the *Times*' failure to investigate

FDA claims on drug testing, Vito now targeted reporters too lazy or indifferent to do their job properly. When he finished with the promise to "kick the shit out of this system," the crowd saluted him with a deafening standing ovation. Pumping one bony arm and fist in the air, he launched his audience on the chant that had become ACT UP's rallying cry: "Act up! Fight back! Fight AIDS!" Vito gave the activists fire for their most ambitious action yet the following morning.

In contrast with the little-noticed Albany demo, the MC ensured that the FDA action received widespread coverage. The group now had sufficient cachet that Susan Sarandon dropped by in preparation for her appearance on *Good Morning America*, where she gave the FDA takeover national publicity. National Public Radio broadcast an ACT UP strategy meeting the week before the demo. Ann Northrup, a former writer for *Good Morning America* and the *CBS Morning News*, helped the MC put together glossy press kits for news media around the country. The committee also began booking speakers on talk shows throughout the United States in advance of the action. When MC chair Michelangelo Signorile turned on the national news on the morning of October 11, he saw images of the FDA bustling with security and buried behind yellow police tape, underscored by the ominous announcement, "Police in Bethesda [Maryland] are gearing up for what is expected to be the largest demonstration since the [1967] storming of the Pentagon!" Mike could hardly contain his glee. The media were parroting the MC's slogan verbatim.

In strategy meetings, a few ACT UP members discussed the logistics of getting themselves locked inside the FDA building over the weekend to examine files and memos. This proposal caught Vito in an ethical dilemma. He felt strongly that no PWA should risk the possibility of a year's incarceration in a federal facility. At the same time, he admitted, "I'm always bitching about us putting our money where our mouths are and showing that we mean business. Somebody is going to have to break the law somehow here if we're not just paper tigers." Vito decided that his own participation would have to be less athletic.

During ACT UP's daylong occupation of the FDA, activists smashed a glass entrance, scaled a marquee to hang a "Silence=Death" banner, and blocked a police bus carting prisoners to jail. Business for the day was shot. Nobody could work with screams of "Fifty-two will die today! Seize control of the FDA!" and "Get to work!" rising from the street. FDA employees stood vigil at their windows while some fifteen hundred activists swarmed before their front doors and burned a rubber effigy of Reagan, whose pants obligingly fell off. Chanting "We are the experts! Let us in!" and "History will recall, Reagan and Bush did nothing at all," the activists lay down on the street with cardboard tombstones reading "Dead from Lack of AL-721," "Dead: As a Person of Color I Was Exempt from Drug Trials," and "AZT Wasn't Enough." To the chant "Drugs for sale," some demonstrators sold tabs of dextran sulfate, available in Japan for twenty years but unauthorized in the United States, for three dollars each. Cops wearing rubber gloves were taunted with the slogan "Your gloves betray your ignorance," while those refusing to show their badges suffered the indignation of "Just call him Mary!"

While all this was going on, Vito marched in a picket line. Along with Ann Northrup and John Thomas, head of the AIDS Resource Center in Dallas, he also spent a fair amount of the day speaking to the media. Mike Signorile knew that Vito had the gift of the sound-bite: the ability to break complex information into "almost insultingly" simple, camera-ready phrases. Standing before a battery of microphones, Vito told reporters that he had come to the FDA because, as he stated simply, "I don't want to die." He went on to reference eighty untested AIDS drugs before spitting, "I'm here today because I don't want a quilt with *my* name on it to be in front of the White House next year!" His remarks were carried in print and television news programs nationally.

The Washington demos exhausted Vito. After his HHS talk, he was "good for shit for a week." Physical woes were certainly part of the problem. During the summer, he'd begun experiencing hip and leg arthritis that made climbing stairs or walking any distance difficult. Shortly before heading to DC, he discovered that his liver function factors had doubled, either as a result of illness or as a side effect of the many drugs he was taking. Hoping for the latter, he spent ten days off all meds, which generated its own anxieties. His peace of mind was destroyed at the end of October when, after returning from a weekend lecture at Yale, he discovered that he had been robbed. Burglars had bent the gates over his kitchen window, entered, and taken his VCR, CD player, Nikon camera, and Burberry raincoat. Vito no longer felt safe sleeping with his windows open—a grave problem in a New York City tenement where the heat worked overtime.

And, of course, the death toll mounted. Vito was shattered by the suicide of his ACT UP friend Steve Webb, with whom he'd been working on a *Village Voice* article about the FDA. On the surface, the handsome young Harvard graduate appeared to have everything. But the day before his death, he hinted to Vito that he was addicted to crack. Whether Vito also knew that Steve was HIV-positive is unclear. A few months later came the suicide of *Very Natural Thing* director Chris Larkin, who'd been struggling with AIDS for years. The spring and early summer also saw the deaths of two Violet Quill members, Michael Grumley and Robert Ferro, who had been a couple for twenty years. Only the previous October, Vito had walked with both men through the first Quilt display in Washington. His anger flared in May when he read Michael's *New York Times* obituary, which omitted mention of Robert. Two months later, Robert called Vito to ask if he would help him gather the pills necessary to kill himself. Vito put him off, and Robert died within a few days of PCP.

In his ragged state, Vito needed a break from ACT UP. Though he appreciated the group's irreverence, he was tiring of the screaming outside and inside meetings. In DC, he had studiously avoided speaking with ACT NOW (AIDS Coalition to Network, Organize and Win) because he had no desire for yet another series of debates on "what [their] priorities should be." And he was sick of the frequent criticism that ACT UP catered mainly to gay white men. Blacks, Vito sniped, were just as capable as whites of getting themselves to the West Village and into meetings. Claims that the gay liberation movement had traditionally been viewed as white and middle-class, or that ACT UP must bear some responsibility for its relative lack of racial and sexual diversity, made him rave. In his twenty years of activism, Vito asserted, "[I have] heard the 'gay white man' speech more times than I care to remember, and I lost my guilt over that about 20 seconds after 1969."

After several months' hiatus from ACT UP, he decided to give the group one more shot. In June 1989, the Fifth International AIDS Conference was held in Montreal. Twenty-three ACT UP members planned to attend in order to protest the never-ending delay in the release of AIDS drugs. One of the demonstrators called Vito, sheepishly confessing that the group hadn't a single PWA among its ranks. With dark amusement, Vito shot back, "What am I, the *token?*" He agreed to go, though he regretted the decision almost immediately.

Scheduled to follow Montreal with "Closet" lectures in San Francisco, Seattle, and Portland, he was already wiped out from the barrage of interviews he was giving for Stonewall 20 festivities. It was exhausting to relate the same story over and over for NBC, *Newsday*, the *Bay Area Reporter*, and the *Seattle Weekly*. Telling it also made Vito feel ancient, cut off from his young ACT UP cohorts. In Montreal, he roomed with Jay Blotcher at the Hotel Royal Rousillon. Twenty-nine and healthy, Jay was constantly on the town, determined to score with as many fellow activists as possible. Observing the younger man's energy, Vito relegated himself to the sexual trash heap. His last two stabs at romance, both with men ten years his junior, were disasters. David Sloan, a rising young executive at ABC, found Vito enchanting but like "a runaway freight train" in his neediness. Vito fared slightly better with Robert Vázquez, a Bronx-born Gran Fury artist. With their exuberant senses of humor, the two men provided each other with a welcome refuge from ACT UP angst. Robert, HIV-positive and asymptomatic, was touched by Vito's desire to protect him from his own advancing illness. But he had lost a lover to AIDS two years earlier and was, he informed Vito, not ready to suffer that pain again.

Vito couldn't dwell on disappointment. His KS was beginning to spread at a terrifying clip. In January, he had undergone seven days of radiation for a jawline lesion; weeks later, he began intralesional therapy to remove other blotches. The therapy, which entailed injection through solid tissue, was very painful.

Treated areas flattened for a time but invariably resurfaced. By the time he reached Montreal, dark patches were blooming all over Vito's body, including a small spot on the tip of his nose. Straining to stay cavalier, he wore shorts and scorned uncomfortable onlookers: "Oh, fuck 'em. If they can't stand it, it's their problem. I'm the one with the disease." But his sexual self-esteem was at its lowest ebb. Watching the young ACT UP guys at play between demos made Vito lament that he could no longer cruise bars or "expect anyone to find [him] desirable." He confessed, "I feel like it's finally over for me in that way." To Allen Sawyer, Vito cried about the lack of touch and intimacy in his life. Allen held his friend and tried to make him feel good about his body.

Vito threw himself into the conference, which opened during a weekend of international chaos. Within a forty-eight-hour period, the Ayatollah Khomeini died, a train derailment in Russia killed hundreds of people, and in Beijing's Tiananmen Square, a military assault resulted in the deaths of thousands of student protesters. In this fractious context, some twelve thousand conference participants—most of them doctors who had paid five-hundred-dollar registration fees—were appalled to see the opening ceremonies hijacked by activists from ACT UP/New York, ACT UP/Montreal, and AIDS Action NOW. As the demonstrators stormed the stage, they chanted, "They say, 'Get back'; we say, 'Fight back!'" and, to the bewildered audience, "Join us!" After declaring the conference open "on behalf of people living with AIDS in Canada and around the world," the activists read a manifesto of their demands. Their cheers shook the hall.

Vito took all this in with immense satisfaction. Leg pains didn't allow him to join his colleagues on the dais, but he felt paternal pride to witness their courage and ingenuity at making the conference their own. "Never again," Vito wrote in a mass mailing for ACT UP, "will anyone try to hold a conference on our lives and our future without incorporating people with AIDS into every level of the decision-making." During a weekend of news overload, the activists received staggering media coverage, including a prominent slot on *ABC World News Tonight*.

After this perfect opening, Vito's investment in the conference shriveled. The panels "Living with AIDS," "Close Friends and Family," and "Self-Help" offered nothing he hadn't already heard a thousand times. He resented listening to batteries of doctors and pharmaceutical agents who were "striking it rich on [his] misery." He also resented Randy Shilts's contention that demonstrators were alienating rather than educating attendees—particularly given Shilts's own tasteless joke that one could catch AIDS from a mosquito only through anal intercourse. Vito was especially nettled to hear doctors making plans for the Seventh International AIDS Conference, to take place in Florence in 1991. If they weren't so unimaginative, he snapped, AIDS "would be over by '91."

Vito was still looking for breakthrough drug information that the conference lacked. For the past twenty months, he had been taking AZT with alternating insomnia and fatigue as side effects. But he feared the drug's potential to render him anemic or damage his bone marrow. Apart from its frequent toxicity, AZT was effective only until the virus developed resistance to it. At a Montreal press conference, Vito stated that when he began taking AZT, he was informed that there would be other, more effective drugs available within two years. Now, with his AZT ride reaching its end, Vito blasted conference doctors who were cheerily predicting a breakthrough in another two years. "That's an unacceptable situation for me," he boomed, "because I'm gonna be dead before two years is up unless they come up with a new antiviral and new treatments."

As summer chilled into autumn 1989, Vito entered one of the busiest and saddest seasons of his life. In August he flew to Stockholm for a successful "Closet" lecture, all the while fighting fatigue and the certainty that he was beginning "a real decline." A week later, he discovered that he had internal candidiasis, evidence that his illness was progressing. His mood nose-dived. He felt like a pariah, albeit in grand Bette Davis, *Now, Voyager* style: "I seem to occupy a space in people's lives reserved for a kind of 'be kind to Aunt Charlotte' attitude." Having begun the '80s as London's prize catch, Vito was ending the decade as an unsexy "elder statesman," respected but never desired. For a time, he tried attending weekend PWAC "teas," designed to match up seropositive men. Tea cofounders Michael Callen and Griffin Gold were determined that PWAs not consider themselves "damaged merchandise" or "factory seconds." Vito put in dutiful appearances, but after Griffin's death at the heartbreaking age of thirty-three, Vito's enthusiasm waned. In nonstop mourning and suffering from an abysmal self-image, he didn't feel attractive enough to make the rounds.

In social and physical decline, Vito became plagued by nightmares. The worst jolted him out of sleep at 3 a.m. and sent him scrambling for his journal, in which he recorded that Ron Grossman told him that he'd exhausted all medical possibilities and the end was drawing near.

Fortunately, for the time being, Vito had plenty of work to keep his mind occupied, and money was not its usual source of anxiety. In 1987, when his annual income dropped to a bare-bones $9,400, Vito began receiving food stamps. He then received a significant boost from Mark Thompson, editor of the *Advocate*, who wanted a film reviewer with "an intensely queer, insider point of view." Mark asked whether Vito could forget his past beefs with David Goodstein (who had died of colon cancer in 1986) and pen a monthly column titled *Russo on Film*. Though he had recently criticized the *Advocate* for turning into a skin magazine devoid of news, Vito accepted. The salary was $500 per column, more than his journalism had ever earned.

In the *Advocate*, Vito proved an unexpected champion of experimental film. In 1987, when Sarah Schulman and Jim Hubbard established the Lesbian and Gay Experimental Film Festival in New York, they hesitantly approached Vito for publicity. Having read *The Celluloid Closet*, Jim felt that Vito was overly focused on gay subtext and straight representations of gay lives; he seemed never to consider "the possibility of an actual homosexual expression" that might diverge from conventional narrative or visual style. Jim was, therefore, astonished when Vito, though almost too ill to sit up, journeyed to Jim and Sarah's work studio on lower Broadway to study several hours of film, including *Assassins* (1987), Todd Haynes's first feature. The form and content couldn't have been less Vito's style, but he promoted experimental film to his readers as "eminently worth [their] time," advising them, "It's rewarding to stretch yourself a little and take a shot at learning a new way to look at images." Sarah and Jim were thrilled. Even the *Village Voice* made them jump through hoops for minimal exposure. Vito simply handed it to them on a platter, without drama. Doing so helped him ease his conscience about not analyzing experimental films in the updated *Closet*, as he had pondered doing.

While Vito was not as socially engaged as he would have liked, professionally he was booked to a crazed degree. He traveled to Washington twice in October 1989: once to serve as a reader at the Quilt, and once to give the keynote address for the National Gay and Lesbian Task Force conference. Failing health did not prevent him from offering a "Closet" lecture in Winnipeg. Nor did it keep him from four weeks of Saturday and Sunday "Closet" presentations at the Public Theater, his first New York lecture in eight years.

After so many years of expanding and refining, the lecture had mushroomed to a full three hours, prompting Karla Jay's jest that it should be retitled "The Marathon Closet." Its current length was perfect for the opening plenary session at "Outside/Inside," Yale University's third annual conference on lesbian and gay studies. Just as Vito was about to break for intermission at the conference, police entered the hall in search of lawyer Bill Dobbs, who had tacked up a series of posters from Boys with Arms Akimbo, a new gay art/activist group, featuring male and female nudes and the slogans "Sex Is" or "Just Sex." When Dobbs was arrested, Vito grabbed the hand of Beryl Normand, a friend and Yale administrative assistant, and exclaimed, "C'mon, let's block that cop car." Despite Vito's painful leg neuropathy, the pair went running out to the street and plunked themselves in traffic, where Beryl confessed to Vito her terror of what they were doing. He responded evenly, "Honey, every time I do it, I'm scared shitless." As the car containing Dobbs inched toward them, cops began swinging nightsticks and arrested nine men, including future Tony-winning actor Stephen Spinella (*Angels in America*). When the police drove off with their prisoners, Vito defiantly followed them to the precinct. One observer, a Yale gay activist who had been cowed by the cops' use of force, "saw Vito Russo striding off with the [other protesters] and his example was what [the spectator] needed" to carry him along with hundreds of demonstrators.

At the Yale conference, Vito enjoyed more than his usual share of celebrity. Two weeks earlier, he had become a media darling with the HBO debut of Rob Epstein and Jeffrey Friedman's documentary *Common Threads: Stories from the Quilt*. Vito served as one of six storytellers who narrate the experiences of loved ones represented in Quilt panels. He was now appearing regularly on television screens across the country.

At the October 1987 Quilt display in Washington, Rob and Jeffrey had stood awestruck by the ocean of memorial fabric at their feet. They determined to make a film not about the Quilt itself, but about its most compelling stories. After reviewing some three thousand letters that had arrived with panels at the NAMES Project, they narrowed their focus to narratives concerning five PWAs: three gay men, an IV drug user, and a hemophiliac child.

To Rob, the inclusion of Vito in *Common Threads* was a "no-brainer." He was not only articulate, but as a PWA who had lost a lover and many friends to the epidemic, he would register with viewers as "a gay male in the eye of the storm." Jeffrey felt that Vito brought the film a necessary "angry activist" voice. The Quilt had been attacked by ACT UP, among other sources, for making AIDS too "cozy and comfortable for Middle America." Vito could talk about his care-taking of Jeff, but he could also discuss his ever-present rage at a society that re-fused to face AIDS until it infected the general population. *Common Threads* had its antidote to coziness.

Rob and Jeffrey shot footage of Vito with Jeff's panel at the October 1988 Quilt display in Washington. They then interviewed him at length a few months later when he was serving as a Regent Professor in the University of California Santa Cruz (UCSC)'s community studies department. Nancy Stoller, his former SFAF colleague, was now a professor in the department and invited Vito to be a guest lecturer. On February 2, he spoke to one of Nancy's classes about his career in activism; he then met Rob and Jeffrey at the home of Carter Wilson, Nancy's colleague in community studies (and cowriter of the narration for both *Harvey Milk* and *Common Threads*). Mindful of his long friendship with Vito and striving for objectivity, Rob asked Jeffrey to conduct the interview. In prelimi-nary remarks, Vito mentioned the long-ago *Closet* inspiration of Willard Van Dyke, his boss at MoMA. As Vito spoke, Jeffrey noticed that the sound man was wiping his eyes. Murray Van Dyke had never realized the profound effect that his father had on Vito's life and career.

All of *Threads'* narratives follow a basic triptych structure: life before AIDS, coping with a loved one's illness, and piecing life together after his death. Ap-pearing on film nearly three years after Jeff's passing, Vito speaks calmly, often humorously, about their shared tastes in movies. When describing the diagnosis, Vito's eyes well and his voice clutches, but he finds a shred of dark humor in Jeff's fanatical belief in the color blue as a cure-all. After describing his lover's passing, Vito waxes philosophic on death, which he depicts as a "state of unconsciousness, and that is it." He continues, "Now that's very hard for me to accept. I would like to believe that consciousness is eternal, and that in some form or another, we exist. I don't think so. Intellectually, I don't buy it. I just think when you're dead, you're dead, and that's it. And that's *why* it's so important to do something while you're here." As the film cuts to footage of the FDA demo, Vito declares in voice-over his determination to "spend most of [his] time educating people, fighting, getting arrested, sitting in the street, blocking traffic to call attention to this issue." Rob and Jeffrey then use Vito's voice to close their film with hope. With the camera gazing panoramically over the Quilt at sunrise, Vito reminds viewers, "Someday this is gonna be over. Someday there's gonna be no such thing as AIDS, and people will just look back and remember that there was a terrible tragedy that we survived."

With the sequence filmed and his lectureship finished, Vito returned to New York. When he described *Common Threads* to Annie, she asked, "Oh, will it be sad?" "No, Mother," he cracked. "It'll be a musical comedy." Jokes aside, his participation in the film gave him pause. He realized that it would bring him a considerably higher profile; "knowing from experience how cruel people can be," he wasn't sure that he wanted such publicity. In September, a few weeks before *Threads'* television debut, he saw a rough cut at HBO and suffered a neck and back spasm so severe that it incapacitated him for a week. The film wasn't the problem. It was the knowledge that through it, he was emerging as "the AIDS poster boy." When one of Annie's brothers saw *Threads*, he and his wife proclaimed that Vito had embarrassed the family—"yet another example," in Vito's opinion, "of why a world filled with stupid people is too dangerous to live in." He received a more positive, if still disconcerting, response from men who'd fallen in lust with him on screen and tracked him down for sex. This wasn't how he had imagined breaking his losing streak.

Threads brought two other unexpected bonuses. In early October, HBO screened the film for members of Congress. Afterward, Vito was riding to a party with coproducer Howard Rosenman, the friend he had once scolded for "selling out" to mainstream Hollywood. By 1989, Howard had made a considerable name for himself in the film industry; he had also secured the pro bono services of Dustin Hoffman as *Threads'* narrator. Duly impressed, Vito remembered his *Celluloid Closet* film, now languishing in preproduction purgatory. In the limo, he turned to Howard and issued a solemn plea: "You're the only one that can get *Celluloid Closet* together. Would you please commit to me that you're going to do that?" Howard knew a deathbed request when he heard one. He promised.

The second bonus came two months later, on December 1, 1989, the second annual World AIDS Day. MoMA held a special screening of *Threads* attended by Elizabeth Taylor, who had contributed an introduction for the film's HBO debut in October. The Lodi teenager who had once bedecked his bedroom wall with *Cleopatra* (1963) posters now had a shot at speaking with Cleo herself. In advance of the screening, Vito spoke with his old NYU classmate John Kane, now a publicist at HBO, and begged to meet Taylor. A phone call to her publicist was all it took.

At the MoMA reception, Vito was escorted to Taylor as if to royalty. After their introduction, he produced a picture of her in full gorgon mode from *Who's Afraid of Virginia Woolf?* (1966). Summoning Martha's corrosive cackle, Vito roared, "I do not bray!" Taylor shrieked with laughter and asked whether he had a more flattering photo for her to sign. "Couldn't you have found something from *BUtterfield 8* [1960]?!" She then turned serious and led him away for a private chat. When he tried to talk movies, she cut him off and asked about his medical care. If he didn't have a good doctor, she could arrange for him to see the best. After seeing *Common Threads*, she wanted to help him in any way possible. Approximately ten minutes later, Vito emerged, profoundly moved that the queen of Hollywood had taken a personal interest in his health. From then on, one of his favorite lines was, "As I was saying yesterday to Elizabeth Taylor . . ." With moments like these, he feared dying only as an impediment to further fun.

As Vito began his final year, death barreled once more into his immediate circle. On January 2, 1990, Sal Licata died of AIDS complications in horrific circumstances. He had spent nine days on a hallway gurney at NYU Medical Center, waiting for a room to become available. Unshaven and covered in spilled food, he lay shivering in the frigid December drafts that blew through the street doors. These conditions would have been unforgivable for any seriously ill person, but they were tragic for the first director of the New York City Department of Health's AIDS Training Institute. Vito hardly knew how to react to Sal's death. "What is there to say that hasn't been said," he reflected. In any case, friends had begun withholding AIDS news from him—a sure sign, he inferred, that everyone now perceived him as a "basket case." He was also beginning to isolate himself from others with operatic flights of self-pity: "I'm wondering when I'm going to die. I wish I could just stop worrying about it all the time. After all, it's such a little thing. Horrible, painful death in the prime of my life. What's the big deal?"

For a time, Vito had toyed with the notion of writing *An Activist Life*, a full-scale autobiography. After almost twenty years of politicking, he had come "to see (and accept) that [his] life and the movement ha[d] been one and the same." As his health failed, he lacked the stamina to take on a book project, but he felt compelled to pass on his wealth of experience and insight. He received the perfect opportunity to do so when Nancy Stoller and Carter Wilson arranged to bring him back to UCSC to teach two courses, Documenting Gay Activism (DGA) and The Celluloid Closet (TCC), for the Winter 1990 quarter. At a salary of fourteen thousand dollars, the courses promised for two months' work almost as much as he had netted during the entire previous year. And the community studies department, which encouraged students to get out of the classroom and into social-change organizations, seemed ideal for Vito. Spouting his usual anti-California rants (nonsmoking houses! omnipresent vegetarianism! ludicrous AIDS "cures"! having to drive everywhere—stick shift!), he settled into the Edric, a harborside motel where he enjoyed a serene water view and his own kitchenette.

Life picked up considerably when classes began the second week of January. Vito was delighted by his DGA students, who brought some surprisingly sophisticated expectations and experiences to the course. In their opening papers, several students wrote candidly of their previous activist work and of their frequent discomfort, in as liberal a school as UCSC, when trying to discuss gay and lesbian issues in other courses. Two avowedly straight male students elected DGA to learn about a culture of which they knew nothing but were curious.

One of those men was Charles Goldman, a San Francisco–born studio art and American studies major who wanted to know more about the gay men with whom he'd grown up. In previous UCSC courses, he'd studied the civil-rights movements of women and African Americans, but never gay men, whom he called his "brothers." For many of Charles's gay classmates, DGA provided their first link to an ancestry that they scarcely knew existed. Janet Myers had always thought that being lesbian meant "playing softball and drinking Coors Light." Through readings about colonial American treatments of gays, the "invention" of homosexuality in the nineteenth century, the Mattachine Society, and Daughters of Bilitis, Vito introduced his students to a cultural history that their high schools had denied them.

For other students, the course provided considerable personal guidance. In 2002, Trev Broudy would achieve unfortunate celebrity as a film and television actor whose brutal attack by gay bashers made national headlines. In 1990, he was a tightly closeted undergraduate who had never felt comfortable talking with other gay men. More than any specific lesson taught in DGA, Trev appreciated that Vito invited him to his apartment to discuss coming out. For already out students, Vito's course provided a focus for anger. George Limperis had done his share of "we're here, we're queer" sloganeering, but Vito helped him put such rhetoric into historic context. Vito also grounded AIDS activism for his students as an outgrowth of the feminist health movement and of battles against racism and classism. He cheered when his students applied these lessons outside the classroom, staging a three-day sit-in at the campus library and forging links between gays and students of color at the UCSC, UC–Berkeley, and UC–Davis campuses.

His other course didn't begin so smoothly. While DGA's enrollment was comfortably capped at thirty students, TCC bulged to nearly two hundred. UCSC assigned Vito four teaching assistants to lead smaller discussion sections. As a visitor to academe, Vito fast lost patience with grad-student presumptuousness. When one TA took it upon herself to promise all-gay discussion sections, Vito saw red. Though he approved the idea, the decision was his to make, not a student's. He also insisted that the course's 16mm films, stored in his apartment, had to stay put. Anyone wishing to view them would have to come to the Edric. Ill and busy, Vito realized that this rule might occasion inconvenience, but he justified its enforcement: "It's too much pressure for me to worry about why you can't accommodate me. Except in extraordinary circumstances you have to. That's why you're a TA."

The TCC students raised their own problems. At the beginning of the course, Vito distributed surveys asking students which of thirty-three gay- or lesbian-themed films they had not previously seen. The responses stunned him: "Please pay close attention here. I've looked at the questionnaires you turned in[;] at first I was quite astonished by the results. More than 85 percent of the class has never seen any of the films on the list." It was no surprise that they were unfamiliar with an oldie like *Rope* or such Stonewall staples as *The Boys in the Band* and *Sunday Bloody Sunday*, which were not yet widely available on VHS. However, the questionnaire also included the recent gay hits *Victor/Victoria*, *Kiss of the Spider Woman* (1985), and *Torch Song Trilogy* (1988), all of which had played in theaters and on cable television during the students' adolescence. Where had they spent the eighties?

No matter. He was there to teach. TA Christina Waters, older and far more experienced than her colleagues, befriended Vito and discussed with him his expectations for the course. More than anything, he wanted students to realize that gay and lesbian film was "not an underground subset of 'decent' society—that [it was], in fact, an artform that has a much longer, older tradition than most people are allowed to know." Accordingly, Vito structured the course as a condensed version of his book. Each week students viewed in class a seminal film (e.g., *Mädchen in Uniform*, *Tea and Sympathy*, *Suddenly Last Summer*) supplemented by a dozen excerpts from narrative films, documentaries, cartoons, and television of the same period. Culled from Vito's private collection, most of this material represented twenty years of stealthy tracking and cataloging. Beyond titles from the *Closet*, Vito also unearthed vintage clips of Jean Genet cavorting with sailors on holiday in Marseilles. For the students, this material was revelatory. It proved to them the existence of open gay sexuality that predated activism. Appropriately, Christina remembers, "a *lot* of people came out during [the] class; it was almost like a ritual." Vito tacitly encouraged this with his passionate "outing" of celebrities (Travolta, Gere, Chamberlain) whose sexuality had long been debated.

As his courses neared completion in mid-March, Vito was desperately depleted. He sometimes began class by announcing, "It's been a tough week for me. I might just take it a little slow tonight." Swathed in scarves, bandages hiding his IV bruises, he gripped the podium and remained standing for a two-hour lecture. In his illness, after much negotiation with American Playhouse, Vito secured a 35mm print of the first studio film to deal with AIDS. At Santa Cruz's Nickelodeon Theater, his students got to see *Longtime Companion* (1990) two months before its commercial release.

Recognizing the extraordinary pains that Vito took on their behalf, his students revered their ailing professor. On the final day of the term, they crammed his classroom "with enough flowers to fill a drag queen's dressing room." Before he entered, still more roses were loaded into his arms. No, he didn't need a vase. "Fuck it, I'll carry them all." Into the hall he wafted, sailing down the aisle "like a Miss America finalist, waving and smiling to a thunder of applause, whistles and yowls of approval." It wasn't merely that Vito was a natural raconteur. He also had the gift of relating to his students as colleagues, making them feel personally invested in the course material. Thanks to Vito, Janet Myers became a sociology professor specializing in AIDS prevention. She describes him as "a Teacher with a capital T. Here was a guy who was dying, and he was teaching; [it] is one of the most profound things he could have done, to take his life's knowledge [as an activist] and give it to younger people." One of his DGA students expressed her affection in a farewell note: "I start to cry when I think of you going back to New York and never seeing you again. You would be shocked to find out how many lesbians have fallen in love with you. HA HA Again, I love you and I will miss you dearly."

Back in New York, Vito scarcely had time to unpack before hitting the road again. In short order, he flew to Dallas to introduce *Common Threads* at the USA Film Festival; a week later, he embarked on a "Closet" tour that included upstate New York, Pittsburgh, Chicago, and Olympia, Washington. He strained to conserve his energy for two upcoming events: ACT UP's massive "Storm the NIH!" demo in May, and June's Sixth International AIDS Conference in San Francisco, where he was invited to deliver a keynote speech.

While preparing for these events, Vito suffered a terrible scare on the 8th Avenue subway platform, one block from his apartment. Drenched with rainwater, he was too distracted to notice a fellow commuter who had spotted his "Silence=Death" button and was now lunging for him. Out of nowhere, Vito heard a roar: "What are you, some kind of *faggot*, you goddamn AIDS-carrying leper?! I oughtta push you on the third rail, you rotten fag sonofabitch!" As the man raised his umbrella to strike Vito, a black teenager and an elderly white woman leapt to his defense, grabbing his shoulders and steering him away from the assailant. Trembling, Vito thought, "Goddammit! Not only do I have to *have* this hideous disease, but I have to be physically attacked on the street by a *stranger* who either doesn't like my politics or is terrified by what I represent."

He fought his fear by reminding himself, "Activism has always been the answer; it's always been the solution in my life. I will never understand how people can lose friends or be sick and not *do* something." Ultimately, he felt, "you either are sad that people you love are dying and you want to do something about it, or you didn't really love them that much and you're just gonna accept that the situation is the way it is."

Unfortunately, Vito didn't get his chance to shine at the NIH or at the International AIDS Conference. On return from Santa Cruz, he entered an immunological spiral. The morning after he watched Rob and Jeffrey receive their Best Documentary Feature Oscar for *Common Threads*, Vito received a blood transfusion for escalating anemia. To prevent the necessity of regular transfusions, he began giving himself daily injections of erythropoietin, a red-cell producer. He stopped taking ddI when it began to harm his pancreas, and a few weeks later, the AZT that he had resumed for lack of any better drug brought him immediate leg pain. His medical options dwindling, Vito panicked that his T cells had dropped to such a level that "anti-virals [wouldn't] really work anymore; then I'll be in deep shit." Worse still, KS had entered his lymph nodes, necessitating chemotherapy. For the time being, Vito chose radiation instead.

His health stabilized until mid-May, when fevers, sweats, and shakes began a daily assault. The trembling became so violent that cabaret diva Morgana King interrupted her own show to ask Vito, seated in the audience, if he was all right. Alarmed by his condition, Arnie gave Vito an alcohol rubdown and helped him accept that his first inpatient hospitalization was inevitable. On June 4, 1990, with his fevers unrelenting, Vito checked into NYU Medical Center's Co-op Care, which attempted to give patients a feeling of hominess. Rooms featured a table and chairs, a private bath, and two beds. Arnie spent occasional nights there to keep his frightened friend company. At Vito's bedside was a small framed picture of himself, Arnie, and Jim from the Halley's comet cruise in 1986. It was, in Arnie's words, "our favorite family photo." But its presence offered cold comfort when Jim failed to visit. Vito didn't realize that Jim was HIV-positive as well and couldn't stand to see one of his dearest friends terminally ill.

After three days of bone marrow biopsies and gallium scans, Vito developed full-blown pneumonia and a fever of 104. Nevertheless, he had one last speaking obligation he was determined to fulfill. From the hospital, a limousine carried him, Arnie, and Larry to the Biograph Theater on West 57th Street, where the New York International Festival of Lesbian and Gay Film was mounting its opening-night celebration. Realizing that Vito would not live to see the 1991 lineup, festival organizers had invited him to be the keynote speaker. Vito based his speech on gay films of the 1980s; otherwise, he contended, "you've got *The Celluloid Closet* all over again and who needs that." The audience laughed appreciatively when Vito promised to stay focused, refraining from "showing [his] favorite scenes from Thelma Ritter movies and explaining why Barbara Nichols was the world's greatest actress, complaining that Helen Hayes stole Maureen Stapleton's Oscar for *Airport*," joking, "I know I can't get away with that tonight." His voice thin, Vito lauded the eighties gay indies and urged his listeners, for the last time, to support gay films and speak out against homophobia in art. He then departed from script to praise lesbians for their contributions to the fight against AIDS. From the epidemic's start, they had tended to the sick, helped staff organizations, and served activist duty alongside their gay brothers. Vito instructed the men present never to forget their debt to women. As he concluded, the audience rose to offer what Larry described as "prolonged, roaring, stomping, shrieking, standing ovations."

Vito's doctors were furious that he had checked himself out of NYU with pneumonia. The moment he stopped speaking—Arnie had put the kibosh on a question-and-answer session—the limo raced him back to the hospital, where he spent the next two weeks. Tests revealed that the KS had spread to his lungs and bone marrow. One week after the festival, Vito was diagnosed with his first case of PCP and began taking Bactrim intravenously. As he prepared to return home, nurses instructed him on how to administer the IV himself. Eager to provide distraction, Arnie read aloud to him from *The Lord of the Rings*. But needles were now part of Vito's daily routine. It was hard to worry about pinpricks when KS gave him horrendous foot pain and swelled his leg to twice its normal size. In agony, Vito had zero patience for Aunt Marie's remark that she was "praying to God why [he] should be punished like this for his lifestyle." And he tried not to notice that while his father was still visiting him, his mother was conspicuously absent. Annie simply couldn't bear to witness her son's decline.

Freed from the hospital, Vito enjoyed a pleasant Gay Pride day watching the march from Larry Kramer's third-story balcony. He tried to keep the day light by joking about his IV: "When I was getting the good drugs, nobody would give me one of these things to be able to hook up instantly!" From the street, hordes of black-shirted ACT UP members spied their favorite uncle above. Screams of "Vito! Vito! Vito! We love you! We love you! We love you!" rose to greet him. Mustering his strength, Vito stood and "waved like Evita" to his multitude of fans. Larry turned to him and whispered, "These are our children." That evening, in homage to Gay Pride, the Empire State Building was illuminated in lavender for the first time.

Vito's spirits plummeted when he realized that he was too sick to enjoy his favorite season. He summoned the courage to discuss his impending death with Charlie and Linda at a West Village restaurant, where Charlie could neither escape nor make a scene. Vito informed his brother that he wished to be cremated and refused to allow any kind of Catholic service. He also asked that Charlie accompany him to speak with Ron Grossman, who had promised Vito that he "wouldn't allow him to linger once the virus [began] to destroy his body and mind." Charlie tried frantically to change the subject, but Vito would not be deterred.

At other times, he was far less stoic about death. Since their breakup twelve years earlier, Vito and Bill had remained friends. With Bill living in the apartment above him, Vito could bang on his steam pipes in the middle of the night if he needed company. Occasionally Vito summoned Bill when the KS in his lungs made breathing difficult and he feared suffocation. Bill would come down and rock him until he fell asleep. At other times, Vito clanged for Bill out of depression. Once he asked him what to expect as his bodily functions successively shut down. Thinking the answer obvious, Bill replied, "Then you die"—rather than "Then the person dies." Vito screamed, "Why would you say something like that to me?" and ordered Bill out. He wasn't quite ready to face the reality of dying.

His fear of death wasn't eased by medical costs that he could ill afford. In order to qualify for Medicaid and Medicare, he had to declare bankruptcy, which left him unable to cover basic expenses. When the NYU Radiology Department attempted to collect on an outstanding bill, he warned, "Don't start dunning me because you're dealing with a person with less than $100 in the bank." Martin Duberman and Lily Tomlin both gave him generous checks in June, but the money seemed never to last.

Panicky over poverty and illness, Vito regularly lashed out. When his *Advocate* columns became sarcastic and belligerent, Mark Thompson requested that he be "a little bit more cheerful" in future writing. Vito agreed to try, though his mood was anything but. With Arnie and Larry, he indulged in some cringe-worthy humor. In the middle of summer, suspecting that he would not live until December, he put on a recording of Bing Crosby's "White Christmas" and remarked, "They should change it to 'I'm dreaming of a Christmas' and make it the new PWA song." Arnie tried to match him in a grim game of one-upmanship that appalled onlookers. When Arnie complained of a headache, Vito countered:

"I have Kaposi's sarcoma in my bone marrow."

"But I feel some nausea, too," Arnie retorted.

"I have AIDS, and I'm going to die."

"But I'm going to lose my best friend."

Arnie and Vito laughed over these outrageous exchanges. But the banter turned vicious a few weeks later when Vito took a trip to Fire Island with Arnie and Charlie. As Arnie rushed to fluff his pillows and fetch whatever he demanded, Vito taunted him about his weight and fashion sense. Socks and shirt the same color? "Nobody's done that since 1963. It's disgusting." Charlie finally exploded and asked Vito how he could be so cruel to the friend who was doing so much to help him. Arnie led Charlie out to the beach and quietly explained that Vito's rudeness meant nothing. He was only venting anger at his illness. When Arnie pledged that he would love Vito no matter how he behaved, Charlie learned a lesson in the nature of "true love and true friendship."

On July 20, Vito gave in to the inevitable and began chemotherapy. Four days later, he received an unexpected phone call. Years after her legal threats and his published accusations of insensitivity, Bette Midler invited Vito to the New York set of her new movie, *Scenes from a Mall*. Chemo or no, he wasn't about to miss this opportunity. *Scenes* was directed by Paul Mazursky, who, despite the recent homophobia of his *Moon over Parador* (1988), was responsible for Vito's beloved *Next Stop, Greenwich Village*. Midler's costar was Woody Allen, of whom Vito had been a passionate fan since *Annie Hall* (1977). On meeting Vito, Allen remarked, "Bette tells me you're ill, and you've been ill for some time. How do you do it?" Vito replied, "You make a movie every year, and I have to see it." The day also gave Vito a chance to lounge in Midler's dressing room and reconnect with an old friend from much happier times.

Side effects from chemo made such days increasingly rare. When Vito's hair thinned, Arnie shaved him bald and tried to cheer him with a pink floral cap. Fighting nausea, diarrhea, and occasional incontinence, Vito grinned and asked, "How do you always know what I want?" At the end of August, Arnie, Larry, and Jim took Vito on a motor trip through New England. A transfusion the day before departure fortified him, but exhaustion and severe leg pain quickly set in. When the crew reached Maine, Vito had to skip their tour of Acadia National Park. It was a drag to have to have his blood tested while on vacation. And he found that he needed escalating doses of Tylenol with codeine to reduce his fever and ease the aches in his legs.

Back in Manhattan, Arnie convened a team of caregivers to check on Vito several times a day. At their first meeting, Vito eavesdropped from his kitchen while baking one of his famous apple pies. Joe De Cola, partners Howard Cruse and Eddie Sedarbaum, Baby Jane Dexter, Eric Myers, Beryl Normand, Don Shewey, Maxine Wolfe, Jan Oxenberg, and a new friend, Gilda Zwerman, were the principal volunteers. Arnie's sole instructions were that Vito be left alone as little as possible and that nobody cry in his presence. Duties ranged from running errands to rubbing Vito's sore feet to simply keeping him company. Gilda received a slew of phone calls in which Vito asked, "Do you want to come over

for a movie and to complain?" She generally did; Vito's rants could be highly entertaining. Unlike some of the other volunteers, Maxine took pity on Vito's need
to smoke. In Co-op Care, he had gone so far as to run his cigarettes under water,
but those noble efforts were now in the past. He told Maxine flatly, "Look, if I
stop smoking, I'm gonna be so anxious. I'm really gonna die, so you know what?
I don't care about PCP. I'm gonna smoke." He also impressed Maxine with his
work ethic. Whenever she came to visit, no matter his physical or emotional state,
he seemed always to be writing and asking her to fetch him more typing paper.

With the help of his care team, Vito tried to hang tough through September
while battling anxieties over becoming "just" a sick person whose endless courses
of painful radiation and chemo would ultimately fail. Arnie once entered Vito's
apartment to find him lying huddled in the dark as Jeff used to, terrified of
death. For as long as possible, Vito tried to derive pleasure from ordinary sights:
a sunset, a flight of birds across the twilight sky, the bronze glint of the sun striking the Empire State Building on an autumn afternoon. But natural beauty
could only lift his spirits so far. On an October weekend trip to Jed Mattes's
home in Philmont, New York, Vito barely noticed the pyrotechnic fall foliage.
One month earlier, he'd been crushed when his friend, artist Mark Mutchnik,
elected to stop all AIDS drugs and die. Now he was strongly considering the
same course. "What's the point of going on?" he asked. "This isn't living."

On October 27, Vito's temperature once again spiked to 104. Arnie spent the
night with him. The following morning, accompanied by Charlie, Larry, Don
Shewey, and Eric Myers, he took Vito back to NYU Medical Center. As the cab
pulled up to the hospital entrance, Vito leaned his head out the window and
shouted, "This *sucks*!" Later, while struggling for breath in the emergency room,
he watched as a young mugging victim came screaming through the door. Vito
turned to Jed, who had rushed to the hospital as soon as he learned of Vito's dire
condition, and remarked, "It breaks your heart, doesn't it?" "Yes," thought Jed,
looking at Vito. "It breaks my heart."

Arnie arranged for Vito to have companions around the clock. During his
first few days in the hospital, it didn't seem that he would need company for
long. On October 29 and 30, he could barely move or speak. For two days and
nights, he could neither eat nor sleep; breathing became impossible unless he
sat straight up, leaving him "gasping like a fish out of water the entire night."
As October turned into November, Vito's liver and kidneys threatened total
collapse, and his doctors surmised that his colon was now invaded by KS or
cytomegalovirus. He suffered a hypoglycemic seizure that turned him blue and
nearly stopped his breathing.

Then came a surprise grace period. Through the intervention of David
Kirby, who had worked for Mayor David Dinkins while Dinkins was Manhattan
borough president, Vito got a private room with a panoramic view of the East

River lit by harvest moon. Reminded of *Moonstruck* (1987), Vicki Russo smiled to see New York adorn itself so opulently for her uncle's farewell. Though Vito's voice was practically gone, he could communicate (with Arnie's help) in a whisper or by writing. Visits were possible once more, and Vito morphed into Elsa Maxwell. He delighted in making sure that everyone in the room knew one another and then tried to facilitate amusing anecdotes among people who hadn't previously met. Gilda Zwerman was incredulous at a death so meticulously orchestrated: "I'd never *seen* anything like it. I had never thought a death like this existed! . . . It was really a moment in history, and [Vito] was very aware . . . that his death was a part of history." He set about ensuring his legacy by delegating future responsibilities to friends: Gilda was to contribute to the gay movement; Beryl Normand was to wear gay-friendly buttons so frightened gay students could always find her; Baby Jane Dexter was to resume her singing after a decade-long hiatus.

On November 2, the day he signed "do not resuscitate" forms," Vito had words of wisdom for visitor Mayor Dinkins. After telling Dinkins that he would have been prouder to meet no other New York City mayor besides Fiorello La-Guardia, Vito counseled him never to sacrifice his own convictions to popular opinion. After an astonished moment, the mayor promised to remember Vito's advice. Vito then grinned and confessed to cribbing his message from the musical *1776*. His room took on greater star power the following day, when Rob Epstein arrived from San Francisco and placed his *Common Threads* Oscar at Vito's bedside.

In the middle of all this frantic socializing, clashes between Vito's biological family and his gay family were brewing. Vito had already warned Charlie that the Russos would not be happy with the bequests in his will. Though he left all publishing royalties to his parents, all his furnishings, electronic equipment, books, and personal papers went to Arnie and Jim Owles. He directed that his ashes be divided in half and scattered in two portions: one on the beach at Fire Island, the other in San Francisco from atop the same hill where Jeff's had been strewn. He further instructed his friends "to terrorize [his] relatives [at his memorial service] by refusing to discuss anything but motion pictures and gay rights." When Vito's friend and lawyer, Lenny Bloom, read the will at his bedside, Charlie swallowed its contents as best he could. It hurt deeply to realize that Vito seemed to value his friends above his family.

Charlie kept control until learning that these friends had turned away relatives at Vito's hospital door. That did it. He had spent weeks watching his only brother waste away. Annie, who hadn't seen Vito in months, was being hospitalized with breathing problems that seemed less like emphysema than inexpressible grief. As Charlie tore between hospital rooms in different states, his work suffered, his marriage suffered, and he hardly had time to see his kids. Now Baby

Jane was telling his cousins they couldn't see Vito? Charlie raced off in search of Arnie, whom he considered the ringleader responsible for the situation. In his rage and grief, he unleashed a torrent of profanity, one word of which caught Arnie's attention: "cocksucker." Charlie was unaware of what he had said until Arnie threw it back at him with its homophobic connotations vividly highlighted. The two men locked in furious stalemate.

They didn't have long to fight. On November 4, Vito accepted the morphine that he knew would dull his brain and might even kill him by depressing his already compromised lungpower. He had to take these risks. The pain was unbearable.

On the drip, he enjoyed his first sleep in days. The next day, his kidney function rebounded. There seemed to be hope for at least several more days. On November 6, Judy Peabody paid for full-time nurses to relieve the exhausted care team.

Shortly after midnight on Wednesday, November 7, Jed Mattes sat at Vito's side. The attending nurse, observing her patient's declining vital signs, remarked quietly to Jed, "I think your friend is leaving."

Peacefully, in his sleep, Vito drew his last breath at 1:40 a.m.

He was forty-four years old.

Afterword

Vito often ended his *GAY* and *Advocate* columns with "Still Shots," gossipy snippets patterned after the Hollywood tabloids of his youth. In his memory, I conclude *Celluloid Activist* in the same fashion.

Hours before Vito's death, Jesse Helms was elected to his third term in the U.S. Senate. Friends joked that Vito would have been only too happy to miss the returns.

On the morning of November 7, Charlie drove to Blueridge Road to tell his parents that Vito was gone. Annie opened the door, saw her son's stricken face, and blurted, "I'll come with you to the hospital today."

The following week, the Bergen *Record* published Annie's letter to the editor. "A better son my husband and I could never find," she wrote. "I have a hole in my heart that cannot be mended." In her grief, Annie adopted Vito's political fury. "I lost the love of my life through neglect, homophobia, and hatred, from the lack of love and compassion of doctors and Jesse Helms."

Obituaries appeared in the *New York Times*, the *Los Angeles Times*, *Variety*, and gay newspapers and magazines across the United States.

Vito was cremated on November 8. The following day, Bill Johnson presided over a "Celebration of the Life and Love of Vito Anthony Russo" at the Rutherford Congregational Church in Rutherford, New Jersey. Bill, Arnie, Vicki, and Charlie offered tributes. Arnie wore a button that read "I Love Vito." Annie's proclaimed "Silence=Death."

At his home in Los Angeles, Craig Zadan hosted a massive memorial for Vito's Hollywood friends. Shortly before Vito's death, Craig asked him why he had never pushed him toward gay activism as he had so many others. Vito smiled and replied that Craig would contribute in his own way and time. With producing partner Neil Meron, Craig went on to helm the lesbian and gay-themed television movies *Serving in Silence: The Margarethe Cammermeyer Story* (1995), *What Makes a Family* (2001), and *Wedding Wars* (2006). He took on these films for Vito. "I made them because he would be proud of me."

Shortly after dawn on December 2, 1990, several of Vito's friends climbed to a hilltop above the Castro to scatter his ashes where Jeffrey's had vanished nearly five years earlier. They then strolled down to the Castro Theatre, where hundreds were gathered for a memorial service organized by Rob Epstein and Frameline director Michael Lumpkin. Eloquent eulogies from Nancy Stoller and Joe Brewer cushioned campy clips from *The Killing of Sister George* and *Caged.* Mourners saw Vito with Bette Midler at the 1973 Gay Pride Gala in Washington Square, and with Lily Tomlin, à la Mrs. Beasley, in *Our Time* clips. Thelma Ritter honked through a *Pick Up on South Street* monologue, Judy Garland soared "Over the Rainbow," and, in a tribute to Jeff, Ethel Waters cooed "His Eye Is on the Sparrow." As directed in Vito's will, Baby Jane Dexter sang Phil Ochs's mournful "When I'm Gone" before slamming "Forever Young" through the far balcony wall—into which Allen Sawyer and Jeffrey Friedman had stashed a small portion of Vito's ashes so that he could watch movies in perpetuity.

At the Castro, Baby Jane was flabbergasted to be approached by Bhavo Michael (Bruce Parker), whom she hadn't seen since his break-up with Vito fourteen years earlier. The pair reminisced about their departed friend and old times. Baby Jane didn't realize that Bhavo also had AIDS. After battling the illness for over fifteen years, he died of lung cancer on September 15, 2000.

Vito's New York memorial took place on Thursday, December 20, at Cooper Union's Great Hall. Arnie served as emcee on the same stage that had been trod by Presidents Lincoln, Grant, Cleveland, Roosevelt (Theodore), Taft, and Wilson. Vito had attended and inspired many an ACT UP meeting there. The capacity audience witnessed much of the same program that had played at the Castro—with one key exception. Larry Kramer took the stage to scream, "We killed Vito. As sure as any virus killed him, we killed him. Everyone in this room killed him. Twenty-five million [gay men and lesbians] outside this room killed him." No one, he argued, had done enough to fight an epidemic that would never have happened had gays and lesbians been more insistent about their rights.

Reaction to Larry's screed was (and remains) sharply divided. Many people present, who had been fighting AIDS since its earliest days, felt attacked. They had devoted their lives to agitating for research, more drugs, education, better care for the sick. How dare Larry accuse them of "killing" Vito? (There are also those who insist that Larry said, "*You* killed Vito," not "*We* killed Vito," as in the speech's published version.) In addition, Vito's aggrieved family sat at Larry's feet; it was in unspeakable taste that he had included them in his roster of murderers.

But Larry also had his defenders. The speech was exactly what everyone expected from him: an in-your-face, over-the-top shriek that contained at least a kernel of truth. More than one person present has remarked that while *they* hated the speech, they were sure *Vito* would have loved it. Larry himself claims that he discussed the eulogy with Vito shortly before his death. Livid at those who weren't actively fighting AIDS, Vito approved Larry's tribute to him.

On the day of the New York memorial, Beryl Normand strolled down Christopher Street past the Oscar Wilde Memorial Bookshop. On an adjacent wall, someone had spray painted "VITO" in six-foot letters. She realized that the gay community "had lost one of their elders, one of their great tribal leaders."

In September 1991, Arnie took the ferry from Sayville, Long Island, out to Fire Island. Along with Larry Mass, Jim Owles, Charlie, and other Russo and Salerno relatives, he scattered a portion of Vito's ashes into the surf. He has not returned to Fire Island since.

Early in 1992, Jim descended into dementia. Toxoplasmosis ravaged his brain, leaving him paranoid and delusional. Arnie watched helplessly as his other best friend succumbed to AIDS on August 6, 1993. To this day, Arnie wears the gold "Lambda" ring given to Jim during his tenure as GAA's first president.

Gay Pride marches have been hard on Arnie since Vito and Jim died. At the 1994 festivities, marking Stonewall's twenty-fifth anniversary, he wailed with grief for his departed friends. In June 2009, I stood with Arnie and thousands of others on lower 5th Avenue as the deafening arrival of Dykes on Bikes announced the start of the Stonewall 40 procession. He turned to me with tears in his eyes and gestured up the avenue at the barrage of floats awaiting their turn. "I still think about the first march in 1970 and wonder what Vito and Jim would have made of all this." From behind, I slipped my arms around his chest and held him. After a moment, he relaxed and smiled.

Institutional tributes to Vito began pouring in soon after his death. In late May 1991, UCSC dedicated the "Vito Russo House," an apartment building reserved for gay, lesbian, and bisexual students. One week later, New York's Lesbian and Gay Community Center inaugurated the Pat Parker/Vito Russo Library, the nation's first gay lending library. That June, the New York International Festival of Lesbian and Gay Film was dedicated in Vito's memory, and in 1994, Los Angeles held the Vito Russo Lesbian & Gay Film Festival. In 1999, GLAAD instituted the Vito Russo Award, given annually to a figure who has excelled in battling homophobia. Recipients have included performers RuPaul, Nathan Lane, Rosie O'Donnell, Cherry Jones, Alan Cumming, and Cynthia Nixon, photographer David LaChapelle, fashion designer Tom Ford, and financial whiz Suze Orman.

Vito's family has honored his legacy as well. Nephew Charlie began college at UCSC, where his first class met in Oakes 105—the very room where Vito taught The Celluloid Closet. Niece Leslie became a writer and eventually ended up on the staff of *Glamour* magazine, where she founded the film series "Reel Moments." Each year, readers submit stories about women's lives; three entries are adapted into short films directed by the likes of Gwyneth Paltrow, Demi Moore, and Jennifer Aniston. Annie always said that Leslie would follow in Uncle Vito's footsteps.

For years, Vito's most important legacy seemed in danger of oblivion. Without funding, the film version of *Celluloid Closet* languished. Following the success of *Common Threads*, Rob Epstein and Jeffrey Friedman were able to secure backing from Channel Four in England, followed by ZDF in Germany, Hugh Hefner, and, finally, HBO. But they knew that the cost of clip rights could run into the millions, far greater than any amount they could hope to raise. They turned to Howard Rosenman for help.

Howard was friendly with studio heads all over Hollywood. Reeling with AIDS grief, he was furious that money problems might prevent Vito's lifework from reaching the screen. He charged into Sid Sheinberg's office at Universal and explained the project. "I said to him, 'I need these clips and I need them for nothing.' And he just said, 'OK, they're yours.'" Mike Medavoy of Orion and Tri-Star Pictures quickly jumped on board, as did Ned Tanen at Paramount. Only Samuel Goldwyn balked when Howard asked for clips from *Hans Christian Andersen* (1952), shrilly proclaiming of the film's star, "My friend Danny Kaye was not gay!"

Times had changed since the seventies, when only a few actors would consent to speak with Vito. In a more progressive era, and with the impetus of Rob's two

Oscars and Howard's industry clout, stars were now much more willing to discuss playing gays or lesbians on film. Tony Curtis, Harvey Fierstein, Whoopi Goldberg, Farley Granger, Harry Hamlin, Tom Hanks, and Susan Sarandon all signed on, as did writers Jay Presson Allen (*Cabaret*), Quentin Crisp, Mart Crowley, Richard Dyer, Armistead Maupin, Paul Rudnick (*Jeffrey* [1995]), and Gore Vidal. Shirley MacLaine—to whom Vito penned his last published lines in a plea for an interview—finally consented to discuss *The Children's Hour*. Cher agreed to talk about *Silkwood* but never showed up. Barbra Streisand refused the invitation altogether. Charlton Heston, approached for permission to use his image as Michelangelo in *The Agony and the Ecstasy* (1965), had a meltdown. To Howard, he grandly and rather oddly proclaimed that he "knew Buonaroti; he was *not* gay." To Rob and Jeffrey, Heston sent a more specific argument: he "knew for a fact" that Michelangelo "wasn't a homosexual but only a misanthrope who cared about nothing but carving marble." The letter still hangs framed on Rob and Jeffrey's office wall. Determined to hang the "pretentious motherfucker," Howard secured homoerotic clips from Heston's Oscar-winning performance in *Ben-Hur* (1959), their overripe subtext acidly elucidated by screenwriter Gore Vidal.

With clips and interviews in place, Rob and Jeffrey hired Armistead Maupin to write the film's narration, which drew on the book's structure and examples but omitted much of its anger. The process went smoothly until the directors began pursuing Lily Tomlin to narrate. Armistead reeled at the irony of naming a star who hadn't declared her lesbianism *The Celluloid Closet*'s official voice. Lily had her own misgivings. She agreed with Armistead that she wasn't "out enough" for the project, and she thought her voice totally wrong: "I narrate horribly. I mean, I become absolutely Detroit. It's so flat and unattractive." But in Vito's memory, she lent her name and her talents to the film.

Armistead went after Lily in Michael Musto's *Village Voice* column and ended up being barred from the opening-night party at the Castro Theatre.

Lily came out in 2000.

When *The Celluloid Closet* premiered in 1995, it attracted its share of criticism. Yes, the film was funny, infuriating, heartbreaking—just like the book—but it was also too Hollywood-focused, too big-budget-obsessed, just like the book. It dropped a nod to New Queer Cinema (*Poison* [1991], *Swoon* [1992], *The Living End* [1992]), but for the most part, it was confined to major studio releases, up through *Philadelphia* (1993). What about experimental film? What about Vito's anger? For that matter, what about Vito himself? Many who remembered his lectures couldn't accept the idea of watching his clips without his voice to string them together.

On the night of October 13, the New York Film Festival audience at Lincoln Center seemed not to share these reservations. Cheers drowned out Rob and Jeffrey as they summarized Vito's career. Before the screening began, the directors brought up the house lights, pointed at the box where the Russos were seated, and announced that it was Annie's seventy-third birthday.

The audience erupted in screams of appreciation. Annie lost her balance as the throng shouted up at her, "Thank you for giving us Vito!"

When the film ended, the Russos slowly made their way downstairs and out to the streets where Annie had roamed as a girl. The echoes of k.d. lang's "Secret Love," played over the closing credits, remained with Vito's mother long after she left the theater.

Notes

Introduction

3   plastered across the first page: Blotcher, "Who in the World Is Vito Russo?" 28.

4   "one of the epicenters of communication in the gay world": Picano, "Imitation of Life," 19.

    "His fans rushed to him": Kramer, Kantrowitz, and Mass, "Remembering Vito Russo," 51.

    "an adoring . . . First Lady [in his presence]": Kantrowitz interview, 5 July 2007.

    starved for "stars" and role models: Kantrowitz interview, 7 August 2006.

    "With Vito, I saw it all the time": Mass interview, 9 August 2006.

5   "You know Vito Russo?": qtd. in Kantrowitz, "Gays in/at the Movies," 22.

Chapter 1. Birth of a New Yorker

6   "from Sicilian thighs": Arnie Kantrowitz, letter to Vito Russo, 8 April 1980, Arnie Kantrowitz Papers.

7   her oldest brothers and sisters: Tramontozzi interview.

    cross for her signature: Tramontozzi interview.

    more careful in future employment: Tramontozzi interview.

    "a chicken in the house and a queen outside": qtd. in Tramontozzi interview.

    while she toiled in the kitchen: Tramontozzi interview.

8   "Grandma called it 'chumbroth'": qtd. in Tozzi, *I Already Am*, 16.

    "I would have enjoyed myself a little bit more": qtd. in Tramontozzi interview.

    "The angels are coming": qtd. in Tozzi, *I Already Am*, 213.

    Annie's moves were attracting attention: Charles Russo interview, 19 October 2007.

    with zoot-suited Angelo (Charles) Russo: Tramontozzi interview.

    on May 21, 1916: Anne Russo, letter to Robert Russo, undated, courtesy of Robert Russo.

    muted by comparison: Charles Russo interview, 18 July 2008.

    work as a stonemason: Charles Russo interview, 18 July 2008.

9   obliged Italians to worship in the basement: Sharman, *Tenants of East Harlem*, 23, 46.

    to work for starvation wages: C. Bell, *Images of America*, 7–8.

    on nearby Pleasant Avenue: Charles Russo interview, 21 November 2008.

    begin supporting his family: Charles Russo interview, 19 October 2007.

    causing his headaches: Charles Russo interview, 21 November 2008.

    targeted with canes: Charles Russo interview, 30 November 2007.

    "I'll Be Seeing You": Antonellis interview.

    "not a dry eye in the house": Tozzi, *I Already Am*, 127.

    St. Matthew's Church one block south: Sally "Anna" Romanello interview.

9   at the nearby Democratic Club: Tramontozzi interview.
     their renditions of popular steps: Sally "Anna" Romanello interview.
10   so that army planes could land safely: Charles Russo interview, 19 October 2007.
     "it had the eyes and everything formed": Tramontozzi interview.
     second child in little over a year: Tramontozzi interview.
     while gossiping with her neighbors: Charles Russo interview, 21 November 2008.
11   "He was too easy": Charles Russo interview, 21 November 2008.
     72 later in the day: *New York Times*, 12 July 1946, 1.
     "[Office of Price Administration, which had ceased operation July 1]": Grutzner,
     "Buyers' Strikes Spreading."
12   lake swimming, and decent food: Coffin, letter to the editor.
     Annie could relax: All narrative relating to Vito's infancy and toddler days is taken from a
     baby book kept by Annie Russo.
13   "Here comes Vito!": Marinaro interview.
     "consume the whole conversation": Antonellis interview.
     He didn't budge for two days: A. Russo, baby book.
     a stick and a piece of wire: Vito Russo interview with Stoller, 2 October 1989.
     pinochle and blackjack: Charles Russo interview, 19 October 2007.
     turn in his own father: Vito Russo interview with Stoller, 2 October 1989.
     "I beat the SHIT out of that woman": qtd. in Tozzi, "Who Is Vito Russo?"
     grounded trains: Antonellis interview.
     sports arena: Charles Russo interview, 21 November 2008.
14   "an amazing, amazing little boy": Antonellis interview.
     clamored over the radio waves: Charles Russo, interviewed in *Vito's Legacy*.
     "a magical time that none of us wanted to have end": Charles Russo memoir.
     beaten for organizing the journey: Charles Russo interview, 19 October 2007.
     where he most wanted to be: Antonellis interview.
15   German artillery in World War II: Charles Russo interview, 21 November 2008.
     all his free time in theaters: A. Russo, baby book.
     "the same movie over and over again": Price, "Coming-Out of Homosexuality."
     an aversion to natural light: remarks for New York City Gay Men's Chorus, "The Movie!"
     Concert, 22 March 1987, Avery Fisher Hall, Lincoln Center for the Performing Arts, Vito
     Russo Papers.
     "I wasn't allowed to go to the movies for a month": V. Russo, "Water in Your Eye."
     "But for a horror movie, I'd go anywhere": Vito Russo interview with Cohen.
16   that a pod doppelgänger wouldn't claim his life: Charles Russo interview, 19 October
     2007.
     that would obsess Vito for the rest of his life: Miller, "Ultimate Movie Lover," 27.
     busy humming "Sophisticated Lady": V. Russo, "Romance on the Range," 21.
     his exasperated father put a stop to it: "Overheard at Julius's."
     George M. Cohan tunes right alongside his brother: Charles Russo interview, 19 October
     2007.
     courting of a new lover: Vito Russo, letter to Bill Johnson, 10 January 1977. Unless other-
     wise noted, all Russo to Johnson letters courtesy of Bill Johnson.
     among her many hated groups: Margolin, "How Films Portray Homosexuals."
     "the greatest performance I'd ever seen": V. Russo, "Baghdad by the Sea," 2.
17   "that I couldn't put my finger on": Vito Russo interview with Cohen.
     pelted them with oil cans: Charles Russo interview, 19 October 2007.

17   cackly imitation ringing in her ear: Antonellis interview.
      "[such] was the entertainment" for the Russos during the 1950s: Charles Russo interview,
      19 October 2007.
18   pulsating soundtrack of fifties pop: Charles Russo interview, 21 November 2008.
      "'Can I please have a chocolate ice cream cone?'": Charles Russo memoir.
      to comfort his wounded client: Charles Russo memoir.
      "he loves it and didn't even miss me": A. Russo, baby book.
      "frequently seem[ed] unhappy": Vito Russo, kindergarten records, Mount Carmel-Holy
      Rosary School, courtesy of Andrea Arce, director of development.
      kept him home and crotchety: Charles Russo, e-mail to Schiavi.
19   twenty-eight dollars per month: Charles Russo interview, 21 November 2008.
      "to teach the world about Catholicism": qtd. in Vito Russo interview with Berkowitz.
      to walk his little brother home: Charles Russo memoir.
20   "Look, here come the Girl Scouts": qtd. in Charles Russo interview, 19 October 2007;
      Charles Russo memoir.
      starting to obsess Vito: Vito Russo interview with Cohen.
      their attacks on Vito: Charles Russo interview, 19 October 2007.
21   served as neighborhood anchors: Sharman, *Tenants of East Harlem*, 29.
      streets became known as "Little Italy": C. Bell, *Images of America*, 8.
      "a piece of the real action in life": V. Russo, "Entertainment."
      "went away to college," the family called it: Charles Russo interview, 30 November 2007.
      or would they all have been killed?: Charles Russo interview, 19 October 2007.
      construction work with his brother Tony: Charles Russo interview, 18 July 2008.
22   not to report what had happened to their father: Charles Russo memoir.
      directly into the Russos' apartment: Charles Russo interview, 21 November 2008.
      the craziness of East Harlem: Vito Russo, letter to Bill Johnson, 22 December 1976.
      the boys' play space increased as well: Charles Russo interview, 21 November 2008.
      Puerto Ricans began arriving en masse: C. Bell, *Images of America*, 8.
23   "Laundromat, bar, and church": Webber, *Flying over 96th Street*, 105.
      "Moody from 100th Street": Webber, *Flying over 96th Street*, 107, 106.
      in the eleven-to-twelve-year-old set: Charles Russo interviews, 19 October and 30 November
      2007.
      "enthusiastic responses to telling scenes": Peter Capra, letter to Vito Russo, 29 March
      1960, courtesy of Charles Russo.
24   "trying to get away from bad things": Charles Russo interview, 19 October 2007.
      "he would just kind of sulk away": Charles Russo interview, 19 October 2007; "'shopping
      bags full of books'": Vito Russo interview with Stoller, 2 October 1989.
      every time such names blasted him: Charles Russo interview, 19 October 2007.
      "Oh, that's glandular": qtd. in Vito Russo interview with Cohen.
      omnipresent on nearby streets: Charles Russo interview, 21 November 2008.
25   bigotry beyond homophobia: Vito Russo interview with Stoller, 2 October 1989.
      "pick up anything near you and use it on them": Charles Russo interview, 21 November
      2008.
      instructed their sons to avoid Charlie: Charles Russo memoir.
      "This is gettin' *bad*, this neighborhood": qtd. in Charles Russo interviews, 19 October
      2007 and 21 November 2008.
      "on Long Island or in Jersey": Webber, *Flying over 96th Street*, 108.
26   to own a home in the suburbs: Charles Russo interview, 19 October 2007.

Chapter 2. Jersey Boy

27   into Jersey on a cloud: Charles Russo interview, 19 October 2007.
28   "and the people I love so well": qtd. in Tozzi, *I Already Am*, 223.
      that dream could become a reality: Charles Russo interview, 30 November 2007.
      innocently plucked flowers from their yards: Robert Russo interview.
29   to become a journalist after attending West Point: Vito Russo, school keepsake book,
      1960, courtesy of Charles Russo.
      the Sharks and Jets opening ballet sequence: "Timeline of a Legend."
      made friends and flourished academically: Sally Romanello interview.
      "without being snobbish or cynical": Toscano, *Lodi in Review, 1956–57*, 2, lines 17–24.
      Lodi Boys' Club: Toscano, *Lodi in Review, 1956–57*, 59, 77.
30   Mamie Van Doren in *Wildcat*: *Lodi Messenger*, 14 September 1961, 28 September 1961, 26
      July 1962.
      "*Ozzie and Harriet* and [*Leave It to*] *Beaver* territory": Charles Russo interview, 21 November
      2008.
      to go home: *Lodi Messenger*, 21 September 1961, 2; 28 September 1961, 1.
      "the king, MR. SINATRA": Charles Russo memoir.
      description of Russo gatherings in Lodi: Charles Russo memoir; Charles Russo inter-
      views, 19 October and 30 November 2007.
31   eclectic materials picked up on construction jobs: Charles Russo interview, 19 October
      2007.
      a unique force had entered Lodi society: Lella interview.
      13.3 percent of New Jersey's teachers lacked certification: *Lodi Messenger*, 7 November
      1963, 3.
      had also earned their masters': *Magic Casements* (Lodi High School yearbook), 1963, Lodi
      Public Library.
      in nearby West Orange: *Magic Casements*, 1964.
      for the Thanksgiving pep assembly: *Magic Casements*, 1963.
32   "Leave that guy alone": qtd. in Charles Russo interview, 21 November 2008.
      "Lots of Dumb Italians": Lella interview.
      "So I got the crap beat out of me regularly": Giles interview.
      already dominating local newspapers: Vito Russo interview with Stoller, 2 October 1989.
      carried off the field on teammates' shoulders: Charles Russo interview, 19 October 2007.
      decked out in corsages: Charles Russo interview, 21 November 2008.
      "a certain reckless hostility": Vito Russo, letter to Bill Johnson, 17 January 1977.
      "just the right mood for the right scene": V. Russo, "Drama Review."
33   "World War III": *Jefferson News*, 7 February 1964, 2, 3.
      playing a tasteless joke: Charles Russo interview, 19 October 2007.
      "When [E. F. Hutton] talks, people listen": qtd. in Giles interview.
      the fair's iconic Unisphere: Kollarik, "Near the Saddle River Waters," 7.
      tossed the case out: Charles Russo interview, 30 November 2007.
      "weekends, N.Y., vacations, and girls": *Magic Casements*, 1964.
34   "I hung on this woman's every word": Vito Russo interview with Cohen.
      also won her no points: Eller interview.
      "He was just his own person": Eller interview.
      for her senior yearbook portrait: *Magic Casements*, 1964.

34 soon exchanged class rings: Eller interview.
"gestures of Judy singing": Eller interview.
nominated for Best Original Screenplay: Eller interview.

35 claimed that they had sex: Vito Russo interview with Cohen.
she wanted the relationship to continue: Eller interview.
devastated that Lucille had dumped him: Lella interview.
"the only one in the world": Vito Russo interview with Stoller, 2 October 1989.

36 switchblade in her back pocket: Vito Russo interview with Cohen.
not quite sure of the cause: Vito Russo interview with Stoller, 2 October 1989.
where she spent the next three years: Salerno interview.
was absolutely "normal": Tozzi, *I Already Am*, 158–60, 11, 209–12.
"It's not a she; it's a he!": Vito Russo interview with Newton.

37 to sell out Carnegie Hall: Lynne Carter obituary.
a second home: Vito Russo interview with Newton.
squid and whale diorama: Vito Russo interviews with Stoller and Newton.
until the police had left: Carter, *Stonewall*, 30.
"too close to the unknown for comfort": Hudson [Hunter], "Scenic Wonders of Central Park."
feeling more cut off than ever: Vito Russo interview with Cohen.
left the order and the Catholic Church: Vito Russo, letter to Bill Johnson, 22 December 1976.

38 "pretty open-minded" for a 1960 nun: Vito Russo interview with Stoller, 2 October 1989.
what he had allegedly done to her son: Charles Russo interviews, 19 October 2007 and 18 July 2008.
after attacking the man on the street: Charles Russo interview, 18 July 2008.
"because [Vito] had sex with him": Vito Russo interview with Cohen.
"it was incredibly traumatic": Praunheim, *Army of Lovers*, 64.
"anything to do with them?": qtd. in Vito Russo interview with Cohen.

39 "couldn't believe a *word* of it": qtd. in Babuscio, "Native New Yorkers," 23.
"this was all just a guilt trip": qtd. in "Faith, Films and the Future.," 3.
"whether to express it openly": qtd. in Marcus, *Making History*, 408.
"just in time for me": Vito Russo interview with Cohen.
"none of which you should see": qtd. in Vito Russo interview with Cohen.

40 suicide sets the story in motion: *Victim*.
"okay to be gay": qtd. in Marcus, *Making History*, 408.
two men kissing on screen: Vito Russo interview with Cohen.
an undeniable erotic charge: V. Russo, "Celluloid Closet," 2nd draft, 392.
"and this is what happened to him": qtd. in Marcus, *Making History*, 407.
the boys of the LHS crowd she shared with Vito were gay: I have omitted these boys' names to protect their privacy.
"never judged [their] friends that way": Lella interview.

41 gay-themed literature with his buddies: Vito Russo interview with Stoller, 2 October 1989.
starlets who played Adler's "girls": V. Russo, "Midnight Shift," 12.
as if they were just anybody: Blauvelt interview.
"already made the decision for you": Adler, *House Is Not a Home*, 40.
"the only real friend" Adler's employees have: Adler, *House Is Not a Home*, 40, 264, 110, 230, 113.

42 lands himself a quarterback hunk: *Our Time*, episode 6, 16 March 1983.
wishing he'd been born a girl: Little, *Maybe—Tomorrow*, 5, 8, 9.
"crabs," "sixty-nine party," and "glory hole": Little, *Maybe—Tomorrow*, 140, 174.
do "what seems natural" for him: Little, *Maybe—Tomorrow*, 184, 156, 185, 190, 189.
"never forgive him he didn't care": Little, *Maybe—Tomorrow*, 283.
"such a thing as a loose man": V. Russo, "Midnight Shift," 12.
"they have confused sex for love": Marlowe, *Mr. Madam*, 12, 23.
test-driving a wide range of peers: Marlowe, *Mr. Madam*, 31, 34.
"You have a kinship": Marlowe, *Mr. Madam*, 46.

43 while dating men every other night: Marlowe, *Mr. Madam*, 134, 159.
"behaved themselves as thinking adults": Marlowe, *Mr. Madam*, 206–8.
getting into gay bars: V. Russo interview with Cohen.
an old, finned old rattletrap: Charles Russo interview, 21 November 2008.
et voilà!: Lella interview.
very different social life than that offered in Lodi: Charles Russo interview, 21 November 2008.
"You were gay": Vito Russo interview with Stoller, 2 October 1989.
"something in common with this person": qtd. in "Faith, Films and the Future," 3.
"the most outrageous drag queen in Bergen County": Vito Russo interview with Stoller, 2 October 1989.
"They couldn't hide it even if they tried": Vito Russo interview with Cohen.

44 "all that stuff you had to know in the '60s": Vito Russo interview with Newton.
"this bitch'll be teasing a bald head": qtd. in V. Russo, "Trip Back in Time."
Asbury Park Y hopped all weekend long: Marlowe, *Mr. Madam*, 167.
"Just a Gigolo" à la Dietrich: Vito Russo interview with Newton.
Robert Treat Hotel: V. Russo, "Trip Back in Time."
"I'll put your lights out": qtd. in Russo, "Trip Back in Time."
"the most amusing boys.": Dennis, *Auntie Mame*, 171.
"and they showed up in swarms": Adler, *House Is Not a Home*, 350.

45 "Oh, *great!*": Vito Russo interview with Newton.
"not be bothered by the straight world?": Vito Russo interview with Newton.
"people having a good time": Vito Russo interview with Newton.

46 the weekend had been "a revelation": Vito Russo interview with Newton.
"virtually no trouble at all": Vito Russo interview with Stoller, 2 October 1989.
collapse on the couch: Charles Russo interview, 19 October 2007.
"So?": Vito Russo interview with Stoller, 2 October 1989.

47 The room fell dead silent: Vito Russo interview with Stoller, 2 October 1989.
accessible at her trailer door: Horrigan, *Widescreen Dreams*, 91.
"We got the tuition!": qtd. in Charles Russo interview, 19 October 2007.
Vito as Inspector Goole: *Castlelight* (Fairleigh Dickinson University yearbook), 1967.

48 The Magnificent Men: *Castlelight*, 1967.
"wasn't that difficult to spot": Russo, "Still Outlaws," 16.
"'and you're talking around me'": Vito Russo interview with Berkowitz.
he knew that he was otherwise inclined: Vito Russo interview with Cohen.
during the World's Fair (April 1964–October 1965): Vito Russo interview with Cohen.
enjoy a drink with his own kind: Vito Russo interview with Stoller, 2 October 1989.

49 "capital of hippiedom," "dilapidated old fire trap," "lost souls and seedy drunks": V. Russo, "Midnight Shift," 12.

49 "you couldn't bend over . . . in any way," "'Keep those doors shut, you queers,'": qtd. in
Praunheim, *Army of Lovers*, 55–56.
more understanding than his own: Russo, "Midnight Shift," 12
"They can't prove a thing": qtd. in Vito Russo interview with Cohen.
so as not to "disgrace" them: V. Russo, "Trip Back in Time."
"'You don't love me'": qtd. in Vito Russo interview with Cohen.

50 "doing this kind of thing for the first time": Vito Russo interview with Cohen.
"Bookshop of the Homophile Movement": Duberman, *Stonewall*, 163, 164, 166.
"previously barred from public discourse": Streitmatter, *Unspeakable*, 17, 20, 26, 18.
"10 percent cause and 90 percent fun": qtd. in Clendinen and Nagourney, *Out for Good*, 23.
suffering under homophobic law: Marotta, *Politics of Homosexuality*, 19, 32.
by a margin of two to one: Eisenbach, *Gay Power*, 43.

51 "on the basis of homosexual solicitation": Carter, *Stonewall*, 53.
"and of laws concerning homosexuality": Bob Stein, letter to Dick Leitsch, 10 November
1966, Mattachine Society Papers.
requested visits as well: letters to and from Dick Leitsch, 5 July, 24 March, 6 August, and
18 August 1967, Mattachine Society Papers.
"leaves me frigid": Carl Otis Gray, letter to Dick Leitsch, 22 September 1965, Mattachine
Society Papers.
"without being subject to attack": Vito Russo interview with Stoller, 2 October 1989.
his free application of "she" and "auntie": Clendinen and Nagourney, *Out for Good*, 23.
for Leitsch to come lecture on campus: Vito Russo interview with Stoller, 2 October
1989.
on March 6, 1968: Dick Leitsch, letter to Vito Russo, 27 February 1968, Mattachine Society
Papers.
"if you push this thing,": qtd. in V. Russo, "Still Outlaws," 16.

Chapter 3. Return of the Native

52 working as a counterman and waiter: V. Russo, "Still Outlaws," 16.
"But I saved your cake for you!": Charles Russo interview, 30 November 2007.
"I don't know how I got into this family": qtd. in Denise Romanello interview.

53 "can't afford to send him": qtd. in Vito Russo interview with Stoller, 2 October 1989.
"why they were treated the way they were": Vito Russo interview with Stoller, 2 October
1989.
on *Texaco Star Theatre*: "Faith, Films, and the Future," 3.
"how things affect[ed] them personally": Vito Russo interview with Stoller, 2 October 1989.
lost in battle: Sciarra, *Lodi as I Remember It*, 61.

54 "questioned everything": Charles Russo interview, 19 October 2007; Charles Russo memoir.
"an old man with a white beard": "Faith, Films and the Future," 3.
an obviously flippant remark: Leslie Russo interview.
The Rose Tattoo: Vito Russo interview with Stoller, 2 October 1989.
Sally Rand's legendary fan dance: Robert Russo interview.
"a white sheet for a dress": Russo, "& The Village."
neatly timed exit wasn't possible: Vito Russo interview with Stoller, 2 October 1989.

55 he was Manhattan bound: Charles Russo interview, 21 November 2008.
the start of his junior year at FDU: Though Vito intended to leave home the day he
turned eighteen (11 July 1964) and often identified this birthday as his date of departure,

evidence suggests that he lived in Lodi longer than he wished. Dianne Wondra Blauvelt, the Russos' neighbor, recalls Vito's living at home for at least his first year at FDU (1964–65), and Vito indicated that he was still living at 24 Blueridge when friends "kidnapped" him for his first trip to Fire Island during the summer of 1966. Furthermore, he recalled living at 77 East Twelfth Street for two years—by which he may have meant two academic years—and in Jackson Heights, Queens, for a year and a half before taking a Chelsea apartment in the early summer of 1969. These dates lead me to the calculation that he moved back to New York near the end of summer, 1966. Blauvelt interview; Vito Russo interview with Newton; Vito Russo interview with Stoller, 2 October 1989; Dick Leitsch, letter to Vito Russo, 27 February 1968, Mattachine Society Papers.

55   "a lot of money": Vito Russo interview with Stoller, 2 October 1989.
evening's honeymoon in Manhattan: Linda Russo interview; Blauvelt interview.
"how bad the food was or the drinks or whatever": Vito Russo interview with Stoller, 2 October 1989.
"Sundays for Mama?": qtd. in V. Russo, "& The Village."

56   Mama paid up: Carter, *Stonewall*, 32, 33.
mortal terror of the word "union": V. Russo, "& The Village."
to retrieve the surplus: V. Russo, "Still Outlaws," 16; Carter, *Stonewall*, 33.
ensemble on Halloween: V. Russo, "Still Outlaws," 16.
"few actual stars of stage and screen": V. Russo, "Still Outlaws," 16.
unknown Robert De Niro playing four different roles: Highberger, *Superstar in a Housedress*, 6, 7.
"hash was hash and slingin' was slingin'!": qtd. in Vito Russo interview with Stoller, 2 October 1989.
unconvincing toupee: Giles interview.

57   "her 'new cunt'": V. Russo, "Still Outlaws," 16.
"occasional sarcasm across the lunch counter": V. Russo, "Still Outlaws," 16.
"until it was light outside again": V. Russo, "& The Village."
"Betty Grable in eyeglasses and I hated her": V. Russo, "Still Outlaws," 16.
"[he didn't] think many of [his] friends shared": Vito Russo interview with Newton.
This was [their] place in society": V. Russo, "Trip Back in Time."

58   "the highest compliment a queen could get": V. Russo, "Trip Back in Time."
asserted a masculinity that they lacked: Vito Russo interview with Berkowitz.
Theater folk and literati . . . were regulars: Vito Russo interview with Stoller, 2 October 1989.
"(Those were the days before we all became gourmet cooks)": Merla, e-mails to Schiavi.
"'What time are you going to the bar tonight?'": qtd. in Vito Russo interview with Stoller, 2 October 1989.
"gay party people at the height of the gay explosion": Vito Russo interview with Stoller, 2 October 1989.

59   "tight gay society of bar people and restaurant people": Vito Russo interview with Newton.
"people used to call Greenwich Village Trash": Vito Russo interview with Stoller, 2 October 1989.
"didn't have a political thought in [his] head": V. Russo, "Still Outlaws," 16.
"'I'm getting outta *here!*'": John Knoebel, Gay Liberation Front panel.
without speaking a word to each other: Vito Russo interview with Stoller, 2 October 1989.
she fell asleep onstage: Frank, *Judy*, 612.
rushed to a hospital: Shipman, *Judy Garland*, 498.

60   "continued to sing about bluebirds and happiness": V. Russo, "Poor Judy," 14.
      "while Judy Garland sang 'The Man That Got Away'": Vito Russo interview with Newton.
      his partner gamely carried on: Kantrowitz interview, 31 July 2007.
      either vodka or gin: Charles Russo interview, 21 November 2008.
      uninformed by personal experience: Ehrenstein interview.
      on Friday, June 27: Shipman, *Judy Garland*, 509.
      to and up Fifth Avenue: Marcus, *Making History*, 409.
      "the old Judy Garland from the MGM musicals": Vito Russo interview with Stoller, 2
      October 1989; makeup man from *The Wizard of Oz* thirty years earlier: Kaiser, *Gay
      Metropolis*, 197.
      an enormous floral rainbow tribute: Vito Russo interview with Stoller, 2 October 1989.
      Lauren Bacall and Mickey Rooney in the crowd: Frank, *Judy*, 635.
      where Vito spent many after-work hours: Vito Russo interview with Stoller, 2 October 1989.
      four days earlier: Carter, *Stonewall*, 124; tonight's customers were actually protesting:
      Duberman, *Stonewall*, 193–94.
61   "Stay away from there": qtd. in Vito Russo interview with Stoller, 2 October 1989.
      "and sheer heaven": V. Russo, "Still Outlaws," 16.
      "who made their fortunes": Duberman, *Stonewall*, 184, 181.
      scrutinized through a peephole: Carter, *Stonewall*, 67–69.
      stolen garments: J. Newton, "Remembering the Stonewall," 19.
      hepatitis outbreak among gay men in 1969: Duberman, *Stonewall*, 81, 72, 181.
      "the hottest dance bar in Greenwich Village": V. Russo, "Still Outlaws," 16.
      dance together unmolested: Duberman, *Stonewall*, 182; "like you were disgusting": qtd. in
      Carter, *Stonewall*, 84.
      under pinspots that made them feel like stars: Duberman, *Stonewall*, 189; Carter, *Stone-
      wall*, 71.
      "the best music": V. Russo, "Still Outlaws," 16; Franco Zeffirelli's *Romeo and Juliet* (1968):
      Carter, *Stonewall*, 73; Mandell, "Stonewall Legacy," 2:9; Duberman, *Stonewall*, 189.
62   "paisley bathing suits and soiled silver g-strings": V. Russo, "Still Outlaws," 16; splashed
      over their taut bodies: Carter, *Stonewall*, 113.
      "very low-class bar[s]": Vito Russo interview with Newton; could enter with little hassle:
      V. Russo, "Still Outlaws," 16.
      "Ladies and gentlemen only!": qtd. in Hudson [Hunter], "Julius'."
      the riot in progress: Vito Russo interview with Stoller, 2 October 1989.
      "whistles and cheers of a large gathering": V. Russo, "Still Outlaws," 16.
      began to march prisoners out of the bar: Carter, *Stonewall*, 141.
      as he later demurred: *Stonewall 20 Years Later*.
      "an Academy Award red carpet walk": Eisenbach, *Gay Power*, 89.
      tearing apart of Stonewall property: Carter, *Stonewall*, 139.
      "applause-meter ratings": Duberman, *Stonewall*, 195.
      "Hello there, fella!": qtd. in Carter, *Stonewall*, 145.
63   felt but never shouted: V. Russo, "Still Outlaws," 16.
      "We Shall Overcome": Carter, *Stonewall*, 147–48.
      "we [were] going to fight for it": qtd. in Carter, *Stonewall*, 149–51, 152, 155, 156, 160.
      shinnied up an elm tree: V. Russo, "Still Outlaws," 16.
      "We're the pink panthers!": Carter, *Stonewall*, 165.
      busted doors and broken windows: Duberman, *Stonewall*, 198; Carter, *Stonewall*, 168.
      ordered his men not to fire their guns: Carter, *Stonewall*, 169; "We'll shoot the first mother-
      fucker that comes through the door": qtd. in Duberman, *Stonewall*, 200.

63   backup forces at 2:55 a.m.: Duberman, *Stonewall*, 200.
      Brandishing nightsticks: Carter, *Stonewall*, 175.
64   "as soon as the Yankees reached Atlanta": V. Russo, "Still Outlaws," 16.
      "We show our pubic hair!": qtd. in Duberman, *Stonewall*, 200–201.
      "the brave few who dared act": V. Russo, "Still Outlaws," 16.
      dismissed this theory as nonsense: Praunheim, *Army of Lovers*, 59; Vito Russo interview
      with Newton; V. Russo, "Still Outlaws," 16; all contemporary gay accounts of the riots:
      Carter, *Stonewall*, 260.
      "owned lock, stock and barrel by straight people": Praunheim, *Army of Lovers*, 59.
      successive evenings' fireworks: V. Russo, "Still Outlaws," 16.
      in flaming tribute: Carter, *Stonewall*, 183, 186, 188.
65   How long could they play before getting arrested?: Vito Russo interview with Stoller, 2
      October 1989.
      "many spirited exchanges": V. Russo, "Still Outlaws," 16.
      "fag follies": Truscott, "Gay Power Comes to Sheridan Square."
      five doors west of the Stonewall: Carter, *Stonewall*, 201.
      "heard that crowd described as beautiful": Truscott, "Gay Power Comes to Sheridan
      Square," 18
      joined the *Voice* protest: Praunheim, *Army of Lovers*, 59.
      frighteningly violent climax: Carter, *Stonewall*, 202, 204.
      "Gestapo!": qtd. in Duberman, *Stonewall*, 209.
      "legs, backs, and necks": Carter, *Stonewall*, 204.
66   "The Hairpin Drop Heard around the World": qtd. in Duberman, *Stonewall*, 206.
      "the third world, the blacks, the workers": qtd. in Clendinen and Nagourney, *Out for Good*,
      23, 26, 29, 31, 32.
      where it held its meetings: Vito Russo interview with Stoller, 2 October 1989.
      "vice cop spilling my drink": V. Russo, "Still Outlaws," 16.
      a softball bat to restore order: Jay, *Tales of the Lavender Menace*, 77, 124–25.
      "listening to Latin music and drinking beer": White, *City Boy*, 83.
      a black and chrome fifties throwback: White and Willensky, *AIA Guide to New York City*, 181,
      182, 186.
67   didn't prettify the picture: Kantrowitz, "Gays in/at the Movies," 18.
      to make it habitable: Tozzi interview.
      "a few discreetly placed mousetraps": Kantrowitz, "Gays in/at the Movies," 18.
      including the bathroom: Kantrowitz, *Under the Rainbow*, 101.
      upstairs in a coma: "500 Angry Homosexuals Protest Raid," 3.
68   "at St. Vincent's immediately after the protest!": qtd. in Teal, *Gay Militants*, 118–19.
      didn't even know it existed: Kantrowitz, *Under the Rainbow*, 92.
      the lint on everyone's sweaters: Vito Russo interview with Stoller, 2 October 1989.
      a "faggot" and a "prick": qtd. in A. Bell, *Dancing the Gay Lib Blues*, 44–45.
      gored his groin and thigh: "500 Angry Homosexuals Protest Raid," 3.
      the silent vigil: Teal, *Gay Militants*, 118, 120.
      "he wouldn't have jumped": qtd. in Marcus, *Making History*, 410.
69   "House of D has got to go": qtd. in Teal, *Gay Militants*, 120.
      "in the history of the homosexual movement in this country": qtd. in "500 Angry Homo-
      sexuals Protest Raid," 3.
      "entirely new to me, and rather scary": Young, e-mail to Schiavi.
      "I don't go to meetings, leave me alone": qtd. in Praunheim, *Army of Lovers*, 60.

70 (he remained a prisoner for resisting arrest): Teal, *Gay Militants*, 117. Vinales spent over three months at St. Vincent's.

"whatever immigration problems the man might have": Leitsch, "Who Did What," 13.

ensured constant admiration: A. Bell, *Dancing the Gay Lib Blues*, 76, 77.

four blocks from Vito's apartment: Praunheim, *Army of Lovers*, 60.

Vito attended his first GAA meeting: This date requires some explanation, as Vito's estimation of when he joined GAA varied over the years. In interviews he gave in 1978 and 1980 (Cohen, Praunheim), he told the story that I have re-created here, which features a two-month gap between the Snake Pit demo and his formal response to it. In interviews from 1987 to 1989 (Newton, Marcus, Stoller), he compressed events considerably: he went to the Snake Pit demo, heard Vinales's tragic story, and joined GAA on the spot. This story makes for good drama but is not entirely credible. I am inclined to favor the earlier version for three principal reasons: (1) Vito told it eight to ten, rather than nearly twenty, years after the events under discussion and was thus likelier to remember the correct chronology; (2) the earlier version is more consistent with Vito's reluctance to join the movement after Stonewall; (3) the earlier version is supported by Arnie Kantrowitz, who did join GAA immediately after the Snake Pit demo and met Vito through Michael Morrissey a "few weeks later," after which Vito joined GAA. As detailed later in the chapter, Vito recalled that Bella Abzug spoke at his first GAA meeting; her speech occurred on May 21, 1970. Kantrowitz, "Gays in/at the Movies," 18.

weekly Thursday-night meetings: A. Bell, *Dancing the Gay Lib Blues*, 24.

71 and part of Chelsea: Ireland interview.

over 200 people came to hear Abzug: Arthur Irving [Arthur Bell], "An Interview with Our President, Jim Owles of Gay Activists Alliance," MS, 29 March 1970, Arthur Bell Papers; "Bella Abzug, Congressional Hopeful," 12.

false arrest of men detained at the Snake Pit: Arnie Kantrowitz, minutes of GAA meeting, 21 May 1970, Arnie Kantrowitz Papers.

a standing ovation: Arthur Irving [Arthur Bell], "Zapping with Carol; Hello Bella," *Gay Power*, qtd. in Teal, *Gay Militants*, 144.

declared police harassment of gays an "outrage": "Bella Abzug, Congressional Hopeful," 3.

under state sodomy laws: Kantrowitz, minutes of GAA meeting, 21 May 1970.

"an active role, an activist role": qtd. in "Bella Abzug, Congressional Hopeful, " 3.

"hooked": Vito Russo interview with Newton.

"in terms that I could understand": Vito Russo interview with Cohen.

"much, *much* more sophisticated than [he] was politically": Vito Russo interview with Stoller, 2 October 1989.

72 activists scrawled "Gay Power!": Tobin, "GAA Confronts Goldberg, Blumenthal."

"more important things to talk about than their civil liberties": qtd. in Teal, *Gay Militants*, 147.

to wait out the day: A. Bell, *Dancing the Gay Lib Blues*, 78.

(symbolizing the exchange of energy): Teal, *Gay Militants*, 152.

"quite a sight for East Fifty-sixth Street": A. Bell, *Dancing the Gay Lib Blues*, 79.

arrested for criminal trespass: Teal, *Gay Militants*, 152, 153.

holding hands in solidarity: A. Bell, *Dancing the Gay Lib Blues*, 80.

"two men in front of a fireplace, 'at home'": A. Bell, *Dancing the Gay Lib Blues*, 78.

NYU's Weinstein Hall: Teal, *Gay Militants*, 324.

while ogling go-go boys: A. Bell, *Dancing the Gay Lib Blues*, 81.

one hundred dollars on the dance: Kantrowitz, minutes of GAA meeting, 11 June 1970; *Gold Diggers of 1933*: Teal, *Gay Militants*, 323.

73   fell early in Pride Week and received scant publicity: A. Bell, *Dancing the Gay Lib Blues*, 77–8; Teal, *The Gay Militants*, 324.

"no gay would remain in the shadows [today]": Teal, *Gay Militants*, 325.

"Suzy Parker breeze": Eben Clark, letter to Arthur Bell, 28 June 1970, reprinted in A. Bell, *Dancing the Gay Lib Blues*, 83.

"I Am a Lesbian, and I Am Beautiful": Kantrowitz, *Under the Rainbow*, 107.

not a silent plea for tolerance: Eisenbach, *Gay Power*, 108.

booked for benefits the same night: Black, "Happy Birthday for Gay Liberation," 58.

slapped with disorderly conduct: Eisenbach, *Gay Power*, 110; Duberman, *Stonewall*, 277.

"don't deserve a reaction": qtd. in Teal, *Gay Militants*, 327.

grabbed by cops or other assailants: anonymous audience member, Gay Liberation Front panel.

74   "'The First Run'": Jerry Hoose, Gay Liberation Front panel.

arriving safely in Central Park: Clendinen and Nagourney, *Out for Good*, 63.

from surrounding rooftops: Carter, *Stonewall*, 253.

happy to see a few hundred people end up on Sixth Avenue: Kantrowitz, *Under the Rainbow*, 106.

Arrest at any moment seemed perfectly possible: Perry Brass, Gay Liberation Front panel.

the only space granted them on the wide boulevard: Teal, *Gay Militants*, 326. According to Arnie Kantrowitz, marchers were permitted no space on Sixth Avenue. They started out walking on the sidewalk before defiantly venturing into the street. Kantrowitz interview, 9 September 2009.

swelled the march's ranks to roughly twenty groups: Carter, *Stonewall*, 254.

"*Twice* as Good": qtd. in Teal, *Gay Militants*, 328; the Village's northern border: Gould, "Out of the Closets," 5.

"give piece a chance": qtd. in Gould, "Out of the Closets," 5.

turned a few observers pale: Teal, *Gay Militants*, 328.

"their sons and daughters in our crowd": Gould, "Out of the Closets," 5.

Streamers showered down at Twenty-second Street: Teal, *Gay Militants*, 328; last summer's cop-tease on Christopher Street: Gould, "Out of the Closets," 6.

the attacks feared back on Waverly Place: Fosburgh, "Thousands of Homosexuals," 1.

75   to float him into the park: Kantrowitz, *Under the Rainbow*, 108.

"Out of the streets and into the bushes!": qtd. in Teal, *Gay Militants*, 329.

sprawling over fifteen blocks: Fosburgh, "Thousands of Homosexuals," 1.

"hugging each other, cheering wildly, applauding": Nichols and Clarke, "Love's Coming of Age."

"who was having the time of his life": Kantrowitz, *Under the Rainbow*, 108, 109.

"Or very stoned": Gould, "Out of the Closets," 5, 6.

unbroken erotic contact for nine hours: Tobin, "World's Kissing Record Broken."

76   "an army of lovers could not fail": Praunheim, *Army of Lovers*, 60.

"TV cameras, tourists, employers, and families": Black, "Happy Birthday for Gay Liberation," 58.

Chapter 4. Birth of an Activist

77   for the next twenty years: Kantrowitz, "Gays in/at the Movies," 18.

"the Bobbsey twins of gay liberation": "Sazlova" [Jim Saslow], letter to Arnie Kantrowitz, 9 November 1990, Arnie Kantrowitz Papers.

"flying in the breeze behind his wiry body": Kantrowitz, "Remembrance of Vito Russo," 72.

77   "who had acted and sung the fantasies [Kantrowitz] had grown up on": Kantrowitz, *Under the Rainbow*, 101.

78   "high school": V. Russo, "Still Outlaws," 17; Praunheim, *Army of Lovers*, 62.
     "the right to make love with anyone, anyway, anytime": Arthur Evans, preamble, Constitution and Bylaws of the Gay Activists Alliance. I am deeply indebted to Hal Offen for lending me the original GAA documents cited in this chapter.
     "rather than theorize about change in the distant future": "The GAA Alternative," 1.
     commitment to nonviolence: preamble, Constitution and Bylaws of the Gay Activists Alliance.
     considered violence integral to political progress: Teal, *Gay Militants*, 104.
     "I could be taken care of after the revolution": qtd. in Van Gelder, "'Gay Bill of Rights' Makes Progress," 16.
     uninhibited anonymous sex: Marotta, *Politics of Homosexuality*, 141.
     first openly gay columnist: A. Bell, *Dancing the Gay Lib Blues*, 21.
     the nation's first lesbian-rights group: Eisenbach, *Gay Power*, 343.
     the anarchy that hampered GLF meetings: A. Bell, *Dancing the Gay Lib Blues*, 23.

79   teenaged Noël Coward wannabe: Steele and Ortleb, "Last Conversations of Arthur Bell," 41, 43.
     "Martha Raye and Frances Faye in *Double or Nothing!*": qtd. in Steele and Ortleb, "Last Conversations of Arthur Bell," 32; "it'll cool you right off": qtd in "Arthur Bell: Two or Three Things," 11; "cast aspersions on people": Kantrowitz interview, 5 July 2007.
     "more about Hollywood movies" than Arthur himself: Fouratt interview.
     resembled Princess Di: Russo and Bell, "Glorious Letdowns," 33.
     while his Nixon-loving parents fumed: Arthur Irving [Arthur Bell], "An Interview with Our President: Jim Owles of GAA," 29 March 1970, MS, Arthur Bell Papers.
     to a Montana base for psychiatric observation: James Owles, personal effects, Arnie Kantrowitz Papers; Tobin and Wicker, *The Gay Crusaders*, 32.
     final shove through the closet door: Kantrowitz, "Jim Owles, 1946–1993," 12.
     stashing of shoplifted steaks: Tobin and Wicker, *Gay Crusaders*, 37, 43; Kantrowitz interview, 5 July 2007.

80   smoothed over any bumps: Kantrowitz interviews, 5 and 18 July 2007.
     for audiences of up to fifteen thousand: Krotz interview, 14 June 2008.
     might recognize him and deny him work: Krotz interview, 14 July 2008.
     "And I would have done it": Krotz, e-mail to Schiavi, 9 August 2007.
     he became "obsessed" with GAA: Krotz interview, 14 June 2008.

81   he attended weekly GAA meetings in silence: Vito Russo interview with Stoller, 2 October 1989.
     a transvestite on litter, Cleopatra-style, down Lexington Avenue: Kantrowitz, minutes of GAA meetings, 16 July 1970, 30 July 1970, 13 August 1970, 22 July 1970.
     membership cards that read Gay "Activist," rather than "Activist*s*," Alliance: Evans, e-mail to Schiavi.
     Encouraged by Arthur Evans: Hudson [Hunter], *Gay Insider USA*, 468; "held hands and embraced as lovers and friends": Kantrowitz, *Under the Rainbow*, 102
     with a passionate liplock: Charles Russo interview, 19 October 2007.
     and exited with Jim: Arnie Kantrowitz, minutes of GAA meeting, 22 August 1970; Teal, *Gay Militants*, 144.
     "just to begin to make ourselves and our issues visible": Vito Russo, classroom lecture, University of California Santa Cruz (UCSC), 2 February 1989, courtesy of Nancy Stoller.

81 "an odd mixture of dead earnestness and high camp": Clendinen and Nagourney, *Out for Good*, 66.
82 inside a circle of protesters: Krotz interview, 17 November 2008.
held her and her husband captive: V. Russo, UCSC lecture.
reeling into an adjacent wall: A. Bell, *Dancing the Gay Lib Blues*, 130; Clendinen and Nagourney, *Out for Good*, 68.
"smile plastered on his face the entire time": Krotz interview, 17 November 2008; joined GAA in the chanting: A. Bell, *Dancing the Gay Lib Blues*, 130.
"at the expense of the city's homosexual community": Nichols and Clarke, editorial, 31 December 1969.
"we needed to go after [it]": Vito Russo interview with Stoller, 17 October 1989.
83 "lived out as part of the pain of the earth": Epstein, "Homo/Hetero," 37, 40, 42, 43, 49, 50, 51.
"very connected to his own balls": Skir, "Breakfast at Harper's," 10.
in response to Epstein's: A. Bell, *Dancing the Gay Lib Blues*, 132.
published in the November issue: Kantrowitz, minutes of GAA meeting, 24 September 1970.
"a living, breathing homosexual": A. Bell, *Dancing the Gay Lib Blues*, 132.
words of actual homosexuals: Eisenbach, *Gay Power*, 148.
plates of donuts and bagels: V. Russo, UCSC lecture.
Israeli cookies and a quart of milk: Skir, "Breakfast at Harper's," 1.
sympathetic to its argument: A. Bell, *Dancing the Gay Lib Blues*, 134.
an army of New York Press was summoned: Skir, "Breakfast at Harper's," 10; V. Russo, UCSC lecture.
"political and social rights for homosexuals": Skir, "Breakfast at Harper's," 10.
84 torched the office: Tobin and Wicker, *Gay Crusaders*, 192.
"open channels to the gay community": Kantrowitz, minutes of GAA meeting, 29 October 1970.
sending GAA information to anyone requesting it: Kantrowitz, minutes of GAA meeting, 29 October 1970.
"apt subjects for a painting depicting Dante's Inferno": qtd. in V. Russo, I'll Take Manhattan, 9.
"Bedroom Busybody of the Week": "5 Arrested in GAA Zap."
"natural" and "unnatural" sexual acts: Wandel, "5 Arrested in Gay Teacher Dispute."
the Fidelifacts "quack-in": Marotta, *Politics of Homosexuality*, 206.
"he probably is a duck": Fisher, *Gay Mystique*, 145.
85 "Sex Life Exposé $12.50": Richard C. Wandel, photograph accompanying Fisher, "Fidelifacts."
"'the cat who won't cop out when there's danger all about'": qtd. in Eisenbach, *Gay Power*, 165.
refused to talk to GAA: Fisher, *Gay Mystique*, 146.
"We don't handle *your* business": qtd. in Fisher, "Fidelifacts."
local TV camera recorded the assault: Fisher, *Gay Mystique*, 145.
to ensure maximum media attention: Vito Russo interview with Stoller, 17 October 1989; V. Russo, UCSC lecture.
"so far as a straight person can understand homosexuality?": Vincent Gillen, letter to Jim Owles, 19 January 1971, reel 3, GAA Papers. .
buying arrest records from the police: "Fidelifacts Pres. Charged with Bribes."

85   at his Church of the Beloved Disciple: Fisher, "Gay Couples Celebrate Engagement," 1.

86   dramatized in the film *Dog Day Afternoon* (1975): Kantrowitz, *Under the Rainbow*, 124.

"a piece of cake at our engagement party": qtd. in interview with Marc Rubin, p. 10, tape 139, Testing the Limits, International Gay Information Center.

"mass cake consumption resumed": Fisher, "Gay Couples Celebrate Engagement," 14.

"[Marriage] wasn't even an option": Krotz interview, 17 November 2008.

"Vito's gregarious personality": Krotz, e-mail to Schiavi, 29 July 2007.

Steve felt like one of the family: Krotz interview, 14 June 2008.

the courage to come out and never look back: Vito Russo interview with Cohen.

87   the other "uncles" he brought to Lodi: Vicki Russo interview; Leslie Russo interview; Charles Russo Jr., interview.

"Vito's your son, too": Tramontozzi interview.

Charles often left the room: Kantrowitz interview, 5 July 2007.

all the Russo family gatherings: Charles Russo interviews, 19 October and 30 November 2007.

401's front door remained unlocked: Krotz interviews, 14 June and July 14 2008.

"Would you change that at all?": qtd. in Arthur Bell, untitled MS, December 1970, box 93, Arthur Bell Papers.

nominate himself for secretary: Krotz interview, 14 July 2008.

nominate him for the vice presidency: Kantrowitz, *Under the Rainbow*, 129.

88   for the presidency: Kantrowitz, minutes of GAA meeting, 17 December 1970.

and *Pink Narcissus* (1971): Praunheim, *Army of Lovers*, 63.

"wonderful crackpots": qtd. in Waters, "In Vito Veritas," *Pacific*, 53.

the first university course in experimental film: Kane interview; Guide to the George Amberg and Robert Gessner Papers 1913–1978.

among Vito's classmates: Kane interview.

FBI-hunted underground-film stash: Guide to the William K. Everson Collection, http://www.nyu.edu/projects/wke/findingaid.htm; Wikipedia, http://en.wikipedia.org/wiki/William_K._Everson (accessed 11 March 2009).

peers and professors alike: Kane interview.

transforming the latter into *After Dark*: Grubb, obituary for William Como.

89   the magazine of his dreams: Pacheco interview; Pacheco, "Before Out Was In."

"and Frequent the West Village": *After Dark*, March 1971, 4.

"the gayest magazine ever published": Zadan interview.

"the most horrifying experience [he had] ever had in [his] life": Vito Russo interview with Berkowitz.

"the broad, changing world of entertainment": qtd. in Hudson [Hunter], *Gay Insider USA*, 185.

"We are an entertainment magazine": qtd. in Vito Russo interview with Berkowitz .

"To penis or not to penis"?: qtd. in Pacheco interview.

"on the same streets as you do": V. Russo, review of *The Panic in Needle Park*, 64, 66.

casual treatment of homosexuality: P. Buckley, "Fresh Faces from the British Cinema."

90   "The mind boggled": V. Russo, "Onstage or Off."

Kay Thompson crossed with Blanche DuBois: Pacheco interview.

the domain of the "Comosexuals": Pacheco, "Before Out Was In."

"let's-dress-straight-enough-to-take-the-boss-out-outfits": V. Russo, "Miss M at Philharmonic Hall," 8.

"and it made me sick": V. Russo, "Onstage or Off."

a screaming match followed: Vito Russo interview with Berkowitz.

90    $125 a week: Pacheco interview.
91   ensured his victory: Eisenbach, *Gay Power*, 163.
      "Right on with this vital work": Vito Russo, letter to gay activists/organizers, 10 November
      1970, reel 13, GAA Papers.
      "in both the gay and the straight press": "Questionnaire for Prominent Political Figures,"
      GAA Papers.
      far better than the GAA leadership expected: Teal, *Gay Militants*, 256.
      Dr. Benjamin Spock: Collected GAA Papers, courtesy of Hal Offen.
      "rather than expanded or continued": reel 11, GAA Papers.
      ancestry, physical handicap, and sex: New York City Council, "Int. No. 475," 6 January
      1971, courtesy of Hal Offen.
      roster of protected minorities: Kantrowitz, *Under the Rainbow*, 129.
      the city's Human Rights Law: Marotta, *Politics of Homosexuality*, 204.
92   solicitation, loitering, and impersonation laws: "Gays March on Albany," 1.
      "level after level of stairs, banners, and banner carriers": Hudson [Hunter], *Gay Insider
      USA*, 453.
      stick handles for signs were verboten: Flyer, "March of the Gay Unveiling: March
      Information Sheet," box 93, Arthur Bell Papers.
      his demand for gay rights: "Gays March on Albany," 8.
      "so damn good to say it out loud": qtd. in Fisher, "3,000 March on N.Y. State Capitol," 8.
      "with all that screeching?": Hudson [Hunter], *Gay Insider USA*, 456.
      to reach full council vote: Marotta, *Politics of Homosexuality*, 207.
      to discuss the stalemate: Kantrowitz, *Under the Rainbow*, 137.
      permitted to come and go: "9 Arrested at City Hall," 4.
      launched his reeking missile at City Hall: "The History of the Struggle for a Gay Rights
      Law in N.Y.C.," 10, reel 1, GAA Papers.
      and was immediately arrested: Kantrowitz, *Under the Rainbow*, 138.
      "herd them away from the front of the building": "9 Arrested at City Hall," 4.
      both men were arrested on the spot: Kantrowitz, *Under the Rainbow*, 138.
93   "my idea of a pleasant afternoon": Kantrowitz, *Under the Rainbow*, 138.
      why they were demonstrating: Kantrowitz, *Under the Rainbow*, 138; Krotz interview, 17
      November 2008.
      "and they're hearing communism": Kantrowitz, *Under the Rainbow*, 139.
      reliving the protest over and over: "9 Arrested at City Hall," 14.
      leading the troops to their East Village destination: Todd interview.
      "heads, necks, crotches, backs": "Intro 475 Now!"
      "a hell of a story in the papers the next day": Silverstein, *For the Ferryman*, 144.
      the pioneering *Society and the Healthy Homosexual* (1972): "Intro 475 Hearings Begin," 8.
      "isn't, aren't, acts of sodomy sins?": qtd. in Katz, "Intro 475"; Skir, "Hearings on Intro 475."
      the bigotry hammering them: Kantrowitz, *Under the Rainbow*, 148.
94   from the Declaration of Independence: "Intro 475—Round 3."
      but were barred: Marotta, *Politics of Homosexuality*, 219.
      Radio City Music Hall: "Lindsay Speech Disrupted by Activists"; GAA Flyer, "Gays
      Know—Lindsay Lies!" Vito Russo Papers.
      a public housing project in Queens: "History of the Struggle," 15.
      boasting *Variety* credentials: A. Bell, "Gays in Chains"; Clendinen and Nagourney, *Out for
      Good*, 55.
      spiraling down to the orchestra seats: "Lindsay Speech Disrupted by Activists."
      who then took shelter in the wings: A. Bell, "Gays in Chains."

94 "and you'd better get used to it!": qtd. in Hudson [Hunter], *Gay Insider USA*, 466.
(7–5, 1 abstention, 2 absences): A. Bell, "Gays in Chains," 20.

95 "'drawing attention to *this* fact?'": qtd. in Bumbalo interview.
Gay American History: Katz interview.
"I will always be grateful to him": Frank Arango, letter to Arnie Kantrowitz, 24 January 1991, Arnie Kantrowitz Papers.
to win the election in a landslide: Phil Eberle, minutes of GAA meeting, 1 June 1972, reel 13, GAA Papers.

96 For $1,100 per month: Clendinen and Nagourney, *Out for Good*, 77.
"love, peace, and homosexuality": "GAA Finds a Home."
Description of Firehouse mural: Tobin and Wicker, *Gay Crusaders*, 175; Kantrowitz, *Under the Rainbow*, 136–37.
description of Firehouse dances: Wicker, "Gay Power Challenges Syndicate Bars"; Silverstein, "For the Ferryman," 146; Krotz interview, 14 July 2008.
"part of something powerful": Kantrowitz, "Day Gay Lib Died," 14; "our people, our troops!": qtd. in Eisenbach, *Gay Power*, 170.
drugs at the Firehouse dances: Wicker, "Randy Wicker's Basket"; Kantrowitz, *Under the Rainbow*, 118.
having to be carried out of the hall: Karaban interview.
lesbians at the Firehouse dances: Rivera (Perotta) interview; Jay interview.
still starkers: Silverstein interview.
he crowed to onlookers: " . . . And the Band Played On."
Firehouse screening of zap footage: Kaiser, *Gay Metropolis*, 263; Clendinen and Nagourney, *Out for Good*, 78.

97 "teaching gay people how to have fun with one another": qtd. in Praunheim, *Army of Lovers*, 61.
"GAA's oftentimes minimized social/cultural programs": Hudson [Hunter], "What Good Is Sitting Alone?" 4.
"Vito Sophia Russo": GAA, Executive Committee attendance sheet, 4 October 1972, reel 3, GAA Papers.
Cabaret schedule and inspiration: Krotz interview, 14 July 2008; Deboske, "Gay Club in SoHo Is Active."
"hiding hiding hiding": Hudson [Hunter], "What Good Is Sitting Alone?" 4.
"love song to a man": qtd. in Deboske, "Gay Club in SoHo Is Active."
Cabaret design: Hudson [Hunter], "What Good Is Sitting Alone?" 5; Krotz interview, 17 November 2008; "and I love it": qtd. in Deboske, "Gay Club in SoHo Is Active."
"totally screwed it up the first time": Krotz interview, 14 July 2008.
reserve judgment for future shows: Hudson [Hunter], "What Good Is Sitting Alone?" 4.

98 to throw struggling performers a lifeline: Hudson [Hunter], *Gay Insider USA*, 64.
"with gay abandon": V. Russo, "Zeffirelli," 12.
"dry seat in the house": "What Good Is Sitting Alone?" 5; Parker's lines: audio tape of GAA Cabaret, 13 November 1973, Rudy Grillo Collection.
to kick off the Flicks: Motions of GAA Meetings, 6 May 1971, reel 3, GAA Papers.
"Well, you just experienced it": qtd. in Evans, e-mail to Schiavi.
"always pulling for the underdog": qtd. in Apple, "Firehouse Flick-Flockers," 11.
denigration of gays and lesbians in Hollywood film: Vito Russo interview with Stoller, 17 October 1989.
Except where otherwise noted, all information about the Firehouse Flicks comes from various GAA flyers and issues of *Gay Activist*.

99 how to edit zap tapes: Vito Russo interview with Stoller, 2 October 1989.
    "fight for their rights themselves": Praunheim, Statement.
    banned it from television: V. Russo, "Premiere!"
    more radical, but now depleted, GLF: Praunheim, e-mail to Schiavi.
    the sheet Vito had been using: Evans, e-mail to Schiavi; information on the screen/sheet
    for Firehouse Flicks screenings: Krotz interview, 14 July 2008; Apple, "Firehouse Flick-
    Flockers," 14; Todd interview; Kantrowitz interview, 5 July 2007.
100 4 a.m. dance riot: V. Russo, "Still Outlaws," 17; only recently released to theaters: Ashkinazy
    interview.
    "Fuck Streisand!": qtd. in Apple, "Firehouse Flick-Flockers,"11.
    and Bill Haley: Allen, "Film Marathon."
    after a film had ended: Karaban interview.
    "I had never in my life experienced such freedom": Goldhaber interview.
    "Save me a breast!": qtd. in Kantrowitz, "Remembrance of Vito Russo," 72.
101 "celebrating the gay image": Goldhaber interview.
    "the people who we're being measured against": Praunheim, *Army of Lovers*, 61.
    their own relationships onscreen: Vito Russo interview with Stoller, 17 October 1989.
    "probably influenced people more directly": Evans, e-mail to Schiavi.
    "maternal role by such encounters": V. Russo, "I Don't Care If You're Gay."
    Roxie Hart: "Firehouse Flicks"; "the women in the community": V. Russo, "Butley, Bette &
    Bijou," 10.
    these singers received at the Firehouse: V. Russo, "I Don't Care If You're Gay."
    Male/female rifts at GAA: Marotta, *Politics of Homosexuality*, 280; Clendinen and Nagourney,
    Out for Good, 167.
    that men read at Firehouse performances: Bumbalo interview.
    women's marginalization at GAA: Kantrowitz interview, 5 July 2007; Clendinen and
    Nagourney, *Out for Good*, 167.
102 "for its transvestite members": Kantrowitz, minutes of GAA meeting, 16 July 1970; to
    wrest attention at meetings from mainstream gays: interview of Sylvia Rivera, p. 8, tape
    113, Testing the Limits, International Gay Information Center; Kaiser, *Gay Metropolis*, 263.
    GAA meetings in chaos: Kantrowitz, *Under the Rainbow*, 121–22; Silverstein interview.
    too conservative: Duberman, *Stonewall*, 232.
    "don't consider ourselves oppressed": qtd. in Hudson [Hunter], *Gay Insider USA*, 101, 102.
    "sanctimonious political bullshit": qtd. in interview of Marc Rubin, p. 4, tape 138, Testing
    the Limits, International Gay Information Center.
    "And humorless": qtd. in Kaiser, *Gay Metropolis*, 263.
    "revival meeting of some sort": Fisher, *Gay Mystique*, 245.
    rule against assassinations/attacks: Steve Krotz, minutes of GAA meeting, 15 April 1971,
    reel 13, GAA Papers.
    for misleading the membership: GAA meeting, 28 April 1971, audiotape, Rudy Grillo
    Collection.
    requiring six stitches: Michaelson, "Charge Police Ignored Beatings."
    "green and purple": Kantrowitz, *Under the Rainbow*, 159.
    had had to field as secretary: Krotz interview, 14 June 2008.
    "known by the company he keeps!": qtd in LeRoy, "Michael Maye."
    "coolie wages": V. Russo, "Still Outlaws," 17; under five hundred dollars per month:
    Vouriotis interview; "spell of perfect weather": V. Russo, "Still Outlaws," 17.
103 "with very famous people": qtd. in Waters, "In Vito Veritas," *Pacific*, 53.

103   referring to movies as "cinema": V. Russo, "Still Outlaws," 17.
       very difficult to obtain: Kardish interview.
       and *Nosferatu* (1922): Vouriotis interview.
       Welles's Oscar for *Citizen Kane*: Kantrowitz interview, 18 July 2007; Pressberger/Powell:
       Waters, "In Vito Veritas," *Pacific*, 53.
       "'let out a squeal at the same time'": Vouriotis interview.
       "missed the moment": Krotz interview, 14 June 2008.
       "'this is *art?*'": qtd. in Veasey, "Books on Gays in Films?"
       "the best tricks": "Daytime Cruising," 2.
104   tassel-twirling stripper: Magliozzi interview.
       "a little uptight" in Vito's presence: Silver interview.
       discuss GAA or his partner Steve at the office: Kardish interview.
       didn't attend parades or Firehouse Flicks either: Vouriotis interview.
       narrowly "tribal" at best: Fulford, "Japan Is His Oyster."
       screenings outside MoMA: Vouriotis interview.
       came back for repeat screenings: Miller, "Ultimate Movie Lover," 27.
       a library, a restaurant, and a cabaret: Lester, "Continental Miracle."
105   "festive wonderland": LeRoy, "Rub a Dub Dub," 3.
       "take a little stroll": *Gay Sex in the '70s*; to a COLT model: Arnie Kantrowitz, journal,
       Spring 1973, Arnie Kantrowitz Papers.
       nonmonogamous relationship: Krotz interview, 14 June 2008.
       an eight-week run: Auer, "Bette at the Bathhouse."
       Midler routine: Mair, *Bette*, 46.
       "I am not from Chicago": qtd. in LeRoy, "Bath Scene."
       distributed poppers between songs: Kantrowitz, interview in *Gay Sex in the '70s*.
       "gay, gay, gay, gay, gay": Richards interview.
106   "back before a straight audience": qtd. in Leitsch, "The Whole World's a Bath!"
       "he'll laugh at anything": Bette Midler at the Continental Baths, 6 September 1971, video-
       tape in private possession.
       "Your mother is gonna hear from me": Bette Midler at the Continental Baths.
       adoring, but unavailable, men: Leitsch, "Whole World's a Bath!"
       "He never went back to guys after me": qtd. in Skir, "Everybody Loves Big-Eyed Bette";
       beyond the gay community: Leitsch, "Whole World's a Bath!"; Skir, "Everybody Loves
       Big-Eyed Bette."
       men making love: Schiff, "Winning Bette," 191.
107   Joseph Epstein and Michael Maye: Hudson [Hunter], "Fag Hag Rag."
       at the Baths: Merla, e-mail to Schiavi, 19 March 2009.
       carry her to her dressing room: Krotz interview, 14 June 2008.
       "not Streisand, *no one*": V. Russo, "Butley, Bette & Bijou," 10.
       "what is liberated and what is not": V. Russo, "I Don't Care If You're Gay."
       "dust from dark closets": Nichols and Clarke, editorial, July 1973.
       "newspaper of record for gay America": Streitmatter, *Unspeakable*, 121; the post-Stonewall
       movement's ferment: Campbell, *Jack Nichols, Gay Pioneer*," 131.
       "Make Men: Avoid the Draft!": *GAY*, 31 December 1969, 1.
108   a regular entertainment column: Vito Russo interview with Berkowitz.
       I'll Take Manhattan: Arnie Kantrowitz, journal, 28 November 1972.
       "alive, well and gay": V. Russo, "In Search of the New Culture," 5.
       farmhouse fell on her sister: V. Russo, "Trip Back in Time," 16.

108   the most objective viewer: V. Russo, "Politics, Actors and the Theatre."
       "to see an ass" on stage: V. Russo, "Tubshit."
       "put to no constructive use": V. Russo, "It's Spring!" 16.
       cry all the harder: V. Russo, "Politics, Actors and the Theatre."
       "treat me for night blindness": V. Russo, "Shelley's New Look!"
       "You'll love it": V. Russo, "It's Spring!" 8.
       snake and a bowl of fruit: V. Russo, "State of Siege," 13.
109   "*Enough!*": V. Russo, "In Search of the New Culture."
       Nixon fallout: V. Russo, "Trip Back in Time," 16; V. Russo, "State of Siege."
       "professional homosexual": V. Russo, I'll Take Manhattan; gay businesses/bars: V. Russo,
       "Miss M at Philharmonic Hall," 8; V. Russo, "Thanks, Brothers, We're Applauding!"
       25,000: Streitmatter, *Unspeakable*, 123.
       power as a voting bloc: V. Russo, "Zeffirelli."
       "It works": V. Russo, "I'm Really Quite Fond."
       Roe v. Wade was signed into law: V. Russo, "It's Poison Pen Time Kiddies," 15.
       "Make every word 'Ha'": V. Russo, "It's Spring!" 16.
110   "not quite what [he] had in mind": Hudson [Hunter], "I Enjoy Being a Girl."
       "Yeah, we're freezing our balls off!": V. Russo, "Thanks, Brothers, We're Applauding!" 14.
       home life on West Twenty-fourth Street: Krotz interviews, 14 June and 14 July 2008.
       "the kind of life I want to live": qtd. in Krotz interview, 14 July 2008.
       "the color of an orange": V. Russo, "Tubshit."
       whose audition left them cold: Katz interview.
       "Psychoanalysis of Edward the Dyke": Tree, "Cruising Off Broadway."
111   thrilled Vito: V. Russo, "Thanks, Brothers, We're Applauding!" 14.
       delayed the opening for months: V. Russo, "It's Poison Pen Time Kiddies."
       that he wanted to break up: Kantrowitz interview, 5 July 2007.
       couldn't give Vito the attention he needed: Krotz interview, 14 June 2008; Krotz, e-mail to
       Schiavi, 15 June 2008.
       staged their own celebrations: Fitzpatrick, "Jerry's Sphere."
       bring entertainers to Washington Square: "Plan Ahead."
       where auditions for gala performers were being held: "Parade Organizers Organize."
       "That would make me very sad": V. Russo, "Tubshit."
112   found a spot on the dais: A. Bell, "Hostility Comes out of the Closet," 1.
       would keep to the rear: Young, "Gay March."
       "live-and-let-live shrug": Darnton, "Homosexuals March Down 7th Avenue."
       whose clothing and throats Sylvia tore: [Wicker], "Behind the Lines."
       twenty thousand strong: Darnton, "Homosexuals March Down 7th Avenue."
       to legitimize gay mental health as well: The American Psychiatric Association removed
       homosexuality from the *Diagnostic and Statistical Manual*'s list of mental disorders on 15
       December 1973.
       that he had donated to the gala: A. Bell, "Hostility Comes out of the Closet," 16.
       "Love Train": David Sasser, Gay Pride Gala footage, 24 June 1973, Queer Blue Light,
       Lesbian Herstory Archives, Brooklyn.
       maintained the crowd's enthusiasm: Gunter, "Looking Back at the Gay Gala."
       "Sing on the *Ed Sullivan Show*": qtd. in A. Bell, "Hostility Comes out of the Closet," 18.
113   "on the same footing": Bowers, e-mail to Schiavi.
       "like Milton Berle in drag": Vito Russo interview with Berkowitz.
       had loved their audition at Brothers and Sisters: Bowers interview.

113   "What the fuck's wrong with you all?!": David Sasser, Gay Pride Gala footage, 24 June
      1973, Queer Blue Light.
      "what the word 'aghast' was made for": Kantrowitz interview, 18 July 2007.
      "can and do show each other who we are": David Sasser, Gay Pride Gala footage, 24 June
      1973, Queer Blue Light.
114   "Who does that drag queen think he is?": qtd. in Newton interview.
      freeing his penis from his pantyhose: Jay interview.
      "already hitting each other": Vito Russo interview with Stoller, 17 October 1989.
      to dress wounds: Clendinen and Nagourney, *Out for Good*, 172.
      "Marilyn Monroe singing in Korea": qtd. in Marcus, *Making History*, 268.
      Mona's Royal Roost: Arnie Kantrowitz, datebook, 24 June 1973, courtesy of Arnie
      Kantrowitz.

Chapter 5. "Professional Movement Flash and Trash"

129   "a Movie Queen before Stonewall": Hudson and Wexler, *Superstar Murder?* 77.
      David Cassidy: Hudson and Wexler, *Superstar Murder?* 222, 194, 347.
      none of Ostrow's business: V. Russo, "Zeffirelli," 12–13.
130   dance nude on their own turf: V. Russo, "Bette Midler," 32.
      "in the zoo?": Arnie Kantrowitz, journal, Spring 1973, Arnie Kantrowitz Papers.
      Bella buttons and nothing else: Ireland interview.
      "turned off by strident shoutings": qtd. in Tobin and Wicker, *Gay Crusaders*, 234.
      Watergate-weary audience: Arthur Bell, letter to Harvey Shapiro, 15 November 1973,
      Arthur Bell Papers.
      "genitals of the same sex": Kantrowitz, journal, 21 November 1972.
      "no other way to do it": qtd. in Rutledge, *Gay Decades*, 60.
      total immunity to outside evil: Vito Russo interview with Newton.
      locked in Suffolk County jail cells: Praunheim, *Army of Lovers*, 56.
      a permanent end on Fire Island: Newton, *Cherry Grove, Fire Island*, 199.
      newly installed *Fire Island Duchess*: Picano, *House on the Ocean*, 9.
      "It's magic": qtd. in Kantrowitz interview, 31 July 2007.
131   on the other side of the bay: Kantrowitz, *Under the Rainbow*, 140–41; Kantrowitz interview,
      31 July 2007.
      GAA politicking in Cherry Grove: Vito Russo interview with Newton; Kantrowitz inter-
      view, 26 June 2008; V. Russo, "Still Outlaws," 17.
      met with dismissal at best: T. Buckley, "Cherry Grove Stays Aloof."
      "Americanized Pines offspring": Newton, *Cherry Grove, Fire Island*, 270.
      nickname of "*After Darkland*": J. Nichols, *Welcome to Fire Island*, 53.
      "the most apolitical place on earth": V. Russo, "Fire Island."
      "animalistic sex in the bushes": qtd. in V. Russo, "Pinin' in the Pines."
      "a lover for 15 years": Vito Russo interview with Newton.
132   description of Bruce Parker's childhood: Gregson Parker interview; Scot Parker interview.
      an engaging film: Thompson, "Erotic Ecstasy," 284.
      validity of gay relationships: Christopher Larkin, program notes, *A Very Natural Thing*
      debut, 25 June 1974, courtesy of Stephen Conte.
      profession renowned for closetedness: V. Russo, "That 'Twinkle in the Eye' Awareness."
133   send it into wide release: Fairbanks, "Naturally, Larkin Does His *Thing*."
      Sophia Loren and Carlo Ponti: Van Dyke interview.

133   Flaherty Seminar summer conference in New Hampshire: Kardish interview.

"write the book on gay film": qtd. in Bowen, "In Vito Veritas," 52.

"The Celluloid Closet: A History of Homosexuality in the Movies": Kantrowitz, "Gays in/at the Movies," 18; V. Russo, *Celluloid Closet*, 1st ed., x; New Line Presentations, promotional material for "The Celluloid Closet," courtesy of Charles Russo.

"that is *not* oppressive": qtd. in Byron, "Finally—Two Films."

134   "*The Boys in the Band*": qtd. in Kantrowitz, journal, 1974.

a dialogue on gay stereotyping: Kennedy, e-mail to Schiavi.

screening of *Boys in the Band* at his apartment: Arnie Kantrowitz, datebook, 24 November 1973, courtesy of Arnie Kantrowitz.

A Very Natural Thing: New Line Presentations, lecture outline for "The Celluloid Closet," courtesy of Charles Russo.

"witty and enthusiastic," if "intense": New Line Presentations, promotional material for "The Celluloid Closet," courtesy of Charles Russo.

piracy of unreleased film scores: V. Russo, I'll Take Manhattan; "Bette Midler's Philharmonic concert": V. Russo, "Miss M. at Philharmonic Hall," 8.

a vast archive: Magliozzi interview.

a clip from Ken Russell's *Valentino* (1977) vanished: Silver interview; presentation that Vito gave at MoMA: Vito Russo, "American Film Criticism," 17 November 1979, flyer, Department of Film, Museum of Modern Art, New York.

135   remove prints from the building: Vouriotis interview.

that Vito had hoarded over the years: Howard Grossman interview.

that he could ill afford: Vito Russo, letter to Bill Johnson, 18 November 1976.

on which he had spent forty-five precious dollars was any good: Vito Russo, journal, 13 February 1979, Vito Russo Papers.

"Women, Blacks and Gays in the Cinema": Bellet, "Russo Decries Image."

description of Rutgers program: Newkirk interview; Vito's fees for Rutgers program: Vito Russo, letter to Bill Johnson, 14 March 1977.

"once I begin" the lecture: Vito Russo, letter to Bill Johnson, 6 April 1977.

its portrayal of gays: Bellet, "Russo Decries Images."

to Fire Island: Vito Russo interview with Newton.

she fell into hysterics: Charles Russo interview, 19 October 2007.

136   remake the paper in his own image: Clendinen and Nagourney, *Out for Good*, 247–48.

"and an inviting home": Goodstein, "Publisher's Opening Space."

"T-shirts and posters": Preston, "Family Matters," 113.

to purchase *After Dark*: Streitmatter, *Unspeakable*, 185.

to tangle with Vito and Dr. Hooker: De Cola interview.

directed the brunt of his on-air bigotry to Vito personally: Vito Russo interview with Berkowitz.

women-in-prison favorite, *Caged*: De Cola interview.

Patrick endorsed Vito for the job: Merla interview, 26 July 2007.

in the paper's eight-year history: Streitmatter, *Unspeakable*, 190.

137   "Yeah, Vito, that's what they all say": qtd. in V. Russo, "Bette Midler," 32.

permanently over: V. Russo, "Bette Midler," 34.

blessing to gay marriage: V. Russo, "Bella! Bella! Bella!"

"a nice guy": V. Russo, "Jerry Rubin Grows Up."

138   "suppressed" in the marketplace: V. Russo, "Brief Encounter with Tennessee Williams."

Vito turned snarky: Vito Russo, letters to Bill Johnson, 5 and 6 March 1977.

138 available in airport bookstores: V. Russo, "Brief Encounter with Tennessee Williams," 20. "He just can't stop writing": qtd. in V. Russo, "Brief Encounter with Tennessee Williams," 20.

"Getting any writing done?": qtd. in Vito Russo, letter to Bill Johnson, 2 April 1977.

"That made me feel better": Vito Russo, letter to Bill Johnson, 12 November 1976.

"The KY Circuit": qtd. in Gavin, *Intimate Nights*, 302, 305.

"what kind of club it [was]": V. Russo, New York, 5 November 1975.

job at Cinema 5: Vito Russo interview with Newton.

"Bye-bye": V. Russo, "It's Gotham!"

the 1973 Gay Pride Gala: V. Russo, "New Hope for Performing Artists."

139 one of Garland's *Oz* pinafores: V. Russo, "Interview with Laura Kenyon."

and Diana Ross: Gavin, *Intimate Nights*, 306, 308, 309.

"think about you guys": qtd. in Richards interview.

finding her way to Reno Sweeney: V. Russo, New York, 27 August 1975, 48.

"in love with the bandleader or something": Dexter interview.

"she's your girl": V. Russo, "Zeffirelli."

140 "gonna break out in headlines!": qtd. in Bush interview.

infamous *Daily News* headline in all caps: 30 October 1975; "changing values and hard times": V. Russo, New York, 17 December 1975.

"New York, New York": V. Russo, New York, 18 June 1975.

Ice Palace performers: V. Russo, New York, 13 August 1975.

"one word or lyric of the show": V. Russo, New York, 30 July 1975.

for the lighting design: V. Russo, "New York City.".

directly into his eyes: V. Russo, "Wanna Dance?"

pre- and post-gay liberation: V. Russo, "Poor Judy," 15.

"'Fine and Mellow'": V. Russo, "I'm Really Quite Fond."

141 "Dead, you know": qtd. in V. Russo, "Poor Judy," 14.

"and get away with it": V. Russo, "I'm Really Quite Fond."

surrounded by gays: V. Russo, "Gay Sensibility."

"where they came from": V. Russo, New York, 24 September 1975.

"unnecessary and unattractive": qtd. in V. Russo, New York, 2 July 1975.

"number of gay men present": V. Russo, New York, 5 November 1975.

"damage [Manilow's] career": qtd. in V. Russo, New York, 27 August 1975, 49.

approached by the *Advocate*: Vito Russo interview with Cohen.

142 and Rex Reed: V. Russo, New York, 16 July 1975.

"Boy in the Band": qtd. in V. Russo, "Onstage or Off."

tacit indication of her lesbianism: Vito Russo interview with Berkowitz. I have omitted the name of this performer, who is still working and still closeted.

necessarily heterosexual: Vito Russo interview with Berkowitz.

"how to lead his life": V. Russo, "Onstage or Off."

Liberace: V. Russo, "New Hope for Performing Artists," 9; V. Russo, "It's Spring!," 8; Anthony Perkins: V. Russo, I'll Take Manhattan, 13 November 1972, 16; V. Russo, "I'm Really Very Fond"; V. Russo, "That 'Twinkle in the Eye' Awareness," 9; Rock Hudson: V. Russo, "Onstage or Off"; Stephen Sondheim: V. Russo, "Tubshit."

who was sleeping with whom: Huston, "Crosstalk."

"and he cleared out": Vito Russo, letter to Lily Tomlin, 28 May 1976. All Russo to Tomlin letters courtesy of Lily Tomlin.

"worry about changing pronouns": V. Russo, review of *Sondheim & Co.*, 30.

143   "that people could be that political": Zadan interview.
"fights with [closeted] people tonight!": qtd. in Vito Russo interview with Berkowitz.
when his career as a film producer . . . took off: Zadan interview.
"people in other walks of life": Pitchford interview.
in Provincetown, Massachusetts: Hudson, "Lily Tomlin . . . Part 1 of 2)," 6.
simple for her to remember him: Vito Russo interview of Berkowitz.

144   to share the story: Tomlin interview, 30 July 2007.
"going to the dogs": Vito Russo, letter to Lily Tomlin, 11 May 1978.
for several years: Hudson, "Lily Tomlin . . . (Second of a Two-Part Series)," 7–8.
she never heard from Johnston again: Tomlin interviews, 30 July 2007 and 24 July 2008.
"most other people have only when *talking*": Wagner, *Search for Intelligent Signs*, 153; Swannack interview.
support her no matter what: Vito Russo interview with Berkowitz. .
"double-edged playing around with the truth": Russo, journal, 28 December 1978; "At least you never have a beard": Swannack interview.

145   "making love to a man on the big screen": Tomlin interview, 30 July 2007.
"and still be perfectly normal": Tomlin, *Modern Scream*.
"more acceptable to me": Tomlin interview, 30 July 2007.
"unless I make the decision to come out": qtd. in Vito Russo interview with Berkowitz.
"or *your* sexuality": qtd. in Hudson, "Lily Tomlin . . . (Second of a Two-Part Series)," 9.
some of which, she believes, he invented: Tomlin interview, 24 July 2008.
"the gay issue": qtd. in V. Russo, "Special Interview by Vito Russo," 28.

146   "those who don't understand": V. Russo, "Special Interview by Vito Russo," 29.
a friend with a great deal to lose: Tomlin interview, 24 July 2008.
"the fag and lezzie baiters": Russo, journal, 26 December 1978.
"a reputable gay archive": Russo, Last Will and Testament, 23 February 1987, Vito Russo Papers.
"New York's notoriously female cabaret circuit": V. Russo, "Fabulous Peter Allen," 20.
didn't mention it overtly: Gavin, *Intimate Nights*, 316.
Charming but evasive chatter ensues: V. Russo, "Fabulous Peter Allen."
"(the mellowness, the sunshine, Taco Bells, and the police)": V. Russo, "Wanna Dance?"
"on a ten-foot screen": Hannaway interview.

147   along with a trove of Vito's favorite Disney films: Hannaway, "Under the Influence."
not completely open about his homosexuality: Hannaway interview.
four others in 1969: Bugliosi, with Gentry, *Helter Skelter*, 8, 305.
the musical director who was renting the house: Hannaway interview.
"the longest laugh in the history of *The Mary Tyler Moore Show*": Harper interview.
"the world [was] changing for the better": V. Russo, "Valerie Harper," 47.

148   that he wasn't alone: Harper interview.
"never have a ring put through my nose": V. Russo, "Interview with Debbie Reynolds," 8, 9, 10, 12.
and the *Los Angeles Times*: Streitmatter, *Unspeakable*, 208.
"'why you should accept us'": Vito Russo interview with Berkowitz.
"from the safety of their closets": Goodstein, "Opening Space."
"to be sure": David Aiken et al., "Rhetoric Shocking."

149   inspired Vito in his own work: V. Russo, "Comments on Gay Conferences."
openness and understanding for gays: *Position of Faith*.
"deep love relationship with another man": qtd. in "Homosexual's Ordination."

150   Bill's own prominence: Johnson, letter to Schiavi.
      though afraid to let himself seem "vulnerable" to Bill: Vito Russo interview with Berkowitz.
      projector during the "Closet" lecture: Vito Russo, letter to Bill Johnson, 12 February 1977.
      his relationship with Bruce was over: Johnson interview, 19 August 2008.
      "if I stifled my feelings out of concern for his": Russo, letter to Johnson, 12 November 1976.
      "I wonder if that's possible": Russo, letter to Johnson, 18 November 1976.
      "whatever he wanted to do in terms of a new relationship": Johnson interview, 19 August 2008.
      Prophet/chart: Vito Russo, letters to Bill Johnson, 19 December 1976 and 6 January 1977.
      their neatly concluded relationship: Johnson, letter to Schiavi.
      thought his life would take a different direction than Bruce's: Vito Russo, letter to Bill Johnson, 2 January 1977.
      "a process, not an 'event'": Vito Russo, letters to Bill Johnson, 5 and 6 January 1977.
      repeatedly threatened to fire him: Johnson interview, 19 August 2008.
      $16 higher than his rent: Vito Russo, letter to Bill Johnson, 25 March 1977.
151   which he longed to show Bill: Vito Russo, letters to Bill Johnson, 5 March 1977, 14 March 1977, 20 December 1976; Johnson interview, 19 August 2008.
      romantic ride down the Pacific Coast Highway: Johnson, letter to Schiavi.
      "a true communion for the first time since childhood": Johnson interview, 8 October 2008; Vito Russo, letter to Bill Johnson, 10 February 1977.
      defiantly apolitical organization: V. Russo, "Blue Flettrich."
      "pornografia for men": Russo, letter to Johnson, 12 February 1977.
      poet Rod McKuen: Vito Russo, letters to Bill Johnson, 16 and 18 February 1977; Islanders Club, Schedule of Activities, 17 February 1977, all courtesy of Bill Johnson.
      on West 13th Street: Vito Russo, letter to Bill Johnson, 13 March 1977.
      "I'll never go for anyone else": Russo, journal, 19 January 1979.
      "without checking with me first": Russo, letter to Johnson, 5 March 1977.
      "the man I love": Stein, "Update."
152   "very creepy": Johnson interview, 19 August 2008; Johnson, letter to Schiavi.
      across the United States: Johnson, letter to Schiavi.
      "unable to give him what he wanted": Johnson, letter to Schiavi.
      "about a lot more than being sexually attracted": Johnson interview, 8 October 2008.
      "He was miserable": Johnson interview, 19 August 2008.
153   "clinically depressed" and "trapped": Johnson, letter to Schiavi.
      "and [Bill's] stuff *stayed* out": Johnson interview, 19 August 2008.
      his own parish: Fosburgh, "From a Quiet Seminarian to Homosexual Spokesman."
      Vito's sophisticated New York friends: Vito Russo, letter to Arnie Kantrowitz, 7 May 1977, Vito Russo Papers.
      the same to him regarding movies: Johnson interview, 19 August 2008.
      "Every time I show up, I'm crying!": qtd. in Kantrowitz interview, 18 July 2007.
      "the first gay television show of any kind": Stavis interview.
      "like a *60 Minutes* thing": Bie interview.
      bicoastal exposure: "Emerald City Expands to West."
154   found himself unemployed: Johnson interview, 19 August 2008.
      their irreconcilable problems: Johnson interviews, 19 August and 8 October 2008; Johnson, letter to Schiavi.
      He moved out immediately: Johnson, letter to Schiavi.
      the previous January: Rutledge, *Gay Decades*, 101.

155   to forget about gay rights: Russo, journal, 19 December 1978; where she worked in food
concession: A. Bell, "My Friend Who Bombed the Waldorf."

"punched out for being a man": Vito Russo, letter to Lily Tomlin, 30 June 1978.

"Go get 'em, Anita!": qtd. in V. Russo, "Still Outlaws," 17.

lunged to punch one boy in the face: Kantrowitz, datebook, 3 December 1979; Offen,
e-mail to Schiavi.

"the deadly QUEER SPEAR": undated flyer in Vito Russo Papers.

occasionally attack gays: Johnson interview, 8 October 2008.

"We hate them": qtd. in V. Russo, "Park Gang: We Hate Fags!"

"different in any way": Russo, letter to Tomlin, 11 May 1978.

moving to Amsterdam: Vito Russo interview with Cohen.

"not willing to be swallowed up": Russo, letter to Tomlin, 11 May 1978.

a "deliberately outrageous" impression on disapproving parents: Boyd interview.

156   to discuss their work: Engstrom interview.

his part in this organization's birth: Reynolds interview; Jerry B. Wheeler, program, AGA
Media Awards, 4 October 1982, courtesy of Charles Russo, Jr.

charging to see unauthorized material: Mayer interview.

a five-thousand-dollar fine or a year in prison: Russo, journal, 6 December 1979.

"understanding what I didn't say": Russo, journal, 14 December 1978.

157   veneer that he was eager to avoid: Russo, journal, 19 December 1978.

"professional movement flash and trash": Russo, journal, 14 and 15 December 1978.

to use sex or an STD as a weapon: Russo, journal, 15, 19, and 25 December 1978.

"'cause you need the quarter": Russo, journal, 4 April 1979.

couldn't even buy food: Russo, journal, 19 and 26 December 1978.

to tide him over for a few days: Vito Russo interview with Stoller, 17 October 1989.

"thank God for the ghetto": V. Russo, *Celluloid Closet*, 1st ed., ix.

Polly Adler's line of work: V. Russo, "Midnight Shift," 12.

$200 in an eight-hour shift: Stoller interview, 17 October 1989.

"the best seat in the house": V. Russo, "Midnight Shift," 12; description of Vito at the St.
Marks: Strub, e-mail to Schiavi, 4 August 2007; V. Russo, "Midnight Shift," 12; Rosenman
interview, 21 August 2007.

158   did not quite meet the ceiling: V. Russo, "Midnight Shift," 13.

"Yes, *Mary!*": qtd. by Arnie Kantrowitz in *Gay Sex in the '70s.*

"not of a specific individual": Kantrowitz, "Boys in the Back Room."

"not as a candy store": Russo, journal, 30 April 1979.

"even intolerance": V. Russo, "Midnight Shift," 13.

find oneself mentally detached from them: Denneny interview.

159   "by the first men with whom they have sex": V. Russo, "Warning," 2.

Cruising's shooting script: Steele e-mail to Schiavi.

prevent the movie from being made: Steele interview.

"try it, don't deny it": Walker, *Cruising,* 171.

"a terrible time": Bell, "Bell Tells."

for appearing in such homophobic trash: Vicki Russo interview.

Vito wielded one of the whistles himself: Steele interview.

if they deemed it objectionable: Kantrowitz interview, 28 September 2007.

160   costly reshoots: Marcus, *Making History,* 413, 414.

"It's the truth": qtd. in V. Russo, "'Cruising," 46, 47, 49.

as the Cockpit scene unfolded onscreen: V. Russo, "Warning," 2.

160   "I didn't notice that": qtd. in Russo, "Warning," 3.

"You scumbag!": qtd. in Steele interview.

"great theatre": Steele interview.

only living convicted blasphemer: Rutledge, *Gay Decades*, 110.

cofounder of London's *Gay News*: Scobie, "Lemon of *Gay News London*," 24.

"patiently and gladly": Kirkup, "Love That Dares to Speak Its Name," 49–50.

161   Lemon's conviction and fines: Gengle, "People," 15.

$350 to his name: Russo, journal, 19 February 1980.

hurled bricks: Scobie, "Lemon of *Gay News London*," 12, 13.

and *The Stepford Wives* (1975): Vito Russo, letter to Arnie Kantrowitz, 25 February 1980, Arnie Kantrowitz Papers.

where Judy Garland had died eleven years earlier: V. Russo, "Poor Judy," 14.

he scribbled to Arnie: Vito Russo, letter to Arnie Kantrowitz, 5 March 1980, Arnie Kantrowitz Papers.

"fell in love with London" and its people: Babuscio, "There Never Have Been Lesbians," 21.

"their American cousins": qtd. in Vito Russo, letters to Russo family, 25 February and 24 March 1980, courtesy of Charles Russo.

"*Gone With the Wind*, jazz, and fist fucking": qtd. in Russo, journal, 4 March 1980.

the U.S. conflict with Iran: Russo, letter to Kantrowitz, 5 March 1980.

162   "boring people to death for the rest of my life": Vito Russo, letter to Arnie Kantrowitz, 2 April 1980, Arnie Kantrowitz Papers.

"I kept pinching myself": Vito Russo, letter to Arnie Kantrowitz, 27 August 1980, Vito Russo Papers.

"I still don't know why myself": Vito Russo, letter to Russo family, 26 August 1980, courtesy of Charles Russo.

"The Battle Hymn of the Republic": V. Russo, "Swedes Chase Lord C."

like "the [Baby] Jane Hudson" of the isle: Russo, journal, 15 and 18 September 1980.

"he could not 'ever accept that [homosexuality] is natural'": qtd. in V. Russo, "Mykonos," 13.

"'What are they [*sic*] for?'": qtd. in Russo, journal, 21 and 22 September 1980.

163   "no way to live": V. Russo, "Baghdad by the Sea," 3, 4.

"as real as it ever gets in Key West": V. Russo, "Key West," 13.

"no intention of letting anyone get that close to me": Russo, journal, 21 February 1980.

alternatives to rigid fidelity: V. Russo, "David Goodstein," 28.

"simply not an option": V. Russo, "Franco Brusati," 18.

"retiring with a good book": V. Russo, review of *States of Desire*, 11.

164   "that was Vito Russo from New York": Timmons interview.

"as unabashedly sexual as I wish": V. Russo, "Glad to Be a Clone," 3, 4.

spat in Vito's face: Babuscio, "There Have Never Been Lesbians," 21.

"sex for the sake of sex!": qtd. in V. Russo, "Alone Again, Naturally," 16.

to clone aesthetics: Your Letters [letters to the editor], *Gay News* (4–17 September 1980), 18.

"exploiting the working classes": Russo, letter to Kantrowitz, 27 August 1980.

"my reaction to" the author: Russo, journal, 2 and 13 March 1980.

"for the Fourth of July": Vito Russo, letter to Arnie Kantrowitz, 16 January 1980, Arnie Kantrowitz Papers.

"live across town": V. Russo, "Alone Again, Naturally," 17.

165   pushed romance so relentlessly: McKerrow interview.

"to make [him] happy, etc.": Russo, journal, 15 September 1980.

"We'd be great": Russo, journal, 16 September 1980.

165 "it won't open till 10": Vito Russo, letter to Arnie Kantrowitz, 25 September 1980, Vito Russo Papers.

"how beautiful Paris was": McKerrow interview.

to gather whatever clues he could in Paris: Babuscio, "There Have Never Been Lesbians," 22.

Chapter 6. Building the Closet

166 were "depressed" over the evening's returns: Arnie Kantrowitz, datebook, 4 November 1980, courtesy of Arnie Kantrowitz; Rutledge, *Gay Decades*, 160.

"eliminates the *need* to do so?": V. Russo, "When It Comes to Gay Money."

167 "payment for work delivered": V. Russo, "When It Comes to Gay Money."

"smooth flesh and bulging sex organs": Streitmatter, *Unspeakable*, 248.

"We are with you all the way": Ann Russo, "Gay Rights" [letter to the editor], *New York Daily News*, 29 November 1980.

left the office without their expected checks: Duane interview.

"New York needs a gay newspaper!": qtd. in Steele interview.

pour out of his typewriter from week to week: Babuscio, "Man Who Blew the Whistle."

"and Arthur Bell is out of town": qtd. in Stern, "From the Closet to the Screen."

168 "they just knew so much": Steele interview.

"end some friendships once and for all": Vito Russo, journal, 31 December 1980, Vito Russo Papers.

"maybe [he's] not taping": Russo and Bell, Russo/Bell Connection, 6–19 April 1981, 14.

shaking Kim Novak's hand: Russo and Bell, Russo/Bell Connection, 23 March–5 April 1981.

"get you well with chicken soup": Russo and Bell, Russo/Bell Connection, 10–24 January 1981.

"quite a good writer": Russo and Bell, Russo/Bell Connection, 23 March–5 April 1981; "the loveliest person": Russo and Bell, Russo/Bell Connection, 9–23 February 1981.

Vito dubbed Arnie "lovely": Russo and Bell, Russo/Bell Connection, 23 March–5 April 1981; and novelist Felice Picano a "doll": Russo and Bell, Russo/Bell Connection, 23 February–8 March 1981.

whom Vito liked: Russo and Bell, "For Fame and Money.".

taunted Arthur about his age: Russo and Bell, "Social History 101.".

"'Living Proof'": Russo and Bell, Russo/Bell Connection, 9–22 March 1981.

"to avoid three local suicides": Russo and Bell, Russo/Bell Connection, 15–28 June 1981, 32.

"Constant writer throws up": Russo and Bell, Russo/Bell Connection, 23 February–8 March 1981.

"nice and little": Russo and Bell, "Wax Dolls.".

169 Friedman's height: Gavin, *Intimate Nights*, 308.

called Tom Steele in a rage: Steele interview.

"and the pothole bill": qtd. in V. Russo, "Playing Politics with Gay Rights."

in the Connection: Russo and Bell, "A Puce Picture.".

Vito's "bitchy" sense of humor: Roskoff interview.

thrilled by the responses: Steele interview; Denneny interview.

"may even be a book someday": Russo, journal, 21 February 1981.

cross-section of gay New York history: Russo and Bell, Russo/Bell Connection, 18–31 May 1981.

self-defense classes offered to gay men at Greenwich House: Russo and Bell, Russo/Bell Connection, 6–19 April 1981, 14.

169   Sisters of Perpetual Indulgence and Bloolips: Russo/Bell Connection, 9–22 March 1981; Russo/Bell Connection, 10–24 January 1981.
      Hellfire, a straight/gay S and M club: Russo, journal, 9 November 1980.
      American debut on the Lower East Side: Bourne interview.

170   Arthur's failing eyesight: Kantrowitz, datebook, 7 March 1981; Judell interview.
      Arthur treated his failing eyesight as a joke: Russo and Bell, Russo/Bell Connection, 18–31 May 1981.
      he hadn't thought "it would ever happen": "Glorious Letdowns," 29.
      "Well, is it done yet?": qtd. in *Celluloid Closet*, 1st ed., ix.
      never being able to finish the book: Kantrowitz, datebook, 29 March 1979; Russo, journal, 24 August 1979.
      like a second skin: Kantrowitz interview, 18 July 2007; Kantrowitz, "Gays in/at the Movies," 21.

171   to many post-Stonewall readers: Sarris, "Aesthete at the Movies."
      all filmed representation of gayness: Tyler, *Screening the Sexes*, xxiv.
      "slander normal sex and completely innocent motives," Tyler, *Screening the Sexes*, 77.
      "an Angel of the Resurrection?," Tyler, *Screening the Sexes*, 122.
      "an incarnation of Homeros," Tyler, *Screening the Sexes*, 125.

172   "the new homosexual militance," Tyler, *Screening the Sexes*, 49.
      "outrage" at the "private and public misfortunes" Tyler, *Screening the Sexes*, 190, 61.
      "inadequate," "esoteric," and "elitist": qtd. in Turner, "Vito Russo and The Celluloid Closet," 23; refused to tackle homophobia: Broderick, "'Stepin Fetchits of the '80s,'" 7; "admit to having gotten through" it: qtd. in Picano, "Imitation of Life," 20.
      a "wider and less specialized audience" than Tyler's: Vito Russo, Harper & Row Book Information Sheet, 7 August 1980, 3, courtesy of Charles Russo Jr.
      "being manipulated" by Hollywood bigotry: qtd. in Veasey, "Books on Gays in Films?"

173   their son is a . . . Communist: Picano, "Imitation of Life," 20.
      a taste of his own medicine: Vito Russo interview with Cole.
      at San Francisco State College (later University): Johnson, letter to Schiavi.
      began to anger him: Vito Russo interview with Berkowitz.
      "not as good as a man": Vito Russo interview with Cohen.
      "lecturer on stereotyped roles": V. Russo, "Men's Liberation?!"
      "hatred of women" among gay men: V. Russo, "Alone Again, Naturally," 16.
      "the necessity of choosing male or female roles": Russo, journal, 28 March 1979.
      "some of the strangest clothes ever assembled": Joe Brewer, remarks at Vito Russo memorial, Castro Theatre, San Francisco, 2 December 1990, courtesy of Joe Brewer.

174   "not like that at all": Guthmann interview.
      Adam Reilly as source for silent films and *Red River*: Engstrom interview; Vito Russo, letter to Bill Johnson, 30 March 1977.
      three titles per day: Waters, "In Vito Veritas," *Pacific*, 54; *Boom!, Performance, Busting*: Vito Russo, letter to Bill Johnson, 20 April 1977.
      "the first time they've let someone in": Vito Russo, letter to Lily Tomlin, 30 June 1978.

175   simply part of the game: Timmons interview. This perception of the Herrick Library protocol is disputed by some researchers, who claim that historically the holdings have been accessible to anyone with a valid project.
      "nothing any of them said was useful": qtd. in C. Taylor, "Fear in Filmdom's Crowded Closet," 22, 21.
      his participation in *Advise & Consent*: Waters, "In Vito Veritas," MetroActiveMovies, 11.

175 cost him the lead in *Love Story*: Russo, *Celluloid Closet*, 1st ed., 213. Subsequent references are cited parenthetically in the text.
"some very polite personal 'no's'": Vito Russo, letter to Lily Tomlin, 11 May 1978.
Attempted Shirley MacLaine interview: Vito Russo, letter to Lily Tomlin, 30 June 1978; Babuscio, "There Never Have Been Lesbians," 22.
lesbian madam in *Walk on the Wild Side*: Russo, letter to Tomlin, 30 June 1978.
sex change and subsequent suicide: Russo, letter to Tomlin, 30 June 1978.
176 to inform him of Whale's homosexuality: Bram interview.
Russo interview of Mart Crowley: Crowley interview; Crowley, letter to Schiavi.
"good and valid points": Crowley, letter to Schiavi; "the first time gay people protested against a Hollywood movie": qtd. in Marcus, *Making History*, 412.
"grab attention at any price": Crowley, letter to Schiavi.
177 "not interested in non-film talk or tumbling": Russo, journal, 16 August 1979.
"'no one will be able to deny it anymore'": Saslow interview.
The Gay Brothers: Russo, journal, 29 May 1980.
"the very first gay liberation statement ever made on film": V. Russo, "Gay Visions in Celluloid," 14.
then screened in Amsterdam: V. Russo, "Gay Visions in Celluloid," 14.
translated it into English for him: Russo, journal, 16 April 1980.
178 two pounds apiece: Russo, journal, 24 February 1980.
British Film Institute: Russo, journal, 17 March 1980.
"They don't make stills of the things I was looking for": Waters, "In Vito Veritas," *Pacific*, 54.
fifty dollars each: Babuscio, "There Never Have Been Lesbians," 21.
homosexual content or innuendo: Picano, "Imitation of Life," 20.
actor Leonard Nimoy: Hochberg interview.
just as Vito was leaving Bruce for Bill: Vito Russo, letter to Bill Johnson, 23 February 1977.
time-consuming articles for the *Advocate*: Vito Russo, letter to Bill Johnson, 18 November 1976.
publishers' rejections of *Celluloid Closet*: Marcus, *Making History*, 411; Picano, "Imitation of Life," 20.
179 "film freaks" of all sexualities": qtd. in Marcus, *Making History*, 411.
recognized the *Closet*'s market appeal and helped Vito to pitch it: Marcus, *Making History*, 411.
half of his five-thousand-dollar payment on signing: Waters, "In Vito Veritas," Metro-ActiveMovies,, 7; a bottle of Korbel champagne: Kantrowitz, datebook, 11 March 1978.
contractual deadline was October 1: Vito Russo, letter to Lily Tomlin, 11 May 1978.
a mass outing of Hollywood stars: Babuscio, "There Never Have Been Lesbians," 21.
"nobody would want to read a yell": qtd. in Babuscio, "There Never Have Been Lesbians," 21.
couldn't help but be political: Turner, "Vito Russo and The Celluloid Closet," 29.
American masculinity and femininity: Turner, "Vito Russo and The Celluloid Closet," 23.
181 did not survive the first edit: V. Russo, "Celluloid Closet," 1st draft, 78–80.
"experiment somewhere else": V. Russo, "Gay Visions in Celluloid," 14.
how gays were viewed in society: "Interview with Author of *The Celluloid Closet*," 9.
billboard over Sheridan Square: Russo, journal, 6 January 1979.
"waiting for the phone to ring": qtd. in Russo, journal, 25 September 1980.
"the genesis of the sissy and not that of the tomboy": V. Russo, "Celluloid Closet," 1st draft, 1. Subsequent references are cited parenthetically in the text as D1.

181   "feminists of both sexes": V. Russo, "Celluloid Closet," 2nd draft, 104. Subsequent references are cited parenthetically in the text as D2.

183   "to bend their meanings to our own purposes": Dyer, introduction, *Gays & Film*, 1.

184   "haven't allowed anything else to get at me": Russo, journal, 2 August 1979.

185   reception of the two films was nearly identical: Russo, journal, 2 August 1979.
      "not exciting and it has to be": Russo, journal, 16 August 1979.
      "a sad day for you people": qtd. in Vito Russo interview with Berkowitz.
      "It's like spic": qtd. in Russo, "Puttin' Down 'The Ritz,'" 45.

186   "the book isn't very good": Vito Russo, letter to Arnie Kantrowitz, 20 March 1980, Arnie Kantrowitz Papers.
      apologized to Howard for his outburst: Rosenman interview, 21 August 2007.
      "the biggest idiot [he had] ever met": Vito Russo, letter to Arnie Kantrowitz, 2 April 1980, Arnie Kantrowitz Papers.
      "keep it light!": qtd in obituary for Homer Dickens, 9.
      "what to say about it or how to promote it": Russo, journal, 29 March 1980.
      before switching the subject to Dietrich: Russo letter to Kantrowitz, 2 April 1980.
      "offhand, breezy writing" he had originally planned: Russo, journal, 6 January 1979.

187   use of his empty Pines house during the fall: Russo, journal, 22 August 1979.
      "not a good place to be poor": Russo, journal, 6 December 1979.
      had drowned there: Tomlin, e-mail to Schiavi.
      last-minute research: Swannack interview.
      "Vito's tobacco smoke permeated every inch of the house": John Morgan Wilson, e-mail to Schiavi.
      significantly sunnier manuscript: Russo, journal, 6 December 1979.

188   "from a certain kind of politically correct gay liberation viewpoint one shouldn't love": Dyer interview.
      sadistic prison matron Hope Emerson: Steele interview.
      Next Stop's first scene for his brother: Don Shewey, journal, 2 November 1990, courtesy of Don Shewey.
      left room for hope: Kantrowitz interview, 18 July 2007.

189   feeling depressed or defensive: Babuscio, "There Have Never Been Lesbians," 22.
      "in a better world of filmdom": Arnie Kantrowitz, letter to Vito Russo, 15 March 1980, Vito Russo Papers.
      a brief fling: Epstein interview.
      suited, straitlaced gay executive: Roggensack, "Inside 'Out.'"
      "*other than* 'gay is good'": Babuscio, "Peter Adair."
      "come to life while still being written": Russo, "'Word Is Out,'" 43.

190   "holding him back" from completing the book: Johnson, letter to Schiavi.
      "it has to be terrific": Russo, letter to Kantrowitz, 20 March 1980.
      "liked [the book] better this reading": Russo, journal, 31 January 1981.
      uniformly positive reviews of *Celluloid Closet*: review of *The Celluloid Closet*, *Booklist*; review of *The Celluloid Closet*, *Christian Century*.
      and *Publishers Weekly*: Russo, journal, 13 June 1981.
      "isn't that just about everyone?": Bell, review of *The Celluloid Closet*.
      "witty, good-tempered survey": French, "Stuff for Buffs"; "that make many of us lose our cool": J. R. Taylor, "Sane Man in a Mad World."

191   "scrupulous research": Harvey, "Hide in Plain Sight."; "wealth of fascinating material": Farber, "From Sissies to Studs," 72; "marvelously bizarre facts": Koenig, "Screening Gays," 38.

191 weigh down the argument: Harvey, "Hide in Plain Sight."

"every one- and two-line fag gag he's ever heard": Koenig, "Screening Gays," 38.

"slavish chronicle of specific movies": Farber, "From Sissies to Studs," 72.

"pulling in opposite directions": Chute, "Velvet Light Trap."

"too-insistent ideology": Koenig, "Screening Gays," 38; "irrelevant sermon on society's mistreatment of gays": Farber, "From Sissies to Studs," 72.

"humanitarianism and art don't proceed from the same impulse or have the same goal": Koenig, "Screening Gays," 40.

"hitherto unsuspected recruits": Conrad, "Conspicuous Liberation."

"who is supposedly homosexual": review of *The Celluloid Closet*, *Choice*.

192 "posturing 'Socialist' German film maker": Rechy, "Cruising Hollywood Attitudes"

Fassbinder: Rechy, "Cruising Hollywood Attitudes"; Harvey, "Hide in Plain Sight"; Eisenstein: Rosenbaum, "They Frighten Horses, Don't They?"; John Waters: Chute, "Velvet Light Trap."

"not a coffee-table book": qtd. in Anderson, "Vito Russo."

"by a liberal gay man": Fleming, "Looking for What Isn't There," 61.

gay and lesbian characters' social class: Fleming, "Looking for What Isn't There," 59, 61.

"instead of being partially ensnared by them": Wood, "Airing the Closet," 35, 36.

"strangely compatible bedfellows": Rosenbaum, "They Frighten Horses, Don't They?"

193 to keep deviants in their social place: Dyer, "Review Essay," 55, 56.

"what it means to be gay": Dyer interview.

"all these deaths of lesbians and gay men in movies": Dyer interview.

194 "everybody has to do what they have to do": Russo, journal, 13 June 1981.

"dull as dishwater but current as hell": Russo, journal, 29 July 1981.

"reaching people with more accessible language": qtd. in Hoctel, "Out of the Closet."

GAU's keynote address: V. Russo, datebook, 9 October 1981; at the Chicago International Film Festival: Siskel, "Movies' Disgrace: Screening Gays."

"like saying we live in a *white* world": qtd. in Babuscio, "There Have Never Been Lesbians," 21.

"blamed [him] for being in town": Russo, journal, 5 June 1981.

195 at New York's GPA conference the previous January: Russo, journal, 5 June 1981.

background on Sean Strub: Clendinen and Nagourney, *Out for Good*, 435, 440; Hammond, "Without a Single Apology."

"a patch of perfect weather": Russo, journal, 5 June 1981.

"Love, Xxx Vito": Strub, e-mail to Schiavi, 3 August 2007.

"at the end of a day like this": qtd. in Russo, journal, 5 June 1981.

"for a long while to come": Russo, journal, 9 June 1981.

196 their exquisitely gay hometown: Russo, journal, 29 June 1981.

eye contact with Jeffrey Allan Sevcik: Epstein interview.

Chapter 7. "A Time of Major Change"

197 "how it feels when the universe reels": Blane and Martin, "Trolley Song."

and introduced the two men: Foto e-mail.

"held each other until morning and my flight to L.A.": Russo, journal, 18 April 1985, Vito Russo Papers.

"just wanted to call and say hello": Jeffrey Sevcik, telephone message to Vito Russo, 24 June 1981, Vito Russo Papers.

198   guy was Manhattan bound: Russo, journal, 29 June 1981.
      Jeff's social circle remained small: Ellsworth interview.
      I'm ready: Sevcik, "That's The Way It Goes," in "Old Shoes," 1–7, 34–37.
      to assert its political voice: Shilts, *Mayor of Castro Street*, 48, 61, 70.

199   Leftover love renewed: Sevcik, "Dreams of San Francisco," in "Thatched Roofs and
      Dreams over Thought," 37–38, 41–43.
      bachelor's degree in January 1980: Jeffrey Sevcik, undergraduate transcript, San Francisco
      State College, 1973–80, courtesy of Suzanne Dmytrenko, Registrar's Office.
      "become [his] tomb": Sevcik, "The darkness," in "Thatched Roofs and Dreams Over
      Thought," 12, 20.
      for upcoming features: Sawyer interview.
      "the light of their lives": Foto e-mail.
      to discuss the poetry of Denise Levertov and Diane Wakoski with him: Kent interview.

200   "but none of us succeeded": Sawyer interview.
      Vito took notice: Russo, journal, 17 July 1981.
      description of Vito and Jeff's early days: Greenbaum interview; Kantrowitz interview, 31
      July 2007; *Common Threads*; Russo, journal, 18 April 1985.
      misgivings of Jeff's San Francisco friends: Foto e-mail; Kent interview.
      Lena Horne and Hedy Lamarr: Russo, journal, 27 July 1981.
      chatting up the new star on a Village street: Sawyer interview.

201   "hardly possible to believe I'm this gone but I am": Russo, journal, 8 August 1981.
      Jeffrey moved to New York and in with Vito: Vito Russo, datebook, 31 August 1981, Vito
      Russo Papers.
      description of Halloween celebration: Vicki Russo interview; Leslie Russo interview.
      "Jeff was still very much that way": Vicki Russo interview.
      "[Jeff] still had that childlike teenage innocence": *Common Threads*.
      "I love him so much": Russo, journal, 28 September 1981.
      "How much time I'm not sure": Russo, journal, 9 October 1981.
      the company's near-pornographic inventory: Judell interview.
      a nerdy bowtie: Greenbaum interview.

202   tapes of Aretha Franklin and his beloved Van Morrison: Lessinger interview.
      but he was in obvious pain: Greenbaum interview.
      "I don't see how such a situation can continue": Russo, journal, 9 December 1981.
      the perfect househusband: Greenbaum interview.
      not a drop of excess water: Kantrowitz interview, 31 July 2007.
      "the kitchen is closed": qtd. in Harding interview.
      "but it's not the meaning of life!": qtd. in Kantrowitz interview, 31 July 2007.
      They needed time apart: Russo, journal, 9 December 1981.
      a "time of major change" in his life: Russo, journal, 21 February 1981.
      bookstores were regularly selling out their stock: Russo, journal, 21 February 1981 and 4
      July 1981.
      a second printing for October: Russo, journal, 16 July and 9 October 1981.
      a lengthy excerpt from the last chapter, "Struggle": V. Russo, "Celluloid Closet—How
      Hollywood Sees Gays."
      the major New York papers were ignoring his work: Russo, journal, 16 July 1981 and 9
      October 1981.
      a gay expert on Stonewall and Judy Garland: Maupin, "Juned In And Gayed Out," A23.
      for his hometown's paper of record: Maupin interview.

203 "enjoy it while it last[ed]": Russo, journal, 4 July 1981.
put him on an unwanted pedestal: Russo, journal, 17 July 1981.
had prized the anonymity of being a writer: V. Russo interview with Stoller, 17 October 1989.
approached him seeking wisdom he didn't have: Russo, journal, 9 June 1981.
an unlisted telephone number: Russo, journal, 31 July 1981.
the most money he had ever received at one time: Russo, journal, 29 June 1981.
his first closet for his ever-expanding film library: Picano, "Imitation of Life," 19.
a bathtub in the living room and no shower: Russo, journal, 13 June 1981.
"the animation sequences from *Mary Poppins*": Russo and Bell, Russo/Bell Connection, 9–22 March 1981.
across his newly finished floors: Charles Russo Jr. interview.
celebrated fashion designer Clovis Ruffin: Russo, journal, 19 July 1979.
"until I met Clovis Ruffin": Russo, journal, 30 July 1979.
Clovis's own sense of superiority: Russo, journal, 2 August 1979.
"but not my values": Russo, journal, 4 August, 2 August, and 30 July 1979.
"like a grown-up": Kantrowitz interview, 5 July 2007.
204 his eighties style: Vito Russo, letter to Arnie Kantrowitz, 6 January 1980, Arnie Kantrowitz Papers.
on the subject of film: Holleran, "Penthouse," 44, 55, 48.
"in a queeny, nasty way": Dexter e-mail.
"modeling clothes for the larger woman these days": qtd. in Picano interview.
rather than suffer any more of his "anti-Semitic shit": Kantrowitz interview, 5 July 2007.
"famous twenty years after you're dead": qtd. in Russo and Bell, Russo/Bell Connection, 9–23 February 1981, 14.
in very distinguished company: Picano, "Rough Cuts from a Journal," 71.
on whom they all agreed: Picano interview.
205 "it has an enormous impact on our culture": qtd. in Russo, *Celluloid Closet*, 2nd ed., 326.
"a lot to do with you here": qtd. in Hofsess, transcript.
why not charge to screen his film of Bette at the baths?: Russo, journal, 19 February 1980.
how her image was shown: Person, "Bette Bites Benefit."
206 nearly brought the police: Vito Russo interview with Berkowitz.
"and dropped the subject": V. Russo, "Too Little, Too Soon," xiii.
a remake she was planning of the B noir classic: Russo, journal, 24 April 1979.
its ceaseless insistence on "killing and killing": Russo, journal, 31 March 1981.
where *Love* director Arthur Hiller was readying an early scene: Russo, journal, 1 April 1981.
"the *Guess Who's Coming to Dinner* [1967] of gay rights": V. Russo, "On the Set [of *Making Love*]."
207 "It meant exposing a lot of nerves": qtd. in V. Russo, "On the Set [of *Making Love*]," 102.
"something more than just making a movie": Sandler interview.
a gay film with a happy ending: V. Russo "On the Set [of *Making Love*]," 103.
as was Kate Jackson: Russo, journal, 1 April 1981.
"if audiences don't like it, screw them": qtd. in Babuscio, "There Have Never Been Lesbians," 22.
"900 more than I have at the moment": Russo, journal, 9 December 1981.
"it fit the very first time around": V. Russo, "Rachel Ward," 14, 16.
"charming, British, well read and sincere": Russo, journal, 26 December 982; V. Russo, "Bowie," 17.

207   the unwed mother of Mikhail Baryshnikov's daughter: V. Russo, "Jessica Lange," 19.
star of the indie smash *Liquid Sky*: V. Russo, "Carlisle and *Liquid Sky*."

208   "fucking up [their] follow up interview": Russo, journal, 5 December 1983; sloshing orange juice over her oatmeal: V. Russo, "Nastassja Kinski," 16.
refusal of the lesbian lead in *The Killing of Sister George*: V. Russo, "All the World's a *Cable Stage*," 27.
"*if* she's gay?": qtd. in Hofsess, transcript.
The Search for Intelligent Signs of Life in the Universe: V. Russo, "Lily!" 44, 43, 47.
"too cozy with a subject": qtd. in Giteck, "Behind the Microphone with Lily."
celebrities' private lives: V. Russo, "Visit with Allan Carr," 36, 35.
"appointments, living style, friendship, etc.": Russo, journal, 29 March 1981.
as *Closet* sales reached thirty-five thousand: Lambda Legal Defense & Education Fund, Inc., program for Seventh Annual Awards Dinner, 18 October 1982, courtesy of Charles Russo Jr.
in *Victor/Victoria* (1982): Jed Mattes, in *Vito's Legacy*.

209   "'and they're all shit'": qtd. in "Give 'Em a Hand," 8.
glared back in steely silence: "Dinner and Debate."
and Edmund White: "Now . . . The Stoneys."
"I would have worn a dress": qtd. in Blotcher, "Pat on the Back."
moving on to some new project: Russo, journal, 14 October 1982.
"Why Is Leather like Ethel Merman?": V. Russo, "Why Is Leather Like Ethel Merman?"
"to beat the living shit": V. Russo, "Why I'm Not Marching."
a book on James Whale: Russo, journal, 29 November 1981; Vito Russo, letter to Rick Mechtly, 7 February 1982, courtesy of Rick Mechtly.

210   "surrounded almost completely by mystery and glamour": Vito Russo, letter to Jed Mattes, 20 May 1982, Vito Russo Papers.
cheerfully sleeping her way to the top: Picano interview.
"test for Mildred Pierce after all those years": Russo, journal, 31 August–1 September 1983.
"every political cause except his own": Wilson, *Street Theater*, 23.
was icing on the cake: Russo, journal, 7 August 1982.
"up the bunghole": Doric Wilson interview.
"and organized religion": *Street Theater*, program, November 1982, Vito Russo Papers.
pronounced his performance "charming": O'Quinn, "Other Side of the Street."
on whom the playwright insisted: Doric Wilson interview.
"no coherent performance style or directorial vision": O'Quinn, "Other Side of the Street."

211   "Love you xx Vito": Doric Wilson interview.
"no danger to nonhomosexuals from contagion": qtd. in Altman, "Rare Cancer."
the number of those afflicted had more than doubled: Kramer, *Normal Heart*, 14.
Nick Rock history: Larry Kramer, 25 July 1990, GMHC Oral History,; Shilts, *And the Band Played On*, 25, 45, 53.
"look and feel like Quasimodo": Harvey, "Defenseless," 1.
he was diagnosed with Kaposi's sarcoma (KS): Jed Mattes, 19 March 1990, GMHC Oral History.
for research funds: Shilts, *And the Band Played On*, 85, 90.

212   "desperately need[ed] research and funds": V. Russo, "Romance on the Range," 22.
"Love Come Down": Cheren, with Rotello and Earle, *My Life and the Paradise Garage*, 314–16.
it simply was "not gonna happen" to him: *Common Threads*.
the world's first article on AIDS: Mass, "Disease Rumors Largely Unfounded."

212   "a variety of past infections": qtd. in Mass, "Cancer in the Gay Community," 21.
      without knowing it: Mass, "Epidemic Q&A."
      lurking in their systems: Mass, "Epidemic Continues," 12.
      "might also seem risky": Mass, "Epidemic Continues," 12.
      "that's bad luck": Kramer, "1,112 and Counting," 18.
213   denying that "immorality" could cause illness: Mass, "Cancer in the Gay Community," 21.
      "be even more genuinely affirmative about [their] sexuality": Mass, "Basic Questions," 21.
      who drew a blank: Arnie Kantrowitz, datebooks, 1 September 1980 and 22 December
      1981, courtesy of Arnie Kantrowitz.
      explain once more how they had met: Kantrowitz, datebook, 28 March 1982.
      to Larry's Chelsea loft: Kantrowitz, datebook, 10 August, 23 August, 20 September 1982.
      Jeff's return to New York: Russo, journal, 24 March 1982; Kantrowitz, datebook, 30 May
      1982.
      more like "playmates" than a well-matched couple: Shewey interview.
      shield him from unnamed fears: Johnson interview, 8 October 2008.
214   never bothered to read The Celluloid Closet: Kantrowitz and Mass interview.
      he needed privacy and space: Russo, journal, 2 May 1983.
      "Drives me nuts": Russo, journal, 26 December 1982.
      Jeff's stony silence when they went out: Russo, journal, 18 July 1983.
      he was feeling the strain: Russo, journal, 26 December 1982.
      that gay men use condoms during sex: Shilts, And the Band Played On, 258.
      gay men parading through Dr. Grossman's office: Ron Grossman interview.
      "it stuck with me": Kirby interview.
215   were "obsessed" with the topic: Russo, journal, 26 December 1982.
      "Our world is going to crumble around us": Kantrowitz, "Family Album," 291; Kantrowitz
      interview, 31 July 2007.
      "make my contribution that way": Russo, journal, 26 December 1982.
      a weekly program on gay and lesbian issues: Wallace, "Our Time."
      he jumped at the opportunity: Siggelkow interview.
      Madeleine Sherwood: DeStefano interview.
      gay youth of all races: Wallace, "Our Time."
216   saw their baby to the screen: Sigglekow interview.
      "That's what this show should be dealing with": qtd. in Siggelkow interview.
      everyone who was anyone in the gay community: Blotcher interview.
      "temperamental": Our Time, episode 1, 16 February 1983 (tape date).
      $30,000 for all salaries: Siggelkow interview.
      and Native journalist: Blotcher interview.
217   for three-quarter-inch videotape: Kerr interview.
      an inauspicious debut: Jay Blotcher, unpublished diary, 27 February 1983, courtesy of Jay
      Blotcher.
      "really has to go": Russo, journal, 26 December 1982.
      he had to pull the plug: Blotcher interview; Blotcher diary, 22 February 1983.
      whom he had been considering for months: Russo, journal, 26 December 1982.
      Pally swallowed her hesitation: Pally interview.
218   "not as nutty and . . . not as comical": Our Time, episode 9, 6 April 1983 (tape date).
      with Eden in hot pursuit: Blotcher interview.
      his acclaimed lesbian drama Lianna (1983): Our Time, episode 2, 18 January 1983 (tape
      date).

218   "I was just jerking off": qtd. in Pally interview.

last-minute replacement: *Our Time*, episode 5, undated.

struggles with alcoholism: *Our Time*, episode 2, 18 January 1983 (tape date); "racism in the gay community": *Our Time*, episode 11, undated.

should return to writing: Blotcher interview.

219   "All of Jerry Falwell's favorite people!": *Our Time*, episode 8, 30 March 1983 (tape date).

anonymous doomsayers: *Our Time*, episode 5, undated.

when Vito spilled the beans: Karla Jay interview; *Our Time*, episode 10.

"I know they can't spell it": *Our Time*, episode 13, 22 May 1983 (air date).

220   "gay men may have no future on this earth": Kramer, "1,112 and Counting," 1.

"I'd like a lot of people in this community angry": *Our Time*, episode 4, 3 March 1983 (tape date).

221   "everyone was a huge *slut*!": Berkowitz interview.

"and other sexually transmitted diseases": Callen and Berkowitz, "We Know Who We Are," 23.

"Did you live like a sex pig, or didn't you?": Berkowitz interview.

who were also falling ill? Mass, e-mail to Schiavi.

didn't lend themselves to monogamy: Jurrist, "In Defense of Promiscuity," 27, 29.

an effort to smear Berkowitz on the air: Berkowitz interview.

an ignorance of death: *Our Time*, episode 4.

222   That much love the show did not receive: Siggelkow interview.

the national anthem: Shilts, *And the Band Played On*, 282, 283.

description of the GMHC benefit: Bush interview; Kantrowitz, datebook, 30 April 1983.

"all the right things": Holleran, "Spectacle at the Bottom."

suicidal depression: Larry Mass, journal, 2 May 1983, courtesy of Larry Mass.

checked himself into St. Vincent's Hospital for treatment: Kantrowitz, datebook, 2, 5, and 17 May 1983.

sent her into hysterics: Russo, journal, 2 May 1983; Kantrowitz, datebook, 12 May 1983.

doctors' offices and emergency rooms: Charles Russo interview, 30 November 2007.

"or so motivated they're never home": Russo, journal, 18 and 25 July 1983.

223   "or a lazy fraud": Russo, journal, 21 January 1985.

catching AIDS from Meat Rack mosquitoes: Umans, "Pines '83."

sparse and subdued: Russo, journal, 28 July 1983.

"and they don't like you": Russo, journal, 30 July 1983.

"Shocking": Russo, journal, 15, 18 August; 31 August–1 September 1983.

convinced himself that he didn't have AIDS: Russo, journal, 18 July 1983.

which even hypnotism couldn't cure: Kantrowitz, datebook, 4 June 1984.

harder for him to cope with stress: Russo, journal, 25 October 1983.

to win Jeff back: Vito Russo, letter to Jeffrey Sevcik, 19 March 1984, Vito Russo Papers.

toward instant marriage: Russo, journal, 20 February 1984.

224   "guilty because I hurt Jeff": Russo, journal, 26 April 1984.

Vito didn't let him down: Epstein interview.

"last days of Cambodia": Russo, journal, 20 and 29 January 1985.

go on to win the Oscar for Best Documentary Feature: *The Times of Harvey Milk*, Disc 2, "San Francisco Premiere."

225   "the courage to be who you are": qtd. in Steele and Ortleb, "Last Conversations of Arthur Bell," 32.

(PCP): Russo, journal, 18 July 1983.

225   referred him to an oral surgeon: Russo, journal, 5 December 1983.
"Or that it could happen to me tomorrow": Russo, journal, 20 February 1984.
allegedly in the works: D'Eramo, "Federal Health Officials."
a disproportionate number of dying young men: Russo, journal, 26 April 1984.
"Everybody was dying": *Common Threads.*
"If I've got AIDS, you've got it": A. Bell, "Mud in Your Eye."
"worse than murderers": qtd. in "Doctor Who Calls Gays 'Worse Than Murderers'"
quarantining people with AIDS: "Falwell Calls for AIDS Quarantine."

226   "until AIDS gets all of them!": qtd. in Paine, "Simon Calls Play 'Faggot Nonsense.'"
devastated him: Russo, journal, 2 and 4 April 1985.
simply wouldn't entertain: *Common Threads.*
Jeff's AIDS fears: Harding interview; Sawyer interview.
"Have I killed Jeff with something inside of myself?": Russo, journal, 18 April 1985.
"if he didn't fight, he would die": *Common Threads.*
he was "committed to fight" the disease: qtd. in Russo, journal, 22 April 1985.

227   "a life thing and not an ending": Russo, journal, 19 and 22 April 1985.
"Do you realize the commitment you're making?" he asked: qtd in *Common Threads.*
whose good intentions he could trust: Russo, journal, 24 April 1985.
for transportation: Russo, journal, 24 April 1985.
financial help from friends: Russo, journal, 6 May 1985; Vito Russo, letter to Arnie
Kantrowitz, 2 June 1985, Vito Russo Papers.
in the Mission District: Bush interview.
had decorated the city for over a year: Shilts, *And the Band Played On,* 416.
they would not take the test: "S.F. Study."
had or would get AIDS: Cole interview.

228   the latest scientific findings: Stoller interview.
Depression at the office was unavoidable: Stoller interview.
"You'll be dead in a year": qtd. in Vito Russo, letter to Ron Grossman, 7 June 1985, this
and all Russo to Grossman letters courtesy of Ron Grossman.
"just as scared as I am": Russo, letter to Kantrowitz, 2 June 1985.
"dread one day at a time": Arnie Kantrowitz, letter to Vito Russo, 10 June 1985, Arnie
Kantrowitz Papers.
possible immune-system boosters: Russo, letter to Grossman, 7 June 1985.
"which is hogwash as far as I'm concerned": Russo, journal, 28 June 1985.
attempts to get Jeff into drug trials: Russo, letter to Grossman, 7 June 1985; Russo, journal,
30 July 1985; Russo, letter to Kantrowitz, 2 June 1985.
Jeff's feelings on blue/yellow: Russo, journal, 14 February 1986; *Common Threads*; Bush
interview.

229   "not a world-class city": Vito Russo, letter to Arnie Kantrowitz, 22 May 1985.
"nothing upsets anyone!": Vito Russo interview with Stoller, 2 October 1989.
"I'm going to start shrieking": qtd. in Jay interview.
at Orphan Andy's on Market Street: Guthmann interview.
for a biopsy: Kantrowitz, datebook, 30 July and 2 August 1985.
a mole, nothing more: Kantrowitz, datebook, 8 August 1985; Kantrowitz interview, 12
October 2007.
"and you do have KS": qtd. in *Common Threads.*
asked her not to tell anyone: Stoller interview.
"The final verdict was that I had AIDS": *Common Threads.*

229   one year: "300 March on Parliament," 2.

230   on a bus back to San Francisco: Kantrowitz interview, 12 October 2007.

"on a cruise to the Caribbean": Russo, journal, 3 and 7 August 1985.

an annual salary of twenty-eight thousand dollars: Vito Russo, letter to Arnie Grossman, 30 August 1985.

still ruled him: Russo, journal, 14 February 1986.

Rock Hudson's death made headlines worldwide: Kantrowitz, datebook, 10 October 1985.

if his suffering became intolerable: Kantrowitz, "Friends Gone with the Wind," 46; Kantrowitz, datebook, 10, 12 and 16 October 1985.

not rumor or speculation: Conant interview.

231   "when most doctors [hadn't] a clue": Ron Grossman interview.

hauled across the border: Bourne interview.

"a daily emotional battle": Vito Russo, letter to Ron Grossman, 18 January 1986.

"doing nothing was not an option": Ron Grossman interview.

"I'm cured": qtd. in Hardy with Groff, *Crisis of Desire*, 49.

"Give me a break here" was his sole reply: Vito Russo, letter to Ron Grossman, 4 February 1986.

his sole weapon against AIDS: Jeffrey Sevcik, letter to Ron Grossman, 29 January 1986, Vito Russo Papers.

Jeff's emotional spiral: Kantrowitz, datebook, 27 October 1985; Russo, journal, 14 February 1986.

232   to leave the apartment on February 1: Kantrowitz, datebook, 1 February 1986.

began seeing a psychotherapist: Russo, letter to Grossman, 4 February 1986.

could still climb stairs: Stoller interview.

took him to San Francisco General: Kent interview.

"breathing his last": qtd. in Kantrowitz, datebook, 5 March 1986; Kantrowitz interview, 12 October 2007.

"I guess that's all there is": qtd. in Bush interview.

he met Joe Brewer for lunch: *Common Threads*.

Vito's learning of Jeff's death: Sawyer interview; Brewer interview.

"I talked to him for a little while": *Common Threads*.

233   they returned home shortly after his death: Ellsworth interview.

Jeff's memorial above the Castro: Harding interview; Bush interview.

before leaving San Francisco: Kantrowitz, "Friends Gone with the Wind," 47, 108.

Chapter 8. The Activist in Wartime

234   second KS lesion; "Time was no longer his friend": Arnie Kantrowitz, datebook, 2 April 1986, courtesy of Arnie Kantrowitz; Vito Russo, journal, 15 March 1986, Vito Russo Papers.

description of Intro 2 celebration: Kantrowitz, datebook, 20 March 1986; Kantrowitz interview, 2 November 2007.

Halley's comet cruise: Kantrowitz, datebook, 11 April 1986; Judell interview.

community film screenings: Luddy e-mail.

as engaging as the film itself: Senak interview.

235   "supposed to believe they're in love": qtd. in Picano interview.

famous for their knowledge of Hollywood arcana: Howard Grossman interview.

235   "I gotta meet this one": Busch interview.

"whose details we all shared": Kantrowitz, "Family Album," 284.

howled over his dastardly moves: Kantrowitz, "Remembrance of Vito Russo," 73.

were less lethal: Kantrowitz, "Family Album," 284.

Sinatra, Garland, Bennett, Vaughan: Kirby interview.

Vito faced frightening depression: Mass, journal, 24 November 1986.

waiting for his sleeping pill to kick in: Russo, journal, 10 March 1989.

provided little comfort: Sloan interview.

236   two bottles of wine and a bag of potato chips: Pitchford interview.

pork: Koestenbaum, "Garbo Index," 146, line 5; "uncooked vegetables": Luddy e-mail.

and pumpkin chiffon pies: Mass, journal, 24 November 1986, 4 December 1988.

of someone on nearly every page: De Cola interview.

Vito stopped taking photos: Russo, journal, 6 January 1988.

depiction of gay sex and violence: "Did You Hear . . . ?"

a raft of roses and cards: Russo, journal, 21 June 1986.

while still alive: Brewer interview.

237   "an anger that has nowhere to go": Russo, journal, 30 April 1986.

"an Epidemic of A.I.D.S. That Will Devastate New York!": qtd. in Schulman, "Anti-Abortion Group Pickets Gay Bathhouse."

"sodomite-anal-pervert": qtd. in Pally and Rist, letter to the editor.

"victimization of other homosexuals": W. Buckley, "Identify All the Carriers."

and Barry Adkins: Kantrowitz, datebook, 30 October 1985.

blistering GAA-style zaps: Clendinen and Nagourney, *Out for Good*, 524.

the Gay and Lesbian Alliance Against Defamation (GLAAD): Fall, "Gay and Lesbian Anti-Defamation League."

238   reopened its doors: Kantrowitz, datebook, 7 and 8 November, 6 December 1985.

"I don't want to take it all back": qtd. in "Interview with Author of *The Celluloid Closet*," 10.

"I do not have the right to control someone else's life": qtd. in "Sex in the Age of AIDS," 46.

a "New Stonewall": Fall, "New Stonewall?"

Arnie accepted the position of secretary: Arnie Kantrowitz, minutes for GLADL Steering Committee meeting, 23 November 1985, Arnie Kantrowitz Papers.

c'est la vie: Kantrowitz, minutes for GLADL Steering Committee, 11 January 1986; Pally interview.

the departure of several radical activists: Wolfe interview.

to make the paper's owners nervous: *Vito's Legacy: A Stronger Community*.

and the editorial brass: Adkins, "Gays at the *Post*," 16.

239   with camera-friendly symbolism: Fall, "Anti-Defamation League Zaps *New York Post*," 10, 11.

maintaining the group's focus on media: *Vito's Legacy: A Stronger Community*.

"and contributions of gay and lesbian people": Kantrowitz, minutes for GLADL Steering Committee meeting, 3 December 1985.

"in a way that made people feel very welcome": Pally interview.

People with AIDS (PWAs): Kantrowitz, minutes for GLAAD Steering Committee meeting, 30 April 1986.

for Vito had lost all meaning: Russo, journal, 14 July 1986.

prejudice them against the cause: Wolfe interview.

240   "abort the Fourth": d'Adesky, "Gays on Two Coasts."

a stirring defense of gay and lesbian rights: Howard Grossman interview.

absence of democracy among the membership: Vito Russo interview with Stoller, 17 October 1989.

241 "bigots, crackpots, and morons": V. Russo, letter to the editor, *New York Native*, 26 January 1987.

"the realm of gossip and innuendo": Russo, *Celluloid Closet*, 2nd ed., 301. Subsequent references are cited parenthetically in the text.

within weeks of Jeff's death: Kantrowitz, datebook, 31 January 1986.

"[didn't] pertain to their own careers": V. Russo, "Russo on Film."

having helped to make bathhouse culture seem like fun: Schiff, "Winning Bette," 190.

242 "she should feel good about the past, present and future ": Vito Russo, letter to Jed Mattes, 12 January 1988, courtesy of Charles Russo Jr.

"disappointed": Praunheim e-mail.

a "fair assessment" of *Making Love*: Sandler interview.

the most (in)famous depictions of gays and lesbians in cinema: Jeffrey Friedman, Commentary track 1, *The Celluloid Closet* DVD.

"entertaining first and worthwhile second": Vito Russo, letter to Rob Epstein and Janet Cole, undated, courtesy of Charles Russo Jr.

243 hoping to "learn": Janet Cole, letter to Vito Russo, 30 April 1988, courtesy of Charles Russo, Jr.

had hardly rushed to depict fairly: R. Epstein and J. Cole, project description, *Celluloid Closet* television special, undated, courtesy of Charles Russo, Jr.

two thousand dollars per minute: Range, "Interview with Vito Russo."

"Insert joke here": Russo, letter to Epstein and Cole.

the use of his name for fundraising: Russo, journal, 29 April 1988.

to secure funding for gay and lesbian projects: "Russo Panels."

244 "in our memory": qtd. in Miller interview.

as a roaring ovation greeted his brother: Charles Russo Jr. interview.

"This is Mrs. Norman Maine": Gelbert, "Movies and Masses."

in the palm of his hand: Moore interview.

description of the concert: New York City Gay Men's Chorus, "The Movie!" 22 March 1987, Avery Fisher Hall, New York City, audiotape courtesy of Fred Goldhaber.

"It Might as Well Be Spring": Mass, *Confessions of a Jewish Wagnerite*, 182.

"and *so* loving!": Mass, journal, 22 March 1987.

245 blew a kiss to his ecstatic mother: Charles Russo Jr. interview; never seen a shorter line for the ladies' room: Vicki Russo interview.

only recently told Charlie that he had AIDS: Russo, journal, 25 February 1987.

might mention his illness to Annie at intermission: Vito Russo, "Coming Out as a PWA," 178.

"Artie Bressan seriously ill with chronic hepatitis": Russo, journal, 7 December 1986.

diagnosed with HIV: Russo, journal, 17 December 1986.

"beaten with a meat cleaver on one side of his face": Engstrom interview.

had appeared in *Variety*: Russo, journal, 3 and 11 May 1987.

addressed the Gay and Lesbian Youth of New York about safe sex: Steinman, "Remembering David Summers."

246 "*one proud faggot!*": *Voices from the Front*.

up to either task: Mass, journal, 30 October 1986.

two more followed within two weeks: Kantrowitz, datebook, 8 November 1986; Mass, journal, 20 November 1986.

"We are not expendable": qtd. in Kantrowitz interview, 2 November 2007.

He dissolved into tears: Kantrowitz interview, 12 October 2007.

by an unseen killer: Senak, *Fragile Circle*, 73.

"and the fear grows": Russo, journal, 27 February 1986.

246   "[they didn't] know if anyone [would] survive": Russo, journal, 5 May 1987.

without a functioning immune system: Kantrowitz, datebook, 9 March 1987.

reported to Ron's office for "misting": Mass, journal, 18 and 21 March 1987.

for a full day: Humble, "Spare Change."

spared him from pneumonia: Mass, journal, 28 and 21 March 1987.

had yet to see one: Russo, journal, 27 February 1988.

possible to dose himself at home: Mass, journal, 28 April 1987.

247   personally treated one hundred: Ron Grossman interview.

"not show [their] grief": qtd. in Bayer and Oppenheimer, *AIDS Doctors*, 218.

"I'd be a moron": Vito Russo, letter to Ron Grossman, 25 April 1987.

and on Fire Island: Bayer and Oppenheimer, *AIDS Doctors*, 114.

calling doctors out of the blue for their advice: Vito Russo interview with Testing the Limits Videotape Collective.

"we're not gonna hurt each other, are we?": qtd. by Marcia Pally, in *Vito's Legacy*.

new underground network that Vito joined: Russo, letter to Grossman, 25 April 1987.

"when the man was trying to save his life?": Kantrowitz interview, 18 July 2007.

a sign of depression: Mass, journal, 3 June 1987.

248   "the hot muscled number on the beach": Licata, "Fire Island Impressions."

"a plumbing problem in my co-op": Russo, journal, 26 October 1987.

to raise his spirits: Kantrowitz, datebook, 11 April 1987.

laziness around the house: Mass, journal, 8 and 9 June 1987.

in the face of the plague: Vito Russo interview with Newton.

their insufficient response to AIDS: Child, "Vito Russo," 2:84; Vito Russo, letter to the editor, *Fire Island News*.

botched tooth extraction in April: Kantrowitz, datebook, 8 April 1987.

further tax his immune system: Russo, journal, 28 July 1987.

the extra time his lover might have enjoyed: "Vito Russo," publication unknown, December 1989, 24, courtesy of Charles Russo Jr.

patients who had avoided PCP: Russo, letter to Grossman, 25 April 1987.

a simple blood test: Ron Grossman interview.

available in pill form: Vito Russo interview with Testing the Limits Collective.

a placebo rather than AZT died: Adkins, "AZT Available to 6,500 AIDS Sufferers."

249   "no such thing as fair": Russo, journal, 28 July 1987.

"concentration camp corpse": Mass, journal, 28 July 1987.

the meaning in so much loss: Licata, "Pines Remembers."

"I could go nuts": Russo, journal, 14 September 1987.

to honor a fallen friend: Jones with Dawson, *Stitching a Revolution*, xiv.

National March on Washington for Lesbian and Gay Rights: d'Adesky and Zwickler, "Names Project," 6.

"so California": "Vito Russo," publication unknown, December 1989, 22, courtesy of Charles Russo Jr.

seventy-nine thousand participants: Williams, "200,000 March."

compromised immune systems: Barker and Wheeler, "Hundreds of Thousands March."

asked his friends not to participate: Kantrowitz interview, 2 November 2007.

austere federal facades: GMHC, "March on Washington," 11 October 1987, videotape, GMHC Oral History Videotape Collection.

tolling the names of those lost: Jones with Dawson, *Stitching a Revolution*, 133, 134.

250   Jeff's Quilt panel: Dexter interview.

250 "I'm sure he would hate this panel": *Common Threads.*
the Quilt's walking paths: Kantrowitz interview, 2 November 2007.
significant drop in his viral load: Russo, journal, 7 November 1987.
to the cocktail: Russo, journal, 2 December 1987.
bereavement-group counseling: Russo, journal, 30 April 1986.
background on Stuart Nichols: S. Nichols, "For Patients and Ourselves"; Gevisser, "New York's Finest," 17.
to help him manage mood swings: Russo, journal, 22 October 1987.
a buffer against the revelation itself: V. Russo, "Coming Out as a PWA," 179.
visible signs of his illness: Antonellis interview.
and niece Vicki: Russo, journal, 16 November 1987.

251 "I hope not": qtd. in Antonellis interview.
"when you were going to decide to tell us": qtd. in V. Russo, "Coming Out as a PWA," 179.
Vito left nonplussed: Russo, journal, 16 November 1987.
"Do you think she didn't care?": qtd. in Antonellis interview.
"He's gonna die!": qtd. in Charles Russo Jr. interview.
"mean-spirited sarcasm": Russo, journal, 7 December 1987.
"in a nice institution far away from *me*": Russo, journal, 29 December 1989.
"I'd rather die in New York than live in New Jersey": qtd. in Antonellis interview.
"Another world": Kramer, *Reports from the holocaust,* xvi.
an occasional Firehouse dance: Kramer interview.
interviewed him about his novel *Faggots*: Kramer interview.
refused to sell the novel at the Oscar Wilde Memorial Bookshop: Kramer, *Reports from the holocaust,* 19.
friends cut Larry dead: Merla, "Normal Heart," 35.

252 the waterfront brawlers of *Min and Bill* (1930): V. Russo, "*Faggots* Reviewed."
seldom attended Vito's film nights: Kramer interview.
"or Judy singing 'Over the Rainbow'": qtd. in Kramer, Kantrowitz, and Mass, "Remembering Vito Russo."
not political strategy: Kramer interview.
and civil disobedience: Kramer, *Reports from the holocaust,* 102, 104, 106, 120–21.
"if they develop": V. Russo, letter to the editor, *New York Native,* 16 February 1987.
ten thousand of them in New York City: Kramer, *Reports from the holocaust,* 127.
"Get your asses into the streets": Russo, letter to the editor, *New York Native,* 16 February 1987, 9.
before slamming down the receiver: Humm interview.

253 "you could be dead in less than five years": Kramer, *Reports from the holocaust,* 128.
over a fire: Kantrowitz, "Enemy of the People," 109.
"Give us the fucking drugs!": Kramer, *Reports from the holocaust,* 131, 132, 136.
the boroughs and New Jersey: Minutes, AIDS Coalition Meeting, 12 March 1987, reel 2, ACT UP Papers.
Priceless publicity: Vito Russo, classroom lecture, University of California Santa Cruz (UCSC), 2 February 1989, courtesy of Nancy Stoller.
shutting down Wall Street: Minutes, AIDS Coalition Meeting, 12 March 1987.
AIDS Coalition to Unleash Power (ACT UP): Clendinen and Nagourney, *Out for Good,* 555.
blacks, Hispanics, Haitians, prostitutes: Minutes, AIDS Coalition Meeting, 12 March 1987.

253   cold concrete of lower Broadway: Mass, journal, 18 March 1987.
254   and hung up: Miller interview.
       "cursing the earliness of it all": Kantrowitz interview, 2 November 2007.
       "Aren't You Worried about Him?": qtd. in Salinas, "Wall Street Closed."
       "Fuck Your Profiteering" on the other: qtd. in Vélez interview.
       debuted two years earlier: Kramer, *Reports from the Holocaust*, 138.
       "This is just the beginning!": qtd. in Salinas, "Wall Street Closed."
       "Silence=Death" coffee mugs?: Russo, UCSC lecture.
       tutorials on drug developments: Child, "Vito Russo: The Impermanence of Vision," 2:86.
       "cynical queers both male and female": Feinberg, *Spontaneous Combustion*, 164.
       often to a wearying degree: Russo, journal, 10 November 1987.
       too bureaucratic: Minutes, ACT UP meeting, 27 April 1987.
255   "True democracy in action": Northrup interview.
       "*éminence grise*": Goldberg interview.
       "save me from ever being seen as one": Russo, journal, 20 January 1988.
       often looked to Vito as a mentor: Blotcher interview; Robbe interview.
       the Macy's Thanksgiving Day Parade: Russo, UCSC lecture.
       description of Vito at ACT UP meetings: Wolfe interview.
       getting drugs into bodies as quickly as possible: Minutes, ACT UP meetings, 30 May 1988.
       "I've heard this for 25 years": Testing the Limits Records, Names no. 5, 9 October 1988, AIDS Activist Videotape Collection.
       MC nightlife: Robbe interview; Russo, journal, 26 March 1988.
256   expanded its horizons: Minutes, ACT UP meeting, 27 April 1987.
       Where were stories of survivors?: V. Russo, "Issues for New York Times Meeting."
       a Harlem drug rehabilitation center: Brozan, "Compassionate Force in the AIDS Battle."
       "It isn't happening to 'them'": Russo, journal, 15 February 1988.
       where the Aids Memorial Quilt lay on display: Wolfe interview.
257   "our queens saw their queens": ACT UP 10th Anniversary Storytelling.
       —"so they don't give a shit": Vito Russo, speech, ACT UP rally, Albany, NY, 7 May 1988, courtesy of Charles Russo Jr.
       before concluding his speech: Goldberg interview.
       "so that this will never happen again": Russo, speech, ACT UP rally.
       "adored" by the membership: Robbe interview.
       financial and emotional support to several ACT UP members: Wolfe, "Mother of Us All," 282; Wolfe interview.
258   "an ability of not making other people as angry as [Larry did]": Kramer interview.
       "Then you have to tell them so!": qtd. in Mass, journal, 12 October 1987.
       some lesbians loved Garland, too: Wolfe interview.
       when court-ordered to do so: Goldberg interview.
       in a hospital: Kramer interview.
       "read the charges" against the government: Testing the Limits Records, National Health and Human Services Rally no. 12, 10 October 1988, tape, AIDS Activist Videotape Collection.
       "exploiting *[his] movement!*": *Common Threads*, DVD, Extra Features, Vito Russo ACT UP speech.
       too lazy or indifferent to do their job properly: Vito Russo, speech, Health and Human Services, Washington, D.C., 10 October 1988, courtesy of Charles Russo Jr.
259   "Act up! Fight back! Fight AIDS!": *Common Threads*, Vito Russo ACT UP speech.

259   Susan Sarandon at ACT UP: Russo, journal, 30 September 1988.

the week before the demo: Mason, "FDA," 13.

parroting the MC's slogan verbatim: Signorile interview.

"if we're not just paper tigers": Russo, journal, 30 September 1988.

rising from the street: Testing the Limits Records, FDA, 11 October 1988, videotape, AIDS Activist Videotape Collection.

whose pants obligingly fell off: Mason, "FDA," 17.

FDA demo actions and slogans: ACT UP at the FDA, 1988, videotape, Royal S. Marks AIDS Activist Videotape Collection.

for three dollars each: ACT UP Action at the FDA and HHS Rally, videotape, Royal S. Marks AIDS Activist Videotape Collection; Kramer, *Reports from the Holocaust*, 207.

260   "Just call him Mary!": Testing the Limits Records, FDA, 11 October 1988.

camera-ready phrases: Signorile interview.

"in front of the White House next year!": Testing the Limits Records, FDA, 11 October 1988.

"good for shit for a week": qtd. in Marcus, *Making History*, 417.

arthritis that made climbing stairs or walking any distance difficult: Russo, journal, 20 June 1988.

which entailed its own anxieties: Russo, journal, 16 October 1988.

where the heat worked overtime: Russo, journal, 31 October 1988.

Steve Webb: Russo, journal, 12 February 1988; Mass, journal, 12 February 1988.

omitted mention of Robert: Russo, journal, 1 May 1988.

Robert died within a few days of PCP: Russo, journal, 13 July 1988.

261   "what [their] priorities should be": Testing the Limits Records, Names no. 5, 9 October 1988.

made him rave: Russo interview with Stoller, 17 October 1989.

"about 20 seconds after 1969": qtd. in Hopkins and Zwickler, "Acting Up or Acting Out?" 38.

"the *token*?": Russo, UCSC lecture.

and the *Seattle Weekly*: Russo, journal, 2 June 1989.

determined to score with as many fellow activists as possible: Blotcher interview.

"a runaway freight train" in his neediness: Sloan interview.

to protect him from his own advancing illness: Vázquez-Pacheco interview.

not ready to suffer that pain again: Russo, journal, 6 July 1988.

to remove other blotches: Russo, journal, 3 and 24 January 1989.

262   "I'm the one with the disease": qtd. in Howard Grossman interview.

"finally over for me in that way": Russo, journal, 10 and 5 June 1989.

to make him feel good about his body: Sawyer interview.

Their cheers shook the hall: Webster CD and Montreal Conference no. 1, Continuation of Montreal Conference no. 1, videotapes, 4 June 1989, Royal S. Marks AIDS Activist Videotape Collection.

"every level of decision-making": Russo, "ACT UP's Report from Montreal," undated, reel 92, ACT UP Papers.

a prominent slot on *ABC World News Tonight*: Blotcher interview.

demonstrators were alienating rather than educating attendees: Shilts, "Politics Confused with Therapy"; through anal intercourse: Jones, *Stitching a Revolution*, 179.

AIDS "would be over by '91": Russo, journal, 3 and 5 June 1989.

263   insomnia and fatigue as side effects: Russo, journal, 31 January and 28 November 1988.

damage his bone marrow: Russo, journal, 1 April 1988.

"a new antiviral and new treatments": Montreal AIDS Conference no. 3, 1989, videotape, Royal S. Marks AIDS Activist Video Collection.

"a real decline": Russo, journal, 14 August 1989.

263   illness was progressing: Kantrowitz, datebook, 24 August 1989.

respected but never desired: Russo, journal, 25 August and 15 September 1989.

"factory seconds": Callen, "Hugely Successful PWA Singles Tea."

didn't feel attractive enough to make the rounds: Russo, journal, 28 May 1989.

the end was drawing near: Russo, journal, 16 October 1989.

Vito began receiving food stamps: Vito Russo, financial papers and datebook, 1987, Vito Russo Papers.

Vito accepted: "Faith, Films and the Future," 4.

$500 per column: Thompson interview.

264   "learning a new way to look at images": Russo, "Different from the Others," 61.

without drama: Hubbard interview; Schulman interview.

as he had pondered doing: Hammer interview.

National Gay and Lesbian Task Force conference: Russo, datebook, 1989, Vito Russo Papers.

"The Marathon Closet": Jay interview.

"Sex Is" or "Just Sex": Hammond, "Yale Campus Police."

"I'm scared shitless": qtd. in Normand interview.

hundreds of demonstrators: Leuze, "9 Arrested."

265   history of *Common Threads*: Zwickler, "Quilt Film Wins Oscar," 16, 17.

"a gay male in the eye of the storm": Epstein interview.

had its antidote to coziness: Friedman interview.

of Carter Wilson: Carter Wilson interview.

Rob asked Jeffrey to conduct the interview: Zwickler, "Quilt Film Wins Oscar," 17.

the sound man was wiping his eyes: Friedman interview.

266   "a terrible tragedy that we survived": *Common Threads*.

"a musical comedy": qtd. in Mass, journal, 19 March 1989.

that he wanted such publicity: Russo, journal, 20 March 1989.

incapacitated him for a week: Russo, journal, 15 September 1989.

"the AIDS poster boy": Greppi, "Painfully Aware."

"too dangerous to live in": Russo, journal, 18 March 1990.

tracked him down for sex: Bowen, "In Vito Veritas," 53.

He promised: Rosenman interview, 1 September 2007.

267   A phone call to her publicist was all it took: Kane interview.

"I do not bray!": qtd. in Sawyer interview.

"something from *BUtterfield 8*?!": qtd. in Howard Grossman interview.

a personal interest in his health: Kane interview.

"As I was saying yesterday to Elizabeth Taylor": qtd. in Ehrenstein interview.

an impediment to further fun: Greppi, "Painfully Aware."

Sal Licata's final days: Brent Nicholson Earle, in *Voices from the Front*.

a "basket case": Russo, journal, 3 January 1990.

"What's the big deal?": Russo, journal, 20 January 1990.

"[his] life and the movement ha[d] been one and the same": Russo, letter to Mattes, 12 January 1988.

268   during the entire previous year: Russo, journal, 28 May 1989.

and into social-change organizations: Stoller interview.

having to drive everywhere—stick shift!: Russo, journal, 1 and 24 January 1990; his own kitchenette: Carter Wilson interview.

but were curious: UCSC course materials, Vito Russo Papers.

268   on Charles Goldman: course materials; Goldman interview.
"and drinking Coors Light": Janet Myers interview.
to discuss coming out: Broudy interview.
in historic context: Limperis interview.
and UC–Davis campuses: Russo, journal, 14 March 1990.

269   "That's why you're a TA.": course materials. Elsewhere, I have discussed Vito's hostile reactions to academe in general, queer theory in particular. See Schiavi, "Looking for Vito."
"any of the films on the list": TCC lecture notes, 17 January 1990, course materials.
"a longer, older tradition than most people are allowed to know": Waters interview.
stealthy tracking and cataloging: The Celluloid Closet, course syllabus, UCSC, Winter 1990, Vito Russo Papers.
"almost like a ritual": Waters interview.

270   (Travolta, Gere, Chamberlain): Waters, "In Vito Veritas," MetroActiveMovies.
"a little slow tonight": qtd. in Limperis interview.
a two-hour lecture: Waters interview.
two months before its commercial release: Schwenterley interview.
"applause, whistles and yowls of approval": Waters, "In Vito Veritas," MetroActiveMovies.
"and give it to young people": Myers interview.
"I love you and I will miss you dearly": course materials.
and Olympia, Washington: Russo, journal, 23 April and 7 May 1990.
invited to deliver a keynote speech: Russo, journal, 20 January 1990.

271   "terrified by what I represent": Vito Russo interview, Testing the Limits Videotape Collective; Mass, journal, 12 April 1990.
"accept the situation the way it is": Vito Russo interview, Testing the Limits Videotape Collective
escalating anemia: Russo, journal, 27 March 1990.
a red-cell producer: Russo, journal, 1 June 1990.
"I'll be in deep shit": Russo, journal, 17 April 1990.
necessitating chemotherapy: Russo, journal, 30 March 1990.
if he was all right: Baby Jane Dexter, in *Vito's Legacy*.
to keep his frightened friend company: Kantrowitz interview, 2 November 2007.
from the Halley's comet cruise in 1986: Mass, journal, 8 June 1990.
"our favorite family photo": Kantrowitz, "Family Album," 281.

272   the keynote speaker: Lunger interview.
speak out against homophobia in art: Vito Russo, Gay Film Festival speech, 7 June 1990, Vito Russo Papers.
never to forget their debt to women: Pally interview.
"standing ovations": Mass, "Vito Russo, 1946–1990."
administer the IV himself: Kantrowitz, datebook, 21 June 1990.
The Lord of the Rings: Kantrowitz, datebook, 25 June 1990.
twice its normal size: Kantrowitz, datebook, 20 June 1990; Mass, journal, 22 June 1990.
"punished like this for his lifestyle": qtd. in Mass, journal, 18 June 1990.
"able to hook up instantly!": qtd. in Swannack interview.
rose to greet him: Kramer, Kantrowitz, and Mass, "Remembering Vito Russo," 52.
to his multitude of fans: McFarlane e-mail.
"These are our children": qtd. in Kantrowitz interview, 31 July 2007.
illuminated in lavender for the first time: Kantrowitz, datebook, 22 June 1990.

273   Vito would not be deterred: Charles Russo memoir.

until he fell asleep: Johnson interview, 8 October 2008.

and ordered Bill out: Johnson, letter to Schiavi.

unable to cover basic expenses: Kramer, "Who Killed Vito Russo?" 27.

"less than $100 in the bank": Vito Russo, letter to NYU [Medical Center] Radiology, 14 July 1990, Vito Russo Papers.

generous checks in June: Kantrowitz, datebook, 17 and 22 June 1990.

in future writing: Child, "Vito Russo," 2:84.

"the new PWA song": qtd. in Mass, "Vito Russo, 1946–1990," 4.

274   "It's disgusting": qtd. in Kantrowitz, "Family Album," 295.

"true love and true friendship": Charles Russo memoir.

began chemotherapy: Kantrowitz, datebook, 20 July 1990.

Scenes from a Mall: Kantrowitz, datebook, 24 July 1990.

"and I have to see it": qtd. in Don Shewey, journal, 2 November 1990, courtesy of Don Shewey.

from much happier times: Russo, journal, 11 August 1990.

"How do you always know what I want?": qtd. in Kantrowitz interview, 2 November 2007

Acadia National Park: Kantrowitz, datebook, 25 and 26 August 1990.

reduce his fever and ease the aches in his legs: Russo, journal, 26 and 29 August 1990.

one of his famous apple pies: Mass, journal, 5 September 1990.

that nobody cry in his presence: Normand interview.

275   Vito's rants could be highly entertaining: Zwerman interview.

those noble efforts were now past: Kantrowitz interview, 18 July 2007.

more typing paper: Wolfe interview.

courses of painful radiation and chemo would ultimately fail: Russo, journal, 11 and 16 September 1990.

terrified of death: Kantrowitz interview, 2 November 2007.

a sunset: Todd interview; across the twilight sky: Mann, "Vito and the Birds"; striking the Empire State Building on an autumn afternoon: Mass, "Vito Russo, 1946–1990."

elected to stop all AIDS drugs and die: Dexter, "Cabaret Singer & Her Friend Vito."

"This isn't living": qtd. in Mass, journal, 22 October 1990.

"This *sucks!*": Eric Myers interview.

"It breaks my heart": Jed Mattes, fax, 14 November 1990, courtesy Charles Russo, Jr.

"gasping like a fish out of water the entire night": Mass, journal, 30 October 1990.

nearly stopped his breathing: Kantrowitz, datebook, 31 October and 1 November 1990.

276   for her uncle's farewell: Vicki Russo interview.

among people who hadn't met previously: Karaban interview.

friends' future responsibilities: Zwerman, Normand, and Dexter interviews.

from the musical *1776*: Kramer, Kantrowitz, and Mass, "Remembering Vito Russo," 52; Mass, journal, 2 November 1990.

at Vito's bedside: Kantrowitz datebook, 3 November 1990.

would not be happy with the bequests in his will: Charles Russo memoir.

"motion pictures and gay rights": Vito Russo, Last Will and Testament, 23 February 1987, courtesy of Charles Russo Jr.

277   until Arnie threw it back at him: Charles Russo memoir.

his already compromised lungpower: Kantrowitz, datebook, 4 November 1990.

"I think your friend is leaving": qtd. in Cruse, "Our Last Night with Vito."

Afterword

278   Sources for the Afterword include: Charles Russo interview, 19 October 2007; Kantro-
       witz, "A Remembrance of Vito Russo," 75; Zadan interview; Mangin, "Tribute to a Gay
       Titan"; Dexter interview; Kramer, "Who Killed Vito Russo?" 26; Kramer interview;
       Normand interview; Kantrowitz interview, 31 July 2007; Charles Russo Jr. interview; Les-
       lie Russo interview; Rosenman interview, 1 September 2007; Epstein interview; Maupin
       interview; Tomlin interview, 30 July 2007; Annie Russo, letter to Vin Tozzi, undated, cour-
       tesy of Vin Tozzi.

Interviews and Personal Communications

Antonellis, Phyllis ("Perky"). Jackson Heights, NY. Telephone, 29 January 2008.

Ashkinazy, Steve. New York, NY. 24 September 2007.

Berkowitz, Richard. New York, NY. Telephone, 15 February 2008.

Bie, Steven. New York, NY. 16 September 2007.

Blauvelt, Dianne Wondra. Hewitt, NJ. Telephone, 10 February 1009.

Blotcher, Jay. New York, NY. 15 July 2008.

Bourne, Bette. London, England. Telephone, 13 July 2007.

Bowers, Michael. Portland, OR. Telephone, 21 October 2007; e-mail to author, 25 November 2007.

Boyd, Malcolm. Los Angeles, CA. Telephone, 17 July 2007.

Bram, Christopher. New York, NY. Telephone, 9 August 2007.

Brewer, Joe. San Francisco, CA. 4 August 2008.

Broudy, Trev. Santa Barbara, CA. Telephone, 17 July 2007.

Bumbalo, Victor. Los Angeles, CA. Telephone, 24 September 2008.

Busch, Charles. New York, NY. 28 July 2008.

Bush, Larry. San Francisco, CA. Telephone, 8 January 2009.

Cole, Janet. San Francisco, CA. Telephone, 7 September 2007.

Conant, Marcus. San Francisco, CA. Telephone, 16 July 2007.

Crowley, Mart. Los Angeles, CA. Telephone, 9 February 2002; letter to author, 27 January 2003.

De Cola, Joe. New York, NY. 16 July 2008.

DeStefano, George. Long Island City, NY. Telephone, 30 August 2008.

Denneny, Michael. New York, NY. 12 July 2007.

Dexter, Baby Jane. New York, NY. Telephone, 20 August 2007; e-mail to author, 3 August 2007.

Duane, Tom. New York, NY. 7 August 2007.

Dyer, Richard. Rome, Italy. Telephone, 19 July 2007.

Ehrenstein, David. Los Angeles, CA. Telephone, 16 July 2007.

Eller, Lucille Sanzero. Cedar Grove, NJ. Telephone, 31 January 2009.

Ellsworth, Adele Sevcik. Phoenix, AZ. Telephone, 21 May 2009.

Engstrom, Everett. Denver, CO. Telephone, 10 October 2008.

Epstein, Rob. San Francisco, CA. Telephone, 16 July 2007.

Evans, Arthur. San Francisco, CA. E-mail to author, 2 August 2007.

Foto, Rink. San Francisco, CA. E-mail to author, 11 March 2008.

Fouratt, Jim. New York, NY. 29 July 2008.

Friedman, Jeffrey. San Francisco, CA. Telephone, 26 June 2007.

Giles, Ronnie. Hasbrouck Heights, NJ. Telephone, 24 November 2008.

Goldberg, Ron. New York, NY. Telephone, 4 December 2007.

Goldhaber, Fred. New York, NY. 29 June 2007.

Goldman, Charles. Brooklyn, NY. Telephone, 18 July 2007.

Greenbaum, Wesley. New York, NY. 28 August 2007.

Grossman, Howard. San Francisco, CA. Telephone, 8 August 2007.

Grossman, Ron. New York, NY. 13 January 2009.

Guthmann, Edward. San Francisco, CA. Telephone, 14 July 2007.

Hammer, Barbara. New York, NY. Telephone, 29 July 2008.

Hannaway, Dorian. Los Angeles, CA. Telephone, 23 August 2007.

Harding, Tom. Portland, OR. Telephone, 3 September 2008.

Harper, Valerie. Santa Monica, CA. Telephone, 29 October 2008.

Hochberg, Fred. New York, NY. 9 November 2007.

Hubbard, Jim. New York, NY. 25 June 2007.

Humm, Andy. New York, NY. Telephone, 10 July 2008.

Ireland, Doug. New York, NY. Telephone, 24 July 2008.

Jay, Karla. New York, NY. 9 August 2007.

Johnson, William. Cleveland, OH. 19 August and 8 October 2008; letter to author, 19 August 2008.

Judell, Brandon. New York, NY. Telephone, 20 August 2007.

Kane, John. Los Angeles, CA. Telephone, 8 September 2008.

Kantrowitz, Arnie. New York, NY. 5, 18, 31 July, 28 September, 12 October, and 2 November 2007, 26 June 2008, 9 September 2009; telephone, 7 August 2006.

Kantrowitz, Arnie, and Larry Mass. New York, NY. 31 July 2007.

Karaban, Jeffrey. New York, NY. 22 September 2008.

Kardish, Laurence. New York, NY. 29 June 2007.

Katz, Jonathan Ned. New York, NY. Telephone, 17 October 2007.

Kennedy, Joe. New York, NY. E-mail to author, 6 August 2007.

Kent, Mary Rose. San Francisco, CA. Telephone, 2 September 2008.

Kerr, Barbara. Plainfield, NJ. Telephone, 25 August 2008.

Kirby, David. Brooklyn, NY. Telephone, 4 December 2008.

Kramer, Larry. New York, NY. Telephone, 30 June 2009.

Krotz, Steve. Tempe, AZ. Telephone, 14 June, 14 July, and 17 November 2008; e-mails to author, 29 July and 9 August 2007, 15 June 2008.

Lella, Carol De Simone. Henderson, NV. Telephone, 1 December 2008.

Lessinger, Natalie. New York, NY. Telephone, 29 September 2008.

Limperis, George. San Francisco, CA. Telephone, 25 July 2007.

Luddy, Tim. San Francisco, CA. E-mail to author, 26 January 2008.

Lunger, Jeff. New York, NY. Telephone, 24 October 2007.

Magliozzi, Ron. New York, NY. 2 July 2007.

Marinaro, Joanie. Fairfield, NJ. Telephone, 21 June 2008.

Mass, Larry. New York, NY. Telephone, 9 August 2006; e-mail to author, 26 February 2008.

Maupin, Armistead. San Francisco, CA. Telephone, 13 October 2008.

Mayer, Tom. San Francisco, CA. Telephone, 31 January 2008.

McFarlane, Rodger. Denver, CO. E-mail to author, 10 July 2007.

McKerrow, Graham. London, England. Telephone, 18 September 2007.

Merla, Patrick. New York, NY. 26 July and 7 August 2007; e-mails to author, 6 and 14 November 2008, 19 March 2009.

Miller, Gary. New York, NY. 19 June 2007.

Moore, Larry. New York, NY. 5 July 2007.

Myers, Eric. New York, NY. 28 July 2008.

Myers, Janet. San Francisco, CA. Telephone, 26 July 2007.

Newkirk, Walter. Chatham, NJ. Telephone, 3 September 2008.

Newton, Esther. Ann Arbor, MI. Telephone, 11 September 2007.

Normand, Beryl. New Haven, CT. Telephone, 5 November 2007.

Northrup, Ann. New York, NY. Telephone, 24 September 2008.

Offen, Hal. San Francisco, CA. E-mail to author, 16 August 2007.

Pacheco, Patrick. New York, NY. 2 September 2008.

Pally, Marcia. New York, NY. Telephone, 5 September 2008.

Parker, Gregson. Portland, OR. Telephone, 6 January 2009.

Parker, Scot. Albuquerque, NM. Telephone, 26 February 2009.

Picano, Felice. San Francisco, CA. Telephone, 5 September 2007.

Pitchford, Dean. Santa Barbara, CA. Telephone, 31 July 2008.

Praunheim, Rosa von. E-mail to author, 12 July 2007.

Reynolds, Dale. Los Angeles, CA. Telephone, 11 July 2007.

Richards, Robert W. New York, NY. 31 August 2007.

Rivera, Corona (Cora Perotta). Oakland, CA. Telephone, 6 November 2007.

Robbe, Scott. Milwaukee, WI. Telephone, 4 September 2008.

Romanello, Denise. Queens, NY. Telephone, 2 February 2008.

Romanello, Sally ("Anna"). Jackson Heights, NY. Telephone, 11 June 2008.

Rosenman, Howard. Los Angeles, CA. Telephone, 21 August and 1 September 2007.

Roskoff, Allen. New York, NY. 15 October 2007.

Russo, Charles (Vito's brother). Glen Rock, NJ. 19 October and 30 November 2007, 18 July and 21 November 2008; e-mail to author, 8 February 2009.

Russo, Charles, Jr. (Vito's nephew). San Francisco, CA. Telephone, 23 October 2007.

Russo, Leslie. New York, NY. 29 February 2008.

Russo, Linda. Glen Rock, NJ. 19 October 2007.

Russo, Robert. Keyport, NJ. Telephone, 7 July 2008.

Russo, Vicki. Greenville, SC. Telephone, 11 February 2008.

Russo, Vito. By Richard Berkowitz. New York, NY. 7 December 1976. Courtesy of Richard Berkowitz.

———. By Leslie Cohen. New York, NY. 19 June 1978. Courtesy of Leslie Cohen.

———. By Janet Cole. San Francisco, CA. 27 June 1988. *The Celluloid Closet*, DVD, extra features.

———. By Esther Newton. Cherry Grove, NY. 25 August 1987. Courtesy of Esther Newton.

———. By Nancy Stoller. New York, NY. 2 and 17 October 1989. Courtesy of Nancy Stoller.

———. By Testing the Limits Videotape Collective. New York, NY. 15 May 1990. Testing the Limits Records.

Salerno, Maria ("Chickie"). La Crescenta, CA. Telephone, 9 June 2008.

Sandler, Barry. Orlando, FL. Telephone, 25 June 2007.

Saslow, James. New York, NY. Telephone, 24 July 2007.

Sawyer, Allen. San Francisco, CA. 5 August 2008.

Schulman, Sarah. New York, NY. Telephone, 18 June 2007.

Schwenterley, Jim. Santa Cruz, CA. Telephone, 16 July 2007.

Senak, Mark. Washington, DC. Telephone, 27 June 2007.

Shewey, Don. New York, NY. 4 June 2007.

Siggelkow, Rick. Nyack, NY. Telephone, 29 September 2008.

Signorile, Michelangelo. New York, NY. Telephone, 1 October 2008.

Silver, Charles. New York, NY. 2 July 2007.

Silverstein, Charles. New York, NY. 22 July 2008.

Sloan, David. New York, NY. 11 July 2008.

Stavis, Gene. New York, NY. 16 September 2007.

Steele, Tom. New York, NY. Telephone, 22 August 2007; e-mail to author, 16 September 2007.

Stoller, Nancy. San Francisco, CA. Telephone, 8 December 2008.

Strub, Sean. Milford, PA. E-mails to author, 3 and 4 August 2007.

Swannack, Cheryl. Washington, DC. Telephone, 5 September 2007.

Thompson, Mark. Los Angeles, CA. Telephone, 13 July 2007.

Timmons, Stuart. Los Angeles, CA. Telephone, 31 August 2007.

Todd, Lew. New York, NY. 24 September 2007.

Tomlin, Lily. Sherman Oaks, CA. Telephone, 30 July 2007 and 24 July 2008; e-mail to author, 9 August 2007.

Tozzi, Vin. Vieques, Puerto Rico. Telephone, 21 February 2008.

Tramontozzi, Jean. Bronx, NY. 5 June 2008.

Van Dyke, Murray. Santa Fe, NM. Telephone, 15 July 2008.

Vázquez-Pacheco, Robert. New York, NY. Telephone, 29 September 2008.

Vélez, Andy. New York, NY. Telephone, 28 July 2008.

Vouriotis, Christine. New York, NY. Telephone, 24 August 2007.

Waters, Christina. Santa Cruz, CA. Telephone, 20 July 2007.

Wilson, Carter. Santa Cruz, CA. Telephone, 25 September 2008.

Wilson, Doric. New York, NY. 29 August 2007.

Wilson, John Morgan. West Hollywood, CA. E-mail to author, 7 August 2007.

Wolfe, Maxine. Brooklyn, NY. 24 July 2007.

Young, Allen. Orange, MA. E-mail to author, 4 September 2007.

Zadan, Craig. Los Angeles, CA. Telephone, 25 August 2008.

Zwerman, Gilda. New York, NY. 22 July 2008.

Bibliography

Archival Collections

ACT UP [AIDS Coalition to Unleash Power] Papers. Astor, Lenox and Tilden Foundations. Manuscripts and Archives Division. New York Public Library.

Bell, Arthur, Papers. International Gay Information Center. Astor, Lenox and Tilden Foundations. Manuscripts and Archives Division. New York Public Library.

Gay Activists Alliance Papers. International Gay Information Center. Astor, Lenox and Tilden Foundations. Manuscripts and Archives Division. New York Public Library.

GMHC [Gay Men's Health Crisis] Oral History. Royal S. Marks AIDS Activist Videotape Collection. Astor, Lenox and Tilden Foundations. Manuscripts and Archives Division. New York Public Library.

Grillo, Rudy, Collection. Astor, Lenox and Tilden Foundations. Manuscripts and Archives Division. New York Public Library.

International Gay Information Center. Astor, Lenox and Tilden Foundations. Manuscripts and Archives Division. New York Public Library.

Kantrowitz, Arnie, Papers. Astor, Lenox and Tilden Foundations. Manuscripts and Archives Division. New York Public Library.

Marks, Royal S., AIDS Activist Videotape Collection. Astor, Lenox and Tilden Foundations. Manuscripts and Archives Division. New York Public Library.

Mattachine Society Papers. International Gay Information Center. Astor, Lenox and Tilden Foundations. Manuscripts and Archives Division. New York Public Library.

Russo, Vito, Papers. Astor, Lenox and Tilden Foundations. Manuscripts and Archives Division. New York Public Library.

Testing the Limits Records. Astor, Lenox and Tilden Foundations. Manuscripts and Archives Division. New York Public Library.

Books, Articles, Films, and Documents

ACT UP 10th Anniversary Storytelling. 21 March 1997. http://actupny.org/divatv/synopsis75.html (accessed 6 July 2009).

Adkins, Barry. "AZT Available to 6,500 AIDS Sufferers." *New York Native*, 13 October 1986, 9.

———. "Gays at the *Post*." *New York Native*, 20–26 January 1986, 16.

Adler, Polly. *A House Is Not a Home*. New York: Rinehart, 1953.

Aiken, David, et al. "Rhetoric Shocking" [letter to editor]. *Advocate*, 11 February 1976, 17.

Allen, Dan. "Film Marathon: 12 Hours on the Firehouse Floor." Publication data unknown. Vito Russo Papers.

Altman, Lawrence K. "Rare Cancer Seen in 41 Homosexuals." *New York Times*, 3 July 1981, A20.

". . . And the Band Played On." *Gay Activist: Newsletter of the Gay Activists Alliance*, June 1971, 5.

Anderson, Scott P. "Vito Russo: The Reel-Life Images of Gays in the Movies." *Advocate*, 15 October 1981, 36.

Apple, Bill. "Firehouse Flick-Flockers." *Gay Activist: Newsletter of the Gay Activists Alliance*, October 1971, 11, 14.

"Arthur Bell: Two or Three Things We Loved about Him." *Village Voice*, 26 June 1984, 11.

Auer, Jeff. "Bette at the Bathhouse." *Gay and Lesbian Review*, May–June 2008, 26–28.

Babuscio, Jack. "The Man Who Blew the Whistle on William Friedkin." *Gay News* (London), 18 September–1 October 1980, 19.

———. "Native New Yorkers." *Gay News* (London), 2–15 November 1978, 23.

———. "Peter Adair." *Gay News* (London), 21 September–4 October 1978, 29.

———. "'There Never Have Been Lesbians or Gay Men in Hollywood Films, Only Homosexuals.'" *Gay News* (London), 1–14 October 1981, 21–22.

Barker, Karlyn, and Linda Wheeler. "Hundreds of Thousands March for Gay Rights." *Washington Post*, 12 October 1987, A1.

Bayer, Ronald, and Gerald Oppenheimer. *AIDS Doctors: Voices from the Epidemic.* New York: Oxford University Press, 2000.

Bell, Arthur. "Bell Tells." *Village Voice*, 16 July 1979, 36.

———. *Dancing the Gay Lib Blues: A Year in the Homosexual Liberation Movement.* New York: Simon & Schuster, 1971.

———. "Gays in Chains." *Gay Activist: News & Opinion from the Gay Activists Alliance*, March 1972, 5.

———. "Hostility Comes Out of the Closet." *Village Voice*, 28 June 1973, 1, 16, 18.

———. "Mud in Your Eye" [letter to the editor]. *New York Native*, 1–14 August 1983, 4.

———. "My Friend Who Bombed the Waldorf." *Village Voice*, 14 September 1978, 71.

———. Review of *The Celluloid Closet. Hollywood Reporter*, 26 June 1981.

Bell, Christopher. *Images of America: East Harlem.* New York: Arcadia, 2003.

"Bella Abzug, Congressional Hopeful, Bids for Gay Vote." *GAY*, 15 June 1970, 3, 12.

Bellet, Pamela. "Russo Decries Image of Gays in Movies as 'Sick or Jokes.'" *Targum* [Rutgers University student newspaper], 11 April 1977, 4.

Black, Jonathan. "A Happy Birthday for Gay Liberation." *Village Voice*, 2 July 1970, 1, 58.

Blane, Ralph (music), and Hugh Martin (lyrics). "The Trolley Song." *Meet Me in St. Louis.* Directed by Vincente Minnelli. Metro-Goldwyn–Mayer, 1944.

Blotcher, Jay. "A Pat on the Back for New York Gays." *New York Native*, 18–31 July 1983, 24.

———. "Who in the World Is Vito Russo?" *Pride '09*, 2009, 28–31.

Bowen, Peter. "In Vito Veritas." *OutWeek*, 26 November 1989, 52–53, 61.

Broderick, Frank. "The 'Stepin Fetchits of the '80s.'" *Au Courant*, 11 January 1988, 6–8.

Brozan, Nadine. "A Compassionate Force in the AIDS Battle." *New York Times*, 13 April 1987, B6.

Buckley, Peter. "Fresh Faces from the British Cinema." *After Dark*, July 1971, 38–41.

Buckley, Tom. "Cherry Grove Stays Aloof from Gay Activists' Cause." *New York Times*, 14 July 1972, 33.

Buckley, William, Jr. "Identify All the Carriers." *New York Times*, 18 March 1986, A27.

Bugliosi, Vincent, with Curt Gentry. *Helter Skelter.* New York: Bantam, 1974.

Byron, Stuart. "Finally—Two Films Dealing with the Issues of Gay Lib." *New York Times*, 18 July 1971, 11.

Callen, Michael. "Hugely Successful PWA Singles Tea to Be Repeated." *PWA Coalition Newsline*, March 1987, 2.

Callen, Michael, and Richard Berkowitz, with Richard Dworkin. "We Know Who We Are: Two Gay Men Declare War on Promiscuity." *New York Native*, 8–21 November 1982, 23, 25, 27, 29.

Campbell, J. Louis, III. *Jack Nichols, Gay Pioneer: "Have You Heard My Message?"* New York: Harrington Press, 2007.

Carter, David. *Stonewall: The Riots That Sparked the Gay Revolution.* New York: St. Martin's Press, 2004.

The Celluloid Closet. 1995. Directed by Robert Epstein and Jeffrey Friedman. DVD. Sony Pictures Classics, 2001.

Cheren, Mel, with Gabriel Rotello, and Brent Nicholson Earle. *My Life and the Paradise Garage: Keep on Dancin'.* New York: 24 Hours for Life, 2000.

Child, Tim. "Vito Russo: The Impermanence of Vision." *Windy City Times,* 21 June 1990, 2:84, 86, 96.

Chute, David. "The Velvet Light Trap." *Film Comment,* September 1981, 78.

Clendinen, Dudley, and Adam Nagourney. *Out for Good: The Struggle to Build a Gay Rights Movement in America.* New York: Touchstone, 1999.

Coffin, Henry Sloane. Letter to the editor. *New York Herald-Tribune,* 11 July 1946, 22.

Common Threads: Stories from the Quilt. 1989. Directed by Robert Epstein and Jeffrey Friedman. DVD. New Yorker Video, 2004.

Conrad, Peter. "Conspicuous Liberation." *Times Literary Supplement,* 4 December 1981, 1423.

Cruse, Howard. "Our Last Night with Vito." Essay. February 1991. Courtesy of Howard Cruse.

d'Adesky, Anne-christine. "Gays on Two Coasts Protest Supreme Court Sodomy Ruling." *New York Native,* 14 July 1986, 8.

d'Adesky, Anne-christine, and Phil Zwickler. "The Names Project: The Quilt That Woke Up America." *New York Native,* 26 October 1987, 6, 8.

Darnton, John. "Homosexuals March Down 7th Avenue." *New York Times,* 25 June 1973, 21.

"Daytime Cruising." *GAY,* 10 May 1971, 2.

Deboske, Su. "Gay Club in SoHo Is Active." Publication data unknown. Vito Russo Papers.

Dennis, Patrick. *Auntie Mame.* 1955. Cutchogue, NY: Buccaneer Books, 2000.

D'Eramo, James. "Federal Health Officials Announce Cause of AIDS." *New York Native,* 7–20 May 1984, 7.

Dexter, Baby Jane. "The Cabaret Singer & Her Friend Vito." *Parlée Plus,* November 1991, 29.

"Did You Hear . . . ?" *New York Native,* 4 May 1987, 4.

"Dinner and Debate." *New York Native,* 8–21 November 1982, 9.

"Doctor Who Calls Gays 'Worse Than Murderers' Dropped by A.P.A." *New York Native,* 5–18 November 1984, 6.

Duberman, Martin. *Stonewall.* New York: Dutton, 1993.

Dyer, Richard. Introduction. *Gays & Film.* Edited by Richard Dyer. 1977. New York: New York Zoetrope, 1984.

———. "Review Essay: Vito Russo, *The Celluloid Closet: Homosexuality in the Movies.*" *Studies in Visual Communication* (Spring 1983): 52–56.

Eisenbach, David. *Gay Power: An American Revolution.* New York: Carroll & Graf, 2006.

"Emerald City Expands to West." *Gaysweek,* 1 May 1978, 19.

Epstein, Joseph. "Homo/Hetero: The Struggle for Sexual Identity." *Harper's Magazine,* September 1970, 37–51.

Fairbanks, Harold. "Naturally, Larkin Does His *Thing.*" *Advocate,* 14 August 1974, 38–39.

"Faith, Films and the Future: A Chat with Vito Russo." *Melbourne Star Observer* (Victoria, Australia), 11 and 25 March 1988, 3–6.

Fall, John A. "Anti-Defamation League Zaps *New York Post.*" *New York Native,* 16–22 December 1985, 10–11.

———. "Gay and Lesbian Anti-Defamation League Changes Name." *New York Native,* 27 January–2 February 1986, 12.

———. "The New Stonewall?" *New York Native,* 25 November–1 December 1985, 11.

"Falwell Calls for AIDS Quarantine." *New York Native,* 15–28 July 1985, 11.

Farber, Stephen. "From Sissies to Studs." *American Film,* September 1981, 72–73.

Feinberg, David B. *Spontaneous Combustion*. New York: Viking, 1991.

"Fidelifacts Pres. Charged with Bribes." *GAY*, 1 March 1971, 12.

"Firehouse Flicks." *Gay Activist: News & Opinion from the Gay Activists Alliance*, December 1971–January 1972, 15.

Fisher, Peter. "Fidelifacts: Sex-Snooping Agency Draws Gay Fire." *GAY*, 15 February 1971, 1.

———. "Gay Couples Celebrate Engagement at Marriage License Bureau." *GAY*, 5 July 1971, 1, 14.

———. *The Gay Mystique: The Myth and Reality of Male Homosexuality*. New York: Stein & Day, 1972.

———. "3,000 March on N.Y. State Capitol." *GAY*, 12 April 1971, 1, 8.

Fitzpatrick, Jerry. "Jerry's Sphere." *GAY*, 7 May 1973, 2.

"5 Arrested in GAA Zap." *Gay Activist: Newsletter of the Gay Activists Alliance*, May 1971, 14.

"500 Angry Homosexuals Protest Raid." *GAY*, 13 April 1970, 3.

Fleming, Martha. "Looking for What Isn't There." *Jump Cut*, 28 April 1983, 59–61.

Fosburgh, Lacey. "From a Quiet Seminarian to Homosexual Spokesman." *New York Times*, 25 January 1977, 16.

———. "Thousands of Homosexuals Hold a Protest Rally in Central Park." *New York Times*, 29 June 1970, 1, 20.

Frank, Gerold. *Judy*. New York: Harper & Row, 1975.

French, Philip. "Stuff for Buffs." *Observer* (London), 6 December 1981, 26.

Fulford, Robert. "Japan Is His Oyster: Decades in Japan Made Donald Richie the Writer He Is Today." *National Post*, 30 November 2004. http://www.robertfulford.com/2004-11-30-richie.html (accessed 18 March 2009).

"The GAA Alternative." Gay Activists Alliance. Typescript, 1970.

"GAA Finds a Home." *Gay Activist: Newsletter of the Gay Activists Alliance*, May 1971, 9.

Gavin, James. *Intimate Nights: The Golden Age of New York Cabaret*. New York: Back Stage Books, 2006.

Gay Liberation Front panel. The Lesbian, Gay, Bisexual and Transgender Community Center. Author's notes. New York, NY. June 26, 2008.

Gay Sex in the '70s. 2005. Directed by Joseph Lovett. DVD. Wolfe, 2006.

"Gays March on Albany." *Gay Activist: Newsletter of the Gay Activists Alliance*, April 1971, 1, 8.

Gelbert, Bruce-Michael. "Movies and Masses." *New York Native*, 13 April 1987, 41.

Gengle, Dean. "People." *Advocate*, 21 September 1977, 15–16.

Gevisser, Mark. "New York's Finest." *7 Days*, 22 June 1988, 14–20.

Giteck, Lenny. "Behind the Microphone with Lily." *Advocate*, 18 March 1986, 5.

"Give 'Em a Hand." *In Touch for Men*, January 1983, 7–8.

Goodstein, D. B. "Opening Space." *Advocate*, 14 January 1976, 5.

———. "The Publisher's Opening Space: Our Challenge." *Advocate*, 29 January 1975, 3.

Gould, Jason. "Out of the Closets, into the Streets." *GAY*, 20 July 1970, 5–6.

Greppi, Michele. "Painfully Aware." *New York Post*, 13 October 1989, 96.

Grubb, Kevin. Obituary for William Como. *New York Native*, 30 January 1989, 8.

Grutzner, Charles. "Buyers' Strikes Spreading as Prices Continue to Rise." *New York Times*, 12 July 1946, 1, 10.

Guide to the George Amberg and Robert Gessner Papers 1913–1978. New York University Archives. http://dlib.nyu.edu/findingaids/html/archives/amberg_content.html (accessed 11 March 2009).

Gunter, Freeman. "Looking Back at the Gay Gala." *Michael's Thing*, 20 August 1973, 28, 31.

Hammond, John. "'Without a Single Apology': Sean O'Brien Strub Runs for Congress." *New York Native*, 17 September 1990, 18.

———. "Yale Campus Police Disrupt Gay and Lesbian Conference." *New York Native*, 13 November 1989, 10.

Hannaway, Dorian. "Under the Influence: A Memoir." Undated manuscript. Courtesy of Dorian Hannaway.

Hardy, Robin, with David Groff. *The Crisis of Desire: AIDS and the Fate of Gay Brotherhood.* Boston: Houghton Mifflin, 1999.

Harvey, Stephen. "Defenseless: Learning to Live with AIDS." *Village Voice,* 21 December 1982, 1, 14, 16, 20.

———. "Hide in Plain Sight: Gays and the Movies." *Village Voice,* 5 August 1981, 30.

Highberger, Craig B. *Superstar in a Housedress: The Life and Legend of Jackie Curtis.* New York: Chamberlain Books, 2005.

Hoctel, Patrick. "Out of the Closet onto the Screen: Gay Film Historian Vito Russo Returns to Roxie." *Bay Area Reporter,* 8 March 1990, 36.

Hofsess, John. Transcript of New Museum "Gay Sensibility" panel, 29 November 1982. Vito Russo Papers.

Holleran, Andrew. "The Penthouse." In *In September the Light Changes: The Stories of Andrew Holleran,* 43–73. New York: Hyperion, 1999.

———. "The Spectacle at the Bottom of the Shaft." *New York Native,* 23 May–5 June 1983, 19.

Homer Dickens obituary. *New York Native,* 27 February 1989, 9.

"Homosexual's Ordination Voted in the United Church of Christ." *New York Times,* 2 May 1972, 28.

Hopkins, Drew, and Phil Zwickler. "Acting Up or Acting Out? Looking Back on ACT UP's First Year." *Village Voice,* 27 June 1988, 33–38.

Horrigan, Patrick E. *Widescreen Dreams: Growing Up Gay at the Movies.* Madison: University of Wisconsin Press, 1999.

Hudson, John Paul. "Lily Tomlin: The First Ten Years (Part 1 of 2)." *Gaysweek,* 9 May 1977, 6–7, 14.

———. "Lily Tomlin: The First Ten Years (Second of a Two-Part Series)." *Gaysweek,* 23 May 1977, 6–8.

———. [John Francis Hunter, pseud.]. "The Fag Hag Rag: Is the New Bette Midler Old Hat?" *GAY,* 7 August 1972, 11.

———. *The Gay Insider USA.* New York: Stonehill, 1972.

———. "I Enjoy Being a Girl." *GAY,* 25 December 1972, 12.

———. "Julius': Uncle Tom's Cabin Revisited." *GAY,* 4 May 1970, 7.

———. "The Scenic Wonders of Central Park." *GAY,* 8 June 1970, 9.

———. "What Good Is Sitting Alone in Your Room? Come to the Cabaret!" *GAY,* 27 November 1972, 4–5.

Hudson, John Paul, and Warren Wexler. *Superstar Murder? A Prose Flick.* New York: Insider Press, 1976.

Humble, Chris. "Spare Change: A Series of Important Questions, Absolute Answers and Free Advice." *PWA Coalition Newsline,* September 1988, 40.

Huston, Bo. "Crosstalk: Vito Russo." *San Francisco Bay Times,* 3 December 1990.

"Interview with Author of *The Celluloid Closet.*" *The Dispatch: The Newsletter of the Center for American Studies, Columbia University,* Fall 1986, 9–10.

"Intro 475 Hearings Begin." *Gay Activist: Newsletter of the Gay Activists Alliance,* November 1971, 8.

"Intro 475 Now! A Plague on Both Their Houses." *Gay Activist: Newsletter of the Gay Activists Alliance,* October 1971, 2.

"Intro 475—Round 3: Is It up to Lindsay?" *Gay Activist: News and Opinion from the Gay Activists Alliance,* February 1972, 3, 8.

Jay, Karla. *Tales of the Lavender Menace: A Memoir of Liberation.* New York: Basic Books, 1999.

Jones, Cleve, with Jeff Dawson. *Stitching a Revolution: The Making of an Activist.* San Francisco: HarperSanFrancisco, 2000.

Jurrist, Charles. "In Defense of Promiscuity: Hard Questions about Real Life." *New York Native*, 6–19 December 1982, 27, 29.

Kaiser, Charles. *The Gay Metropolis, 1940–1996*. Boston: Houghton Mifflin, 1997.

Kantrowitz, Arnie. "The Boys in the Back Room." *Advocate*, 31 May 1978, 40.

———. "The Day Gay Lib Died." *New York Native*, 2–15 November 1981, 1, 14–15.

———. "An Enemy of the People." In Mass, *We Must Love One Another or Die*, 97–114.

———. "Family Album." In *Friends and Lovers: Gay Men Write about the Families They Create*, edited by John Preston, with Michael Lowenthal, 281–300. New York: Dutton, 1995.

———. "Friends Gone with the Wind." *Advocate*, 2 September 1986, 42–47, 108–9.

———. "Gays in/at the Movies: An Appreciation of Vito Russo." *White Crane* 72 (Spring 2007): 18–22.

———. "Jim Owles, 1946–1993." *Village Voice*, 24 August 1993, 12.

———. "A Remembrance of Vito Russo." *Advocate*, 18 December 1990, 72–75.

———. *Under the Rainbow: Growing Up Gay*. 1977. New York: St. Martin's Press, 1996.

Katz, Phil. "Intro 475: Round 2." *Gay Activist: News & Opinion from the Gay Activists Alliance*, December 1971–January 1972, 4.

Kirkup, James. "The Love That Dares to Speak Its Name." 1976. *Annoy.com*. http://www.annoy.com/history/doc.html?DocumentID=100045 (accessed 6 April 2009).

Koenig, Rhoda. "Screening Gays." *New Republic*, 30 September 1981, 38–40.

Koestenbaum, Wayne. "The Garbo Index." *New Yorker*, 21 March 1994, 146.

Kollarik, Mary. "Near the Saddle River Waters." *Lodi Messenger*, 6 February 1964, 7.

Kramer, Larry. *The Normal Heart*. New York: Samuel French, 1985.

———. "1,112 and Counting." *New York Native*, 14–27 March 1983, 1, 18.

———. *Reports from the holocaust: The Making of an AIDS Activist*. New York: St. Martin's Press, 1989.

———. "Who Killed Vito Russo?" *OutWeek*, 20 February 1991, 26–27.

Kramer, Larry, Arnie Kantrowitz, and Larry Mass. "Remembering Vito Russo." *Village Voice*, 20 November 1990, 51–52.

Leitsch, Dick. "Who Did What with Whom to Whom: The Snake Pit Raid—Some Afterthoughts." *GAY*, 13 April 1970, 13.

———. "'The Whole World's a Bath!' A Chat with Bette Midler." *GAY*, 15 January 1973, 11.

LeRoy, John P. "The Bath Scene." *GAY*, 9 January 1971, 2.

———. "Michael Maye: Soap Opera in Court Continues." *GAY*, 10 July 1972, 10.

———. "Rub a Dub Dub, 3,000 Men in a Tub—New York: Bath Capital of the World." *GAY*, 7 February 1972, 3.

Lester, Barry. "The Continental Miracle." *GAY*, 21 December 1970, 1.

Leuze, Robert. "9 Arrested: Homophobic Overreaction to Posters?" *New York City Yale GALA Newsletter*, November 1989, 4.

Licata, Sal. "Fire Island Impressions." *PWA Coalition Newsline*, November 1987, 36.

———. "The Pines Remembers." *PWA Coalition Newsline*, November 1987, 37.

"Lindsay Speech Disrupted by Activists." *GAY*, 21 February 1972, 1

Little, Jay. *Maybe—Tomorrow*. 1952. New York: Paperback Library, 1965.

Lynne Carter obituary. *New York Native*, 28 January–10 February 1985, 15.

Mair, George. *Bette: An Intimate Biography of Bette Midler*. New York: Birch Lane Press, 1995.

Mandell, Jonathan. "The Stonewall Legacy." *New York Newsday*, 8 June 1989, 2:8–9, 14, 15.

Mangin, Daniel. "Tribute to a Gay Titan: Castro Memorial Honors Vito Russo." *Bay Area Reporter*, 6 December 1990, 33–34, 44.

Mann, William J. "Vito and the Birds." *Metroline*, 30 November 1990, 10.

Marcus, Eric. *Making History: The Struggle for Gay and Lesbian Equal Rights, 1945–1990—An Oral History*. New York: Harper Perennial, 1992.

Margolin, Michael H. "How Films Portray Homosexuals Is Author's Topic." *Oakland Press*, 22 February 1983, A-11.

Marlowe, Kenneth. *Mr. Madam: Confessions of a Male Madam*. Los Angeles: Sherbourne Press, 1964.

Marotta, Toby. *The Politics of Homosexuality*. Boston: Houghton Mifflin, 1981.

Mason, Kiki. "FDA: The Demo of the Year." *New York Native*, 24 October 1988, 13, 17.

Mass, Lawrence, MD. "Basic Questions, Basic Answers about the Epidemic." *New York Native*, 3–16 January 1983, 21, 23, 25.

———. "Cancer in the Gay Community." *New York Native*, 27 July–9 August 1981, 1, 20–21, 30.

———. *Confessions of a Jewish Wagnerite*. New York: Cassell, 1994.

———. "Disease Rumors Largely Unfounded." *New York Native*, 18–31 May 1981, 7.

———. "The Epidemic Continues." *New York Native*, 29 March–11 April 1982, 12–15.

———. "An Epidemic Q&A." *New York Native*, 21 June–4 July 1982, 11.

———. "Vito Russo, 1946–1990." *New York Native*, 19 November 1990, 4.

———, ed. *We Must Love One Another or Die: The Life and Legacies of Larry Kramer*. New York: St. Martin's Press, 1997.

Maupin, Armistead. "Juned In and Gayed Out." *New York Times*, 27 June 1981, A23.

Merla, Patrick. "A Normal Heart: The Larry Kramer Story." In Mass, *We Must Love One Another or Die*, 23–70.

Michaelson, Judith. "Charge Police Ignored Beatings at Hilton Gala." *New York Post*, 18 April 1972, 4.

Miller, Peter. "The Ultimate Movie Lover: An Interview with Vito Russo." *New York Native*, 11 December 1989, 27, 39.

Newton, Esther. *Cherry Grove, Fire Island: Sixty Years in America's First Gay and Lesbian Town*. Boston: Beacon, 1993.

Newton, Jeremiah. "Remembering the Stonewall." *New York Native*, 12 June 1989, 17–20. Nichols, Jack.

Nichols, Jack. *Welcome to Fire Island: Visions of Cherry Grove and The Pines*. New York: St. Martin's Press, 1976.

Nichols, Jack, and Lige Clarke. Editorial. *GAY*, 31 December 1969, 2.

———. Editorial. *GAY*, July 1973, 2.

———. "Love's Coming of Age: June 28, 1970." *GAY*, 20 July 1970, 2.

Nichols, Stuart, MD. "For Patients and Ourselves: AIDS Support Services." *New York Native*, 11–24 October 1982, 15.

"9 Arrested at City Hall." *Gay Activist: Newsletter of the Gay Activists Alliance*, August 1971, 4, 14.

"Now . . . The Stoneys." *New York Native*, 25 April–8 May 1983, 13.

O'Quinn, Jim. "The Other Side of the Street." *New York Native*, 20 December 1982–2 January 1983, 43.

Our Time. Manhattan Cable Television. WNYC-TV. 1983.

"Overheard at Julius's: A Conversation between Arthur Bell, Doric Wilson and Vito Russo." Manuscript. 1981. Individuals, Ephemera, Vito Russo. International Gay Information Center. Astor, Lenox and Tilden Foundations. Manuscripts and Archives Division. New York Public Library.

Pacheco, Patrick. "Before Out Was In: Life after Dark with Arnold, Bette, the Baths, and the Boys." Lecture, New York Public Library for the Performing Arts. 25 September 2008.

Paine, Tom. "Simon Calls Play 'Faggot Nonsense.'" *New York Native*, 25 March–7 April 1985, 18.

Pally, Marcia, and Darrell Yates Rist. Letter to the editor. *New York Native*, 6–12 January 1986, 4.

"The Parade Organizers Organize: Christopher Street Beat." *GAY*, 4 June 1973, 17.

Person, Glenn. "Bette Bites Benefit." *New York Native*, 15–28 March 1982, 7.

Picano, Felice. *A House on the Ocean, a House on the Bay: A Memoir*. Boston: Faber & Faber, 1997.

———. "Imitation of Life: Interview with Vito Russo." *Christopher Street*, July 1981, 18–25.

———. "Rough Cuts from a Journal." 3 March 1981. In *The Violet Quill Reader: The Emergence of Gay Writing after Stonewall*, edited by David Bergman, 28–74. New York: St. Martin's Press, 1994.

"Plan Ahead for the Christopher Street Parade!" *GAY*, 7 May 1973, 17.

A Position of Faith. 1973. Directed by Michael Rhodes. VHS. McGraw-Hill.

Praunheim, Rosa von. *Army of Lovers*. London: Gay Men's Press, 1980.

———. Statement. "West Germany: Das Neue Kino, March 16–April 9, 1972." Department of Film, Museum of Modern Art, New York.

Preston, John. "Family Matters." In *Long Road to Freedom: The* Advocate *History of the Gay and Lesbian Movement*, edited by Mark Thompson, 113–14. New York: St. Martin's Press, 1994.

Price, Deb. "The Coming-Out of Homosexuality in Movies." *Detroit News*, 29 October 1993, 1F.

Range, George. "An Interview with Vito Russo." *Chorus Lines*, February 1987, 2.

Rechy, John. "Cruising Hollywood Attitudes." Books, *Los Angeles Times*, 16 August 1981, 4.

Review of *The Celluloid Closet*. *Booklist*, 15 July 1981, 1428.

Review of *The Celluloid Closet*. *Choice*, March 1982, 932.

Review of *The Celluloid Closet*. *Christian Century*, 23 December 1981, 1348.

Roggensack, David. "Inside 'Out': An Interview." *Gaysweek*, 15 May 1978, 13.

Rosenbaum, Jonathan. "They Frighten Horses, Don't They." *Soho News*, 4 August 1981, 39.

Russo, Angelina ("Annie"). Baby book for Vito Russo. 1946–50. Courtesy of Charles Russo.

———. "Gay Rights" [letter to the editor]. *Daily News*, 29 November 1980.

Russo, Charles. Memoir. Undated manuscript. Courtesy of Charles Russo.

"Russo Panels." *The Dispatch: The Newsletter of the Center for American Studies, Columbia University*, Fall 1986, 8, 11.

Russo, Vito. "All the World's a *Cable* Stage." *On Cable*, January 1984, 25–27.

———. "Alone Again, Naturally." *Gay News* (London), 18 September–1 October 1980, 16–17.

———. "& The Village." *Advocate*, 22 October 1975, 47.

———. "Baghdad by the Sea." *Gay News Special Report* (London), 12–25 June 1980, 2–4.

———. "Bella! Bella! Bella!" *Advocate*, 24 September 1975, 13–14.

———. "Bette Midler: An Exclusive Interview." *Advocate*, 23 April 1975, 31–34.

———. "Blue Flettrich: His Business Is Other People's Pleasure." *Advocate*, 16 June 1976, 15.

———. "Bowie." *Moviegoer*, August 1983, 15–18.

———. "A Brief Encounter with Tennessee Williams." *Advocate*, 20 April 1977, 19–20.

———. "Butley, Bette & Bijou." I'll Take Manhattan, *GAY*, 11 December 1972, 10, 16, 23.

———. "Carlisle and *Liquid Sky*." *Moviegoer*, July 1984, 8–11.

———. "The Celluloid Closet: Homosexuality in the Movies." 1st draft. Manuscript. Courtesy of Charles Russo.

———. "The Celluloid Closet: Homosexuality in the Movies." 2nd draft. Manuscript. Courtesy of Charles Russo.

———. *The Celluloid Closet: Homosexuality in the Movies*. 1st ed. New York: Harper & Row, 1981.

———. *The Celluloid Closet: Homosexuality in the Movies*. 2nd ed. New York: Harper & Row, 1987.

———. "The Celluloid Closet—How Hollywood Sees Gays: An Excerpt from a New Book." *US*, 23 June 1981, 51–52.

———. "Coming Out as a PWA to One's Family." In *Surviving and Thriving with AIDS: Collected Wisdom*, edited by Michael Callen, 2:178–79. New York: PWAC, 1988.

———. "Comments on Gay Conferences." *Advocate*, 14 January 1976, 34.

———. "'Cruising': The Controversy Continues." *New York*, 13–20 August 1979, 46, 47, 49.

———. "David Goodstein." *Gay News* (London), 17–30 April 1980, 28–29.

———. "Different from the Others." *Advocate*, 24 October 1988, 61.

———. "Drama Review." *Jefferson News*, 7 February 1964, 2. Courtesy of Charles Russo.

———. "Entertainment." *GAY*, November 1973, 17.

———. "The Fabulous Peter Allen." *Advocate*, 13 July 1977, 19–20.

———. "*Faggots* Reviewed." *Gay News* (London), 10–23 July 1980, 21.

———. "Fire Island." *Advocate*, 11 August 1976, 28.

———. "Franco Brusati." *Gay News* (London), 26 June–9 July 1980, 17–18.

———. "Gay Sensibility: The Disney Version" [letter to editor]. *Village Voice*, 14 July 1975, 4.

———. "Gay Visions in Celluloid." *Gay News* (London), 15–28 May 1980, 13–14.

———. "Glad to Be a Clone." *Gay News Special Report* (London), 21 August–3 September 1980, 2–4.

———. "I Don't Care If You're Gay. Can You Sing?" *GAY*, 4 September 1972, 11.

———. I'll Take Manhattan, *GAY*, 13 November 1972, 9, 16.

———. "I'm Really Quite Fond of You Boys." I'll Take Manhattan, *GAY*, 12 March 1973, 15.

———. "In Search of the New Culture." *GAY*, 30 October 1972, 5.

———. "An Interview with Debbie Reynolds." *Christopher Street*, November 1976, 7–12.

———. "An Interview with Laura Kenyon: Laura Isn't Only a Dream." *GAY*, 18 June 1973, 13, 16.

———. "Issues for New York Times Meeting." Manuscript. January 1988. Courtesy of Charles Russo Jr.

———. "It's Gotham! It's Grossman! It's the Entertainment Liberation Front." *GAY*, March 1974, 8.

———. "It's Poison Pen Time Kiddies." I'll Take Manhattan, *GAY*, 26 February 1973, 15.

———. "It's Spring! Who [*sic*] Do I Hate?" *GAY*, 4 June 1973, 8, 16.

———. "Jerry Rubin Grows Up." *Advocate*, 24 July 1976, 35–36.

———. "Jessica Lange." *Moviegoer*, February 1983, 14–19.

———. "Key West." *Gay News Supplement* (London), 22 January–4 February 1981, 12–13.

———. Letter to the editor. *Fire Island News*, 13–19 August 1987, 2.

———. Letter to the editor. *New York Native*, 26 January 1987, 52.

———. Letter to the editor. *New York Native*, 16 February 1987, 8–9.

———. "Lily!" *Advocate*, 18 March 1986, 42–47.

———. "Men's Liberation?!" *Bell Telephone Magazine*, Spring 1978, 24–26.

———. "Midnight Shift." *Gay News Supplement* (London), 13–26 November 1980, 12–13.

———. "Miss M at Philharmonic Hall." I'll Take Manhattan, *GAY*, 12 February 1973, 8–9.

———. "Mykonos." *Gay News* (London), 30 October–12 November 1980, 12–13.

———. "Nastassja Kinski." *Moviegoer*, April 1984, 15–19.

———. "New Hope for Performing Artists." *GAY*, 26 March 1973, 8–9.

———. New York, *Advocate*, 18 June 1975, 18.

———. New York, *Advocate*, 2 July 1975, 32.

———. New York, *Advocate*, 16 July 1975, 38.

———. New York, *Advocate*, 30 July 1975, 34.

———. New York, *Advocate*, 13 August 1975, 49.

———. New York, *Advocate*, 27 August 1975, 48–49.

———. New York, *Advocate*, 24 September 1975, 19.

———. New York, *Advocate*, 5 November 1975, 43.

———. New York, *Advocate*, 17 December 1975, 38.

———. "New York City." *Advocate*, 7 April 1976, 39.

———. "Onstage or Off: I'm Straight!" *GAY*, 12 February 1973, 11.

———. "On the Set [of *Making Love*]." *Esquire Film Quarterly*, October 1981, 102, 103.

———. "Park Gang: We Hate Fags!" *Soho Weekly News*, 20 July 1978, 4.

———. "Pinin' in the Pines: Confessions of the Last 'Rose' of Summer." *GAY*, September 1973, 11.

———. "Playing Politics with Gay Rights." *Soho News*, 1 April 1981, 5.

———. "Politics, Actors and the Theatre." I'll Take Manhattan, *GAY*, 21 May 1973, 12.

———. "Poor Judy." *Gay News Supplement* (London), 11 December 1980–7 January 1981, 14–15.

———. "Premiere! Gay Liberation from German with Reluctance." *Gay Activist: News & Opinion of the Gay Activists Alliance*, April 1972, 9.

———. "Puttin' Down 'The Ritz.'" *Advocate*, 22 September 1976, 40, 45.

———. "Rachel Ward." *Moviegoer*, June 1982, 14–16.

———. Review of *The Panic in Needle Park*. *After Dark*, July 1971, 64, 66.

———. Review of *Sondheim & Co. Advocate*, 23 April 1975, 30.

———. Review of *States of Desire*. *Gay News* (London), 3–16 April 1980, 11.

———. "Romance on the Range: Two-Stepping to the Music at the National Gay Rodeo." *New York Native*, 5–18 October 1981, 21–22.

———. "Russo on Film: Vanities of the Nitwits." *Advocate*, 7 June 1988, 59.

———. "Shelley's New Look!" I'll Take Manhattan, *GAY*, 15 January 1973, 10.

———. "A Special Interview by Vito Russo, Starring Lily Tomlin." *Advocate*, 14 January 1976, 23–29.

———. "State of Siege—Richard M. Nixon and the Arts." I'll Take Manhattan, *GAY*, 7 May 1973, 13.

———. "Still Outlaws." *Gay News* (London), 28 June–11 July 1979, 16–17.

———. "Swedes Chase Lord C." *Gay News* (London), 18 September–1 October 1980, 1, 2.

———. "Thanks, Brothers, We're Applauding!" I'll Take Manhattan, *GAY*, 25 December 1972, 14, 16.

———. "That 'Twinkle in the Eye' Awareness." I'll Take Manhattan, *GAY*, 9 April 1973, 8–9.

———. "Too Little, Too Soon: The Premature Biography of Bette Midler." *Gay News Supplement* (London), 20 March–2 April 1980, xiii.

———. "A Trip Back in Time." I'll Take Manhattan, *GAY*, 27 November 1972, 9, 16.

———. "Tubshit—A Parade of Tight Asses." I'll Take Manhattan, *GAY*, 18 June 1973, 14.

———. "Valerie Harper: 'Gays Have to Get That It's Good to Be Who They Are.'" *Advocate*, 14 February 1976, 46–47.

———. "A Visit with Allan Carr: Hollywood's Can't-Stop Mogul." *Advocate*, 12 June 1984, 34–36.

———. "Wanna Dance? Get Wrecked to the Ass!" *Advocate*, 13 August 1975, 41.

———. "Warning: This Film Could Seriously Damage Your Health." *Gay News Special Report* (London), 1–14 May 1980, 2–4.

———. "Water in Your Eye, Mice in Your Hair, Girls in Your Lap." *In Cinema*, April/May 1981, 18.

———. "When It Comes to Gay Money—Gay Lib Takes Care of the Pennies; Will Big Business Take Care of the Pounds?" *Gay News* (London), 2–15 April 1981, 16–17.

———. "Why I'm Not Marching." *New York Native*, 20 June–3 July 1983, 46.

———. "Why Is Leather Like Ethel Merman?" *Village Voice*, 15–21 April 1981, 37.

———. "'Word Is Out.'" *Advocate*, 5 April 1978, 30–31, 43.

———. "Zeffirelli—Nice Asses and No Talent." I'll Take Manhattan, *GAY*, 23 April 1973, 12–13.

Russo, Vito, and Arthur Bell. "For Fame and Money." The Russo/Bell Connection, *New York Native*, 1–14 June 1981, 31.

———. "Glorious Letdowns." The Russo/Bell Connection, *New York Native*, 13–26 July 1981, 31, 33.

———. "A Puce Picture." The Russo/Bell Connection, *New York Native*, 4–17 May 1981, 31.

———. The Russo/Bell Connection, *New York Native*, 10–24 January 1981, 19.

———. The Russo/Bell Connection, *New York Native*, 9–22 February 1981, 14.

———. The Russo/Bell Connection, *New York Native*, 23 February–8 March 1981, 28.

———. The Russo/Bell Connection, *New York Native*, 9–22 March 1981, 30.

———. The Russo/Bell Connection, *New York Native*, 23 March–5 April 1981, 30.

———. The Russo/Bell Connection, *New York Native*, 6–19 April 1981, 14, 33.

———. The Russo/Bell Connection, *New York Native*, 15–28 June 1981, 32.

———. "Social History 101." The Russo/Bell Connection, *New York Native*, 18–31 May 1981, 31.

———. "Wax Dolls." The Russo/Bell Connection, *New York Native*, 25 January–8 February 1981, 14.

Rutledge, Leigh W. *The Gay Decades: From Stonewall to the Present, the People and Events That Shaped Gay Lives*. New York: Plume, 1992.

Salinas, Mike. "Wall Street Closed for 15 Minutes by Angry Gays." *New York Native*, 6 April 1987, 9.

Sarris, Andrew. "An Aesthete at the Movies." *Commentary*, February 1971, 84.

Schiavi, Michael. "Looking for Vito." *Cinema Journal* 49, no. 1 (Fall 2009): 41–64.

Schiff, Stephen. "Winning Bette." *Vanity Fair*, December 1987, 142, 190–91.

Schulman, Sarah. "Anti-Abortion Group Pickets Gay Bathhouse." *New York Native*, 30 September–6 October 1985, 17.

Sciarra, Felix. *Lodi as I Remember It*. 1994. Lodi Public Library, Lodi, NJ.

Scobie, W. I. "Lemon of *Gay News London*." *Advocate*, 13 December 1979, 24–26.

Senak, Mark. *A Fragile Circle*. Los Angeles: Alyson, 1998.

Sevcik, Jeff. "Old Shoes." Undated poetry collection. Courtesy of Allen Sawyer.

———. "Thatched Roofs and Dreams over Thought." Undated poetry collection. Courtesy of Allen Sawyer.

"Sex in the Age of AIDS." *Advocate*, 8 July 1986, 42–47.

"S.F. Study Shows Gay Men Reluctant to Take HTLV-III Antibody Test." *New York Native*, 23–29 September 1985, 12.

Sharman, Russell Leigh. *The Tenants of East Harlem*. Berkeley: University of California Press, 2006.

Shilts, Randy. *And the Band Played On*. New York: St. Martin's Press, 1987.

———. *The Mayor of Castro Street: The Times of Harvey Milk*. New York: St. Martin's Press, 1982.

———. "Politics Confused with Therapy." *San Francisco Chronicle*, 26 June 1989, A4.

Shipman, David. *Judy Garland: The Secret Life of an American Legend*. New York: Hyperion, 1992.

Silverstein, Charles. "For the Ferryman." Undated memoir. Courtesy of Charles Silverstein.

Siskel, Gene. "Movies' Disgrace: Screening Gays." *Philadelphia Inquirer*, 6 December 1981, 1-I.

Skir, Leo. "Breakfast at Harper's: An Inside View of a Sit-In." *GAY*, 23 November 1970, 1, 10.

———. "Everybody Loves Big-Eyed Bette: The Toast of the Tubs Goes Big Time." *GAY*, 11 October 1971, 5.

———. "The Hearings on Intro 475: Part III." *GAY*, 24 January 1972, 4.

Steele, Tom, and Chuck Ortleb. "The Last Conversations of Arthur Bell." *Christopher Street*, November 1984, 32–46.

Stein, Ruthe. "Update: The First Gay Ministry." *San Francisco Chronicle*, 2 March 1977, 21.

Steinman, Wayne. "Remembering David Summers." *New York Native*, 8 December 1986, 9.

Stern, Alan. "From the Closet to the Screen: Vito Russo on Gays in Films." *Boston Phoenix*, 3 November 1981, 15.

Stonewall 20 Years Later. Gay Cable Network. 1989.

Streitmatter, Rodger. *Unspeakable: The Rise of the Gay and Lesbian Press in America*. Boston: Faber & Faber, 1995.

Taylor, Clarke. "Fear in Filmdom's Crowded Closet." *Los Angeles Times*, Calendar, 9 August 1981, 21–22.

Taylor, John Russell. "Sane Man in a Mad World." *Gay News Literary Supplement* (London), 17–30 September 1981, 10.

Teal, Donn. *The Gay Militants*. New York: Stein & Day, 1971.

Thompson, Mark. "Erotic Ecstasy: An Interview with Perusha the Androgyne." In *Leatherfolk: Radical Sex, People, Politics and Practice*, edited by Mark Thompson, 284–93. Boston: Alyson, 1991.

"300 March on Parliament." *Melbourne Star Observer* (Victoria, Australia), 11 March 1988, 2.

"Timeline of a Legend." Liner notes. *West Side Story*, DVD Collector's Set. Metro-Goldwyn-Mayer Home Entertainment, 2003.

The Times of Harvey Milk. 1984. Directed by Robert Epstein and Richard Schmiechen. DVD. New Yorker Films, 2004.

Tobin, Kay. "GAA Confronts Goldberg, Blumenthal." *GAY*, 29 June 1970, 12.

———. "World's Kissing Record Broken." *GAY*, 20 July 1970, 2.

Tobin, Kay, and Randy Wicker. *The Gay Crusaders*. New York: Paperback Library, 1972.

Tomlin, Lily. *Modern Scream*. 1975. Laugh.com. 2003.

Toscano, Lawrence C. *Lodi in Review, 1956–57*. Lodi, NJ: Paci Press, 1956.

Tozzi, Vincent. *I Already Am*. New York: iUniverse, 2004.

———. "Who Is Vito Russo and Why Are They Saying Those Wonderful Things about Him?" Publication data unknown. Vito Russo Papers.

Tree, Ian J. "Cruising Off Broadway . . ." *GAY*, 24 July 1972, 13.

Truscott, Lucian, IV. "Gay Power Comes to Sheridan Square." *Village Voice*, 3 July 1969, 1, 18.

Turner, Dan. "Vito Russo and The Celluloid Closet." *Bay Area Reporter*, 18 June 1981, 23, 29.

Tyler, Parker. *Screening the Sexes: Homosexuality in the Movies*. 1972. New York: Da Capo Press, 1993.

Umans, Richard. "Pines '83: Back to the Beaches." *New York Native*, 6–19 June 1983, 40.

Van Gelder, Lindsay. "'Gay Bill of Rights' Makes Progress." *New York Post*, 5 November 1970, 16.

Veasey, Jack. "Books on Gays in Films? Vito's Gives You Freedom of Choice." *Philadelphia Gay News*, 29 May–11 June 1981, 6.

Victim. 1961. Directed by Basil Dearden. Screenplay by Janet Green and John McCormick. DVD. HVE, 2002.

Vito's Legacy: A Stronger Community. Produced by Raymond Jacobs. Directed by Joe Nicola. Gay Cable Network. 20 December 1990.

Voices from the Front. Directed by Robyn Hutt, David Meieran, and Sandra Elgear. VHS. Testing the Limits Video Collective, 1992.

Wagner, Jane. *The Search for Intelligent Signs of Life in the Universe*. New York: Harper & Row, 1986.

Walker, Gerald. *Cruising*. 1970. New York: Fawcett Crest, 1971.

Wallace, John. "'Our Time': TV on Our Terms." *New York Native*, 28 February–13 March 1983, 13.

Wandel, Richard C. "5 Arrested in Gay Teacher Dispute." *GAY*, 24 May 1971, 1.

Waters, Christina. "In Vito Veritas." *Pacific*, 1990, 53–55.

———. "In Vito Veritas." MetroActiveMovies. http://www.metroactive.com/papers/cruz/04.11.96/celluloid-9615.html (accessed 19 March 2009).

Webber, Thomas L. *Flying over 96th Street: Memoir of an East Harlem White Boy*. New York: Scribner, 2004.

White, Edmund. *City Boy: My Life in New York during the 1960s and '70s*. New York: Bloomsbury USA, 2009.

White, Norval, and Elliot Willensky. *AIA Guide to New York City*. 4th ed. New York: Crown, 2000.

[Wicker, Randy]. "Behind the Lines on Gay Pride Sunday." *GAY*, August 1973, 3.

Wicker, Randolfe. "Gay Power Challenges Syndicate Bars: Dances Draw Large Crowds." *GAY*, 21 June 1971, 1.

———. "Randy Wicker's Basket." *GAY*, 15 July 1971, 4.

Williams, Lena. "200,000 March in Capital to Seek Gay Rights and Money for AIDS." *New York Times*, 12 October 1987, A1.

Wilson, Doric. *Street Theater*. In *Out Front: Contemporary Gay and Lesbian Plays*, edited by Don Shewey, 1–77. New York: Grove Press, 1988.

Wolfe, Maxine. "The Mother of Us All." In Mass, *We Must Love One Another or Die*, 282–86.

Wood, Robin. "Airing the Closet." *Canadian Forum*, February 1982, 35–36.

Young, Tracy. "Gay March: 'How Dare You Assume I'm Heterosexual.'" *Village Voice*, 28 June 1973, 17.

Zwickler, Phil. "Quilt Film Wins Oscar." *PWA Coalition Newsline*, May 1990, 16–17.

Index